CRIMINAL JUSTICE
IN AMERICA

CRIMINAL JUSTICE IN AMERICA

A Critical View

RANDALL G. SHELDEN

University of Nevada, Las Vegas

WILLIAM B. BROWN

Western Oregon University

Boston   New York   San Francisco
Mexico City   Montreal   Toronto   London   Madrid   Munich   Paris
Hong Kong   Singapore   Tokyo   Cape Town   Sydney

Series Editor: *Jennifer Jacobson*
Editorial Assistant: *Elizabeth Lee*
Executive Marketing Manager: *Brad Parkins*
Editorial-Production Service: *Omegatype Typography, Inc.*
Composition Buyer: *Linda Cox*
Manufacturing Buyer: *Andrew Turso*
Cover Administrator: *Kristina Mose-Libon*
Electronic Composition: *Omegatype Typography, Inc.*

For related titles and support material, visit our online catalog at www.ablongman.com.

Between the time Website information is gathered and published, some sites may have closed. Also, the transcription of URLs can result in typographical errors. The publisher would appreciate notification where these errors occur so that they may be corrected in subsequent editions.

Library of Congress Cataloging-in-Publication Data

Shelden, Randall G.
    Criminal justice in America : a critical view / Randall G. Shelden, William B. Brown.
       p. cm.
    Includes bibliographical references and index.
    ISBN 0-205-37464-6
      1. Criminal justice, Administration of—United States.   I. Brown, William B. (William Bud). II. Title.

HV9950 .S543 2003
364.973—dc21

                                      2002026143

Printed in the United States of America

10 9 8 7 6 5 4 3 2 1   07 06 05 04 03 02

CONTENTS

CHAPTER FOURTEEN

Women and the Criminal Justice System   357

CHAPTER FIFTEEN

**Making Changes: Reforming Criminal Justice
and Seeking Social Justice   382**

PREFACE

In this text we are offering an alternative interpretation of criminal justice that is rarely presented either in traditional textbooks or in the media. It is normal that whenever one focuses on any public issue there are many emotions involved. The problem of crime touches many lives and is the subject of many heated debates, especially around election time. Many different points of view are offered during these debates. When writing about crime and criminal justice it is impossible to be purely objective. Even if we merely presented facts, some subjectivity and some values enter the picture. This is because (to quote an old saying) "facts never speak for themselves." More than this, though, is that in a world filled with an endless variety of facts, not every one of these facts can be selected and placed into a text—or any piece of writing. Many facts are often conveniently omitted (sometimes by accident, sometimes through carelessness, sometimes on purpose).

We should make clear that what we are presenting in this book is not the only possible view of the subject. There is no rigidly defined correct way of interpreting anything in life. There is no right or wrong way of interpreting a poem, a painting, a photograph, a movie, or any work of art. In fact, there is no correct way to view or interpret an individual human being.

Our purpose in writing this book is to present an alternative interpretation of the criminal justice system. To present every possible interpretation would take literally several thousand pages (and no student would want that). We do offer a few interpretations that differ from our own, for it would be impossible not to do so. However, the overall thrust of the book is, as you will soon realize, very critical and quite at variance to what one normally receives in standard texts, in the media, from politicians, and from criminal justice officials. Whether each person who reads this agrees with our interpretation is irrelevant. All we expect from you, the reader, is that you try to understand this interpretation, then read the interpretations of others (and we give numerous references to other views), and then come to your own conclusion and act accordingly.

As an example, we refer to *Bury My Heart at Wounded Knee*. This book was written about thirty years ago by Dee Brown, a Native American. In this book he made clear his bias. He said that traditional American history was written "looking westward." His book was to be written from the perspective of "looking eastward." Think about that for a moment. The traditional textbook was written from the point of view of those coming in a western direction, namely the Europeans who set out to conquer the west and in the process decimated most of the Native American population. But, Brown asked, what did this history look like from the point of view of those who already lived here? Obviously this view was quite different. But which interpretation is the correct one? Both are correct. They are different. Each is a view on the same events and covers the same period. It is just that each side sees things differently. We are certain that American history is also viewed differently by women and men, by African Americans and Mexican Americans and whites, by the rich and by the poor. Likewise, crime and criminal justice can be seen from different perspectives. For example, recall the different interpretations of the O. J. Simpson case.

One final point is in order. Many will, no doubt, notice that we express a great deal of anger and passion throughout this book. This is simply because, as human beings, we are angered about what we perceive to be gross injustices in this country and passionate about writing and talking about them and about wanting to do something. We cannot and we will not control our anger and passion and hide behind the so-called objectivity of the social sciences. We are both humanists at heart and are proud of it. We hope that those who read this text will also be angered and passionate and take some appropriate action to correct the problem.

This is a book about America's response to the problem of crime. The position taken by the authors is that the response is itself criminal, for we act violently against violence, we act with hate against actions which are hateful, we inflict pain and suffering on those who inflict pain and suffering on others. Today we live in a world that is filled with violence and exploitation. Indeed, we do not have to look very far to find this: from Bosnia to the Middle East, from Central America to South America, from the streets of Los Angeles to the streets of Miami, and in Afghanistan and wherever there are alleged terrorist activities. America's response to war and violence abroad mirrors its response to war and violence on our city streets and within our own homes. We fight fire with fire, violence with violence, cruelty with cruelty. This, unfortunately, is the nature of our criminal justice system.

Most Americans, and unfortunately most of the "experts" on crime and criminal justice, do not see the crime problem and our response to it from this perspective. However, we believe it is time for a new perspective on what passes for criminal justice in our society. We base this belief in part on the fact that despite the huge expenditures for our "war on crime," the vast majority of citizens still believe crime is our number one problem. Clearly something is amiss.

This book presents an alternative perspective to business as usual. The student that reads this book will, of course, develop an understanding of the general principles of the criminal justice system. That is, the student will become knowledgeable about the "nuts and bolts" of the criminal justice system in American society. However, we will clearly offer a challenge to "what is" and offer "what could be." We hope you will be challenged by what we are saying.

ACKNOWLEDGMENTS

We would like to offer our thanks to several people. First, to Jennifer Jacobson at Allyn and Bacon, who has supported us throughout this project, and to Shannon Foreman at Omega-type Typography, Inc., for her excellent assistance in the always-important editorial stages. Thanks also to the reviewers of this book: Florence Ferguson, State University of West Georgia; Marianne Fisher-Giorlando, Grambling State University; Shaun Gabbidon, Pennsylvania State University–Harrisburg; Tara Gray, New Mexico State University; Jacqueline Huey, Grambling State University; James Nolan, West Virginia University; Everette B. Penn, Prairie View A&M University; Larry Tifft, Central Michigan University; Robert Weiss, State University of New York at Plattsburgh.

Special thanks should be extended to several fellow academics who have helped shape our view of the world and whose works are cited throughout this book, especially Richard Quinney, Noam Chomsky, Meda Chesney-Lind, and Howard Zinn. Finally, a special thanks to Judy Brown, Virginia Gray, and Marcie Collins for their support throughout this project.

CRIMINAL JUSTICE
IN AMERICA

CHAPTER ONE

AN OVERVIEW OF THE CRIMINAL JUSTICE SYSTEM

In recent years millions of people—in the United States and other countries—watched in fascination some of the most famous cases in the history of U.S. criminal justice. The names of Rodney King, O. J. Simpson, Timothy McVeigh, Susan Smith, and Ted Kaczynski, and the impeachment trial of President Bill Clinton, come immediately to mind. Fictional accounts of crime and criminal trials have been among the most popular best-selling books and movies, such as the books by John Grisham and the movies based on them (e.g., *The Firm, A Time to Kill, The Rainmaker*) and the most-watched television programs (e.g., *Cops, Law and Order, America's Most Wanted*). People are fascinated by crime, especially violent crime. Yet the picture of the U.S. criminal justice system that emerges from those cases and fictional accounts is grossly distorted. Those few "celebrated" cases provided the highly unusual and completely atypical examples of the daily operation of the criminal justice system. While they were being played out in the media, literally millions of routine cases were quickly processed rather unceremoniously through the various stages of the criminal justice system.

What highly publicized cases and the entertainment media have done perhaps more than anything else is increase the public's concern about and fear of crime, despite little evidence of any significant increase in most types of crime during the past couple of decades. In fact, by all official accounts, rates of many serious crimes have decreased. Unfortunately, at the same time, we have spent billions of dollars fighting crime but have achieved only modest gains in crime reduction. For instance, between 1982 and 1996 the money spent on the U.S. criminal justice system increased from about $35 billion per year to more than $120 billion per year. This reflects nearly a 400 percent increase over a period of less than 15 years![1] Such an increase might not seem particularly alarming if there were a significant decline in crime rates during this period. But no significant decline can be found. In 1982 the crime rate was 5,603.6 per 100,000 population. In 1996 the rate was 5,086.6 per 100,000. This modest reduction constitutes a decline of about 517, or less than 10 percent—following an *$85 billion increase* in criminal justice expenditures. In taxpayer dollars, this amounts to $164,410,058 per declining point in the crime rate. If we wanted to cut the crime rate by one-half (from 1996 figures), it would cost nearly half a trillion dollars more.

It appears that such logic has been adopted in the formulation of crime policies today—more police, more courts, more prisons. Although a half-trillion-dollar increase in the criminal justice budget may sound absurd, one can only wonder what a proposed $85 billion increase in criminal justice spending sounded like to a 1982 audience. A half-trillion-dollar budget increase in criminal justice spending would place a severe strain on the U.S. economy. Much of the funding would probably come from property taxes and increases in the costs for using public institutions (e.g., universities). We might be able to cover this cost by increasing property taxes and tuition by 400 to 500 percent. Such an economic environment, however, might force more and more people to turn to crime to meet their basic subsistence needs, in which case such a costly attempt to reduce crime may spur an increase in crime.

There is presently what some have termed a "criminal justice industrial complex" or a "crime control industry" that has, in a sense, a vested interest in maintaining a certain level of crime. After all, crime is profitable. The only question to be answered is "for whom?"[2] We currently house more people in prisons and jails and process more through the criminal justice system than ever before. Some inmates find themselves housed in "corporate" prisons, or prisons operated by private corporations. Indeed, the latest figures show that nearly 6 million citizens are in prison, in jail, on probation, or on parole—largely because of the "war on drugs," which has contributed more than any other offense in recent years to the increasing numbers caught up in the criminal justice system.

This is a book about the United States' response to the problem of crime. That response takes place mostly within the *criminal justice system,* which has three major components: law enforcement, the courts, and prison. "System" is perhaps a misnomer, for as many have noted what exists is really a mishmash or a "loosely articulated hierarchy of subsystems."[3] To describe criminal justice in the United States merely as a "system" with three "components" is barely to scratch the surface of what is going on.

You already have some knowledge of the criminal justice system. You have seen police cars driving around (perhaps, unfortunately, you have taken a ride in the back seat with your hands cuffed behind you). You may have visited a courthouse (perhaps to pay a traffic fine). You may have seen a prison somewhere or even visited a local jail to help a friend post bail. Maybe while you were in high school you had the occasion to visit a juvenile court. In all likelihood you probably have formed some impressions from these limited experiences, as you have from watching television or movies. However, there's a lot more to this system than you may realize. Understanding the criminal justice system requires taking a sort of journey that includes many detours along the way. Like any journey, it must begin with the first step, which takes us to the ultimate source of the criminal justice system. So, before going any further in this introductory chapter, let us begin this journey at the ultimate source of the criminal justice system. For this we need to review, briefly, the constitutional basis of this system.

THE CONSTITUTIONAL BASIS OF THE CRIMINAL JUSTICE SYSTEM

On what authority does the American system of criminal justice exist? Where does this system come from? The ultimate source of authority for our criminal justice system is the U.S. Constitution, which provides for the creation of laws by state legislatures and Congress. In essence, "Law is the formal statement of authority that is exercised by the state."[4] Executive branch officials, and the courts, are given authority, through provisions in the Constitution, to enforce or interpret these laws. Those provisions are founded on the principles of security for individuals and for the nation as a whole. The criminal justice system is the *instrument* designated by executive-branch officials to enforce laws that pertain to criminal behavior.

The basis of the U.S. criminal justice system is found within the **three branches of the U.S. government:** legislative, executive, and judicial. The legal authority to establish an official response to crime comes from this structural arrangement. "Legal authority, like other forms of authority, may be enforced by threatening or physically coercing people to comply or by economic rewards."[5] Rarely do we reward people for *not* committing a crime.[6] Legal authority may also be a product that is marketed in such a way that people tend simply to accept law as a cultural obligation—they accept the law because they have been trained to accept the law. The legislative branch (federal and state legislatures) defines what behaviors are to be prohibited by the criminal law it enacts and how individuals who are convicted are to be punished. The judicial branch (e.g., the U.S. Supreme Court, state supreme courts, and various appellate courts) interprets these laws and determines whether they are constitutionally valid. The executive branch (comprised of such public officials as presidents, governors, and mayors) creates the official response in terms of agencies, personnel, and the like, in addition to reviewing the decisions of other branches (e.g., an appeal of a conviction or an arrest).

The legislative branch is perhaps the most important of the three branches because it is here where behaviors officially become defined as "crime." Of particular importance are legislatures at the state and local levels, for most "criminal acts" are violations of state and local laws. In fact, state and federal legislatures have, in effect, created two major criminal justice systems: state and federal. Thus, we have state and federal law enforcement systems, state and federal courts, and state and federal prison systems. You should be aware of who the individuals are who constitute the legislature, both at the state and local and at the federal level.

In theory, each of these branches "represents" the general public. In practice, however, as many studies have shown, these groups do not necessarily represent all of the population. The majority of the people who occupy legislative seats (especially at the federal level, in the U.S. Congress and the Senate) are white males from upper-middle-class or upper-class backgrounds. Much legislation and much of the law itself reflect the values and interests of this class, and not necessarily those of other social classes.[7] For example, sidewalk vendors in New York, who sell everything from used magazines to used neckties from their makeshift "booths," are in constant struggle with legislators who pass laws that deny them a means of subsistence. Their struggle is compounded by the police, who often engage in various forms of harassment as they interpret and selectively enforce those laws.[8] This behavior helps explain what many citizens believe—namely, that "money talks," especially when it comes to being accused of a crime, and the criminal laws are selectively enforced.

Criminal law is the body of laws that justify the existence of a criminal justice system. Without criminal law there would be no purpose for a criminal justice system. (Criminal law is thoroughly examined and discussed in Chapter 3.) The criminal justice system is the apparatus used to enforce the standards of conduct, reflected in criminal law, established by a legislative body for a given society.

THE CRIME CONTROL INDUSTRY

Law enforcement, the courts, and the prison system—the three major components of the criminal justice system—are discussed in much more detail in subsequent chapters. At this point, it should be noted that this system is rather large and very expensive. Expenditures are roughly $150 billion annually. Over 50,000 different governmental agencies employ close to 2 million people in this system who share a payroll amounting to more than $5 billion per month.[9] We suggest that this system is part of a much larger system known as the **crime control industry.**[10]

The crime control industry consists of a lot more than the criminal justice system itself. It includes a number of businesses that profit either directly or indirectly from the existence of crime and from attempts to control crime. Examples include private security firms (which provide not only security police but also an abundance of security hardware), a "prison-industrial complex" (providing plenty of investment opportunities as well as profits from hundreds of businesses), drug-testing firms, and gun manufacturers, plus colleges and universities that offer criminal justice degrees and media that depend a lot on stories about crime and criminals (ranging from stories on the 11 o'clock news to "real cop stories" on television and in major motion pictures).

The *control* of crime—often expressed as a "war on crime" (including the "war on drugs" and the "war on gangs")—has become a booming business. Literally hundreds of companies, large and small, are itching for a slice of the growing pie of profits. Employment in this industry offers careers for thousands of young men and women, many with college degrees in criminal justice programs at more than 3,000 colleges and universities. The criminal justice system provides a steady supply of career possibilities (police officers, correctional officers, etc.), with good starting pay and benefits, along with job security. Many groups within this system have formed very powerful unions.

One of the first scholars to recognize the existence of the crime control industry was Richard Quinney in his book *Class, State and Crime,* first published in 1977. Quinney wrote that there is a "social-industrial complex," of which a "criminal justice industrial complex" is a part. This much larger complex is "an involvement of industry in the planning, production, and operation of state programs. These state-financed programs (concentrating on education, welfare, and criminal justice), as social expenses necessary for maintaining social order, are furnished by monopolistic industries." Large corporations, Quinney suggested, have found a new source of profit in this industry, with the criminal justice industry leading the way. Private industry, in short, has found that there is much profit to be made as a result of the existence of crime.[11]

Part of the reason for the growth of the crime control industry is policy makers' decision that a technocratic solution to the crime problem would offer the best course. This perspective suggests that the solution to crime requires a combination of science and technology. Such a position was stated well by the President's Crime Commission in 1967:

> More than 200,000 scientists and engineers have applied themselves to solving military problems and hundreds of thousands more to innovation in other areas of modern life, but only a handful are working to control the crimes that injure or frighten millions of Americans each year. Yet the two communities have much to offer each other: Science and technology is a valuable source of knowledge and techniques for combating crime; the criminal justice system represents a vast area of challenging problems.[12]

It is obvious that the government took up the challenge, for since 1967 the crime control industry has become enormous. It is so huge that to estimate the amount of money spent and the profits made is almost impossible.

If we focus on the annual expenditures of the three main components of the criminal justice system, we can begin to understand how huge this industry is. Table 1.1 shows these expenditures covering the years 1982 and 1996 (the latest figures available from the Department of Justice). In 1996 total expenditures exceeded $120 billion, an increase of 235

TABLE 1.1   Criminal Justice Expenditures, Fiscal Years 1982 and 1996

	1982	1996	PERCENT INCREASE
Total	$35,840,000,000	$120,194,000,000	235
Police	19,022,000,000	53,007,000,000	179
Judicial	7,771,000,000	26,158,000,000	236
Corrections	9,047,000,000	41,029,000,000	356

Source: McGarrell, E. F. and T. J. Flanagan (eds.). *Sourcebook of Criminal Justice Statistics—1985.* Washington, D.C.: U.S. Department of Justice, 1986, p. 2; Maguire, K. and A. L. Pastore (eds.). *Sourcebook of Criminal Justice Statistics—1998.* Washington, D.C.: U.S. Department of Justice. 1999, online version, Table 1.2.

percent over 1982. The largest increase went toward the correctional system, going up 356 percent.[13] At least two writers estimate that total expenditures as of 1999 were in excess of $150 billion; by 2005 annual expenditures might be more than $200 billion.[14]

Employment within the crime control industry is growing rapidly, providing many career opportunities for college students and high school graduates. The most recent data show that in fiscal year 1993 there were just over 1.8 million employed within this system, a 65 percent increase from 1982. (As of October 1995—the most recent data available—there were 584,925 sworn police officers, up 27 percent from 1980.)[15] The largest component is within the corrections category, with just over 1.4 million, representing an increase of over 90 percent from 1982. The U.S. Census reports that the hiring and training of correctional officers is the "fastest-growing function" of all government functions. More people are working in corrections than are employed in any Fortune 500 company except General Motors.[16]

A multitude of businesses large and small have found a steady market for goods and services. Examples can be seen in advertisements found in journals, newspapers, and elsewhere. An advertising brochure from an investment firm called World Research Group states: "While arrests and convictions are steadily on the rise, profits are to be made—profits from crime. Get in on the ground floor of this booming industry now!"[17] Other examples come from two major journals serving the correctional industry, *Corrections Today* and *The American Jail* (*Corrections Today* is the leading prison trade magazine, and the amount of advertising it carried tripled in the 1980s). We sampled a few issues of these two journals and found advertisements everywhere. Among the companies advertising their products are the following:[18]

> Prison Health Services, Inc., a company that has, since 1978, "delivered complete, customized healthcare programs to correctional facilities only. The first company in the U.S. to specialize in this area, we can deliver your program the fastest, and back it up with services that are simply the best."

> Southwest Microwave, Inc., manufactures fence security. Their latest invention, known as "Micronet 750," is "more than a sensor improvement"; it is "a whole new paradigm in fence detection technology."

> Acorn Engineering, Inc., makes stainless steel fixtures known as "Penal-Ware" (lavatories, toilets, showers, etc.) and the "Master-Trol" electronic valve system.

> Rotondo Precast, Inc., boasts "over 21,000 cells…and growing."

> Nicholson's BesTea provides "tea for two or…two thousand."… "Now mass-feeding takes a giant stride forward."

> Northwest Woolen Mills manufactures blankets. Their slogan is "We've got you covered."

> "Prison on Wheels" from Motor Coach Industries offers an "Inmate Security Transportation Vehicle."

We found more than two hundred different companies listed in these sources. But that is a mere sampling, for there is now a Web site known as "Corrections Yellow Pages" (http:// www.correctionsyellowpages.com; see also http://www.corrections.com). There are at least a thousand different ads on this site.

The American Jail Association, during its annual meeting, advertised many new products. (The annual meeting of the American Correctional Association has an even greater display of advertisers.) Advertising included lines such as "Tap into the Sixty-Five Billion Local Jails Market" and "Jails Are BIG BUSINESS."[19] The Correctional Medical Services company provides medical care to around 150,000 inmates, three times as many as the company "served" in 1987, as reported in a *USA Today* article appropriately titled "Prison Business Is a Blockbuster."[20]

You can get some idea of the magnitude of this industry and the profits to be made by thinking of all the businesses involved in planning, building, and operating a typical jail, prison, courthouse, or police department. Included would be architects, structural and mechanical engineers, electrical contractors, landscaping firms, security firms, bankers/ mortgage companies, furniture suppliers, food service vendors, linen services, bedding manufacturers, toiletries, medical personnel (doctors, nurses, etc., on call), and automobile companies (e.g., police cars, prison transportation vans), to name a few.

Another large component of the crime control industry is the private security industry, which includes (1) private security police ("rent-a-cops"), (2) security devices (locks, burglar alarms, auto alarms, electrified fences), and (3) gated communities.[21] Other components of this industry that might be included are the following: (1) the profits made by hospitals and insurance companies (from, for instance, hospital emergency-room visits, doctors' fees, and premiums on auto insurance and other insurance covering crime) and the salaries of those who deal with victims (e.g., doctors, nurses, paramedics, insurance adjusters); (2) the profits from the sale of books (e.g., college textbooks, trade books), magazine and journal articles, newspaper coverage (and the advertisers who profit from crime stories), television crime shows (and their advertisers) and movies about crime (with the enormous salaries paid to actors and actresses who star in them); (3) the money collected by courts through various fines (especially traffic tickets), special courses defendants can enroll in as a condition of (or in lieu of) their sentence (e.g., traffic schools, petty larceny programs); (4) the money collected by bail bondsmen; (5) the money to be made in urine testing; (6) the gun industry.

It is difficult to provide accurate dollar estimates of the money involved and the profits made by businesses in this industry, but we estimate that the total comes to at least $300 billion per year (and this is probably a gross underestimate), almost as high as the Pentagon budget. To say the least, controlling crime, both directly and indirectly, is certainly a huge and very profitable enterprise. One can easily conclude that reducing crime by any significant amount would cut a wide swath into these profits.

Because this book is about the criminal justice system—the police, courts, prisons—we provide in the next section a rough sketch of this system.

A THUMBNAIL SKETCH OF THE CRIMINAL JUSTICE SYSTEM

The criminal justice system is very complex. Criminal justice is so much more than simply making an arrest, taking the defendant to court, and sentencing him or her to prison or probation. Each subsequent chapter explores the details of this system. For now, however, let us take a brief view of this system's major components.

The Police

There are roughly 20,000 police departments, ranging from small town departments with one officer to large urban departments with 1,000 or more officers. There are nearly 1 million law enforcement employees who share a monthly payroll of more than $2 ½ billion.[22] Police agencies today can be divided into the three major branches of government: federal, state, and local (city and county). The federal law enforcement system includes well-known agencies such as the FBI, National Park Service, Border Patrol, U.S. Marshals Service, and U.S. Postal Inspector.

Law enforcement on the state level includes the state police or highway patrol, drug control agencies, fish and game control agencies, investigative bureaus (the state equivalent of the FBI), among others. County and municipal police agencies (local government) are by far the largest law enforcement group. These agencies include municipal (or city) police, county sheriffs' offices, constables, and village police departments.

The police engage in a wide variety of duties, many of which are not directly related to the control of crime (e.g., traffic control). The essential role of the police officer is both *proactive* and *reactive*. The former refers to providing routine patrol in communities in order to identify potential criminal activities and generally maintain "order" (a rather vague term that we discuss in Chapter 7). The latter refers to reacting after a crime occurs, typically by arriving at the scene, interviewing witnesses, collecting evidence, attempting to locate or identify a suspect, making the arrest, and transporting the suspect to the local jail. Also, police officers are often called on to testify during the court trial.

The Courts

It is within the court system that some key decisions are made following an arrest. In the United States there are two major court systems: federal and state. Within each system there are two general types of courts: trial and appellate. This is what is known as the *dual court system.* Trial courts are used to hear cases and decide on guilt or innocence. Appellate courts are used to hear appeals, to ensure that laws are properly interpreted, and "to devise new rules, reexamine old ones, and interpret unclear language of past court decisions or statutes."[23] In essence, the appellate courts "police" the behavior of the trial courts.

Most criminal and civil cases in the United States come before the state court system. Most of the criminal cases are heard in *trial courts of limited jurisdiction,* more commonly known as **lower courts.** These courts are variously called municipal, justice of the peace, city, magistrate, or county courts. They are usually created by local governments (cities or counties) and are not part of the larger state court system. Within these courts are heard misdemeanors, traffic cases, city ordinance cases, minor civil disputes, and the like. They are also responsible for initial appearances and preliminary hearings for felony cases. They are certainly the most numerous of the courts; they number almost 14,000 and collectively represent 84 percent of all state judicial bodies. The number of judges serving in these courts, according to the most recent count, is 18,272. They dispose of about 71 million cases each year.[24]

These lower courts are the courts most citizens come in contact with if they run afoul of the law. Cases are heard in a rather perfunctory manner (many are handled by clerks as traffic cases and many are settled by the payment of a small fine), often taking as little as a minute. It is also the ultimate in assembly-line justice. Technological advancements are constantly used to upgrade or streamline the assembly line in order to make it more efficient.

Within the court system are four crucial stages of the criminal justice process:

1. *Initial appearance.* The main purpose of this hearing is to arrange for some form of pretrial release, usually through some form of bail.
2. *Preliminary hearing.* One of the major aims of this hearing, often referred to as the "probable-cause hearing," is to determine whether there is probable cause to believe that a crime was committed and the defendant committed it.
3. *Arraignment.* During this hearing the defendant first enters a plea.
4. *Trial.* A relatively rare event (occurring in less than 10 percent of all criminal cases), this is an *adversary* procedure between the prosecutor and the defense attorney.

The Prison System

The prison system consists of a vast array of institutions designed to supervise and control convicted persons, either on a temporary basis (jails) or for a longer term (prisons) ranging from one year to life. Prison administrators, in certain jurisdictions, are given the responsibility for carrying out state-sanctioned killing (execution) under the order of a court. The prison system also consists of two very important components, *probation* and *parole*. Probation is a status reserved for persons who have been convicted but whose sentence to jail or prison has been suspended for a certain period of time, during which they are to be supervised in the community by a probation officer. Parole is a post-prison status: the person is released prior to the expiration of the sentence and technically serves the remainder of the sentence under the supervision of a parole officer. Probation is a result of a court action after conviction but in lieu of an actual term of incarceration. Parole, a prison administrative action, follows a period of incarceration. The general purpose of both is to supervise and control behavior. In some jurisdictions probation/parole officers have both probationers and parolees on their caseloads.

Correctional institution is a relatively recent term (becoming popular after World War II) and applies to jails, detention centers, reception centers, state and local prisons, and federal prisons, and the like. In recent years the number of correctional institutions has grown tremendously. Whereas in 1990 there were 1,287 prisons (80 federal and 1,207 state prisons), by 1996 there were 2,499 state prisons and 385 federal prisons, for a grand total of 2,884, an increase of 124 percent. Also, there were 2,297 state and 98 federal juvenile correctional facilities (125 federal and 1,375 state prisons).[25] The South has 629 state prison facilities, the Midwest 275, the West 267, and the Northeast 204.[26] There are more than 3,000 jails in the United States today.[27]

What is the main difference between prisons and jails? A jail serves as a *short-term* or temporary housing facility. About half of the persons in jail are awaiting their court appearance or trial; the other half are serving sentences of less than one year. A prison holds persons serving sentences of one year or more. In some instances, and generally for logistical or economic reasons, some convicted persons do much of their prison sentence in jails because of overcrowded prison facilities.

This, then, is a very brief look at the basic components of the criminal justice system. It is, in a sense, an overview of the *structure* of the system. There is, however, a *process* that takes place. Crimes are reported, arrests are made, and defendants are booked and charged with specific offenses and processed through various stages of the system. Two models attempt to describe what the criminal justice system looks like and what actually takes place within it. These two models, the *President's Commission model* and the *wedding cake model,* are the subjects of the next section.

TWO TRADITIONAL MODELS OF THE CRIMINAL JUSTICE SYSTEM

The President's Commission Model

More than thirty years ago the President's Commission on Law and Administration of Justice provided a view of the criminal justice system as a sequence of stages through which cases are processed. The **President's Commission model** of the criminal justice system has been reproduced in scores of introductory criminal justice and criminology textbooks, so there is no need to reproduce it once again. This model does little more than outline the steps or stages of the process. It suggests that the system is an efficient one in which cases are processed in a more or less orderly manner from the beginning to some point at a later stage, sometimes getting to the very end but most of the time falling out somewhere along the way.

This model is both a description of how the system is supposed to work and a prescription of how it can be improved. From this view, the system is seen as "fragmented" and even considered as a "non-system" with little coordination among the different parts. It emphasizes "efficiency" and "cost-effectiveness" as the major goals, rather than justice.[28] Also, the "Custer syndrome" operates here, which means that as long as you don't lose, you win. This outlook is typical of the mentality that drives workers within bureaucracies to keep their heads above water and maintain some semblance of control. Why else would most call this "crime control"?

The President's Commission model is misleading in other ways. It ignores the social context of the system—that is, how and why cases move through the system the way they do. It ignores the role of race, gender, and social class as determinant factors. More important, it ignores legislative process in which certain behaviors are defined as "criminal" while others are not.

The Wedding Cake Model

In contrast to the President's Commission model of criminal justice, Samuel Walker proposed what he called the **wedding cake model.** This model depicts the criminal justice system as consisting of four layers, as on a wedding cake. Walker's assumption is that the system handles different kinds of cases differently. The differences reflect disparities between cases in the four layers.[29]

The first layer consists of the small number of "celebrated" cases. The O. J. Simpson case comes to mind immediately, along with Susan Smith (convicted of killing her two sons), the Oklahoma City bombing case, the Menendez trial, and the Rodney King case, among others. Two major types of cases fall within this category. The first type involves the rich and famous (or someone whose intended victim was famous, as in the John Hinckley case, in which the victim was U.S. president Ronald Reagan). The O. J. Simpson case is the most famous example in recent history. Also included would be various examples of white-collar or corporate crime such as the savings and loan scandal and the Ford Pinto case. The second type of "celebrated" case involves individuals, such as Dolree Mapp, Ernesto Miranda, and Danny Escobedo, at the lowest end of the class system whose case ends up as a landmark Supreme Court decision. "Celebrated" cases, though constituting a minute proportion of all cases, tend to capture the public imagination and have an enormous impact on public perceptions of how the criminal justice system works. Many people conclude that they indicate how the system works, yet the exact opposite is true. The majority of cases are handled in a routine manner in a matter of minutes, and it is a rare case that ever goes before a jury.

The second and third layers consist of what Walker calls "heavy duty" felonies and "lightweight" felonies. The "heavy duty" felonies of the second layer are usually the most violent crimes (e.g., murders, robberies, rapes, and assaults) and major property crimes (e.g., burglary and grand theft). One variable that separates the two layers is whether the victims are strangers to the offender. If prosecutors believe that a particular crime is a private matter among acquaintances, the crime will be considered a "lightweight" (third-layer) felony. If the case involves a repeat offender, the case will be handled as a serious matter (a second-layer felony). In rape cases, when there has been some prior relationship between the victim and the offender, the case is viewed as a third-layer case (and often the result is dismissal of the case). Many serious cases of spouse abuse (including ex-husbands tracking down, stalking, attacking, and even killing their ex-wives) also are treated as third-layer felonies or perhaps are even relegated to the fourth layer. Several research studies have demonstrated that most of the cases in which the victims and offenders know one another either end with a dismissal or are not prosecuted as vigorously as cases involving strangers.[30]

The fourth layer is, in Walker's words, "a world unto itself." These are the cases that fill the lower courts. These are the millions of misdemeanor cases that the criminal justice system handles each year. The bulk of such cases involves public-order violations (e.g., drunkenness, disorderly conduct) or minor thefts (e.g., shoplifting). In a fascinating study Feeley found that the lower courts provide the classic illustration of assembly-line justice. Many defendants are arraigned *en masse* without the assistance of a lawyer, each case is disposed of in a matter of minutes, and the sentence is usually a light fine and rarely jail time. Feeley concluded that in such cases the "process is the punishment"—merely being present in court is punishment enough.[31] You may have experienced fourth-layer proceedings if you ever went to court to pay a traffic ticket, especially if you wanted to plead your case to the judge in the hope of leniency (or a reduction of the fine in return for attending traffic school).

Although the wedding cake model correctly points out that many different kinds of cases are processed through the criminal justice system, the focus of the model is mostly toward (1) the decisions of those who work in the system—particularly actors of the court (e.g., prosecutors, defense attorneys, and judges)—and (2) the relationship between victims and offenders. We glimpse the role of power and status in such decisions and see that race, class, and gender may influence outcomes, but such factors are not often made explicit and do not form the centerpiece of the model. Further, like the President's Commission model, the wedding cake model does not direct us into an inquiry into the lawmaking process—that is, into how certain behaviors come to be defined as "criminal" while others are not. Also, the surrounding economic and political systems, with their class, racial, and gender inequalities, are taken for granted. Neither the wedding cake nor the President's Commission model addresses the question of why the defendants (and many victims as well) are disproportionately racial minorities and the poor, especially those that end up doing time in jails and prisons.

For those and related reasons we offer a theoretical explanation of criminal justice that illuminates the underbelly of the system. Such an explanation must not be confined to the promotion of efficiency, and it must not be limited to how an institution ought to operate. Such an explanation should not be limited to explaining the obvious but should venture into that which is not obvious. Thus, our real goal in writing this book is the furtherance of social justice. It is to this goal that we now turn.

THE CRIMINALIZATION MODEL

There is a lot of truth to the saying "Money talks." "Money" was the title of a song originally made popular in 1960 by Barrett Strong. One line of this song says that money doesn't buy everything, but what it doesn't buy is of little use. In general, we can say that the greater the amount of money and other resources you have at your disposal, the greater will be the likelihood of getting your way in spite of opposition. This applies not only to receiving justice but also to getting elected to office, getting a good education, being healthy, becoming wealthy, and and enjoying thousands of other aspects of the good life, however you define it.

In common parlance the "other aspects" include things like connections, "juice," contacts. What this boils down to is social class. As one writer puts it, class counts.[32] Social class determines nearly everything that matters in a capitalist society, so why should it not affect criminal justice? This simple idea forms the basis of our **criminalization model.**

Whether a certain behavior is considered "criminal," whether a person is arrested and charged with a "crime," and a person's fate after being arrested and charged depend largely on social class. However, as so much research has demonstrated (much of it to be reviewed in subsequent chapters), race and gender also have a significant bearing on criminal justice outcomes. When we examine various stages of the criminal justice system in detail, you will see that the odds of being arrested, charged, convicted, and sentenced to prison (or death) are greater the lower a person is in the social class hierarchy, and greater still for persons who are racial minorities, especially males. Women do not fare too well either, especially those who are poor and racial minorities.[33]

The Process of Criminalization

A complete understanding of criminal justice requires, initially, a description of the process itself. Indeed, before we can realize a truly just legal system, we must comprehend what this system really is and how it works on a daily basis. The remainder of this chapter is devoted to the beginnings of this task as we describe the modern response to crime by the criminal justice system. Criminal justice is not always about responding to crime per se, but rather is about the processing of certain kinds of defendants accused of committing certain kinds of crimes. The effect of such processing amounts to *criminalization*—defining certain behaviors and persons as "criminal." Criminal justice is like a *homogenization process:* the offenses and offenders become more and more alike (in social class, race, gender, and other characteristics) the farther a person goes into the system.[34]

The criminalization process recognizes most of the major stages of the criminal justice system. It also draws attention to the political process and to the involvement of powerful interest groups and lawmakers with the selection of behaviors defined as criminal, with administrative and legislative responses to those behaviors, with the policies adopted to control predefined criminal behavior, and with the transformation of responsibility for making public policy by legislators and senior jurisdictional administrators (e.g., presidents and governors) to criminal justice officials who assume the responsibility for interpretation and implementation of those policies. In addition to the typical stages set forth in traditional models of criminal justice, which reflect much of what is normally regarded as the criminal justice process itself, we exhibit the enhanced likelihood of reentry for convicted persons and convicts back into the system—not because of the crimes they commit, or because of special attention directed toward them by criminal justice officials, but because of diminished opportunities resulting from social stigmatization and alienation.[35]

The remaining chapters of this text are devoted to a detailed examination of all of these stages. For the present, we note that the various crime control policies established at both the national and the local level ultimately determine the structure and operations of the entire criminal justice system as well as what laws are enforced. It is by definition a very political process, as many have noted.[36] These policies determine what sorts of behaviors should be considered criminal and what kinds of specific actions the criminal justice system should take. Here we find the beginning of what Quinney once referred to as the process of creating a "social reality of crime."[37] Most important perhaps is that these policies and these "realities" help determine not only the response of the major actors in the criminal justice system (police, courts, prisons) but also what kinds of persons and what sorts of acts are labeled "criminal." During certain periods of time, certain specific behaviors are singled out for special attention. The "war on drugs" and the "war on gangs" are recent examples. Many of these policies are part of what some researchers have called "moral panics," defining certain behaviors as "problems" in proportions far greater than the actual threat, and groups who are deemed offensive or threatening to those in power are targeted.[38]

A related concept that helps explain this political process is "symbolic politics."[39] This term refers to a "technique" that directs attention to certain "problems" (for instance, crime, drugs, or gangs) and simultaneously diverts the focus from larger social issues that may actually create the problems that we now concentrate on. The larger social problems that we are talking about include inequality, poverty, racism, and sexism. Declaring wars on crime, drugs, and gangs is easy for policy makers and powerful interest groups when public attention is distracted from the true causes of problems related to these phenomena. Scheingold observes that to "politicize crime" in this way diverts attention away from structural reforms, which would be far more costly, and toward individual "deviants" or the "dangerous classes."[40] Quoting Murray Edelman, Scheingold notes that "The appeal of an emphasis upon the pathologies of criminals and the utility of punishing them lies partly in what it negates: the tracing of crime to pathological social conditions." Scheingold further observes that "the power of these symbols is that they are deeply rooted in America's individualistic culture, which *increasingly* generates the kinds of insecurities that promote a yearning for scapegoats."[41] One effect of this tendency is that the criminal justice system becomes a mechanism for controlling these scapegoats, in particular members of the "underclass" or the "dangerous classes."

It is the poor, the young, ethnic minorities, and women who have the least vocal representation in both federal and state legislatures. These groups have a minimal political voice and the least amount of political influence. Consequently, these groups become easy targets for those whose interest it is to create and develop scapegoats (i.e., large businesses and corporations striving for more profit and for influence with the legislators and administrators their campaign contributions purchase). They also become easy targets for those whose function it is to control politically weak groups (i.e., the criminal justice system), and for those who implement public policies that are created and enacted by various legislative and administrative bodies. Figure 1.1 illustrates this model.

Stages in the Criminalization Process

The criminalization process begins with the legislation. During stage 1, laws are passed that determine what sorts of behaviors are deemed criminal, along with the corresponding punishments, plus state, local, and national criminal justice policies. We begin our critique by noting the influence of the persons responsible for passing such legislation and formulating social policies. A great deal of research has shown that they enjoy money and power and occupy the highest rungs in society.[42] In 1996 winners of a seat in the U.S. House of

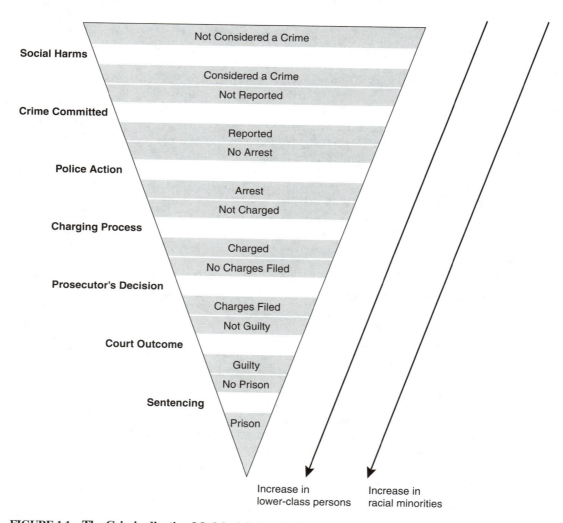

FIGURE 1.1   The Criminalization Model of Criminal Justice

Representatives spent on average $673,000 on their campaigns.[43] Soft money—campaign contributions beyond the control of campaign finance rules—as well as thousands of lobbying groups (most under the control of large corporations),[44] and many special-interest groups that do not represent the poor or minorities,[45] has had a profound impact on the drafting and passing of legislation and on public policy. The linkage between powerful interest groups and political influence lies in the control of purse strings before, during, and after elections, which often determines whether a politician keeps or loses his or her job.

Through a political process, public policies are discussed and formulated. The passage of legislation and the formulation of public policies, particularly crime policies, are often preceded by a barrage of marketing techniques directed toward the public. Isolated incidents (serial murders, school shootings, deaths resulting from illegal drugs, drive-by shootings, etc.) are amplified to the general public through elaborate media presentations (e.g., newspapers, magazines, television, radio). Nauseating details about relatively rare forms of crime are presented in a manner that leads an unquestioning public to believe that such forms of crime are commonplace. Some observers might argue that the media, protected under the First Amendment, are an unbiased entity, but we have yet to find any major media source that is not linked to a major corporation. Typically, after a media blitz attempting to persuade the public that more stringent social control measures are needed, laws become easier to pass and policies easier to craft and implement. It seems that when lawmakers are satisfied that the public is adequately frightened and willing to surrender rights for imaginary safety, laws are passed and policies established. At this juncture, the establishment of crime policy, the formal criminal justice process begins. It is important to note that in American society numerous acts result in harms done to individuals and to society as a whole. We call these behaviors *social harms*. Some of them may be treated as criminal acts.[46]

When a legislative body (e.g., state legislature) passes a law that defines a certain behavior as "criminal," it provides an agenda for persons who work within the criminal justice system. This is important to understand, because the criminal law lies at the heart and is indeed the foundation of the criminal justice system. After all, the agents of the criminal justice system (e.g., police, judges, prosecutors) are empowered to enforce criminal law (not civil law or any other form of law). For the most part, the decisions that determine what constitutes a crime are based on narrow vested interests, such as class, racial, and gender interests. Criminal laws "are formulated by those segments of society which have the power to shape public policy." Thus, lawmaking "represents the translation of specific interests into public policy."[47]

It should be noted that legislation in general (not just that which defines behavior as "criminal") involves interest groups and rarely is any piece of legislation not the product of some powerful interest group. Interest groups are organized groups of individuals who try to influence public policy decisions. Most interest groups disproportionately include people of high social standing and represent powerful corporations, rather than average citizens.[48] In many if not most cases, these are the interests of white, upper-class males who together constitute what some believe to be a "ruling class" in American society.[49] It is not by accident that many harmful acts engaged in by those of high social standing are considered misdemeanors or are not considered criminal. The people who pass these laws are predominantly individuals of high social standing (in many cases they are quite wealthy; some are even classified as millionaires), specifically upper-middle-class and upper-class white males.

Stage 2 involves the commission of a criminal act. An act that is defined as criminal and is observed by a citizen is likely to generate several responses. It is either reported or not reported to the police. (There are a number of reasons why people report and fail to report crimes they observe. We cover these reasons later.) If the act is reported, the police appear to have discretionary power to respond in one of two ways: either conducting an investigation or ignoring the report altogether.

In the aftermath of a police investigation—stage 3—the police may either make an arrest or not make an arrest. As a general rule, the more serious a violation is, the more likely the police are to make an arrest if they have a "suspect." It is not necessary to arrest the actual perpetrator, but rather a highly probable suspect. Probability may rest on detailed information, social stereotypes, or administrative pressure to "clear the case." A case is cleared by making an arrest—any arrest.

If an arrest is made, the police have the discretion to file a formal charge. Here, in stage 4, we are actually dealing with two theoretically separate substages: (1) The police are the first to charge a defendant (this procedure is commonly known as booking). (2) The district attorney's office then decides whether to accept the original charges, alter some or all of the charges, or dismiss one or more or even all of the charges. That last alternative is known as *denying the charge*. At stage 5, if the prosecutor feels the evidence against the suspect is relatively strong, court processes are likely to begin.

Stage 6 involves various court decisions. Several different court processes (or substages) may occur. One is the *initial appearance* (usually within a short time following an arrest, such as 48 or 72 hours), where it is determined whether there is sufficient evidence to hold a defendant for further action. Another hearing, known as a *preliminary hearing,* may be held. It is a sort of mini-trial in which the prosecutor and the defense attorney present some of their evidence to a judge, who then determines whether the case can be processed further. If the case is accepted, there is usually an *arraignment,* where the defendant is required to enter a plea. More often than not, a guilty plea as a result of some form of *plea bargaining,* is entered, and there is no trial. A *trial* occurs only if the defendant pleads not guilty. During the trial, the defendant's guilt or innocence is determined.

If the verdict is guilty, then the defendant moves on to stage 7, which is sentencing. During the sentencing stage the convicted person is given some form of sanction, usually probation, intermediate sanction (e.g., community service, restitution, drug treatment), or incarceration in a prison or jail.

The criminal justice process is often viewed as terminated when the final disposition of a case is reached. But the process continues, for criminal justice agents often continue to be involved in the life of the convicted person. There may be one of two forms of supervision in the community—probation (if this is the sentence established during the sentencing stage) or parole (if the individual was sentenced to prison or jail). *Probation* is formally a sentence that places the convicted offender under some form of supervision in the community for a certain period of time in lieu of going to prison or jail. *Parole* is a period of supervision in the community *following* a period of time spent in jail or prison. An offender on parole technically serves a part of the jail or prison sentence in the community. (More is said about probation and parole in Chapters 10 and 12). The individual either completes his or her period of supervision successfully or is brought back to court (in the case of probation) or to the parole board (in the case of parole) as a result of violating probation or parole or committing some other offense.

This brings to an end the formal criminal justice process, but it may not be the end for an offender. He or she may have probation or parole revoked because of the violation of some rule or the commission of a new offense. A defendant who is placed on probation must follow a number of rules and regulations. If one of these rules is violated, the state may revoke probation and send the defendant to jail or prison. A defendant who is sentenced to prison is likely to be released on parole prior to the expiration of the sentence. If parole rules are violated, the defendant may have his or her parole revoked and may be put back in prison to serve out the remainder of the original sentence, or the defendant may be given "another chance" to continue his or her community supervision. If the individual commits another crime and is caught, he or she moves into yet another stage (which could also, of course, be reached even if the individual successfully completes the period of supervision on parole or probation) and reenters the system through arrest.

Even after a conviction, every defendant has the right to file an appeal of the decision to a higher court (e.g., court of appeals, supreme court). This court (called an *appellate court*) either affirms or reverses the conviction. (More is said about these kinds of courts in Chapter 8.) If the conviction is reversed, the case goes to trial again, and the process begins again.

The foregoing presentation describes what is *supposed* to happen. What really happens varies in both time and space. As our discussion indicates, there are several critical stages during which important decisions are made.

As we examine each stage of the system, we see that the number of people involved as defendants declines. We also see increasing homogeneity among the people involved. They become more alike in age (younger), sex (more are males), race (increasingly non-white), social class (increasing numbers of lower- and working-class people and the poor), and offense (offenses typically associated with the poor and the powerless), and more have previous experience with the criminal justice system. At stage 7, we see the most homogeneous grouping: the vast majority of the people incarcerated in the nation's prisons and jails are poor, unskilled, uneducated, and well experienced in crime and have had much contact with the criminal (and juvenile) justice system.

This sifting and sorting is often based on legal criteria such as offense (especially its seriousness) and past record, but nonlegal variables such as class, race, and sex become "proxy variables" and play an important role as well. An inmate at a women's prison told Kathryn Watterson: "Money talks, bullshit walks."[50] This statement illustrates a strong feeling among many inmates (and noninmates) that if you have money and power you may never go to prison no matter what kind of offense you commit. There is certainly much truth to this notion. Money does in fact buy a person's freedom, and in many cases a lot of money has to be spent to prove one's innocence.

Reiman argues that "the criminal justice system effectively weeds out the well-to-do, so that at the *end of the road in prison,* the vast majority of those we find there come from the lower classes." He further asserts:

> This "weeding out" process starts before the agents of law enforcement go into action.... [O]ur very definition of crime *excludes* a wide variety of actions at least as dangerous as those included and often worse.... Even before we mobilize our troops in the war on crime, we have already guaranteed that large numbers of upper-class individuals will never come within their sights.... At each step, from arresting to sentencing, the likelihood of being ignored or released or lightly treated by the system is greater the better off one is economically.[51]

One important factor that is linked to class position and criminal justice is **power.** Michael Parenti gives as good a definition as anyone:

> By "power" I mean the ability to get what one wants, either by having one's interests prevail in conflicts with others or by preventing others from raising their demands. Power presumes the ability to manipulate the social environment to one's advantage. Power belongs to those who possess the resources that enable them to shape the political agenda and control the actions and beliefs of others, resources such as jobs, organization, technology, publicity, media, social legitimacy, expertise, essential goods and services, organized force, and—the ingredient that often determines the availability of these things—money.[52]

Power can be achieved either by force or by being able to get someone "to think and believe in accordance with your interests."[53] Power achieved in the latter way is more long lasting. Those who have this type of power are able to influence legislation to their own advantage or to the disadvantage of others. Power also allows certain individuals with "pull" to avoid detection of criminal acts, prevent acts from being defined as criminal, or, if caught, avoid or at least minimize punishment.

Traditional models of criminal justice fail to address most of the issues brought forth by our critical model—which leads us to ask, What sort of theoretical perspectives have generally been used to explain the criminal justice system? How have academics and practitioners explained the criminal justice system? Traditionally, two perspectives have been used: the *classical* and the *positivist* schools of thought, which also happen to be the two most popular schools of criminology used to explain criminal behavior. Chapter 3 reviews these two views. After that review we discuss further our own *critical* perspective on criminal justice.

We would be remiss, in this opening chapter, not to give at least a brief summary of the concept of social class and a sketch of the class structure of U.S. society. It is also appropriate to review the extent of social inequality in the United States, given that social inequality stems directly from the class structure. We do so in the next section.

SOCIAL INEQUALITY AND CLASS STRUCTURE IN THE UNITED STATES

U.S. society is characterized by a tremendous amount of inequality. The share of the total wealth (land, stocks, bonds, etc.) going to the top wealth-holders has increased in recent years. One percent of the households got 40 percent of all household wealth in 1997, doubling from about 20 percent in 1976. The largest increases came during the boom years of the 1980s (going from about 25% to about 36% during the decade). During this same period, all other households received proportionately less.[54] Overall inequality, measured by what is known as the **Gini Index of Inequality** (a scale where 0 means everyone earns the same amount and 1 means one person earns all), has gone up since the late 1960s. In 1970 the index for the United States was 0.353; in 1996 it was 0.425, higher than for any other industrialized nation.[55]

The super-rich reaped the most benefits from the trickle-down economics of the 1980s. The wealthiest 10 percent received 85 percent of the stock market gains between 1989 and 1997. According to *Business Week*'s annual survey of executive salaries, the average CEO (chief executive officer) earned 419 times the pay of the average worker in 1998, up from a ratio of 42 to 1 in 1980! Indeed, the rich are getting richer and practically everyone else is getting poorer.[56] And most of the increase has been the result of the tax reforms of the Reagan–Bush years in the 1980s, resulting in an estimated $1 trillion going to the very rich.[57] One study found that between 1977 and 1994 the share of after-tax-income of the top 1 percent of all families increased by 72 percent, compared to a decrease of 16 percent by the bottom 20 percent of all families.[58]

As measured in real dollars (what money will actually buy), the paycheck of the average American worker has shrunk. In 1973 the average weekly paycheck was $502 (in 1998 dollars); by 1998 it had shrunk by 12 percent to $442. Meanwhile, what these workers actually produced (their productivity) increased by about one-third. In other words, workers produced more for the owners while getting proportionately less. And, as previously suggested, the owners gained quite a bit, to say the least! Between 1977 and 1994, for instance, the top 1 percent of families saw their after-tax income go up by 72 percent, while the bottom 20 percent of families saw theirs *decrease* by 16 percent.[59]

As of 1995, 18.5 percent of all households had either zero or negative net worth, up from 15.5 percent in 1983. In 1976, 10 percent of the population owned 49 percent of all wealth; by 1999, 10 percent owned 73 percent of all wealth![60] Meanwhile, the savings rate among Americans dropped, going from around 11 percent in 1984 to about 2 percent in 1999; correlated with this decline is the rising number of personal bankruptcy filings, doubling from 1990 to 1999 while personal debts doubled from 1990 to 1997 (from $243 billion to $560 billion).[61]

Likewise, the proportion of Americans living in poverty has increased. As inequality has grown, the social conditions of the most disadvantaged sectors of society have worsened. Massive cutbacks on social spending for programs for the poor have been especially devastating to children. Indeed, one of the most striking facts is that more than one in five children (and over half of all African American children) now live in poverty. Millions more live in near-poverty conditions. The definition of *poverty* is based on a certain amount of money needed for a low standard of living—typically a bare-bones minimum level such as $16,450 for a family of four as of 1998. According to this criterion, 13.3 percent of all Americans were living in poverty as of 1997; for children (under 18) the rate was 20 percent. Not surprisingly, racial differences are significant. For both African Americans and Hispanics the rate was about 27 percent, more than double the rate for whites (11 percent). For African American and Hispanic children the rates were about 37 percent.[62]

This cutoff point has been based on the same rationale since the 1960s. It was calculated by taking the amount of money needed for a "subsistence diet" and multiplying it by 3, updated for inflation. However, as many critics point out, food costs now constitute a much smaller share of family budgets, and rent and transportation costs have increased and now constitute a larger share of household expenditures. Most critics contend that the official poverty rate should be raised by at least 50 percent. If this standard were used, the official poverty rate would increase to 22.5 percent, and the percentage of the poor under 18 would jump up to about 31 percent. For African Americans and Hispanics, the rates would be 40 and 43 percent, respectively; for African American and Hispanic children, the rates would be 52 and 56 percent, respectively.[63]

The distribution of wealth and income is directly connected to the social class structure of the United States. There are many definitions of the term *social class*. Sociologists do not agree on a single definition. Also, there is little agreement among sociologists about what the class structure looks like—that is, about how many social classes there are. Nevertheless, we need to provide some kind of definition, knowing full well that it will not satisfy everyone. We draw from the definitions given by two different sociologists, Robert Rothman and Martin Marger. By **social class** we mean groups of individuals or families who have about the same income and occupation and have a similar position within the larger system of economic production in an industrial society.[64]

The class structure of the United States can be seen as a system consisting of six major classes (see Table 1.2). These social groupings are differentiated mainly by the amount of income and wealth families or individuals have, by the sources of such income

TABLE 1.2 The American Class Structure

CLASS	PERCENTAGE	SALARY RANGE	SOURCE OF INCOME	TYPICAL OCCUPATION
Upper	1–2	>$1 million	Assets*	Investors, corporate executives
Upper-middle	14–20	$80,000–$1,000,000	Salaries	Upper-level managers, professionals, small-business owners
Lower-middle	25–30	$35,000–$75,000	Salaries and wages	Lower-level managers, semiprofessionals, small-business owners, craftspersons
Working	20–30	$25,000–$40,000	Wages	Low-skilled workers, clerical, retail sales, some service workers
Working poor	10–15	$12,000–$25,000	Wages	Lowest-level skills, low-level service, unskilled workers
Underclass	8–12	<$12,000	Public assistance; "underground economy"	Unemployed

*Assets include mostly stocks and bonds and other investments, land, companies owned, and so on. Most of the very rich got their start from inheritances.

Source: Rothman, R. A. *Inequality and Stratification* (3rd ed.). Upper Saddle River, NJ: Prentice-Hall, 1999, p. 7; Marger, M. N. *Social Inequality.* Mountain View, CA: Mayfield, 1999, p. 28; Gilbert, D. *The American Class Structure* (5th ed.). Belmont, CA: Wadsworth, 1998, p. 15.

and wealth (mostly from earned income but at the upper level from assets such as land, stocks, and bonds), and by the amount of education individuals have.

In the context of crime and criminal justice it is important to note that a person's social class—plus race and gender—has direct and indirect consequences, especially on what sociologists refer to as **life chances.** We are referring to a person's or a family's odds for having a supply of goods and services, living conditions, and various personal life experiences. Life chances include infant mortality, the opportunity to go to college (and, more important, to what kind of college), choice of occupation, income and wealth, health and longevity (class relates to all sorts of physical and mental illnesses), the risk of being a victim of a crime, the likelihood of being an offender, and, if an offender, the chances of getting arrested, being convicted, going to jail or prison, and receiving the death penalty.

It is certainly true that in the United States, in contrast to most other societies, there is greater mobility between classes, and most of the movement is *upward*—from one class to the class immediately above it. In the six-class structure indicated in Table 1.2, most mobility would occur from the lower-middle class to the upper-middle class and from the working class to the lower-middle class. It should also be pointed out that in recent years there has been a great deal of *downward* mobility. On the whole, however, most people born into a certain social class tend to remain in that class their entire lives. Whatever movement takes place, either upward or downward, results mostly from a combination of structural changes in the economy beyond the control of the average person (e.g., corporate downsizing, technological changes that eliminate jobs), the accident of birth, situational factors (being in the right place at the right time), educational attainment (which directly relates to class and race), and plain old-fashioned luck.[65]

What needs to be underscored is the power-plus-privileges that goes with being among the small percentage of upper-class people. Those in the top 1 or 2 percent essentially run the country. They pass most of the laws, they create all sorts of social policies (both foreign and domestic), they help themselves and their "classmates" get elected (look at the close correlation between campaign contributions and social class), and they control the lion's share of the country's assets. Little wonder that this class is often given names "ruling class," "dominant class," "governing class," or simply "the powers that be."[66]

Several other things should also be noted. People at the bottom of the social class structure—the working poor and the underclass—have practically no power and no resources, both of which are necessary to resist being labeled "criminal." The lower you go on this social class structure, the more likely you are to find racial minorities. African American families, for example, are about three times more likely than white families to be living in poverty.[67] Gender also strongly relates to inequality. Women are far more likely than men to be single parents and to be poor if they are single parents. Women earn far less than men. One reason for this disparity is that they so often work part time. Another is that they are employed in occupations with the lowest earnings, such as clerical and secretarial work.[68]

Given such huge disparities in wealth and power, is it possible to have anything resembling "equal justice"? As David Cole notes in his book *No Equal Justice,* there are two systems of justice in the United States: one for the privileged, another for the nonprivileged.[69]

SUMMARY

We began this chapter with the observation that the basis of the U.S. system of criminal justice is found within the legislative, executive, and judicial branches of U.S. government. The U.S. Constitution provides for the creation of laws by state legislatures and Congress. Executive-branch officials and the courts are given authority, through provisions in the Constitution, to enforce these laws. The criminal justice system is the instrument designated by executive-branch officials to enforce laws that pertain to criminal behavior.

We described the basic components of the criminal justice system: the police, (including a vast array of local, state, and federal agencies), the courts, and the prison system. Each component is involved in different stages of the criminal justice process.

We reviewed two traditional models of the criminal justice system. The President's Commission model does little more than outline the steps or stages of the process. It suggests that the system is an efficient one in which cases are processed in a more or less orderly manner from the beginning to some point at a later stage, sometimes getting to the very end but most of the time falling out somewhere along the way. The wedding cake model, proposed by Samuel Walker, depicts the criminal justice system as consisting of four layers, as on a wedding cake. Walker's assumption is that the system handles different kinds of cases differently. The differences reflect disparities between cases in the four layers.

We set forth our criminalization model. We view criminal justice as a process that is not always about responding to crime per se, but rather is about the processing of certain kinds of defendants accused of committing certain kinds of crimes. The effect of such processing amounts to criminalization—defining certain behaviors and persons as "criminal." The criminal justice process also results in "homogenization": the offenses and offenders become more and more alike (in social class, race, gender, and other characteristics) the farther a person goes into the system. A key variable in understanding the criminalization model is power. Essentially, power or the lack of it determines how one is processed. Differences in power (based on criteria such as race, sex, and social class) determine what kinds of behavior and which people are deemed criminal and thus processed through the system. Social class, race, and gender have significant consequences on individuals' life chances, including the likelihood of getting arrested, being convicted, going to prison, and receiving the death penalty.

KEY TERMS

crime control industry   4
criminalization model   10
Gini Index of Inequality   16
life chances   18

lower courts   7
power   15
President's Commission model   8
social class   17

three branches of the U.S. government (executive, legislative, judicial)   3
wedding cake model   9

NOTES

1. See *Trends in Justice Expenditure and Employment.* Washington, DC: U.S. Department of Justice, Bureau of Justice Statistics, NCJ 178268, 2000 (Online).

2. See Shelden, R. G., and W. B. Brown. "The Crime Control Industry and the Management of the Surplus Population." *Critical Criminology* 9: 39–62 (Spring 2001).

3. Hagan, J. "Why Is There So Little Criminal Justice Theory?" *Journal of Research in Crime and Delinquency* 26: 116–135 (1989).

4. Zalman, M., and L. Siegel. *Cases and Comments on Criminal Procedure.* St. Paul: West, 1994, p. 13.

5. Turkel, G. *Law and Society: Critical Approaches.* Boston: Allyn and Bacon, 1996, p. 200.

6. The only instance in which we can remotely identify rewards for not committing crimes might be found in "weapons buy-back" programs that have taken place in some inner cities. In these instances, people may bring in handguns (legal or illegal) to the police and receive payment for their effort without *any questions*. Such programs might be considered rewarding people for turning in registered or unregistered firearms.

7. Domhoff, W. *Who Rules America? Power and Politics in the Year 2000.* Mountain View, CA: Mayfield, 1998; Domhoff, W. *The Power Elite and the State.* New York: Aldine de Gruyter, 1990; Bennett, W. L. *Inside the*

System: Culture, Institutions, and Power in American Politics. New York: Harcourt Brace, 1994, pp. 439–442.

8. Duneier, M. *Sidewalk.* New York: Farrar, Straus and Giroux, 1999.

9. Maguire, K., and A. L. Pastore (eds.). *Sourcebook of Criminal Justice Statistics—1998.* Washington, DC: U.S. Department of Justice, Bureau of Justice Statistics, 1999.

10. Shelden and Brown, "The Crime Control Industry"; Parenti, C. *Lockdown America: Police and Prisons in the Age of Crisis.* New York: Verso, 1999.

11. Quinney, R. *Class, State and Crime* (2nd ed.). New York: Longman, 1980, p. 133.

12. President's Commission on Law Enforcement and Administration of Justice. *The Challenge of Crime in a Free Society.* Washington, DC: U.S. Government Printing Office, 1967, p. 1.

13. Maguire and Pastore, *Sourcebook of Criminal Justice Statistics—1998.*

14. Chambliss, W. J. *Power, Politics, and Crime.* Boulder, CO: Westview Press, 1999, p. 5; Dyer, J. *The Perpetual Prisoner Machine.* Boulder, CO: Westview Press, 2000.

15. Maguire and Pastore, *Sourcebook of Criminal Justice Statistics—1998.*

16. Shelden, R. G. *Controlling the Dangerous Classes: A Critical Introduction to the History of Criminal Justice.* Boston: Allyn and Bacon, 2001, ch. 7.

17. Silverstein, K. "America's Private Gulag." In D. Burton-Rose (ed.), *The Celling of America: An Inside Look at the U.S. Prison Industry.* Monroe, ME: Common Courage Press. 1998, p. 156.

18. *Corrections Today,* August 1996.

19. Donziger, S. *The Real War on Crime.* New York: Harper/Collins, 1996, p. 93.

20. Meddis, S. V., and D. Sharp. "Prison Business Is a Blockbuster." *USA Today* (December 1994, p. 13).

21. See Shelden and Brown, "The Crime Control Industry," for a more complete listing.

22. Maguire and Pastore, *Sourcebook of Criminal Justice Statistics—1998.*

23. Neubauer, D. W. *America's Courts and the Criminal Justice System* (5th ed.). Belmont, CA: Wadsworth, 1996, p. 45.

24. Ibid., p. 51.

25. Rush, G. *Inside American Prisons and Jails.* Incline Village, NV: Copperhouse, 1997, p. 157.

26. Maguire and Pastore, *Sourcebook of Criminal Justice Statistics—1998.*

27. Allen, H. E., and C. E. Simonsen. *Corrections in America* (8th ed.). Englewood Cliffs, NJ: Prentice-Hall, 1998, p. 170.

28. Walker, S. *Sense and Nonsense about Crime and Drugs* (4th ed.). Belmont, CA: Wadsworth, 1997, p. 15.

29. Ibid., p. 16.

30. Ibid.

31. Feeley, M. *The Process Is the Punishment.* New York: Russell Sage Foundation, 1979.

32. Wright, E. O. *Class Counts.* New York: Cambridge University Press, 2000.

33. For documentation see Shelden, *Controlling the Dangerous Classes.*

34. Newton, C. H., R. G. Shelden, and S. W. Jenkins. "The Homogenization Process within the Juvenile Justice System." *International Journal of Criminology and Penology* 3: 213–227 (1975); Shelden, R. G. *Criminal Justice in America: A Sociological Approach.* Boston: Little Brown, 1982.

35. Irwin, J. *The Felon.* Englewood Cliffs, NJ: Prentice-Hall, 1970. Terry, C. M. "Beyond Punishment: Perpetuating Differences from the Prison Experience." *Humanity and Society* 24:108–135 (2000); Richards, S. C. *Structure of Prison Release: An Extended Case Study of Prison Release, Work Release, and Parole.* New York: McGraw-Hill, 1995.

36. Scheingold, S. A. *The Politics of Law and Order: Street Crime and Public Policy.* New York: Longman, 1984; Scheingold, S. A. *The Politics of Street Crime.* Philadelphia: Temple University Press, 1991.

37. Quinney, R. *The Social Reality of Crime.* Boston: Little, Brown, 1970.

38. Cohen, S. *Folk Devils and Moral Panics: The Creation of the Mods and Rockets.* London: MacGibbon and Kee, 1972; Hall, S., C. Critcher, T. Hefferson, J. Clarke, and B. Roberts. *Policing the Crisis: Mugging, the State, and Law and Order.* New York: Holmes and Meier, 1978; Goode, E., and N. Ben-Yehuda. *Moral Panics: The Social Construction of Deviance.* Cambridge, MA: Blackwell, 1994.

39. Edelman, M. *Constructing the Political Spectacle.* Chicago: University of Chicago Press, 1988; Scheingold, *The Politics of Street Crime;* Gordon, D. *The Justice Jug-gernaut.* New Brunswick, NJ: Rutgers University Press, 1990.

40. Gordon, D. *The Return of the Dangerous Classes: Drug Prohibition and Policy Politics.* New York: Norton, 1994.

41. Scheingold, *The Politics of Street Crime,* p. 173.

42. Domhoff, *Who Rules America?* See also Domhoff, W. *The Powers That Be.* New York: Random House, 1979; Quinney, R., *Critique of Legal Order: Crime Control in Capitalist Society.* New Brunswick, NJ: Transaction Books, 2002 (originally published in 1974); Chambliss, W. J., and M. S. Zatz (eds.). *Making Law: The State, the Law, and Structural Contradictions.* Bloomington: Indiana University Press, 1993.

43. Harrigan, J. *Empty Dreams, Empty Pockets: Class and Bias in American Politics.* New York: Addison-Wesley Longman, 2000.

44. Simon, D., and J. Hagan. *White Collar Deviance.* Boston: Allyn and Bacon, 1999.

45. Domhoff, *Who Rules America?*

46. Michalowksi, R. *Order, Law and Crime.* New York: Macmillan, 1985; and Reiman, J. H. *The Rich Get Richer and the Poor Get Prison* (6th ed.). Boston: Allyn and Bacon, 2001.

47. Quinney, *The Social Reality of Crime,* p. 43.

48. Janda K., J. M. Berry, and J. Goldman. *The Challenge of Democracy: Government in America* (3rd ed.). Boston: Houghton Mifflin, 1993, pp. 339–368; see also Bennett, *Inside the System,* p. 304.

49. For documentation of the existence of this "ruling class" see, e.g., Mills, C. W. *The Power Elite.* New York: Oxford University Press, 1956; Domhoff, *Who Rules America?* and *The Powers That Be;* and Domhoff, W. *The Higher Circles.* New York: Random House, 1970.

50. Watterson, K. *Women in Prison: Inside the Concrete Womb.* Boston: Northeastern University Press, 1996, p. 18.

51. Reiman, *The Rich Get Richer and the Poor Get Prison,* 110.

52. Parenti, M. *Democracy for the Few* (7th ed.). Boston: Bedford/St. Martin's, 2002, p. 4.

53. Eitzen, D. S., and M. B. Zinn. *In Conflict and Order* (8th ed.). Boston: Allyn and Bacon, 1998, p. 403. Getting someone to think and believe in accordance with your own interests suggests the use of propaganda as a method of thought control. On this subject see Chomsky, N. *Necessary Illusions: Thought Control in Democratic Societies.* Boston: South End Press, 1989; and Parenti, M. *Power and the Powerless.* New York: St. Martin's Press, 1978; and Parenti, M. *Land of Idols: Political Mythology in America.* New York: St. Martin's Press, 1994.

54. Sklar, H. "Let Them Eat Cake." *Z Magazine* (November 1998); Collins, C., B. Leondar-Wright, and H. Sklar. *Shifting Fortunes: The Perils of the Growing American Wealth Gap.* Boston: United for a Fair Economy, 1999, p. 10. See also Heintz, J., N. Folbre, and the Center for Popular Economics. *The Ultimate Field Guide to the U.S. Economy.* New York: New Press, 2000; and Collins, C., and F. Yeskel. *Economic Apartheid in America.* New York: New Press, 2000.

55. Miringoff, M., and M. Miringoff. *The Social Health of the Nation.* New York: Oxford University Press, 1999, p. 105.

56. Sklar, H. "For CEO's, a Minimum Wage in the Millions." *Z Magazine* (July/August, 1999). See also the following studies for further confirmation of the increase in inequality: Collins et al., *Shifting Fortunes,* pp. 11–13; Wolff, E., "Trends in Household Wealth in the United States, 1962–83 and 1983–98." *Review of Income and Wealth* (Series 40, no. 2), June 1994; Wolff, E., *Top Heavy: A Study of Increasing Inequality of Wealth in America.* New York: Twentieth Century Fund Press, 1995; Phillips, K. *The Politics of the Rich and the Poor.* New York: Random House, 1990; Domhoff, *Who Rules America?*

57. Bartlett, D. L., and J. B. Steele. *America: What Went Wrong?* Kansas City, MO: Andrews and McMeel, 1992. Bartlett and Steele note that as a result of the 1986 "Tax Reform Act" the average 1989 tax savings for those earning $1 million or more came to $281,033 (a tax cut of 31%), compared to $37 for those earning less than $10,000 (an 11% tax cut). They also found that during the 1980s the increase in salaries of people earning more than $1 million per year came to 2,184 percent.

58. Shapiro, I., and R. Greenstein. "Trends in the Distribution of After-Tax Income: An Analysis of Congressional Budget Office Data." Washington, DC: Center on Budget and Policy Priorities, August 14, 1997.

59. Collins et al., *Shifting Fortunes,* pp. 27–32.

60. Collins and Yeskel, *Economic Apartheid in America,* p. 55.

61. Ibid., pp. 19–21.

62. Collins et al., *Shifting Fortunes,* p. 29.

63. Ibid. See also Heintz et al., *The Ultimate Field Guide to the U.S. Economy,* pp. 106–108.

64. Rothman, R. A. *Inequality and Stratification* (3rd ed.). Upper Saddle River, NJ: Prentice-Hall, 1999, p. 5; Marger, M. N. *Social Inequality.* Mountain View, CA: Mayfield, 1999, p. 364. For a variation, see Gilbert, D. *The American Class Structure* (5th ed.). Belmont, CA: Wasworth, 1998, p. 15.

65. Marger, *Social Inequality,* pp. 153–157.

66. Numerous citations can be given to document these assertions. See the works cited in notes 49, 53, 59, and 60. See especially Parenti, *Democracy for the Few,* ch. 2.

67. Rothman, *Inequality and Stratification,* p. 91.

68. Ibid., pp. 83–84.

69. Cole, D. *No Equal Justice: Race and Class in the American Criminal Justice System.* New York: New Press, 1999, p. 9.

CHAPTER TWO

THE PROBLEM OF CRIME IN AMERICAN SOCIETY

DEFINITIONS OF CRIME

If you stop people on the street and ask them what "crime" is or ask them to give an example of crime, they would probably mention murder, robbery, rape, and burglary. We frequently ask students this question in our criminal justice courses. Students mention those offenses most often. Drunk driving, domestic violence, and drug-law violations are other crimes included in their responses.

These responses are not surprising, for we are confronted day and night by newspaper and television stories about murder, robbery, illegal drug sales, drunk driving, and so on. Local police and other criminal justice agencies furnish crime statistics about these kinds of offenses, and we hear ghastly details on the evening news or read about them in our local newspapers. However, as Bourdieu points out, "a very high proportion of the population reads no newspaper at all and is dependent on television as their sole source of news."[1] Television crime shows and major motion pictures reinforce our perceptions of crime by focusing much of their attention on murder and other violent offenses. Since the late 1960s politicians, in the true fashion of demagogues, have been creating fear among members of society by promoting the notion that we are at great risk of being victimized at any time by a murderer, rapist, burglar, or robber. This fear mongering is particularly evident during election years. Candidates for public office decry the breakdown in "law and order" and urge crackdowns on "street crimes." All of these factors contribute to and reinforce the popular image of crime. "We ought to have concerns about crime, drug addiction, child abuse, and other afflictions," argues Glassner; but he also asks, "How have we gotten so mixed up about the true nature and extent of these problems?"[2] The answer to Glassner's question rests within the notion of distortion—distorting the reality of crime.

The popular image of crime is, as Reiman says, like the image in a "carnival mirror" that distorts reality. When we think of a criminal, often the first image that comes to mind is a young minority male who commits a murder, robbery, rape, or some other "popular" criminal act. However, the threat posed by the "typical criminal," as Reiman notes, "is not the gravest threat to which we are exposed."[3] The acts of a street criminal are not the only ones that put us in danger, nor are they the ones that are most threatening. The costs of crimes committed by wealthy and powerful people far exceed those that are reflected in the popular image of crime.

As previously mentioned, the media, officials of the criminal justice system, and politicians reinforce stereotypes of "typical criminals" and "typical crimes" on a daily basis. More than twenty years ago, Richard Quinney wrote, "The social reality of crime is basically constructed from the criminal conceptions held by the most powerful segments of society."[4] You don't find many corporate offenders portrayed on *America's Most Wanted, NYPD Blue, CSI (Crime Scene Investigation), The Agency, The District, Law and Order,* and so on. In "infotainment" programs such as those, you are not likely to see corporate offenders on the hoods of police cars, lying face-down in the street with a police officer's foot on their back, or in the booking room. Those shows, with few exceptions, reinforce popular images of crime. Real life is different. High-ranking executives of Enron Corporation were charged with serious crimes, yet none was approached by the police and taken away in handcuffs.

We are told that the goal of the criminal justice system is to protect us from the most serious threats. If we, as a society, believe this claim and watch as the criminal justice system directs its resources to street crimes, we begin to believe the distortion that crimes such as murder, robbery, and burglary actually pose the gravest threats to our well-being. But thousands of people die each year from unnecessary surgeries and wrongly prescribed drugs, and many more die, or are injured, from occupational accidents and diseases that result from negligent employers.[5] Thus, we are deceived into thinking about the dangers associated with street crime while the larger dangers remain obscured. In this way the criminal justice system contributes to popular images of crime.

The concept of crime has many different meanings. It may mean one thing to the average citizen and quite another to people who work within the criminal justice system (police, lawyers, judges). The concept of crime also has different meanings to those who study the crime problem: criminologists.

The most common definitions of crime come from the law itself, in particular the criminal law. Criminologists state quite categorically that crime exists only in the legal codes of the state. One such classic definition came in the 1930s from two criminologists who wrote that "the most precise and least ambiguous definition of crime is that which defines it as behavior which is prohibited by the criminal code."[6] Thus, crime is defined as a violation of criminal law. This legalistic definition has been the subject of extensive criticism.

Some critics suggest that there are two basic concepts of crime—the legal concept and the social/popular concept. The **legal concept of crime** refers to crime as a "legal category assigned to conduct by authorized agents of the state." Legislators are the authorized agents of the state who introduce and enact laws. The **social/popular concept of crime** refers to "conduct that does not necessarily involve either the violation of a criminal law or the application of the legal category to the conduct."[7] Some have suggested that criminology should not be limited to the study of the violation of criminal laws but instead should examine the violation of "conduct norms."[8] The American criminologist Edwin Sutherland once argued that criminologists should expand their focus to include illegal corporate behavior.[9] Other criminologists argue that there should be a "human rights" definition of crime. Such a definition would include many behaviors, in addition to certain structural features of modern society, that result in tremendous harm to people. The "human rights" definition would include institutional arrangements in society that violate basic human rights. Among these human rights violations are sexism, racism, and imperialism. Additional violations include unsafe working conditions, inadequate opportunities for employment and education, substandard housing, and lack of access to medical care.[10]

Many other critics have argued for extending the definition of crime to those areas.[11] However, we must avoid expanding the definition to include what some critics refer to as an "everything-but-the-kitchen-sink" list of all theoretically possible harms.[12] Instead, we must consider the acts that pose the gravest threats to human beings. Perhaps the real question, in response to those critics, is which threats and which human beings. If you are rich or well-to-do, you are more likely to enjoy the lion's share of human rights. When these rights are applied to the working and lower classes, concern about the kitchen sink comes to the forefront. We say more on this topic shortly. Our point here is that the agreement about what constitutes a crime is far from universal. Many acts, some of them falling under the criminal law, are committed by people of wealth and power and do far more damage to society and to other people than do murder, robbery, burglary, and other commonly accepted "crimes."

However, for our purposes here, we need to focus first on the legalistic definition because this definition represents the foundation of the criminal justice system. It is the source of the behaviors that call forth responses from the various components of this system.[13]

In seeking understanding of the problem of crime and hence the criminal justice system, it is first necessary to go to the ultimate source, the criminal law, because according to the legalistic definition **crime** is a violation of a criminal law or statute. Thus, in a sense, crime is actually "created" through the passage of criminal laws. However, it is not as simple as this, for, as Reiman notes, the label "crime" is often misapplied. The "decisions as to what to label and treat as crime are not compelled by objective dangers, and thus to understand the reality of crime, we must look to the social processes that shape those decisions."[14] One of our major goals in writing this book is to examine the processes that help shape the reality of crime and criminal justice. In Chapter 3 we begin this understanding by distinguishing between criminal law, which defines what behaviors are crimes and determines the activities of the criminal justice system, and other forms of law, especially civil law. For now, however, it is imperative that we develop an understanding of how crimes and criminal become classified.

CLASSIFICATIONS OF CRIME

Criminal behavior includes a wide variety of acts prohibited by legal codes. These acts range from the most serious, such as homicide and rape, to the most innocuous, such as loitering. There are several ways to classify crimes and simplify an understanding of the problem of crime. Some common methods of classifying crime are now discussed.

Felonies and Misdemeanors

One of the most common methods of classifying crimes is to distinguish between felonies and misdemeanors. A **felony** is a crime punishable by a year or more in prison. Some common examples of felonies are homicide, rape, and robbery. A **misdemeanor** is a crime punishable by a fine, forfeiture, or less than one year in a jail. Misdemeanors include such acts as disorderly conduct, vandalism, shoplifting, and prostitution. Theoretically, these two categories reflect the extent of harm done and the degree of moral outrage by society that such acts elicit. But in many cases this is simply not true, as is the case with many drug laws. Most offenders who are sentenced in felony cases to terms of imprisonment go to a state or federal prison. Those sentenced to confinement in misdemeanor cases are placed in local jails. In some states, such as Nevada, some crimes are classified as *gross misdemeanors,* which are offenses punishable by a term of imprisonment ranging from six months to one year, usually in a local jail.

Mala in Se and *Mala Prohibita* Crimes

Another method of classification is the common-law distinction between *mala in se* and *mala prohibita* crimes. **Mala in se crimes** are acts that are considered wrong in and of themselves. These crimes assault the moral conscience of society. They include offenses such as murder, rape, arson, and burglary. **Mala prohibita crimes** are prohibited acts or acts of omission that in and of themselves are not criminal. These acts have been criminalized through legislation. Examples of *mala prohibita* crimes include most of the so-called victimless crimes, such as prostitution, public drunkenness, drug offenses, and failure to file income-tax returns. *Mala in se* crimes are said to be morally wrong because every society considers these acts "evil" without requiring legislation to demonstrate their abomination. But, what a society considers to be inherently evil can change.

Classification by Governmental Jurisdiction

Jurisdiction is both a geographical area of authority where a court has the power and authority to hear and determine judicial proceedings, and the power to render a particular judgment. There are three principal jurisdictions in the United States: federal, state, and local. Each one has its own legal codes and procedures for enforcing those codes.

Federal offenses are offenses committed within federal territories, such as national parks; crimes that occur in two or more states, such as interstate transportation of stolen goods; and attempts to assassinate a government official, such as the president or a senator. State crimes are crimes described in state *penal codes.* This generic term refers to compilations of laws and corresponding punishments published by every state and going by such titles as "California Penal Code" and "Nevada Revised Statutes." Local crimes are those that apply to cities, townships, counties, and the like. These are usually called *ordinances.* An example is traffic laws.

It is important to be aware of this classification because there are, correspondingly, three types of criminal justice systems. For instance, a person charged with a federal offense would be prosecuted by a federal prosecutor and, if sentenced to prison, would go to a federal prison. A person charged and prosecuted for a state crime would be processed through a state court system and, if found guilty, may be sentenced to a state prison. Failing to stop for a red light can draw the attention of a city police officer and result in a summons to appear at a city or municipal court. Ignoring that summons could result in a fine or jail time within that local jurisdiction.

FBI Classifications of Crime

We now turn to the classification that is a major source of statistics on crime: the categories used by the Federal Bureau of Investigation in its annual report *Crime in the United States,* often referred to as the **Uniform Crime Report.** It should be noted at the outset that these statistics are among the most unreliable of all crime statistics, and they are easily manipulated by criminal justice officials and politicians.[15] This problem is addressed later in this chapter.

The FBI publishes *Crime in the United States* every year. In this report we find statistical data on crime in America during the previous year. Two major sections of the report focus on "crimes known to the police" (offenses that come to the attention of police, usually through calls from citizens) and "persons arrested" (suspects placed under arrest). Two categories of offenses are reported: Part I or index crimes and Part II offenses.

Index crimes are divided into eight categories: (1) homicide, (2) forcible rape, (3) robbery, (4) aggravated assault, (5) burglary, (6) larceny–theft, (7) motor-vehicle theft, and (8) arson. These offenses are listed as "index crimes" because the FBI considers them to be the most serious crimes in U.S. society. Using an index to summarize the extent of crime is sort of like using the Dow Jones Industrial Average to summarize what the stock market did yesterday.[16] Why these and not other crimes are labeled "index crimes" is an interesting question and tells us much about the popular images of crime. Quite often the FBI, local law enforcement, or newspapers report that "serious crime" increased by such and such an amount or the rate of "serious crime" decreased or increased by such and such an amount. The term *serious crime* refers to index crimes. The contention that these crimes are more serious than Part II crimes has been criticized because some index crimes may be less serious than many Part II crimes.

Part II crimes include drug-law violations, fraud, embezzlement, and driving under the influence. In terms of monetary losses and deaths and injuries, many Part II offenses are a great deal more serious than many index crimes.

A list of Part I offenses, accompanied by definitions, is reprinted in Figure 2.1. It should be noted that many of these offenses are not specific crimes but rather are *categories* of crimes. For example, there is no such crime as "aggravated assault." This is usually referred to in state legal codes as "felonious assault." This particular offense should be distinguished from the Part II category "other assaults," which is a catch-all term referring to a variety of altercations or threats (ranging from a brawl to a couple of teenagers fighting after school). The category "all other offenses" includes public nuisance, failure to appear on a warrant, bigamy, and, strangely enough, kidnapping, which can carry a penalty harsher than murder or rape if there is a ransom (and supports our contention that Part II offenses are not always less serious than Part I offenses).[17]

Another method for examining the nature of crime is to focus on the actual behaviors that come under the general heading of crime. Many criminologists use typologies of criminal behavior.

Typologies of Criminal Behavior

Criminologists often use typologies to better understand crime. Usually, typologies classify crimes according to similarities in behaviors or in the persons who generally commit crimes. Through the years many typologies have been used. The categories shown in Figure 2.2 are adapted from a book by Marshal Clinard and Richard Quinney called *Criminal Behavior Systems: A Typology,* originally published in 1967 and presently in its third edition.[18] As these authors note, typologies are common in all of the sciences. The goal of such classification schemes is to bring some order to the study of a wide variety of phenomena. The typology depicted in the figure closely follows Clinard and Quinney's scheme, with a few minor changes (especially in category 5). Although not exhaustive, their categories cover most forms of criminal behavior.

Inevitably, crime typologies are incomplete and far from perfect. As Miethe and McCorkle note, part of the problem is "the fact that the very definitions of crime and criminals are volatile social constructs that vary according to the prevailing social, economic, and political conditions in a society."[19]

Notice that the term **white-collar crime** is not used in Figure 2.2. The reasons are many and varied, but the principal reason is the vagueness of the term and the lack of a clear definition. Generally, various frauds, crimes committed by persons of high social standing, and crimes committed by corporations are subsumed under this category. But many so-called white-collar crimes are committed by persons of relatively low social status. We include the category "Frauds by Individuals" (category 6) to help distinguish between crimes by persons of high social status and crimes involving fraud by all others.

FIGURE 2.1   A Profile of Index Crimes

Homicide. Homicide is the killing of an individual by the act, procurement, or omission of another individual. The perpetrator must knowingly, purposely, recklessly, or negligently cause the death of another human being. Homicides, in addition to other violent crimes, tend to occur most often between people of the same age group, sex, race, and social class, with one exception: when females are murdered and raped, the offenders usually are male. On the other hand, when females commit murder, the victims are male about 35 percent of the time. Also, the majority of the victims have had some relationship with the offender. At least one-third are members of the same family, and the majority of these crimes occur in the context of minor arguments. A good proportion could be included within the context of "domestic violence." African Americans have a much higher rate of involvement in homicide.

Robbery. The act of robbery includes the felonious taking of anything of value that is in the possession of someone else and against his or her will. Furthermore, in order for an act to be considered a robbery, that which is taken must be in the immediate possession of the victim, and the act must include force or the threat of force by the perpetrator. Several different types of robberies can be noted. The most common type is one that occurs on the streets or highways and is most often referred to as "mugging." Ranked next in frequency is robbery of a "commercial house" (such as a restaurant), followed by a residence, a convenience store (such as a 7-Eleven store), gas stations, and banks (which fall victim to less than 1 percent of all robberies). The weapon most likely to be used is the offender's hands or feet, followed closely by the use of a firearm. Robbery is largely a young man's crime, as the majority of those arrested are under 25 years of age. African Americans are almost twice as likely as whites to be arrested.

Rape. Rape is unlawful intercourse without the consent of the victim. The act of rape is usually accompanied by the threat or use of force. The victims are overwhelmingly female, and those arrested usually are male. Most of those arrested are over 21, and African Americans and whites each constitute about 50 percent of those arrested. About one-third of the victims are under 18, and over half of the victims know their offenders, at least casually. There is still considerable debate on the subject of rape. This is particularly so with regard to the actual number of rapes committed during the course of a year. Some estimates suggest that only one of every ten rapes is reported.

Aggravated Assault. This offense is an assault in which the intention is to commit another crime. Aggravated assault is almost by definition accompanied by the use of a dangerous or deadly weapon, usually a firearm. The relationship between victims and offenders is about the same as that for homicide—that is, they are likely to be friends or acquaintances—and the assault occurs in the context of a minor argument. Almost 90 percent of those arrested are young males, with the 18–21 and 25–29 age groups being predominant. African Americans are arrested for this crime in disproportionate numbers.

Burglary. This is defined as an unlawful entry into any structure for the purpose of committing a felony or theft. It also includes attempted forceful entry. The word "structure" is important because it includes not only residences, but also businesses. Technically, a person who shoplifts can be said to be committing burglary because they entered a structure (a retail store) in order to commit a theft. Burglary is most commonly a young adult's crime, with about 20 percent involving persons under 18. A slight majority of these crimes (53 percent in 1998) are committed during the daytime. (About 60 percent of residential burglaries occur in the daytime, while people are at work.) The majority of those involved in burglaries are white males.

Larceny–Theft. This offense is most often characterized by the unlawful taking of property with the intention to deprive the lawful owner of the property permanently. The most common example within this broad category is that of shoplifting. Other offenses within this category include thefts of motor-vehicle accessories (tires, batteries, etc.) and thefts *from* motor vehicles (purses, clothing, etc.). Most of those arrested are young (it is the most common offense for teens) and male, although it should be noted that this is the offense for which females are most often arrested (usually for shoplifting).

Motor Vehicle Theft. This is largely a young man's crime. More than one-third of those arrested are under 18, and about another 25 percent are between 18 and 21. Consistent with the age factor is the fact that the most common type of motor-vehicle theft is known as "joyriding." Typically, this offense is characterized by a group of teenagers who find a car with the keys in and go for a ride. This seems to be an overwhelming white and male offense. A few offenders are engaged in rather sophisticated auto-theft rings, stealing expensive cars, stripping them, and selling the parts individually (usually the total value of the parts is more than the value of the car itself).

Arson. At common law, arson was confined to the malicious burning of another's residence. This description has been broadened by state statutes and criminal codes. For example, many criminal codes define arson as the malicious act of burning anyone's property, or burning one's own property if the purpose is to collect insurance. The definition of arson is quite complex. First-degree arson is usually the burning of an occupied residence, second-degree arson is the burning of property at night, and third-degree arson is the burning of property not included in first- or second-degree categories. The most common forms of arson are the burning of a single residence and the burning of motor vehicles. As with other property crimes, this offense is a young man's crime. Most of those arrested for these offenses are white males.

FIGURE 2.2 A Typology of Criminal Behavior

1. ***Violent Crime.*** This category includes homicide, rape, aggravated assault, manslaughter, and robbery. There is some debate over the inclusion of robbery. Some believe that because the major motive is the theft of property, robbery should be considered as a property crime. Others, including the FBI, argue that because there is force or at least the threat of force, robbery should be a violent crime. Also, during the past ten years or so it has become alarmingly clear that there is a great deal of violence in the home that is not usually included in this category. Thus, we should also include child abuse and spouse abuse. It should be noted that a good deal of violence has historically been committed by organized nation-states or persons representing them, including the U.S. government. The criminal justice system does not deal with these crimes in any way. These crimes are included within category 5 below.

2. ***Major Property Crime.*** Included in this category are at least four major types: grand larceny (theft of money or property in excess of a certain dollar value, which varies from state to state—usually $400–$500, which indicates a "felony" and anything under this amount is classified as a "misdemeanor"), burglary, motor-vehicle theft, and arson.

3. ***Petty Property Crime.*** This category includes such offenses as shoplifting (unless the value exceeds the amount designated under grand larceny), stolen-property offenses (buying, receiving, possession), and a form of motor-vehicle theft commonly known as "joyriding" (usually involving a group of teenagers who "borrow" a car and drive it for a few miles). It should be emphasized that some stolen-property offenses could easily be placed within the major property-crime category, especially when the value exceeds the monetary amount that distinguishes between petty and grand larceny, which varies from state to state. The distinction between both categories of property crime is somewhat arbitrary. Some criminologists have distinguished between the "occasional property offender" and the "professional" or "career property offender." The former is usually a one-time offender; the latter is a persistent violator. Even this distinction is somewhat arbitrary. Some states have passed "habitual criminal" laws and usually have defined "habitual criminal" as someone who has been arrested three times or convicted of at least three felonies.

4. ***Public Order/Victimless Crime.*** These offenses are so called because they either occur in public view or are "victimless" in that there are no *complaining* victims. In the former category we have public drunkenness, disorderly conduct, disturbing the peace (in many jurisdictions one or all of these three may be subsumed under another), and vagrancy (many states

have either eliminated this category because courts have ruled such laws to be unconstitutional or the same behavior is subsumed under another category). In the latter group we have such offenses as drug-law violations, prostitution, gambling, and homosexuality (in many areas some or all of these are either legal or have been "decriminalized," that is, dealt with through small fines or a no-arrest policy).

5. ***Crimes of the State: Government and Political Crime.*** This category includes offenses committed by or against the government. In the former category we have police corruption, crimes by the CIA, FBI, etc., bribery, and the like. These would also include violations of international human rights laws, such as activities of the CIA, and other U.S.-sponsored violence in foreign countries. Crimes against the state include treason and conspiracy to overthrow the government.

6. ***Frauds by Individuals.*** These are offenses that involve attempts by individuals to obtain money or property "under false pretenses" and usually involve face-to-face encounters with the victim but with no physical force (as in a robbery). Included are such crimes as confidence games (such as the "big con" or "sting"), swindles, insurance frauds, credit-card frauds, and check frauds (passing bad checks). Income-tax evasion (or simply cheating on income taxes) should also be included and would be an example of a fraud not involving any face-to-face encounter with the victim.

7. ***Occupational Crime.*** These are offenses that are directly related to a person's occupation. Generally there are two major types: (1) crimes committed by employees against their employers (employee pilferage, embezzlement, etc.) and (2) crimes (usually fraud) committed in the course of normal occupational pursuits (maintenance and repair fraud, health care fraud, Medicare and Medicaid fraud, fee splitting and unnecessary surgeries by doctors, land sales fraud, etc.).

8. ***Corporate Crime.*** These offenses are acts by large corporations that do physical or economic harm to the environment, to employees, or to customers. Such crimes "arise from the ownership or management of capital or from occupancy of positions of trust in institutions designed to facilitate the accumulation of capital."* Examples include creating occupational health hazards, price fixing, manufacturing unsafe products, pollution, price gouging, false advertisement, economic exploitation of employees, and corporate stealing from employees, unfair labor practices.†

9. ***Organized and Professional Crime.*** This category refers to persons whose criminal behavior is viewed as a "career" or "profession." There are two major categories. First, there are individuals who are

(continued)

FIGURE 2.2   A Typology of Criminal Behavior

involved in criminal behavior, whether alone or in concert with others. A small number specialize in one major crime (pickpockets, safe-crackers, etc.). However, most commit a wide variety of crimes, mostly major property offenses. Second, there are individuals who belong to organized criminal "syndicates" or "crime families." Included here is the legendary "Mafia" or "La Costra Nostra" and similar organizations that engage in crimes such as loan-sharking, drug smuggling, and racketeering.

*Michalowski, R. *Order, Law and Crime.* New York: Macmillan, 1985, p. 314.
†Friedrichs, D. D. *Trusted Criminals: White Collar Crime in Contemporary Society.* Belmont CA: Wadsworth, 1996, pp. 65–95.

Source: Adapted from Clinard, M. B., R. Quinney, and J. Wildeman. *Criminal Behavior Systems* (3rd ed.). Cincinnati: Anderson, 1994.

MEASURING CRIME

Youth gang activity has long been viewed as criminal behavior. In April 2001 the Office of Juvenile Justice and Delinquency Prevention (OJJDP) released a report claiming that gang problems for communities increased by more than 1,000 percent between 1970 and 1998.[20] Such figures are alarming only to individuals not inclined to think critically. Applying a minimal amount of critical thought to this issue generates some obvious questions. How can these data be collectivized when the simple definition of *gang* varies across jurisdictional lines? Where did the researchers find a "list" of gangs to consider? The numbers were generated largely from law enforcement agencies—the same agencies that increase their chances of receiving more funding by making a case that their communities have gang problems. The fact is, many of the youth who have been labeled as gang members in this study are probably not gang members at all. Some of the activities are not even related to youth gang activities and may be acts committed by persons legally classified as adult. And, as revealed in a recent police scandal in Los Angeles (centering around a special gang unit in the Rampart Division, which covers an area that includes Hollywood), some of the activities may never have occurred at all. The point to be made at this juncture is: Beware of state-sponsored reports, and apply critical thinking before arriving at conclusions.

The actual amount of crime committed in the United States today is not known and is probably unknowable, despite the vast technology that is available. There are several reasons for this. First, literally hundreds of actions are prohibited by law. Many of them, such as "disorderly conduct" and "disturbing the peace," lack precise definition.[21] Second, many illegal acts, such as possession or sale of illegal drugs, are committed out of public view. These and other so-called victimless crimes often do not involve a complaining victim. Third, in order for the true extent of crime to be known, each individual would have to be monitored twenty-four hours a day. The only realistic sources of information are crimes that come to the attention of local police or other authorities (from actual observation or reports by citizens) and crimes admitted by perpetrators or described by victims to sources other than criminal justice practitioners (interviewers conducting victimization surveys, friends and family members, etc.).

These sources have yielded five measuring methods used to find how much crime there is: (1) official statistics, such as the FBI's annual report; (2) surveys of citizens who have been the victims of a crime (whether or not they reported it); (3) self-report studies asking groups of people about unlawful behavior they have engaged in; (4) observations of criminal activity by field researchers or other persons (such as those who observe delinquent gang activities or people who "blow the whistle" on illegal corporate behavior or organized crime); and (5) reports from private businesses on employee theft or from the Securities and Exchange Commission on corporate crimes. In this chapter we concentrate on the first three because they are the most common types.

The FBI Uniform Crime Reports

Since 1930 the Federal Bureau of Investigation has been publishing statistics on crime in the United States. These reports began as a monthly publication, became a quarterly in 1932, and since 1959 have been published annually. The Uniform Crime Reports (UCRs) are based on data sent to the FBI by local police departments representing about 93 percent of the population. Much of the data are channeled through state-level UCR programs (there are forty-one). However, the accuracy of the data depends primarily on local police departments and how well they adhere to reporting procedures suggested by the FBI in their annual publication *Uniform Crime Reporting Handbook.*

Two major sections in the Uniform Crime Report called *Crime in the United States* are "crimes known to the police" and "persons arrested." These are crimes that are reported to, or otherwise come to the attention of, local police departments. The first category consists of index crimes only. The second category includes both index and Part II crimes.

Detailed summaries are given for all of the "crimes known to the police" (types of victims and offenders, geographic locations, the time of day, etc.). Two kinds of data are presented: (1) the actual number known to the police and (2) the crime rate per 100,000 people in the general population (based on the most recent census). The crime rate is established by dividing the number of crimes by the size of the population and multiplying by 100,000. For instance, if a particular area has a population of 350,000 and 30,000 crimes were known to the police during the year, the crime rate would be 8,571.4. For arrests, data are given for all persons arrested and include both Part I and Part II offenses. The FBI breaks this information down according to age, sex, race, and location (urban, rural, suburban, etc.). There is a breakdown of arrests by race, sex, age, and so on, but the FBI does not provide cross-tabulations of race and age and race and sex. We do not know, for example, how many black males or white females are arrested. Neither do we know the arrest rate of black males between the ages of 15 and 17.

Hispanics are essentially invisible in the FBI report, for they are grouped with whites and are not in a separate category. Thus, we do not know the extent of criminal involvement by Hispanics. This reporting method tends to tone down the disparity between the numbers of whites (non-Hispanic) and ethnic minorities who are arrested. As we explain in Chapters 10–12 however, prison statistics have recently begun to be broken down by race so as to include the Hispanic population.

The report also includes a section called "crimes cleared by an arrest," which consists of the percentage of the crimes "known to the police" that result in (or are "cleared" by) an arrest. What is noteworthy is that relatively few crimes known to the police are ever cleared by an arrest. In fact, in spite of steady improvements in technology and in police professionalism, the percentage of crimes cleared by an arrest has been declining over the years. According to the most recent figures, about one in every five reported crimes is cleared by an arrest. The percentage varies according to the type of crime committed. For instance, about two-thirds of all reported homicides but just under half of all rapes are cleared by an arrest. Slightly more than 28 percent of all robberies, less than 14 percent of all burglaries, and less than 15 percent of all reported motor-vehicle thefts are cleared by an arrest.[22]

Other kinds of UCR data include changes over time (both for crimes known to police and for persons arrested), geographic location (crime by state, region, etc.), the number of full-time law enforcement personnel, and the number of police officers killed. (A copy of the FBI's Uniform Crime Reports can be found in most public and university libraries.) FBI data should be interpreted with extreme caution because there are a number of shortcomings.[23] Indeed, serious criticisms have been leveled at these statistics.

Critique of the FBI Uniform Crime Reports

The first and most important problem, in our view, is that the accuracy of UCR data depends on the work done by local police departments. This fact in and of itself leads us to seriously question official reports of crime. Law enforcement agencies (like other bureaucracies) have a need to protect themselves, to put forth an image that convinces the public that they are doing their job. And they are not above manipulating crime statistics in order to obtain more local, state, or federal funding, or to improve their public image.

Crime statistics are among the easiest statistics to manipulate. Some crimes are never counted officially. In one study, an audit of arrests by 196 police departments found an error rate of around 10 percent and found that almost all police departments make numerous errors in their UCR reporting procedures.[24] Another study found serious problems in the reporting of arson, for many fire departments do not report suspicious fires to the UCR and many departments that do report them omit many fires that may have been set by arsonists.[25] Some police administrators may knowingly falsify crime reports by undervaluing the cost of stolen goods, or report as a "robbery" a "larceny from a person" that was an ordinary pickpocketing (especially if they want to show that "violent crime" is rising so as to justify an increase in the police budget), or even exaggerate the number of gangs, gang members and gang-related crime in order to get federal funding to create or increase the size of a "gang unit" or to divert the public's attention away from problems within the police department.[26]

A recent example emerges in a study from New York City. Brownstein found that a relatively modest fluctuation in reported crime was exaggerated by the media, politicians, and criminal justice officials, largely to advance private and political ambitions. His analysis demonstrates how easily local data throughout the state of New York could be miscounted and left open to wide interpretation. Data are sent on a monthly basis from more than six hundred local law enforcement agencies to one central data collection agency, the Division of Criminal Justice Services (DCJS). At the time of the study (mid-1990s) DCJS had a staff of four data entry clerks, one supervisor, and one administrator, who collectively had to handle about eight hundred forms every month. Brownstein (who was the head of that unit for several years) reports that there were major staff cutbacks during the early 1990s, including field staff who trained UCR clerks in local police departments. Thus, many local clerks never got any training. Another problem was constant turnover in several positions. Not surprisingly, there were several problems with the UCR data, not the least of which was the constant backlog of forms submitted to the DCJS. And as the deadline for submitting the forms neared, stress levels increased. As Brownstein notes, "Even diligent and hardworking people have difficulty maintaining their usual standard of quality control under these circumstances."[27]

Space does not permit a complete reporting of Brownstein's fascinating study, but one item he notes is worthy of mention because it casts serious doubt on official statistics on the type of crime that is perhaps most easily manipulated—drug offenses. Brownstein notes that in New York City in 1980 there were a reported 14,339 arrests for drug sales but in 1981 there were only 4,317—a decrease of 70 percent. After doing some checking, Brownstein dismissed the charge that the low number must have been a misprint, for in 1979 there were a reported 14,007 arrests for drug sales (almost identical to the 1980 number), and in 1982 the number was 3,950 (very close to the 1981 number). It turned out that "two informal, unwritten policy-shifts around that time" essentially "refined how drug sales were counted." One change was linked to no longer counting phone calls from citizens reporting drug sales. The other change was that instead of counting the arrest of one drug dealer as one crime, the police began counting each drug sales *scene* as one crime, *no matter how many people were arrested.* So think critically when considering official reports of drug arrests. Critically analyze all official reports on crime, because crime reporting and data collection are human enterprises and hence subject to ordinary human error.

A 1998 report revealed scandals in police departments in cities such as Philadelphia, Boca Raton, Florida, Atlanta, and Buffalo, New York. The report noted that during 1998 police departments in these cities were accused of falsely reporting crime statistics. Some high-ranking police officials resigned or were demoted.

A police captain in Boca Raton downgraded property crimes like burglary to less serious misdemeanors like vandalism and trespassing, lowering that city's felony rate by 11 percent. Philadelphia had to withdraw the city's crime figures from the FBI reports for

1996, 1997, and the first half of 1998. Philadelphia accounts for 2 percent of all homicides in the United States and thus can have a significant impact on the national homicide rate. Also in Philadelphia, a police captain reported an 80 percent decrease in serious crime in his district, caused in part by his downgrading many robberies, burglaries, and thefts to missing-property cases. In Boca Raton a police official downgraded 385 felonies (11% of the total serious crime). In one instance, he reclassified as "vandalism" a case in which a burglar stole $5,000 in jewelry and did more than $25,000 in damage.[28]

In Detroit, the FBI is investigating inflated crime numbers. In 1999 Detroit had 415 killings and made 1,152 murder arrests. In 2001 the *Detroit Free Press* said, "Experts say the number of murders and arrests should be about equal. Detroit has reported similar numbers to the FBI for years."[29] Officials in Detroit blamed outdated computers for their problems. We wonder whether such an excuse satisfies the innocent people who experienced the trauma of being booked for murder in that city. Critical thinking forces us to question the issues raised here. Are Detroit, Boca Raton, Philadelphia, and New York isolated cases, or are they only the jurisdictions that have been exposed to date?

A second problem with UCR data is that many crimes are never reported to the police. It has been estimated that more than twice as many index crimes are committed than are actually reported to the police. It should be noted that most unreported crimes are relatively minor. Many citizens are reluctant to report crimes, for several reasons. Some believe that nothing can be done or that the police do not want to be bothered. Some fear reprisal or consider whatever happened as essentially a private matter. Rape victims fear (justifiably so) that the criminal justice system will not take their victimization seriously and in effect further victimize them by blaming them for what happened.[30] This problem is even more significant when we consider the Part II offenses. Our only measurement for the extent of these crimes is through arrest data, which leave much to be desired. How many frauds and embezzlements really occur each year? How many DUIs occur? How many drug offenses are committed? How many minor assaults ("other assaults") actually occur? How much domestic violence happens? Nobody has any idea!

A third problem with UCR data revolves around the arrest figures. If someone is arrested and charged with more than one crime, only the most serious of these crimes is counted in the final tabulation of arrest data. Further, in some cases each *act* is counted as a separate offense; in others, multiple acts are counted as a single offense. Several people may be robbed in a restaurant, and these acts would be counted as one robbery. However, if the same offender physically attacked four people, these acts would be listed as four assaults. In the case of an arrest for the crime of murder, you should keep in mind the fact that the data pertain to persons arrested, not to the number of murders. We have no idea how many murders the person arrested actually committed. This becomes a problem when we consider the problem of serial killers. The arrest of Ted Kaczynski (the "Unabomber") or David Berkowitz (the "Son of Sam") or Andrew Cunanan or John Wayne Gacy, among others, will be listed as one person arrested for *one homicide,* not several homicides.

The fourth problem is that we have no idea, from reading the FBI's reports, what eventually happened to each arrest. Were any charges dropped by the police department or the district attorney? In many cases *all* charges are dropped. What does that tell us about the arrest figures? Moreover, was the person convicted and if so of what crime? As we note in Chapter 9, on prosecution, the vast majority of all arrests are dismissed by the district attorney's office, or the original charge is reduced to some lesser charge. Further, many arrestees are *overcharged* by the police because they anticipate that the district attorney will "bargain down" the charges. Thus, we have no idea how many of the millions of arrests the police make each year are a true reflection of what really happened in the field.

The fifth problem with UCR data is the interpretation of crime *rates.* First, these rates are based on the *total* population (in the most recent reports this meant about 230 million people), which is far different from the population *at risk* of a particular crime (that is, the population of potential victims). For instance, rates of forcible rape should be based on the number of *women* in the population (because they are the major at risk group). Because women are about 50 percent of the population, the actual rate of reported rapes should be about double the rate reported by the FBI. Similarly, motor-vehicle theft should be based on the number of motor vehicles, because not every person owns a motor vehicle. At the very least, this rate should be based on the population ages 16 and over. Second, changes in crime rates may be more a reflection of changes in the population or in various demographic characteristics (e.g., increases or decreases in the proportion of youth), than of changes in the amount of crime committed. Quite often the actual *number* of specific crimes increases while the *rate* decreases during a given period (and vice versa).

The sixth problem with UCR data is the exclusion of several types of crimes. Federal crimes are excluded. More important, the reports focus almost exclusively on traditional "crimes," particularly the "one-on-one" direct harms, and largely ignore corporate crimes and crimes of the state, even though crimes committed by corporations and by the state do far greater harm to people than any of the common "crimes" committed by ordinary people. Why does the criminal justice system prefer to ignore such crimes? Could it have anything to do with the fact that the common definitions of crime, and the popular images of crime are shaped and determined by the dominant classes in society and by the state itself, which helps to perpetuate their influence? It would not make sense for them to define some of their own harmful behaviors as "crimes," nor would it seem logical for the state to define itself as "criminal." There are built-in class and racial biases in the very definition of crime.

In response to many of these criticisms the FBI developed the **National Incident-Based Reporting System (NIBRS).** The goal of this program is to develop a form to be filled out by local police departments that has enough room for a much wider variety of data. All crimes would be reported, not just the index crimes, and attempted crimes would be distinguished from completed crimes. Some states already have such a system, but it is still far from uniform. Such a huge database, however, presents many potential problems, and most of this new system does not ensure against misuse by police departments. Too much information on citizens is a problem waiting to happen. We have seen how databases on "gangs" can be misused, especially on minorities.[31]

Tables 2.1a through 2.6 present crime data covering several time periods, starting with 1971 and running through the year 2000. We discuss these data in more detail starting on page 37. We begin with a thirty-year look at "crimes known to the police." We then move on to a discussion of recent trends in arrests according to race, gender, and age. As noted, there has been a great deal of fluctuation in crime and arrest rates throughout these time periods, partly attributed to changing definitions of some crimes, especially aggravated assault. Some of the increases in aggravated assault were in effect a "paper increase" rather than any real increase.

Victimization Surveys

Every year, a national representative sample of citizens is asked a series of questions regarding their experiences as victims of crime. Since 1972 a version of the original survey, known as the **National Crime Victimization Survey (NCVS),** has been conducted each year. The surveys focus on a "National Crime Panel" of about 50,000 households drawn through a random sampling procedure. More than 100,000 persons 12 years of age and older are asked about their experiences with crime, including whether they reported a crime if they were victimized and if they did not, why not. They also are asked to describe their offenders (in cases of personal crimes) and how they (the survey respondents) reacted (did they resist, etc.).

The National Crime Victimization survey focuses on rape, robbery, assault, larceny (both personal larceny and larceny without contact), burglary, larceny from respondents' homes, and motor-vehicle theft. The results consistently show some rather significant differences from the FBI's annual *Crime in the United States* report. In Table 2.1a and Table 2.1b we compare the FBI's "crimes known to the police" with NCVS results for 2000 (the latest

TABLE 2.1a Number of Crimes Known to the Police, 1971–2000

CRIME	1971	1975	1980	1985	1990	1995	2000
Murder	17,780	20,510	23,040	18,976	23,438	21,606	15,517
Rape	42,260	56,090	82,990	87,671	102,555	97,470	90,186
Robbery	387,700	470,500	565,840	497,874	639,271	580,509	407,842
Aggravated assault	368,760	492,620	672,650	723,246	1,054,863	1,099,207	910,744
Burglary	2,399,300	3,265,300	3,795,200	3,073,348	3,073,909	2,593,784	2,049,946
Larceny–Theft	4,424,200	5,977,700	7,136,900	6,926,380	7,945,670	7,997,710	6,965,957
Motor-vehicle theft	948,200	1,009,600	1,131,700	1,102,862	1,635,907	1,472,441	1,165,559
Arson*							
Total	8,588,200	11,292,400	13,408,300	12,430,357	14,475,613	13,862,727	11,605,751
Total violent crime	816,500	1,039,710	1,344,520	1,327,767	1,820,127	1,798,792	1,424,289
Total property crime	7,771,700	10,252,700	12,063,700	11,102,590	12,655,486	12,063,935	10,181,462

*Insufficient data to estimate totals, according to the FBI.

Source: U.S. Department of Justice, Bureau of Criminal Justice Statistics, 1999 (Online).

TABLE 2.1b   Crimes Known to the Police, 1971–2000 (rates per 100,000)

CRIME	1971	1975	1980	1985	1990	1995	2000
Murder	8.6	9.6	10.2	8.0	9.4	8.2	5.5
Rape	20.5	26.3	36.8	36.8	41.1	37.1	32.0
Robbery	188.0	220.8	251.1	209.3	256.3	220.9	144.9
Aggravated assault	178.8	231.1	298.5	304.0	422.9	418.3	323.6
Burglary	1,163.5	1,532.1	1,684.1	1,291.7	1,232.2	987.0	728.4
Larceny–Theft	2,145.5	2,804.8	3,167.0	2,911.2	3,185.1	3,043.2	2,475.3
Motor-vehicle theft	459.8	473.7	502.2	463.5	655.8	560.3	414.2
Arson*							
Total	4,164.7	5,298.5	5,950.0	5,224.5	5,802.7	5,274.9	4,124.0
Total violent crime	396.0	487.8	596.6	558.1	729.6	684.5	506.1
Total property crime	3,768.8	4,810.7	5,353.3	4,666.4	5,073.1	4,590.5	3,617.9

*Insufficient data to estimate totals, according to the FBI.

Source: U.S. Department of Justice, Bureau of Criminal Justice Statistics, 1999 (Online).

year for which comparisons can be made as of this writing). Homicide and arson are not listed because they do not appear on the NCVS (which doesn't affect the overall results because they are few in number). Larceny–theft is not listed because the FBI data combine household and business theft and the NCVS includes only household theft.

According to these figures, the amount of crime that is actually occurring is about twice the amount that is reported to the police. However, we must recognize some methodological problems with the NCVS. For instance, many of the "crimes" noted by survey respondents may not have been crimes after all. A door left open may have been interpreted as a "burglary." Some of the offenses may have been rather minor, such as the theft of a child's tricycle from the driveway (though technically a larceny).

A major problem with the National Crime Victimization Surveys, as with the FBI data is that many crimes are underreported. There are several reasons for underreporting. Crime is obviously a sensitive topic, and many people may choose to keep some information away from the police and from researchers. Respondents who live in areas where there is a lot of crime might have a hard time remembering details about many of these crimes. When it comes to crimes committed by family members, individuals are likely to be reluctant to be honest or even to consider such behavior as criminal (especially when the victims are children). Women who are victims of abuse by their husbands often rationalize or minimize such behavior, or it may occur so often that they consider it normal. Women who are raped are often reluctant to report such incidents, even to researchers. Many people do not get an opportunity to be counted through such surveys because of their habits of mobility. Someone who moves frequently, is homeless, or is a runaway is likely to be at a risk for victimization but not likely to be included in these surveys.

A common criticism of the National Crime Victimization Survey is that many of the questions are about relatively minor offenses. The same also can be said about the FBI data, the bulk of which is about relatively minor offenses. Survey respondents are never asked "if toxic chemicals were dumped in the creek behind their house, if they were cheated out of a month's rent by the local bank or rental agent, if their children were made sick by companies selling lead-based crayons, or if they lost their union retirement benefits when the local savings and loan closed down after the president left for the Cayman Islands with $100 million"; nor are they asked about racial or sexual harassment in their schools, at work, or even on the street.[32] Moreover, children are never asked whether their parents or some other adult sexually or physically abused them. Why are such offenses omitted? Does this omission reflect class or racial bias? Perhaps we can conclude that both the NCVS and the FBI's annual report help perpetuate traditional images of crime—namely as acts committed by certain classes or racial groups.[33]

Self-Report Studies

One of the most popular methods of determining the extent of crime is the **self-report survey.** These are surveys that ask people to talk to a researcher about the crimes they have committed. Since the 1940s there has been a rather large number of such studies, and the studies have taken several different forms. First, there are those that rely on anonymous questionnaires. Second, there are those that are based on anonymous questionnaires that have been validated through checks with police records or follow-up interviews. Third, there are questionnaires that ask people to confess their offenses and to sign their names, after which researchers check police records. Fourth, some researchers check the accuracy of answers to questionnaires with follow-up interviews and the threat of the use of lie-detector tests (a rather dubious method). Fifth, some researchers use the interview method plus validation by looking at police records.[34]

In general, self-report studies demonstrate that nearly everyone has committed some act that could be designated as "criminal" or "delinquent," but few people have been caught. Most people have not committed serious forms of criminal or delinquent behavior, and they have not committed these acts on a regular basis. Self-report studies show that crime and delinquency are distributed throughout the social class structure and that blacks and whites have about the same average of deviance. Class and racial differences become most apparent when "serious" (a term, as we have noted, that may itself be class or racially biased) and persistent forms of lawbreaking are considered. Unfortunately, with few exceptions, the majority of self-report surveys are taken by school-age children. Some national self-report surveys of adults focus specifically on drug usage and the abuse of wives by their husbands.[35]

Self-report studies can be criticized on several grounds. In the first place, most of them have been conducted on adolescents rather than adults. Second, and more important, there are many problems in the research methods used. The social settings where the research is conducted differ (some in high school classrooms, some at institutions, some in the home, etc.). Also, there are problems inherent in asking people questions about their past behavior. This is especially the case when asking about behaviors that violate the law. There is the problem of the loss of memory (e.g., we often tend to forget an experience that was unpleasant). Some people like to lie or exaggerate (e.g., youths may want to seem "tough"). The wording of questions and even the meaning of different acts may be interpreted differently by different people. And there is always the problem of bias on the part of the interviewer. A third problem is that of how to measure social class. Researchers use different methods. Some use income levels of individuals (or their parents), some use median income of census tracts, and some use occupation.

Perhaps a more fundamental problem with self-report studies (and, for that matter, all studies of crime) is that what is regarded as "criminal" and what is regarded as a "serious" offense is not a constant. Is stealing a car more serious than manufacturing thousands of unsafe cars that cause serious injuries or even deaths? A related problem is that no study has yet focused on the (undetected) deviant activities of corporate executives or other high-status persons. Instead, self-report studies focus almost exclusively on conventional criminal and delinquent behavior.

THE EXTENT OF CRIME

How much crime is there in American society? No one knows for sure. All we can say for certain is that a lot of different types of harms are being committed against a lot of people. It should be emphasized that there is a lot of media hype about crime and that the most popular images of crime center on crimes that make the headlines—mostly violent crimes, especially homicide. In fact, it has been documented on several occasions that homicide is the crime most commonly reported on the evening news, portrayed on television shows and in feature-length movies, and written about in local newspapers, although in fact it is one of the least likely of all crimes to actually occur.[36] The news media are less interested in reporting news than they are in *making* news, shaping public opinion ("manufacturing consent"), and perpetuating a certain view of "reality," a view that tends to serve mostly the wealthy and powerful.[37]

As you read the following sections you should be aware of the contrast between crimes associated with the lower classes and the crimes of the rich and powerful, including crimes of the state. Always ask this question: "What are they *not* telling us about crime?" The answer simply put, is: "A lot!" The next logical question to be asked is: "*Why* are they not telling us this?"

The Official Crime Picture Painted by the Department of Justice

In Tables 2.1 through 2.6 we provide summaries of the extent of crime, *according to official sources.* We will begin with a discussion of the FBI's annual report, *Crime in the United States,* which is derived from the Uniform Crime Reports (UCR).

Crimes Known to the Police.   In 2000, 11,605,751 index crimes were known to police—a rate of 4,124 per 100,000 in the population. Looking at crime rates over the past thirty years we see that the current crime rate is nearly identical to the crime rate in 1971, in which there were 8,588,200 index crimes known to the police—a rate of 4,165 (see Tables 2.1a and 2.1b, pages 33 and 34). Of course, the U.S. population for 1971 was about 206 million[38] compared to 281 million in 2000.[39] Therefore, the number of crimes known to police increased by over 26 percent from 1971 to 2000 and the population of the United States increased by over 26 percent during that same period. Such figures are completely at odds with the common notion that the United States experienced a crime wave in the past three decades. In fact, controlling for population increases, we are at exactly the same place we were in 1971 with the following exceptions: There has been a 1,264 percent increase in criminal justice expenditures, the prison population has increased more than 800 percent, and the overall incarceration rate has increased almost 500 percent.[40] Moreover, if we broaden our examination of official data that center on crimes known to police, we see that property-crime rates have decreased about 4 percent since 1971. In 1971 property-crime rates stood at 3,768 compared to 3,618 in 2000. The burglary rate has decreased by about 37 percent since 1971. Motor vehicle–theft rates experienced a more modest decline of 9 percent, while the larceny–theft rate increased about 13 percent during the same period. Comparing total violent-crime rates for this time period reveals a different picture. The total violent-crime rate for 1971 was 396 per 100,000 compared to 506 per 100,000 in 2000—an increase of almost 22 percent. Murder and robbery rates declined 36 percent and 23 percent, respectively. In contrast, rape and aggravated assault rates rose by 36 percent and 45 percent.

The category "crimes known to the police" should not be passed over lightly, for it represents perhaps the ultimate source of the popular image of crime in U.S. society. Indeed, as already noted, whenever the media (or local politicians, especially during an election year) discuss the "crime problem," and especially when the discussion turns to the success or failure of local police efforts to deal with crime, this is the source of the data cited. For all practical purposes, the "crime problem" is measured almost entirely by reference to "crimes known to the police." A closer look at the data suggests that using these figures to determine the extent of the "crime problem" is at best woefully inadequate and at worst a gross distortion of reality.

To begin with, the category "crimes known to the police" is not a real measure of *criminal behavior.* Rather it is a measure of the extent to which certain crimes come to the attention of local police departments, whether from citizens who call 911 or crimes observed by the police. Even taken at face value, it tells us that violent crime (especially homicide) represents a small percentage of the total number of crimes "known to the police." The vast majority of crimes, as reflected in Tables 2.1a and 2.1b, are property crimes, with the category "larceny–theft" heading the list.

Arrests.   Perhaps the most revealing figures from the FBI reports are those pertaining to the category "persons arrested." Arrest does not mean guilt—it simply means arrest. You should not assume that because an arrest is made the person arrested is guilty. You could get arrested for failing an "attitude test"—by not showing the degree of respect that an officer believes is appropriate. As shown in Table 2.2, the vast majority of arrests involve Part II crimes. This remains consistent in each of the years exhibited in Table 2.2. Leading the pack is the category "all other offenses," which consists of mostly local ordinances, violation of probation and parole regulations, failure to appear, and even kidnapping. Driving under the influence (DUI) has typically held second place (except in 1996, when DUI fell behind drug-abuse violations and larceny–theft arrests). If you look closely at Table 2.2 you can see that four of the top five arrest offenses are Part II crimes. This is consistent in each of the years presented in Table 2.2. The only index crime that is situated in this top five is larceny–theft. Notice the offense "other assaults." This category includes mostly minor fights that usually involve no weapons and result in only slight injuries. Also included are the many cases of domestic violence, an offense that accounts for large numbers

TABLE 2.2   Estimated Number of Arrests in the United States, Selected Years (1987–2000)

OFFENSE CHARGED	NUMBER ARRESTED					
	1987	*1990*	*1993*	*1996*	*1999*	*2000*
Total Arrests	12,711,600	14,195,100	14,036,300	15,168,100	14,031,070	13,980,297
PART I/INDEX CRIMES						
Murder	19,200	22,990	23,400	19,020	14,790	13,227
Rape	36,310	39,160	38,420	33,050	28,830	27,469
Robbery	138,290	167,990	173,620	156,270	108,850	106,130
Aggravated assault	352,450	475,330	518,670	521,570	483,530	478,417
Burglary	443,400	432,600	402,700	364,800	296,100	289,844
Larceny–Theft	1,469,200	1,554,800	1,476,300	1,486,300	1,189,400	1,166,362
Motor-vehicle theft	169,300	211,300	195,900	175,400	142,200	148,225
Arson	18,000	19,100	19,400	19,000	16,800	16,530
PART II CRIMES						
Other assaults	787,200	1,014,100	1,144,900	1,329,000	1,294,400	1,312,169
Forgery and counterfeiting	93,900	94,800	106,900	121,600	106,900	108,654
Fraud	341,900	291,600	410,700	465,000	363,800	345,732
Embezzlement	12,700	15,300	12,900	15,700	17,100	18,952
Stolen property	139,300	165,200	158,100	151,100	121,900	118,641
Vandalism	273,500	326,000	313,000	320,900	278,200	281,305
Weapons	191,700	221,200	262,300	216,200	172,400	159,181
Prostitution	110,100	111,400	97,800	99,000	92,100	87,620
Sex offenses (except rape and prostitution)	100,100	107,600	107,100	95,800	92,400	93,399
Drug abuse violations	937,400	1,089,500	1,126,300	1,506,200	1,532,200	1,579,566
Gambling	25,400	19,300	17,300	21,000	10,400	10,842
Offenses against family and children	58,700	85,800	109,100	149,800	151,200	147,663
Driving under the influence	1,727,200	1,810,800	1,524,800	1,467,300	1,511,300	1,471,289
Liquor laws	616,700	714,700	518,500	677,400	657,900	683,124
Drunkenness	828,300	910,100	726,600	718,700	656,100	637,554
Disorderly conduct	698,700	733,000	727,000	842,600	633,100	638,740
Vagrancy	36,100	38,500	28,200	27,800	30,000	32,542
All other (except traffic)	2,836,700	3,267,800	3,518,700	3,786,700	3,728,100	3,710,434
Suspicion*	13,500	22,200	14,100	4,900	7,500	5,682
Curfew and loitering	89,500	80,800	100,200	185,100	167,200	154,711
Runaways	160,400	174,200	180,500	195,700	148,300	141,975

*Suspicion not included in total.

Source: U.S. Department of Justice, Bureau of Criminal Justice Statistics, 1999 (Online).

of arrests for this category, along with the category "aggravated assault," during the past decade.

A large proportion of arrests are directly related to the use of drugs and alcohol; many more are indirectly related.[41] Those directly related include drug-abuse violations, driving under the influence, drunkenness, and liquor-law violations, which together constituted 31.2 percent of all arrests in 2000. If we add disorderly conduct (which usually involves drinking or drug use), the percentage rises to 35.8. Thus, more than one out of three arrests directly relate to the use or abuse of drugs or alcohol. However, the connection between crime and drugs or alcohol may be even greater, for about one-half of all murders are drug or alcohol related and at least the same proportion of other crimes of violence have a similar relationship with drugs or alcohol. Then, too, substantial numbers of property crimes are at least indirectly related to drugs or alcohol, although the research is not as consistent as is the case for violent crimes. Some research suggests that the drug–crime connection is not a clear-cut causal one and that in many cases criminal behavior may *precede* the drug use.[42]

As with crimes known to the police, arrest figures do not tell very much about the real extent of law violations. For example, there is no way of knowing how many people drove a car after drinking a "few too many" and hence are guilty of driving under the influence. Likewise, there is no way of knowing how many people have possessed illegal drugs, but have never been arrested. The same can be said of the possession of illegal firearms. Examples could be cited endlessly. The point that needs to be stressed, however, is that arrests for these offenses are more of a measure of police activity, and of the visibility of certain groups of people, than a measure of criminal behavior itself. In this context, a remark by Chambliss seems appropriate. He notes that

> the transgressions of lower-class persons are much more visible than are the transgressions of middle-class persons. Crowded living conditions create an environment in which most behavior, even that which occurs in one's own home, is susceptible to screening by the neighbors and by law enforcement officials. Domestic disputes, drinking to excess and other quasi-illegal acts are much more likely to be seen in the lower classes than in the middle classes.[43]

Indeed, police officers are under enormous pressure to make arrests. They look for situations that make an arrest highly likely. Most of these Part II offenses, especially drug dealing and public disturbances, are highly visible in lower-class and minority communities, where, incidentally, the greatest amount of police patrol.

As noted in Table 2.2, the really "serious" crimes do not rank among the top five in terms of persons arrested. As noted in this table, the catch-all category "all other" offenses leads the way, accounting for more than a quarter of all arrests (26.5%). Larceny–theft, which encompasses a wide variety of property offenses (the most common of which is shoplifting), hardly represents what most would consider "serious crime," especially if it is lumped together (as it usually is) with murder, rape, and robbery. Larceny–theft accounts for more than half of all index-crime arrests (51.9%).

Looking at the total arrest picture, we can summarize as follows: (1) The majority of all arrests are for relatively minor offenses. (2) Most arrests involve either property crimes or public-order and victimless crimes. (3) At least half may be drug or alcohol related.

Before we move on, it is important to discuss the practice of clearing (or solving) a case through arrest. When a case is cleared by an arrest, that does not necessarily mean that the person who committed the crime is sitting in jail awaiting trial or sentencing. It simply means the police made an arrest and believe the person they arrested committed a particular crime. In essence, the clearance rate is the proportion of cases solved or cleared through an arrest. The argument could be made that clearance rates are more about politics than about fighting or solving the problem of crime. Clearance rates are about law enforcement taking credit for doing its job. Sometimes credit is warranted; at other times, as in the case of the Los Angeles Rampart scandal, it is premature. (For a discussion of this scandal, see Chapter 7.) Table 2.3 shows clearance rates between 1971 and 2000.

As demonstrated in Table 2.3, the criminal justice system, and particularly law enforcement, has little to boast about when it comes to clearance rates. If we go back to 1971, we find that the percentage of cases cleared by arrest was about 20 percent when computers and other contemporary state-of-the-art technology were not available. In 2000, when law enforcement agencies were not experiencing a shortage of high-tech equipment and personnel, the overall clearance rate was lower than in 1971. Despite the spending of tens of billions of dollars to upgrade equipment and hire numerous additional officers, in an environment in which crime either declined or remained constant the overall clearance rate declined. The decline in overall clearance rates has been constant since 1990 (see Table 2.3).

TABLE 2.3 Total Number of Offenses Known to the Police and the Percentage Cleared by an Arrest, 1971–2000

	1971	1975	1980	1985	1990	1995	2000
Total offenses known to police	5,377,735	8,198,613	12,483,038	11,762,540	13,468,228	11,859,129	9,366,936
Percentage cleared by an arrest	(20.9%)	(21.0%)	(19.2%)	(20.9%)	(21.6%)	(21.2%)	(20.5%)
Total violent crimes known to police	473,126	797,688	1,242,511	1,240,134	1,700,303	1,531,703	1,131,923
Percentage cleared by an arrest	(46.5%)	(44.7%)	(43.6%)	(47.6%)	(45.6%)	(45.4%)	(47.5%)
Total property crimes known to police	3,126,936	7,400,925	11,240,527	10,522,406	11,767,925	10,327,426	8,235,013
Percentage cleared by an arrest	(15.7%)	(18.5%)	(16.5%)	(17.8%)	(18.1%)	(17.6%)	(16.7%)

Source: U.S. Department of Justice, Bureau of Criminal Justice Statistics, 1999 (Online).

Racial Distribution of Arrests.   Racial bias permeates the legal system, from the making of laws (and hence the definition of crime) to the interpretation and application of laws. This bias is evident in the patterns of arrests, as reported in the annual *Uniform Crime Reports.* Table 2.4 shows this distribution.

African Americans, while constituting around 12 percent of the U.S. population, account for nearly 28 percent of all arrests. They are particularly overrepresented for violent crimes, especially homicide and robbery. African Americans account for about half of all homicide and robbery arrests since 1990. However, this picture is highly misleading. In many jurisdictions, African Americans are especially likely to be singled out as suspects of a crime. Remember, these data concentrate on arrests and reflect police behavior, not a determination of guilt or innocence. Also remember that UCR data lump together whites and Hispanics (for statistical purposes we suppose). If we could separate Hispanics from the "white" category, the proportion of African Americans arrested would probably be more striking.

Gender Distribution of Arrests.   In 1985, female arrestees accounted for 21.4 percent of all people arrested for index crimes. By 2000, female arrestees accounted for 26.4 percent of all people arrested for index crimes. As Table 2.5 demonstrates, between 1985 and 2000 women maintained high arrest rates for crimes such as fraud, forgery and counterfeiting, embezzlement, and larceny–theft. Women have always led their male counterparts in both runaway and prostitution arrests, but as the table shows, men have been closing the gap on the latter since 1985. A broader and more comprehensive discussion of women and crime is offered in Chapter 14.

Age Distribution of Arrests.   As indicated in Table 2.6, arrests vary by age and by offense. In 1985, 17.2 percent of those arrested were under the age of 18. In 1990 and 1995 juveniles accounted for 15.6 percent and 18.3 percent, respectively, of all arrests in the United States. In 2000, those under 18 accounted for 17.1 percent of all arrests. Hence, the percentage of those people under the age of 18 is nearly identical to the same population group in 1985. These data contradict the popular conception that juvenile crime is out of control. Indeed, the majority of those arrested are, and always have been, adults. As can be seen in Table 2.6, older persons are far more likely than juveniles to be arrested for index crimes, with the exception of arson. A broader and more comprehensive presentation of juvenile crime is offered in Chapter 13.

TABLE 2.4   Persons Arrested by Race, 1985–2000 (percent)

Offense	1985			1990			1995			2000		
	White	Black	Other	White	Black	Other	White	Black	Other	White	Black	Other
TOTAL	**71.0**	**27.3**	**1.7**	**69.2**	**28.9**	**1.9**	**66.8**	**30.9**	**2.2**	**69.7**	**27.9**	**2.4**
INDEX CRIMES												
Homicide	50.2	48.2	1.5	43.7	54.7	1.6	43.4	54.4	2.2	48.7	48.8	2.5
Rape	52.9	45.8	1.4	55.1	43.2	1.7	55.6	42.4	2.1	63.7	34.1	2.2
Robbery	39.1	59.9	0.9	37.7	61.2	1.2	38.7	59.5	1.8	44.2	53.9	1.8
Aggravated assault	58.1	40.3	1.6	59.9	38.4	1.7	59.6	38.4	2.0	63.5	34.0	2.4
Burglary	65.9	32.5	1.3	68.1	30.1	1.8	67.0	31.0	2.0	69.4	28.4	2.1
Larceny–Theft	65.4	32.5	2.1	67.2	30.5	2.3	64.8	32.4	2.7	66.7	30.4	2.9
Motor-vehicle theft	63.8	34.5	1.7	59.4	38.4	2.2	58.5	38.3	2.0	55.4	41.6	3.0
Arson	69.3	29.2	1.4	75.2	23.0	1.8	74.2	23.7	2.0	76.4	21.7	1.9
Violent crime	52.6	46.0	1.4	53.7	44.7	1.6	54.3	43.7	2.0	59.9	37.8	2.3
Property crime	65.5	32.7	1.9	66.7	31.1	2.2	64.7	32.6	2.7	66.2	31.0	2.8
Total crime index	62.3	35.9	1.7	63.6	34.4	2.1	61.9	35.7	2.4	64.5	32.9	2.7
PART II CRIMES												
Other assaults	65.6	32.7	1.7	64.1	33.9	2.0	63.0	34.7	2.3	66.0	31.5	2.6
Forgery and counterfeiting	65.5	33.4	1.1	64.7	34.0	1.3	65.0	33.1	2.0	68.0	30.0	2.0
Fraud	68.0	31.2	0.8	66.1	33.2	0.8	64.0	34.7	1.3	67.3	31.5	1.3
Embezzlement	70.1	28.5	1.3	66.4	32.1	1.6	64.9	33.1	2.0	63.6	34.1	2.3
Stolen property	61.2	37.7	1.0	57.5	41.2	1.3	58.6	39.4	1.9	58.9	39.1	1.9
Vandalism	75.4	22.9	1.7	75.5	22.6	1.9	73.4	23.9	2.7	75.9	21.6	2.5
Weapons	64.3	34.4	1.4	58.6	39.8	1.6	59.4	38.8	1.9	61.3	36.8	1.9
Prostitution	55.4	43.0	1.5	59.8	38.9	1.3	60.9	36.8	2.2	58.0	39.5	2.5
Sex offenses (except rape and prostitution)	79.5	19.0	1.5	78.7	19.5	1.9	75.0	22.6	2.4	74.4	23.2	2.4
Drug abuse violations	67.9	31.1	0.9	58.5	40.7	0.7	62.1	36.9	1.1	64.2	34.5	1.2
Gambling	45.8	49.4	4.7	47.2	47.5	5.2	53.3	41.3	5.4	30.7	64.4	4.8
Offenses against family and children	63.6	35.0	1.4	65.7	30.3	3.9	65.2	32.2	2.7	67.6	29.6	2.8
Driving under the influence	88.5	9.8	1.7	89.5	8.7	1.8	86.4	10.9	2.7	88.2	9.6	2.2
Liquor laws	80.5	16.0	3.5	87.3	9.6	3.1	79.6	17.3	3.1	85.6	10.6	3.8
Drunkenness	79.9	17.6	2.5	79.3	18.2	2.4	80.8	16.4	2.8	84.7	13.7	1.6
Disorderly conduct	67.2	31.1	1.8	65.8	32.4	1.9	62.9	35.1	1.9	65.3	32.6	2.1
Vagrancy	66.5	29.8	3.7	56.8	40.8	2.0	52.4	45.0	2.7	53.6	43.4	3.1
All other (except traffic)	64.2	34.3	1.6	63.4	34.7	2.0	63.1	34.7	2.1	65.8	31.6	2.6
Suspicion	43.3	55.8	0.9	42.0	57.1	0.9	51.9	47.5	0.6	69.0	29.6	1.5
Curfew and loitering	x	x	x	78.9	17.7	3.3	75.8	21.3	2.9	72.2	24.7	3.1
Runaways	x	x	x	80.2	16.4	3.3	76.9	19.0	4.1	76.3	17.9	4.4

Source: U.S. Department of Justice, Bureau of Criminal Justice Statistics, 1999 (Online).

TABLE 2.5 Persons Arrested by Sex, 1985–2000 (percent)

Offense	1985 Male	1985 Female	1990 Male	1990 Female	1995 Male	1995 Female	2000 Male	2000 Female
TOTAL	**82.6**	**17.4**	**81.4**	**18.4**	**79.6**	**20.4**	**77.8**	**22.2**
INDEX CRIMES								
Homicide	87.6	12.4	89.6	10.4	90.5	9.5	89.4	10.6
Rape	98.9	1.1	98.9	1.1	98.8	1.2	98.9	1.1
Robbery	92.4	7.6	91.7	8.3	90.7	9.3	89.9	10.1
Aggravated assault	86.5	13.5	86.7	13.3	82.3	17.7	79.9	20.1
Burglary	92.6	7.4	91.2	8.8	88.9	11.1	86.7	13.3
Larceny–Theft	69.0	31.0	68.0	32.0	66.7	33.3	64.1	35.9
Motor-vehicle theft	90.7	9.3	90.0	10.0	86.9	13.1	84.2	15.8
Arson	86.9	13.1	87.0	13.0	84.3	15.7	84.9	15.1
Violent crime	89.1	10.9	88.7	11.3	85.1	14.9	82.6	17.4
Property crime	76.0	24.0	74.7	25.3	72.7	27.3	70.1	29.9
Total index	78.6	21.4	78.1	21.9	76.1	23.9	73.6	26.4
PART II CRIMES								
Other assaults	84.6	15.4	83.9	16.1	80.4	19.6	77.0	23.0
Forgery and counterfeiting	66.8	33.2	65.4	34.6	64.1	35.9	61.0	39.0
Fraud	57.4	42.6	55.8	44.2	59.0	41.0	55.1	44.9
Embezzlement	64.4	35.6	58.8	41.2	56.4	43.6	50.0	50.0
Stolen property	88.2	11.8	88.0	12.0	85.8	14.2	82.6	17.4
Vandalism	90.0	10.0	89.2	10.8	86.4	13.6	84.5	15.5
Weapons	92.4	7.6	92.6	7.4	92.1	7.9	91.9	8.1
Prostitution	30.5	69.5	36.0	64.0	38.9	61.1	37.9	62.1
Sex offenses (except rape and prostitution)	92.6	7.4	92.3	7.7	92.0	8.0	92.6	7.4
Drug abuse violations	86.2	13.8	83.2	16.8	83.3	16.7	82.4	17.6
Gambling	85.4	14.6	86.2	13.8	84.8	15.2	89.0	11.0
Offenses against family and children	87.3	12.7	82.2	17.8	79.8	20.2	77.6	22.4
Driving under the influence	88.4	11.6	87.2	12.8	85.4	14.6	83.6	16.4
Liquor laws	83.6	16.4	81.3	18.7	81.1	18.9	77.0	23.0
Drunkenness	91.1	8.9	90.0	10.0	88.2	11.8	86.9	13.1
Disorderly conduct	81.3	18.7	80.9	19.1	78.3	21.7	77.2	22.8
Vagrancy	88.3	11.7	87.4	12.6	80.6	19.4	79.1	20.9
All other (except traffic)	84.4	15.6	83.4	16.6	81.6	18.4	79.1	20.9
Suspicion	85.1	14.9	85.0	15.0	84.8	15.2	80.4	19.6
Curfew and loitering	75.3	24.7	72.0	28.0	70.4	29.6	68.7	31.3
Runaways	42.7	57.3	43.6	56.4	42.6	57.4	41.2	58.8

Source: U.S. Department of Justice, Bureau of Criminal Justice Statistics, 1999 (Online).

TABLE 2.6   Persons Arrested by Age, 1985–2000 (percent)

	1985		1990		1995		2000	
Offense	*Under 18*	*18 and Over*	*Under 18*	*18 and Over*	*Under 18*	*18 and Over*	*Under 18*	*18 and Over*
TOTAL	**17.2**	**82.8**	**15.6**	**84.4**	**18.3**	**81.7**	**17.1**	**82.9**
INDEX CRIMES								
Homicide	8.3	91.7	14.0	86.0	15.3	84.7	9.3	90.7
Rape	15.1	84.9	14.9	85.1	15.8	84.2	16.4	83.6
Robbery	25.0	75.0	24.2	75.8	32.3	67.7	25.2	74.8
Aggravated assault	13.8	86.2	13.6	86.4	14.7	85.3	13.9	86.1
Burglary	38.0	62.0	32.9	67.1	35.1	64.9	33.0	67.0
Larceny–Theft	32.8	67.2	30.0	70.0	33.4	66.6	31.2	68.8
Motor-vehicle theft	38.0	62.0	43.3	56.7	42.0	58.0	34.3	65.7
Arson	41.2	58.8	43.8	56.2	52.3	47.7	52.9	47.1
Violent crime	16.8	83.2	16.2	83.8	18.7	81.3	15.9	84.1
Property crime	34.4	65.6	31.9	68.1	34.7	65.3	32.0	68.0
Total Index	30.8	69.2	28.1	71.9	30.2	69.8	27.5	72.5
PART II CRIMES								
Other assaults	15.2	84.8	14.9	85.1	16.7	83.3	18.0	82.0
Forgery and counterfeiting	10.4	89.6	9.1	90.9	7.2	92.8	6.9	93.1
Fraud	6.2	93.8	3.4	96.6	5.8	94.2	3.1	96.9
Embezzlement	7.1	92.9	7.2	92.8	8.2	91.8	10.3	89.7
Stolen property	25.1	74.9	25.9	74.1	25.7	74.3	23.4	76.6
Vandalism	44.8	55.2	40.4	59.6	44.9	55.1	40.6	59.4
Weapons	16.4	83.6	18.2	81.8	23.1	76.9	23.6	76.4
Prostitution	2.4	97.6	1.4	98.6	1.3	98.7	1.5	98.5
Sex offenses (except rape and prostitution)	17.18	2.9	15.9	84.1	17.0	83.0	18.6	83.4
Drug abuse violations	11.4	88.6	7.4	92.6	12.9	87.1	12.9	87.1
Gambling	2.7	97.3	5.2	94.8	8.3	91.7	14.2	85.8
Offenses against family and children	4.9	95.1	4.0	96.0	4.8	95.2	6.4	93.6
Driving under the influence	1.4	98.6	1.1	98.9	1.0	99.0	1.4	98.6
Liquor laws	25.1	74.9	22.1	77.9	20.2	79.8	23.3	76.7
Drunkenness	2.9	97.1	2.7	97.3	2.9	97.1	3.4	96.6
Disorderly conduct	14.3	85.7	16.6	83.4	23.2	76.8	25.9	74.1
Vagrancy	9.1	90.9	8.1	91.9	13.5	86.5	9.3	90.7
All other (except traffic)	13.1	86.9	9.7	90.3	10.9	89.1	11.2	88.8
Suspicion	23.1	76.9	17.4	82.6	16.9	83.1	21.1	78.9
Curfew and loitering	x	x	x	x	x	x	x	x
Runaways	x	x	x	x	x	x	x	x

Source: U.S. Department of Justice, Bureau of Criminal Justice Statistics, 1999 (Online).

There is a great deal more to the present "crime problem" than what has been presented so far. We now will take a different look at crime, with a view that presents a picture radically different than that given to us by the media and official statistics. This will entail a close examination of so-called "upperworld" crimes of the state, corporations, and people of high social standing. As will be shown, these crimes cause far more harm (both financially and physically) than the crimes mentioned so far.

The Other Side of the Crime Picture: Corporate, White-Collar, and State Crimes

Who are the dangerous people in society? Who threatens us most with death and serious bodily injury? Who poses the greatest threat to our money or property? There is no question that we would be frightened if faced with a robber on the streets, and coming home to find that some stranger has broken into the house would be rather scary too. We do not want to downplay the significance of these "traditional" crimes of violence, for they do create much fear and concern. But these kinds of crimes are only one side of the crime picture. Let's look closely at the other side.

Statistically speaking, the gravest threats come not from robbers, burglars, rapists, and the like, but from people who wear business suits or white medical coats to work or who occupy plush offices in corporate headquarters or hold powerful positions within the government. Their weapons are ballpoint pens, scalpels, computers, and merely their words.

According to FBI figures, about two people will be murdered within the next hour (probably with a gun or knife). However, according to one recent study, about 56,000 Americans die on the job every year or from occupational diseases such as black lung, brown lung, asbestosis, and cancers associated with various occupations (about six per hour).[44] Another estimate puts the number of annual deaths from work-related causes at 100,000, with deaths from job-related diseases ranging from a low of 136,800 to a high of 390,000. Work-related accidents kill an estimated 10,700, and there are 1.8 million disabling injuries each year.[45] One author estimates that the overall work-related death rate is around 115 per 100,000, compared with a homicide rate of around 8 per 100,000.[46]

The most recent case (as of this writing) is the Enron case. Most commentary and reporting focus on the alleged connection with the White House and politicians who received over $1 million in campaign contributions from Enron in recent years. The news media are having a field day trying to turn this event into another Watergate scandal; some call it "Enrongate." But in our opinion, a terse comment by Treasury Secretary Paul O'Neill points to where the analysis of this case should be going. He is quoted as saying that he was not too surprised at Enron's downfall: "Companies come and go. It's…part of the genius of capitalism." Senator Joseph Lieberman called O'Neill's remarks "cold-blooded."[47] Lieberman, however, supports the very system O'Neill is praising. His role as a senator is essentially to represent big business and the "genius of capitalism." Part of the so-called genius of capitalism is, of course, greed, with profits going to a narrow group of individuals being the only goal. Too bad the workers and most of the stockholders get shortchanged. Corporate decision making is corporate predatory behavior at its best but merely masks what really goes on within corporate America: criminal behavior, pure and simple.

The Enron case is merely the tip of the iceberg. **Corporate crime** has been part and parcel of the capitalist system since day one. In fact, we can say that capitalism and corporate crime are synonymous. After all, how can such huge profits continue to grow without a good deal of deviance?

Consider too the case of the Ford Explorer and of thousands of Firestone tires. At least 103 deaths have been attributed to defects in some Firestone tires, particularly on Ford Explorers. Another recent scandal involves one of the largest pharmaceutical companies, Abbott Laboratories. An investigation into drug prices by the *New York Times* found that Abbott paid off some competitors for *not* producing some generic—and hence cheaper—drugs and thus keeping them away from consumers for an entire year. One drug was Hytrin, used to treat high blood pressure and prostate enlargement. It costs patients around $30 per month. Abbott was able to reap profits of around $1 million each day the generic version of Hytrin was off the market. Abbott paid producers of the less expensive generic drug around $6 million per month.[48]

There have been many warnings throughout the past two hundred years. Both Adam Smith and Thomas Jefferson warned of dire consequences from the concentration of power in the hands of a few corporations. John Dewey stated that government (or politics) is but the "shadow cast upon society by big business."[49] More recently, in his book *Corporation Nation,* Charles Derber argued that corporate power is the "new problem with no name" (borrowing Betty Friedan's words describing women's secondary status in America).[50] Corporate decision making, usually behind closed doors, determines what is produced, how it is produced, how profits are distributed, who may work, whether jobs will be moved to foreign lands, and much more. It is certainly not an example of true democracy.

Such cases go back many years. In March 1976, twenty-six miners were killed by a methane gas explosion. During the previous six years the company that owned the mine had been cited for 1,250 safety violations, 57 of which had resulted in the temporary closing of the mine by the federal government. On 21 separate occasions federal inspectors believed that there was "imminent danger to the lives of the miners working there."[51]

In the now-famous Ford Pinto case, an internal memo showed that Ford Motor Company executives knew about the potentially lethal design defect in the Pinto's fuel system. The memo showed that correcting the problem would cost the company $137 million. Ford decided not to correct it. An estimated 500 people died because of the defect.[52] According to one recent study, as many as 140,000 Americans have died in auto accidents because auto companies' "legislative privilege effectively thwarted all efforts to develop and legally mandate" front air bags.[53]

The National Safety Council estimated that since the passage of the Occupational Safety and Health Act in 1970, 250,000 workers have died on the job. The death of a worker in a chicken-processing plant in Florida prompted an investigation by the Occupational Safety and Health Administration (OSHA). It was discovered that the company had been cited for six violations of federal worker safety laws, and a $530,000 fine was recommended. However, the fine eventually was reduced to $30,000, and the violations were reduced from "willful violations" to "serious violations." Because only "willful violations" can be prosecuted, the company was never prosecuted. Yet the worker was just as dead as if he'd been the victim of a drive-by shooting.[54]

Here are additional cases. The three largest manufacturers of infant formula (together accounting for around 90% of the market) were charged with fixing prices, costing the government (in other words, taxpayers) about $25 billion. The savings and loan bankruptcy case cost taxpayers more than $1 billion. The owner of one of the savings and loans, Vernon Savings and Loan in Dallas, used money stolen from savers to purchase a $1.9 million chalet in Colorado, plus a $1 million home in California and a $2.6 million yacht in Florida.[55] Still other examples include the 500 deaths and 200,000 or more injuries because of a chemical gas leak in India caused by the criminal negligence of Union Carbide; the Oraflex arthritis drug (estimated to be responsible for the death of at least 49 elderly people); the Dalkon Shield (responsible in the death of at least 17 women and the injury of at least 200,000 more); deaths from asbestos, estimated at 170,000.[56] Tables 2.7 and 2.8 illustrate various causes of death due to corporate criminality.

The property crimes reported to the FBI cost the American people an estimated $3 billion to $4 billion per year. In contrast, the most recent estimate of the yearly costs of corporate and white-collar crime is in excess of $200 billion, or 500 times more.[57] Table 2.9 lists many of these crimes and their costs. However, the list of specific crimes seems endless. It includes bribery of government officials, defense contract fraud, health care provider fraud, and corporate tax evasion. Moreover, the corporate share of the tax burden has declined from around 25 percent in the 1950s to less than 10 percent today.[58] The list of corporate and white-collar crimes also includes price-fixing (costing consumers over $100 million each

TABLE 2.7   Death and Injury from Selected Corporate Crimes

CORPORATION/INDUSTRY	PROBLEM	EXTENT OF DEATH AND INJURY
Union Carbide	Chemical gas leak in Bhopal, India	500 deaths and 200,000 injuries
Miscellaneous	Asbestos	Estimated 100,000 workers may eventually die
Pharmaceutical	Oraflex (arthritis drug)	Killed at least 49 elderly
Firestone	Firestone 500 tires	Loss of tread believed to have resulted in 41 deaths
General Motors	Faulty breaks	Estimated 13 people killed
Ford Pinto and Mercury Bobcat	Exploding fuel tanks	Estimated more than 50 killed
Pharmaceutical	Dalkon Shield contraceptive	Estimated to have killed 17 women and injured as many as 200,000

Source: Miethe, T., and R. McCorkle. *Crime Profiles.* Los Angeles: Roxbury Press, 1998, ch. 7.

year), price-gouging ("systematic overcharging" with markups as high as 7,000 percent),[59] false advertising and product misrepresentation, corporate stealing from employees (cheating workers out of overtime pay, violations of minimum wage laws, etc.), unfair labor practices, surveillance of employees, theft of trade secrets, monopolistic practices, and defrauding investors (e.g., the equity funding case, in which a corporation inflated stock prices by claiming $200 million in nonexistent assets).[60] And all of this does not even include various forms of so-called occupational crime, such as retail fraud by small businesses, service business fraud (especially prevalent in the car repair industry), and various forms of medical crime, especially Medicaid and Medicare fraud, which is estimated to be as high as $25 billion per year.[61] A list of some corporate lawbreakers is presented in Figure 2.3. These examples come from a study by Irwin Ross appearing in *Fortune* magazine in 1980; the study included corporations convicted in federal courts during the 1970s—117 different offenders, representing 11 percent of the largest corporations.[62]

Keep in mind that the offenses noted here are based, in many cases, on estimates because hard data are difficult to come by. By the same token, much of what is reported by the FBI in its annual report is based on estimates. It is entirely possible that the estimates on corporate crime represent only the tip of the iceberg, because so much illegal behavior goes unreported. And it is not that corporate crime is of recent origin. The extent of corporate crime was noted in a now-classic study by Edwin Sutherland, published in 1949 under the title *White Collar Crime.* Sutherland focused on law violations by 70 corporations and

TABLE 2.8   How Americans Are (Really) Murdered

CAUSE	DEATHS
Occupational hazard and disease	34,100
Knife or other cutting instrument, including scalpel	14,538
Firearms	13,673
Other weapons: club, poison, hypodermic prescription drug	4,650
Personal weapons (hands, fists, etc.)	1,182
Total	68,143

Source: Reiman, J. H. *The Rich Get Richer and the Poor Get Prison* (5th ed.). Boston: Allyn and Bacon, 1998, p. 80.

TABLE 2.9 The Cost of White-Collar and Corporate Crime (in billions of dollars)

OFFENSE	ESTIMATED COST
Corporate crime (fraud, antitrust violations, bribery, corruption, price-fixing, illegal mergers, etc.)	$700+
Embezzlement (employee theft)	$6–435
Tax fraud	$100–300
Money laundering	$100–300
Computer-related, high-tech crime	$.1–200
Consumer/personal fraud (telemarketing)	$40–100
Health care fraud (Medicare, Medicaid)	$10–100
Insurance fraud	$18–31
Savings and loan bailout	$8–15
Check fraud	$10
Phone and cellular fraud	$.5–9
Credit/debit/charge/bank-card fraud	$.75–1.5
Total estimated costs	$993.35–$1,491.5

Sources: Coleman, J. W. *The Criminal Elite* (3rd ed.). New York: St. Martin's Press, 1994; Friedrichs, D. O *Trusted Criminals: White Collar Crime in Contemporary Society.* Belmont, CA: Wadsworth, 1996; Green, G. S *Occupational Crime.* Chicago: Nelson-Hall, 1990; Miethe, T., and R. McCorkle. *Crime Profiles.* Los Angeles Roxbury Press, 1998.

found 980 specific violations, about one-third of which were restraint of trade.[63] About twenty years later, another study documented the extent of corporate violations. Clinard and Yeager found that over a two-year period more than 60 percent of the 582 largest corporations had at least one violation. Automobile, oil-refining, and drug companies accounted for about half of all violations. Unfortunately, this study excluded the banking, insurance, transportation, and communications industries and utilities.[64] At about the same time, a very detailed case study of a mining company discovered that for several years the company had used a nearby stream to dump waste material, which eventually piled and created a large dam with a lake behind it. When the dam collapsed during a rainstorm, 125 people died and an entire community was almost literally washed away. Most of the people who died had worked for the company.[65]

State crime is rarely discussed (it is virtually ignored in standard criminal justice books), yet the death toll and economic devastation of crimes committed by the state are beyond description. State crimes include several different harmful behaviors that have at least one thing in common: they are generally committed against powerless people and are rarely, if ever, called crimes. Although there are several definitions, we generally accept one offered by Kramer and Michalowski, who use the term "state–corporate crime" because there is some relationship between corporations and the government, as when "one or more institutions of political governance pursue a goal in direct cooperation with one or more institutions of economic production and distribution."[66] Admittedly this definition is a little vague, so let's just say that **state crimes** involve harmful behaviors committed by the government itself (e.g., the CIA, the State Department), sometimes in collusion with private corporations, on the national level or on the state and local levels. Most of the literature on this subject focuses on the national level.

Examples of these harms include the following: the violation of environmental, safety, and health standards at federal nuclear weapons production facilities by private contractors; the Iran-Contra affair (cooperation between the CIA and private arms dealers);

FIGURE 2.3   A "Criminal Class"? Some Illustrations of Corporate Crime (a small sample of a total of 117)

Allied Chemical	Price-fixing and tax fraud related to paying kickbacks.
American Airlines	Illegal campaign contributions of $55,000.
Archer-Daniels-Midland	Defrauding grain buyers by short-weighing.
Ashland Oil	Illegal political contributions of $100,000 and fixing prices of resins used to make paint; Ashland-Warren subsidiary pleaded guilty in three cases involving bid-rigging in highway construction and was fined $1.5 million.
Bethlehem Steel	Two cases of fixing prices of steel reinforcing bars; mail fraud related to bribes paid for ship-repair business.
Braniff International	Illegal campaign contributions ($40,000); slush fund of $900,000; criminal restraint-of-trade charges.
Chemical Bank of New York	Money-laundering for drug dealers.
Consolidated Foods	Price-fixing of sugar.
Du Pont	Price-fixing of drugs.
Equity Funding	SEC charges related to $2 billion in fictitious insurance policies.
Firestone	Slush fund and illegal contributions of $330,000; false tax returns related to $13 million in "set-aside income."
Genesco	Price-fixing of women's clothing.
Hammermill Paper	Price-fixing of paper products.
Walter Kidde	SEC charges related to $2.5 million in illegal rebates by subsidiary U.S. Lines.
J. Ray McDermott	SEC charges related to slush fund of more than $800,000 used for commercial bribes and illegal contributions; wire fraud and racketeering charges filed.
Owens-Illinois	Fixing prices of corrugated containers.
Pepsi-Co	Frito-Lay subsidiary fixed prices of snacks; parent company fixed prices of sugar; bribery of union officials.
Phillips Petroleum	Illegal campaign contributions of $100,000; SEC charges related to $2.8 million slush fund; fixing prices of gasoline; tax evasion.
Joseph Seagram	Over $1 million in illegal rebates; bribery of and illegal payments to state liquor officials.
Time, Inc.	Price-fixing.
United Brands	Improper use of funds to pay $1.2 million bribe to Honduran official (charged with wire fraud).

Source: Green, G. S. *Occupational Crime.* Chicago: Nelson-Hall, 1990, pp. 111–119.

and the intervention by the U.S. government into the affairs of third-world countries in support of dictatorships and the overthrow of democratically elected governments, all in support of private corporate interests. The last category is particularly interesting, because the U.S. government is supposedly making the world "safe for democracy." Specific examples of these interventions include Guatemala (1950s), Zaire (1960s), Dominican Republic (1961–1962), Indonesia (including East Timor, 1960s–1970s), Greece (1967), Chile (1973), Angola (1975), Libya (1980), Grenada (1980s), El Salvador (1980s), Nicaragua (1980s), Haiti (late 1980s, early 1990s)—to name only a few in a long list of mostly CIA-backed atrocities in the name of private profit and political domination.[67]

The U.S. government has made it a practice to support all sorts of dictators who think nothing of violating human rights. The government does so mostly in the name of profit for major corporations that have interests in foreign lands. Noam Chomsky succinctly summarized the U.S. government's role:

> Or consider US-backed dictators like Trujillo in the Dominican Republic, Somoza in Nicaragua, Marcos in the Philippines, Duvalier in Haiti and a host of Central American gangsters through the 1980s. They were all *much* more brutal than Noriega, but the United States supported them enthusiastically right through decades of horrifying atrocities—as long as profits were flowing out of their countries and into the US. George Bush's administration continued to honor Motubu, Ceausescu and Saddam Hussein, among others, all far worse criminals than Noriega. Suharto of Indonesia, arguably the worst killer of them all, remains a Washington-media "moderate."[68]

A particularly gruesome example—almost completely ignored by the mainstream press—occurred in East Timor, a portion of Indonesia, north of Australia. Rich in oil and other resources, East Timor became a pawn of the Indonesian dictator Suharto (who had overthrown the democratically elected President Sukarto with CIA backing). Suharto, using weapons from the United States, killed around 200,000 innocent citizens (out of a population of around 600,000) in what has been described as the worst example of genocide (on a per capita basis) since the Holocaust.[69] All of the foregoing cases are examples of criminal offenses or at least violations of international human rights laws, but they were not committed by unemployed black teenagers who had dropped out of school. These offenders came from the highest echelons of society, were pillars of the community, or agents of the U.S. government. And in the minds of most people they were not really "criminals" or at least were not perceived as "dangerous." Yet collectively these particular offenses cost thousands of lives and several hundred billion dollars each year. For the most part, these are indeed *white*-collar crimes, for they are committed overwhelmingly by wealthy white males. In fact, there is no way anyone can argue that the worst crimes are committed by racial minorities. Nevertheless, racial minorities are overwhelmingly subjected to the actions of the criminal justice system and fill the jails and prisons. It is a rare occurrence when the perpetrator of a corporate or state crime goes to prison.

One reason these offenses are not part of the popular image of "crime" and "criminals" is that those labels are the result of a conscious social process. They are not inherent in the behaviors themselves and certainly not the result of some mysterious force. Further, it must be more than merely a coincidence that the offenders mentioned above come from the same social class as those who own the news media (especially newspapers and television), which help create and perpetuate the popular images of crime and criminals. And they are from the same social class as legislators who pass laws making behaviors "criminal" and judges who interpret the laws and hand out sentences.

In one sense these acts *are* different from street crimes. Reiman explains this by distinguishing between *one-on-one harms* and *indirect-harms*. **One-on-one harms** are acts, such as robbery, rape, and burglary in which one or more specific individuals seek to intentionally harm one or more specific victims—that is, the mugger who terrorized you in the parking lot set out to harm *you*. These offenses involve some force or at least the threat or potential of force (even the so-called nonviolent burglar may think nothing of using violence if you come home while he is burglarizing your house). **Indirect-harms** do not involve direct threats to individuals. The owners of the mine mentioned earlier did not set out to harm a specific person, nor did Ford Motor Company executives. What they wanted was quite legitimate. They simply wanted to maximize profits and minimize costs.[70]

SUMMARY

This chapter focused on the problem of crime in America today. Crime ranges from ordinary street crimes, such as those reported by the FBI in its annual report *Crime in the United States,* to corporate, white-collar, and state crimes, which rarely are reported anywhere.

Several sources of crime data were summarized and critiqued. The typical methods of measuring crime utilize FBI reports, victimization surveys, and self-report studies. Each of these contains several flaws. The FBI reports have great potential for abuse, especially at the local level.

The extent of crime was noted and summarized, covering "crimes known to the police" and "persons arrested," two major UCR categories. Victimization surveys were summarized, and it was noted that a great deal more crime is committed than is reported to local police departments. Self-report studies, though focusing mostly on the behavior (often minor) of school-age children, reveal a great deal of criminal behavior that never gets reported.

We presented data on the "official" crime picture according to conventional sources. We followed this with a presentation of a vast array of data on harmful (not always officially labeled "criminal") behavior among the rich and powerful. Crimes among those of high social standing, corporations, and members of the U.S. government range from price-fixing and various forms of fraud to murder and genocide. The last two are not the one-on-one harms defined by Reiman, which is one reason why they do not fall within the popular conception of crime. Nevertheless, the toll they exact is enormous.

KEY TERMS

corporate crime 45	*mala prohibita* crimes 25	one-on-one harms 50
crime 24	misdemeanor 24	self-report survey 36
felony 24	National Incident-Based	social/popular concept of
index crimes 26	Reporting Program	crime 23
indirect-harms 50	(NIBRS) 32	state crime 48
legal concept of crime 23	National Crime Victimization	Uniform Crime Report 25
mala in se crimes 25	Survey (NCVS) 32	white-collar crime 26

NOTES

1. Bourdieu, P. *On Television.* New York: New Press, 1998, p. 18.

2. Glassner, B. *The Culture of Fear: Why Americans Are Afraid of the Wrong Things.* New York: Basic Books, 1999, p. 23.

3. Reiman, *The Rich Get Richer and the Poor Get Prison,* p. 53.

4. Quinney, *The Social Reality of Crime,* p. 302.

5. Reiman, *The Rich Get Richer and the Poor Get Prison.*

6. Michael, J., and M. J. Adler. *Crime, Law and Social Science.* New York: Harcourt, Brace, 1933, p. 5.

7. Quinney, R., and J. Wildeman. *The Problem of Crime: A Peace and Social Justice Perspective* (3rd ed.). Mountain View, CA: Mayfield, 1991, p. 4.

8. Sellin, J. T. *Culture, Conflict and Crime.* New York: Social Science Research Council, 1938.

9. Sutherland, E. *White Collar Crime.* Chicago: University of Chicago Press, 1949.

10. Schwendinger, H., and J. Schwendinger, "Defenders of Order or Guardians of Human Rights." *Issues in Criminology* 5: 113–146 (1970).

11. Michalowski, *Order, Law and Crime;* Reiman, *The Rich Get Richer and the Poor Get Prison;* Quinney, *Class, State and Crime,* Lynch, M. J., and R. Michalowski. *A New Primer in Radical Criminology* (3rd ed.). New York: Harrow and Heston, 2000.

12. Turk, A. "Prospects and Pitfalls for Radical Criminology: A Critical Response to Platt." *Crime and Social Justice* 4: 41–42 (1975); Bohm, R. "Radical Criminology: An Explication." *Criminology* 19: 565–589 (1982).

13. We want to bring up an important point at this juncture (which will be covered again in subsequent chapters). Because the criminal law dictates the specific behaviors that will result in processing by the criminal justice system, it is obvious that serious social harms not covered by the criminal law go virtually ignored by the criminal justice system. Some of these harms may be responded to by the civil court system or some other court system, but on these occasions the punishment is extremely light in comparison with that imposed by the criminal justice system. The fact that these behaviors are committed by those of high social standing, and the fact that the behaviors that come to the attention of officials of the criminal justice system are committed primarily by persons of low social standing, mean that there are obviously two separate and distinct systems of justice in our society: one for the rich and powerful and one for everyone else. Even when ordinary crimes are charged to persons of high social standing, the criminal justice system usually treats them lightly. For examples see Reiman, *The Rich Get Richer and the Poor Get Prison.* Also see Cole, D. *No Equal Justice: Race and Class in the American Criminal Justice System.* New York: New Press, 1999.

14. Reiman, ibid., p. 60.

15. Brownstein, H. H. *The Rise and Fall of a Violent Crime Wave: Crack Cocaine and the Social Construction of a Crime Problem.* Guilderland, NY: Harrow and Heston, 1996; Scheingold, *The Politics of Street Crime.*

16. DeKeseredy, W. S., and M. D. Schwartz. *Contemporary Criminology.* Belmont, CA: Wadsworth, 1996, p. 112.

17. Legal codes distinguish between "assault" and "battery" as specific crimes. A simple example will help. If someone comes up and threatens you with bodily harm, technically the act is an "assault" because all that is necessary is the threat. For example, someone says, "Next time you cross me, I'll bash your face in!" If that person carries through on this threat, it is "assault and battery." If there was no threat but someone simply attacked you without a weapon, the charge would be "battery" (but for statistical purposes would be counted as an "assault"). Also, if someone points a gun or other weapon at you and threatens you, a charge of "assault with a deadly weapon" can be made. If the threat is carried out, it can result in a charge of "felonious assault."

18. Clinard, M. B., R. Quinney, and J. Wildeman. *Criminal Behavior Systems* (3rd ed.). Cincinnati: Anderson, 1994.

19. Miethe, T., and R. McCorkle. *Crime Profiles: The Anatomy of Dangerous Persons, Places, and Situations.* Los Angeles: Roxbury, 1998. These authors identify seven major crime categories that deviate from more conventional types: (1) homocide and aggravated assault, (2) sexual assault, (3) personal and institutional robbery, (4) residential and nonresidential burglary, (5) motor-vehicle theft, (6) occupational and organizational crime, and (7) public-order crime.

20. Miller, W. B. *The Growth of Youth Gang Problems in the United States: 1970–98.* Washington, DC: U.S. Department of Justice, Office of Justice Programs, Office of Juvenile Justice and Delinquency Prevention, April 24, 2001.

21. The concept of high crimes and misdemeanors went through a very heated debate among politicians considering the impeachment of President Bill Clinton. The fact that interpretations often vary according to political party alignment demonstrates not only the inherent vagueness of the concept of crime but the political nature as well. Incidentally, "high crimes and misdemeanors" are not covered in state criminal codes and hence are not within the purview of the criminal justice system.

22. Pastore, A. L., and K. Maguire (eds.). *Sourcebook of Criminal Justice Statistics—1999.* Washington, DC: U.S. Department of Justice, Bureau of Justice Statistics, 2000, pp. 369–370.

23. When we were writing this chapter, in February 2002, the most recent report was the one released in October 2000, which presents crime data from 1998. The data were nearly two years old when the report was published. Lack of timeliness is one of the problems with the Uniform Crime Reports.

24. Sherman, L., and B. Glick. "The Quality of Arrest Statistics." *Police Foundation Reports* 2: 1–8 (1984).

25. Jackson, P. "Assessing the Validity of Official Data on Arson." *Criminology* 6: 181–195 (1988).

26. This assertion is based on our own observations and on confidential conversations that we have had with members of police departments in two different cities and on internal memos that we have obtained. Documentation about using "gangs" to divert attention away from internal problems is found in Miethe, T., and R. McCorkle, "The Political and Organizational Response to Gangs: An Examination of a 'Moral Panic' in Nevada." *Justice Quarterly* 15: 41–64 (March 1998).

27. Brownstein, *The Rise and Fall of a Violent Crime Wave,* p. 22.

28. Butterfield, F. "Possible Manipulation of Crime Data Worries Top Police." *New York Times,* August 3, 1998, as reported on the *New York Times* Web site (http://www.nytimes.com).

29. "Detroit's Crime Totals Still a Mystery." *Detroit Free Press,* May 4, 2001.

30. Allison, J., and L. Wrightsman. *Rape: The Misunderstood Crime.* Newbury Park, CA: Sage, 1993; Madigan, L., and N. Gamble. *The Second Rape: Society's Continual Betrayal of the Victim.* New York: Lexington Books, 1989.

31. R. G. Shelden, S. K. Tracy, and W. B. Brown. *Youth Gangs in American Society* (2nd ed.). Belmont, CA: Wadsworth, 2001.

32. DeKeseredy and Schwartz, *Contemporary Criminology,* pp. 132–133.

33. It should also be added that such images are continually reinforced in the news media. For an illustration of how the television news reinforces these images see Klite, P., R. A. Bardwell, and J. Salzman. *Not in the Public Interest: Local TV News in America.* Denver: Rocky Mountain Media Watch, 1998.

34. DeKeseredy and Schwartz, *Contemporary Criminology,* p. 135.

35. National Institute on Drug Abuse. *National Household Survey on Drug Abuse: Highlights 1990.* Washington, DC: U.S. Government Printing Office, 1991; Straus, M., and R. Gelles. *Physical Violence in American Families.* New Brunswick, NJ: Transaction Books, 1986.

36. Klite, Bardwell, and Salzman, *Not in the Public Interest: Local TV News in America.*

37. This charge has been systematically documented in numerous studies. See, for example, Herman, E., and N. Chomsky. *Manufacturing Consent: The Political Economy of the Mass Media.* New York: Pantheon, 1988; Chomsky, N. *Necessary Illusions: Thought Control in Democratic Societies.* Boston: South End Press, 1989; Postman, N. *Amusing Ourselves to Death.* New York: Penguin Books, 1985; B. Bagdikian, *The Media Monopoly* (2nd ed.). Boston: Beacon Press, 1987.

38. 1971 U.S. population was calculated from 1970 Census Bureau data by increasing the total U.S. population by .0134 (the yearly population increase average over the previous decade). *1990 Census of Population and Housing: Population and Housing Unit Counts.* U.S. Department of Commerce, Economics and Statistics Administration, Washington, D.C.: Bureau of the Census. (Table 2) 1990.

39. U.S. Census Bureau. Internet Release Date: December 28, 2000.

40. These figures are based on the following: total expenditures are from 1973 (1971 and 1972 figures not available), which came to $11 billion (Hindelang, M. J., C. S. Dunn, L. P. Sutton, and A. L. Aumick. *Sourcebook of Criminal Justice Statistics—1975.* Washington, D.C.: U.S. Department of Justice, 1976, p. 46; most recent expendi-

tures are from 1996 and were about $150 billion (see Chapter 1); prison population was 198,000 in December, 1971 (*Sourcebook of Criminal Justice Statistics—1975,* p. 641); prison population reported here was as of 2000 and was about 1.3 million (rate of about 464), plus another 621,000 jail prisoners, which brings the overall incarceration rate to about 700 (Bureau of Justice Statistics, *Sourcebook on Criminal Justice Statistics—2000,* on-line version.

41. McCaghy, C. H., and T. A. Capron. *Deviant Behavior: Crime, Conflict and Interest Groups* (3rd ed.). New York: Macmillan, 1994.

42. Many years of research have confirmed the relationship between drugs and alcohol and violent crime. See discussions in Miethe and McCorkle. *Crime Profiles;* McCaghy and Capron, *Deviant Behavior;* Clinard, Quinney, and Wildeman, *Criminal Behavior Systems.* For a good review of the drug–crime connection see Currie, E. *Crime and Punishment in America.* New York: Metropolitan Books, 1998, and *Reckoning: Drugs, the Cities, and the American Future.* New York: Hill and Wang, 1993.

43. Chambliss, W. J. (ed.). *Criminal Law in Action.* New York: McGraw-Hill, 1984, p. 201.

44. Mokhiber, R. "Corporate Crime: Underworld U.S.A." In K. Danaher (ed.), *Corporations Are Gonna Get Your Mama: Globalization and the Downsizing of the American Dream.* Monroe, ME: Common Courage Press, 1996, p. 62.

45. Friedrichs, D. O. *Trusted Criminals: White Collar Crime in Contemporary Society.* Belmont, CA: Wadsworth, 1996, p. 80.

46. Michaloski, *Order, Law and Crime,* pp. 325–338.

47. *Las Vegas Review-Journal,* January 14, 2002. See also the following sources: Hedges, S. J., and F. James. "Playing Politics Not New to Enron." *Las Vegas Review-Journal,* January 13, 2002; Huffington, A. "Compassionately Conserving Enron." *Los Angeles Times,* January 10, 2002; Scheer, R. "Connect the Enron Dots to Bush." *Los Angeles Times,* December 11, 2001; Oppel, R. A., and D. Van Natta. "Bush and Democrats Disputing Ties to Enron," *New York Times,* January 12, 2002; Corn, D. "Enron and the Bushes." *The Nation,* February 4, 2002; Geider, W. "Crime in the Suites." *The Nation,* February 4, 2002.

48. Mokhiber, R., and R. Weissman. "The 10 Worst Corporations of 2001." *The Progressive Populist,* February 1, 2002.

49. Quoted in Chomsky, N. *Class Warfare.* Monroe, ME: Common Courage Press, 1996, p. 29.

50. Derber, C. *Corporation Nation.* New York: St. Martin's Press, 1998.

51. Reiman, *The Rich Get Richer and the Poor Get Prison,* p. 35.

52. Michalowski, *Law, Order and Crime,* p. 357; Cullen, F. T., B. G. Link, and C. Polanzi. *Corporate Crime under Attack: The Ford Pinto Case and Beyond.* Cincinnati: Anderson, 1987.

53. Mokihber, "Corporate Crime," pp. 62–63.

54. Ibid., p. 64.

55. Geis, G. "A Base on Balls for White Collar Criminals." In D. Shichor and D. K. Sechrest (eds.), *Three Strikes and You're Out: Vengeance as Public Policy.* Thou-

sand Oaks, CA: Sage, 1996, pp. 245–246. See also Calavita, K., and Pontell, H. N. "The State and White Collar Crime: Saving the Savings and Loans." *Law and Society Review* 28 (1994): 297–324; Poveda, T. G. *Rethinking White Collar Crime.* Westport, CT: Praeger, 1994.

56. Calavita and Pontell, "The State and White Collar Crime."

57. Mokhiber, "Corporate Crime," p. 61; Clinard, Quinney, and Wildeman, *Criminal Behavior Systems,* p. 192.

58. Friedrichs, *Trusted Criminals,* p. 85.

59. Mokhiber, "Corporate Crime," p. 87.

60. Friedrichs, *Trusted Criminals,* pp. 83–93.

61. Ibid., p. 104.

62. Ross, I. "How Lawless Are Big Companies?" *Fortune* (December 1, 1980), pp. 55–61, cited in Green, G. S. *Occupational Crime.* Chicago: Nelson-Hall, 1990, pp. 111–119.

63. Sutherland, E. *White Collar Crime.* Chicago: University of Chicago Press, 1949.

64. Clinard, M. B., and P. C. Yeager. *Corporate Crime.* New York: Free Press, 1980.

65. Erickson, K. T. *Everything in Its Path: Destruction of Community in the Buffalo Creek Flood.* New York: Simon & Schuster, 1976. It is interesting to note that nearly all of the tobacco companies have significantly increased the marketing of their product overseas and toward the young in the United States. Given that tobacco is directly related to between 300,000 and 400,000 deaths each year, one could reasonably argue that these companies are among the biggest drug traffickers in the world. The same can be said about the liquor industry. However, largely because of the collective power of these companies, such behaviors are not labeled "crimes," while the mere *possession* of marijuana is a felony in some states (such as Nevada)!

66. Kramer R., and R. Michalowski, "State-Corporate Crime." Paper presented at the annual meeting of The American Society of Criminology, November, 1990.

67. A complete listing and detailed discussion of these and other state crimes could fill an entire book—in fact they fill several books. See, for example, the following works: Parenti, M. *Against Empire.* San Francisco: City Lights Press, 1995; Chomsky, N. *Year 501: The Conquest Continues.* Boston: South End Press, 1993; Zepezauer, M. *The CIA's Greatest Hits.* Tucson, AZ: Odonian Press, 1994; Barak, G. (ed.). *Crimes by the Capitalist State.* Albany: State University of New York Press, 1991. U.S. policies that led to various crimes by the American state are concisely summarized in Chomsky, N. *What Uncle Sam Really Wants.* Tucson, AZ: Odonian Press, 1992.

68. Chomsky, ibid., pp. 54–55.

69. Extensively documented in Chomsky, N., *Powers and Prospects.* Boston: South End Press, 1996, ch. 7; Parenti, M. *Against Empire.* San Francisco: City Lights Press, 1995, pp. 26–27; Zepezauer, *The CIA's Greatest Hits,* pp. 30–31.

70. Reiman, *The Rich Get Richer and the Poor Get Prison,* pp. 60–61.

CHAPTER THREE

PERSPECTIVES ON CRIMINAL JUSTICE AND LAW

Why do we have a criminal justice system? What is the overall purpose of this system? What does it really do? Is it supposed to impose sanctions after the fact? Is its purpose to act as a deterrent, to prevent crime from occurring in the first place? Is this system a truly equal system, or does it dispense biased justice? Whose interests does the system serve, all of the people or only some of the people? And how should we measure its effectiveness? These are a few of the questions that people routinely ask about the American system of criminal justice.

As Cullen and Gilbert note, two different perspectives have been offered over the past two hundred or so years in an attempt to address those questions.[1] This chapter reviews those perspectives, known as the *classical* and the *positivist* schools of thought. Then we offer our own perspective on crime and criminal justice, which differs significantly from them.

THE CLASSICAL SCHOOL

The **classical school** of thought about crime and criminal justice emerged during the late eighteenth century with the work of an Italian named **Cesare Beccaria** and an Englishman named Jeremy Bentham. Classical thinking derives core ideas from the Enlightenment period, which first emerged in France during the early eighteenth century and was represented by thinkers such as John Locke (1632–1704), Jean-Jacques Rousseau (1712–1778), Charles Louis Montesquieu (1689–1755), and Thomas Hobbes (1588–1679). This period has been described as one of tremendous changes in traditional thinking about human nature and society.

According to the classical school, an unwritten social contract emerged during the Renaissance (1300–1600). This was a vast social movement that swept away feudal customs and institutions, made for gains in intellectual development, and paralleled the emergence of capitalism throughout the Western world. According to the emerging view of the social contract (perhaps best illustrated by the writings of Hobbes and Rousseau), humans originally lived in a state of nature, grace, or innocence, and their escape from this state resulted from the application of reason. In other words, humans were essentially rational people whose reasoning powers placed them far above animals. Also, this perspective stressed that humans have free will and theoretically there was no limit to what they could accomplish. Furthermore, it was asserted that humans were essentially hedonistic—that humans, by their very nature, freely choose actions that maximize pleasure and minimize pain. Social contract thinkers claimed that the main instrument of the control of human behavior is fear, especially fear of pain. Punishment, as a principal method of operating to create fear, is seen as necessary to influence human will and thus to control behavior. Also, society had a right to punish the individual, and to transfer this right to the state. Finally, some code of criminal law, or some system of punishment was deemed necessary to respond to crime.[2]

The classical school derives mainly from the work of Cesare Beccaria (1738–1794), whose influential book *On Crimes and Punishment* was first published in 1764.[3] Beccaria and other liberal thinkers believed that the major principle that should govern legislation was "the greatest happiness for the greatest numbers" (this supports the view that government should be "of the people, by the people, for the people"). This philosophical doctrine is known as *utilitarianism,* the idea that punishment ought to be based on its *usefulness* or *utility* or *practicality.* In his book, Beccaria noted, "For a punishment to attain its end, the evil which it inflicts has only to exceed the advantages derivable from the crime." In other words, punishment should not be excessive; *it should fit the crime.*

The book *On Crimes and Punishment* was the first to provide a basic outline of what turned out to be the modern system of criminal justice. Several of his recommendations provide good summaries of his perspective. Perhaps most notable is the following, from the last page of his classic book: "In order for punishment not to be, in every instance, an act of violence of one or of many against a private citizen, it must be essentially public, prompt, necessary, the least possible in the given circumstances, proportionate to the crimes, dictated by the laws."[4] Beccaria also argued that punishment that closely follows the commission of a crime will be more just and useful. In other words, punishment should be "swift and certain." The major thrust of the classical school, however, is that the purpose of the criminal justice system is to prevent crime through deterrence. According to this line of thinking, a potential criminal will decide against committing a crime because the punishment would be too costly.

Jeremy Bentham (1748–1832), one of Beccaria's contemporaries, suggested that criminal behavior (like all human behavior) is a rational choice, born of free will. To prevent crime, we must make the punishment (i.e., pain) greater than the criminal act.

In summary, the classical school makes these assumptions: (1) All people are by their nature self-seeking and therefore liable to commit crime. (2) In order to live in harmony and avoid a "war of all against all" (as Hobbes stressed), people agree to give up certain freedoms in order to be protected by a strong central state. (3) Punishment is necessary to deter crime, and the state has the prerogative (which has been granted to it by the people through a social contract) to administer it. (4) Punishment should fit the crime and not be used to rehabilitate the offender. (5) Use of the law should be limited, and due process rights should be observed. (6) Each individual is responsible for his or her actions, and thus mitigating circumstances or excuses are inadmissible.[5]

The classical school of thought has generally given rise to two contrasting models of the criminal justice system that are roughly the equivalent of two differing political ideologies—namely, conservatism and liberalism.[6] From the conservative ideology comes the **crime control model.** It is based on the assumption that the fundamental goal of the criminal justice system is the repression of crime through aggressive law enforcement and harsh punishments, including the death penalty. From this point of view, protecting citizens from crime is more important than protecting the civil liberties of citizens. Supporters of this model would prefer that few criminals be set free on so-called technicalities, even at the expense of depriving innocent persons of their constitutional rights. Thus, the concern is more public safety than individual rights.

From the liberal ideology comes the **due process model.** If the crime control model resembles an "assembly line," the due process model resembles an "obstacle course." The due process model stresses the importance of individual rights and supports the general belief that it is better to let several criminals go free than to falsely imprison an innocent person. This model is based on the assumption that the criminal justice process is plagued by human error and that at each stage individual rights need to be safeguarded. The accused should be accorded legal counsel and equitable treatment, and the discretion of criminal justice personnel, especially the police, should be limited.

The classical school, as well as its modern derivatives, is subject to several criticisms. First, the assumptions that people always act rationally and that all people are hedonists and self-serving can be challenged. In fact, over one hundred years of social science research has demonstrated that this is clearly not the case, that humans are much more complex than such a simplistic view implies.[7]

Second, the assumption that people are equal in the narrow sense of being able to reason and are equally as likely to commit a crime can also be challenged. In point of fact, people in society (especially when the classical school emerged) are hardly equal by any method of measurement. Thus, you can hardly have "equal justice" in an unequal society. Appropriate here is the statement by French philosopher Anatole France, who once praised the "majestic equality of the law" because it "forbids rich and poor alike to sleep under bridges, to beg in the streets and to steal bread."[8]

This point leads us directly to the third objection—namely, that the classical school does little to address the causes of crime. As Taylor, Walton, and Young note, the classical writers particularly avoided any discussion of the relationship between inequality and crime and instead focused on problems associated with the control of crime.[9] Criminology became, in the words of George Vold, "administrative and legal criminology" during which justice became "an exact scale of punishments for equal acts without reference to the nature of the individual involved and with no attention to the question of special circumstances under which the act came about."[10]

The problems associated with the classical approach as proposed by Beccaria was felt as soon as legislatures began to adopt it. The French Code of 1791 tried to adopt, almost literally, Beccaria's proposals. This legislation tried to fix an exact amount of penalty to every crime and left nothing for the courts to do except to determine guilt. No attempt was made to allow for extenuating circumstances. The Code was impossible to enforce on a daily basis.[11] More important, it was nearly impossible to ignore the various social determinants of human behavior "and to proceed as if punishment and incarceration could be easily measured on some kind of universal calculus."[12] What eventually occurred was the rise of what criminologists have called the neoclassical school. Lawyers and jurists, mostly in Europe, attempted to revise the classical approach to account for the practical problems in the administration of justice according to Beccaria's plan. Certain reformers attacked the French Code as unjust because of its rigidity and called for a "need for individualization and for discriminating judgement to fit individual circumstances."[13] Among other things, the past record, the degree of incompetence, the insanity, and so on, of the offender and the impact of age on criminal responsibility would be taken into consideration.[14] In short, there was recognition that all offenders did not possess the same degree of "free will" and not every offender was suitable for imprisonment.

It is important to note, however, that the basic thrust of the classical school's vision of human beings and the proper response to crime was, for all practical purposes, left unchanged. As Vold and Bernard have observed:

> The doctrine continued to be that humans are creatures guided by reason, who have free will, and who therefore are responsible for their acts and can be controlled by fear of punishment. Hence the pain from punishment must exceed the pleasure obtained from the criminal act; then free will determines the desirability of noncriminal conduct. The neoclassical school therefore represented primarily the modifications necessary for the administration of the criminal law based on classical theory that resulted from practical experience.[15]

More important, the administration of justice continued to be guided, as it is today, by one overriding principle: that human behavior—in this case, criminal behavior—can be shaped, molded, changed, and so on, through the fear of punishment and that all that is needed to prevent people from committing crime is to make the punishment (or rather the pain associated with it) exceed the pleasure (or profit from the crime). This, along with most of the other assumptions of the classical school, was already beginning to be challenged almost at the same time that Beccaria's proposals were being debated. The challenge came from the positivist school.

THE POSITIVIST SCHOOL

The **positivist school** of thought about crime and criminal justice originated in the nineteenth century out of the scientific revolution, especially the discoveries of Charles Darwin and subsequent scientific advances. This revolution represented a sharp break from the past. Answers to fundamental questions about human beings and the universe began to be presented through the means of an "objective" science instead of religious beliefs or armchair philosophy. In *On the Origin of Species* (1859), Darwin presented evidence that "humans were the same general kind of creatures as the rest of the animals, except that they were more highly evolved or developed." Most important, humans were beginning to be "understood as creatures whose conduct was influenced, if not determined, by biological and cultural antecedents rather than as self-determining beings who were free to do what they wanted."[16] It was at this time that the first "scientific" studies of crime and criminal behavior began.

Positivism is a method of inquiry that attempts to answer questions through the scientific method. The researcher examines the real world of empirical facts through the testing of hypotheses. The main goal is to arrive at the ultimate "truth" and to derive "laws" (e.g., the law of falling bodies, the law of relativity). The positivist mode of inquiry gained respectability in the social sciences largely through the work of Auguste Comte (1798–1857), often credited as being the founder of positivism and the founder of the discipline known as sociology. According to Comte, knowledge passes through three stages: theological, metaphysical, and positive or scientific. The positive or scientific is the highest or final stage of knowledge. At this stage human beings are able to discover among social phenomena regularities resulting in the establishment of predictability and control.[17]

The positivist school of criminology argues that humans do not have free will and that human behavior is determined by various biological, psychological, and sociological factors. Thus, responsibility for one's actions is diminished. The solution to the problem of crime, from this perspective, is to eliminate the various factors that are thought to be the most likely causes of it. Such a task might include, but certainly is not limited to, psychiatric and/or psychological testing and treatment, dietary monitoring and supplements or adjustments, and the reduction of poverty or greater emphasis on education. The criminal justice system has attempted to accomplish the goal of reducing crime by making the punishment *fit the offender* (rather than fit the crime, as the classical school proposes). Subscription to this goal directs the criminal justice system to rehabilitate the offender, rather than punish, and do this through the wide exercise of discretion by criminal justice officials and some form of indeterminate sentence.

The scientific study of crime began with **Adolphe Quételet** (1796–1874), a Belgian mathematician, and **Andre-Michel Guerry** (1802–1866), a French statistician, in Europe during the 1830s and 1840s, plus several English writers, such as Henry Mayhew, during the 1840s and 1850s.[18] Quételet laid the foundation for positivist criminology through his work in statistics. His quest for identifying lawlike regularities in society, using traditional scientific methods, resulted in an interest in studying crime by studying rates of crime. Quételet looked at official crime data for France and found striking regularities within the French criminal justice apparatus. He found consistencies in the number of defendants who failed to appear in court. Certain courts also were found to be more likely to impose particular sanctions for particular offenses. Looking at different types of crimes committed in France between 1826 and 1829, he concluded, "So, as I have had occasion to repeat several times before, one passes from one year to the other with the sad perspective of seeing the same crimes reproduced in the same order and bring with them the same penalties in the same proportions."[19]

Identifying a correlation between crime and the ability to read and write, Quételet found that as reading and writing proficiency increased, the frequency of criminal acts decreased. Looking at the years 1828 and 1829, he was able to identify over 2,000 crimes against the person committed by people who could not read or write. He noted that during the same period only 80 similar offenses were committed by people who received "superior" academic instruction. He found that those with superior education were much less likely to be involved in property crimes than their uneducated counterparts. He identified 206 property offenses committed by the well educated and 6,617 property offenses committed by illiterate offenders during the same time period. Quételet explained these phenomena as follows:

> It is possible, in fact, that individuals of the knowledgeable class of society, while committing fewer manslaughters, murders, and other serious crimes than those individuals who have not received any instruction, nevertheless commit even fewer crimes against property.... This conjecture likewise becomes probable if one considers that the knowledgeable class implies more affluence and, consequently, less need to resort to the different varieties of theft which make up a great part of crimes against property; while affluence and knowledge do not succeed as easily in restraining the fire of the passions and sentiments of hate and vengeance.[20]

Later, Quételet turned his attention to propensities for crime and found striking correlations between crime and independent variables such as climate and the age, sex, and socioeconomic status of offenders. Young males between the ages of 21 and 25 were found to have the highest propensity for crime; women had the lowest. When Quételet compared female and male offenders, he discovered that males committed nearly four times as many property offenses as women and were involved in over six times more violent offenses. He also noted that violent offenses were most likely to occur in the summer months, and property offenses during the winter. The poor and the unemployed were found to have a higher propensity for crime than members of the working and upper classes. Quételet also discovered that economic changes were related to crime rates, and he surmised that society itself, through its economic and social attributes, was responsible for crime. Although people may have free will, there nevertheless were scientific laws to which criminal behavior was responsive.

Recognizing that all people had the "capacity" to commit crime (an idea that would later be adopted by neo-Freudians), Quételet argued that the average person rarely transformed that option into action. He eventually turned away from the social influences of criminal behavior (as most contemporary criminologists have done) and focused on the correlation between crime and morality, suggesting that certain "types" of people (e.g., vagabonds, Gypsies, and others with supposedly "inferior moral stock") were more prone to criminal behavior than others.

The big breakthrough as far as positivist criminology is concerned was made by an Italian doctor named **Cesare Lombroso** (1835–1909). In 1876 he published *Criminal Man,* which earned him the dubious title "father of criminology." In this work Lombroso emphasized the *biological* basis of criminal behavior. He argued that a person is "born" criminal and can be distinguished from noncriminal persons by the presence of certain physical characteristics, especially those Lombroso called **stigmata**—characteristics that are throwbacks to "primitive" people. Criminals, said Lombroso, are essentially biologically inferior.

Since Lombroso's time, positivist criminology has branched out into psychological and sociological approaches. *Biological* positivism (which began with Lombroso) locates the causes of crime within an individual's physical makeup; *psychological* positivism suggests the causes are faulty personality development; *sociological* positivism stresses social factors within one's environment or the surrounding culture and social structure.[21]

The positivist approach suffers from several problems. First, it assumes that pure objectivity is possible, that research can be value free or without any bias. The German sociologist Max Weber, perhaps fully understanding the potential for intellectual and academic arrogance, strongly cautioned researchers about the assumption of objective or value-free research. Second, positivism takes for granted the existing social and economic order—that is, it generally accepts the status quo and the official definition of reality. Because the state's definition of crime is part of the accepted reality, positivists have focused their research on people who violate the criminal law, rather than on the law itself; positivists' efforts are aimed at controlling or changing the lawbreaker, not changing the law or the social order of which it is a part. Third, positivists assume that the scientific method offers the only way of achieving knowledge, of arriving at the truth. Fourth, positivism provides no assistance in the search for alternatives to the present social and economic order and hence to the present method of responding to crime.[22]

There is also a more frightening implication of the positivist orientation. Two of Lombroso's followers, Enrico Ferri (1856–1928) and Raffaele Garofalo (1852–1934), became supporters of fascism. For Ferri especially, the positivist orientation justified elevating the authority of the state over the "excesses of individualism." As Vold and Bernard note, what happened to Ferri

> highlights one of the problems of positivistic theory, namely the ease with which it fits into totalitarian patterns of government. It is centered on the core idea of the superior knowledge and wisdom of the scientific expert who, on the basis of scientific knowledge, decides what kind of human beings commit crimes, and prescribes treatment without concern for public opinion and without consent from the person so diagnosed (i.e., the criminal). There is an obvious similarity between the control of power in society advocated in positivism and the political reality of centralized control of the life of the citizen by a governmental bureaucracy indifferent to public opinion.[23]

Like the classical school, positivism is primarily concerned with the *control* of crime, rather than with the amelioration of the social conditions that foster crime. Although positivism does pay lip service to the causes of crime, positivists have been most interested in the offender and how he or she can be controlled or changed. What is needed is a method of thinking and inquiry that allows us to question the taken-for-granted assumptions of both the positivist and the classical schools of thought. We need a method that allows us to conceive of something other than the status quo and to seek alternatives to the business-as-usual approach of the modern criminal justice system. Thus, we now turn to our own critical perspective on the criminal justice system.

A CRITICAL PERSPECTIVE ON CRIMINAL JUSTICE

At the heart of our approach to the criminal justice system is **critical thinking,** with which we attempt to look beyond the current social order and institutional arrangements. Thinking critically, we no longer merely accept what is. Rather, we attempt to visualize what could be. To paraphrase the late senator Robert Kennedy, some may think about what is and ask "why" while others—that is, critical thinkers—think about what could be and ask "why not." Our **critical perspective** encourages us to *question authority* and ask, "Says who?"

Many of the beliefs that you hold reflect the views of people in authority—parents, teachers, political leaders, academics, "experts." But how do you know they are right? The best thing to do is to find out for yourself, through your own research. (We encourage readers to challenge us, the authors of this text—check our sources—and to challenge the person teaching the class you are taking!) The historian Howard Zinn once suggested not merely checking out what people in authority say but wondering what they are *not* saying. What are they hiding? Are they omitting certain facts? Are they covering up something? The livelihoods and careers of individuals in positions of authority are often at stake, and they have a lot to lose by telling the truth.

Standard treatments of the criminal justice system rest on a number of rarely questioned assumptions. They take the law for granted and treat the criminal justice system in a social, political, and economic vacuum. They tend to ignore critical issues such as class, race, and gender. Racism, inequality, poverty, and class conflict are rarely raised, or are raised merely in passing, as if they were aberrations.

A critical perspective utilizes what C. Wright Mills called the **sociological imagination.** The best way to understand the world around us, Mills said, is to "grasp history and biography and the relations between the two within society." Through the use of this method "the individual can understand his own experience and gauge his own fate only by locating himself within his period [of history]." Using the sociological imagination lets us distinguish between what Mills called "personal troubles of milieu" and "public issues of social structure." By "personal troubles" Mills meant those very personal, private matters that "occur within the character of the individual and within the range of his immediate relations with others." A problem becomes a "public issue of social structure" when the issue has to do with "matters that transcend those local environments of the individual" and when "some value cherished by publics is felt to be threatened."[24]

By *social structure* we mean the basic institutions of society, such as the economy, family, education, law, and government. We all work and live every day of our lives within these institutions and often are constrained by roles created for us. Individual police officers, for instance, may be sensitive to the issues of racism and the racist nature of the drug laws but are nevertheless required to enforce the law. Police officers are products of a police subculture that helps shape their attitudes, values, and views of the world. In short, they are constrained by "the system." It may be fruitless to deal with issues like police brutality or racial profiling by blaming individual police officers. After all, they are, in a sense, *ordered* to patrol mostly poor and minority communities.

Viewed from this perspective, humans are products of the larger social environment in which they live and work, but they have the power and ability to make significant changes even while working within the system. Karl Marx once wrote that human beings "make their own history" but "do not make it just as they please; they do not make it under circumstances chosen by themselves, but under circumstances directly encountered, given and transmitted from the past. The tradition of all the dead generations weighs like a nightmare on the brain of the living."[25] Students who hope to work within the criminal justice system need to keep this perspective in mind so they will not be overwhelmed by the problems they face.

Key Assumptions of the Critical Perspective

Our critical approach to the criminal justice system rests on several key assumptions. Here are those that we consider most important:

1. The current *social order and the nature of this order* helps determine the nature of the law and therefore the definitions of crime. Thus, for instance, in a feudal system, law concerns mostly issues of land tenure and inheritance; in a capitalist system, the law is concerned mostly with private property.[26]

2. The *legal institution* (including lawmaking bodies and agencies that enforce the law, such as police, courts, and penal systems), as do other social institutions (e.g., education, politics), ultimately helps to support and perpetuate the existing social order. In modern American society the legal institution helps support and perpetuate a capitalist order. Because modern capitalist societies are based on the private ownership of capital by a relatively small class of people—that is, a "ruling" or "upper" class, which has created a great amount of structured social inequality (based on social class, race, and gender)—it follows that the legal institution helps to perpetuate such inequality, at least indirectly.[27]

3. A capitalist system such as American society is based not only on the above-noted inequalities, but such inequalities result from an unequal distribution of resources (e.g., wealth, education), which in turn creates an unequal distribution of power (and with it the ability to control others).[28]

4. It follows that, in general, the legal institution tends to operate in a way that favors those with the most resources and power.[29]

From those general assumptions we offer three propositions that together constitute our operating theory of the criminal justice system:

1. *Role of the State.* The state (which includes legal institutions), while representing the long-term interests of the ruling class and the capitalist system, does not always act as a mere instrument of the ruling class. The state often acts as an autonomous unit and against the interests of the ruling class. Thus, state definitions of crime do not always reflect the interests of the ruling class.[30]

2. *Definition of Crime.* The defining of behaviors as criminal by the state and the application of such definitions are exercises in power; the ability to define behaviors as criminal and to resist such definitions varies with the degree of power one has. Crime describes behaviors that are most likely to correspond to behaviors committed by groups with the least amount of power in society. Similar behaviors committed by those with the most power are the least likely to be defined as a crime.[31]

3. *Application of Criminal Definitions.* At each stage of the criminal justice process, key decisions are made by agents of the state to either dismiss the case or process it further. At each stage, *the probability of advancing further into the system increases as the degree of powerlessness by defendants decreases.* At each stage, those who are left become more and more homogeneous in social class, race, and other social demographic characteristics. By the time a case reaches the final stage, sentencing, the group that has the least amount of power is the most likely to receive a prison sentence or the sentence of death. It is this group that is most homogeneous.

Is the Criminal Justice System Designed to Fail?

Our critical perspective challenges conventional wisdom about the criminal justice system by arguing that the system not only fails to provide protection from crime and make people feel safe but is *designed to fail*. In making this argument, we are borrowing the ideas of Jeffrey Reiman, who calls this view of criminal justice the **Pyrrhic defeat theory.** In military terminology, a Pyrrhic victory is a victory won at such a great loss of life that it amounts to a defeat. Reiman suggests that "the failure of the criminal justice system yields such benefits to those in positions of power that it amounts to success."[32] Such "success" manifests itself comes in the following ways:

1. By focusing primarily on the crimes of the poor and racial minorities, the criminal justice system distorts the crime picture by deflecting the discontents and anger of middle-class Americans toward the poor and racial minorities, rather than toward those in positions of power above them.

2. The American criminal justice system, in its "war on crime," makes it look as if the most serious threat comes from the crimes of the poor and racial minorities, when in fact the greatest harms, in terms of both life and property, come from the crimes of the very rich.

3. By focusing on crime control and the punishment of *individual offenders,* the system fails to address some of the major causes of crime. Focusing exclusively on the individual offender diverts attention away from institutions, away from consideration of whether institutions themselves are wrong or unjust or indeed "criminal." It diverts attention from the evils of the social order.[33]

Debra Seagal's comments about a prime-time television "real crime" show based on videotapes of real police arrests are appropriate here. Seagal discusses how focusing on individual criminals diverts attention away from the social context of crime and, indeed, communicates the idea that these offenders exist in a social vacuum:

> By the time our 9 million viewers flip on their tubes, we've reduced fifty or sixty hours of mundane and compromising video into short, action-packed segments of tantalizing, crack-filled, dope-dealing, junkie-busting, cop culture. How easily we downplay the pathos of the suspect; how cleverly we breeze past the complexities that cast doubt on the very system that has produced the criminal activity in the first place.[34]

In a similar vein, one writer noted that the hoopla about "family values" by Dan Quayle over the riots in Los Angeles following the Rodney King verdict and an episode of the television series *Murphy Brown* in which the main character decides to have her baby out of wedlock and raise the child by herself, completely ignored the "social context" of the lives of most women and most inner-city African Americans. This writer further noted that

> the erasure of the L.A. uprising in the *Murphy Brown* incident moved the debate away from issues of race, from the condition of inner cities, and from the deteriorating economic base in the United States, to a much safer, symbolic ground. By shifting the debate from the material conditions of inner cities to the discursive field of "family values," both parties occupied a much more comfortable terrain for debate.[35]

This is an example of "symbolic politics."[36] Similarly, TV crime shows constantly inform the public about the dangerous criminals in our midst but make no attempt to account for their presence. Of course, we understand that television is not really concerned with providing in-depth analysis of social problems; it is interested principally with ratings. Nevertheless, viewers are left with the impression that these criminals come out of nowhere!

It should be emphasized that there is an important difference between *understanding* or *explaining* certain behaviors (like crime) and *justifying* or *excusing* such behaviors. We can certainly condemn the rapist, the murderer, and even the corporate offender, but it is also important to develop an understanding of *why* these behaviors occur, for understanding may lead to some solutions. Similarly, we rightly condemn the terrorist attacks of September 11, 2001, as totally unjustifiable, but we need to understand why they happened in order to prevent anything similar from occurring again. If a police officer is facing a man who is wielding a gun in a threatening manner, it is of little use for the officer, *while facing the point of a gun,* to try to understand why the man is behaving in this way. But eventually it may be important for that officer to develop some understanding of why someone might resort to such behavior. Understanding may help to save a life if it leads to preventive measures.

Critical thinking and sociological imagination help to keep us informed about what is going on. Reiman suggests the following:

> To look only at individual criminality is to close one's eyes to social injustice and to close one's ears to the question of whether our social institutions have exploited or violated the individual. *Justice is a two-way street—but criminal justice is a one-way street.* Individuals owe obligations to their fellow citizens because their fellow citizens owe obligations to them. Criminal justice focuses on the first and looks away from the second. *Thus, by focusing on individual responsibility for crime, the criminal justice system literally acquits the existing social order of any charge of injustice.*[37]

Reiman is not suggesting (and neither are we) that the crimes of the poor and racial minorities do not constitute a major problem. Indeed, those who are the most likely to be victimized come from the ranks of the urban poor and racial minorities. We cannot ignore the human wreckage that occurs every day in urban areas in the form of violence and predatory crime, including crimes against women and children (usually falling within the category "domestic violence"), not to mention the devastating effects of drugs and alcohol. However, we agree with Reiman when he writes, "On the other hand, there are enough benefits to the wealthy from the identification of crime with the poor and the system's failure to reduce crime that those with the power to make profound changes in the system feel no compulsion nor see any incentive to make them."[38]

It should be noted that we are not claiming that many who work within the criminal justice system do not try their best to deal with people fairly and equitably. We have met many who do (though certainly not enough). Our point is that *the system itself* and most of the people who ultimately control it (and control the major institutions in society, especially economic and political institutions) have become part of the problem and help perpetuate the crime problem.[39]

Throughout this book you will view the criminal justice system from a variety of perspectives, identify the relationship between the various facets of that system, evaluate the assumptions underlying each perspective, and weigh the evidence presented. Thus, you are challenged to use different colored lenses to examine many topical areas surrounding the criminal justice system and to question, and consider alternatives to, the existing system of criminal justice in America.

Before moving ahead, we need to begin to take a critical view of the basic foundation of the criminal justice system, the criminal law. Without the criminal law there is, technically, no "crime." This is more than an academic exercise, for to examine this idea is to begin to expose the law and legal system as an important aspect of social life. In the next section we consider common perspectives on the criminal law.

PERSPECTIVES ON CRIMINAL LAW

Why does the law prohibit some behaviors but not others? It doesn't take much analysis to figure out that some very harmful behaviors are perfectly legal—such as the possession and consumption of cigarettes and alcohol, not to mention addictive prescription drugs. Marijuana, heroin, and cocaine are illegal yet not nearly as harmful as cigarettes and alcohol. Laws prohibit the killing ("homicide" or "murder") of another human being, but in some contexts the taking of a human life can be perfectly legal, such as a police officer killing a citizen who threatens his life, the application of the death penalty, killing in time of war, and the controversial actions of Dr. Jack Kevorkian, the so-called suicide doctor.

Moreover, even if there is clear evidence that someone probably took another person's life or committed some other crime, there may be different interpretations of whether a law was violated. These interpretations may come from a variety of criminal justice "actors," such as the police (who may look the other way at certain violations) and district attorneys (who decide that some act wasn't really a crime).[40]

Finally, we have behaviors that do tremendous harm mostly to women—namely, rape and battering. In theory, rape is universally condemned, yet numerous studies document how in so many instances men accused of rape are not arrested or not prosecuted if arrested or if prosecuted are acquitted, often because certain key actors in the criminal justice system decided that "she deserved it," or "she led him on," and so on. Similar conclusions also have been reached with regard to battering.[41]

Thus, we can conclude that the law is more than words on paper. It has a dynamic quality of its own. It is a reflection of a particular society at a particular time. As Quinney writes, the law "is also a method or *process* of doing something. As a process, law is a dynamic force that is continually being *created and interpreted.* Thus, law in action involves the making of specialized (legal) decisions by various *authorized agents.*"[42] Law is a creation of specific people holding positions of authority; it is not the creation of a divine authority, as people once believed.

The law, because it is a *social* product, must be viewed *sociologically,* for the law is first and foremost a social institution complete with a system of roles and status positions (lawyers, judges, legislators, police officers). Also, it contains an ideology, a set of values supportive of the legal system and the existing social order.[43] The law, moreover, is a *social process*—many different people interpret and apply the law in various social contexts. How the law is interpreted and applied depends on many extralegal factors, such as class and race.

A question that has concerned scholars for many years is that of the origins and functions of criminal law. Through the years scholars have offered a variety of perspectives on the law. These perspectives have been called by various names, such as "consensus," "societal needs," "pluralist," "interactionist," "interest group," "conflict," "elite theory," "ruling class theory," and "Marxist." For purposes of simplification, we reduce all of these perspectives to three main views: (1) consensus/pluralist, (2) interest group/conflict, and (3) critical/Marxist.[44]

Consensus/Pluralist Model

According to the **consensus/pluralist model,** legal norms are a reflection of the values held in common by the majority of the population. In other words, legal norms reflect the will of the people. This is perhaps the oldest and most articulated perspective on criminal law. A variation of this view is that criminal law merely makes official what are common norms or rules of everyday behavior. In other words, what has been custom (e.g., rules followed because everybody has always followed them) eventually becomes the law. From this perspective the criminal law reflects the social consciousness of a society and the kind of behavior a community universally condemns. Thus, the criminal law (and law in general) represents a synthesis of the most deeply held moral values and beliefs of a people or society. The violation of such laws serves, in effect, to establish the "moral boundaries" of a community or society, according to nineteenth-century sociologist Émile Durkheim.[45]

Another variation of this view is that the law functions to achieve social equilibrium or to maintain order. The law is an instrument used to resolve conflicting interests in a society. The legal philosopher Roscoe Pound believed that the law is a specialized organization of social control as well as a form of "social engineering" in a "civilized" society. Without organized social control, said Pound, people's aggressive self-assertions would prevail over their cooperative social tendencies, and civilization would come to an end. Hence, criminal law serves as a sort of social "glue." Pound also suggested that the law adjusts social relationships in order to meet prevailing ideas of fair play.[46]

Another way of expressing the consensus view is the common phrase "there ought to be a law," meaning that people "rise up" and demand that a certain form of behavior be outlawed. This model is based on the assumption that there is a common consensus by the majority of the people in a society on what is good and proper conduct, an assumption that is highly suspect.

This model makes three main points. First, law helps to maintain social order, and it is the best way to do so. In other words, the only way to maintain order in society is through the law or, as commonly phrased, the **rule of law.** Second, law reflects a more or less universal consensus on what is or is not "proper" behavior. Third, law and the criminal justice system protect public, not private, interests. In other words, the law is neutral and helps to resolve conflicts between competing interest groups (and it follows that those who uphold and interpret the law—police, courts, and so on—are neutral as well).

This view also argues that a society needs not only law but a strong, centralized state to prevent people from becoming barbarians and engaging in what seventeenth-century philosopher Thomas Hobbes described as a "war of all against all." Such a view assumes that once upon a time humans were simply mean and nasty to one another, thinking only of themselves in a selfish way, and that there was constant civil strife and war. This, we are told, is just "human nature." Yet such a view is contradicted by years of anthropological and historical research, which has proved that prior to our modern era thousands of human societies existed (beginning some 40,000 to 50,000 years ago) in small, economically co-operative groups. This research shows us that state-created law is not the only way to maintain order and peace. But in modern capitalist societies, based as they are on competitive social relations and class (as well as racial and gender) inequalities, the view of "human nature" as self-centered and in need of control becomes a rationalization for a capitalist order and leads inevitably to the idea that we need law in order to restrain people's "naturally wicked" ways.[47]

Interest-Group/Conflict Model

The consensus/pluralist model assumes that law is a reflection of societal needs. This assumption leads us to ask, "Whose needs?" The answer "society" is far too general and vague. Such a view assumes that what is good for one group or segment is good for all segments. In a society segmented along class, racial, and gender lines, this is clearly not an appropriate view. The **interest-group/conflict model** attempts to answer these kinds of questions. This view begins with the basic fact of modern industrialized societies, which are highly stratified and unequal in the distribution of power and in life chances. Using this base, conflict theorists contend that the law reflects the interests of some groups at the expense of others. Quinney's *The Social Reality of Crime* perhaps best exemplifies this approach. Quinney states that society is characterized by diversity, coercion, change, and conflict. Law is a *result* of the operation of *interests.* More specifically, "law incorporates the interests of specific persons and groups.... Law is made by men, representing special interests, who have the power to translate their interests into public policy."[48]

Quinney's model is based on a conception of society as segmental rather than singular. In a singular society there is a common value system to which all persons conform. The law reflects these common values (this is what the consensus/pluralist model supports). In a segmental society there are numerous segments, each having its own values and interests. Thus, "some values of a segment may be incorporated into some of the criminal laws." Moreover, many segments are in conflict with one another, some segments having values and interests that conflict with other segments. The passage of laws, therefore, is primarily the outgrowth of these conflicting interests. These laws are the product of interest groups who are aware of what their true interests are and organize to promote these interests. The important point here is that the *interest structure* in modern American society is character-ized by an unequal distribution of *power and economic resources* and those who have the greatest amount are most able to have their interests represented by the law. Indeed, those groups that have little or no power will have little or no opportunity to have their interests represented by the law and public policies in general. Powerless groups such as women, minorities, youth, and poor people are rarely represented.[49] Quite often, laws are passed after vigorous campaigning by various interest groups (or perhaps even one group) or by what one writer has called "moral entrepreneurs."[50] These groups lobby Congress, write letters to newspapers, and engage in other activities in order to get a piece of legislation written into law. Such groups do not necessarily represent "the people"; more often than not, they represent themselves or some other small but powerful group.[51]

A Critical/Marxist Model

Our **critical model** derives from the theories of Karl Marx and modern-day Marxist writings. It resembles the interest-group/conflict model in its focus on group conflict and power as important variables, but it differs in many important ways. This theory challenges us to view the law and the legal order in a specific social and historical context. Such a view argues that the law—and in fact the entire legal system—is one of many institutions that are part of what Marx called the *superstructure* of society and therefore operates to help support and perpetuate the *substructure* or economic base—namely a capitalist economic and social system.[52]

Variations of the critical perspective can be categorized into two approaches: (1) instrumentalist and (2) structuralist.

The Instrumentalist Perspective.   Marx himself set forth the **instrumentalist perspective** when he asserted that law and the legal order (in fact the state itself) serves mostly as an "instrument" or tool through which the ruling class (the relatively small group that owns and controls most of the wealth in society—or what Marx called the "means of production") dominates society. Marx and Engels summarized this position simply in *The Communist Manifesto* when they wrote that "the executive of the modern state is but a committee for managing the common affairs of the whole bourgeoisie."[53]

One of the best illustrations of the instrumentalist position in recent years was postulated by Richard Quinney in *Critique of Legal Order.* Quinney asserted: "Criminal law is used by the state and the ruling class to secure the survival of the capitalist system, and, as capitalist society is further threatened by its own contradictions, criminal law will be increasingly used in the attempt to maintain domestic order."[54] The legal order, in short, is used to help keep the ruling class in power. The legal order is also used to keep the subordinate classes "in their place" (i.e., to perpetuate a social class system) by defining some of their behaviors as "criminal" while ignoring similar or identical behaviors among members of the ruling class or other powerful individuals.

Critics of this position maintain that it is too extreme, that it exaggerates the cohesiveness of the ruling class and its use of the legal order. Not every law is passed to preserve the current social order, nor is every law passed solely to represent the interests of the ruling class, for clearly some legislation favors groups other than the dominant class. Often even subordinate classes are represented in legislation, although it can be said that much of this legislation nevertheless does not threaten the basic social order and the class that rules that order. Also, according to critics, the instrumentalist position ignores the many occasions when even members within the ruling class have conflicting interests and thus not all of their interests are going to be reflected in law. It may be true that the instrumentalist position is most helpful for analyzing the relationship between social class and law in earlier periods of American development, but as "the relationship between law and the state changes over time," other perspectives need to be considered. In short, say critics, the law does not always support economic interests alone.[55]

The Structuralist Perspective.   The **structuralist perspective** suggests that law is the result of contradictions inherent in the capitalist system, which in turn create problems that even the ruling class cannot easily manipulate. Thus, the nature of the capitalist economic system is that law might sometimes operate against the short-term interests of the ruling class but in favor of the long-term interests of the capitalist system as a whole. A classic example is the passage of antitrust laws in the early 1900s and laws against discrimination in employment, minimum-wage laws, consumer protection laws, and laws supporting labor unions.[56] The ruling class does not always get its way.

Those supporting this position also maintain that the state often acts independently of the ruling class, rather than being a mere "instrument" of that class. To be sure, the law can and will be used when the capitalist system appears to be threatened. However, in day-to-day affairs, the various parts of the "superstructure" (e.g., law, ideology, politics, education, media) have a lot of autonomy. Thus, not every political decision, not everything that is taught in school, and not every law is a reflection of the narrow interests of capitalists.

Some Concluding Thoughts on Critical Law Perspective

Having said this, how can we summarize what a critical perspective of the law and legal order has to say? Our position is that the law is not some mystical force beyond human comprehension and control. Too often the law is thought of as a cure-all for societal ills. Also, it has been said that society is ruled by law, not by men. On the contrary, we would argue that society is ruled by men and that the law serves to legitimate and sometimes obscure this rule (the Watergate scandal during the Nixon administration and the Clinton impeachment hearings demonstrated that very powerful men run the country, not some abstraction called "the law"). Moreover, it has been commonly believed that the law serves as a protective device that shields the victim and punishes the offender, that it is capable of righting wrongs, and that it is impartial, incorruptible, and equitably applied, providing equal justice for all. In the review that follows, however, we cite instances in which this has not been the case, and we show that this view is largely a fiction.

It needs to be pointed out that this society is characterized by a tremendous amount of inequality and that a very small proportion of the population does in fact own whatever one calls the "means of production." As noted in Chapter 1, the gap between the very rich and the rest of the population has grown in recent years; most of the wealth is held by fewer and fewer hands. Also, corporate power is very concentrated. For instance, in 1995 the top 100 industrial corporations held 30 percent of the assets of all nonfinancial corporations and the largest 5 percent of banking organizations owned 52 percent of all the banking assets.[57] Given this amount of wealth and the power that comes with it, it logically follows that the legal order, in the final analysis, is controlled by this small proportion of the population because of the simple fact that they own and control most of the nation's assets.

It really doesn't matter that the law does not always side with these rulers. It doesn't have to, as long as profits can be made and the capitalist system survives. And it is not as if no one else but this small group of capitalists receives the benefits of capitalism, for a lot of other people do as well. Howard Zinn illustrates this in his analysis of the passage of the U.S. Constitution. He notes that the Constitution and the Bill of Rights were primarily passed to protect private property. Because so many people at that time owned property, it was in the interests of a lot of people to have property protected. But although a lot of people owned property, most owned only a little property and only a small group owned a lot (as they still do today). Zinn notes:

> The Constitution, then, illustrates the complexity of the American system: that it serves the interests of a wealthy elite, but also does enough for small property owners, for middle-income mechanics and farmers, to build a broad base of support. The slightly prosperous people who make up this base of support are buffers against the blacks, the Indians, the very poor whites. They enable the elite to keep control with a minimum of coercion, a maximum of law—all made palatable by the fanfare of patriotism and unity.[58]

The Bill of Rights gave just enough liberties to the masses to build support for the ruling class of the period and the government. But, as Zinn notes, what was never made very clear "was the shakiness of anyone's liberty when entrusted to a government of the rich and the powerful."

This was shown, for instance, when Congress passed a law that essentially abridged freedom of speech guaranteed by the First Amendment. This was the Sedition Act of 1798.[59]

Thus, the law and the legal order favors especially the very wealthy, but it favors enough of the rest of the population to appear to be equal. Yet the law clearly has never done a good job supporting the most marginalized sectors of the population: the poor in general, and African Americans, Native Americans, and other minorities.

We next present a more detailed review of the criminal law itself. The criminal law is the foundation of the entire criminal justice system. Why? For the simple reason that the criminal justice system is in charge of the *enforcement* of criminal law and the *punishment* of individuals who violate it. Moreover, without criminal law, there would, by definition, be no crime.

THE NATURE OF CRIMINAL LAW

Law: What Is It?

Law is a concept that most people think they understand. But if you were asked to provide a definition of law, how would you respond? Over the years, this problem has haunted legal scholars. Law, in its generic sense, can be viewed as rules of action or conduct that are prescribed by a controlling authority that has enforcement power. Thus, law is that which must be obeyed and followed by citizens who are subject to sanctions or legal consequences. The American jurist Benjamin Cardozo described law as: "A principle or rule of conduct so established as to justify a prediction with reasonable certainty that it will be enforced by the courts if its authority is challenged."[60] Oliver Wendell Holmes, another American jurist, argued that law is that which judges make: "The prophecies of what the courts will do in fact, and nothing more pretentious, is what I mean by law."[61] Donald Black, a leading law and society scholar, argues that "Law is the normative life of a state and its citizens, such as legislation, litigation, and adjudication."[62] Thus, according to Black, law is government social control.

Following the work of Lisa J. McIntyre,[63] who identified scores of definitions of law in her research, we might conclude that there are as many definitions as there are legal scholars. This does not mean that the concept is undefinable, but it does suggest that there is little agreement on its definition. Law can be viewed as an abstract concept and as such takes on different meanings for different audiences. To someone in the legal profession, law may be seen as a concept that explains social behavior as being either black or white or right or wrong. In other words, behavior either complies with the law or it does not. To the sociologist, law may be a topic of inquiry that often leads researchers into the domain of power, influence, and the relativity of law to the real world. Sociologists ask, Who benefits from law, and does law reflect the desires and needs of the majority? To criminal justice practitioners, law might represent a foundation from which political and tactical decisions are constructed and implemented, or law may simply serve as legitimation for engaging in daily routines (e.g., police officers arresting homeless people or "shaking down" young black males in the inner city). We support the notion that law is a formal institution that continuously reifies itself and its importance while it simultaneously engages in legitimating state social control. Thus, law controls the lives of individuals who live under the jurisdiction of law.

Law often seems estranged from other parts of life, yet everyone is affected by law in nearly all aspects of life—beginning at birth. Here are some everyday examples. Parents are required by law to "register" their newborn child with the state by filling out the appropriate documentation for a birth certificate and to secure a Social Security number for their newborn child. Law follows the child to first grade and dictates the age that the child must be in order to begin compulsory education. Law also prescribes the minimum number of years the child must attend school. The law establishes age and knowledge requirements before a driving license can be issued. As a young woman or man matures into adulthood and decides to get married, the law requires that certain criteria first be met (age requirements, medical tests, licensing procedures, etc.). Law governs contracts that a person may enter into as he or she goes through life (financing a car or a home, regulations for licensing a new business, etc.). Near the end of one's life journey, in many cases, law specifies whether a person can die quickly or must linger in pain and suffering (regulation of life support apparatuses, physician-assisted suicide, etc.). Law even follows the individual after death (the administration of estates and wills is regulated by law). Like it or not, law is an integral part of life.

If you now find yourself somewhat overwhelmed by the law, you are not alone. Many people are intimidated by the complexity and the apparent mystique of law. Although many would rather distance themselves from any personal involvement in law, they cannot divorce their lives from law. Most people agree with the assumption that in order for society to exist we must have an institution of law. To support this claim, they often rely on an explanation such as "We cannot exist as a society without formal written laws." This claim is debatable. Earlier societies managed to flourish without formal written laws.

Throughout world history, human behavior has been subject to a variety of social control mechanisms other than formal law. There is nothing inevitable about the "need" for people to be controlled by a formal legal system. For example, if we take a close look at the history of Native Americans, predating European intervention, we find no evidence of written laws or of an elaborate legal system. This does not mean that Native Americans did not have rules. They had rules, and everyone knew those rules. They generally were based on religious beliefs rather than on secular principles (to regulate commerce, contracts, etc.) and were strictly enforced. Despite the absence of written laws and elaborate legal systems, Native Americans developed and maintained diversified cultures, formed communities, developed personal relationships, and raised families. They appear to have thrived until Europeans introduced formal (written) law and an elaborate legal system that they believed provided justification for the dislocation and mass murder of hundreds of thousands of Native Americans in the name of progress and prosperity.[64]

Law and Social Norms

Today, most human behavior is regulated by rules that are unwritten or otherwise informally expressed. These rules are called **social norms,** and they can be defined as the expectations and rules, both spoken and universally understood, that direct human behavior in a society. There are two basic categories of social norms: folkways and mores. **Folkways** are society's conventional rules that we deal with every day. In many ways our compliance with folkways (rules of etiquette, dress, language, etc.) seems almost automatic. This conformity generally results from informal methods of social control (gossip, ridicule, ostracism, etc.). Folkways are not believed to be essential to the survival of the group. Although we may get upset at someone for violating a folkway, we probably would not express disgust or indignation for such a violation.

Mores, in contrast, are stronger norms that reflect the moral judgments of society. Violations of mores are subject to stronger sanctions because they are believed to threaten group survival. The violation of mores prohibiting murder, rape, incest, and assault usually calls forth moral indignation and can result in severe punishment.[65] Mores are frequently codified into laws; folkways are not.

To illustrate possible responses to the violation of a folkway or of mores, imagine that you are dining out with a business client at a restaurant. After reviewing the menu, you decide to order spaghetti with tomato sauce. When the waiter serves your meal, you set your fork and spoon aside and begin to eat with your hands. Other diners, who direct their attention to you, shake their heads at such a display of bad and unacceptable manners. Moreover, you probably do not impress your business guest favorably. This is quite possibly the last time your guest will accept a dinner invitation from you. Now suppose that in the same restaurant you become irritated at the service you and your guest receive. To express your irritation, you stand up and turn over the table. As dishes and glasses break when they hit the floor, all of the other diners shake their heads in dismay at your display of anger. It is quite possible that your behavior could result in a formal criminal charge of "disturbing the peace" or "destruction of private property" and you could end up being arrested. Clearly, there is a distinction in the seriousness of these two forms of behavior. In the former case (bad manners), you are violating a folkway. In the latter case (disturbing the peace or destroying private property), you are violating mores and quite possibly are in violation of a codified or written law. Such a violation might be sufficient to launch formal social control measures, such as the owner of the restaurant calling the police and demanding your arrest.

Formal Social Control

Formal social control measures (e.g., summoning the criminal justice system into action) are often adopted and used when informal social control measures (e.g., being ridiculed or ostracized) prove to be inadequate to maintain conformity. The adoption of formal social control measures is most likely to occur as societies become more diverse and social class distinctions become more prevalent. Hallmarks of formal social control include systems of specialized agencies (e.g., law enforcement agencies), the application of standardized techniques (e.g., court procedures), and the general predictability of universal sanctions (e.g., probation or prison). Thus, **formal social control** consists, ideally, of (1) explicit rules of conduct, (2) planned use of sanctions, and (3) designated officials to interpret and enforce the rules.[66]

There are two types of formal social control: political and nonpolitical. The first type, **political social control,** is most relevant to the study of criminal justice. It is characterized by the state's authority to use force, if the state deems it necessary, to ensure conformity to established rules that are germane to the authority bestowed on the state. Donald Black identifies four styles of political social control germane to state law:

1. *Penal* social control views the offender as a violator of a prohibition and subjects her or him to condemnation and punishment.
2. *Compensatory* social control occurs when the offender is considered to have contractual obligations and is expected to pay restitution to the victim.
3. *Therapeutic* social control occurs when the offender's behavior is perceived to be abnormal and calling for psychiatric help or treatment.
4. *Conciliatory* social control may be applied when the offender's behavior reflects a dimension of a social conflict to which the state responds without consideration of who is right or who is wrong.[67]

The second type of social control, *nonpolitical social control,* is used by institutions that are not a direct part of the state's political social control apparatus (e.g., the church or the university). This type of social control employs either rewards or punishments to elicit conformity to the institution's rules, because these kinds of institutions do not have the authority to use force. For example, a university may have a policy that places students on the dean's list when they achieve a designated grade point average in a given semester. The university may also place a student on academic probation if the student's grades fall below a prescribed level. In the first situation, students are rewarded for their compliance with university academic standards; in the second instance, a penalty is bestowed on students for failing to meet university standards. The university, however, cannot place a student with a lower-than-required grade point average in prison for noncompliance with its academic standards.

TYPES OF LAW

There are many types of law in U.S. society—for example, administrative law, absolute law, canon law, constitutional law, civil law, criminal law, general law, foreign law, international law, case law, maritime law, organic law, military law, municipal law, and statutory law. A person might reasonably arrive at the conclusion that the United States is a society with an endless set of laws. Because the list is so extensive, we limit our discussion to the types that have the greatest impact on the American criminal justice system.

Civil Law

The other day you may have read in the newspaper about someone filing a suit against someone else because the victim (called a **plaintiff** in civil suits) was harmed in some way. The plaintiff may be suing for damages due to libel (e.g., a magazine or newspaper published something that harmed the reputation of the victim) or for being fired because of sex or race. These are only two of the many kinds of cases that are germane to civil law. **Civil law** focuses on rules and procedures that regulate relationships between individuals. Violations of civil law are usually referred to as *civil wrongs*.

One of the most celebrated civil cases of the twentieth century was the case brought against O. J. Simpson by the families of Ron Goldman and Nicole Brown. They won the civil suit, and Simpson was ordered to pay several million dollars. You, too, might face a civil suit someday. Suppose you invite a guest to your house for dinner and upon entering he trips over your son's tricycle and breaks his leg. Your guest gets angry and calls his lawyer, who in turn brings suit against you for damages. The purpose of this civil suit is to seek restitution (e.g., payment of medical bills) from you (or your insurance company) due to your negligence. After all, you should have moved the tricycle before your guest arrived!

Civil law consists of several different subtypes, such as tort law, corporate law, contract law, and divorce law. Of particular importance to the study of crime is the law of torts. **Torts** are acts "that cause injury to the financial, physical, emotional, or psychological well-being of some individual."[68] A tort can also be defined as "a wrongful act that does not violate any enforceable agreement but that nevertheless violates a legal right of the injured party."[69] Common examples of torts include wrongful death (which applies to the O. J. Simpson case), intentional or negligent personal injury, destruction of property, trespassing, and defaming someone's character. In such cases the injured party seeks compensation or restitution, but no one is sent to jail or prison.

This raises some interesting questions, for the distinction between *criminal law* (and thus *crime*) and *civil law,* especially torts (and thus *wrongs*), is rather curious. Under criminal law, the "state," which theoretically is synonymous with or representative of "the people," assumes the role of the victim, and prohibited acts are those that are supposedly threats to society as a whole or to the "social order." In contrast, torts constitute a general class of harms done to *individuals* rather than to "society" or to the "state," and, unlike crimes, torts do not harm "society" or pose a threat to the "social order." More important, suits under tort law do not carry the stigma associated with the criminal law—the perpetrator is not viewed as part of some dangerous class or criminal class. Nevertheless, the harm done by many persons who violate tort law (especially corporate, occupational, and political crimes) clearly exceeds the harm done by those who violate criminal law.

Is it any accident that the distinctions between civil and criminal law have been created by the sorts of powerful and influential people who are most likely to commit the torts that do so much harm to society? As one writer notes:

> Socially recognized harms in America have been divided into civil and criminal wrongs in a way that generally protects middle-class and elite Americans from being stigmatized as "criminals" for the harms they are most likely to cause. In contrast, nearly all those forms of harm that the working class and the underclass can commit bear the full weight of criminal stigma.[70]

Civil law and criminal law often overlap. Like O. J. Simpson, a person may stand trial for the criminal charges of murder and also be held accountable for civil damages resulting from the same act (e.g., the wrongful taking of life). A successful conviction for criminal offense demands criminal sanctions (e.g., prison), whereas in a civil case the court is likely to order monetary rewards to the "winner."

Criminal Law

Suppose someone stops you on the street and, at gunpoint, demands your wallet. After recovering from the initial shock, you probably will call the police. The police will arrive and take down any relevant information you can give them (e.g., a description of the suspect). From this information they may attempt to locate the person who held you up and make an arrest. If apprehended by the police, the holdup man will be brought to court and (you hope) convicted and sent to prison as punishment. Obviously you can see the difference between your holdup man and the guest who tripped over your son's tricycle. The holdup man violated a *criminal* law and committed a *crime*.

Criminal law defines specific behaviors that are prohibited and prescribes sanctions for the violation of those forbidden behaviors. When someone violates a criminal law, it is said that he or she has harmed the "state" or "the people." From a strictly legal standpoint, crime is considered a harm to the *public* rather than a harm to an *individual* (as in a civil suit), even though an individual is harmed in both instances. Thus, instead of an individual or a group taking action against a *defendant* (as in a civil suit), the state (specifically, representatives of the state, such as police and prosecutors) takes action against an *offender*. Instead of the victim taking personal action against the offender (with the help, let us say, of an attorney or a group of the victim's friends) and seeking either compensation (your wallet that was stolen by the holdup man) or revenge (you and your friends go out and beat up the holdup man), the offender is *punished* by the state (e.g. through fine, probation, or imprisonment) because "society" or the "public" is considered to have been harmed. The agents of the state are acting as your representatives in the arrest and prosecution of offenders (in contrast to your lawyer representing you in the civil suit). Often it is said that the "state" is the victim, and the criminal case may be described as "The State of Michigan v. Jones," where "the state" is the *plaintiff* and Jones is the *defendant*.

Criminal law outlines proper procedures for the state to follow if an offense comes to the attention of the authorities. Thus, criminal law is divided into two subsets: substantive law and procedural law. **Substantive law** is a written body of rules specifying the **elements of a crime,** which is a legal way of describing in some detail such offenses as homicide and robbery and sanctions for committing those offenses. **Procedural law** consists of a body of rules specifying the conditions required before, and the manner in which, the state may proceed against an alleged offender. Procedural laws include laws on search and seizure, rules of evidence, and laws concerning proper arrest procedures. Included within procedural laws are the fundamental rights of the accused guaranteed by the U.S. Constitution.

A *constitution* is the fundamental law of a state or a nation that establishes the character and conception of government. For example, assume that a state or nation claims to promote equality, freedom of speech, and freedom of movement for all citizens within its boundaries. Ideally, each of these concepts must be stipulated in that state's or nation's constitution to ensure that all citizens can practice free speech, move about freely, and be treated equally. A constitution regulates the organization, powers, and framework of government, as well as the relationship between the government and citizens. The constitution must also specify procedures for subsequent amendments to its own text.

Constitutional law ensures that all amendments and subsequent laws (enacted after the adoption of a constitution) comply with that state's or nation's fundamental law (constitution). Suppose that a legislative body (e.g., the U.S. Congress) passes a particular law. That law is subject to a constitutional test or interpretation by the court (e.g., the Supreme Court) to ensure that it conforms to the fundamental law contained within the U.S. Constitution. If it fails that test, the law is considered unconstitutional and not binding on or applicable to the citizens bound by the Constitution. Constitutional law also applies to the **Bill of Rights,** the first ten Amendments to the U.S. Constitution, which safeguards individual rights and freedoms and offers protection from governmental abuse of power. Because these are such important topics, a detailed discussion is warranted.

Procedural Law: The Rights of the Accused

In theory, individuals sworn to uphold the law are required to follow certain rules. After all, the United States is supposed to be a nation under the "rule of law." Most textbooks on criminal justice say that the U.S. Constitution and the Bill of Rights guarantee equality under law or, as one notes, that the Bill of Rights guarantees that "citizens are protected from the arbitrary abuse of power by any single element of the law" (the police, the courts, etc.) and also guarantees that "no one branch of government can in and of itself determine the fate of those accused of crimes" and, further, that these rights were added "to prevent any future government from usurping the personal freedom of citizens."[71] Millions of African American and other minority citizens might be tempted to roll over with laughter when reading such words! On a daily basis such rights are virtually ignored on the streets of urban ghettos.

Procedural law in general and the Bill of Rights in particular must be placed within a larger social and historical context. We also must consider that the basis of the legal system itself is the U.S. Constitution. Indeed, all law, and in fact the entire criminal justice system, is derived from the Constitution. The Bill of Rights, as a set of amendments to the Constitution, was the result of often intense struggle in the years following the American Revolution.[72] It can be demonstrated empirically that the Constitution itself was based on and reflective of very narrow class interests. As Howard Zinn observes, when economic interests are seen within the political clauses of the Constitution, then this body of work is "not simply the work of wise men trying to establish a decent and orderly society, but the work of certain groups trying to maintain their privilege, while giving just enough rights and liberties to enough of the people to ensure popular support." It is true that the Constitution protected property for the people during that time who owned property. However, as we said before, a few people owned a lot of property while most owned little or no property (African slaves and Native Americans were completely propertyless, and women had no property rights at all). Thus, the Constitution illustrates the complexity of the capitalist system in that it serves the interests of a small wealthy elite but also does just enough for small property owners and for middle-income people so as to build up a small base of support. The members of this small, slightly prosperous group serve as a buffer against those who have little or nothing. They, in turn, "enable the elite to keep control with a minimum of coercion, a maximum of law—all made palatable by the fanfare of patriotism and unity."[73]

The U.S. Constitution was made even more acceptable to the general public by the passage of the Bill of Rights. And here is the essence of how a small group of extremely wealthy and powerful people rule: they do so by making it appear that the government, and also the law, is the guardian of *all* the people and of their basic rights—to bear arms, to petition, to worship, to assemble, to speak, to be tried fairly by a "jury of their peers," and so on. What was never made clear, notes Zinn, "was the shakiness of everyone's liberty when entrusted to a government of the rich and the powerful." Indeed, to protect everyone's "contract" does

> seem like an act of fairness, of equal treatment, until one considers that contracts made between rich and poor, between employer and employee, landlord and tenant, creditor and debtor, generally favor the more powerful of the two parties. Thus to protect these contracts is to put the great power of the government, its laws, courts, sheriffs, police, on the side of the privileged—and to do it not, as in premodern times, as an exercise of brute force against the weak but as a matter of law."[74]

Zinn goes on to note that not too long after the passage of the First Amendment of the Bill of Rights, Congress in 1798 passed the Sedition Act, which abridged the freedom of speech protected by the First Amendment!

As these passages suggest, the men of power at the time of the writing of the Constitution and the Bill of Rights (we really are talking here about *white men*—women and African slaves and Native Americans were totally excluded) wanted a system of laws that would enable them to pursue their own interests. They believed that their interests were the interests of everyone, as in the sayings "What's good for General Motors is good for America" and "The business of America is business." They were certainly mindful that there were scores of people below them, people over whom they exercised power and control. They knew they wielded power and control, believed they deserved this power and control, and wanted to keep it that way—and still do today. But they needed the "consent of the governed," and they needed to convince the majority that this was the "best of all possible worlds." So they created and perpetuated the myths of "equal justice for all" and "a government of laws, not men." This became a very convenient ideology of class (not to mention race and gender) control, all under the "color of law." They created a "legal order," an order that continues to mask its class basis.

Key Constitutional Amendments That Apply to Criminal Justice

Several amendments directly apply to the criminal justice system. Let's consider the Fourth, Fifth, Sixth, Eighth, and Fourteenth Amendments in turn.

The Fourth Amendment.   The **Fourth Amendment** states:

> The right of the people to be secure in their persons, houses, papers, and effects, against unreasonable searches and seizures, shall not be violated, and no warrants shall issue, but upon the probable cause, supported by oath or affirmation, and particularly describing the place to be searched, and the persons or things to be seized.

It should be obvious that the writers of this statement were most concerned that the British had subjected the colonists to a great deal of interference and that there had been little freedom under British rule. Little did these writers realize that this amendment would become the subject of great controversy some two hundred years later, as the police engaged in systematic violations, especially when it came to the behaviors of minority citizens. And the police complain that they are "handcuffed" by an overly broad interpretation of the Fourth Amendment and that too many criminals are "let off" through "technicalities." It is curious that protection from one of the ultimate freedoms people might have (simply to be left alone and to have their privacy) is called a "technicality"!

The Fifth Amendment.   The **Fifth Amendment** also relates to police behavior, specifically the behavior of the police toward citizens placed under arrest. It pertains to the right against "self-incrimination," and it is supposed to protect a person who has been placed under arrest from a confession coerced by the police. But it says a lot more:

> No person shall be held to answer for a capital, or otherwise infamous crime, unless on a presentment or indictment of a Grand Jury, except in cases arising in the land or naval forces, or in the militia, when in actual service in time of war or public danger; nor shall any person be subject for the same offense to be twice put in jeopardy of life or limb; nor shall be compelled in any criminal case to be a witness against himself; nor be deprived of life, liberty, or property, without due process of law; nor shall private property be taken for public use, without just compensation.

First, if a charge is very serious (especially an offense punishable by death), there must be a "presentment or indictment of a grand jury."[75] Second, the famous "double jeopardy" clause is found here (which is why O. J. Simpson cannot ever be brought to trial again in a *criminal* case for killing Nicole Brown and Ron Goldman, even if additional incriminating evidence is discovered). Third, in a trial you do not have to be a witness against yourself; you do not have to take the witness stand in your own trial. Fourth, you cannot be deprived of life, liberty, or property without due process. The due process clause is crucial, for it suggests that the state (especially the police) cannot arrest you, charge you, hold you in jail, bring you to court, and so on, unless they abide by all the applicable rules of procedure, including all of the relevant Bill of Rights. This, essentially, is the concept of *due process of law.* One particular case that is related to this amendment is *Miranda v. Arizona* (1966), the result of which is the so-called Miranda warnings that the police have to give someone who is under arrest. More is said about this case in Chapter 5.

The Sixth Amendment.   The **Sixth Amendment** says that the accused must receive a "fair trial," is entitled to know the charges set forth by the state, and has the right to legal representation (a lawyer). The amendment states:

> In all criminal prosecutions, the accused shall enjoy the right to a speedy and public trial, by an impartial jury of the state and district wherein the crime shall have been committed, which district shall have been previously ascertained by law, and to be informed of the nature and cause of the accusations; to be confronted with the witnesses against him; to have compulsory process for obtaining witnesses in his favor, and to have the assistance of counsel for his defense.

As in the Fifth Amendment, there's a lot going on here. First, a person has the right to a "speedy" as well as a "public" trial. This requirement has been subject to a lot of interpretation over the years. What is a *speedy* trial? Is it 30, 60, 90, or 180 days? Also, what is meant by *public*? Does this mean that everyone has a right to be a spectator? If everyone cannot attend, does it mean that television must be allowed to take the proceedings into everyone's home (as was done in the Simpson criminal trial)? Then there's the issue of "impartial jury" and the issue of venue. Does the trial always have to be where the crime occurred? Third, there's the critical issue of the right to counsel, which has been extended to earlier stages of the process (including immediately after the arrest). Does this mean that everyone is entitled to an F. Lee Bailey or a Johnnie Cochran? Should such high-powered attorneys provide cut-rate prices for indigent defendants? These and related issues are discussed in Chapter 9.

The Eighth Amendment.   The **Eighth Amendment** states:

> Excessive bail shall not be required, nor excessive fines imposed, nor cruel and unusual punishments inflicted.

The term *bail* refers to a bond the accused puts up in order to obtain his or her freedom while awaiting trial. It is meant to ensure that the accused shows up and does not skip town, but the issue is complex, as we discuss in Chapter 9. Notice that this amendment does not guarantee that a person receives bail; it only protects against "excessive" bail. But what constitutes "excessive"? This is largely a *class* issue. Five hundred dollars may not be a lot to you, but for a homeless or otherwise poor person, it very well may be too much. The mere existence of a bail system guarantees that jails become poorhouses.

Another critical issue contained within this amendment is the phrase "cruel and unusual punishment." What punishments are "cruel" and "unusual"? This issue has yet to be settled. Although the Supreme Court has ruled that capital punishment is neither cruel nor unusual, it is interesting that the United States is the only industrialized nation that added execution-efficiency to its list of accomplishments in recent years. If the death penalty is not cruel and unusual punishment, then what is? This issue is explored in Chapter 10.

The Fourteenth Amendment.   The **Fourteenth Amendment** says that the Bill of Rights is applicable to all of the states:

> All persons born or naturalized in the United States, and subject to the jurisdiction thereof, are citizens of the United States and of the state wherein they reside. No state shall make or

enforce any law which shall abridge the privileges or immunities of citizens of the United States; nor shall any state deprive any person of life, liberty, or property, without due process of the law; nor deny to any person within its jurisdiction the equal protection of the laws.

This amendment was adopted in 1868, following the Thirteenth Amendment (which abolished slavery), so it figures prominently in the battle for civil rights. The key phrase here is that no state can "deprive any person of life, liberty, or property, without due process of the law." In other words, every state must act in accordance with the Bill of Rights. The civil suit filed by Rodney King charged that he had been deprived of his rights by the police officers who beat him—a violation of the Fourteenth Amendment.

Although the Bill of Rights seems sound in principle and is stated in relatively straightforward wording, it nevertheless remains controversial. The point we want to make here is that these are mere words on paper. What occurs in the real world is what really matters. It is true that if your rights have been violated you can seek redress for these violations, but if you are poor, your "freedom" to do so will be restricted by your class background, unless (as in the case of Rodney King) you become a sort of celebrity and attract the attention of lawyers willing to take your case for free. The real question is: For every Rodney King, how many others are similarly abused but never gain celebrity status and never have their cases heard in a civil court?

Other Forms of Law

Laws govern just about every imaginable human behavior. What is not covered under civil or criminal law is covered under other forms of law. One of the most important is **administrative law** (or *regulatory law*)—rules, regulations, orders, and decisions issued by administrative agencies to carry out their regulatory powers and duties. The relationship between administrative law and criminal justice is often ignored. However, this body of law includes regulations and rules that, if violated by citizens or organizations, carry criminal penalties. Thus, administrative agencies have the authority to "create" crimes without direct legislative action. Moreover, administrative law can impact the personnel configuration of organizations and agencies (e.g., criminal justice agencies) through the establishment of regulations and rules that oversee hiring practices and procedures (e.g., through affirmative action programs, which are required by federal statutes, and regulations designed to remedy discrimination practices in hiring minorities and women).

There are several regulatory agencies set up to oversee the activities of corporations and, especially, to protect consumers. The Interstate Commerce Commission regulates various types of transportation businesses and intervenes on behalf of consumers when complaints occur. Other regulatory agencies include the Federal Communications Commission, the Securities and Exchange Commission, and the National Labor Relations Board. Many forms of corporate crimes are handled by these and other agencies.[76] Only on rare occasions is the criminal justice system involved in the processing of corporate offenders.[77]

Another form of law is what is known as **case law** or **common law.** This is law that has been created as a result of court decisions. This becomes what is called *stare decisis,* or a policy of interpreting laws according to previous court decisions (e.g., decisions by the U.S. Supreme Court). **Legislative law,** the most commonly recognized form of law, consists of the laws passed by special legislative bodies at all governmental levels. The resulting legal rules are called **statutes** if passed on the state or federal level and **ordinances** if passed on the local level. Elected officials, such as state legislators or congressional representatives, pass most of the laws (and decide their corresponding punishments as well). Statutory law is most important for the criminal justice system because most of the "crimes" that this system deals with are violations of state and federal laws passed by legislative bodies. At the state level such laws (both substantive and procedural) are published in state penal codes (e.g., the California Penal Code, the Nevada Revised Statutes).[78] In the past, criminal codes were often drafted ad hoc, in response to highly publicized incidents or in the aftermath of anticrime crusades.

We now turn to the central or essential elements of crime.

ESSENTIAL ELEMENTS OF CRIME

A crime is committed when an actor satisfies all of the elements stipulated in the definition of the crime. There is much debate over what elements are essential, but we believe that the introductory course in criminal justice should not mire students down in this debate. Therefore, we address what we consider the three the most important elements: (1) a voluntary act (*actus reus*), (2) omission, and (3) culpable intent (*mens rea*).

A Voluntary Act: *Actus Reus*

A crime begins with a *voluntary* act. Generally, that act can be any bodily movement. Therefore, any voluntary bodily movement is conduct that qualifies for criminal liability. There are, however, exceptions. If the act is not of the actor's own volition, if the act is reflexive or convulsive, or if the act is performed while the actor is asleep or otherwise unconscious, criminal liability is not established.

Suppose you are standing behind someone on the curb waiting for a bus. Someone behind you shoves you, causing you to push the person in front of you under the front wheel of the arriving bus, resulting in that person's injury. Does your act ground criminal liability? Of course not. The act was not a result of your own volition.

Let us now consider an individual who experiences an epileptic seizure and during this episode injures another person. Again, criminal liability is not grounded.

Finally, suppose that you are sound asleep at home. You get up and begin sleepwalking. Remaining asleep, you walk into the guest room and begin to strangle an overnight visitor who is also sound asleep. Criminal liability is not grounded in this example either. But suppose you become very sleepy during a lecture at school and then, on your way home, you fall asleep at the wheel and your car crashes into another car, injuring the driver of the other vehicle. In this instance, you satisfy the criminal liability requirement.

In theory at least, people cannot be arrested, charged, and convicted for merely talking about violating a law unless they take steps toward the furtherance of the crime. In theory, this rule places a check on the arbitrary power of the state. In reality, this principle is violated on numerous occasions. For instance, people (especially those who fit the stereotype of the "criminal," such as young black males) are often arrested on "suspicion" or on a charge of "vagrancy" (it should be noted that although most vagrancy laws have been ruled unconstitutional, many police departments still make arrests for identical behavior stipulated by vagrancy laws but charge such persons with "disorderly conduct," "trespassing," and the like). Charging a person with conspiracy is another way the state circumvents this principle. This has been done repeatedly against certain groups demanding social and political changes, beginning with the indictment of the leaders of the International Workers of the World (a socialist labor organization) in 1917 and the arrests of the "Chicago 8" during the 1968 Democratic Convention (they were indicted for "conspiracy to incite a riot").[79]

For an act to be considered a crime, it must be *specifically* prohibited by law—that is, the act must be specified in such a way that the average person will know that it is illegal. The legal term for this act is **actus reus,** "guilty act." A closely related concept is expressed by the Latin phrase *nullum crimen, nulla poena, sine lege,* which means "there is no crime, there is no punishment, without law." This is one of the unique features of Western legal systems, for there is an emphasis on the elimination of vaguely worded statutes. Under such a system individuals are to "be given the maximum legal protection to conduct their lives as they see fit." Such an emphasis is not without its problems, however.[80]

From a critical perspective, an emphasis on such legal specificity tends to separate "moral obligations" from "legal obligations." As Michalowski notes: "No legal system can specifically enumerate every possible violation of a general moral standard. As a result, where the law emphasizes specificity a proportion of moral violations will always fall beyond the law's reach."[81] One result is that certain moral violations common to groups that are involved in legislative actions resulting in the defining of certain behaviors as illegal are not likely to define their own morally questionable actions as illegal (e.g., certain immoral but perfectly legal "sharp" business practices).

Another problem is that such legal specificity "reduces the power of community and social groups to influence and control the behavior of their members," for only "legally prohibited" behavior can be acted upon and then only by "authorized agents" of the state (e.g., police, courts). One primary example is the reluctance of the police and the courts to take seriously the crime of spouse battering, especially after the couple has divorced. In such cases, the woman who is being victimized may have to resort to the civil law and hire her own attorney to take some action because neither the legal system nor community resources have much power over the offending ex-husband. Yet this is problematic, because in many cases the person victimized has neither the time nor the resources to take the perpetrator to court, as shown in numerous cases in which a woman tries to obtain a restraining order against an abusive ex-husband or an ex-husband who is behind in his child support payments. A woman whom we know complained that juvenile court was "like a lion with no teeth!" The key point here is the power differences between men and women.

Relatedly, legal specificity helps perpetuate the cultural emphasis on "self-oriented" rather than "altruistic" behavior because individuals will tend to "identify their obligations toward others as legal and specific rather than moral and general." It then "becomes difficult to motivate people to engage in altruistic acts that may benefit others or society as a whole" because people may come to feel that as long as they are obeying the "letter of the law," under the current ideology of the "rule of law," they are "meeting their obligations as citizens."[82] Also, there is a tendency to overrely on authorized agents of the state (police, courts, etc.) to solve problems that may more easily be solved by citizens.

Omission: Failure to Comply with the Legal Duty to Act

The *actus reus* requirement signifies that in most situations, criminal liability is not grounded for an *omission* to act. American criminal law has no provisions that stipulate a legal duty to rescue. In certain circumstances, however, there may be a *legal duty to act.* There are five circumstances in which a person has a legal duty to act.

The first circumstance is *statutory:* a legal requirement, based on legal statutes, requires individuals to act. For example, there are statutes (federal, state, or city) that stipulate that people must file income-tax returns and pay income tax. The second circumstance there is *contractual:* there is an obligation to act when there is a distinct relationship between one's "profession" and an existing "situation." For example, a licensed paramedic with certified training in CPR has a legal obligation to act in many emergency situations. The failure to act in an emergency situation may be grounds for criminal liability.

The third circumstance in which there is a legal requirement to act arises when the legal obligation is based on the *relationship between parties.* For example, parents have a legal obligation to protect their children. The fourth circumstance arises when someone *voluntarily assumes a duty of care toward another person.* Suppose you are at the beach with several friends. All of a sudden you hear someone in the water yell for help. You tell your friends that you are going to swim out and assist the person who yelled. You enter the water and begin swimming. Just as you are about to reach the person, you recognize him. You don't like him, and you say to yourself, "I don't like that person, and I'm not going to save him." You turn around and swim back to shore. The person drowns, and you are criminally responsible because you "voluntarily" assumed the legal duty of care of another individual.

The fifth circumstance requiring you to act arises if your *conduct created the peril.* Although you have no legal obligation to rescue, you may be criminally liable if, after creating a peril, you fail to act or respond. Suppose you are at a poolside party and you bump into someone and she falls into the water. Neither you nor the person whom you knocked into the water can swim. You are not required by law to jump into the water, but you are required to go and seek help.

Culpable Intent: *Mens Rea*

When criminal law developed in England, it emerged as common law (judge-made law or case law). Although the roots of U.S. criminal law were propagated in common law, most jurisdictions in the United States have codified their original common-law crimes into statutes. However, we continue to cling to one of the most important artifacts of common law—the doctrine that most crimes require a true **mens rea,** a "guilty mind." In other words, before someone can be convicted of a criminal act, there must be proof, in most cases, that the accused "had in mind" (mental state) to cause harm or to violate the law. Under common-law standards, there are four mental state requirements: (1) general intent, (2) specific intent, (3) malice, and (4) strict liability.

For most crimes under common law, the offender's **intent** is inferred from the act itself. These acts are known as *general intent crimes. General intent* means intent to do that which the law prohibits. Nearly all crimes in today's state criminal codes are general intent crimes. A general intent crime "refers to an actor's physical conduct in the sense that the actor intends the consequences of his or her voluntary actions."[83] In contrast, *specific intent crimes* require proof that the accused desired to do something to further the basic criminal act (*actus reus*). For example, to substantiate common-law burglary (a specific intent crime), the state must show that the offender not only intended to break and enter the residence of A but intended to steal something once inside A's residence. Specific intent crimes are crimes in which the defendant "intends a particular result."[84] Hence, whereas general intent means that the offender intended to commit a specific act (i.e., crime), specific intent means that the offender intended to accomplish a particular result.

Malice, the third mental state under common law, is the commission of an intentional wrongful act, without just cause or excuse, with the intent to inflict an injury, or an act that by its very nature implies evil intent. Malice in law does not necessarily assume hatred or ill will against a particular individual by the offender; rather it is the offender's state of mind that is viewed as reckless of law itself or of the legal rights of individuals. Under common law, there are only two malice crimes: murder and arson.

The final common-law mental state is *strict liability.* Strict liability offenses are generally crimes that endanger the public welfare. These crimes are typically in the administrative, regulatory, or morality area of law, and their elements do not require criminal intent or *mens rea.* Suppose that X, an adult, purchases alcohol for Y, who is a minor. The intention of X, who provided the alcohol, is not a legal consideration; the law does not care what X's intention was. The law is concerned only that X purchased alcohol for Y, who is a minor. Other examples of strict liability crimes include statutory rape (an adult having intercourse with a minor), illegal dumping of toxic wastes (pollution), and concealing a weapon while boarding an aircraft. Again, as in the case of X purchasing alcohol for Y, the state is not required to center its attention on the intent of the defendant who is charged with statutory rape, polluting the water, or having a concealed weapon at the terminal gate. The state needs to prove only that the offender committed the acts that he or she is charged with.

Today, many jurisdictions have moved away from the ambiguities of general and specific intent. These jurisdictions reject the common-law terms of intent and instead stipulate four mental states: (1) purposely, (2) knowingly, (3) recklessly, and (4) negligently. *Purposely* and *knowingly* are equal to specific intent at common law; *recklessly* and *negligently* are not equal to specific intent at common law.

When an individual *consciously desires* to engage in an illegal act, and is *aware* of the *probable consequences,* it is argued that he or she acted *purposely.* Suppose you are provided with evidence that shows A was extremely angry at B and had a conscious desire to kill B. A purchased a gun and ammunition, loaded the gun, drove to B's house, pointed the loaded gun at B's head, and pulled the trigger. Instantly, B died. It can be argued that A consciously desired to kill B. Furthermore, A was aware of the probable consequences—death—associated with shooting B in the head. Thus, you can, with some degree of certainty, successfully argue that A acted purposely.

Closely related to *purposely* is the mental state *knowingly.* The principal difference between them rests with the *consciously desired* result of the act. For example, A wants to kill B so that he can collect insurance money. A places a bomb on an airplane where B is a passenger. Shortly after takeoff, the bomb explodes. B is killed, along with the other passengers. Did A purposely kill the other passengers? It can be argued that A *purposely* killed B, because that was his conscious desire. It can be argued that A *knowingly* killed the other passengers, because he lacked the conscious desire to kill them but was aware that it was practically certain that they would die in the explosion.

A person is said to act *recklessly* if he or she "consciously disregards a substantial and unjustifiable risk" and the risk is "of such a nature and degree that, considering the nature and purpose of the actor's conduct and the circumstances known to him [or her], its disregard involves a gross deviation from the standard of conduct that a law-abiding person would observe in the actor's situation."[85] For example, assume that L is late for work this morning. As she drives down the very familiar street to work, she seems to be "hitting" every possible red light. Looking at her watch, L realizes that she has only ten minutes left to drive twenty blocks. All of a sudden she finds herself stopped behind a school bus with blinking red lights. L looks carefully and decides that she cannot afford to wait any longer. With the red light still flashing she passes the school bus. Out of nowhere a child steps in front of L's car. She slams on the breaks, but it is too late. The child dies instantly. Clearly, L's behavior grossly deviated from the norm; she made a conscious decision to disregard a substantial and unjustifiable risk. It is assumed that law-abiding people understand that small children are likely to be present when a school bus has its red lights flashing. Thus, L is criminally liable for the child's death. The law applies an objective standard to the mental state *negligently.* A person is negligent

> when he [or she] should be aware of a substantial and unjustifiable risk.... The risk must be of such a nature and degree that the actor's failure to perceive it, considering the nature and purpose of his [or her] conduct and the circumstances known to him [or her], involves a gross deviation from the standard of care that a reasonable person would observe in the actor's situation.[86]

Recall our previous example, in which you become sleepy during a lecture, leave the lecture hall, get into your car, and begin to drive home. You fall asleep while driving and hit another vehicle. The act is negligent: you should have pulled off the road and taken a nap.

Most courts require a greater degree of culpability for criminal negligence (typically gross negligence) than for civil negligence. The law clearly defines each category of culpability, in contrast to common-law interpretations of specific intent and general intent, which have caused much confusion across legal jurisdictions. Yet, as Scheb and Scheb note, in reading cases, you will find that most courts cling to the common-law classifications of "specific and general intent."[87]

CRIMINAL DEFENSES

A defendant who is presented with formal charges has three legal options from which a response to those charges can be made:

1. The defendant can plead guilty to the formal charges or plead guilty to a lesser charge resulting from plea-bargain negotiations. In such cases, defense is a nonissue; most criminal defendants choose this course of action to respond to the criminal charges.

2. The defendant can plead *nolo contendere,* which in essence means "I will not contest the charge(s)." The defendant is neither admitting to nor denying the charges. The court must give its consent before a defendant can plead *nolo contendere.* The legal effect of a *nolo contendere* plea is similar that of a guilty plea: as soon as the plea is made, the defendant proceeds to the sentencing phase of the court process.

3. The defendant can plead not guilty to the formal charges. In such cases, the defendant must present a defense to the charges.

The two principal categories of criminal defense are *denial of the charges,* in which the defendant purports that factual allegations presented by the state (prosecutor) are wrong, and the *affirmative defense,* in which the defendant introduces new factual allegations that may constitute a defense to the criminal charges. In an affirmative defense, the defendant does not necessarily dispute all or most of the facts presented by the prosecutor but aims to provide an explanation (sometimes referred to as *excuse*) in the form of evidence. In essence, the defendant is saying, "Yes, I did it, *but....*" When using an affirmative defense, the defendant has the burden of proof that will allow him or her to escape conviction, even though the prosecution is able to prove all the elements of the crime.

In the remainder of this section we discuss several affirmative defenses: infancy; duress; intoxication; entrapment; use of force in defense of self, others, and property; insanity; and the battered-person syndrome. This collection of defenses is by no means exhaustive, but it does lay the groundwork for a general understanding of criminal defenses and their applications.

Infancy

One of the most important assumptions in Western law is that an individual has free will and is capable of knowing right from wrong. We may assume that in the absence of the ability to distinguish between right and wrong, the *mens rea* element of a crime cannot be satisfied. The belief that persons under a certain age do not have the capacity to know the difference between right and wrong is one of the oldest traditions in Western law. Roman law and then common law operated on the assumption that an individual cannot tell right from wrong before reaching the "age of reason"—age 7 (age 7 is still considered the minimum).[88] At common law, children between the ages of 7 and 14 were presumed not to have the capacity to commit crimes. Western law ruled that between the age of 7 and 14 a child's capacity to know right from wrong needed to be proved, and prosecutors were given the opportunity to rebut the infancy defense and introduce evidence demonstrating that a child did possess the mental capacity to fulfill the necessary culpable intent element of a crime.

During the nineteenth century, the number of offenders between ages 7 and 14 increased, and more and more attention was directed to the issue of capacity. With the creation of the first juvenile court in 1899 in Chicago, it was determined, through the passage of the Juvenile Court Act, that children below the age of 16 could not be convicted of a criminal act, regardless of whether they knew right from wrong (Ill. Laws 131 1899). The intent of such legislation was *preventive.* The goal of the nineteenth-century reformers was to reduce a juvenile's chances of entering into a life of crime, and such measures were a form of protection. Under the new juvenile court system, a juvenile would be rehabilitated rather than punished (see Chapter 13).

Duress

Duress is an unlawful threat or coercion used by someone to induce another person to act in a way in which he or she would not normally act. In the case of crimes of omission, an unlawful threat or coercion used to induce a person *not* to act as he or she normally would act is also considered duress. A defendant must establish five elements of the duress defense:

1. There was a *threat* by a third party.
2. The threat produced a reasonable *fear* in the defendant.
3. The defendant was in *imminent danger* at the time of the alleged duress.
4. Failure to comply would have resulted in *serious bodily injury or death.*
5. There was *no opportunity to escape* the duress without committing the crime.

In order for this defense to be successful, the defendant must show that the harm that he or she was likely to experience was greater than the harm experienced by the victim(s) of the crime committed by the defendant. Thus, duress is not likely to be a successful defense in the case of intentional murder.

Suppose that E pulls out a gun and threatens F, saying, "If you don't go into this store and help me rob the clerk, I'm going to kill you." F then accompanies E into the store and holds open a paper bag as the clerk fills it with money. After they leave the store, E looks at F, says, "Thanks, stupid," and runs away. Several minutes later the police arrive and arrest F for robbery. In this instance, duress is clearly a viable defense.

Now suppose that X joins a youth gang because, among other reasons, he wants to be cool. One day, several members of the gang tell X that they are going to steal a car. X tells the other gang members that he does not want to go with them and steal a car. Z, the leader of the group, takes out a gun and says to X, "I'm going to shoot you if you don't come with us." Reluctantly, X accompanies the other gang members. They steal a car and shortly afterward are arrested by the police. Can X claim duress as a defense? The correct answer is probably not. Many states deny the defense of duress to an individual,

Intoxication

Intoxication is the result of ingesting alcohol or other drugs. Two types of intoxication may be used as a defense: voluntary and involuntary. *Voluntary* (self-induced) intoxication was rarely considered a viable defense under common law. Today, most jurisdictions recognize voluntary intoxication as an acceptable defense if it negates an element of the offense, but this only applies to specific intent crimes (robbery, burglary, larceny, etc.). No jurisdictions allow voluntary intoxication as a defense for general intent crimes.

The *involuntary* intoxication defense is rarely used but is appropriate when the defendant became intoxicated through coercion or deception. Some courts have allowed the involuntary intoxication defense in cases in which the defendant mistakenly became intoxicated or was ignorant about the pharmacological properties of the intoxicating substance. The latter option is, of course, limited to prescription drugs.[89]

The law suggests that intoxication cannot be a defense for the crime of drunk driving, because alcohol is obviously an element of the crime. The language also places full responsibility for becoming intoxicated, and for the effects resulting from intoxication, on the individual. This issue is obviously questionable in the cases of alcoholics and drug addicts. who, it might be argued, have physical dependencies on their respective substances. It seems dubious also for youngsters who consume alcohol, given that the justification for liquor laws stems from the inability of minors to handle alcohol responsibly.

Entrapment

The entrapment defense is very narrow and almost never available to the defendant. Let's face it: in the eyes of the police, one of their principal roles is to trap people. The only defendant who is going to benefit from this defense is someone who can prove no predisposition or desire to commit the offense of which he or she is charged. *Entrapment* became a household word during the ABSCAM investigations in the late 1970s. These investigations, conducted by the FBI, were directed against elected officials in the U.S. Congress, who claimed that the FBI had entrapped them—meaning that were it not for the FBI's tactics, the defendants would have committed no crimes.[90]

Generally speaking, entrapment can occur in only two ways. Entrapment occurs when law enforcement or informants induce a person to engage in criminal activities by (1) "making knowingly false representations designated to induce the belief that such conduct is not prohibited" or (2) "employing methods of persuasion or inducement that create a substantial risk that such an offense will be committed by persons other than those who are ready to commit it" (M.P.C. 2.13:1:a:b). The defense can be successful only if the defendant can prove by a preponderance of the evidence that his or her behavior was a result of the entrapment. A major reason why this defense is rarely successful is that determining the validity or truthfulness of testimony of witnesses often boils down to the question of "Who is telling the truth, the police or the defendant?" There is an overwhelming tendency for juries and judges to take the word of police officers over defendants.

Use of Force in Defense of Self, Others, and Property

Under certain conditions, the law provides individuals with the opportunity to protect themselves, other people, and property against unlawful threats or force. There are, however, limitations that are contingent on the level or severity of the unlawful threat or force confronting the defender. In the case of self-defense, two types of force may apply to a given situation. First, individuals may use *nondeadly* force in self-defense any time they believe force will be used against them, and further believe that the use of force is necessary for protection. Second, most jurisdictions allow individuals to employ *deadly* force in self-defense any time they believe that deadly force is about to be used against them. Some jurisdictions, however, stipulate that in certain conditions the defender must *retreat to the wall,* or break contact with the threat if such a movement can be accomplished with complete safety. In three situations, however, the retreat rule does not apply: (1) inside one's own home, (2) if one is the victim of a rape or robbery, and (3) if one is a police officer—police officers have no duty to retreat.

Essentially, the same rules apply in situations in which one is compelled to use force in order to protect others. Under common law, a special relationship must exist between the parties in question before protective force could be used, and a person may use force to protect another person if the situation is such that the defender would be justified to use force if it were he or she who was subjected to the threat. Finally, the defender must believe that her or his intervention is necessary for the protection of the other person. The retreat requirements for self-defense also apply to the use of force for the protection of another person.

Although many people subscribe to the notion that they have a legal right and moral duty to kill someone who violates their property, deadly force may never be used solely to defend one's property. Short of deadly force, most jurisdictions stipulate that one may use reasonable force necessary to protect property from immediate criminal acts. However, if the protection of property can be fulfilled by simply using verbal instructions, the use of force is not permissible.

Concerning the use of devices to protect one's property: First, the device that is used must not be designed to cause, or be known to create, a significant risk of death or substantial bodily injury. Second, the actor's use of a device to protect her or his property from entry or trespass must be reasonable under the circumstances. Finally, the device used is one that is customarily used for the specified purpose, or reasonable care has been taken to alert probable intruders that such a device is being employed.

Insanity

The insanity defense is perhaps one of the most controversial issues of capacity, largely because of some rather sensational cases of recent years (e.g., John Hinckley, who attempted to assassinate President Ronald Reagan). The courts have generally attempted to measure a person's "mental capacity" through one of five major tests: (1) the M'Naughten rule,

(2) the "irresistible impulse" test, (3) the Durham rule, (4) the Model Penal Code rule, and (5) the Insanity Defense Reform Act passed by Congress in 1984.[91]

The **M'Naughten rule** came from an English case in 1843. The accused was charged with murdering Edward Drummond, the private secretary of the prime minister of England, Sir Robert Peel, believing that he was actually killing Peel (the accused fired the shot as the victim was leaving the prime minister's home). The defense claimed insanity based on the belief that the accused suffered from "delusions," so much so that he did not know what he was doing at the time of the crime. He was found not guilty by reason of insanity. After the verdict the queen of England demanded that a law be provided that furnished some guidelines for the insanity defense. The House of Lords passed the M'Naughten rule, which provided that

> it must be clearly proved that, at the time of committing the act, the party accused was labouring under such a defect of reason, from disease of the mind, as not to know the nature and quality of the act he was doing; or, if he did know it, that he did not know what he was doing was wrong.[92]

Hence, under the M'Naughten rule, the defendant, because of his or her mental state, must show that he or she lacks awareness of the wrongfulness of his or her act(s), or fails to understand the nature and quality of the act(s). In the United States this rule is used in thirty states; however, in many of these states an additional test, known as the *"irresistible impulse" test,* is used. It considers a person's emotions and self-control or volition. Under this rule, it is held that there are forms of "mental illness" that reduce a person's ability to control his or her behavior but do not reduce the ability to "distinguish right from wrong." In other words, an accused cannot be held criminally liable if it can be proved that he or she was suffering from such illnesses that "rendered them incapable of controlling their actions."[93]

The **Durham rule** arose from a case in 1954 (*Durham v. United States*)[94] in which a federal judge, David Bazelon, ruled that an accused person cannot be held liable "if his [or her] unlawful act was the product of mental disease or mental defect."[95] This ruling opened the door for the consideration of all sorts of mental and emotional problems as they relate to criminal behavior.

The test of insanity proposed by the American Law Institute in the "Model Penal Code" has been increasingly used by some courts.[96] The *Model Penal Code rule,* often referred to as the *"substantial capacity" test,* states: "A person is not responsible for criminal conduct if at the time of such conduct as a result of mental disease or defect, a person lacks substantial capacity either to appreciate the wrongfulness of his conduct or to conform his conduct to the requirements of the law."[97]

The most recent federal standard, the *Insanity Defense Reform Act of 1984,* provides that in federal courts:

> It is an affirmative defense to a prosecution under any Federal statute that, at the time of the commission of the acts constituting the offense, the defendant, as a result of a severe mental disease or defect, was unable to appreciate the nature and quality or the wrongfulness of his acts. Mental disease or defect does not otherwise constitute a defense.[98]

It should be noted that the courts continue to struggle with this problem, and one of the latest methods is to use the verdict "guilty but mentally ill" when the defendant's insanity has been established but the person nevertheless will be subject to some form of incarceration and treatment. Perhaps as long as certain forms of behavior are subject to the criminalization process, the issue of insanity will be with us.

Battered-Person Syndrome

Domestic violence is a relatively new legal concept. The concept *child abuse* did not surface, and become a household term, until the 1960s. Historically, women and children were treated, legally, as property of males, who had the right to do with their property as they saw fit. Although laws were enacted to dispel the woman-and-children-as-property notion, not until 1994 did Congress finally get around to passing the Violence against Women Act, which provides civil rights relief for women who are victimized by males.

The **battered-person syndrome** is a relatively new legal defense tool. Originally referred to as the *battered-wife syndrome,* the term was changed to *battered-person syndrome* to accommodate children who, after years of abusive treatment at home, assault or kill their parent(s). This term is employed in all cases where evidence of long-term battering is presented in defense of a criminal act, or as mitigating circumstances in the negotiation of a sentence or a plea for clemency following a conviction.[99] The battered-person syndrome is often used by defendants to shore up a self-defense strategy.

Domestic, or family, violence frequently emerges out of power struggles in which individuals are quarreling over resources and benefits. These struggles originate not only from personal aspirations but also from changing social norms and social conditions. The state has always been reluctant to intervene in the domain of the family. This reluctance stems from the public versus the private use of law, whereby the latter purports that individuals should be free to act without public intervention. In other words, what happens behind closed doors is not the law's business. Historically, the state has been slow in responding to the needs of children and women who find themselves in brutal family situations. Until recently, welfare laws provided a vehicle for women to escape abusive family environments. However, with new welfare laws making it more difficult for women to receive benefits, coupled with time constraints, there is a possibility that more women may feel that violence is the only alternative to abusive treatment at home.

SUMMARY

In this chapter we described two traditional perspectives on crime and criminal justice and presented our alternative, critical perspective. The classical approach assumes that people have free will and that most offenders act rationally, focuses on the crime itself, and argues that in order to reduce crime punishments must be "proportionate to the offense." In contrast, the positivist approach stresses various biological, psychological, and sociological factors determining human behavior and argues that crime is not necessarily rational behavior, that it is caused by factors external to the individual. Instead of punishment, positivists generally favor social reform or rehabilitation.

The classical and positivist approaches generally take the existing social and economic order for granted. Our critical approach challenges this view. Our focus is on the inherently unequal distribution of resources within a capitalist society and on the relationship between this inequality and crime and criminal justice.

We discussed three perspectives on criminal law: the consensus/pluralist model, the interest-group/conflict model, and our critical model of law. We pointed out that the criminal law is the basis of the criminal justice system. This system exists to enforce the *criminal* law, not other forms of law. Thus, under normal circumstances when a corporation dumps toxic chemicals into a river or engages in price-fixing or other harmful acts, the criminal justice system is rarely involved in the case. You are not likely to see the police handcuff and take to jail the CEO of a corporation on the 11 P.M. news even though his actions, or inactions, could have resulted in the deaths of many people. A rather obvious class bias is built into the legal system. There is one system of justice for the rich and powerful (civil law, administrative law, etc.) and another system (criminal law and the criminal justice system) for the rest of the population.

We described the nature of criminal law, types of law, the essential elements of crime, and the most common criminal defenses.

KEY TERMS

actus reus   77
administrative law   76
Adolphe Quételet   58
Andre-Michel Guerry   58
battered-person syndrome   85
Bill of Rights   72
case law/common law   76
Cesare Beccaria   55
Cesare Lombroso   59
civil law   71
classical school   55
consensus/pluralist model   64
constitutional law   72
crime control model   56
criminal law   72
critical model   66
critical thinking   60

critical perspective   60
due process model   56
Durham rule   84
Eighth Amendment   75
elements of a crime   72
Fifth Amendment   74
folkways   69
formal social control   70
Fourteenth Amendment   75
Fourth Amendment   74
instrumentalist perspective   66
intent   79
interest-group/conflict model   65
legislative law   76
M'Naughten rule   84
mens rea   79
mores   69

ordinances   76
plaintiff   71
political social control   70
positivist school   57
procedural law   72
Pyrrhic defeat theory   61
rule of law   65
Sixth Amendment   75
social norms   69
sociological imagination   60
statutes   76
stigmata   59
structuralist perspective
   of law   66
substantive law   72
torts   71

NOTES

1. Cullen, F., and K. Gilbert. *Reaffirming Rehabilitation.* Cincinnati: Anderson, 1982, p. 27.

2. Social contract theorists based their theories on some unproven assumptions about human nature, yet their views were taken as given by the new bourgeois governments in the seventeenth and eighteenth centuries. Social contract became a convenient ideology justifying a strong central government or state that is ultimately concerned with protecting the interests of private property and profits. The social contract theory in turn justified the build-up of police forces and other formal methods of handling conflicts and disputes—in short, a formal criminal justice system. (Also included was a definition of crime as a harm to the state and the people—often used interchangeably.) Ironically Rousseau wrote that the ultimate source of inequality was man taking a plot of ground and claiming it as his own. This is exactly what happened during the infamous *Enclosure Movements* in England during the sixteenth century. Powerful landlords built fences around common ground (land formally used by all and not legally owned) and claimed it as their own or charged rent in the name of private property. This resulted in thousands of vagrants (homeless people) invading European cities in search of work and eventually being labeled the *dangerous classes* (or worse) by the privileged. The Elizabethan Poor Laws were passed during the sixteenth century and declared two kinds of poor: (1) the worthy—those who can be reformed and be useful to society, and (2) the unworthy—those who are unreformable, useless, requiring sentence to the poorhouse/workhouse (early forms of jails and prisons). The prevailing view of crime was that it is a voluntary violation of the social contract and became an essential idea in much of the subsequent thinking about crime, especially classical views. Such a view largely ignored the gross inequalities existing at the time. With such inequality came illiteracy, leading us to question whether the people in these new social orders unanimously agreed on the social contract, since so few could read or write.

3. This classic book is available in many bookstores and libraries. See Beccaria, C. *On Crimes and Punishment.* New York: Bobbs-Merrill, 1963.

4. Beccaria, C. *On Crimes and Punishment.* Indianapolis: Bobbs-Merrill, 1963, p. 99 (originally published in 1764).

5. Taylor, I., P. Walton, and J. Young. *The New Criminology.* London: Routledge & Kegan Paul, 1973, p. 2.

6. Packer, H. L. *The Limits of the Criminal Sanction.* Palo Alto, CA: Stanford University Press, 1968.

7. For a good discussion of human nature and the fact that humans are not inherently hedonistic see Michalowksi, *Order, Law and Crime,* ch. 3. See Taylor, Walton, and Young, *The New Criminology,* for a critique of the classical school of thought. For an excellent discussion of deterrence (a central feature of the classical school) see Zimring, F. and G. J. Hawkins. *Deterrence: The Legal Threat in Crime Control.* Chicago: University of Chicago Press, 1973.

8. Quoted in Burtch, B. *The Sociology of Law.* Toronto: Harcourt Brace Jovanovich, 1992, p. 6.

9. Taylor, Walton, and Young, *The New Criminology,* p. 5.

10. Vold, G., and T. J. Bernard. *Theoretical Criminology* (3rd ed.). New York: Oxford University Press, 1986, p. 25.

11. Ibid., pp. 25–26,

12. Taylor, Walton, and Young, *The New Criminology,* p. 7.

13. Vold and Bernard, *Theoretical Criminology,* p. 26.

14. Taylor, Walton, and Young, *The New Criminology,* p. 8; Vold and Bernard, *Theoretical Criminology,* p. 26.

15. Vold and Bernard, *Theoretical Criminology,* p. 27.

16. Ibid., p. 36.

17. Bottomore, T., L. Harris, V. G. Kiernan, and R. Miliband (eds.). *A Dictionary of Marxist Thought.* Cambridge, MA: Harvard University Press, 1983, p. 382.

18. Vold and Bernard, *Theoretical Criminology,* pp. 131–132; Quinney and Wildeman, *The Problem of Crime,* pp. 48–50.

19. Quételet, A. *Research on the Propensity for Crime at Different Ages.* Cincinnati: Anderson, 1984, p. 69 (originally published in 1831).

20. Ibid.

21. Cullen and Gilbert, *Reaffirming Rehabilitation,* p. 33.

22. Quinney and Wildeman, *The Problem of Crime,* pp. 32–33.

23. Vole and Bernard, *Theoretical Criminology,* p. 42.

24. Mills, C. W. *The Sociological Imagination.* New York: Oxford University Press, 1959, pp. 5–8.

25. Marx, K. *The 18th Brumaire of Louis Bonaparte.* New York: International Publishers, 1963, p. 15 (originally published in 1852).

26. Michalowski, *Order, Law and Crime,* pp. 14, 22–23.

27. See the discussion on social class and social inequality in Chapter 1. For further elaboration and documentation see the endnotes in that chapter. See especially Parenti, *Democracy for the Few,* ch. 2.

28. Ibid.

29. We elaborate on this theme throughout the text. For supporting evidence see the following: Chambliss, W., and R. Seidman. *Law, Order and Power* (2nd ed.). Reading, MA: Addison-Wesley, 1982; Chambliss, W., and M. S. Zatz (eds.). *Making Law: The State, the Law, and Structural Contradictions.* Bloomington: Indiana University Press, 1993; Reiman, J. *The Rich Get Richer and the Poor Get Prison* (6th ed.). Boston: Allyn and Bacon, 2001.

30. Lynch, M. and R. Michalowski. *A New Primer in Radical Criminology* (3rd ed.). New York: Harrow and Heston, 2000.

31. Quinney, *The Social Reality of Crime.*

32. Reiman, *The Rich Get Richer and the Poor Get Prison,* p. 5.

33. Ibid., p. 156.

34. Seagal, D. "Tales from the Cutting-Room Floor: The Reality of 'Reality-Based' Television." *Harper's Magazine,* November 1993, quoted ibid, p. 157.

35. Stabile, C. A. "Feminism without Guarantees: The Misalliances and Missed Alliances of Postmodernist Social Theory." In A. Callari, S. Cullenberg, and C. Biewener (eds.), *Marxism in the Postmodern Age.* New York: Gulliford Press, 1995, p. 289.

36. See Gordon, *The Return of the Dangerous Classes,* p. 4.

37. Reiman, *The Rich Get Richer and the Poor Get Prison,* p. 157.

38. Ibid., p. 6.

39. Reiman (ibid., pp. 18–27) suggests that those in positions of power who could do a lot to reduce crime tend to come up with "four excuses that don't wash." These excuses are (1) we are too soft on crime; (2) crime is inevitable in a complex society such as ours; (3) crime is the fault of young people or, rather, too many in the "crime prone years"; and (4) we don't know how to reduce crime. Each of these excuses is very lame.

40. Sudnow, D. "Normal Crimes: Sociological Features of the Penal Code in a Public Defender's Office." *Social Problems* 12: 255–276 (Winter 1965).

41. The research on this topic is far too numerous to cite here. For a good summary see Belknap, J. *The Invisible Woman: Gender, Crime, and Justice.* Belmont, CA:

Wadsworth, 1996, ch. 7; Swisher, K., C. Wekesser, and W. Barbour (eds.). *Violence against Women.* San Diego: Greenhaven Press, 1994; Muraskin, R. and T. Alleman (eds.). *It's a Crime: Women and Justice.* Englewood Cliffs, NJ: Prentice-Hall, 1996, section 7.

42. Quinney, *The Social Reality of Crime,* p. 37.

43. Quinney, *Critique of Legal Order.*

44. See the following for extended discussions of these theories: Chambliss, W. J. "On Lawmaking" and "The Creation of American Law and Crime Control in Britain and America," in Chambliss and Zatz, *Making Law;* Quinney, *The Social Reality of Crime* and *Class, State and Crime;* Michalowski, *Order, Law and Crime;* Lynch and Michalowski, *A New Primer on Radical Criminology;* J. A. Whitt, "Toward a Class-Dialectical Model of Power: An Empirical Assessment of Three Competing Models of Political Power," in Chambliss and Zatz, *Making Law.*

45. Durkheim, E. *The Division of Labor in Society.* Glencoe, IL: Free Press, 1947 (originally published in 1893).

46. Pound, R. *An Introduction to the Philosophy of Law.* New Haven: Yale University Press, 1922; Pound, R., *Social Control through Law.* New Haven: Yale University Press, 1942; Geis, G. "Sociology and Jurisprudence: Admixture of Lore and Law." *Kentucky Law Journal* 52: 267–293; (Winter 1964); Quinney, *The Social Reality of Crime,* p. 33.

47. Michalowski, *Order, Law and Crime,* pp. 47–48.

48. Quinney, *The Social Reality of Crime,* p. 35.

49. Ibid., pp. 39–41.

50. Becker, H. S. *Outsiders: Studies in the Sociology of Deviance.* New York: Free Press, 1963.

51. For an excellent critique of this model see the following studies by G. W. Domhoff: *Who Really Rules: New Haven and Community Power Re-Examined.* New Brunswick, NJ: Transaction Books, 1978; and *The Powers That Be.* New York: Random House, 1979.

52. There are literally hundreds of books and articles by and about Karl Marx. See for instance Giddens, A. *Capitalism and Modern Social Theory.* New York: Cambridge University Press, 1971 (reprinted in 1994). For an informal and enjoyable summary of Marx's thinking see Ruis, *Marx for Beginners.* New York: Pantheon Books, 1989.

53. Marx, K., and F. Engels. *The Communist Manifesto.* Arlington Heights, IL: Crofts, 1955, pp. 11–12 (originally published in 1848).

54. Quinney, *Critique of Legal Order,* p. 16.

55. Lynch and Michalowski, *A New Primer in Radical Criminology,* pp. 44–58.

56. Chambliss and Seidman, *Law, Order and Power;* Greenberg, D. (ed.). *Crime and Capitalism* (rev. ed.). Philadelphia: Temple University Press, 1993; O'Connor, J. *The Fiscal Crisis of the State.* New York: St. Martin's Press, 1973.

57. Folbre, N., and the Center for Popular Economics. *The New Field Guide to the U.S. Economy.* New York: New Press, 1995.

58. Zinn, H. *A People's History of the United States* (2nd ed.). New York: Harper, 1995, pp. 98–99.

59. Ibid., p. 99.

60. Cardoza, B. N. *The Growth of the Law.* New Haven: Yale University Press, 1924, p. 52.

61. Holmes, O. W. "The Path of the Law." *Harvard Law Review* 10: 461 (March 1897).

62. Black, D. *The Behavior of Law.* New York: Academic Press, 1976, p. 2.

63. McIntyre, L., *The Public Defender: The Practice of Law in the Shadows of Repute.* Chicago: University of Chicago Press, 1994.

64. Zinn, *A People's History of the United States;* pp. 1–7, 13–32. See also Chomsky, *Year 501;* Deloria, V. *Custer Died for Your Sins.* New York: Macmillan, 1969; Burns, H., "Racism and American Law." In R. Quinney (ed.), *Criminal Justice in America.* Boston: Little, Brown, 1974.

65. For the classic statement on folkways and mores see Sumner, W. G. *Folkways.* Lexington, MA: Ginn, 1906.

66. Quinney, *The Social Reality of Crime,* p. 36. See also Sutherland, E., and D. Cressey, *Criminology* (10th ed.). Philadelphia: Lippincott, 1978, pp. 5–7.

67. Black, *The Behavior of Law.*

68. Michalowski, *Order, Law and Crime,* p. 139.

69. Scheb, J. M., and J. M. Scheb, II. *Criminal Law and Procedure* (4th ed.). St. Paul: West, 2000, p. 7.

70. Michalowski, *Order, Law and Crime,* p. 141.

71. Senna, J. J., and L. J. Siegel. *Introduction to Criminal Justice* (7th ed.). St. Paul: West, 1996, pp. 170–171.

72. Zinn, *A People's History of the United States,* pp. 98–101.

73. Ibid., pp. 97–99.

74. Ibid., p. 99.

75. The Supreme Court has ruled that states are not bound to provide grand juries. Thus, only federal cases now require grand jury indictments to proceed with prosecution.

76. Kerper, H. B. *Introduction to the Criminal Justice System* (2nd ed.). St. Paul: West, 1979, p. 26.

77. See Chambliss and Seidman, *Law, Order and Power;* and Reiman, J. H. *The Rich Get Richer and the Poor Get Prison* (5th ed.). Boston: Allyn and Bacon, 1998. For a perfect example of how corporate offenders are dealt with we need only cite the savings and loan scandal, for which taxpayers will have to pay most of the estimated $500 billion by the year 2021 to bail out insolvent savings and loan institutions. See Calavita, K., and H. N. Pontell. "'Other People's Money' Revisited: Collective Embezzlement in the Savings and Loan and Insurance Industries." In Chambliss Zatz, *Making Law.*

78. Rush, G. E. *Dictionary of Criminal Justice.* Boston: Holbrook Press, 1977.

79. Michalowski, *Order, Law and Crime,* pp. 153–154.

80. Scheb and Scheb. *Criminal Law and Procedure.*

81. Michalowski, *Order, Law, and Crime,* p. 155.

82. Ibid., p. 156.

83. Scheb and Scheb, *Criminal Law and Procedure* (4th ed.).

84. Ibid.

85. Ibid.

86. Ibid.

87. Ibid., p. 77.

88. Ibid., ch. 14.

89. Ibid.

90. Ibid.

91. Michalowski, *Order, Law, and Crime,* pp. 161–163; Scheb and Scheb, *Criminal Law and Procedure* (4th ed.), pp. 339–342.

92. Scheb and Scheb, ibid., p. 272.

93. Michalowski, *Order, Law, and Crime,* p. 162; Scheb and Scheb, ibid., p. 273.

94. 214 F.2d 862, 876 (D.C. Cir. 1954).

95. Michalowski, *Order, Law, and Crime,* p. 162.

96. The "Model Penal Code" was a proposal put together in 1962 by the American Law Institute, an organization of distinguished judges, lawyers, and academics. It consisted of several provisions concerning criminal liability, sentencing, defenses to crime, and several other important criminal law matters. It is not a law per se but rather a model that has been adopted by most states.

97. Scheb and Scheb, *Criminal Law and Procedure* (4th ed.), p. 273.

98. Ibid., pp. 273–274.

99. Ibid., ch. 14.

CHAPTER FOUR

THEORIES OF CRIME

Theory is an important part of any academic discipline, including criminal justice. In Chapter 3 we examined the classical and positivist perspectives on crime and criminal justice. The classical perspective has dominated theories of the criminal justice system; the positivist paradigm has dominated theories of criminal behavior. In this chapter we review three categories of theories within the positivist paradigm, plus a popular extension of the classical approach, rational choice theory. The three perspectives—biological, psychological, and sociological—correspond to three categories of factors or variables that have been used to explain or account for crime and criminal behavior: the offender's body (biological), mind (psychological), or environment (sociological). Once upon a time, extraterrestrial factors were often cited (and sometimes even today are cited), such as phases of the moon, but these have been discredited over the years.

BIOLOGICAL THEORIES[1]

The central thesis of biological theories is that criminals are biologically different from noncriminals. More than this, however, is the assumption that these individuals are inferior to noncriminals, presumably because their biological characteristics are themselves inferior. The most famous representative of this perspective was **Cesare Lombroso.**

Lombroso's Views

Lombroso (1836–1909), along with two of his followers, Enrico Ferri (1856–1928) and Raffaele Garofalo (1852–1934), are often referred to as the "Italian School" (because all three were from Italy). Lombroso and his followers put forth the notion that the criminal was a "biological throwback" to some form of "primitive" man or woman who had certain "atavistic" physical features.

Lombroso's theory included five propositions: (1) Criminals are, at birth, a distinct type of human being. (2) This "type" can be recognized by certain **stigmata,** such as high cheekbones, large jaws, deformed or oddly shaped ears, and excessive body hair. (Lombroso arrived at these and other conclusions as a result of his work doing autopsies on the bodies of hundreds of Italian prisoners who had died in confinement. It never dawned on him that the physical conditions of these prisoners could have been the *result of their confinement* rather than the *cause* of their criminal behavior, an especially appropriate explanation given the horrible conditions in Italian prisons and jails of the time.) (3) The "criminal type" can be clearly distinguished if a person exhibits five or more of these stigmata. (Lombroso believed that women offenders were worse in many ways than their male counterparts, mainly because they had "fallen from grace" so far that they were inferior even to male criminals.) (4) These stigmata do not so much cause criminal behavior as they indicate that someone is *predisposed* to becoming a criminal. (5) Because of their personal natures, such offenders cannot help but become criminals unless they grow up under extremely favorable conditions.[2]

Although the popular notion that a person can spot a criminal because of certain physical features has been thoroughly rejected within academic circles, certain variations of it exist today.[3] Also, it is interesting to note that within American society there continue to be stereotypes of what criminals look like (the media play a major role in this). Unfortunately many of the stereotypes center on race (mostly African American and Hispanic) and class (mostly lower class or the underclass).

Lombroso's views are not one-dimensional, for several variations can be distinguished, and his initial research findings were followed by several notable researchers. It is to this topic we now turn.

Variations of Lombroso's Views

One famous variation of Lombroso's views is the general theory of *body types* (sometimes referred to as *physiognomy*), which gained popularity during the first half of the twentieth century. According to this view, humans can be divided into three basic body types, or **somatotypes,** which correspond to certain innate *temperaments.* The first type is the **endomorph,** characterized by excessive body weight and described as being "soft" and having an extroverted personality (the stereotype of the "jolly fat man" comes to mind). The second type is the **mesomorph,** who is athletically built and muscular. These individuals are described as being active and behaving aggressively. They are also said to be most likely to be involved in serious criminal activity and to join gangs. The third type is the **ectomorph,** described as thin and delicate and having an introverted personality. These individuals are said to be loners and hence not likely to engage in crime. Studies by Sheldon and Eleanor Glueck, William Sheldon, and Ernest Hooton expanded on these ideas.[4] The works of these scholars were taken seriously by others in the field, no doubt in part because of the fact that they all were on the faculty of Harvard University at one time.

Another variation of Lombroso's views is that criminal behavior is somehow genetically transmitted from one generation to another. Throughout the twentieth century various researchers claimed to have found evidence in support of this view, especially evidence that bases the claims on studies of twins. Correlations have been found in studies of identical twins raised in different geographical locations, but the samples have been much too small to be able to generalize. Such studies tend to ignore social and cultural factors and the fact that the vast majority of offenders have predisposing genetic "traits," although criminality in a family is correlated to an individual's becoming an offender (having a father with a criminal record is highly correlated with delinquency, but this finding may have less to do with genes than with the modeling of the father or lack of parenting skills).

An additional view holds that certain men have an extra Y chromosome and this genetic abnormality makes them "supermales" who exhibit more aggressive behavior than normal. However, an extra Y chromosome is found in only about one male out of every thousand. Despite the hoopla surrounding this research "find" (including the fact that these individuals are overrepresented in the criminal justice system), the vast majority of male offenders (including most violent offenders) do not have an extra Y chromosome.[5]

Still another variation of Lombroso's views focuses on women offenders and *premenstrual syndrome (PMS)*. Simply put, PMS is thought to cause crime among women. There is virtually no research indicating that PMS is a factor, even though it is used as a form of insanity defense in France and has been used as a defense in both England and the United States. Part of the problem is the lack of precise definition of the term itself.[6]

One final variation focuses on the functioning of the central nervous system. The central nervous system is involved in conscious thought and voluntary motor activities. Abnormal brain-wave patterns, measured with electroencephalographs (EEGs), have been associated with various abnormal behavioral patterns in individuals. Some studies find that offenders have an excessive amount of slow brain-wave activity; other studies find the opposite—fast brain-wave activity. Still other studies examined the role of epilepsy and certain forms of brain damage but report mixed or inconclusive results.[7]

We agree with Vold and Bernard's conclusion that the evidence is not sufficient "to conclude that biological differences can be found in the majority of criminals, and where those differences are found, the causal linkages to criminal behavior are still weak."[8] Instead, we think that biological factors should be viewed as simply influencing behavior, along with other factors. They certainly do not influence whether certain behaviors will be *defined by society as criminal*. Perhaps more important, we want to make clear that these kinds of theories, based as they are on notions of biological inferiority, have been used to describe, more often than not, people of certain races and ethnic groups (e.g., European immigrants, African Americans). African American children in the United States are often labeled as "born to be disruptive."[9]

RATIONAL CHOICE THEORY

A theory that became popular in the 1970s and 1980s took the position that crime is a product of "rational" choices and decisions that people make in their daily lives. Various terms have been used, almost interchangeably, for this idea, such as *criminal opportunity theory* and *routine activity theory*.[10] This kind of thinking originated with the classical school of criminology, which was discussed in Chapter 3.

In the last half of the twentieth century the classical approach to crime has reemerged. However, most modern versions avoid the mistakes of the past. Beccaria and Bentham erroneously assumed that all humans behave "rationally" all the time, that they carefully calculate the pros and cons of their behaviors. Rational choice theory recognizes that many choices are not based on pure reason and rationality but rather are determined by a host of factors. Constraints on our choices include lack of information, various moral values, the social context of the situation, and other situational factors. In short, not everyone acts logically and rationally all the time, especially young offenders.[11]

Modern rational choice theory still makes the assumption that people freely choose to commit crime because they are goal oriented and want to maximize their pleasure and minimize their pain. In short, they are acting out of self-interest. One modern variation, *routine activities theory,* suggests that criminals plan very carefully by selecting specific targets based on such things as vulnerability (e.g., elderly citizens, unguarded premises, lack of police presence) and commit their crimes accordingly. Thus, people who engage in certain "routine activities" every day place themselves at risk of being victimized—activities such as being in high-crime areas at night, not locking your doors, leaving keys in your car, and working at certain jobs during certain hours of the day (e.g., as a late-night clerk at a 7-Eleven store). Active criminals select such targets carefully, weighing the odds of getting caught. One flaw, among others, in such thinking is the implicit assumption that people should stay home more often to avoid being victims, when in fact certain groups (especially women and children) seem to be much more vulnerable at home than anywhere else.[12]

One example of rational choice theory is that of a young person joining a gang. There are many logical reasons why someone may want to join a gang—for protection from rival gang members, for a feeling of belonging, for respect, for the prospects of earning a little money, and for fun and companionship. Thus, rational choice theory may be quite suitable in explaining this. But it does not logically follow that the threat of punishment (e.g., so-called enhancement statutes that increase the penalty for the commission of a crime if a person is a gang member) will deter such a person. One of the best comments on this problem comes from Malcolm Klein, one of the most respected gang researchers. Klein used a crackdown on gangs by the Los Angeles Police Department known as Operation Hammer to illustrate the problem of deterrence. This operation resulted in mass arrests of almost 1,500 individuals who were subsequently booked at a "mobile booking" unit next to the Los Angeles Memorial Coliseum. About 90 percent were released with no charges filed; there were only 60 felony arrests, and charges were eventually filed on about half of these. Klein uses a hypothetical example of a gang member arrested and booked during such an operation. There are two possible scenarios as the gang member, immediately after his release, returns to his neighborhood and his gang. Klein writes as follows:

> Does he say to them [his homies], "Oh, gracious, I've been arrested and subjected to deterrence; I'm going to give up my gang affiliation." Or does he say, "Shit man, they're just jivin' us—can't hold us on any charges, and gotta let us go." Without hesitation, the gangbanger will turn the experience to his and the gang's advantage. Far from being deterred from membership or crime, his ties to the groups will be strengthened when the members group together to make light of the whole affair and heap ridicule on the police.[13]

In other words, human behavior is far more complex than the rather simplistic notion that "we all make choices" with our "free will."

PSYCHOLOGICAL THEORIES

Psychological theories of criminal behavior tend to focus on the link between crime and such factors as intelligence, personality, and various abnormalities of the brain. As biological views stress that criminals are biologically inferior, psychological views stress that criminals are psychologically or mentally inferior.

Feeblemindedness and Crime

Early in the twentieth century the psychologist Henry Goddard began to study intelligence and argued that there was a correlation between low intelligence and crime. He was one of the first to use the term **feeblemindedness** and associate this condition with a certain intelligence level as measured by IQ tests (in theory, IQ is a measure of a person's "mental age"). Goddard administered an IQ test to inmates at the New Jersey Training School for the Feebleminded. He found that none of the inmates scored higher than a mental age of 13. Because these individuals were in a "school" for the "feebleminded," he came to the conclusion that an IQ score of 13 indicated feeblemindedness, since, after all, a person would not be in such an institution if he or she were not feebleminded! The only problem was that no one had any measure of feeblemindedness, so how could anyone tell whether these inmates were in fact feebleminded?

Over the years, this view has been totally discredited because of poor measurement tools and the linkage of such testing and attempts to control or even eliminate certain "undesirables." During the early twentieth century much was made of the claim that various racial and ethnic minorities were inferior and even dangerous and needed to be either controlled or eliminated. This was the general aim of the so-called eugenics movement, which led to the sterilization of certain "defective" people, who were more often than not southern European immigrants. In this way "science" lent credibility, once again, to class and racial control.[14]

Lest you think that this line of thinking is dead, we should cite the work of Wilson and Herrnstein called *Crime and Human Nature,* with its arrogant subtitle *The Definitive Study of the Causes of Crime.*[15] This book uncritically reviews research that ostensibly claims that "criminals" are biologically predisposed to commit crime largely because of their low IQs and mesomorphic body types. Such theories are essentially racist and sexist. They have been used repeatedly as methods of class, race, and gender control. It is easier to control or even eliminate people if they are "proved" to be inferior. The Nazi genocides, the practice of slavery, and the eugenics movement and more recent rationalizations of sterilization have all been justified on the basis of "scientific" theories and research.[16]

Psychoanalytic Theories

Psychoanalytic theories are credited to Sigmund Freud, the founder of the psychoanalytic school of psychology. Although Freud did not concentrate on criminal behavior, a good deal of what he had to say has been used to explain this kind of behavior. Essentially, this view maintains that crime is a symptom of deep-seated mental problems stemming from personality defects. Freud's major insights include his work on human personality and his differentiation of the id, ego, and superego. The problems that Freud noted and that are often said to cause criminal behavior include (1) difficulties or problems during one of the psychosexual stages of development (e.g., anal, phallic, oedipal); (2) an inability to sublimate (or redirect) sexual and aggressive "drives" or "instincts"; (3) an inability to successfully resolve the *oedipal* complex (in men) or *electra* complex (in women); and (4) an unconscious desire for punishment.[17]

Some researchers claim that specific crimes are associated with certain stages of development. For example, problems occurring during the so-called *phallic* stage, in which a child begins to understand the pleasure associated with his or her sexual organs, can be related to such crimes as sexual assault, rape, or prostitution. Problems occurring during the *oral* stage may result in crimes associated with alcoholism or drug addiction. Other work that is related to criminal behavior and that can be linked with Freud includes studies of such personality types as sociopaths and psychopaths and, in general, studies of persons having antisocial personalities. These people are characterized as lacking any sense of guilt and any sense of right and wrong.[18]

Personality Trait Theories

Many researchers have resurrected some of the old IQ and feeblemindedness tests and applied them to the study of personality traits. Various standardized tests have been devised for this purpose. The most famous is the **Minnesota Multiphasic Personality Inventory (MMPI),** which consists of over 500 true and false questions. Several different scales are used, corresponding to the responses to certain questions. One scale is the "psychopathic scale" or "Scale 4." A problem here is that this test asks questions about the test taker's involvement with the criminal justice system. Such involvement often causes inmates and former inmates to score lower on this test, thus "proving" they are "different" from the rest of us. A variation is the California Psychological Inventory (CPI).[19]

Part of the problem with personality trait theories is the assumption that we can easily distinguish between "criminals" and "noncriminals." If we give the MMPI or CPI or some other test to a group of prison inmates and to a group of college or high school students, how do we know the extent of the test takers' involvement in crime? Simply put, we don't! Self-report studies indicate that most high school and college students have done something that could have landed them in jail, yet they are viewed, during these kinds of research projects, as the "nonoffender" control group! We agree with Akers's conclusion that "The research using personality inventories and other methods of measuring personality characteristics have not been able to produce findings to support personality variables as major causes of criminal and delinquent behavior."[20]

Mental Illness and Crime

Over the years much has been made of the claim that offenders are suffering from some sort of mental illness. Although it is true that some offenders have, to put it bluntly, "lost it," these kinds of individuals are a rare minority within the total criminal population, which is why they get the most attention from the news media. It is often incorrectly assumed that they are "typical criminals," which they are not, as numerous studies have shown. In fact, offenders are not more "mentally ill" than the general population.[21]

Part of the problem here is that there have been several famous examples in the news over the years. People like David Berkowitz (the "Son of Sam"), Jeffrey Dahmer, Ted Bundy, and the Menendez brothers, to name just a few, capture the public limelight but shed little real light on the problem of crime because such individuals are so rare. Yet at the same time, our culture supports such a view and popularizes this theory in movies like *The Texas Chainsaw Massacre* and the *Friday the 13th* movies, along with various "slasher" movies in which the victims are almost always women, plus such favorites as *Basic Instinct, The Hand That Rocks the Cradle,* and *Fatal Attraction.*

What can be said about psychological and biological theories in general? Many questions remain unanswered. One problem is that cross-cultural research has failed to arrive at findings similar to those in the United States. Crime in the United States tends to be concentrated in the inner cities and in poor areas heavily populated by racial minorities. Why don't the same biological and psychological traits turn up in the inner cities of other countries? Why is the risk of being a crime victim higher in the United States than in most other countries? Is there an "American crime gene" or "American personality trait"? One problem of these types of theories is what Currie has called the "fallacy of autonomy"—the idea that people act totally on their own, uninfluenced by others and unaffected by the surrounding culture and social institutions.[22] If crime were caused by some inferior gene or by a certain personality trait, then how would we explain the high rate of corporate and white-collar crime committed by supposedly "normal" upper-class white males? Why have crime rates remained highest in certain parts of large urban areas, regardless of the kinds of people who live there, over about a hundred-year period? Why are crime rates higher in urban than in rural areas, and why do males have a crime rate about four times the rate of females? For some answers to these and other questions, we turn to sociological theories of crime.

SOCIOLOGICAL THEORIES

The sociological theories to be reviewed here[23] are grouped into seven categories: (1) social disorganization/social ecology, (2) strain/anomie, (3) cultural deviance, (4) control/social bond, (5) social learning, (6) labeling, and (7) critical/Marxist perspectives. Figure 4.1 provides a brief summary of these perspectives.

Social Disorganization/Social Ecology Theory

The Chicago School.   **Social disorganization theory** is one of the most popular and enduring sociological theories of crime and delinquency. This theory is also called **social ecology theory** because it has a lot to do with the spatial or geographical distribution of

FIGURE 4.1 Sociological Perspectives on Crime

THEORY	MAJOR POINTS/KEY FACTORS
Social Disorganization/ Social Ecology	Crime stems from certain community or neighborhood characteristics, such as poverty, dilapidated housing, high density, high mobility, and high rates of unemployment. *Concentric zone theory* is a variation that argues that crime increases toward the inner-city area.
Strain/Anomie	Cultural norms of "success" emphasize goals such as money, status, and power, but the means to obtain such success are not equally distributed. As a result of blocked opportunities, many among the disadvantaged resort to illegal means, which are more readily available.
Cultural Deviance	Certain subcultures, including a gang subculture, exist within poor communities and foster values, attitudes, beliefs, and norms that run counter to the prevailing middle class culture. An important feature of this subculture is the absence of fathers, resulting in female-headed households, which tend to be poorer than traditional two-parent families. Youths are exposed to this subculture early in life and become *embedded* into it.
Control/Social Bond	Delinquency persists when a youth's bonds or ties to society are weak or broken, especially bonds with family, school, and other institutions. When this occurs, a youth is likely to seek bonds with other groups, including gangs, in order to get his or her needs met.
Social Learning	Delinquency is *learned* over time through association with others, especially gang members. Delinquency results from a process that includes the acquisition of attitudes and values, the instigation of a criminal act based on certain stimuli, and the maintenance or perpetuation of such behavior.
Labeling	Definitions of delinquency and crime stem from differences in power and status in the larger society. Youths without power are most likely to have their behaviors labeled as "delinquency." Delinquency may be generated, and perpetuated, through negative labeling by significant others and by the judicial system. A person may associate with others similarly labeled, such as gangs.
Critical/Marxist	Crime is an inevitable product of social (and racial) inequality brought about by capitalism itself; power is unequally distributed and those without power often resort to "criminal" means to survive.

crime, delinquency, and gangs.[24] Modern versions of this perspective began with the work of several sociologists at the University of Chicago during the first three decades of the twentieth century. The original idea behind the spatial distribution of crime can be traced back to the mid-nineteenth century, in the work of Adolphe Quételet (1796–1874) and Andre-Michel Guerry (1802–1866). They were the first scientists who collected and analyzed various crime data and examined the residences of offenders, matching them with socioeconomic variables such as poverty, infant mortality, and unemployment. Thus began what became known as the **cartographic school** of criminology—in other words, mapmaking, plotting on a city map the location of criminals and various social indicators. Many police departments use colored pins or dots to mark the locations of certain crimes, such as serial rapes, or the locations of a series of muggings, auto thefts, and so on.[25]

This kind of mapmaking and the general notion that crime is spatially distributed within a geographical area became hallmarks of what came to be known as the **Chicago School** of sociology (many researchers in the sociology department at the University of Chicago during the early twentieth century were involved in this work). Within Chicago (and other major cities) researchers noticed that crime and delinquency rates varied from one area of the city to another. The highest rates of crime and delinquency were found in areas exhibiting high rates of other social problems, such as single-parent families, unemployment, multiple-family dwellings, welfare cases, and low levels of education.

A key hypothesis of the social ecology theory of crime is that high rates of crime and other problems persist within neighborhoods over long periods of time *regardless of who lives there.* As several researchers have noted, some gangs in certain neighborhoods have existed for fifty or more years, often spanning three generations. This has been especially the case in East Los Angeles.[26] Perhaps there is something about the *places,* something about the *neighborhoods,* rather than the people, that produces and perpetuates high crime rates.[27]

The social ecology perspective borrows concepts from plant biology, specifically studying human life and problems using notions derived from studies of the interdependence of plant and animal life. From this perspective, people are seen as being in a relationship to one another and to their physical environment. Further, just as plant and animal species tend to *colonize* their environment, humans colonize their "geographical space."[28] One of the most important ideas originating from these Chicago sociologists (specifically Robert Park and Ernest Burgess) is the **concentric zone model** of city life (see Figure 4.2).[29] Researchers identified five zones emanating outward from the center of the city: (1) central business district, or "Loop"; (2) zone in transition, (3) zone of workingmen's homes, (4) residential zone, and (5) commuter zone.

According to this theory about city life and land use patterns, growth is generated (from mostly political and economic forces) outward from the central business district. Such expansion occurs in concentric waves and affects neighborhood development and patterns of social problems. Studies of the rates of crime and delinquency, especially by the sociologists Henry Shaw and David McKay, demonstrated that over an extended period of time, the highest rates were found within the first three zones, *no matter who lived there.*

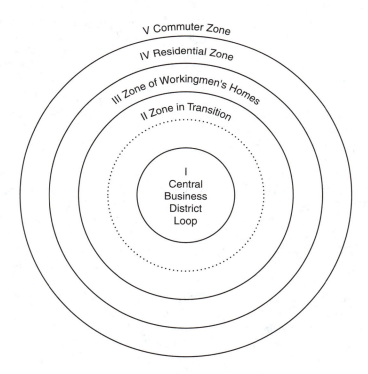

FIGURE 4.2   Concentric Zones

Source: Burgess, E. W. "The Growth of the City." In R. E. Park, E. W. Burgess, and R. D. McKenzie (eds.), *The City.* Chicago: University of Chicago Press, 1925.

These high rates were strongly correlated with mental illness, unemployment, poverty, infant mortality and many other social problems.[30]

Such a distribution is caused by the breakdown of institutional, community-based controls, which in turn is caused by three factors: industrialization, urbanization, and immigration. People living within the first three zones often lack a sense of community because the local institutions (e.g., schools, families, churches) are not strong enough to provide nurturing and guidance for the area's children. Important political and economic forces also are at work here. The concentration of human and social problems within these zones is not the inevitable, "natural" result of any abstract laws of nature but rather results from the actions of powerful groups in a city (urban planners, politicians, wealthy business leaders, etc.) who place limitations on where people can buy homes and on wages.

Thrasher's Classic Study of the Gang.   Within such environments a subculture of criminal values and traditions replaces conventional values and traditions and persists regardless of who lives in the area. One of the classic works about gangs from a social disorganization perspective was written by Frederic Thrasher. His book, *The Gang,* published in 1927, seems as relevant today as it was when originally published. Thrasher said that gangs originate from

> the spontaneous effort of boys to create a society for themselves where none adequate to their needs exists. What boys get out of such associations that they do not get otherwise under the conditions that adult society imposes is the thrill and zest of participation in common interests, more especially in corporate action, in hunting, capture, conflict, flight, and escape. Conflict with other gangs and the world about them furnishes the occasion for many of their exciting group activities.[31]

Thrasher's view of gang causation is consistent with social disorganization theory. Gangs develop within the most impoverished areas of a city. Thrasher noted that gangs tend to flourish in areas he called *interstitial,* areas that lie within a city's "poverty belt" and are "characterized by the deteriorating neighborhoods, shifting populations, and the mobility and disorganization of the slum...Gangland represents a geographically and socially interstitial area in the city."[32] These areas have been given many names: zones in transition, slums, ghettos, and barrios.

In Chicago, Thrasher found evidence of at least 1,313 gangs with an estimated 25,000 members. No two of these gangs were alike; they reflected the great diversity of the city itself in the 1920s (today Chicago and the gangs of Chicago are no less diverse). Much like today, gang delinquency when Thrasher was doing his research ranged from the petty (e.g., truancy and disturbing the peace) to the serious (e.g., serious property crime and violent crime).

Thrasher's theory of why gangs exist and what functions they perform is summarized in the following quotation from *The Gang:*

> The failure of the normally directing and controlling customs and institutions to function efficiently in the boy's experience is indicated by the disintegration of family life, inefficiency of schools, formalism and externality of religion, corruption and indifference in local politics, low wages and monotony in occupational activities; unemployment; and lack of opportunity for wholesome recreation. All these factors enter into the picture of the moral and economic frontier, and, coupled with deterioration in the housing, sanitation, and other conditions of life in the slum, give the impression of general disorganization and decay.
>
> The gang functions with reference to these conditions in two ways: It offers a substitute for what society fails to give; and it provides a relief from suppression and distasteful behavior. It fills a gap and affords an escape.[33]

According to Thrasher, by being in a gang a young man acquires a personality and name for himself; he acquires a sort of status and has a role to play. The gang "not only defines for him his position in society...but it becomes the basis for his conception of himself." The gang becomes the youth's reference group—that is, the group from which he obtains his main values, beliefs, and goals. In a sense the gang becomes his family. Moreover, these groups of youths tend to progress from what Thrasher called spontaneous play groups to gangs when they begin to receive disapproval from adults. When this occurs, particularly if disapproval is coupled with legal intervention, the youths become closer and develop a "we" feeling.[34]

Thrasher clearly believed that gangs provided certain basic needs for growing boys, such as a sense of belonging and self-esteem. This perspective is consistent with Abraham Maslow's hierarchy of needs.

Extensions of the Chicago School Tradition.   Several subsequent studies focus on the community or neighborhood as the primary unit of analysis. This focus begins with the assumption that crime and the extent of gang activities vary according to certain neighborhood or community characteristics.

In his book *Racketville, Slumtown and Haulberg* (1964), Irving Spergel reported that the three neighborhoods he studied varied according to a number of criteria and had different kinds of traditions, including delinquent and criminal norms. Racketville, a mostly Italian neighborhood, had a long tradition of organized racketeering. Gangs in this neighborhood were likely to be involved in the rackets because this was where the criminal opportunities were to be found.[35] Slumtown was primarily a Puerto Rican neighborhood with a history of conflict and aggression. Gangs in this area were likely to be involved in various conflict situations with rival gangs (usually over turf). Haulberg was a mixed ethnic neighborhood (Irish, Germans, Italians, and others) with a tradition of property crimes. A theft subculture flourished there.

A more recent variation of this theme can be seen in the ethnographic fieldwork of Mercer Sullivan. *Getting Paid* (1989), his study of three neighborhoods in Brooklyn provides important new information about the relationship between social, cultural, and economic factors and gangs. The three neighborhoods that Sullivan studied varied according to several socioeconomic indicators and had significantly different patterns of crime. Hamilton Park had the lowest rate, Projectville ranked first, and La Barriada ranked second. La Barriada ranked the highest for crimes of violence.

La Barriada was a mixed Latino and white area; Projectville was a largely African American neighborhood; Hamilton Park was predominantly white. Projectville and La Barriada, the neighborhoods with the highest crime rates, also had (1) the highest poverty level, with more than half of the families receiving public assistance; (2) the highest percentage of single-parent families; (3) the highest rate of renter-occupied housing; (4) the highest rate of school dropouts; (5) the lowest labor-force participation rates (and correspondingly highest levels of unemployment).[36] Sullivan suggests that these differences can be explained by noting

> the concentration in the two poor, minority neighborhoods [La Barriada and Projectville] of sustained involvement in high-risk, low-return theft as a primary source of income during the middle teens. The primary causes for their greater willingness to engage in desperate, highly exposed crimes for uncertain and meager monetary returns were the greater poverty of their households, the specific and severe lack of employment opportunities during these same mid-teen years, and the weakened local social control environment, itself a product of general poverty and joblessness among neighborhood residents.[37]

A key to understanding these differences, argues Sullivan, is personal networks, rather than merely human capital. He explains that these

> personal networks derived from existing patterns of articulation between the local neighborhoods and particular sectors of the labor market. These effects of labor market segmentation were important for youth jobs both in the middle teens and during the ensuing period of work establishment. The Hamilton Park youths found a relatively plentiful supply of

temporary, part-time, almost always off-the-books work through relatives, friends and local employers during the middle teens, most of it in the local vicinity.[38]

When youths from Hamilton Park reached their late teens, they were able to make use of these contacts to get more secure and better-paying jobs. The minority youths from Projectville and La Barriada never developed such networks.

Sullivan discusses at length what motivated these youths to get involved in crime. He maintains that, because of the unusual risks associated with crime (including, it should be added, the risk of injury or even death), the unpredictability of criminal endeavors, and the fact that most crime is considered immoral, such a decision is influenced by a number of social factors, not merely economic considerations. According to Sullivan's analysis, certain characteristics of the neighborhood in which a youth grew up played a key role in influencing the decision to get into crime. Crime patterns "were related to the ways in which each neighborhood environment both generated and controlled different types of crime." The major types of crimes the youths became involved in included street fighting, burglaries of factories and residences, street robberies, auto theft, drug dealing, and running errands for older professional or organized criminals, among others. These types were not distributed randomly by neighborhood.[39]

Sullivan found that among the precursors to a criminal career among most of the youths he studied was involvement in some gang or clique of youths. This gang involvement typically began with fighting with and against other youths. Street fighting was mostly motivated by status and territory. Beginning in their early teens, these youths would spend a great amount of time within what they considered to be their own territory or turf. The cliques and gangs these youths belonged to "were quasi-familial groupings that served to protect their members from outsiders."[40]

Strain Theories

Anomie. *Strain* theory originated with Robert Merton, who borrowed the term *anomie* from the nineteenth-century French sociologist Émile Durkheim and applied it to the problem of crime in the United States.[41] The term **anomie** refers to inconsistencies between societal conditions and opportunities for growth, fulfillment, and productivity within a society (the term *anomia* has been used to refer to the condition of those who experience personal frustration and alienation as a result of anomie within a society). Anomie also involves the weakening of the normative order of society—that is, norms (rules, laws, etc.) lose their impact on people. The existence of anomie within a culture can also produce a high level of flexibility in the pursuit of goals, even suggesting that it may at times be appropriate to deviate from norms concerning the methods of achieving success.

Durkheim, writing during the late nineteenth century, suggested that under capitalism there is a more or less chronic state of "deregulation" and that industrialization had removed traditional social controls on aspirations. The capitalist culture produces in humans a constant dissatisfaction resulting in a never-ending longing for more and more. And there is never enough—whether money, material things, or power. There is a morality under capitalism that dictates "anything goes," especially when it comes to making money (it certainly applies to the modern corporation).

What Durkheim was hinting at but (unlike Marx) not saying was that a very strong social structure is needed to offset or place limits on this morality. In other words, strong institutions—the family, religion, and education—are needed to place some limits on us. The failure of these institutions is evident in high crime rates and the fact that the economic institution has become so powerful that it has "invaded" and become dominant over other institutions.

The basic thesis of **strain theory** is this: Crime stems from the lack of articulation or "fit" between two of the most basic components of society, culture and social structure.[42]

Here we refer to **culture** as consisting of (1) the main value and goal orientations, or "ends," and (2) the institutionalized or legitimate means for attaining these goals. **Social structure,** as used here, consists of the basic social institutions of society, especially the economy but also such institutions as the family, education, and politics, all of which are responsible for distributing access to the legitimate means for obtaining goals.

According to Merton, this lack of fit creates strain for certain groups and individuals, who respond with various forms of deviance. Thus, people who find themselves at a disadvantage relative to legitimate economic activities are motivated to engage in illegitimate activities (perhaps because of the unavailability of jobs, lack of job skills, lack of education, and other factors). Within a capitalist society like America, the main emphasis is on "success" goals; less emphasis is on legitimate means to achieve these goals. Moreover, success goals have become institutionalized in that they are deeply embedded in the psyches of everyone via a powerful corporate propaganda.[43] The legitimate means are not as well defined or as strongly ingrained. In other words, there is a lot of discretion and a lot of tolerance for deviance from the means but not from the goals. One result of such a system is high levels of crime.

Another important point made by strain theory is that American culture contributes to crime because the opportunities to achieve success goals are not equally distributed. There is a strong class structure and incredible inequality within American society, which means that some people confront extreme disadvantages.[44] Here is another way of saying this: *Culture promises what the social structure cannot deliver*—namely, equal access to opportunities to achieve success. People faced with this contradiction face pressures or "strains" to seek alternatives.

Merton identifies five alternatives, which he calls "modes of adaptation":

1. *Conformity*—accepting both the legitimate means and the success goals.
2. *Ritualism*—accepting the means but rejecting the success goals. (A person goes to work every day but has given up the goal of success.)
3. *Innovation*—accepting the success goals but rejecting the legitimate means to obtain them.
4. *Retreatism*—rejecting both the success goals and the means and more or less dropping out of society (to become, for instance, part of a drug subculture).
5. *Rebellion*—rejecting both the success goals and the means and, instead of retreating, substituting *new* definitions of success and new means to achieve it.

Obviously, the adaptation known as *innovation* directly relates to criminal activity, including gang activities. Thus, anomie/strain theory suggests that participating in gang-related activities is an example of being *innovative* in the pursuit of success.

According to Messner and Rosenfeld, in a recent revision of anomie theory, such strain explains high rates of crime not only among the disadvantaged but also among the more privileged, who are under "strains" to make more money, often "by any means necessary." This theory can certainly help explain the large amount of corporate crime in the United States.[45] Messner and Rosenfeld's revision of strain theory contains an important component usually missing from writings on this particular theory: emphasis on the importance of social institutions and the relationship with what is normally called the American Dream. In the next section we pursue this idea in more detail.

Strain Theory and the American Dream.   The **American Dream** is deeply embedded in American culture. Generally, it refers to a commitment to the goal of material success that is to be pursued by every- one. Within a capitalist society, everyone is supposed to act in his or her own self-interest in this pursuit, and self-interested behavior is supposed to promote the "common good." Somehow, the fruits of individual pursuits in this "free market" system eventually will "trickle down" to benefit others. At the heart of the American

Dream are four core values: (1) achievement, (2) individualism, (3) universalism, and (4) fetishism of money (see Figure 4.3).

There is, however, a "dark side" to the American Dream, which stems from a contradiction in American capitalism: the forces that promote "progress" and "ambition" also produce a lot of crime because there is such pressure to succeed at any cost. The emphasis on competition and achievement also produces selfishness and drives people apart, weakening a collective sense of community. Because monetary rewards are such a high priority, tasks that are noneconomic receive little cultural support (e.g., housewives, child care workers). Even education is seen as a means to an end—the end being a high-paying job or any secure job (one university in its advertising urges people to "Go back so you can get ahead"). The existence of such a high degree of inequality produces feelings of unworthiness. Those who fail are looked down upon. And their failure too often is seen as an individual failure, rather than a failure attributable to institutional and cultural factors.

One of the keys to understanding the linkage of the American Dream and crime is understanding the meaning and importance of social institutions. A **social institution** can be defined as a persistent set of organized *methods* of meeting basic human needs. Gradually over time, relatively stable groups and organizations, with various norms and values, statuses, and roles, have arisen to meet fundamental human needs. The human needs that these social institutions seek to meet are the needs (1) to "adapt to the environment," (2) to "mobilize and deploy resources for the achievement of collective goals," (3) and to "socialize members to accept the society's fundamental normative patterns." The most important of these institutions are (1) the economy, (2) the family, (3) education, and (4) politics. Other important institutions include health care, the media, religion, and the legal institution (many would place the last within the much larger political institution).[46]

When these institutions fail to meet the needs of members of society—or at least the needs of a sizable proportion of the population—alternative methods will begin to develop. If the prevailing economic system is failing, more and more people will find alternative ways to earn a living. If organized religion is not providing answers to fundamental life questions, people will seek out unorthodox religious forms (e.g., cults like the Branch Davidians or Heaven's Gate). If the legal institution is not perceived as providing "justice," people may decide to take the law into their own hands. If the mainstream media provide too much disinformation and do not allow dissenting views, alternative media will emerge.

FIGURE 4.3 Adapted from Core Values of American Culture

1. *Achievement* According to this value, one's *personal worth* is typically evaluated in terms of one's monetary success or how "famous" one has become. This stems from a culture that emphasizes "doing" and "having" rather than "being." Failure to achieve is equated with failure to make a contribution to society. This value is highly conducive to the attitude "It's not how you play the game; it's whether you win or lose." A similar attitude is "Winning isn't everything; it's the *only* thing."
2. *Individualism* According to this value, individuals are supposed to "make it on your own." This value discourages cooperation and collective action. The "rugged individualist" is perhaps the most famous representation of this cultural value. A corollary is "I don't need any help." Messner and Rosenfeld comment that: "The intense individual competition to succeed pressures people to disregard normative restraints on behavior when these restraints threaten to interfere with the realization of personal goals."
3. *Universalism* According to this value, everyone is suppose to strive for the American Dream, and everyone has the same opportunity to succeed, as long as you "work hard." Part of the value of individualism stems from the Protestant work ethic.
4. *Fetishism of Money* Money is so important in American culture that it often overrides almost everything else. Money is the measure of just about everything. The worship of money has created a *consumerist culture* in which everyone is socialized, almost from birth, to be first and foremost a consumer. (Witness the emergence of corporate-sponsored programs within elementary schools, including the ever-present McDonald's.)

Source: Messner, S., and R. Rosenfeld. *Crime and the American Dream* (2nd ed.). Belmont, CA: Wadsworth, 1997, pp. 62–64.

As Messner and Rosenfeld suggest, what is unique about American society is that the economic institution almost completely dominates all other institutions. This was once expressed by the American philosopher and educator John Dewey, who said that politics (or government) "is but the shadow cast upon society by big business."[47] American capitalism, unlike capitalism in other countries, emerged with virtually no interference from previously existing institutions. In the United States, no institutions could tame or offset the economic imperatives. European and Japanese cultures, in contrast, give almost equal importance to the family, religion, education, and other institutions. In the United States, those institutions are subordinate to the economic one: the goal is to make a profit, and everything else is of secondary importance. Over time, the U.S. society has become a "market society" in contrast to a "market economy." Under American capitalism, the pursuit of private gain dominates all other pursuits (e.g., the arts, family support).[48]

Differential Opportunity Structures.   A variation of strain theory comes from the work of Cloward and Ohlin in *Delinquency and Opportunity*.[49] These authors argue that (1) blocked opportunities cause poor self-concepts and feelings of frustration and (2) this frustration leads to delinquency, especially within a gang context. A key concept here is *differential opportunity structure,* which is an uneven distribution of legal and illegal means of achieving economic success, especially as they are unequally available according to class and race. Cloward and Ohlin argue that although legitimate opportunities are blocked for significant numbers of lower-class youths, the same cannot be said for illegitimate opportunities (e.g., selling drugs and other crimes). Their major thesis is that

> The disparity between what lower class youth are led to want and what is actually available to them is the source of a major problem of adjustment. Adolescents who form delinquent subcultures, we suggest, have internalized an emphasis upon conventional goals. Faced with limitations on legitimate avenues of access to these goals, and unable to revise their aspirations downward, they experience intense frustrations; the exploration of nonconformist alternatives may be the result.[50]

Among the specific assumptions of this theory is that blocked opportunities (or aspirations) create feelings of frustration and low self-esteem, which in turn often lead to delinquency and gang behavior.

Cloward and Ohlin postulate that three different types of gangs emerge and that these types correspond with characteristics of the neighborhoods (which affect opportunities to commit different types of crimes) rather than of the individuals who live there. *Criminal gangs* are organized mainly around the commission of property crimes and exist in areas where relatively organized forms of adult criminal activity are already in existence. Thus, adult criminals are seen as successful role models by youths who live there. *Conflict gangs* engage mostly in violent behavior, such as gang fights over turf. These gangs exist in neighborhoods where living conditions are for the most part unstable and transient, resulting in the lack of any adult role models, whether conventional or criminal. *Retreatist gangs* engage in mostly illegal drug use and exist in neighborhoods dominated by a great deal of illegal drug activity. Retreatist gang youths are described as double failures by Cloward and Ohlin.

Social Embeddedness.   One of the most interesting new variations of strain theory comes from Hagan.[51] He uses the term *social embeddedness* to describe a developmental view of involvement in delinquency.

Hagan notes that instead of unemployment preceding involvement in criminal behavior (a common view in criminology), for young offenders the reverse is actually the case. For these youths, involvement in crime begins before they can legally be involved in the labor market. Becoming a regularly employed person depends on much more than an individual's skills and education. It requires being connected to a social network of contacts that accrue over time, usually from a relatively early age. In other words, to become involved in the labor market, a person needs to be socialized into this market starting at an early age. A youth needs to earn money doing odd jobs such as mowing lawns, baby-sitting, washing windows, shoveling snow, and delivering papers long before turning 16. Through such activities a youth begins a process of social embeddedness early in life. For those youths who do poorly in school or drop out, such contacts become difficult to establish.[52]

Hagan argues that, just as one can become socially embedded in the world of regular job contacts and the world of work, so too can one become embedded in a network of crime and deviance. In most of the high-crime, inner-city neighborhoods, the odd jobs available to middle-class youths do not exist in large number (for example, in the projects there are no lawns to be mowed). He notes that parental involvement in crime will integrate youths into networks of criminal opportunities. Likewise, association with delinquent peers or contacts with drug dealers can integrate youths into criminal networks. Moreover, delinquent acts tend to cause youths to become further isolated from networks of employment. A sort of snowball effect takes place, whereby each delinquent act or contact with the world of crime further distances a youth from the legitimate world of work. Thus, the perspective of social embeddedness identifies "a process of separation and isolation from conventional employment networks" that has a time sequence with a "lagged accumulation of effect that should build over time."[53]

Several examples of ethnographic research on delinquency (mostly work on gangs) support this view.[54] All of these studies find evidence of the socialization of inner-city youths (especially minority youths) into the world of criminal opportunities and their subsequent isolation from the social networks of legitimate work.

Data from a London cohort of youths originally studied by West and Farrington[55] further document this perspective. Among a group of white, working-class youths, these researchers found that "early embeddedness among delinquent friends and in continuing delinquent behavior leads to adult unemployment." Hagen also notes that "parental criminality plays a more salient role in the development of early adult unemployment than parental unemployment" and further that "parental criminal conviction interacts with early adolescent delinquency conviction to produce later adolescent delinquency and adult unemployment." Thus, "This chain of effects embeds youth crime within a context that joins parent, peer, and court contacts in a process leading to adult unemployment. Criminal youths are embedded in contexts that isolate them from the likelihood of legitimate adult employment."[56]

Cultural-Deviance Theory

Cultural-deviance theory proposes that delinquency is a result of a desire to conform to cultural values that are to some extent in conflict with the values of conventional society. In part, this perspective is a direct offshoot of social disorganization theory, which suggests that criminal values and traditions emerge within the communities most affected by social disorganization.

Cohen's Culture of the Gang.   One of the most popular accounts of cultural-deviance theory is Albert Cohen's work, *Delinquent Boys: The Culture of the Gang.*[57] Cohen's view incorporates the following assumptions: (1) A high proportion of lower-class youths (especially males) do poorly in school. (2) Poor school performance relates to delinquency. (3) Poor school performance stems from a conflict between the dominant middle-class values of the school system and the values of lower-class youths. (4) Most lower-class male delinquency is committed in a gang context, partly as a means of meeting some basic human needs, such as self-esteem and belonging.

Two key concepts in Cohen's theory are (1) reaction formation and (2) the middle-class measuring rod. *Reaction formation* is open rejection of what a person wants or aspires to but cannot achieve or obtain. The *middle-class measuring rod* consists of evaluations of school performance and behavior within the school that are based on norms and values thought to be associated with the middle class, such as punctuality, neatness, cleanliness, nonviolent behavior, drive and ambition, achievement and success (especially at school), and deferred gratification. Cohen argues that delinquents often develop a culture that is at odds with the norms and values of the middle class, which they turn upside down and rebel against.

Lower-Class Focal Concerns.   Still another variation of this perspective comes from the work of Walter B. Miller, an anthropologist from Harvard University, who has published extensively on the topic of gangs for the past thirty years. His theory includes an examination of what he calls the *focal concerns* of a distinctive lower-class culture. Miller argues that (1) there are clear-cut focal concerns (norms and values) within the lower-class culture and (2) *female-dominated households* are an important feature within the lower class and are a major reason for the emergence of street-corner male adolescent groups in these neighborhoods.[58]

Two key concepts here are (1) *focal concerns,* which include trouble, toughness, smartness, excitement, fate, and autonomy (see Figure 4.4); and (2) *one-sex peer units* that serve as alternative sources of companionship and male role-model development outside the home. These focal concerns are often at odds with mainstream middle-class society. The one-sex peer group is important to Miller's theory in the sense that gangs provide male members opportunities to prove their own masculinity in the absence of an adequate male

FIGURE 4.4   Miller's "Focal Concerns" of Lower-Class Culture

1. *Trouble* is a dominant feature of lower-class life. The major axis is law-abiding/non-law-abiding behavior. Unlike the middle class, where judgment is usually based on one's achievements (e.g., education, career advancement), the lower-class concern is whether one will pursue the law-abiding route or its reverse. Further, membership in a gang is often contingent on demonstrating a commitment to law-violating behavior, acts that carry much prestige.
2. *Toughness* is associated with stereotypical masculine traits and behaviors, featuring mostly an emphasis on a concern for physical prowess, strength, fearless daring, and a general macho attitude and behavior (or machismo). It also includes a lack of sentimentality, a disdain for art and literature, and a view of women as sex objects. Concern over toughness may derive from being reared in a female-headed household and lack of male role models. The concern with toughness precludes males from assuming roles that might be seen as feminine, such as caring for one's children and acting responsibly toward fathering children out of wedlock.
3. *Smartness* revolves around the ability to con or outwit others, to engage in hustling activities. Skills in this area are continually being tested and honed, and the really skillful have great prestige. Many leaders of gangs are valued more for smartness than for toughness, but the ideal leader possesses both qualities.
4. *Excitement* refers to the lifestyle within the lower class that involves a constant search for thrills or kicks to offset an otherwise boring existence. Alcohol, sex, and gambling play a large role here. The night on the town is a favorite pastime involving alcohol, sex, and music. Fights are frequent, so "going to town" is an expression of actively seeking risk and danger, hence excitement. Most of the time between episodes of excitement is spent doing nothing or hanging around—common for gang members.
5. *Fate* involves luck and fortune. According to Miller, most members of the lower class believe that they have little or no control over their lives, that their destiny is predetermined. Much of what happens is determined by luck, so if one is lucky life will be rewarding; if one is unlucky then nothing he does will change his fate, so why bother working toward goals?
6. *Autonomy* is reflected in a contradiction of sorts. On the one hand there is overt resentment of external authority and controls ("No one is going to tell me what to do!"), and on the other hand there are covert behaviors that show that many members of the lower class do want such control. They recognize that external authority and controls provide a somewhat nurturing aspect to them. So, if one is imprisoned and subjected to rigid rules and regulations, one may overtly complain while locked up but upon release may soon behave in such a way as to ensure reimprisonment and its corresponding nurturance. Rebellion over rules is really a testing of the firmness of the rules and an attempt to seek reassurance that nurturing will occur. Youngsters often misbehave in school because they do not get such reassurance.

Source: Adapted from Miller, W. B. "Lower Class Culture as a Generating Milieu of Gang Delinquency." *Journal of Social Issues* 14: 5–19 (1958).

role model within their family of origin. The principal unit in lower-class society is an age-graded, one-sex peer group constituting the major psychic focus and reference group for young people. The adolescent street-corner group is one variant of the lower-class structure, and the gang is a subtype distinguished by law-violating activities. For boys reared in female-headed households, the street-corner group provides the first real opportunity to learn essential aspects of the male role—by learning from other boys in the group with similar sex-role identification problems. The group also acts as a selection process in recruiting and retaining members.

Echoing Thrasher's work, Miller states that two central concerns of the adolescent street-corner group are belonging and status. One achieves belonging by adhering to the group's standards and values and continues to achieve belonging by demonstrating such characteristics as toughness, smartness, and autonomy. When there is conflict with other norms—for example, middle-class norms—the norms of the group are far more compelling because failure to conform means expulsion from the group. Status is achieved by demonstrating qualities that adolescents value (smartness, toughness, etc., as defined by lower-class culture). Status in the adolescent group requires *adultness*—that is, the material possessions and rights of adults (a car, the right to smoke and drink, etc.)—but not the responsibilities of adults. The desire to act like an adult and avoid "kid stuff" results in gambling, drinking, and other deviant behaviors and compels the adolescent more than the adult to be smart, tough, and so on. He or she will seek out ways to demonstrate these qualities, even if they are illegal.

There is also a pecking order among different groups, defined by one's "rep" (reputation). Each group believes its safety depends on maintaining a solid rep for toughness compared with other groups. One's rep refers to both law-abiding and law-violating behavior. Which behavior will dominate depends on a complex set of factors, such as which community reference groups (criminals or police) are admired or respected, or the individual needs of the gang members. Above all, having status is crucial and is far more important than the means selected to achieve it.

Control/Social Bond Theory

The essence of **control/social bond theory** is that the weakening, breakdown, or absence of effective social control accounts for delinquency. A unique feature of this perspective is that instead of asking "Why do they do it?" it asks "Why *don't* they do it?" Control theory wrestles with what it is that keeps or prevents people from committing crime. In this sense, it is really a theory of prevention.

The basic assumption of control theory is that proper social behavior requires proper socialization. Proper socialization leads to conformity; improper socialization leads to nonconformity. Criminality is one consequence of improper socialization. According to control theory, delinquent behavior occurs because it is not prevented in the first place.

There are several versions of this theory. According to one, the delinquent lacks either strong *inner* controls or strong *outer* controls.[59] The former refers to things such as a positive self-image or strong ego; the latter, to strong family controls, community controls, legal controls, and so on. According to another version of the theory, many youths commit delinquent acts because they rationalize deviance before it occurs—that is, they neutralize the normal moral beliefs they have learned while growing up. For instance, they deny that there is a victim by saying things like "He had it coming," or they deny that there was any real harm by saying something like "No one was really hurt" or "They won't miss it."[60]

The most popular version is the one put forth by the sociologist Travis Hirschi. According to Hirschi, all humans are basically antisocial, and all are capable of committing a crime. What keeps most of us in check (that is, prevents us from deviating) is what he calls the social bond to society, especially the norms of society that we have internalized. Hirschi identifies four elements of this bond: attachment, commitment, involvement, and belief (see Figure 4.5).[61]

FIGURE 4.5   Hirschi's Four Elements of the Social Bond

1. *Attachment.* This refers to ties of affection and respect between kids and parents, teachers and friends. Attachment to parents is most important because it is from parents that kids obtain the norms and values of the surrounding society, which they internalize. This is similar to Freud's concept of superego but more conscious than his term.
2. *Commitment.* This is similar to Freud's concept of ego except it is expressed in terms of the extent to which kids are committed to the ideal requirements of childhood, such as getting an education, postponing participation in adult activities (working full time, living on their own, getting married, etc.), and dedication to long-term goals. If kids develop a stake in conformity, engaging in delinquent behavior would endanger their future.
3. *Involvement.* This is similar to the conventional belief that "Idle hands are the devil's workshop." Large amounts of unstructured time may weaken the social bond; kids busy doing conventional things, such as chores at home, homework, sports, camping, working, and dating, do not have time for delinquency.
4. *Belief.* This refers simply to belief in the law, especially the morality of the law (e.g., belief that stealing is just plain wrong).

Source: Adapted from Hirschi, T. *Causes of Delinquency* (3rd ed.). Berkeley: University of California Press, 1969.

This theory is very popular (although many do not call it "control theory"), for most people share traditional beliefs about what is and is not appropriate role behavior for young people. Everyday, juvenile justice workers put this theory into practice as they try to, in a sense, *reattach* delinquents to family, school, and so on; convince them to *commit* themselves to the demands of childhood; *involve* them in conventional activities; and help them acquire a *belief* in and respect for the law.

Social Learning Theory

According to **social learning theory,** people learn to be delinquent or criminal through the same kind of process in which they learn anything else. Individuals learn behavior in the same way they learn values, beliefs, and attitudes—through association with other human beings. One of the earliest variations of social learning theory as it applies to crime and delinquency was the theory of *differential association* originally developed by Edwin Sutherland.[62] According to Sutherland's theory, a person becomes a delinquent or criminal through contact not only with others who are delinquent but also through exposure to values, beliefs, and attitudes supportive of criminal or delinquent behavior, and to the various techniques used to commit such acts. One of the central points of this theory is the proposition that one becomes a delinquent or criminal "because of an excess of definitions favorable to violation of law over definitions unfavorable [to violation] of law."[63] In other words, a young person becomes delinquent through his or her association with delinquent youths. Together these delinquents reinforce beliefs, values, and attitudes that lead to, and perpetuate, delinquency.

Social learning theory suggests that there are three related processes that lead a person to become a delinquent or criminal: (1) acquisition, (2) instigation, and (3) maintenance.[64] *Acquisition* refers to the original learning of behavior. The key to this process is reinforcement through the modeling influences of one's family and the immediate subculture (especially the peer subculture) and symbolic modeling (for example, via television). A child who witnesses violence within the home is likely to engage in violence later in life, especially if violence within the home is rewarded or no sanctions are applied. Children tend to acquire behaviors they observe in others and behaviors that they see rewarded.

Instigation refers to the process whereby once a person acquires a behavior, certain factors work to cause or instigate a specific event—in this case, an act of delinquency. Learning theory suggests five factors as major instigators:

1. *Aversive* events—events such as frustration, relative deprivation, and, of particular importance in gang violence, verbal insults and actual assaults. Threats to the reputa-

tion and status of an individual who is especially violent, especially threats occurring in public, are very important instigators of violent acts.

2. *Modeling influences*—actually observing delinquent or criminal behavior by someone who serves as a role model.

3. *Incentive inducements*—anticipated rewards. A person can be motivated to commit a crime by some perceived reward, usually monetary.

4. *Instructional control*—following orders from someone in authority. A gang member, for instance, may obey a direct order from a leader within the gang.

5. *Environmental control*—factors in one's immediate environment, such as crowded conditions (including traffic), extreme heat, pollution, and noise. Each of these can cause someone to "lose it" and act out, sometimes in a violent manner.

In order for delinquent or criminal behavior to persist, there needs to be consistent *maintenance*, or reinforcement. Social learning theory suggests four kinds of reinforcement: (1) direct reinforcement, (2) vicarious reinforcement, (3) self-reinforcement, and (4) neutralization of self-punishment. *Direct reinforcement* refers to extrinsic rewards (money, recognition, etc.) that correspond to an act. *Vicarious reinforcement* occurs from seeing others get rewards or escape punishment for delinquent or criminal acts. For example, a youth sees someone carrying a lot of money obtained by selling drugs. *Self-reinforcement* means that a person derives his or her self-worth or sense of pride as a result of criminal acts. *Neutralization* is the process whereby one justifies or rationalizes delinquent acts.

A long-standing sociological theory is commonly referred to as *techniques of neutralization*.[65] The authors of this perspective suggest that delinquents often come up with rationalizations or excuses that absolve them of guilt. A youth may say that no one was harmed or that the victim deserved it ("He had it coming to him"). Or a youth may condemn persons who condemn him or her—for example, by saying that adults do these kinds of things, too. Other techniques are to appeal to higher loyalties ("I'm doing it for the 'hood'"), or to blame external factors. Such techniques of neutralization dehumanize the victim, and there is a gradual desensitization regarding the use of violence or other means of force to get one's way.

The sociological theories summarized so far tend not to seriously question the existing social order, although social disorganization and strain theories to some extent provide at least an indirect critique of the existing order. The next two sociological perspectives that we discuss question social order, specifically the social order of advanced capitalism in the late twentieth century. Instead of focusing on how offenders and potential offenders or at-risk youths can be made to accommodate to the existing social order, the labeling and critical/Marxist perspectives call for changing the social order so that fewer people will be drawn into criminal behavior.

Labeling Theory

Labeling theory (also known as the *societal reaction perspective*) does not address in any direct way the causes of criminal or deviant behavior but rather focuses on three interrelated processes: (1) how and why certain behaviors are defined as criminal or deviant; (2) the response to crime or deviance by authorities; and (3) the effects of such definitions and official reactions on the person or persons so labeled.[66] The key to this perspective is reflected in a statement by Becker: "Social groups create deviance by making the rules whose infraction constitutes deviance, and by applying those rules to particular people and labeling them as outsiders."[67] Advocates of labeling theory insist that the criminal justice system itself (including the legislation that creates laws and hence defines crime and criminals) helps to perpetuate crime and deviance.

One of the most significant analyses of crime and criminal behavior to emerge from the labeling tradition is Quinney's theory of the *social reality of crime*. In a landmark textbook on crime and criminal justice, Quinney organized his theory around six interrelated propositions, listed in Figure 4.6.

An important component of Quinney's theory is four interrelated concepts: (1) process, (2) conflict, (3) power, and (4) social action.[68] By *process,* Quinney is referring to the fact that "all social phenomena…have duration and undergo change." The *conflict* view of society and the law is that in any society "conflicts between persons, social units, or cultural elements are inevitable, the normal consequences of social life." Further, society "is held together by force and constraint and is characterized by ubiquitous conflicts that result in continuous change." *Power* is an elementary force in our society. Power, says Quinney, "is the ability of persons and groups to determine the conduct of other persons and groups. It is utilized not for its own sake, but is the vehicle for the enforcement of scarce values in society, whether the values are material, moral, or otherwise." Power is important if we are to understand public policy. Public policy, including crime control policies, is shaped by groups with special interests. In a class society, some groups have more power than others and therefore are able to have their interests represented in policy decisions, often at the expense of less powerful groups. For instance, white upper-class males have more power than working- or lower-class minorities and women, and their interests are more likely to be represented. Finally, by *social action,* Quinney is referring to the fact that human beings engage in voluntary behavior—behavior that is not completely determined by forces beyond their control. Thus, individuals are "able to reason and choose courses of action" and are "changing and becoming, rather than merely being." It is true that people are shaped by their physical, social, and cultural experiences, but they also have the capacity to change and achieve their maximum potential and fulfillment.

An important aspect of labeling theory is the distinction between **primary and secondary deviance.**[69] *Primary deviance* includes acts that the perpetrator or others consider alien to, or at odds with, a person's true identity or character. In other words, an act is "out of character," (or a behavior is "not like you.") Such acts have only marginal implications for one's status and psychic structure. They remain primary deviance as long as the individual can rationalize or otherwise deal with the behavior and still maintain an acceptable self-image and an image acceptable to others. *Secondary deviance,* in contrast, refers to a process whereby the deviance takes on self-identifying features—that is, deviant acts begin to be considered indicative of a person's true self, of the way someone "really" is. Deviance becomes secondary "when a person begins to employ his deviant behavior or a role based upon it as a means of defense, attack, or adjustment to the overt and covert problems created by the consequent societal reaction to him."[70]

Labeling theory led some scholars to begin to question not only the criminal justice system but also the social structure and institutions of society as a whole. In particular, some research in the labeling tradition directed attention to such factors as class, race, and

---

FIGURE 4.6   Quinney's Social Reality of Crime Propositions

1. Crime is a definition of human conduct that is created by authorized agents in a politically organized society.
2. Criminal definitions describe behaviors that conflict with the interests of the segments of society that have the power to shape public policy.
3. Criminal definitions are applied by the segments of society that have the power to shape the enforcement and administration of criminal law.
4. Behavior patterns are structured in segmentally organized society in relation to criminal definitions, and within this context persons engage in actions that have relative probabilities of being defined as criminal.
5. Conceptions of crime are constructed and diffused in the segments of society by various means of communication.
6. The social reality of crime is constructed by the formulation and application of criminal definitions, the development of behavior patterns related to criminal definitions, and the construction of criminal conceptions.

Source: Quinney, R. *The Social Reality of Crime.* Boston: Little, Brown, 1970, pp. 15–25.

sex not only in the formulation of criminal definitions but also as major causes of crime it-self. This in turn led to a critical examination of existing institutions of American society and to a critique of the capitalist system itself. A critical/Marxist criminology emerged from such efforts.

Critical/Marxist Theory

Quinney and Wildeman place the development of a **critical/Marxist theory** in the histori-cal and social context of the late 1960s and early 1970s:

> It is not by chance that the 1970s saw the birth of critical thought in the ranks of American criminologists. Not only did critical criminology challenge old ideas, but it went on to in-troduce new and liberating ideas and interpretations of America and of what America could become. If social justice is not for all in a democratic society—and it was clear that it was not—then there must be something radically wrong with the way our basic institutions are structured.[71]

In *Class, State and Crime* Quinney outlined his own version of a critical or Marxist theory of crime. He linked crime and the reaction to crime to the modern capitalist political and economic system. This viewpoint suggests that the capitalist system itself produces a number of problems that are linked to various attempts by the capitalist class to maintain the basic institutions of the capitalist order. These attempts lead to various forms of accom-modation and resistance by people who are oppressed by the system, especially the work-ing class, the poor, and racial and ethnic minorities. In attempting to maintain the existing order, the powerful commit various crimes, which Quinney classified as crimes of control, crimes of economic domination, and crimes of government. At the same time, oppressed people engage in various kinds of crimes related to accommodation and resistance, includ-ing predatory crimes, personal crimes, and crimes of resistance.[72]

Much of what is known as gang behavior, including gang-related crime, can therefore be understood as an attempt by oppressed people to accommodate and resist the problems created by capitalist institutions. Many modern gang members adapt to their disadvantaged positions by engaging in predatory and personal criminal behavior. Much of their behavior, moreover, is in many ways identical to normal capitalist entrepreneurial activity. For in-stance, drug gangs engage in buying and selling drugs, like any other commodity in the eco-nomic system. They seek "market share" on certain street corners and in certain parks and alleys, not unlike typical legitimate businesses. Moreover, the famous law of supply and demand exists: drugs (or other illegal commodities, such as stolen goods) are in high de-mand, and thus someone will always find a way to provide the goods.[73]

A critical/Marxist perspective goes even further by focusing on "those social struc-tures and forces that produce both the greed of the inside trader as well as the brutality of the rapist or the murderer. And it places those structures in their proper context: the mate-rial conditions of class struggle under a capitalist mode of production."[74] The material conditions include the class and racial inequalities produced by the contradictions of capi-talism (which produce economic changes that negatively affect the lives of so many peo-ple, especially the working class and the poor).

Lanier and Henry identify six ideas common to critical/Marxist theories of crime and criminal justice. These are shown in Figure 4.7.[75]

The importance of the capitalist system in producing inequality and hence crime is apparent when we examine recent economic changes in American society and the effects of these changes. In recent years, particularly, many scholars have begun to seek an expla-nation of gangs (and crime in general) by examining changes in the economic structure of society and how such changes contribute to the emergence of what some have called an un-derclass that in many ways resembles what Marx called the "surplus population" and to the "lumpenproletariat."[76] In many ways, this perspective is an extension of some of the basic

FIGURE 4.7   Crime and Capitalism

1. *Capitalism shapes social institutions, social identities, and social action.* In other words, the actual "mode of production" in any given society tends to determine many other areas of social life, including divisions based on race, class, and gender, plus the manner in which people behave and act toward one another.

2. *Capitalism creates class conflict and contradictions.* Because a relatively small group (about 1–2% of the population) owns or controls the "means of production," class divisions have resulted and the inevitable class conflict over control of resources. The contradiction is that workers need to consume the products of the capitalist system, but in order to do this, they need to have enough income to do so and thus increase growth in the economy. However, too much growth may cut into profits. One result is the creation of a *surplus population*—a more or less steady supply of able workers who are permanently unemployed or underemployed.

3. *Crime is a response to capitalism and its contradictions.* This notion stems in part from the second theme in that the "surplus population" may commit crimes to survive. These can be described as crimes of *accommodation.* Crimes among the more affluent can also result (see next point), in addition to crimes of *resistance* (e.g., sabotage and political violence).

4. *Capitalist law facilitates and conceals crimes of domination and repression.* The law can often be repressive toward certain groups and engage in the violation of human rights (*crimes of control and repression*). Crimes of *domination* also occur with great frequency as corporations and their representatives violate numerous laws (fraud, price-fixing, pollution, etc.) that cause great social harms but are virtually ignored by the criminal justice system.

5. *Crime is functional to capitalism.* There is a viable and fast-growing *crime control industry* that provides a sort of "Keynesian stimulus" to the economy by creating jobs and profits for corporations (e.g., building prisons, providing various products and services to prisons, jails, police departments, courthouses).

6. *Capitalism shapes society's response to crime by shaping law.* Those in power (especially legislators) define what is a "crime" and what constitutes a threat to "social order" and, perhaps more important, *who* constitutes such a threat (usually members of the underclass). Various "problems" that threaten the dominant mode of production become "criminalized" (e.g., the use of certain drugs used by minorities, rather than drugs produced by corporations, such as cigarettes, prescription drugs, and alcohol).

Source: Adapted from Lanier, M., and S. Henry. *Essential Criminology.* Boulder, CO: Westview Press, pp. 256–258.

assumptions and key concepts of the social disorganization/ecology, strain, and cultural deviance theories.

SUMMARY

This chapter reviewed several different theories of crime. Three major perspectives were reviewed. Biological perspectives stress certain physical features of human beings as causal factors in crime, paying special attention to body types and various "abnormalities" such as Lombroso's "stigmata." Also important from this perspective are defects in the central nervous system and the premenstrual syndrome (PMS), in addition to extra Y chromosomes in certain males. Most of the research into this perspective has challenged such views, and to date there is little empirical support.

Psychological theories stressed the mental makeup of human beings and various abnormalities that appear to cause criminal behavior. Starting with Freud's views of unresolved childhood issues and continuing with low intelligence and defective personalities, these theories, like their biological counterparts, largely ignore social and cultural factors. Little empirical support exists for most of them.

Several themes emerge from our review of sociological theories. First, the external socioeconomic environment is of major significance. Social disorganization/social ecology theory (especially the early work of Thrasher) links crime to such environmental factors as poverty, social inequality, lack of community integration, lack of meaningful employment and educational opportunities, as well as to the larger economic picture of a changing labor market and the corresponding emergence of an underclass mired in segregated communities.

A second theme is that adolescents who grow up in such environments are faced with the struggle everyday for self-esteem, a sense of belonging, protection from outside threats, and some sort of family life. These and other basic human needs are not being met by social institutions such as the family, the school, the church, and the community.

A third theme is that becoming a "delinquent" or "criminal" is a social process that involves learning various roles and social expectations within a given community. It involves the reinforcement of these expectations through various rationalizations or "techniques of neutralization," in addition to the perpetuation of various lifestyles, attitudes, and behaviors by the significant others in the lives of these youths. Over time (beginning at a very early age) a youth becomes "embedded" in his or her surrounding environment and cultural norms, and it becomes increasingly difficult to leave the world of crime.

A fourth theme is that crime and delinquency are shaped to a large degree by the societal reaction to such behavior and to the kinds of individuals who engage in such behavior. Such a response helps to perpetuate the very problem that we are trying to solve.

A fifth theme is that one cannot possibly explain crime without considering the economic context of capitalism. Most criminal activity is consistent with basic capitalist values, such as the law of supply and demand, the need to make money, and the desire to accumulate consumer goods. As the economy continues to pass over the most disadvantaged segments of the population, crime will continue to be an alternative lifestyle.

KEY TERMS

American Dream   100
anomie   99
cartographic school   95
Cesare Lombroso   89
Chicago School   95
concentric zone model   96
control/social bond theory   105
critical/Marxist theory   109
cultural-deviance theory   103
culture   100

ectomorph   90
endomorph   90
feeblemindedness   92
labeling theory   107
mesomorph   90
Minnesota Multiphasic Personality Inventory (MMPI)   93
primary and secondary deviance   108

social institution   101
social disorganization/social ecology theory   94
social learning theory   106
social structure   100
somatotypes   90
stigmata   90
strain theory   99

NOTES

1. Thanks are extended to UNLV graduate student Erin Reese for her research assistance on biological and psychological theories.

2. Bohm, R. M. *A Primer on Crime and Delinquency.* Belmont, CA: Wadsworth, 1997, p. 35. See also Vold, G., and T. J. Bernard. *Theoretical Criminology* (3rd ed.). New York: Oxford University Press, 1986.

3. Vold and Bernard, ibid.

4. Glueck, S., and E. Glueck. *Physique and Delinquency.* New York: Harper & Row, 1956; Sheldon, W. *Varieties of Delinquent Youth.* New York: Harper, 1949; Hooton, E. A., *The American Criminal: An Anthropological Study.* Cambridge, MA: Harvard University Press, 1939.

5. DeKeseredy, W. S., and M. D. Schwartz. *Contemporary Criminology.* Belmont, CA: Wadsworth, 1996, p. 180.

6. Ibid.

7. Ibid.

8. Vold and Bernard, *Theoretical Criminology,* p. 107.

9. See especially: Bregin, P. R., and G. R. Bregin, *The War against Children of Color.* Monroe, ME: Common Courage Press, 1998.

10. Some illustrations of this approach can be found in Cook, P. J. "The Demand and Supply of Criminal Opportunities." In M. Tonry, and N. Morris (eds.), *Crime and Justice,* vol. 7. Chicago: University of Chicago Press, 1986; Cohen, L., and M. Felson. "Social Change and Crime Rate Trends: A 'Routine Activities' Approach." *American Sociological Review* 44: 588–608 (1979).

11. For a good discussion of this issue see Bartollas, C. *Juvenile Delinquency* (5th ed.). New York: Macmillan, 2000, pp. 111–112.

12. Mesner, S., and K. Tardiff. "The Social Ecology of Urban Homicide: An Application of the Routine Activities Approach." *Criminology* 23: 241–267 (1985); Maxfield, M. "Household Composition, Routine Activities, and

Victimization: A Comparative Analysis." *Journal of Quantitative Criminology* 3: 301–320 (1987).

13. Klein, M. *The American Street Gang.* New York: Oxford University Press, 1995, p. 163.

14. Rafter, N. H. (ed.). *White Trash: The Eugenic Family Studies, 1899–1919.* Boston: Northeastern University Press, 1988.

15. Wilson, J. Q., and R. Herrnstein. *Crime and Human Nature: The Definitive Study of the Causes of Crime.* New York: Simon & Schuster, 1985.

16. Kraska, P. "The Sophistication of Hans Jurgen Eysenck: An Analysis and Critique of Contemporary Biological Criminology." *Criminal Justice Research Bulletin* 4(5): 1–7 (1989).

17. Bohm, *A Primer on Crime and Delinquency,* p. 51; DeKeseredy and Schwartz, *Contemporary Criminology,* pp. 182–183.

18. Ibid.

19. DeKeseredy and Schwartz, ibid, pp. 183–184.

20. Akers, R. L. *Criminological Theories: Introduction and Evaluation.* Los Angeles: Roxbury Press, 1994, p. 88.

21. Vold and Bernard, *Theoretical Criminology.*

22. Currie, E. *Confronting Crime.* New York: Pantheon, 1985.

23. Much of this material is adapted from Shelden, Tracy, and Brown, *Youth Gangs in American Society,* ch. 7.

24. Lanier, M. M., and S. Henry. *Essential Criminology.* Boulder, CO: Westview Press, 1998, ch. 9; Stark, R. "Deviant Places: A Theory of the Ecology of Crime." *Criminology* 25: 893–909. (1987).

25. For a detailed discussion of the work of Guerry and Quételet and the Chicago School, see Lanier and Henry, *Essential Criminology,* pp. 183–192; see also Quinney, R., and J. Wildeman. *The Problem of Crime: A Peace and Social Justice Perspective* (3rd ed.). Mountain View, CA: Mayfield, 1991, pp. 48–50.

26. See Moore, J. W. *Homeboys: Gangs, Drugs, and Prisons in the Barrio of Los Angeles.* Philadelphia: Temple University Press, 1978, and *Going Down to the Barrio: Homeboys and Homegirls in Change.* Philadelphia: Temple University Press, 1991, for documentation of this phenomenon.

27. Stark, "Deviant Places."

28. Lanier and Henry, *Essential Criminology,* p. 182. Lanier and Henry also note that the term "social" or "human" ecology comes from the Greek word *oikos,* which translates roughly into "household" or "living space."

29. Burgess, E. W. "The Growth of the City." In R. E. Park, E. W. Burgess, and R. D. McKenzie (eds.), *The City.* Chicago: University of Chicago Press, 1925.

30. Shaw, C., and H. D. McKay. *Juvenile Delinquency in Urban Areas.* Chicago: University of Chicago Press, 1942.

31. Thrasher, F. *The Gang.* Chicago: University of Chicago Press, 1927, pp. 32–33.

32. Ibid., pp. 20–21.

33. Ibid., p.33.

34. In his study of Hispanic gangs in Los Angeles, Vigil concludes that the gang provides many of the functions that a family provides: "The gang has become a 'spontaneous' street social unit that fills a void left by families under stress. Parents and other family members are preoccupied with their own problems, and thus the street group has arisen as a source of familial compensation." Vigil notes that about half of those he interviewed mentioned how im-portant the group was to them, that the gang was something they needed, and that it gave them something in return. Close friends become like family to the gang member, especially when support and love are missing from one's real family. See Vigil, J. D. *Barrio Gangs.* Austin: University of Texas Press, 1988, pp. 89–90.

35. Spergel, I. A. *Racketville, Slumtown and Haulberg.* Chicago: University of Chicago Press, 1964.

36. Sullivan, M. L. *Getting Paid: Youth Crime and Work in the Inner City.* Ithaca, NY: Cornell University Press, 1989, pp. 21–27, 98.

37. Ibid., p. 203.

38. Ibid., p. 103.

39. Ibid., p. 108.

40. Ibid., p. 110.

41. See Merton, R. K. *Social Theory and Social Structure.* New York: Free Press, 1968.

42. The reader is encouraged to browse through any introductory sociology textbook to find numerous references to culture and social structure. In fact, one definition of *sociology* could easily be "the study of culture and social structure."

43. For an excellent discussion of the role of corporate propaganda see the following: Herman, E. and N. Chomsky, *Manufacturing Consent* (2nd ed.). New York: Pantheon Books, 2002; Chomsky, *Necessary Illusions;* Fones-Wolf, E. *Selling Free Enterprise.* Indianapolis: Indiana University Press, 1994; Carey, A. *Taking the Risk out of Democracy.* Chicago: University of Illinois Press, 1995.

44. For a quick and easy look at inequality see Folbre and the Center for Popular Economics, *The New Field Guide to the U.S. Economy.* See also Domhoff, *Who Rules America?;* and Rothman, *Inequality and Stratification.*

45. Messner, M., and R. Rosenfeld. *Crime and the American Dream* (3rd ed.). Belmont, CA: Wadsworth, 2001.

46. Ibid., pp. 65–66.

47. Quoted in Chomsky, N. *Class Warfare.* Monroe, ME: Common Courage Press, 1996, p. 29.

48. Messner and Rosenfeld, in *Crime and the American Dream,* p. 73, note that the United States lags far behind other countries (whose economic institutions are not nearly as dominant) in paid family leave.

49. Cloward, R., and L. Ohlin. *Delinquency and Opportunity.* New York: Free Press, 1960.

50. Ibid., p. 86.

51. Hagan, J. "The Social Embeddedness of Crime and Unemployment." *Criminology* 31: 465–491 (1993).

52. Although not mentioned by Hagan (ibid.), to become embedded in the labor market, one also needs social or cultural capital. For those who lack the necessary social or cultural capital, being involved in the labor market with steady employment is quite difficult.

53. Hagan, ibid., p. 469.

54. See Shelden, Tracy, and Brown, *Youth Gangs in American Society,* for a summary of these studies.

55. West, D. J., and D. P. Farrington. *The Delinquent Way of Life.* London: Heinemann, 1977.

56. Hagan, "The Social Embeddedness of Crime and Unemployment," pp. 486–487.

57. Cohen, A. *Delinquent Boys: The Culture of the Gang.* New York: Free Press, 1955.

58. Miller, W. B. "Lower Class Culture as a Generating Milieu of Gang Delinquency." *Journal of Social Issues* 14: 5–19 (1958).

59. Reckless, W. *The Crime Problem* (3rd ed.). New York: Appleton-Century-Crofts, 1961.

60. Sykes, G., and D. Matza. "Techniques of Neutralization." *American Journal of Sociology* 22: 664–670 (1957).

61. Hirschi, T. *Causes of Delinquency.* Berkeley: University of California Press, 1969.

62. Sutherland E. H., and D. R. Cressey. *Criminology* (8th ed.). Philadelphia: Lippincott, 1970.

63. Shoemaker, D. J. *Theories of Delinquency* (3rd ed.). New York: Oxford University Press, 1996, pp. 152–153.

64. Goldstein, A. P. *Delinquent Gangs: A Psychological Perspective.* Champaign, IL: Research Press, 1991, pp. 55–61.

65. Sykes and Matza, "Techniques of Neutralization."

66. Schur, E. *Labeling Deviant Behavior.* New York: Harper & Row, 1971.

67. Becker, H. *Outsiders,* New York: Free Press, 1963, pp. 8–9.

68. The following quotes are taken Quinney, *The Social Reality of Crime,* pp. 8–15.

69. Lemert, E. *Social Pathology.* New York: McGraw-Hill, 1951.

70. Ibid., p. 76.

71. Quinney and Wildeman, *The Problem of Crime,* p. 72.

72. Quinney, *Class, State and Crime,* pp. 33–62.

73. Shelden, Tracy, and Brown, *Youth Gangs in American Society,* ch. 4.

74. Quinney and Wildeman, *The Problem of Crime,* p. 77.

75. Lanier and Henry, *Essential Criminology,* pp. 256–258.

76. It is important to emphasize, however, that Marx did distinguish between these two terms. The *lumpenproletariat* was seen by Marx as the bottom layer of society, the "social junk," "rotting scum," "rabble," etc. In short, they were described as the "criminal class." *Surplus population* referred to working-class men and women who, because of various fluctuations in the market (caused chiefly by contradictions within the capitalist system), were excluded, either temporarily or permanently, from the labor market.

CHAPTER FIVE

A HISTORICAL OVERVIEW
OF AMERICAN POLICING

With the red and blue lights fully engaged, and flashing brightly, the scout car executed an abrupt U-turn and sped after the light blue Caprice. The driver of the Caprice pulled over to the side of the road and stopped. Both officers approached the car. One officer moved close to the driver's side of the Caprice and instructed the driver to provide his driver's license, registration, and proof of insurance. The other officer stood at the passenger side of the vehicle; his right hand rested on his service weapon. The driver of the Caprice asked the officer why he was being pulled over. The officer did not provide an answer. The driver was then instructed to get out of his vehicle and move to the back of the car. He was further instructed to place both hands on the trunk of the Caprice, spread his legs, and remain in that position. After patting-down the driver, presumably for weapons, the two officers then returned to the scout car, opened their respective doors, and got in.

It was raining very hard. One officer used the unit's mobile computer to seek information about the driver and the vehicle he was driving. Within several minutes the information had been retrieved from the central computer and sent back to the scout car. The suspect had no warrants. His driver's license was current, and the vehicle was properly registered to the driver who had been stopped. Both officers remained in the car for more than 30 minutes after the information about the driver and the vehicle had been relayed back to them. They were engaged in a discussion about their favorite basketball team. Finally, one officer got out of the car, walked toward the Caprice, and "flipped" the driver's license, registration, and insurance card toward the driver, and said, "Have a nice evening." All three documents landed in the pool of water the driver had been standing in. Completely soaked, the driver of the Caprice looked pathetic in the glare of the scout car's headlights as he reached into the water to retrieve his documents. Later in the shift, the officers were asked why they had stopped the Caprice. One officer stated, in a quite matter-of-fact manner, "He knew he wasn't supposed to be here this time of night." The answer was spontaneous and was offered in such a way that no further explanation occurred to either officer. The driver was a black male, it was late at night, and he was in an all-white suburb of Detroit.[1]

Policing can been defined as "the use of state power by delegated authorities for the purposes of law enforcement and the maintenance of order."[2] This definition raises two questions: What is law enforcement? What is the maintenance of order? In the most simplistic terms, law enforcement is the enforcement of enacted laws derived through a democratic process and designed to accommodate the majority of the people. Maintenance of order is simply maintaining the status quo by keeping so-called problem components of the population under control. The status quo can be defined as those in whose interest it is to keep social, economic, and political arrangements at their current status or level. Problem components include ethnic/racial minorities, homeless people, young people, or people who simply seem to be "out of place" or those who resist the status quo. Historically, problem components have included civil rights advocates (e.g., Martin Luther King, Jr.), labor leaders (e.g., Eugene Debs, a labor movement activist during the early twentieth century), antiwar protesters, university students, workers on strike, and many others who dared to question or contest the status quo. Many have been jailed, beaten, or killed by police and other social control agents of the state (e.g., the Ohio National Guard, which opened fire on students at Kent State University in 1970, killing four) as they attempted to exercise their constitutional rights as American citizens.

The hallmark of American policing is reflected in synthesis of two concepts, *law* and *order,* which implies the maintenance of order within the framework of law. The concept of law and order has contributed to media sound bites and infotainment that promote the legitimation of policing policies through slogans like "You are in danger and you need protection." These sound bites are often adopted by politicians who weave law and order into slogans that legitimate their own political agendas (claiming, for instance, that more police will result in more protection, contrary to research). This sound-bite strategy is useful in the artificial creation of people's needs as well as proposed solutions to those needs, and this scheme has been successful for businesses and corporations that sell products through advertisements provided by mass media conglomerates (e.g., major radio and television networks and magazine and newspaper companies).

The media's preoccupation with profit promotes concern about ratings and the revenue generated through the sale of commercial spots on television, on the radio, and in newspapers and magazines. The media constantly package and sell myths of crime to the public. Often, these myths are packaged as entertainment that provides excitement for the targeted audience, the American consumer. By and large, the public has been willing to purchase these mythical products.[3] Politicians have been successful in their sales of crime-fighting methods that, under close scrutiny, are social and fiscal failures. The constant message is that more and more police is the answer to people's fear of crime. Yet, as many suggest, crime is largely nothing more than a symptom of larger social problems that have been carefully compacted into the conceptual illusion called crime.[4] Crime has become a political product, carefully crafted, marketed, and sold by the media (consisting of a small number of corporate conglomerates). The media and the political figures have, through the successful sales of their products, managed to create a public addiction for stronger social control measures, and a public that is apathetic over issues related to individual rights.[5] In many instances, this addiction has resulted in a reduction of individual liberties for all.[6] In essence, police have become commodity products used to promote the sale of the mythical notion that more police necessarily results in less crime.[7]

American Policing is vital to the operation of the criminal justice system. It is not too far-fetched to suggest that the police are to criminal justice what procurers of raw materials such as steel and plastic are to the automobile industry. Corporations cannot sustain an industry without raw materials, and the criminal justice system cannot operate its industry without criminal defendants. From this perspective, prosecutors, judges, and wardens need police to procure "warm bodies" for their respective criminal processing roles within the criminal justice system. Today, in pursuit of the "warm bodies" necessary for criminal justice processing, American policing faces a dilemma. Confronted with two conflicting roles, American policing must decide on an image to offer to the public. As agents of the state, the police must perform their principal role as social control agents. To a large degree, this role is accommodated through widespread visible police presence. This presence is often amplified by a vast assortment of paramilitary gear worn by police officers who often project the image of combat soldiers or occupation forces ready for a major foreign enemy attack. In a sense, this is true, because we have declared a "war on crime," "war on drugs," and "war on gangs" and therefore are fighting many "enemies." Thus, it is not surprising to find a great deal of "collateral damage"—to borrow a war phrase—such as innocent people being locked up or even killed.[8] One recent example includes the activities and presence of the Seattle Police Department during a World Trade Organization meeting. Peaceful demonstrators, with relatively few exceptions, who were opposed to the unfair labor practices and human rights violations committed by many of the visiting nations, were met with tear gas and a 7 P.M. curfew instituted by police sporting the "latest fashions" in "look tough" riot attire.[9]

History (including recent history as reflected in the Rampart investigations in Los Angeles) demonstrates that police, concurrent with their visible public presence, are often willing to break laws in the name of winning their war against crime. As the Rampart investigation disclosed, the police seem willing even to make up crimes to win the war against crime.[10] Furthermore, as social control agents, police are authorized to intervene, without invitation, in disputes between citizens. They also can deprive citizens of their freedom through detainment or arrest (as vividly shown in the story that began this chapter). And, committing a crime is certainly not a prerequisite for anyone to experience intervention, detainment, or arrest. In fact, police intervention in disputes has become part of American culture. If someone is playing a stereo too loud, people call the police rather than go and ask the person to turn the volume down. The state-defined role of policing is simply "enforcing the laws of the state." Keep in mind that laws are not necessarily laws of the people; instead they are often rules that protect a privileged class in American society. The higher your position on the social ladder, the more likely it is that laws will ensure your security.[11]

Police, through their widespread and visible contact with citizens, must be creative and must attempt to present a positive image of the institution of police and also of the state. People, as a general rule, tend to respond more favorably to that which is presented as legitimate and in their interest. In addition to long-range public relations campaigns, the police institution is able to control the flow of information about crime and its performance as a social control apparatus. Allowing police to keep track of crime and of their responses to that social problem is problematic. As demonstrated in Philadelphia, Boca Raton, and elsewhere, police often underreport crime to make communities appear safe—often for the benefit of the tourist and recreation industries. And the police argue that they are entitled to receive credit for this illusion of safety.[12] Their preoccupation with credit-entitlement is linked to funding. Other jurisdictions engage in the practice of **arrest-overkill,** the arrest of many suspects for an individual crime. A story in the *Detroit Free Press* illustrates that the Detroit police have engaged in arrest-overkill for years. The story draws attention to the number of arrests for murder in the city of Detroit. In 1999, Detroit police made 1,152 murder arrests for 415 killings. Typically, there is one arrest for each murder, but the Detroit police arrest about three suspects for each murder.[13] While Detroit police demand credit for fighting crime in that city, we can only wonder why so many innocent people have been degraded and humiliated by suffering the experience of arrest and incarceration.

The mass media consist of profit-oriented enterprises of information delivery. This enterprise has done much to enhance the image of police in ways that are entertaining to an audience that is neither familiar with, nor willing to engage in, the rigors of critical inquiry and, as a result, is susceptible to the seductive qualities of this infotainment (e.g., an almost endless display of mindless programs such as *Cops, America's Most Wanted,* and tapes of wild police chases). Typically, the image of the institution of police that mass media present is that law enforcement exists to *serve* and *protect* the public (and always "get their man"). The mainstream presentation of police is that of the crime-fighter. Recently released Javier Francisco Ovando, a young man who was shot by Los Angeles police officers, framed, and sentenced to twenty-three years in prison might not agree with the "serve and protect" image of American law enforcement.[14] People often view the police as crime-fighters, but maintaining order has always been the primary goal of the police institution.[15]

The state is typically portrayed as a just entity that, though imperfect, can and must be trusted. The police often define themselves as the "thin blue line" between "civilization" and "anarchy." Of course, the much-shown video recording of police in Los Angeles beating Rodney King begs for a definition of what police actually mean when they refer to "civilization."

Within the criminal justice system, the institution of policing receives the lion's share of funding. Yet the police, as an institution of social control and as an occupational subculture, seem to be not well understood. To develop an understanding of American policing, we must first trace the historical development of this unique institution. How did we get from the initial conception of policing to stopping young African American males for simply being in the wrong part of town at the wrong time of day? Is such an act indicative of progress, stagnation, or regression? Or, perhaps, it has always been this way. Policing did not simply emerge from a vacuum. The practice of governments policing citizens is not a new activity, but policing as an institution is a relatively recent creation that is unique to industrialized societies. Let us now turn our attention to the emergence of the institution of policing.[16]

EARLY POLICE SYSTEMS

Derived from the Greek term *politeia,* the term *police* often had a very broad meaning. In the early seventeenth century, the verb *policier* meant "to order, govern, rule advisedly," and the term *police* meant "civil government." Regardless of the term's origin, contemporary policing is an artifact of nineteenth century empires and nation-states.[17] There were, however, forms of policing that predated the nineteenth century.

Mysticism, superstition, and scores of romantic characterizations obscure the origins of policing. "When one attempts to trace the evolution of law enforcement from antiquity to modern times, it becomes impossible either to completely or absolutely identify the origins of this practice."[18] Systems of police seem to be linked to the historical, prevailing economic and political landscape. In other words, it is possible to study the emergence of police by looking closely at historical social, political, and economic factors germane to the period being studied. We know that during ancient times social control was sustained through patriarchal rule. Today, some, perhaps correctly, argue that policing continues to be an extension of social control through patriarchal rule.[19]

All societies have not had organized police systems, certainly not in the context that we think of policing today. "As a general rule, the more stratified a society, the greater will be the reliance on formal methods of social control."[20] It is argued that as societies became more and more class graded, reliance on or acceptance for organized police forces grew. As a corollary to this general principle, police forces in stratified societies have tended to help preserve class differences. Members of the privileged class have always understood that the best way to preserve their power is to ensure that conflict exists between the various groups located beneath them. The preservation of class differences serves the interests of dominant groups.[21] The institution of American policing has developed, at least in part, in response to organized threats against class domination of a relatively small ruling class.

During ancient times clan and tribal members served as the police and security force of their respective groups. The clan or tribal leader retained complete control. Those members of the community who were given enforcement power did not compose an organized police force. One of the earliest known police systems existed in Babylonia at the time when the Code of Hammurabi was instituted (2181–2123 B.C.). During this period, the monarchs, or ruling class, enjoyed control of the police. "The Babylonian monarchs possessed vast landed estates, the feoffee [a person invested with a grant of land, as a "fief"] being bound to come up when summoned and serve as soldier or slave-driver or policeman."[22] Later, some societies, usually ruled by kings and monarchs, had strong, efficient central governments that maintained order with a totalitarian police force as well as standing armies.[23] Today, it appears that efficiency continues to play a key role, for the police often behave like soldiers in the "war" on drugs.[24]

The Roman Empire adopted forms of policing that relied on a police force and a standing army. Rome had many of the characteristics of stratified societies elsewhere. The inequalities that existed within the Roman Empire created wars, internal strife, and riotous behavior among the masses. As Reith describes:

> Successful wars and the loot and wealth with which they provided some Romans in the capital altered and enhanced the status and divisions and power of classes and factions in the Roman community. Abundance and cheapness of slaves enabled the rich to exploit the land, dispossess the older class of peasant farmers, and, in consequence, Rome became crowded with an increasingly large population of aimless, workless, discontented, and often hungry malcontent, for the control of whose power of insurrection there was only the weak machinery of oratory.... Against the activities of swarms of discontented slaves, only repressive measures were possible.[25]

Following years of strife, Augustus (63 B.C.–A.D. 14) took control and maintained "law and order" with *vigiles,* an imperial force of police and firemen. Among the expressed goals of the *vigiles* was that of arresting thieves and returning fugitive slaves.[26] Augustus had a police force of 10,000 in a city (Rome) with a population of about three-quarters of a million, or one policeman for every 75 citizens.[27] By comparison, today we have one police officer for every 400 or 500 citizens.[28] Many politicians are frantically attempting to reduce this ratio. It is not known whether these political figures want to reduce America's police-to-citizen ratio to Roman standards, one officer per 75 citizens, but it might be useful to consider that soon after Rome reached this ratio, the Roman Empire collapsed.

A common interpretation of the rise of Roman police is provided by Kelly, who suggests that it stemmed from the need to control "crime in the streets," which he argues was rising quite rapidly. But he does not provide any supporting data or documentation. He goes on to suggest that among the specific causes of crime include inadequate street lighting, inefficient law enforcement, "minority problems" (not defined), and the existence of swamps outside the city which "made of [sic] a perfect hideaway for the marauders and fugitives who victimized Rome."[29] This kind of interpretation lends support for those in power, for "crime in the streets" often consisted of riots and rebellions launched by slaves and other oppressed people. Given the degree of inequality that existed in Rome during this period, one of the principal functions of the police was to protect the property and the powerful positions of the rulers.[30] Hence, the role of police was to maintain the interests of the status quo.

A POLICE INSTITUTION EMERGES IN ENGLAND

Prior to the Norman invasion by William the Conqueror, policing in England was a community responsibility. Villages throughout England were divided into **tythings,** units of ten families. A **tythingman** within these units was responsible for keeping order in his section of the village. These sections are comparable to police beats or police sectors in contemporary American policing. A system known as the **mutual pledge system** emerged whereby small sums of money were awarded to citizens who reported crimes to the tythingman or responded to the tythingman's **hue and cry** (an announcement that a crime had occurred). In addition to catching thieves, the tythingman also reimbursed individuals who lost property.[31] The mutual pledge system and other forms of citizen participation in crime control were forerunners of the vigilantes and bounty hunters that would eventually play significant roles in American culture and history. The practice of reimbursing lost property reaches back to the Code of Hammurabi. One section of that code stipulated that if a robber was not caught, and if the victim swore under oath the amount lost, the community was obliged to compensate the victim.

As villages grew, tythings were combined into **hundreds** (each hundred consisted of ten tythings), policed by **constables.** The hundreds eventually were combined to form **shires** (similar to present-day counties). Each shire was policed by a **shire-reeve,** or sheriff. The Normans introduced **vicecomes,** which replaced the shire-reeve. One historian of the police notes, "The shire court of the vicecomes became, often, merely an instrument for collecting unjust and oppressive fines and taxes."[32] The tythingman later become known as the *chief pledge.* The chief pledges came under the authority of the knights of the shire, later known as **justices of the peace,** who were under the direct authority of the king. By the fourteenth century the chief pledge was known as the *petty constable* and later as the *parish constable.* Thus, early policing in England was community based: policing was a responsibility of the community. Then, as class distinctions became more defined, and as social structures became less bearable for the masses, policing gravitated toward the interests of the powerful.

The constabulary system was the dominant form of policing in England until early in the nineteenth century. This system became influential in America. As Parks notes, "The constable did not use his power to discover and punish deviation from the established laws. Rather, he assisted complaining citizens if and when they sought his help."[33] The constable performed his duties during the day while citizen volunteers took turns performing their duties at night, during what was known as the *night-watch.* Policing still was considered a community responsibility and was under the control of the community members. The constable was not concerned with crime prevention as we know it today. He did not spend his time looking for potential criminals. Then, in the face of rapid population growth, more pronounced class divisions, and emerging capitalism, the *voluntary observance* of law no longer seemed able to hold the social order together, and community-responsibility policing changed. Reith points out that such a system of social control seems never to survive:

> in effective form, the advent of community prosperity, as this brings into being, inevitably, differences in wealth and social status, and creates, on this basis, classes and parties and factions with or without wealth and power and privileges. In the presence of these divisions, community unanimity in voluntary law observance disappears, and some other means of securing law observance and the maintenance of authority and order must be found.[34]

Of course, authority and order are defined by those in power. To keep the masses under control, those in power in England created definitions of behavior that they considered deviant or criminal. Further, the broader the gap between the rich and the poor, the less likely it is that the poor will be satisfied with their place in society. As the poor seek some form of social satisfaction (e.g., food and adequate shelter), those in power often resort to formal social control approaches—the police—to protect their own social satisfaction (e.g., wealth).

THE METROPOLITAN POLICE OF LONDON: MODERN ROOTS OF POLICING

By the end of the fifteenth and sixteenth centuries, as capitalism began to claim its place as the dominant economic form, feudal society in England came to an end. As the sixteenth century came to a close, large landowners realized the economic advantage of raising sheep for wool rather than using the land to raise food. This agricultural shift from crop land to pasture displaced serfs and spurred the migration of landless people from rural hamlets and villages to urban centers in search of employment.[35]

By the end of the seventeenth century, the enclosure acts and other similarly repressive actions by the emerging bourgeoisie had forced many landless peasants to live in substandard housing (those "lucky" enough to have housing) and work for virtually starvation wages (those fortunate to find jobs).[36] As might be expected, the masses of propertyless peasants began to engage in various types of revolt and criminal activity in response to the situation they found themselves in. They soon became part of what was known as the "dangerous classes."[37] Anxious to protect their property, the propertied classes attempted to contain this revolt and discontent and to restore order. The best way for the wealthy to contain lower-class disruption and restore order was to create a social control apparatus that would protect the interests of the powerful. By the mid-eighteenth century, that apparatus was the Bow Street Runners.

The Bow Street Runners: Managing Class Struggle

The creation of the **Bow Street Runners** by Henry Fielding, police reformer, was one of the first organized attempts to maintain order and control the peasant class.[38] The Bow Street Runners emerged during the 1740s, a period when new criminal careers were emerging, such as pirating, highway robbery, and begging. Eighteenth-century British law allowed these entrepreneurial thief-takers to prosper. A thief-taker was "commissioned" to recover the property of a victim. Often, it was difficult to distinguish between the thief-taker and the thief. Generally, the distinction was determined by whoever made a contractual arrangement with the victim to recover stolen property. Jonathan Wild, called the Thief-Taker General, was occasionally forced to hand over one of his confederates to mask relationships between the thief-takers and the "criminals."[39] We suppose that one might consider this simply a tradeoff so business could continue.

Economic conditions in England began to worsen, and by 1770 prices were rising much faster than wages. People who worked could not support their families. The Gordon Riots reflect the response of the working class to this economic situation. Alarmed by the presence of mobs in the streets, Parliament and property owners (often indistinguishable) pointed to the inability of police to control the mobs and called for military intervention. The police often were sympathetic toward the working class; after all, most of the police officers came from the ranks of the working and lower classes. Thus, in the minds of the powerful owners, the police were not neutral enough. The military provided the neutrality that satisfied those who believed their property was at risk.[40]

In the early nineteenth century, uniformed policemen were dispatched to provide supervision on main roads and city streets—particularly in the hours of darkness. Attention was directed to the unemployed, the idle, and the poor. There seemed to be little interest in dispatching policemen to businesses where the economic changes of the nineteenth century offered new and ample opportunities for business fraud.[41] As in the eighteenth century, police officers continued to be hired by private individuals to recover stolen property and solve whatever crime had been committed. In 1821 a local magistrate stated that "officers in abundance are loitering about the police offices, in waiting for hire. Protection is reserved for individuals who will individually pay for it."[42]

Economic conditions remained unsettled in England. In 1807, England blockaded French ports. The result was rising unemployment and an increase in hunger and poverty among English workers and their families. The severe winter of 1810 and the harvest failure of 1812 compounded the problems confronting the working class and the poor. Moreover, the use of machinery by factory owners began to displace skilled workers or reduce them to the status of mere appendages to the machines. Men, women, and children worked up to 18 hours per day under grueling conditions in these factories, and they worked for wages which were insufficient to support themselves and their families. Not surprisingly, the workers began to protest. One of the most famous revolts was the Luddite Riots of late 1811 and early 1812. Workers attacked the machines that were displacing them, and they generally disrupted the oppressive factory system.

The British government's response was to make the destruction of machines punishable by death! The War of 1812 with the United States resulted in increased profits and thus temporarily reduced the tension between workers and owners as unemployment decreased. Then, between 1815 and 1822, hard times for the poor returned. An economic depression once again brought widespread unemployment and worker unrest. In 1815, Parliament enacted the Corn Laws, and the price of bread, a staple food of the poor, increased. The result was more poverty and rioting in the streets. Once again, the British government responded with a series of repressive measures. The Six Acts (known also as the Riot Acts) authorized the seizure of "seditious and blasphemous literature." Similar laws had been passed to control the American colonists shortly before the American Revolution.[43]

Bobby Peel and Preventive Policing

Although the depression temporarily ended around 1822, a financial panic occurred in 1825 when many of the banks closed. This resulted in the lowering of wages and increased unemployment, which sparked a new wave of riots and protests by workers.[44] At this time, Sir Robert Peel (known as "Bobby," after whom the London "bobbies" were named) became the Home Secretary of England. For several years he and his supporters advocated the creation of a new police force. Finally, after years of debate, the **Metropolitan Police Act** was passed in 1829.

Immediately preceding the formation of the police force there was an apparent increase in crime. Most of the crime, as indicated in arrests and court appearances, was of a petty nature and emerged out of the class conflicts of the period. For example, the rate of males going to trial increased from 170 per 100,000 population in 1824 to 250 by 1830. The proportion committed for vagrancy increased by 34 percent between 1826 and 1829 and rose by 65 percent between 1829 and 1832. Over half of the prison population during this period were persons convicted of vagrancy, poaching, petty theft, disorderly conduct, and public drunkenness.[45] Only 25 percent of those awaiting trial in local jails or serving actual sentences were being held for indictable crimes; deserters and debtors constituted the remainder.[46] The new police increased the already growing crackdown on minor offenses. Thus, during the 1830s about 85 percent of all arrests were for drunkenness, disorderly conduct, and similar minor offenses.[47] The severe emphasis on minor offenses, committed primarily by the poor and the working classes, reflected the trend toward the regulation and control (i.e., repression) of the laboring population so often referred to as the "dangerous classes." They *were* dangerous, because they had the capacity to disrupt business and production and thus cut into the profits of the owners.

There was strong resistance to the creation of an organized, twenty-four-hour police force in the early years of the nineteenth century. Some of this resistance was most likely due to the English tradition of handling offenses as private matters. Moreover, "full-time" policing was associated with police practices in France, and the British were skeptical of adopting any practices condoned by the French.[48] The formation of the Metropolitan Police of London was supported because of concerns by the wealthy and powerful about the presence of mobs. Such a concern is not unique; many police forces have been established for this reason. Bordua and Reiss note:

> The paramilitary form of early police bureaucracy was a response not only, or even primarily, to crime per se, but to the possibility of riotous disorder. Not crime and danger but the "dangerous classes" as part of the urban social structure led to the formation of uniformed and military organized police. Such organizations intervened between the propertied elites and the propertyless masses who were regarded as politically dangerous as a class.[49]

Another historian notes that "By the late 1820s the fear of crime and disorder overshadowed the potential threats to liberty inherent in an organized police, at least for the politically dominant upper classes."[50]

Peel faced stiff opposition to his version of an organized police force. However, events during the 1820s convinced Parliament and other powerful leaders that armed intervention of the military was most damaging. In essence, such intervention undermined the legitimacy of Parliament and the existing police. The death of eleven and wounding of more than five-hundred citizens peacefully attending a lecture, labeled a "mob" by local magistrates, convinced the majority that some alternative was necessary. The Metropolitan Police Act passed in 1829 without serious opposition.

Peel took his case for legitimating his police force to the people, and he argued that the police would serve the interests of all the people. He stressed that the new role of the police would be the prevention of crime through increased patrols. This claim rested on the premise that more police would automatically result in less crime. The police would have a civilian character because members would be recruited from the ranks of the working class, and the police would be service oriented.[51] The beat policeman came from the working or peasant classes in the nineteenth century, and although he aspired to respectable status, his job was, by and large, unskilled. The pay was less than a respectable working-class level, but it was regular. There were additional benefits as well. For instance, the uniform saved on clothing, and some officers received housing allowances. Although there was talk about a pension, it did not materialize until the twentieth century.[52] Another explanation for the passage of the Metropolitan Police Act has been offered by Alan Silver. He suggests that it shielded the rulers from the masses:

> If the power structure armed itself and fought a riot or a rebellious people, this [would create] more trouble and tension than the original problem. But, if one can have an independent police which fights the mob, then antagonism is directed toward the police, and not the power structure. A paid professional police force seems to separate "constitutional" authority from social and economic dominance.[53]

The recruitment of police from the lower classes provided an additional shield for the ruling class. Police brutality would simply be the brutalization of the lower classes by other members of the lower classes—the police. This strategy is in practice today in England and in the United States. As in time of war, the hands of the ruling class always appear clean.

Thus, with the enactment of the Metropolitan Police Act, control of policing shifted from the community (i.e., the constabulary system) to control by the state, which was under the control of the ruling class. The notion that the presence of the police in the streets would prevent crime was a critical break from the past. This shift paved the way for the police practice later called selective enforcement. The concern over the presence of mobs and radical protests and political parties helps explain the formation of the Metropolitan Police of London. The police could now serve more direct class functions, as well as more routine functions, by patrolling communities where the poorest and most oppressed people resided, thus reducing the potential for organizational activities associated with riots, rallies, and demonstrations. The police were now able to, as Chomsky says, keep the rabble in line.[54]

There is much evidence that the wealthy classes, on one hand, and the working classes and the poor, on the other, had different views of the police. Richardson notes that a "parliamentary committee of 1834 noted the possibility of abuses of power; still it found the Metropolitan police 'well calculated to maintain peace and order...' and further found that the police were 'one of the most valuable of modern institutions.'" In contrast, the poor and the working classes "considered the police more as an element of control than as a group of protectors. In a sense the police monitored the behavior of the dangerous classes so that the comfortable and satisfied could sleep more soundly at night or not be annoyed by the sight of public drunkenness."[55] Following a major corruption scandal within the detective department of the London Metropolitan Police in 1877, the English middle class became suspicious of police who wore plain clothes and who, in the eyes of the middle class, spent too much time posing as political spies.[56] Nevertheless, the London Metropolitan Police emerged as an institution and served as a model for future police institutions in America.

Several characteristics of the London Metropolitan Police stand out. First, there was a striking attempt to make policing strong enough to maintain order but restrained in its response to political conflict. To accomplish this goal, the London police was founded on military principles, observed strict rules of conduct, and used management practices that were well defined.[57] Second, police in London tended to refrain from personalization in their functions of policing. One method employed to accomplish this goal was to recruit officers from outside London—officers who had no personal ties to those whom they would be policing. Finally, in London, police represented the legal system. Of course, the ruling class remained in control of defining criminal behavior as well as making and implementing laws.

AMERICAN POLICING EMERGES

Four theories are useful to explain the development of police in America:[58]

1. **Disorder control theory.** This is the notion that police developed in response to the threat and actions of mob violence. To be certain, early America had mobs and mob violence. The issue at this juncture is the motivation for the emergence of the mob and its subsequent violence. Typically, the motivation was oppression by the ruling class.
2. **Crime control theory.** This is the notion that a significant increase in criminal activity preceded the development of significant policing approaches. This theory presupposes a climate of fear within the citizenry over threats to the social order. Of course, as noted previously, in the absence of critical thinking, people often believe what they hear or read.
3. **Class control theory.** This is the notion that the growth of police and class-based economic exploitation occurred simultaneously. Subscribers to this theory also posit the idea that police were created as instruments of the ruling class for the primary purpose of controlling the so-called dangerous classes.
4. **Urban dispersion theory.** This is the notion that significant numbers of municipal police departments emerged in copycat fashion—other cities have police departments, so we want one.[59] In other words, elected government officials wanted a police department; there was no linkage to crime increases at all.

We concede that each theory has merit. Before you subscribe to one or more of these theories, you should consider the validity of the data supporting each theory.

We divide the emergence of American policing into four periods. The first period, the *colonial pre–post revolutionary* period, encompasses the earliest forms of American policing and extends into the first couple of decades of the nineteenth century. Policing during this time was largely a community affair. From about 1840 and extending into the early decades of the twentieth century we have the *political era,* in which policing took the initial steps toward becoming an institution and the linkage between politics and police was quite overt. During this era, police catered to the whims of those who held political office, and their allegiance changed with the changing of political party victory at the polls. The next period, the *professional model era,* lasted from about 1920 into the 1970s. This period is characterized by progressive training and educational programs for police officers and by innovative technology. The final period, the *early police state era,* begins in the early 1970s and continues to this day. This period has been characterized by increased surveillance and control over U.S. citizens. Many criminologists insist that since the 1970s *community policing* has been the watchword of American policing. We admit that an illusion of community policing exists, but we have found no substantial data to support the notion that any type of egalitarian partnership between police and members of the community exists. In fact, as we point out in Chapter 6, the concept of community policing is at best ambiguous. Police are reluctant to accept citizens as members of review boards, and when citizens are allowed to occupy seats on these boards, they have very little if any authority. In many law enforcement institutions, as in the military, nonsocial control agents and nonmembers of the ruling class are referred to as "civilians." Furthermore, the common belief among law enforcement agencies is that civilians *need* to be policed.

The Colonial and Pre–Post Revolution Period

English customs and traditions accompanied the early colonists to America, and English-style policing was among the traditional practices brought to American shores. Early colonial policing was founded on punishment rather than policemen. Public punishments—the ducking stool for people who gossiped, the stocks for petty thieves, the branding iron for thieves, the gallows for murderers—were shaming devices employed as both general and specific deterrents. Jails, often a social control tool associated with police, were used only for the temporary detention of suspects between arrest and trial, or those convicted between trial and sentencing. Jails were not places where punishment or rehabilitation occurred. Before the emergence of large cities and the mass immigration in the nineteenth century, policing was largely dependent on community consensus and citizens who were willing to assist in capturing criminals. In the seventeenth century, people living in the Puritan New England colonies were dependent on each other to watch their neighbors' behavior and report any and all deviations. Sin and crime were interchangeable concepts in Puritan New England.[60]

Policing in the South was somewhat different. The middle and southern colonies adopted policing methods quite similar to those found in the countryside of England where many of these early settlers originated. The county court was the dominant institution and was controlled by local elites, but people in the southern colonies, who often lived in the countryside, preferred resolving disputes themselves rather than relying on the court. This self-reliance probably stems from their origins in rural England.[61] African slaves in the South had no rights, were viewed as property, and were under constant surveillance by slave patrols and local militia.[62]

Constables were the first form of law enforcement in the American colonies. They were not professional police, nor were they always volunteers. They were elected or often drafted into service.[63] Policing was largely viewed as a community obligation. The night-watch system was used in the colonies and remained a component of American policing until the mid-1800s.

The first night-watch was organized in Boston in 1631. Citizens were expected to serve on the night-watch, although many prosperous citizens paid others to take their place. Failure to serve or to pay a surrogate could result in a stiff penalty, and in some cases, night-watch became a punishment at sentencing time.[64] New Amsterdam (New York), under Dutch control until 1664, instituted a paid night-watch in 1658. This night-watch was known as the *rattle watch* because of the wooden rattles shaken by its members to make their presence known. By 1700, Philadelphia had created its own night-watch, and in 1712 Boston adopted a paid (50 cents per night), full-time night-watch. Other cities followed these early examples (e.g., Cincinnati in 1803, New Orleans in 1804).[65] The silence of darkness was broken by night-watchmen calling out the hour and sometimes giving weather reports as they performed the task of watching for suspicious characters.

The role of the early American colonial constable centered on assisting citizens in resolving disputes, bringing alleged offenders to court, tax collection, collecting fines, and, in some instances, dispensing corporal punishment to the convicted. Private police became popular in the later colonial years, and from time-to-time the wealthy would "hire out" their private police to the community. Periodically, the militia was called upon to suppress disorders, common during the late eighteenth century. For the most part, however, policing in early America was at the community level, with some form of constabulary system dominant. During the colonial period constables were citizen police. They had no formal training; any training they received was probably limited to on-the-job training.[66]

Whereas the northeastern part of America relied on the constable/night-watch approach to law enforcement, the South relied on county sheriffs and slave patrols. The first sheriff appeared in Virginia in 1634. It is quite possible that this early reliance on the sheriff accounts for the power enjoyed by that office throughout the South today. Performing night-watch services and serving on the slave patrol was considered a community obligation. And, of course, whites were the only ones considered members of the community. Slave patrols had a dual purpose: to apprehend runaway slaves and to ensure that slaves did not revolt.

Regardless of the geographic region, early American policing was community centered, and participation in law enforcement was considered a community obligation for citizens. Certainly policing, in both North and South, was of particular benefit to wealthy landowners, businessmen, and others who had the most to lose amid an angry citizenry. While the level of citizen participation varied over space and time, it seems reasonable to assume that the legacy of this participation has been carried into various police auxiliary organizations today.

Politics and Police: The Political Era of Policing (1840–1920)

Between the 1830s and 1850s, many cities began to consider the constable/night-watch system inadequate in both organization and personnel. The population of New York City quintupled between 1790 and 1830. The arrival of new immigrants was the principal contributor to this population explosion. Many of these new immigrants found themselves forced to seek residence in New York's Five Points slum district. The exodus of the middle and upper classes from the older areas of New York provided little space to accommodate the vast number of arriving immigrants. New York's rapid urbanization was generated by economic and industrial developments that greatly benefited the owners; the workers were often left to the "mercy" of merciless owners. Rioting was just about the only viable means of protest available to poor and lower-class laborers. In 1834, New York experienced what was later called the "year of riots" (the Stonecutter's Riot, the Five Points Riot, the Chantham Street Riots, etc.).[67] By 1845 New York had one hundred marshals and a part-time watch of nearly a thousand men known as constables. These police officers were not paid a salary, but they received fees for recovering stolen property and for providing other police duties. During the night a group of volunteers served as watches.[68] According to most historians, the growth of population, increased immigration, the emergence of class divisions, and urban disorder were the major factors associated with the rise of an organized police force.[69]

Writing about New York, Richardson says that between 1830 and 1845 there was "a marked upsurge in crime, vice, and disorder" in addition to "rapid population growth with sharp increases in immigration, heightened distinctions between class, ethnic, and religious groups with consequent social strain, and a dizzy economic cycle of boom and bust." The city was no longer a "homogeneous community with a common culture and a shared system of values and moral standards."[70] Lane points out that Boston was plagued with some of the same changes: "Riot, one of the first problems recognized as beyond control, dramatized the need for force. The leaders of government were firmly set against popular violence as a means of political and social protest."[71] The leaders of the American Revolution had supported popular violence as a means of political and social protest. Apparently, those leaders, and the subsequent generation, did not apply the same logic to the protests of other oppressed groups. Historians such as Richardson and Lane fail to point this out.

Most police historians, including Richardson and Lane, argue that the changes noted above were inevitable and were a result of a breakdown in normal mechanisms of social control and the development of a full-time organized police force. Kalmanoff captures the conventional view of the rise of the American police:

> While the need for social control diminishes in the presence of increasing stability, rapid or extensive change will necessitate the development of new or improved mechanisms of maintaining social order. As in England, the Industrial Revolution in the United States was accompanied by profound and rapid social change. Traditional social patterns were disrupted by the migration from rural to urban areas, the inevitable competition for employment, and the pressures of urbanization. The problems of transition were aggravated by the extremely heterogeneous nature of American society and by the constant influx of new immigrants from Europe and other areas. Social dislocation, economic development, and a growing class structure in the United States demonstrated the inadequacy of the prevailing methods of social control, particularly in rapidly developing urban areas.[72]

This view accepts capitalism as a given and never considers that such a system (with its inevitable inequality) might be a cause of these problems. This point of view also accepts the popular consensus argument by suggesting that "the people" were actually supportive of the newly created police forces during the mid-nineteenth century.

In point of fact, however, the organization of a full-time organized police force was the result of actions promoted and taken by business and political leaders in large cities in the North. There was a great deal of opposition and resistance to organized policing by the working class: "Workers did not always accept such exploitive conditions (i.e., union busting, depressing wages and other practices on the part of employers) without resistance. This took its most organized form in labor strikes which directly threatened the high profit levels that employers maintained through the exploitation of workers."[73] For instance, in Lynn, Massachusetts, workers on several occasions organized to defeat shoe manufacturer mayors; in Lynn the largest issue was the strikebreaking activities of the police.[74]

Two studies challenge some of the conventional interpretations of the rise of the police. One study focused on the rise of the Buffalo police,[75] another on the Milwaukee police.[76] Although it is true that the rise in disorder required new methods of social control, it is equally true that the new methods were those perceived as necessary by people in power. Business leaders in the major cities of the North felt threatened by the specter of urban disorder, the presence of "mobs," and the "dangerous classes." Their attitude toward these groups, and toward the working class in general, was similar to white attitudes toward blacks in the South: they feared that these powerless groups would somehow seize power. The studies of Buffalo and Milwaukee present evidence that (1) the size of the police force increased more rapidly than both the rise in population and the increase in crime, (2) "crime" was primarily of the public-order variety (disorderly conduct, vagrancy, etc.), and (3) the police were created by and under the strict control of business and political leaders.

Lane and Richardson argued that in New York and Boston the rise of a full-time police force in the 1840s and 1850s followed a rapid increase in crime and disorder. There is, however, no evidence to support this claim. In fact, there is no evidence to support the notion that there was any more crime and disorder during this period than in earlier periods. The period preceding the American Revolution and the decades that immediately followed it witnessed a great deal of crime and disorder (e.g., Shays's Rebellion). Moreover, the population of eastern cities was not as homogeneous prior to the 1840s as Lane and Richardson suggest. Rather, these cities were quite heterogeneous, having a well-defined class structure, numerous ethnic groups, and slums.[77] Thus, Lane's and Richardson's view, that the police arose because of increasing heterogeneity, the growth of slums, and increasing crime and disorder lacks credibility. In Boston as well as in Buffalo, the rise in police personnel did not correspond to a rise in crime.[78]

The importance of urban disorder, particularly that which is typically referred to as "rioting," is contained in the conventional analysis of the rise of police. Strikes and disgruntled workers, however, were not the only motivations for riots. Throughout the 1830s and 1840s there were many riots in large cities such as Philadelphia, Baltimore, New York, and St. Louis. "Some of these were race riots: vicious mobs ran wild in the black sections of town. Savage anti-Catholic mobs burned the Ursuline Convent near Boston in 1834."[79] It is, however, quite likely that many of these instances were linked to conflict between competing groups (the poor, the unemployed, new immigrants, ethnic groups, racial groups, etc.), insecurity, and the horrible conditions of city life, to the creation of which the wealthy played a significant role. Riots were matters of concern during the American Revolution and in the South especially before the Civil War. They were of particular interest to those who held positions of economic and political power: during the Revolution, the British; in the North, manufacturers; in the South, white plantation owners.

Throughout the nineteenth century there was widespread political turmoil and resistance as workers sought to gain some form of democratic control of their lives, especially in the workplace. Capitalist owners used various techniques to keep workers in line, such as hiring scabs to fill the jobs of striking workers, token advancement of leaders, and the use of private and public police forces. In many instances, the police were simply tools used by the owners to break up strikes and arrest workers on vague charges such as disorderly conduct. Such arrests increased during periods of rioting and declined sharply after the turmoil ceased.

We have mentioned the connection between police and politics. In many large cities during the mid-1800s, party politics played a significant role in policing. The Republican Party, being partial to business, opted for more state control over police. The Democratic Party was partial to local control. State control meant control by large business; local control translated to control by local businesses. In New York, Cleveland, Detroit, and several other large cities during the mid-1800s the state took control of the police. However, when the Democrats regained power, the police were once again under local control.[80] But whether under Republican Party or Democrat Party "rule," the common people never had much to say or played an active role in the control of police (in this respect, not much has changed).

Before the close of the nineteenth century nearly every large city in America had a police force. Rural areas had a sheriff as the chief law enforcement official. Federal marshals were the mainstays of law enforcement in the territories in the West. The discovery of gold in California prompted more than 100,000 people to migrate to California by 1850, and the number exceeded 300,000 by 1851. As the population of the West rapidly expanded, there was a need to provide supplies, and security was deemed necessary for the timely delivery of supplies. The U.S. Army provided some security, particularly after the Civil War, but much of their time was devoted to breaking treaties with Native Americans and displacing them into regions that most whites did not, at the time, want.[81] Private police began to flourish in the mid-1800s. Wells Fargo became one of the largest private security companies. With the western migration also came the railroad, which solicited the service of private police organizations like the Pinkerton detective agency.[82] **Pinkertons**—employees of the agency—were also deeply involved in strikebreaking during the late 1800s. Contracted by mine owners in Pennsylvania, the Pinkertons infiltrated the Molly Maguires, an organization of coal miners said by the mine owners to have committed a number of "terrorist activities." The testimony of an undercover Pinkerton agent resulted in the hanging of nineteen men later found to be innocent. Their skills at union organizing—not "terrorism"—had resulted in their deaths.[83]

Private security firms were not always as "colorful" as the Pinkerton agency, and many were actually innovative in their efforts to prevent crime. Edwin Holmes was responsible for the first burglar alarm in 1858, and Washington Perry Brink began a truck package-delivery service in Chicago in 1859. Brink eventually expanded his business to provide security for payroll deliveries. Following an episode where two employees were gunned down in 1917, Brink developed the armored car.[84] By the close of the nineteenth century, private security firms—or private police—had carved out a formidable niche for themselves politically, socially, and, of course, economically.

For the police, the early years of the twentieth century proved disastrous for public relations. Race riots seemed beyond control. Such riots had occurred before the twentieth century. For example, in 1866 during a race riot in Memphis, forty-six African Americans were murdered, five African American women were raped, twelve churches and four schools were burned. In 1908, several thousand whites assaulted African American neighborhoods in Springfield, Illinois. Homes were burned, stores were looted, and two elderly African Americans were mutilated and lynched. The police did nothing. In 1917, after African Americans had been hired in a factory holding government contracts, several thousand whites stabbed, clubbed, and hanged dozens of African Americans in East Saint Louis. More than 6,000 African Americans were driven from their homes. The police did nothing. In 1918, sixty-four lynchings were attributed to Ku Klux Klan activities. That number increased to eighty-three in 1919, and there were race riots in Washington, D.C., Arkansas, Tennessee, and Texas.

The year 1919 was also the year of the Chicago race riot. Rapid population increases in South Chicago (the African American population increased from 44,000 in 1910 to nearly 110,000 in 1920), coupled with discriminatory hiring practices, unemployment, and horrible poverty, set the stage. The murder of a young African American swimming in a "whites only" area of Lake Michigan and the refusal of police to arrest the killers sparked the riot. Chicago was under siege for thirteen days, in spite of efforts by the state militia to control the angry mobs. At the end of the thirteen-day ordeal twenty-three African Americans and fifteen whites were dead, over five hundred people were injured, and more than a thousand African American families were homeless. United States president Woodrow Wilson pointed the finger at whites and accused them of being the aggressors. Again, the police did nothing. Some believed that it was time to rethink American policing.

The Professional Model Era (1920 to the 1970s)

Since shortly after the turn of the twentieth century, professional status had been a goal within much of the institution of policing in America. The argument for professional status was based on changes in the administrative and operational functions of police—recruitment, training, and the adoption and implementation of scientific crime-detection and crime-fighting technology. Newly recruitment practices placed more emphasis on education and psychological evaluations. Training was instituted throughout most of American policing, and national training academies (e.g., the FBI National Academy) emerged. Scientific technology was integrated into American policing: mobile methods of patrolling, radio communications, modernized fingerprint identification methodologies, and more modern methods of record-keeping. American policing had charted a course that would accommodate the acquisition and use of massive amounts of high-tech equipment in the 1980s and 1990s.

EARLY LEADERS IN MODERN AMERICAN POLICING

Many individuals associated with policing contributed significantly to law enforcement. Three, however, stand out, and their influence and impact on modern American policing are unchallenged. They are August Vollmer, Orlando Winfield Wilson, and J. Edgar Hoover. Although their personalities, philosophies, and approaches to modernizing American policing differed, their fingerprints are present on many aspects of American policing today. Each had a profound effect on the direction of law enforcement.

August Vollmer

August Vollmer has been called the father of modern American policing. Most changes that occurred in policing during the late 1800s and early 1900s were influenced by the activities of special-interest groups, politicians, and the like. Vollmer was among the first to initiate change from within the institution of policing. The changes that he launched occurred during a period when policing was mired in external politics and strongly affiliated with political figures.

Berkeley, California, represents one geographic location where the seeds for professional status recognition for modern American policing were sown. As the chief of police in Berkeley, California, from 1905 through 1932, Vollmer had an insider's knowledge of policing. Following the policing model established by Sir Robert Peel in London, Vollmer began the first American police training school in 1909. His officers patrolled first on bicycles, then on motorcycles in 1911, and then in cruisers with radios by 1913. To Vollmer's credit, the Berkeley police force was completely mobile by 1920. The development of the police call box and the creation of one of the first fingerprinting bureaus in the United States are additional accomplishments including Vollmer's interest in professionalizing American policing.

Central to Vollmer's philosophy on policing was the notion that police should be the vanguard for the socialization of America's youth. Police officers, he argued, should also take a more active part in casework for social agencies. He was adamantly opposed to unorthodox behavior by police officers. As a member of the Wickersham Commission, a commission formed to investigate police misconduct, Vollmer helped to expose brutality and other unconstitutional practices police officers had engaged in.[85] Vollmer promoted higher education for his own officers in Berkeley, and he organized the first college-level police course at the University of California at Berkeley. He was the author of the 1931 Wickersham Commission report on police administration. Vollmer's influence on policing produced a reform agenda for professionalizing in policing. The agenda included

1. Elimination of political influence
2. Appointment of qualified chief executives
3. Establishment of a mission of nonpartisan public service
4. Raising personnel standards
5. Introduction of the principles of scientific management
6. Emphasis on military-style discipline
7. Development of specialized units[86]

Law enforcement and political critics of Vollmer viewed many of these goals as overly idealistic and impractical. Nevertheless, many of Vollmer's students went on to become reform chiefs of police.

A new generation of police executives emerged in the 1930s, and many set out to implement the reform agenda established by Vollmer.[87] This new generation of police executives demonstrated willingness to confront issues associated with citizen abuse by police officers, and they instituted formal internal affairs units intended to investigate citizen reports of police abuse.[88] One of Vollmer's students, Orlando Winfield Wilson, was a leader among the reform police executives.

Orlando Winfield Wilson

Orlando Winfield Wilson was a police officer under Vollmer's command for almost four years and received his degree from the University of California at Berkeley. His first position as chief of police was in Fullerton, California. Community leaders there, however, believed that his reform methods were too "radical," and he was fired after one year. Wilson then became chief of police in Wichita, Kansas. Wilson's ideas about accountability and ethics really were radical. After several years of implementing progressive policing ideas in Wichita, he was again fired. Wilson returned to California and took a position teaching in the School of Criminology at the University of California at Berkeley.

Wilson was especially interested in the efficiency of police management. He strived to reduce response time (the time between the report of a crime and the time of arrival by law enforcement) and to maximize police coverage—to place police officers in vehicles and offer more geographic coverage based on a formula taking into account, among other factors, crime reports in each sector beat (designated area of operation).[89] Wilson also was an advocate for police accountability, particularly as it applied to the abuse of power.[90] In 1960, Wilson left the University of California and accepted a position as police commissioner of Chicago. He remained in that position until his retirement in 1967. One year later, the Chicago police made international headlines with their brutal performance at the 1968 Democratic National Convention.

J. Edgar Hoover: Targeting "Subversives"

Born in Washington, D.C., on January 1, 1895, **John Edgar Hoover,** while working as a messenger boy at the Library of Congress, studied law at George Washington University. In many ways, Hoover was strikingly different from Vollmer and Wilson. Although their views on the importance of law enforcement efficiency were parallel, Hoover's methods and objectives were sharply different. All three, however, wanted professional status for the police (or perhaps for themselves?).

After graduation in 1917, Hoover secured employment with the Department of Justice. Alexander Palmer, the U.S. attorney general, recruited Hoover, and together, under the pretense of enforcing the Espionage Act (1917) and the Sedition Act (1918), the two initiated campaigns against anyone they considered radical or sympathetic with left-wing ideas. This meant anyone who supported organized labor, women's suffrage, and other progressive causes that could be labeled "communist conspiracies." Working as Palmer's special assistant, Hoover gathered evidence on suspected subversives, communists, and others with left-wing leanings. The purpose of the investigations was to legitimate the arrest and deportation of these "suspects." Clearly influenced by his work at the Library of Congress, Hoover created extensive card files on those who had leftist views. In a few years Hoover indexed more than 450,000 names and compiled detailed biographies on nearly 60,000 of the individuals whom he considered the most dangerous.

Many lawyers found themselves listed in Hoover's file because they were willing to represent radicals such as Eugene Debs, an organized-labor activist, and Emma Goldman, who promoted women's rights and birth control.[91] Clarence Darrow, a famous defense attorney, was placed in Hoover's file because of an article he wrote for the May 1936 issue of *Esquire* magazine. In this article, Darrow criticized the jury selection process and mentioned the futility of the state fighting crime while ignoring social and economic issues related to crime and criminal defendants. Hoover added Darrow to his list of unscrupulous criminal lawyers who "stimulate disrespect for law and influence crime conditions."[92]

Palmer and Hoover's attempts to purge people with left-wing views had a withering effect on the Communist Party of the United States. Membership declined from an estimated 80,000 to fewer than 6,000. Hoover was rewarded for his efforts by being appointed assistant director of the Bureau of Investigation. The function of the Bureau was to investigate violations of federal law and assist other law enforcement agencies throughout the United States. In 1924, Hoover was appointed director of the Bureau. As director, Hoover paid close attention to the organization and training of Bureau agents. The Bureau's power, however, was limited—agents were not allowed to carry weapons or authorized to arrest suspects. Hoover viewed this limitation of power with disdain and complained to Congress regularly. In 1935, Congress established the Federal Bureau of Investigation (FBI), and Hoover's agents were permitted to carry weapons and arrest citizens. In addition, Hoover was responsible for the creation and implementation of the FBI National Academy.[93]

Hoover wanted much more than armed agents, authority to make arrests, and a federal law enforcement academy. He wanted power and seemed willing to go to any extremes to gain it. Many people in the government feared Hoover. They knew that he collected information that could be used to humiliate and embarrass those whose political and moral views differed from his.

In the 1940s, Hoover became convinced that communists were plotting to overthrow the U.S. government. In 1947 the FBI—that is to say Hoover—opened a file regarding the petition of the Spanish artist Pablo Picasso for a visitor's visa. The FBI did not want to allow

Picasso, who was sympathetic to left-wing politics, into the United States even for a short visit. In a very short period of time, Picasso's FBI file had more than 180 pages.[94]

During the 1950s, Hoover played an instrumental role in the House Un-American Activities Committee hearings. The committee relied extensively on information provided by Hoover's FBI. Hoover insisted that the committee investigate the entertainment industry. He was sure that this industry was corrupting the minds and souls of American citizens. By the late 1950s, more than three-hundred artists had been blacklisted from the entertainment industry pending a hearing before the House Un-American Activities Committee. As early as 1945 President Harry S. Truman had complained that Hoover was exceeding his authority by collecting information on the sexual behavior of targeted individuals and using that information to blackmail powerful figures in government and in business. By the end of 1959 Hoover had 489 agents spying on "suspected" communists but only 4 agents assigned to investigate Mafia activities.[95]

The list of "suspects" in Hoover's FBI files seems endless: John Lennon, Albert Einstein, W. E. B. Du Bois, Amelia Earhart, Jacqueline Kennedy, Mickey Mantle, George Orwell, Eleanor Roosevelt, Jackie Robinson, John Steinbeck, and thousands upon thousands of others who may have criticized Hoover at some time or may have attended a meeting that Hoover and the FBI did not approve of or may have done any number of other things. Many of the people named in his files had connections to the Mafia, the Black Panther Party, the Students for a Democratic Society, and other organizations that were defined by the FBI as criminal, subversive, and so on. But individuals did not have to engage in criminal behavior to become part of Hoover's list. All that they needed to do was express views in opposition to Hoover's.

The civil rights movement and the Vietnam War were hallmarks of the 1960s. Hoover launched campaigns to undermine both the civil rights and the antiwar movements. He empowered agents to use paid informants to infiltrate civil rights and left-wing organizations. Hoover ordered Martin Luther King Jr. placed under FBI surveillance. More than 16,000 pages of King's FBI file have been released through the Freedom of Information Act, in comparison with 2,397 pages on Al Capone and 588 pages on the Ku Klux Klan. It is important to recognize that the purpose of the Freedom of Information Act, at least in part, is to allow disclosure to the public of the activities of the FBI and other federal law enforcement agencies. It is equally important to understand that the release of FBI records for public scrutiny is subject to FBI approval. We reviewed thousands of pages of released documents and discovered hundreds of "blackened out" pages. The truth about the behavior of the FBI and other agencies, in all probability, lies behind those lines concealed by Magic Markers.[96]

Hoover's greatest accomplishments and contributions to modern American law enforcement were his control and manipulation of politics/politicians and media/journalists. His influence in the manipulation of political figures is linked to his success at blackmailing politicians who disagreed with him. His influence over the media and journalists had similarly chilling effects. When Ray Tucker wrote an article for *Collier's* magazine about Hoover's homosexuality, various aspects of Tucker's private life were leaked to the media. This most certainly made other journalists think twice before criticizing Hoover.[97]

Another skill perfected by Hoover was the manipulation of public opinion. For example, Hoover argued that the value of the stolen property recovered by the FBI was greater than the agency's entire budget. Hoover often "legitimated" this claim by pointing to the FBI's role in recovering stolen vehicles. He conveniently neglected to mention that local police recover the vast majority of stolen vehicles and that most stolen vehicles are used for joyriding and eventually are returned to their owners. (The FBI would be able to draw a valid comparison between its budget and the value of recovered stolen vehicles only if all of the recovered stolen vehicles became property of the federal government.)[98]

There was an obsessive side to Hoover's FBI during the 1960s. In 1956, Richard Berry, an African American musician from Los Angeles, wrote and recorded the song "Louie Louie." Berry's recording sold about 40,000 copies. In 1963, the Kingsmen made another recording of "Louie Louie" with lead singer Jack Ely controlling the vocals. Ely, who was suffering from fatigue and having problems with the braces on his teeth, slurred the lyrics. Many of the lyrics were incomprehensible. Parents and clergymen criticized the Kingsmen's new release. "J. Edgar Hoover's FBI soon took up the case. Following more than two years of an investigation that employed the latest in audio technology, the bureau concluded that the lyrics were 'unintelligible at any speed.' Remarkably, no agent ever questioned Jack Ely."[99]

Subsequent investigations of the FBI's activities against the Black Panther Party revealed evidence of the agency engaging in burglary, illegal wiretapping, illegal mail tampering, and conspiracy to murder (as in the case of Fred Hampton, a Black Panther leader in Chicago, and one of the pioneers of the Panthers' breakfast program).[100] In a 1976 subcommittee hearing, the FBI admitted to more than ninety false allegations (Hoover had died in 1972). Yet, today, in the aftermath of investigations and findings of flagrant law enforcement abuses under the leadership of J. Edgar Hoover, his name remains on FBI headquarters in Washington, D.C. Perhaps changing the name would cost too much money. Or perhaps nothing has really changed.

Clandestine activities against American citizens have been an important part of the FBI's history. COINTELPRO, one of the FBI's most notorious programs, involved systematically eliminating the Black Panther Party, among other groups.

COINTELPRO: Neutralizing the Black Panthers and Other Radical Groups.   From 1956 through 1971 the FBI, under the close scrutiny and direction of J. Edgar Hoover, waged a war against African American groups striving for civil rights. Within the FBI, a program known as **COINTELPRO** (Counterintelligence Program) targeted many civil rights organizations and their leaders across America. Dr. Martin Luther King Jr. became a principal target. The FBI tapped his telephone conversations, threatened his life, committed blackmail to discredit him, and even sent him a letter suggesting that he commit suicide. A Senate report in 1976 points out that the FBI set out to destroy King.[101]

The FBI launched a major offensive against the Black Panther Party. By the mid-1960s, peace marches and peaceful demonstrations for civil rights clashed with the less patient, more confrontational strategies of organizations like the Black Panther Party (BPP). In 1965 Malcom X was assassinated. He had long spoken of strong resistance by blacks against white oppression. He had even advocated the creation of a separate black nation. Huey P. Newton, Bobby Seals, Eldridge Cleaver, and other leaders of the BPP embraced the words of Malcom X, and they began to promote the notion of self defense as means to attain civil rights. To a power structure that was well enmeshed in the practice of economic and racial exploitation and oppression, talk about self-defense by the lower classes, and particularly blacks, was frightening. In fact, when members of the BPP began arming themselves, within the parameters of California law, the power structure was more than frightened—they were terrified. Ronald Reagan, then governor of California, urged the state legislature to quickly change the law and "disarm" the BPP.[102]

The Civil Rights Act of 1967, prompted by inner-city riots, offered minimal protection for blacks. This act provided for stronger penalties for the violation of people's civil rights. However, despite those stronger penalties, it did not include the violence committed by social control agents like the military, the National Guard, and the police.[103] In fact, this act failed to address or offer a remedy to two of the major problems facing African Americans in the 1960s—abuse of power by law enforcement and police brutality.

As to the attack on the Black Panther Party, FBI files made available to the public through the Freedom of Information Act reveal that the file on the BPP in Winston-Salem, North Carolina, had accumulated nearly 2,900 pages. There were Black Panther Party affiliates in most cities across the United States during the 1960s and early 1970s. This suggests that tens of thousands of pages on the Black Panther Party, as a whole, may have been collected.

In 1970, Huey Newton, one of the leaders of the Black Panther Party, during a SECHABA (the National African Congress of South Africa—in exile) meeting, was asked about Black Panther Party resistance. Newton responded, "Repression breeds resistance."[104] Clearly, the continued FBI "investigation" of BPP activities such as the breakfast program, which provided nourishing meals for large numbers of African American children in the inner cities, could be construed as repression.

Antiwar organizations, such as Students for a Democratic Party (SDS), were also targeted by law enforcement.[105] Abbie Hoffman, a leader in the antiwar movement, had more than 13,000 pages in his FBI file released through the Freedom of Information Act. Blackmail, illegal surveillance tactics, arson, perjury, smear campaigns, and allegations of assassination were a few of the "repressive" methods used by the FBI and local law enforcement against civil rights and antiwar movement members.[106] The war waged against the BPP was perhaps the bloodiest of all against targeted dissident groups during the 1960s and early 1970s. In fact, someone reviewing the tactics employed by federal and local law enforcement against the BPP might conclude that those tactics were quite similar to the Nazis' tactics revealed in William Shirer's book *The Rise and Fall of the Third Reich*.[107] Consider these examples of state oppression and injustice in America noted by Howard Zinn:

1. In the 1967 riots in Detroit, three black teenagers were killed in the Algiers Motel. Three Detroit policemen and a black private guard were tried for this triple murder. The defense conceded, a UPI dispatch said, that the four men had shot two of the blacks. A jury exonerated them.
2. In Jackson, Mississippi, in the spring of 1970, on the campus of Jackson State College, a Negro college, police laid down a 28-second barrage of gunfire, using shotguns, rifles, and submachine guns. Four hundred bullets or pieces of buckshot struck the girls' dormitory and two black students were killed. A local grand jury found the attack "justified" and U.S. District Court Judge Harold Cox (a Kennedy appointee) declared that students who engage in civil disorders "must expect to be injured or killed."
3. In Boston in April 1970, a policeman shot and killed an unarmed black man, a patient in a ward in the Boston City Hospital, firing five shots after the black man snapped a towel at him. The chief judge of the municipal court of Boston exonerated the policeman.
4. In April 1970, a federal jury in Boston found a patrolman had used "excessive force" against two black soldiers from Fort Devens, and one of them required twelve stitches in his scalp; the judge awarded the servicemen $3 in damages.[108]

Shirer offers many similar examples of state abuse and oppression in Germany throughout the 1930s and early 1940s.[109] In the early 1970s the Vietnam War ended, the leadership of the BPP was neutralized (killed or imprisoned with the efforts of American law enforcement), and Watergate became an icon in American politics. "Order" had been restored. At least that is what people wanted to believe, so they believed it.

The Whole World Is Watching

In the summer of 1968, the Vietnam War continued, the civil rights movement seemed stalled, and President Lyndon Johnson's Great Society program was floundering. Civil rights activists, university students, antiwar demonstrators, and others disgruntled with the direction in which policy makers were taking America took to the streets in Chicago to protest racial segregation and discrimination, the Vietnam War, and other social injustices at home and abroad. The demonstrators knew they would have a worldwide audience because the Democratic Party was holding its national convention in Chicago to nominate a presidential candidate. Tensions were high because the convention was being held in the aftermath of the Martin Luther King and Robert Kennedy assassinations earlier in 1968. For several days the demonstrators held rallies in the parks, and marched in the streets. Some groups obtained permits to march and hold rallies in strategic locations. Groups unable to obtain permits nevertheless held their rallies and marched in the streets. Most of the demonstrators wanted to exercise their constitutional right to protest government policies they believed were wrong.

After several days of demonstrations, Mayor Richard Daly and his law enforcement apparatus had had enough. Chicago police officers engaged in numerous incidents of kicking and clubbing unarmed demonstrators lying on the ground trying to protect themselves from the blows. Demonstrators, hands cuffed behind their backs, were beaten as police officers forced them into waiting police vans to take them to jail. Tear gas was frequently used. Televised images of these events were projected around the world. Many of the demonstrators chanted "The whole world is watching!" Indeed, the whole world *was* watching—and did not like what it was witnessing.

On television screens at home and abroad people watched in horror as America demonstrated how its social control apparatus brutalized citizens as they exercised their constitutional right to assemble peacefully and voice their objections to government policies and practices. Contrary to official accounts, the demonstrations were peaceful. It was provocation by the Chicago Police Department that made them appear violent. Most of the violence was attributed to acts of police brutality. For many, the true nature of American "democracy" had been revealed. There were some in Europe who remembered that Hitler's brown-shirt thugs, S.S. troops, and Gestapo had brutalized and terrorized Europeans in a similar manner some thirty years earlier.

Law enforcement learned a lesson from events at the 1968 Democratic National Convention in Chicago: if citizens are going to be brutalized, it must be done outside the view of television cameras. With isolated exceptions, such as the beating of Rodney King, the lesson was learned well. In 1992, South Central Los Angeles erupted in reaction to the "Simi Valley" verdict in which an all-white jury exonerated police officers involved in the Rodney King beating (and once again abuse of power and inexcusable brutality by the police were "endorsed" by the courts). The police backed away and did nothing, allowing people to pillage and burn at will. Of course, neither brutalization of citizens nor ignoring violent acts provided strong support for the notion of police professionalism.

THE SUPREME COURT AND AMERICAN POLICING: POLICING THE POLICE

Throughout the 1960s the U.S. Supreme Court rendered a series of decisions that addressed constitutional issues related to American policing. These decisions often placed the U.S. Supreme Court at odds with American law enforcement. We focus here on three that have had the most impact on American policing.

Mapp v. Ohio

Mapp v. Ohio (1961) dealt with the issue of *search* and *seizure*. Three Cleveland police officers arrived at Miss Darlee Mapp's home on May 23, 1957. Their purpose was to conduct a search of the premises for a person wanted in connection with a recent bombing. They also claimed that they had information indicating that a substantial amount of policy paraphernalia concerning a numbers game was stored in the home. Following a demand by police to open the door, Miss Mapp immediately called her attorney, who instructed her to ask the police for a search warrant. The police did not have a search warrant, and the officers withdrew; however, they did place the residence under surveillance after notifying headquarters. Several hours later, four additional officers arrived at the scene. When Mapp failed to respond immediately to another knock on the door by police, the door was forcibly opened and the police gained entrance to the residence. Mapp again asked to see a warrant. One officer held up a piece of paper, stating that it was a warrant. She grabbed the paper to look at it, and officers forcibly took the piece of paper away from her and placed her in handcuffs. In court, a search warrant was never produced, nor was any explanation offered as to why a search warrant was not entered as prosecutorial evidence. *Perhaps there never was a search warrant.*

Shortly after the police entered the premises, Mapp's attorney arrived. He was not allowed to enter the house, nor was he allowed to see his client. In the basement of the two-story dwelling, after a widespread search, the police found some contraband materials that were considered obscene under Ohio's Revised Statutes. The police failed to find anyone hiding in the house or any policy paraphernalia. Mapp was convicted on the basis of the obscene material found in the basement.

The U.S. Supreme Court overturned Mapp's conviction and in the process applied the Fourth Amendment exclusionary rule to the state courts through the Fourteenth Amendment. In essence, this ruling suggests that the suspect may be freed because of mistakes made by law enforcement. Justice Benjamin Cardozo recognized the impact of such a mistake by state officials but also noted that the imperative of judicial integrity must also be a consideration. If the guilty are set free, it is the law that sets them free. In addition, he contended, nothing can destroy a government more quickly than its failure to observe its own laws or disregarding the charter of its own existence. Therefore, and at the heart of the exclusionary rule, illegally obtained evidence cannot be used against a defendant.[110]

The *Escobedo, Gideon,* and *Miranda* Decisions

In *Escobedo v. Illinois* (1964), the Supreme Court recognized the right to counsel by suspects during police interrogation. This ruling reinforced the Court's 1963 ruling in **Gideon v. Wainwright** that a defendant charged with a crime has a fundamental right to an attorney.[111] In anticipation of criticism of this ruling from law enforcement, Justice Arthur Goldberg stated, "If the exercise of constitutional rights will thwart the effectiveness of a system of law enforcement, then there is something very wrong with that system."[112] In 1966 the U.S. Supreme Court rendered a landmark decision that reinforced its earlier ruling in the *Escobedo* case. In **Miranda v. Arizona,** the Court argued that suspects held in custody cannot be interrogated before they are warned of their rights to remain silent and to have an attorney present during questioning.[113]

American police desperately objected to the U.S. Supreme Court decisions in *Mapp v. Ohio* (1961), *Escobedo v. Illinois* (1964), and *Miranda v. Arizona* (1966). These decisions touched on issues related to evidence (searching for and seizing evidence) and on the treatment of suspects at the start of the criminal investigation process (conducting interrogations). As Justice Goldberg anticipated, police objected to these rulings. American law enforcement took the position that these rulings would hinder their battle against crime.

Hollywood came to the aid of law enforcement in the 1970s and reflected police dissatisfaction with these rulings in, among many other "cop hero" movies, the "Dirty Harry" films, starring Clint Eastwood. Eastwood portrayed a San Francisco detective who was constantly pitted against the dregs of San Francisco society. In most cases, Eastwood projected the notion that the only way to protect innocent victims was to violate the constitutional rights of suspects. Much of the American audience applauded—the films were box-office hits.

In reality, these 1960s U.S. Supreme Court decisions did more to advance the American policing crusade for professional status than the policies and practices introduced by law enforcement agencies themselves. Police were required to substantiate information and to be specific about what they were looking for when requesting a search warrant. Deceit and unconstitutional law enforcement practices of earlier years might indeed turn the suspect free. The right to have an attorney present undoubtedly had an impact on "station-house" interrogations—it is more difficult to use excessive force on a suspect when his or her attorney is present. The suspect, according to the U.S. Supreme Court, must now be treated as a human being with constitutional rights. And through the *Miranda* ruling, law enforcement was required to inform a suspect of his or her rights. However, the pendulum was about to shift.

The Erosion of Constitutional Rights

In 1984 the U.S. Supreme Court decision in *United States v. Leon* weakened the Court's earlier decision in *Mapp v. Ohio*. Throughout the 1970s the U.S. Supreme Court began its journey down the road to erode the *exclusionary rule*. In 1974, in *United States v. Calandra*, the Court ruled that illegally obtained evidence could be used to obtain grand jury indictments.[114] The exclusionary rule was weakened further in *Michigan v. DeFillippo* (1979), when the Court ruled that evidence obtained during a lawful arrest could be admitted even though the dynamics surrounding the arrest are deemed unconstitutional.[115] The real benefit to law enforcement did not occur until 1984, when, in United *States v. Leon,* the Court held that evidence obtained on the basis of a search warrant that is later held to be invalid may be admitted into evidence at trial if the law enforcement official who conducted the search relied on the warrant in "*good faith.*"[116] The problem was, Who was going to make a determination on what constituted good faith? The criminal justice system relied on judges appointed by conservative Republican presidents, Nixon and Reagan, to make that determination.

The U.S. Supreme Court has remained consistent with its rulings in *Escobedo v. Illinois* (1964) and *Gideon v. Wainwright* (1963) concerning the Sixth Amendment right to an attorney for criminal defendants. But more is at stake than simply having right to counsel and the state's compliance with that right. What about quality? As Cole points out, "Former President Ronald Reagan…spent half a million dollars on legal advice to respond to an investigation of his activities in connection with the Iran Contra affair."[117] Few defendants can afford *that* kind of counsel. In addition, and this is particularly true in capital offense cases, many states do not provide attorneys during the appeal process. Discussing the Supreme Court's 1970s and 1980s rulings undermining the rights afforded in *Gideon,* Cole notes,

> First, the Court denied the right to counsel when many defendants most needed it—before they were indicted, but after the state had singled them out for investigation and arrest. Second, the Court retreated from the equality principle reflected in *Griffin* and *Douglas* [two earlier decisions] holding that the state need not provide appointed counsel for most appeals. Third…the Court adopted an "effective assistance of counsel" standard so low that as a practical matter states need not insure that defendants are appointed competent attorneys.[118]

Police are aware of the differences in the quality of counsel. They are also aware that certain behaviors that would raise doubt in an appellate court may pass quite easily in a local court. The knowledge that the state does not necessarily have to provide counsel for appeals facilitates the potential to introduce questionable evidence and misleading statements concerning probable cause.

The U.S. Supreme Court has not yet reversed its decision in *Miranda v. Arizona* (1966). In 2000, in **United States v. Dickerson,** the issue of *Miranda* rights was raised, and justices Antonin Scalia and Clarence Thomas voted to reverse *Miranda*. Given the conservative trend in recent appointments to the Court, sufficient votes for overturning *Miranda* likely to be present in a few years. The problem with overturning *Miranda* is, perhaps, political. Most people who watch television or go to the movies may not be aware of other rights, but they know they have *Miranda* rights. It might be a political disaster for the Court to take away the one set of rights that most people know they have. Besides, even though most people are aware of their *Miranda* rights, they frequently waive their rights and tell the police everything they want to know.[119]

THE EARLY POLICE STATE ERA

In the 1970s an investigation of police corruption in New York City began. The Knapp Commission found corruption to be widespread in this city. Soon it was discovered that such corruption was spread all across the country. The fallout of the Knapp Commission report raised serious questions about the course charted by American police in its struggle for professional status. Once again, as in the final years of the political era, some believed that it was time to rethink American policing. Throughout the 1970s and early 1980s American police chose a course that would lead them toward the status of "enforcers of the police state." Attempts were made to continue the pursuit of professional status, but eventually the police proclaimed themselves professionals.

As the police state emerged, four things became clear. First, external funding had to be made available to assist police agencies to turn the institution of policing into something less transparent. Education and specialized training, and research influenced by the police, were some of the tools used to accomplish this task. Second, police operations needed at least the illusion of a science-through-research stamp, which would provide the legitimacy necessary to carry out those operations. The police subculture, that unique social phenomenon which facilitates the "us versus them" mind-set, attempted to legitimate itself through the adoption of police unions, which found homes throughout American policing in the 1970s. The illusion of police accountability came into being. One of the best ways to sell the police state to the public is to convince people that law enforcement will actively and diligently police the police. Of course, the courts would also assist in accountability; as already noted, by the early 1970s the U.S. Supreme Court was already preparing the groundwork for that judicial role.

Third, every successful police state must equip its enforcement apparatus with the latest, most technologically advanced police gadgets. Fourth, it was imperative that this "package" be accepted by the general public without significant citizen objection. Even totalitarian regimes understand that persuasion is the preferred means to rule. It is less expensive than force and more pleasing to those who control the state from behind the scenes. The distinction between totalitarian regimes and democratic societies seems to lie in the fact that democratic regimes are much less willing to resort to force than their totalitarian counterparts.[120]

Unions as a Means to Protect Law Enforcement from the Courts

In the aftermath of U.S. Supreme Court decisions in the 1960s, particularly those that pertained to the Fourth Amendment, American law enforcement officers felt a need for protection. Protection would not be such an issue if police were operating within the parameters of the U.S. Constitution. Protection was, however, necessary if police continued to operate outside the parameters of the Constitution. As Walker noted, "Police officers were angry and alienated over Supreme Court rulings, criticism by civil rights groups, poor salaries and benefits, and inept management practices."[121] As a result of the unionization of American law enforcement, police received higher pay, representation in disciplinary hearings, and protection against innovative strategies and efforts to improve police–community relations.[122] The arguments in favor of unions, however, seem at odds with the arguments in favor of professionalism.[123]

Of course, the solution to the professional status recognition problem proved to be rather simple: call yourself a professional, and if you do this long enough, the public will simply accept the notion. The notion that police felt alienated by the U.S. Supreme Court decisions is a bit murky. After all, police are sworn to uphold the law. The U.S. Constitution is the foundation for American law. Why would law enforcement officials feel alienated from that of which they are a part?

Police Accountability—Selling It to the Public

Police accountability is an interesting, multidimensional concept. Accountability suggests that police must explain or rationalize their actions. A police officer who shoots and kills an unarmed person has to explain why. The police officer may face department charges, criminal charges, and civil charges. On the surface, this seems to meet the necessary criteria for police accountability. The problem is that juries and judges tend to give the testimony of police officers greater credibility than the testimony of citizens, the complainant (in civil action), and suspects. Thus, the police seem to have a built-in advantage in the courts.[124]

Another dimension of law enforcement accountability rests with production versus cost. What are police doing with all of that money provided by American taxpayers? In most instances, the public allows the police to keep *production records,* and by and large, the public seems willing to accept the "executive summaries" provided by management. This differs significantly from the management–stockholder arrangement common to the corporate world. Law enforcement has received gargantuan funding increases while demonstrating little, if any, *production gains.*

High-Tech Advancements: New Toys for the Boys

The benefits of high-tech equipment appear endless for police.[125] The polygraph machine, introduced in the 1930s, undoubtedly amazed law enforcement. Today, there are so many new technologically advanced pieces of equipment available to police that we hardly hear about the polygraph machine, which has, by the way, been improved significantly. Microwave surveillance equipment, Bradley military vehicles, armored personnel carries, helicopters equipped with night-vision technology, state-of-the-art wiretapping devices, radar, automatic weapons, the latest computers—the list goes on. It is sometimes hard to understand why American law enforcement claims that it is outgunned by the "bad guys." To date, we have not heard about, or witnessed, any youth gangs with helicopters (with or without night-vision technology), nor have we seen youngsters driving around in armored personnel carriers. And we cannot forget about the change in styles of uniforms. Many agencies within law enforcement have adopted elite military attire and project a very scary image. Yet what would one expect in a society that is transforming into a police state?

Ironically, despite all this new technology, the percentage of crimes "cleared by an arrest" has gradually declined over the past forty years. The new technology has not improved the chances of catching criminals. Nor has it made citizens feel any safer from crime.

SUMMARY

The historical course of policing has been anything but smooth. Policing has been plagued with episodes of graphic brutality, extensive corruption, and vivid campaigns that depreciate the rights of citizens. These episodes have been interrupted by reform movements, political and judicial activism, and other crusade-like attempts to control the image of police. But one must recognize that the general goal and purpose of police is social control. History prohibits any other conclusion. History reminds us of Augustus reviewing his legions of *vigiles* in Rome or sitting in some elaborately constructed Roman building as he placed his official seal on a document ordering his police to control unruly slaves. We are also reminded of the energy expended by sheriffs in England who terrorized British peasants as they clandestinely searched for food in a forest owned by a lord in order to feed their family. In this case, we can select a book by Howard Pyle and be taken back to the days of the fictional character Robin Hood, as he and his merry band stole from the rich to give to the poor.[126] History reminds us of the bullies who filled the ranks of the Bow Street Runners who brutalized members of the "dangerous classes."

Closer to home, history reminds us of the American South and the use of fire hoses and German shepherd dogs by police against civil rights marchers in Birmingham, Selma, and countless other places. History also requires that we look back at the Chicago Police Department in 1968, as officers clubbed unarmed demonstrators in the streets and in front of television news cameras. We are also reminded of the Hoover era at the FBI, when Americans were subjected to unconscionable tactics. Countless Americans were subjected to violations of the Bill of Rights by Hoover's FBI. Certainly most have viewed the

Rodney King film, and the behavior of the Los Angeles Police Department during the 1992 riots in South Central. Also in 1992, in Detroit, several officers beat Malice Green to death with a long-handled flashlight as he lay pinned beneath the steering wheel of a car while neighbors looked on. More recently, many Americans are familiar with the activities of the Rampart unit in Los Angeles. Bribery, framing innocent defendants, committing perjury in court, drug sales, and murder are but a few of the activities thus far revealed in the investigation of this American law enforcement component. Today, we worry about the implications of legislation enacted after the events of September 11, 2001. The "USA Act of 2001" provides law enforcement with legislative authority to do legally what Hoover and other law enforcement entities have had to conceal.[127] Even though the Hoover era has technically come to an end, many of the problems that originated during his time continue. We explore this new legislative authority in the next chapter.

KEY TERMS

arrest-overkill   116
August Vollmer   128
Bow Street Runners   120
class control theory   123
COINTELPRO   132
constable   119
constabulary system   119
crime-control theory   123
disorder control theory   123
Escobedo v. Illinois   135

Gideon v. Wainwright   135
hue and cry   119
hundred   119
J. Edgar Hoover   130
justices of the peace   119
Mapp v. Ohio   134
Metropolitan Police Act   121
Miranda v. Arizona   135
mutual pledge system   119
Orlando Winfield Wilson   129

Pinkertons   127
shire-reeve   119
shire   119
tythingman   118
tything   118
United States v. Dickerson   136
urban dispersion theory   123
vicecomes   119
vigiles   118

NOTES

1. Generated from the field notes of W. B. Brown, who conducted numerous "ride-alongs" throughout the Detroit Metropolitan region from 1992 to 1998.

2. Michalowski, *Order, Law and Crime,* p. 170.

3. Fromm, E. *Escape from freedom.* New York: Henry Holt, 1994.

4. Numerous studies can be cited (referenced in earlier chapters), but see especially Currie, *Crime and Punishment in America;* Greenberg, *Crime and Capitalism;* Chambliss, *Power, Politics and Crime.*

5. Staples, *The Culture of Surveillance.*

6. Ibid. If you are interested in the extent of the decline of individual rights, go to www.supremecourtus.gov/ where you will find thousands of pages of recent U.S. Supreme Court decisions related to criminal justice topics that impact individual rights.

7. Documented in Bayley, D. H. *Police for the Future.* New York: Oxford University Press, 1994; see also Walker, S. *Sense and Nonsense about Drugs and Crime* (5th ed.). Belmont, CA: Wadsworth, 2001.

8. For elaboration on this theme with regard to gangs, see Shelden, Tracy, and Brown, *Youth Gangs in American Society.*

9. This sort of "fashion statement" may have been on the minds of people in seventeenth-century Boston when they expressed their concern about police wearing police uniforms as that institution emerged in their city. See Friedman, L. M. *Crime and Punishment in American History.* New York: Basic Books, 1993.

10. "Outside Probe Sought in LAPD Scandal." *Los Angeles Times,* February 11, 2000; "LAPD Corruption Case Keeps Growing." *Washington Post,* February 13, 2000.

11. For further documentation, see Shelden, *Controlling the Dangerous Classes.*

12. McCorkle, R., and T. Miethe. "The Political and Organizational Response to Gangs: An Examination of a Moral Panic." *Justice Quarterly* 15: 41–64 (March, 1998); Brownstein, H. H. *The Rise and Fall of a Violent Crime Wave: Crack Cocaine and the Social Construction of a Crime Problem.* Guilderland, NY: Harrow and Heston, 1996, p. 22; F. Butterfield. "Possible Manipulation of Crime Data Worries Top Police." *New York Times,* August 3, 1998, as reported on the *New York Times* Web site http://www.nytimes.com

13. "Detroit's Crime Totals Still a Mystery." *Detroit Free Press,* May 4, 2001.

14. "Police Version of Killing Apparently Unraveling." *Los Angeles Times,* November 23, 1999.

15. Friedman, *Crime and Punishment in American History.*

16. Some of the following is an updated version of Shelden, *Controlling the Dangerous Classes,* ch. 2.

17. Emsley, C. *Policing and Its Context: 1750–1870: Themes in Comparative History.* London: Macmillan, 1983; Emsley, C. *Crime and Society in England: 1750–1900.* Essex: Longman, 1990; Emsley, C. *The English Police: A Political and Social History* (2nd ed.). London: Longman, 1996.

18. Berg, B. L. *Law Enforcement: An Introduction to Police in Society.* Boston: Allyn and Bacon, 1992, pp. 13–14.

19. Parenti, C. *Lockdown America: Police and Prisons in the Age of Crisis.* New York: Verso, 1999; Cole, *No Equal Justice;* Shelden and Brown, "The Crime Control Industry and the Management of the Surplus Population."

20. Chambliss and Seidman, *Law, Order and Power,* p. 34.

21. Bacon, S. "The Early Development of American Municipal Police." Unpublished Ph.D. diss., Yale University, 1939.

22. Reith, C. *The Blind Eye of History: A Study of the Origins of the Present Police Era.* Montclair, NJ: Patterson Smith, 1975, p. 179 (originally published 1952).

23. Ibid.

24. Baum, D. *Smoke and Mirrors: The War on Drugs and the Politics of Failure.* Boston: Little, Brown, 1996; Scott, J. C. *Seeing like a State.* New Haven: Yale University Press, 1998; Parenti, *Lockdown America;* Miller, *Drug Warriors and Their Prey.*

25. Reith, *The Blind Eye of History,* p. 226.

26. Kelly, R. M. "Increasing Community Influence over the Police." In A. W. Cohn and E. C. Viano (eds.), *Police Community Relations.* Philadelphia: Lippincott, 1975, p. 9.

27. Ibid.

28. Bayley, *Police for the Future.*

29. Kelly, "Increasing Community Influence over the Police," p. 6.

30. Wolff, H. J. *Roman Law: An Historical Introduction.* Norman: University of Oklahoma Press, 1951.

31. Reith, *The Blind Eye of History,* p. 26.

32. Ibid., p. 28.

33. Parks, E. L. "From Constabulary to Police Society: Implications for Social Control." In J. F. Galliher and J. L. McCartney (eds.), *Criminology: Power, Crime and Criminal Law.* Homewood, IL: Dorsey Press, 1977, p. 196.

34. Reith, *The Blind Eye of History,* p. 210.

35. Such a shift might be compared to modern-day urban renewal (occasionally called *negro removal*—see Hendrickson, W. W. (ed.). *Detroit Perspectives: Crossroads and Turning Points.* Detroit: Wayne State University Press, 1991), in which the poor and disadvantaged who live in urban settings are forcibly removed from their homes (or from the streets), often without any consideration of where they might go to live. Often urban renewal programs are initiated in order to accommodate the construction of some "social necessity" or "social improvement" (e.g., a new baseball stadium, a new jail), or to accommodate developers who speculate on the gentrification of older regions within the city. See Massey, D. S., and N. A. Denton. *American Apartheid: Segregation and the Making of the Underclass.* Cambridge, MA: Harvard University Press, 1993.

36. Trattner, W. L. *From Poor Law to Welfare State* (5th ed.). New York: Free Press, 1994.

37. Germann, A. C., F. D. Day, and R. J. Gallati. *Introduction to Law Enforcement and Criminal Justice.* Springfield, IL: Thomas, 1974; J. L. Lyman. "The Metropolitan Police Act of 1829." In G. F. Killinger and P. Cromwell (eds.), *Penology.* St. Paul, MN: West, 1973; Elmsley, *The English Police;* Elmsley, *Gendarmes and the State in Nineteenth-Century Europe.*

38. Reith, *The Blind Eye of History;* Lyman, 1975; Lee, W., and L. Melville. *A History of Police in England.* Montclair, NJ: Patterson Smith, 1971.

39. Elmsley, *The English Police.*

40. Lyman, "The Metropolitan Police Act of 1829"; Critchley, T. A. "The New Police in London, 1750–1830." Both in J. Skolnick and T. Gray (eds.), *Police in America.* Boston: Little, Brown, 1975; Elmsley, *The English Police;* Elmsley, *Gendarmes and the State in Nineteenth-Century Europe.*

41. Elmsley, *The English Police.*

42. Richardson, J. F. *Urban Police in the United States.* Port Washington, NY: Kennikat Press, 1974, p. 7.

43. Shelden, R. G. *Criminal Justice in America: A Sociological Approach.* Boston: Little Brown, 1982, pp. 91–92.

44. Lyman, "The Metropolitan Police Act of 1829," pp. 21–28; Elmsley, *The English Police.*

45. Recent research has documented the fact that the vast majority of those incarcerated in prisons and jails today were convicted of relatively minor offenses. This is not surprising, for the majority of those arrested are charged with minor offenses, including disturbing the peace and similar public-order crimes. See, for instance, Irwin, J., and J. Austin. *It's about Time: America's Incarceration Binge* (3rd ed.). Belmont, CA: Wadsworth, 2001; and Irwin, J. *The Jail: Managing the Underclass in American Society.* Berkeley: University of California Press, 1985.

46. Ignatieff, M. *A Just Measure of Pain.* New York: Pantheon, 1978, p. 179.

47. Ibid., p. 185.

48. Elmsley, *The English Police* and *Gendarmes and the State in Nineteenth-Century Europe.*

49. Quoted in Parks, "From Constabulary to Police Society," p. 199.

50. Richardson, *Urban Police in the United States,* p. 11.

51. Lyman, "The Metropolitan Police Act of 1829," pp. 33–36.

52. Elmsley, *Gendarmes and the State in Nineteenth-Century Europe.*

53. Silver, A. "The Demand for Order in Civil Society." In D. Bordua (ed.), *The Police: Six Sociological Essays.* New York: Wiley, 1967, pp. 11–12.

54. Chomsky, N. *Keeping the Rabble in Line.* Monroe, ME: Common Courage Press, 1994.

55. Richardson, *Urban Police in the United States,* p. 14.

56. Elmsley, *The English Police.*

57. Roberg, R. R., and J. Kuykendall. *Police and Society.* Belmont, CA: Wadsworth, 1993.

58. Ibid.

59. Mokkonen, E. *Police in Urban America.* Cambridge, MA: Harvard University Press, 1981.

60. Friedman, *Crime and Punishment in American History.*

61. Berg, *Law Enforcement.*

62. Friedman, *Crime and Punishment in American History.*

63. Michalowski, *Order, Law and Crime;* Friedman, *Crime and Punishment in American History.*

64. Berg, *Law Enforcement.*

65. Ibid.

66. Parks, "From Constabulary to Police Society"; Center for Research on Criminal Justice. *The Iron Fist and the Velvet Glove* (2nd ed.). Berkeley: Center for Research on Criminal Justice, 1977.

67. Costello, A. E. *Our Police Protectors: A History of New York Police.* Montclair, NJ: Patterson Smith, 1972 (originally published in 1885).

68. Richardson, *Urban Police in the United States.*

69. Bacon, "The Early Development of American Municipal Police 1939; Lane, R. *Policing the City: Boston,*

1822–1885. Cambridge, MA: Harvard University Press, 1967; Richardson, ibid.; Silver, "The Demand for Order in Civil Society."

70. Richardson, J. F. "The Early Years of the New York Police Department." In J. Skolnick and T. Gray (eds.), *Police in America.* Boston: Little, Brown, 1975, p. 16.

71. Lane, *Policing the City,* pp. 24–25.

72. Kalmanoff, A. *Criminal Justice: Enforcement and Administration.* Boston: Little, Brown, 1976, p. 36.

73. Center for Research on Criminal Justice, *The Iron Fist and the Velvet Glove,* p. 24.

74. Ibid.

75. Harring, S., and L. McMullen. "The Buffalo Police: Labor Unrest, Political Power and the Creation of the Police Institution." *Crime and Social Justice* 4: 5–14 (1975).

76. Harring, S. "The 'Most Orderly City in America': Class Conflict and the Development of the Police Institution in Milwaukee, 1880–1914." Paper presented at the annual meeting of the American Sociological Association, September 1978.

77. Harring, S. "The Development of the Police Institution in the U.S.," *Crime and Social Justice* 5: 55 (1976).

78. Ferdinand, T. N. "The Criminal Patterns of Boston Since 1849," *American Journal of Sociology* 73: 84–99 (1967).

79. Friedman, *Crime and Punishment in American History,* pp. 68–69.

80. Ibid.

81. Zinn, *A People's History of the United States.*

82. Berg, *Law Enforcement.*

83. Zinn, *A People's History of the United States.*

84. Berg, *Law Enforcement.*

85. Walker, S. *Popular Justice: A History of American Criminal Justice* (2nd ed.). New York: Oxford University Press, 1997.

86. Walker, S. *The Police in America.* (3rd ed.). New York: McGraw-Hill, 1999.

87. Fogelson, R. *Big City Police.* Cambridge, MA: Harvard University Press, 1977.

88. President's Commission on Law Enforcement and Administration of Justice. *Task Force Report: The Police.* Washington, DC: Government Printing Office, 1967.

89. Wilson, O. W. *Police Administration.* New York: McGraw-Hill, 1950.

90. President's Commission, *Task Force Report: The Police.*

91. Gentry, C. *J. Edgar Hoover: The Man and the Secrets.* New York: Norton, 1991. Also see Powers, R. G. *Secrecy and Power: The Life of J. Edgar Hoover.* New York: Free Press, 1987.

92. Hoover memorandum dated June 24, 1936, which initiated the FBI file of Clarence Seward Darrow. Released via Freedom of Information Act.

93. Keen, M. F. *Stalking the Sociological Imagination: J. Edgar Hoover's FBI Surveillance of American Sociology.* Westport, CT: Greenwood Press, 1999; Gentry, *J. Edgar Hoover;* Powers, *Secrecy and Power.*

94. Hoover memorandum dated February 27, 1950, which discussed the visa request for Picasso. FBI file of Pablo Picasso. Released via Freedom of Information Act.

95. Powers, *Secrecy and Power;* Theoharis, A. *From the Secret Files of J. Edgar Hoover.* Chicago: Ivan R. Dee, 1991.

96. Ibid.

97. Ibid.

98. Chambliss, *Power, Politics and Crime.*

99. Isserman, M., and M. Kazin. *America Divided: The Civil War of the 1960s.* New York: Oxford University Press, 2000, p. 163.

100. Newton, H. P. *To Die for the People.* New York: Writers and Readers, 1999, p. 200 (originally published in 1973); Zinn, *A People's History of the United States;* Wilkins, R., and R. Clark. *Search and Destroy: A Report by the Commission of Inquiry into the Black Panthers and the Police.* New York: Metropolitan Applied Research Center, 1973; Kennebeck, E. *Juror Number Four: The Trial of Thirteen Panthers as Seen from the Jury Box.* New York: Norton, 1973.

101. Zinn, *A People's History of the United States.*

102. Newton, *To Die for the People;* Wilkins and Clark, *Search and Destroy.*

103. Ibid.

104. Newton, *To Die for the People,* p. 200.

105. Students for a Democratic Society was one of several radical college campus political groups around the country during the 1960s. SDS was perhaps the most popular of such organizations.

106. Powers, *Secrecy and Power;* Theoharis, *From the Secret Files of J. Edgar Hoover;* Newton, *To Die for the People;* Newton, H. P. *War against the Panthers: A Study of Repression in America.* New York: Harlem River Press, 1996.

107. Shirer, W. *The Rise and Fall of the Third Reich.* New York: Simon & Shuster, 1960.

108. Zinn, *A People's History of the United States,* pp. 462–463.

109. Shirer, *The Rise and Fall of the Third Reich.*

110. Supreme Court of the United States, 1961. 367 U.S. 643, 81 S.Ct. 1684, 6 L.Ed.2d 1081.

111. Supreme Court of the United States, 1963. 372 U.S. 335, 344, S.Ct. 792, 796 9 L.Ed.2d 799, 805.

112. Supreme Court of the United States, 1964. 378 U.S. 478, 84 S.Ct. 1758, 12 L.Ed.2d 977.

113. Supreme Court of the United States, 1966. 384 U.S. 436, 86 S.Ct. 1602, 16 L.Ed.2d 694.

114. Supreme Court of the United States, 1974. 414 U.S. 338, 94 S.Ct. 613, 38 L.Ed.2d 561.

115. Supreme Court of the United States, 1979. 443 U.S. 31, 99 S.Ct. 2627, 61 L.Ed.2d 343.

116. Supreme Court of the United States, 1984. 486 U.S. 897, 104 S.Ct. 3405, 82 L.Ed.2d 677.

117. Cole, *No Equal Justice,* p. 71.

118. Ibid.

119. Parenti, *Lockdown America;* Cole, *No Equal Justice.*

120. Fanon, F. *The Wretched of the Earth.* New York: Grove Press, 1963; Robertson, G. *Crimes against Humanity: The Struggle for Global Justice.* New York: New Press, 2000.

121. Walker, *The Police in America.*

122. Juris, H. A., and P. Feuille. *Police Unions.* Lexington, MA: Lexington Books, 1973.

123. Terry, C. W. *Policing Society.* New York: Wiley, 1985.

124. Barker, T., and D. L. Carter. *Police Deviance.* Cincinnati: Anderson, 1991.

125. Shelden and Brown, "The Crime Control Industry and the Management of the Surplus Population."

126. Pyle, H. *The Merry Adventures of Robin Hood.* New York: Scribner, 1900.

127. H.R. 3108, 107th Congress, U.S. Congress.

CHAPTER SIX

AMERICAN LAW ENFORCEMENT IN THE TWENTY-FIRST CENTURY

In 1992 Kansas City, Missouri, police set up a fake crack house selling imitation crack. Customers were thereupon arrested, even though the police admitted they did not know if such a purchase violated any law. Police explained that victims merited arrest even if their actions were legal. Such forthright application of the educational nature of law is inspired by the war on drugs, but as in [Nazi] Germany, once the principle is established, its application will cover more and more areas of citizen conduct.[1]

We are certain that any reference to Nazi Germany in a discussion of American policing will draw disdain from our more conservative critics. We invite their critique. In fact, we believe that if such critiques are amplified, a dialogue among critical thinkers could possibly result in a more enriched inquiry into the politics and methodologies pertinent to American policing.

In 1933, traditional laws in Germany were replaced with laws that gave full power to various individuals and agencies. We now understand that many of these laws emerged as a result of government propaganda and official manipulation of information delivered to the German people. By 1935, the Nuremberg Decree virtually legalized the profiling of

Jews and other *government-defined* allegedly "dangerous" groups throughout Germany. Concentration camps were created primarily to control the dangerous classes and ethnic groups propagandized as unsavory, and as a deterrent to other social and economic groups as well.[2] Special favors were given to many university faculty members who assisted in the legitimation of totalitarian rule throughout Germany. Often, university faculty members simply responded to governmental requests in order to elevate their own status and the prestige of their respective institution—they conducted research that reified Nazi propaganda, and they ignored the ethical guidelines and rigors of scientific inquiry.[3]

On the surface, criminal justice under Nazi rule continued to function in a more or less traditional manner by controlling traffic, arresting thieves, and so on. Beneath the surface, criminal justice duties included the deprivation of the rights of targeted citizens and the promotion of terror aimed at particular groups throughout Germany. Habitual criminal laws were passed that provided the illusion that traditional crime was a primary target of criminal justice responses. The implementation of the death penalty was increased.[4]

We are not suggesting that American policing has reached the point of policing that existed within the Third Reich. We are, however, wondering how many more rights people are willing to relinquish (privacy, search and seizure protection under the fourth Amendment, etc.). We also wonder how many more intrusive laws the American public is willing to accept (e.g., civil forfeiture of property without due process). Finally, we wonder how much more militaristic American policing will become (e.g., SWAT units dressed in G. I. Joe costumes). In the aftermath of the tragedy in New York City on September 11, 2001, the need for answers to these questions is crucial.

There is a tendency to mythologize policing in America. The most popular myth about policing is that it is an institution composed of crime fighters.[5] In fact, research reveals that many police officers actually perpetuate this myth. They believe that crime fighting is what they do, and many select policing as an occupation because of a desire to become crime fighters.[6] Contained within this myth are the notions that police spend most of their time enforcing criminal law and waging war against various types of crime (the drug war, the war against gangs, etc.). This perception of policing is clearly a myth, for most police officers, particularly those officers assigned to patrol, spend very little time fighting crime, making felony arrests, shooting criminals, and so on. Police spend about one-third of their time enforcing criminal laws. Most police officers never fire a weapon in the line of duty, and few officers make more than an occasional felony arrest.[7]

Another prevailing myth is that police protect and serve the public. It is our contention that while certain segments of the public certainly benefit from police presence—they may indeed be protected and served—there are other segments of society that receive relatively few services and even less protection from American law enforcement. This is particularly the case in areas that sociologists call the lower socioeconomic neighborhoods often found in America's inner cities, where police tend to be viewed as occupational forces.[8] Police provide protection and services for the state. They also appear to provide ample protection for major businesses, corporations, and industries. During the 1990s, New York City police, with the blessing of Mayor Rudoloph Giuliani, set out to rid the city of "riffraff" (the homeless, the mentally ill, etc.).[9]

The stated purpose of this policy—to eliminate violence—was rationalized through the logic of the **broken windows** theory. According to this theory, broken or boarded-up windows suggest that residents don't care about their neighborhood. This in turn leads to other residents neglecting their property and law-abiding people begin to move out. In time, the entire neighborhood becomes a slum, which results in an increase in crime, starting with minor crimes and escalating to major crimes. The theory suggests that police intervene at the earliest stages of the deterioration process to ensure the safety of residents. The problem with this view is that there is no empirical support for it. Moreover, there is no explanation for why such neighborhoods begin to deteriorate in the first place. Little, if any thought was given to serving or protecting the homeless or mentally ill, or wondering where they might go after expelling them from the inner-city of New York.[10]

In Los Angeles, police sweeps of alleged gang members became institutionalized in the 1980s. During one operation (Operation Hammer) conducted in 1988 more than fourteen hundred youth were rounded up. Over 90 percent were released without charges. The apparent purpose of this sweep was to start a "file" on inner-city youth in South Central Los Angeles.[11] Although Miller compares such operations to Vietnam military strategies (i.e., search and destroy missions), they are also strikingly similar to Gestapo tactics in Nazi-controlled Europe in the 1930s and early 1940s. Similarities between American police tactics and the tactics used by the Nazi law enforcement apparatus can be readily identified through the documentation offered in the various studies of the Third Reich.[12]

PROMOTING FEAR AND SELLING THE ILLUSION OF PROTECTION

Scholars have argued that economic power facilitates control in capitalist societies.[13] Much of their research shows that one way for those with economic power to maintain control in a capitalist society is to wield their influence over the institutions that control information.[14] At the state level, subsidies can be provided to those who both control and distribute information. One way to subsidize these information "producers" is for the state, through its legislative power, to "give away" the airwaves to broadcasting corporations. Another way to subsidize information producers is to provide selected info-peddlers with insider information.[15]

Richard Miller points out that President Richard Nixon actually met with almost fifty television producers to convince them to promote his version of the drug war. Several were production representatives of *Dragnet, Hawaii Five-O, The Storefront Lawyers, I Spy, Felony Squad, The FBI, Mod Squad, Marcus Welby, M.D.,* and other television shows. Jack Webb, producer of *Dragnet,* proceeded to dramatize federal drug squads.[16] Clearly, when the president of the United States turns to Hollywood to promote a political agenda, one can clearly surmise that the state is influential in the *construction* of information delivered through mass media.

In the late 1980s and early 1990s, corporations such as Philip Morris (tobacco manufacturer), RJR Nabisco (tobacco manufacturer), Anheuser-Busch (alcohol producer), Bristol-Myers Squibb (drug producer), Johnson & Johnson (drug producer), and Du Pont (manufacturer of defoliants used in the Vietnam War) were contributors to an organization called Partnership for a Drug-Free America. This organization managed to isolate tens of thousands of people who used drugs from mainstream society. This foundation's goal was not to educate people about drugs but rather to promote propaganda that supported the state's drug war. ABC's Peter Jennings, NBC's Tom Brokaw, and others promoted the drug war in nightly broadcasts.[17] When nightly news broadcasts tell people they should be afraid, and when nightly television sitcoms let them know whom they should fear, people seem to believe the filtered information they receive. Regarding violent crime, research has revealed that the mass media grossly exaggerate incidents of violence in the United States. For example, Graber found that murder accounted for 0.2 percent of all crimes recorded by police. Yet stories about murder in the *Chicago Tribune* accounted 26.2 percent of all crime reports.[18] In general, all crimes involving some form of violence are overreported, whereas property crimes are significantly underreported.

According to Schlesinger and Tumber, journalist often know more about crime than the police do. In fact, they found that many police department headquarters are designed to accommodate journalists and that some major media outlets have their own facilities inside police headquarters buildings.[19] The media have been particularly helpful to law enforcement as they wage war against children—particularly when those children have darker skin, or if they happen to be from families living in the lower-income neighborhoods of U.S. society.[20] Crime stories are easy stories. By and large, reporters only have to pay proper homage to local law enforcement, and the whole idea of investigative journalism becomes obsolete. A reporter only needs to practice proper etiquette: Get the information from a police contact person or in certain cases from the police information officer, and make law enforcement look good. A crime reporter who practices good *support-the-police* etiquette need never worry about missing deadlines.

In most instances, law enforcement reaps benefits from mass media. The popular television program *NYPD Blue* continues to promote an image of law enforcement that captures the attention of audiences across the country, an audience that continues returning to watch the next episode. Police are often portrayed as the underdog in a society where hardened criminals lurk behind every shadow. The police are portrayed as though they alone stand between the American public and all of those hardened criminals hidden in those shadows. To be certain, it appears that much of America has bought into this fantasy portrayal of American policing. A. M. Rosenthal, a senior executive of the *New York Times,* expressing his views in support of the drug war, stated,

> Inevitably the time will come when the people of the country will no longer stand for it. They will seek the solution in death penalties and martial force. They will stop caring how many prisoners are crowded into a cell or how they are treated, just as long as they are off the streets. They will support judges and legislators and politicians who understand their sense of hopelessness against drugs and who will support repression as a national policy. Repression will satisfy a totally understandable and justifiable public sense of fury and frustration.[21]

From most accounts, it appears that Rosenthal may be correct. People are afraid. After all, they have been told to be afraid for at least the past couple of decades. We are not certain whether they are completely willing to succumb to the type of repression Rosenthal suggests. One thing is certain, however. Rosenthal's statement clearly opens the door for an official police state. At the present time, many in America seem oblivious to the prospects of a police state. An analysis of public perceptions of American law enforcement may explain, at least in part, the apparent ignorance by citizens of the potentiality of an emerging police state.

As we have already suggested, the media has the means to shape public opinion. A considerable amount of literature reflects the notion that police officers subscribe to the notion that they must envelop themselves in the waiting arms of the police subculture because they do not receive the proper respect from citizens. We are not certain how police justify this notion. Perhaps this notion is similar to the pouting child who wants more parental attention. In an attempt to secure more attention or to get his or her way, the child accuses the parents of not exhibiting sufficient amounts of love. There is simply a lack of hard evidence to support any notion that American policing is not given substantial respect by the public. To the contrary, data support the notion that police*men,* as the Gallup pollsters refer to all police officers, have been held in high esteem for decades by those whom police often refer to as *civilians who do not understand us* (police officers).

Data collected by Gallup Polls between 1977 and 2000 reflect that, according to respondents, *policemen* have occupied solid positioning in the upper echelon of occupations in the area of honesty and ethical standards (see Table 6.1). In addition, since the disaster in New York City on September 11, 2001, they have been elevated to an even higher position, according to a Gallup poll taken on November 26–27, 2001 (see Table 6.2).

These data fail to provide justification for police to take the position that they operate in an atmosphere lacking in public support. After all, the respondents indicate that they believe police officers are more honest, and have higher ethical standards, than the doctor who might perform surgery on them, the dentist who examines their teeth, and the clergy who offer religious support. This is clearly a lofty position for an occupation that has in its history the police response at the 1968 Democratic National Convention held in Chicago, the beating of Rodney King and its aftermath, recent developments in the Los Angeles Rampart Division, and numerous investigations,[22] as well as cases of civil rights violations filed against various local and state agencies by the Department of Justice.[23] More recent public opinion data demonstrate that, among the respondents who participated in Gallup

TABLE 6.1   Gallup Poll Results of Selected Occupation Ratings of Very High/High for Honesty and Ethical Standards by Respondents (selected years between 1977 and 2000)

	1977 (%)	1983 (%)	1988 (%)	1993 (%)	1998 (%)	2000 (%)
Druggists/pharmacists	NA	61	66	65	64	67
Medical doctors	51	52	53	51	57	63
Clergy	61	64	60	53	59	60
College teachers	46	47	54	52	53	59
Dentists	NA	51	51	50	53	58
Engineers	46	45	48	49	50	56
Policemen	37	41	47	50	49	55
Bankers	39	38	26	28	30	37

Source: Gallup Poll [Online]. http://www.gallup.com/poll/releases/pr001127asp [January 21, 2002].

Polls, policemen assume a status position directly behind the U.S. military forces.[24] Of course, this may be a reflection of media control of information. By November 2001, a number of college teachers and clergy had started to criticize U.S. policy in Afghanistan as well as the diminishing rights of American citizens following the New York disaster. This criticism may account for the fall of these two occupations to positions below policemen—in Gallup's late-November survey (see Table 6.2).

It is also important to point out that the public's perceptions of police honesty and ethical standards seem to be subject to various individual characteristics. Race and age influence views of police honesty and ethical standards. Among whites (the Department of Justice fails to indicate whether this category also includes Hispanics) there is a strong tendency to rank police officers very high/high in the area of honesty and ethical standards (59%); blacks are more reluctant to offer a very high/high rating (32%). Younger respondents (18–29 years of age) tend to rate police honesty and ethics somewhat lower than do older respondents.[25] There is also some differentiation over time regarding the level of respect people have for police in their own area. In 1965, 70 percent of respondents indicated they had a great deal of respect for police. By 1991 that percentage had declined to 60 percent, and remained at that level in 2000.[26] It is not our intention to question the reliability of the Gallup Polls, although you may indeed feel the need for such questions; it is our intention to draw attention to the lack of supporting evidence for the contention that police are not supported by the public they are supposed to serve.

AMERICAN POLICING: THE FIFTH ARMED FORCE?

Over the years, law enforcement in America has been presented as a quasi-military, multidimensional organization structured in such a way that each dimension is often an independent entity under the authority of an assigned or claimed jurisdiction.[27] American law

TABLE 6.2   Top 10 Rated Occupations Rated Very High/High for Honesty and Ethics by Respondents, November 26–27, 2001

1. Firefighters	90%	6. Medical doctors	66%
2. Nurses	84%	7. Clergy	64%
3. U.S. military	81%	8. Engineers	60%
4. Policemen	68%	9. College teachers	58%
5. Pharmacists	68%	10. Dentists	56%

Source: Gallup Poll [Online]. http://www.gallup.com/poll/releases/pr001127asp [January 21, 2002].

enforcement has emerged in the twenty-first century as the **fifth armed force** of the United States. It is not exactly clear why American law enforcement has achieved that status. Perhaps the U.S. government now believes that the traditional armed forces (Army, Navy, Air Force, Marines, Coast Guard) no longer provide sufficient security for America's interests.

Or the government may feel that American law enforcement can improve its image by going global. American law enforcement agents have, for many years, crossed international boundaries to expand the war against drugs (DEA activity in Bolivia, Colombia, Panama, etc.).[28] More recently, the war against terrorism has been used to deploy domestic law enforcers abroad (e.g., FBI in Afghanistan). Although it is quite likely that some of these incursions across sovereign international boundaries by America's *domestic* police may be violations of international law, it is unlikely that the governments of these countries will protest loudly. The United States is in firm control of institutions such as the International Monetary Fund (IMF), the World Bank (WB), and the World Trade Organization (WTO).[29] Protests by the governments of violated countries would simply result in one or more of these U.S.-controlled institutions exerting pressure on the protesting government until compliance or silence was achieved. This is one of the benefits of being the biggest world bully. Of course, America does not use the term *bully;* rather it alludes to the concept *leader of globalization*—which by some accounts amounts to a twenty-first-century version of colonization.[30]

Nearly all law enforcement agencies in the United States have embraced, and adopted, to varying degrees, characteristics that are common to the military. These characteristics include but are by no means limited to the distribution and differentiation of policing areas/jurisdictions, clothing/uniforms, divisions of labor based on job classifications and personnel location within a hierarchy of command, the authorization and use of high-tech equipment, and operations/strategies. *Jurisdiction* in law enforcement is similar to the military's *areas of operation* or *theaters of operation* (sectors, zones, regions, continents, etc.).

Law enforcement officials are often attired in uniforms that highlight distinctions not only between law enforcement officials and civilians but also among the various police organizations (e.g., state police, sheriff's deputies, and city police), in the same way that the U.S. military establishes individual branch distinctions with uniforms (e.g., Army, Navy, Air Force, Marines, and Coast Guard). Moreover, uniforms and insignia identify unique units within individual law enforcement agencies (e.g., SWAT and typical patrol officers) in the same way that they identify individual units within a particular branch of the military service (e.g., U.S. Army Rangers, Special Forces; U.S. Navy SEALS; U.S. Marines Recon). Distinctive uniforms for individual units authorized by the various branches of the U.S. military often amplify the special nature of those units and promote esprit de corps. Many law enforcement organizations use military-style ranks (captain, lieutenant, sergeant, etc.) to accommodate and differentiate their hierarchal command structures. Often these ranks are differentiated by insignia quite similar to those worn by military personnel (stripes, bars, oak leaves, stars, etc.). American law enforcement has managed to acquire and deploy vast amounts of assault weaponry found in the U.S. military arsenal (AR-15 assault rifles, helicopters, armored personnel carriers, etc.). These weapons are now mainstays of both military and police operations.[31]

JURISDICTIONAL CONSIDERATIONS

Many argue that American policing is a complex, fragmented, assortment of agencies without central control.[32] This is not particularly true in the twenty-first century. There is a hierarchy of jurisdictional control or responsibility. We would argue that there is more centralized control of policing than we have been led to believe. Our position on this issue stems from jurisdictional responsibility, authority, and autonomy.

Most law enforcement agencies are confined to specific jurisdictions.[33] The term **jurisdiction** refers to a legal or judicial area or boundary of authority (e.g., townships, cities, counties, states, nations, and territories).[34] The concept *jurisdiction* also has political implications and often funding implications as well. Funding for the drug war is often based on intelligence reports pertaining to the illegal drug trade, interdiction performances of one agency or another, and so on. These reports are often linked to jurisdictional control (federal jurisdictional control/authority, state or local jurisdictional control/authority, etc.). There is a similitude between the various dimensions of American law enforcement, and substantial evidence supports the notion that each dimension may complement or compete with other dimensions of law enforcement.[35] The competition we are referring to is often linked to funding and jurisdictional "rewards" given to the "victorious" (e.g., federal funding for youth gang interdiction).[36]

Although local law enforcement agencies (municipal police, township police, etc.) are usually confined to their respective jurisdictions, there are times and situations in which they encroach into the jurisdiction of another agency. One such impingement might occur in an emergency situation (e.g., a high-speed chase involving an armed robbery suspect), or by invitation from an agency with jurisdictional control (e.g., to assist in an emergency situation). When these jurisdictional encroachments occur, they usually reflect some formally agreed-upon arrangement. Law enforcement procedures or methods generally fall under the rules set forth by the jurisdiction's controlling agency. Let us return to the high-speed chase example. Some jurisdictions place significant limitations on high-speed chases by law enforcement because of the potential danger to innocent citizens. Other jurisdictions are more "officer friendly" in high-speed chase situations. If a patrol car from one jurisdiction chases a suspect across a jurisdictional boundary, the officers in the chase car are bound by the high-speed-chase rules of the jurisdictional area they entered. Each agency sets and is in control of its own standard operating procedures. This example provides support for those who subscribe to the fragmented, decentralized structure and control description of American law enforcement.

Now suppose that a state law enforcement official is engaged in a high-speed chase but is not necessarily bound by the restraints outlined in local jurisdiction's high-speed chase procedures. The state police officer in this case may choose not to follow the local jurisdiction's procedures. The fact that the state police can choose to follow or disregard local procedures supports the notion that a hierarchy of law enforcement exists and that police power is indeed more centralized than we are led to believe.

Further evidence of centralized control of policing can be found in the 1994 Violent Crime Control and Law Enforcement Act.[37] This legislation authorizes the U.S. Justice Department to investigate local law enforcement agencies and, as in Pittsburgh, Pennsylvania, bring suit and take control of agencies that abuse their authority. In this instance, the U.S. Justice Department becomes the central authority.

We are not suggesting that America's law enforcement apparatus is centralized to the extent that Great Britain's and France's law enforcement systems are structured.[38] We are suggesting that American law enforcement may be much more centralized than most criminal justice "experts" would have us believe. One advantage of promoting the decentralized perspective is that each agency is perceived as establishing its own standards and policies. Such a perspective releases agencies with encroachment power from responsibility when the lower agency violates citizens' rights, harbors discriminatory practices, engages in acts of brutality or corruption, and so on. For example, most state police agencies have the power, often under the authority of the governor, to intervene into the affairs of local law enforcement. They may or may not be involved in the constitutional violations practiced by a local agency. However, if local law enforcement gets "caught," state agencies back away and claim no knowledge or no responsibility. That being said, we turn now to the general structural characteristics of American law enforcement.

AMERICAN LAW ENFORCEMENT: STRUCTURE, COMPOSITION, AND PERSONNEL

What do we really know about the structure and organization of American law enforcement? The structure of American law enforcement can be viewed from several vantage points. The three we have chosen are: (1) jurisdiction (e.g., legal authorized geographic area of operation); (2) composition (e.g., configuration of internal components); and (3) personnel (e.g., race, sex, training).

Imagine driving south on Interstate 75 near Detroit, Michigan (or on any other freeway near an urban setting in America). You are likely to witness or experience one or more of the following scenes: A Michigan State Police vehicle, lights flashing, is parked behind a vehicle that was stopped by an officer. One mile farther south, a Troy police vehicle is parked by the side of the road, and an officer is aiming a speed-detecting device toward oncoming traffic. A couple miles farther south, a Detroit police officer is peering into the window of an apparently abandoned vehicle. One-half mile farther south, a Wayne County deputy sheriff is handing a speeding ticket to a disgruntled motorist. If you follow Interstate 94 north through Chicago, you are likely to see similar scenes orchestrated by the Illinois State Police, Chicago police, Lynwood police, South Holland police, Dolton police, Lincolnwood police, Skokie police, Morton Grove police, Glencoe police, Highland Park police, Northbrook police, and a host of other law enforcement agencies. Each of these agencies is operating in its own jurisdiction. Assuming that each agency is handing out tickets to motorists, you can safely say that each is making money for its respective government body. You might consider that each police agency is, in and of itself, unique. To understand this uniqueness, you need to have a general understanding of how American policing is structured.

Today, the United States has nearly 700,000 sworn law enforcement officers, and more than 17,000 federal, state, and local law enforcement agencies, within its overall policing apparatus. In addition, nearly 200,000 employees work for law enforcement agencies at the state and local levels but do not have sworn-officer status.[39] The distinction between sworn officers and other police employees is that only sworn officers are authorized to carry firearms and make arrests. From 1990 to 1999 local police employment increased by approximately 97,000 (21%), including an increase of 73,000 full-time sworn officers. Between 1997 and 1999 the number of full-time local police employees increased by 25,000, and 16,000 of these new employees were sworn officers. In June 1999, New York City had 39,009 full-time officers and rightfully claimed the title of America's largest police department. The number of full-time officers in New York City is almost three times greater than the number of full-time officers in the second largest police department—Chicago.[40] The number of federal officers authorized to carry firearms and make arrests is over 85,000.[41] In sum, policing has increased dramatically in America over the past few years.

The structure of American law enforcement can be viewed in the context of levels of government authority or jurisdiction. There are five levels of government-authorized law enforcement agencies: (1) townships and special districts; (2) municipal or metropolitan police; (3) county law enforcement; (4) state police; and (5) federal police. The demographic characteristics of law enforcement personnel, the operations and strategies employed by various levels of law enforcement, and the politics associated with law enforcement become more obscure as one moves up the hierarchical scale of American law enforcement. In other words, there appears to be a great deal of information available to the public about law enforcement at local levels of jurisdiction (city police, sheriff's departments, etc.). This may be attributed to visibility and the fact that many local law enforcement personnel are drawn from local labor pools. For example, it is certainly not uncommon for deputy sheriffs to have attended schools in the jurisdictions they now police. Conversely, state and federal law enforcement officials are more likely to be transplants into the communities they now police.

It is common to find more than one agency competing with another agency over the same turf, or jurisdiction, or embroiled in disputes over the same crime or offense. Specialized police often add to the confusion. To illustrate, Hoffman describes Washington, D.C., as "America's most policed city." In addition to the nearly 5,000 District of Columbia police department officers, there are 1,100 uniformed Secret Service officers, more than 1,200 U.S. Capitol police officers, 76 Supreme Court officers, over 150 Library of Congress police officers, over 250 Federal Protective Service police officers, and nearly 275

Metro Transit police officers. Finally, there are 35 Amtrak police officers and 20 Smithsonian Institution–National Zoo Police officers.[42] Imagine what a criminal investigation of a murder at the National Zoo might look like, particularly if the perpetrator escaped through the Smithsonian Institution and continued his escape using the subway and tried to hide behind some bushes near the White House. Who would have control over the investigation?

In 1997, the Department of Justice identified 1,332 "special police" agencies within the state and local law enforcement complex across the United States. They employed more than 61,000 full-time employees, including more than 44,000 sworn officers.[43] Clearly, jurisdiction is an issue in policing that should receive more attention by researchers. In a study of Clark County, Nevada, researchers found evidence that even local agencies (prosecution, law enforcement, etc.) had much difficulty sharing information within a single jurisdiction.[44]

Local Law Enforcement

We include townships and special district police, municipal or metropolitan police, and county law enforcement in the category of **local law enforcement.** This is due to the fact that each of these finds itself with local jurisdictional overlaps and shared tax bases. For example, municipal or metropolitan police agencies and township police are located in counties with a sheriff's department. Ideally, these entities would rely on each other to provide collective services, thereby reducing the cost of duplicate resource requirements for local communities; sheriff's offices would provide jails, or detainment facilities, thereby allowing other local agencies the freedom to focus their resources on patrol. In reality, local agencies compete for scarce community resources, and there is not always a friendly relationship among them. The sheriff wants a new jail furnished with the most technologically advanced surveillance equipment and also wants a very expensive oak desk for his or her office. The chief of police wants new patrol cars and new uniforms for his or her officers. Taxpayers, however, have limited resources. So interagency competition for resources begins.

Local Police Departments.   Local police departments include township and special district police, constables, and municipal or metropolitan police departments. Some areas have local marshals who serve as bailiffs and perform other court duties such as serving subpoenas and writs and transporting prisoners to and from court. Local marshals are either appointed or elected. These agencies can be viewed as local police department agencies because they operate in restricted jurisdictions and are under the control of some form of local government (mayor, township supervisors, city council, etc.) There are more than 13,500 local police departments that employ over 550,000 full-time employees, including about 436,000 sworn officers. In addition, there are more than 63,000 part-time employees in local law enforcement, including 27,824 sworn officers.[45] More than 40 departments employed 1,000 or more officers. These departments account for almost one-third of all local police officers.[46] The cost of operating local law enforcement agencies throughout the United States, on average, is about $150 per resident.[47] Local policing costs have increased significantly. In 1982 municipal law enforcement cost taxpayers $805,378,000. By 1997 that expenditure had increased by nearly 250 percent, to over $2 billion.[48]

There are nearly 19,000 townships across America. Most of these townships, particularly those in rural areas, offer limited police services. Townships that border large metropolitan areas typically offer a broader range of policing services. Small communities often run into problems as they enter the law enforcement arena. Generally, funding shortages create hardships, and coordination is problematic. Many townships have only one officer, who is on call twenty-four hours a day. In 1999, nearly 800 departments employed only one officer.[49]

Municipal or metropolitan police agencies range in size from organizations having fewer than ten officers and providing limited services, to organizations having thousands of officers and offering a wide range of services. Small municipal agencies often have problems finding resources to provide emergency-oriented services. In many instances, the qualifications of officers in small municipal agencies are lacking compared to their counterparts employed in larger metropolitan police agencies. Some small municipal officers have no academy training, and the supervision in these small communities is questionable. In contrast, many metropolitan police agencies have large pools of applicants from which they can select candidates, and many have their own training academies. Because many large urban police departments are confronted with diverse populations, as well as contrasting social situations, they often are able to provide a wide range of policing services. In addition, large urban police agencies are confronted with a disproportionate amount of criminal behavior. Six of the largest police departments (New York, Chicago, Los Angeles, Houston, Philadelphia, and Detroit) are responsible for less than 8 percent of the U.S. population but contend with nearly 25 percent of all reported violent crimes.[50]

Local Police Departments and Women.   Women compose about 10 percent of all sworn local law enforcement officers. Local law enforcement agencies that serve larger populations tend to hire a larger proportion of women officers. In 1997, women accounted for nearly 16 percent of all sworn officers in local law enforcement agencies serving populations of a million or more. In local law enforcement agencies serving populations between 10,000 and 24,999, women accounted for 5.3 percent of sworn officers. In agencies serving fewer than 2,500 citizens, women made up only 3.1 percent of all sworn officers in 1997.[51] Clearly, the number of women in local law enforcement fails to reflect the number of women in American society. The 1972 Equal Employment Opportunity Act, which extended coverage of Title VII of the 1964 Civil Rights Act to include state and local governments, applies to local law enforcement agencies. There should be concern that agencies given the responsibility to enforce laws seem to violate, or at least circumvent, federal employment laws. We discuss gender discrimination in policing later in this chapter.

Race and Ethnicity in Local Police Departments.   Department of Justice data indicate that the racial/ethnic composition of local law enforcement agencies is largely contingent upon the size of the agency. Larger police departments tend to have more minority sworn officers than smaller departments. Departments that serve populations of a million or more have about a one-third representation of minorities as sworn officers. Departments that serve populations of fewer than 10,000 have fewer than 11 percent minority sworn officers. African American and Hispanic sworn officers in local agencies represent 17.8 percent and 15.6 percent, respectively, of the total sworn-officer population. In departments that serve fewer than 50,000 citizens, African Americans and Hispanics account for between 8 and 10 percent of sworn officers.[52]

Educational Requirements and Local Police Departments.   The education requirements for new recruits in local law enforcement vary from department to department. The size of the agency reflects differences in educational requirements. For example, about 85 percent of all local law enforcement agencies serving less than 25,000 citizens require high school diplomas, compared with 63 percent of the agencies that serve populations of half a million or more citizens. According to Department of Justice data, no local law enforcement agencies that serve half a million or more citizens require a college degree.[53] Some critics argue that requiring college degrees would limit the pool of applicants and discriminate against minorities who have been victims of inferior schooling.[54] We find such an argument quite weak. The obvious solution is to end the inferior schooling of ethnic minorities. To do less is to support such practices.

Local Police Department Training.   Local law enforcement agencies often establish their own training requirements, sometimes within state guidelines. Nearly 75 percent of all large metropolitan police departments operate their own training academies; smaller agencies tend to rely on state-operated academies.[55] Police training can be divided into classroom and field instruction. Smaller police departments as a general rule require the fewest hours of combined classroom and field training for recruits. For example, local law enforcement agencies serving fewer than 25,000 citizens require, on average, around 700 hours of combined classroom and field training, compared with 1,200 combined training hours for larger departments that serve more than 100,000 citizens.[56] The police academy serves a number of functions. It provides formal training for recruits. Today, this training is likely to include fundamental aspects of law enforcement along with other skills that introduce the recruit to areas such as domestic violence, ethics, and constitutional law. In addition, the academy socializes the recruit into the police subculture. We discuss the subculture of law enforcement shortly.

County Law Enforcement

The personification of **county law enforcement** is the county sheriff. There are also county police departments, but they compose less than 1 percent of county law enforcement. Two examples of large county police departments are the Nassau County Police Department and the Suffolk County Police Department. Combined, they employ more than 5,600 sworn officers. The functions performed by these types of county law enforcement agencies are most aligned with agencies located in city or metropolitan police departments.[57]

There are obvious differences in the types of duties performed by county sheriff's departments. However, one constant exists in this category of law enforcement. Except in counties in Rhode Island and Hawaii, the chief officer is an *elected* sheriff. Many state constitutions proclaim sheriffs the chief law enforcement officials of the counties within their jurisdiction. The fact that sheriffs are elected means that sheriffs play an important role in politics and law enforcement. Folley points out,

> The office of sheriff is probably the most obvious example of mixing police and politics. This office was integrated into the American police system with little change from what it was in England. Today the office of sheriff is subject to popular election in almost all counties throughout the United States…. [W]hen a new sheriff is elected he will repay political debts by appointing new deputies and promoting others already employed…This constant change of leadership and manipulation of the hierarchy has not been conducive to the provision of efficient police services.[58]

The sheriff, as an elected official, often must repay political debts—particularly if he or she has a desire to secure funding to hold his or her office through the reelection process. Such a debt may open the door for questionable law enforcement practices. But because the sheriff is an elected official, he or she enjoys a certain amount of autonomy denied to law enforcement officials who are appointed.

County sheriffs perform a number of functions, many of which are at least influenced through state legislation. The sheriff appoints deputies to assist in carrying out the responsibilities of the office. In small county sheriff's offices, deputies are often selected because of their political support, as well as state-defined attributes (education, training, etc.). An obvious responsibility is keeping the peace. In some jurisdictions the sheriff is principally an officer of the court. Some sheriff's offices are involved in criminal investigations and traffic duties. Often, the geographic location of a sheriff's office determines the types of duties and responsibilities expected of that office. In the northern United States, sheriff's offices do little criminal investigation. Instead, they perform mostly courtroom and processing duties. In the southern and the southwest sections of the United States, the sheriff may be the primary criminal investigator. In unincorporated sections of a county, the sheriff works closely with municipal police departments, as well as with state law enforcement agencies.

There are more than 3,000 sheriff's offices across the United States, and the operational costs of maintaining these offices is, on average, $49 per resident.[59] Over the years, the cost of county law enforcement has increased significantly. In 1982, county law enforcement cost taxpayers $472,129,000. By 1997, that cost had increased to more than $1.5 billion—an increase of more than 300 percent.[60] One of the principal functions of the sheriff's office is maintaining and managing county jails.[61] The number of persons held in jails increased from 541,913 in 1995 to 687,033 in 2000.[62]

County Police and Women.   Women make up about 15 percent of all sworn officers in sheriff's departments across the United States. As in local law enforcement, the percentage of women who are sworn officers in sheriff's departments is greater in those departments serving populations with half a million or more citizens. In 1997, women accounted for between 17 and nearly 20 percent of sworn officers in larger sheriff's offices, compared with around 12 percent in offices that served populations with fewer than 25,000. The representation of women in sheriff's departments is somewhat better than in local law enforcement but remains well below the level of women's representation in the general society.

Race and Ethnicity in County Policing.   Department of Justice data indicate that the racial/ethnic composition of sworn employees in sheriff's departments is very similar to minority representation in local law enforcement agencies. Larger sheriff's departments tend to have more minority sworn officers than smaller departments. In departments that serve populations of a million or more, minorities make up about one-third of all sworn officers. In departments that serve populations of fewer than 10,000, less than 7 percent of all sworn officers are minorities. In large departments, African Americans account for about 17 percent of sworn officers; Hispanics, about 13 percent. Racial politics is alive and well in county law enforcement, especially in small county sheriff's departments, where African Americans and Hispanics make up only 2.2 percent and 3.7 percent, respectively.[63]

Educational Requirements and County Policing.   The educational requirements for new recruits in sheriff's departments vary from department to department, according to the size of the department. About 90 percent of all sheriff's departments serving fewer than 25,000 citizens require high school diplomas. The same requirements are evident in departments serving a million or more citizens. About 78 percent of those departments serving 50,000 to 99,999 citizens require high school diplomas, compared with 63 percent of the agencies that serve populations of half a million or more citizens. According to Department of Justice data, no sheriff's departments that serve a million or more citizens require a college degree.[64] Notice again the sad state of affairs concerning educational requirements. Surely if law enforcement is becoming more complex, as many suggest, minimum educational requirements must be increased to meet the needs of law enforcement.

County Police Training.   Sheriff's departments often establish criteria for training requirements. In many jurisdictions the state establishes general guidelines for training. As in local law enforcement training, sheriff's department training can be divided into classroom and field instruction. Small departments, as a general rule, require the fewest hours of combined classroom and field training for recruits. Departments serving fewer than 25,000 citizens require between 441 and 521 hours of combined classroom and field training. Departments that serve more than 500,000 citizens require between 804 and 1,003 combined hours of training.[65] Again, as in the training of local law enforcement recruits, police academies that service sheriff's departments perform a number of functions. These functions range from providing technical skills to familiarizing recruits with constitutional restraints and other procedural law requirements typically employed by law enforcement officials. And, as in the case of local law enforcement, the academy socializes the recruit into the law enforcement subculture.

State Law Enforcement

State law enforcement emerged in a clouded atmosphere of apprehension and contempt. There are several reasons that have been used to legitimate the creation of state police: (1) to assist local law enforcement, which lacked satisfactory training and resources; (2) to bridge jurisdictional law enforcement problems whereby criminal behavior fluctuated across jurisdictional boundaries; (3) to provide services to rural areas lacking local law enforcement services.[66] Despite these politically correct reasons supporting the creation of state law enforcement, many people were apprehensive that state governors would have too much power with their own private police forces, and that a state law enforcement agency would encroach on sacred local law enforcement jurisdictions. Many local law enforcement agencies, though scarred with corruption and evidence of ineffectiveness, adamantly opposed the organization of state law enforcement agencies. Sheriffs—powerful political figures within their own jurisdictions who often had different political views than reigning governors—viewed state police agencies as extensions of control from the governor's office.[67]

In spite of the resistance raised by local law enforcement agencies, state law enforcement did emerge and spread across the American landscape. The earliest state law enforcement agency was the Texas Rangers in 1836. In 1865, the Massachusetts legislature created a state police force with general law enforcement responsibilities. Its primary concern was to enforce vice laws. This agency was disbanded in 1875 as a result of controversy about its operations in cities. In Colorado, the state police was disbanded after demonstrating its preference to support industrial interests with brutal strikebreaking. In 1905, the first state police agency with general law enforcement capabilities came into being in Pennsylvania. This agency emerged in the aftermath of a brutal coal miners strike in 1902 in which the Army was ordered to seize and operate the coal mines until the owners were willing to arbitrate the conflict with mine workers.[68] By the 1960s, all states, with the exception of Hawaii, had adopted and instituted some form of state-level law enforcement.[69]

State law enforcement in America is partitioned into two structural types: (1) state police and (2) highway patrol. State police typically have more general policing powers that often reflect many of the duties of local law enforcement, but the jurisdictional boundaries of state police agencies encompass the entire state. There are 23 states that have state police organizations, compared to 26 states with highway patrol organizations. Highway patrol organizations tend to focus attention on the operation of motor vehicles on public highways and interstate freeways. Many states have also added law enforcement capabilities beyond the state police–highway patrol organization. Some states have their own Bureau of Investigation and Bureau of Narcotics and Dangerous Drugs (e.g., Oklahoma), and other states have created agencies like Gaming Control (e.g., Michigan and Nevada) to police the gaming industry within state jurisdiction.

In total numbers of sworn officers, state law enforcement has the lowest growth rate of all law enforcement agencies. In 1980, there were 50,672 sworn state law enforcement officers. By 1997, that number had increased to 56,023—an increase of less than 10 percent.[70] However, between 1982 and 1997, the price tag of state law enforcement increased from $577,808,000 to $1,956,789,000—nearly 400 percent.[71] In 1999, there were 55,892 sworn state police officers in America, and this figure reflects a loss of nearly 200 sworn-officer positions since 1997.[72] Today, on average, there are about 21 sworn state police officers per 100,000 residents across America. Delaware has 81 state police officers per 100,000 residents; Wisconsin has 9 per 100,000 (See Table 6.3).

State Police and Women.   The representation of women in the ranks of sworn officers in state police agencies across America is far lower than in local law enforcement. A recent study shows that women make up approximately 14.5 percent of sworn officers in municipal police agencies, 13.5 percent of sworn officers in county law enforcement, and only 6.8 percent of sworn officers in state police agencies. There are many possible explanations for this apparent exhibit of sexual discrimination by law enforcement in general and state law enforcement in particular.

As exhibited in Table 6.4, state police agencies such as the Alabama Department of Public Safety, Louisiana State Patrol, New Mexico State Police, North Carolina State Highway Patrol, South Dakota Highway Patrol, West Virginia State Police, and Wyoming Highway Patrol have less than 3 percent of their sworn-officer positions filled by women. Wyoming and

TABLE 6.3   Number of Sworn State Police Officers (1999) per 100,000 (1999), and Percentage Change (1997–1999)

AGENCY	SWORN OFFICERS	STATE POPULATION	OFFICERS PER 100,000	PERCENTAGE CHANGE
Alabama Dept. of Public Safety	600	4,287,178*	14	−16
Alaska State Troopers	332	604,966	55	+3
Arizona Dept. of Public Safety	1,025	4,434,340	23	+6
Arkansas State Police	561	2,506,293	22	+11
California Highway Patrol	6,597	31,857,646	21	+1
Colorado State Patrol	700	3,816,179	18	+23
Connecticut State Police	1,046	3,267,293	32	+11
Delaware State Police	587	723,475	81	+5
Florida Highway Patrol	1,766	14,418,917	12	+8
Georgia State Patrol	778	7,334,274	11	−6
Idaho State Police	273	1,187,597	23	+40
Illinois State Police	1,931	11,845,316	16	−2
Indiana State Police	1,277	5,828,090	22	+5
Iowa State Patrol	432	2,848,033	15	0
Kansas Highway Patrol	474	2,579,149	18	+10
Kentucky State Police	984	3,882,071	25	+7
Louisiana State Police	1,058	4,340,818	24	+16
Maine State Police	351	1,238,566	28	+4
Maryland State Police	1,574	5,060,296	31	+4
Massachusetts State Police	2,191	6,085,395	36	−14
Michigan State Police	2,065	9,730,925	21	+1
Minnesota State Patrol	539	4,648,596	12	+8
Mississippi Highway Safety Patrol	541	2,710,750	20	+4
Missouri State Highway Patrol	964	5,363,669	18	−9
Montana Highway Patrol	206	876,684	23	−3
Nebraska State Patrol	447	1,648,696	27	−4
Nevada Highway Patrol	405	1,600,810	25	+8
New Hampshire State Police	302	1,160,213	26	+4
New Jersey State Police	2,699	8,001,850	34	+6
New Mexico State Police	589	1,711,256	34	+35
New York State Police	4,139	18,134,226	23	+4
North Carolina State Highway Patrol	1,303	7,309,055	18	0
North Dakota Highway Patrol	127	642,633	20	−3
Ohio State Highway Patrol	1,430	11,162,797	13	+6
Oklahoma Highway Patrol	799	3,295,315	24	+7
Oregon State Police	844	3,196,313	26	−22
Pennsylvania State Police	3,987	12,040,084	33	−3
Rhode Island State Police	205	988,283	21	+5
South Carolina Highway Patrol	909	3,716,645	24	+16
South Dakota Highway Patrol	158	737,561	21	+3
Tennessee Dept. of Safety	888	5,307,381	17	−3
Texas Dept. of Public Safety	3,107	19,091,207	16	−13
Utah Highway Patrol	396	2,017,573	20	+2
Vermont State Police	296	586,461	50	+13
Virginia State Police	1,812	6,666,167	27	+9
Washington State Patrol	932	5,519,525	17	0
West Virginia State Police	648	1,820,407	36	+ 7
Wisconsin State Patrol	466	5,146,199	9	−6
Wyoming Highway Patrol	152	480,011	32	−3
Total	55,892	263,457,184		

*Population data based on U.S. Census Bureau estimates April 1, 1996.

Source: U.S. Department of Justice, Bureau of Justice Statistics. *Sourcebook of Criminal Justice Statistics, 2000* (2001), p. 48.

TABLE 6.4   Women in the State Police, 2000

AGENCY	TOTAL SWORN OFFICERS	TOTAL WOMEN SWORN OFFICERS	PERCENTAGE OF WOMEN SWORN OFFICERS
Alabama Dept. of Public Safety	636	18	2.8
Alaska Dept. of Public Safety	331	24	7.3
Arizona Dept. of Public Safety	1,047	80	7.6
Arkansas State Police	559	31	5.5
California Highway Patrol	6,564	571	8.7
Colorado State Patrol	696	32	4.6
Connecticut Dept. of Public Safety	689	43	6.2
Florida Highway Patrol	1,748	170	9.7
Idaho State Police	268	14	5.2
Indiana State Police	1,285	70	5.4
Illinois State Police	2,047	191	9.3
Iowa State Patrol	451	15	3.3
Kansas Highway Patrol	457	15	3.3
Kentucky State Police	937	32	3.4
Louisiana State Patrol	1,037	26	2.5
Maine Dept. of Public Safety	344	14	4.1
Maryland State Police	1,611	159	9.9
Massachusetts State Police	2,228	218	9.8
Michigan State Police	2,102	259	12.3
Minnesota State Police	553	47	8.5
Missouri Highway Patrol	1,083	41	3.8
Montana Highway Patrol	235	21	8.9
Nebraska State Patrol	356	16	16.0
Nevada Highway Patrol	429	24	5.6
New Hampshire State Police	313	26	8.3
New Mexico State Police	483	14	2.9
New York State Police	4,105	320	7.8
North Carolina State Highway Patrol	1,336	24	1.8
North Dakota Highway Patrol	125	6	4.8
Ohio State Highway Patrol	1,408	130	9.2
Oregon State Police	798	72	9.0
Pennsylvania State Police	4,134	166	4.0
Rhode Island State Police	219	19	8.7
South Carolina Dept. of Public Safety	1,109	52	4.4
South Dakota Highway Patrol	157	2	1.3
Tennessee Dept. of Public Safety	899	45	5.1
Texas Dept. of Public Safety	3,121	163	5.2
Utah Highway Patrol	406	14	3.4
Vermont State Police	292	21	7.2
Virginia State Police	1,821	74	4.1
Washington State Patrol	989	66	6.7
West Virginia State Police	682	17	2.5
Wisconsin State Patrol	508	71	14.0
Wyoming Highway Patrol	147	4	2.7

Source: Equality Denied: The Status of Women in Policing: 2000, Penny E. Harrington, director, National Center for Women and Policing, a division of the Feminist Majority Foundation (April 2001).

South Dakota combined have only six women who are sworn state law enforcement officers. Apparently out of a total population of more than 1.2 million in both Wyoming and South Dakota only six women are qualified or want to be sworn state law enforcement officials. Of course, many in the dominant male majority in law enforcement have long argued that policing is too dangerous for women or that women are not capable of performing police duties as well as men. Research has proved both arguments to be nothing more than mythical reflections without sufficient data.[73] However, women officers do seem to lag behind their male counterparts in the areas of police brutality and other forms of misconduct.[74] Because American policing often seems to compare itself with the military, the following data may support an argument against sex discrimination at all levels of law enforcement.

Nearly 10,000 women served in Vietnam, and their service, like that of many women in law enforcement today, has passed unnoticed.[75] Women came home from Vietnam with post-traumatic stress disorder (PTSD).[76] These women saved countless lives.[77] Eight military nurses died in Vietnam (seven Army nurses and one Air Force nurse). Ironically, these 10,000 women served in the Vietnam War at a time when many male police officers used their occupation as a means to avoid the military draft. On March 31, 1997, more than 165,000 women were serving in America's armed forces. We believe that *any* excuse offered by law enforcement to continue blocking women from pursuing careers as sworn law enforcement officers is a clear civil rights violation committed by the institution of policing in America.

Federal Law Enforcement

Federal law enforcement emerged from congressional power provided by the U.S. Constitution. Section 8:1 of the U.S. Constitution gives Congress the power to "Lay and collect Taxes, Duties, Imports and Excises, to pay the Debts and provide for the common Defence [sic] and general Welfare of the United States." Section 8:6 gives Congress the power to "provide for the Punishment of counterfeiting the Securities and current Coin of the United States." Thus, under the banner of common defense and general welfare of the United States, the federal law enforcement apparatus emerged, expanded, and has flourished into a lucrative component of the criminal justice industrial complex. As of June 2000, there were more than 88,000 full-time federal law enforcement officers authorized to make arrests and carry firearms in nearly 70 federal law enforcement agencies. These agencies also employed nearly 72,000 support personnel and operated on a combined budget of approximately $18 billion.[78] In federal law enforcement agencies that employed 500 or more there were 79,718 officers with arrest power and authorization to carry a firearm.[79] This figure reflects an increase of more than 5,200 from 1996,[80] and an increase of nearly 14,000 since 1993.[81] There are nearly 60 federal law enforcement agencies. In this chapter, we limit our scope to agencies that employ 500 or more sworn officers.

About 41 percent of federal officers are involved in criminal investigation. Police response and patrol account for 19 percent; corrections, 18 percent. About 13 percent are in noncriminal investigation and inspection duties, 4 percent in court operations, and 3 percent had duties in security and protection.[82] We limit our discussion to the largest agencies within the two principal federal law enforcement employers—the Department of Justice and the Department of the Treasury.

Department of Justice. The **Department of Justice** was created in 1870 and was given the responsibility of enforcing federal laws. Today, with a budget of more than $20 billion, and over 127,000 authorized positions, the Department of Justice houses one of the five largest federal law enforcement agencies.[83] The attorney general, a presidential appointee requiring confirmation by the Senate, heads the Department of Justice. Protection, law enforcement, and punishment are included in the mission statement of the Department of Justice:

> To enforce the law and defend the interests of the United States according to the law, to provide Federal leadership in preventing and controlling crime, to seek just punishment for those guilty of unlawful behavior, to administer and enforce the Nation's immigration laws fairly and effectively, and to ensure fair and impartial administration of justice for all Americans.[84]

Most large organizations have mission statements. Compliance with those statements is another matter. Historically, agencies throughout the federal law enforcement apparatus— including the Department of Justice—often fail to live up to their lofty creeds. Forfeiture laws, "snitch programs," illegal surveillance programs, and so on, have prevented the Department of Justice from living up to its own mission statement. After years of research focusing on J. Edgar Hoover's activities in the FBI, Americans may be confused about who the "bad guys" actually are. The Department of Justice is a complex apparatus with a direct link to the president of the United States.

The current U.S. attorney general, John Ashcroft, asked for, and apparently won the endorsement of George W. Bush to receive (reflected in the 2003 FY U.S. Budget proposal), $30.2 billion to prevent and combat terrorism, continue the fight against drugs, and ensure civil rights. The irony to this request is that simultaneously, the Department of Justice is currently being criticized for violating the civil rights of many who are being detained without charges in relation to the traumatic events of September 11, 2001.[85] In addition, this is the same department of the federal government that, with the assistance of J. Edgar Hoover, spent a decade violating the civil rights of African American leaders,[86] critical congressmen,[87] organizations such as Vietnam Veterans against the War,[88] and others during the 1960s and 1970s.[89]

U.S. Marshals Service. The **U.S. Marshals Service** was the first federal law enforcement agency. It was established by the Judiciary Act of 1789. This element of federal law enforcement was not given agency status, however, until 1969 and in 1974 was recognized as a federal bureau.[90] Early accounts of the U.S. marshals tended to focus on colorful characters such as Bat Masterson and Wyatt Earp, who became legends often portrayed in "pulp paperback" books depicting U.S. marshals as principled upholders of the law in the west.[91] Over the course of history the U.S. Marshals Service was assigned to the presidency, the Treasury Department, the War Department, Department of State, and Department of Interior, before finding its present home in the Department of Justice. Berg refers to this agency as the "National Sheriff."[92] United States marshals were deployed to provide security for James Meredith at the University of Mississippi. Ironically, U.S. marshals were directed to protect Dr. Martin Luther King through much of the civil rights movement, while J. Edgar Hoover simultaneously authorized the FBI to violate King's constitutional rights.[93]

The duties of the U.S. Marshals Service include providing security for federal courts. This security assignment extends to federal judges, court officials, witnesses, and jury members. With more than 2,000 federal judicial officers operating in more than 700 locations, this is certainly a complex assignment. Following the enactment of the 1984 Comprehensive Crime Control Act, which contained provisions for forfeiture of assets, the U.S. Marshals Service was given the responsibility for the maintenance, inventory, and disposal of seized property ordered by the federal courts.

United States marshals are responsible for the transportation of prisoners to federal courts, and with assistance from the federal Bureau of Prisons (BOP) they transport federal prisoners between BOP institutions. The U.S. Marshals Service handles the custody of approximately 27,000 detainees who are confined in local, state, and federal facilities across America. The U.S. Marshals Service contracts with nearly 1,200 state and local governments for the custody of federal prisoners. The Witness Security Program is operated by the U.S. Marshals Service. Following authorization from the attorney general, witnesses are provided with federal court-ordered identity changes, relocation, job training, medical coverage, and so on. The U.S. Marshals Service also provides 24 hour protection for witnesses still in what is called a "threat" area. United States marshals execute federal fugitive warrants, making approximately 55 percent of all arrests of federal fugitives. Fugitive investigations conducted by the U.S. Marshals Service are conducted within the United States and abroad and are assisted by surveillance and analytical support units with this agency.

The U.S. Marshals Service engages in special operations assignments by deploying special operations groups that respond to emergency situations around the world. One of these special operations duties is the Missile Escort Program, which entails providing security for the movement of nuclear warheads by the Department of Defense and the U.S. Air Force.[94] This assignment raises the issue of the conflict between the U.S. military and law enforcement. Is it possible that the Department of Defense and the U.S. military are no longer capable of providing security for their own operations? Is it possible that American law enforcement is now in the business of providing security for the U.S. military, or does this shift in responsibility provide an opportunity to present a more acceptable image of law enforcement in general?

Operating with a $570 million budget (fiscal 2000), the U.S. Marshals Service has 92 U.S. marshals, appointed by the president, and more than 2,700 officers authorized to carry a firearm and make arrests. Less than 18 percent of the more than 2,700 officers are ethnic minorities, and only 12 percent are women.

Drug Enforcement Administration. In the aftermath of the Harrison Act, passed in 1914, a branch of the Internal Revenue Service, the Miscellaneous Division, was charged with enforcing drug enforcement laws generated by that act. The responsibility for federal drug enforcement was transferred in 1930 to the Federal Bureau of Narcotics (FBN). In the late 1960s, the FBN was shifted from the Treasury Department to the Department of Justice and combined with the Bureau of Drug Abuse Control to form the Bureau of Narcotics and Dangerous Drugs. The **Drug Enforcement Administration (DEA)** was created in 1973.[95] Through the efforts of the producers of *Miami Vice,* a colorful television cop show, the DEA became glorified throughout America. Others have portrayed the DEA in less flattering ways. For instance, Levine, a retired federal drug agent, argues that the DEA is "more about politics than drug interdiction," and Miller suggests this agency is simply another link in the attempt to create a police state in America.[96] Regardless of the degree of accuracy presented by Levine and Miller, there are data that certainly call into question the legitimacy of this agency and its mission. Here is the DEA's mission statement:

> The mission of the Drug Enforcement Administration (DEA) is to enforce the controlled substances laws and regulations of the United States and bring to the criminal and civil justice system of the United States, or any other competent jurisdiction, those organizations and principal members of organizations, involved in the growing, manufacture, or distribution of controlled substances appearing in or destined for illicit traffic in the United States; and to recommend and support non-enforcement programs aimed at reducing the availability of illicit controlled substances on the domestic and international markets.[97]

The duties assigned to the DEA include assisting in the investigation and prosecution of major drug-law violators within the United States and in other countries. The DEA has more than 20 domestic division offices throughout the United States (including Washington, D.C.) and branch offices in more than 200 major cities. This agency also has 78 offices in 56 countries around the world (see Figure 6.1). This agency is also responsible for the collection and management of illegal drug trafficking intelligence, seizure and forfeiture of assets linked to the illegal drug trade, coordination of drug enforcement with local and international law enforcement agencies, and a laundry list of other drug-related duties.[98]

The level of drug abuse in America has been relatively stable over the past few years according to data provided by the University of Michigan's Institute for Social Research. These data reveal that drug abuse did not decline or increase significantly among eighth, tenth, and twelfth graders between 1997 and 2001. Some rather interesting facts do surface from these data. Over the past five years, MDMA (the drug ecstasy) has enjoyed a remarkable increase in popularity among the age groups targeted by these studies. Another category, tranquilizers, has also experienced an appreciable increase as an abused drug. Cocaine use, both crack and powder forms, and the use of marijuana have declined ever so slightly over the past five years (see Table 6.5).[99]

In 1997, the U.S. federal drug control budget exceeded $14 billion, and DEA's share of that budget was about $1.1 billion.[100] By 2001, the U.S. federal drug control budget had risen to more than $18 billion, and DEA's portion of that budget had grown to more than $1.6 billion—a $500 million increase.[101] During the period 1997–2001, the federal drug control budget consumed more than $82.7 billion.[102] These data prompt the question, *Was*

FIGURE 6.1 DEA Foreign Offices

EUROPE/MIDEAST/AFRICA	FAR EAST	SOUTH AMERICA	CENTRAL AMERICA	CARIBBEAN
Vienna, Austria	Canberra, Australia	Buenos Aires, Argentina	Belize City, Belize	Freeport, Bahamas
Brussels, Belgium	Rangoon, Burma	Cochabamba, Bolivia	San Jose, Costa Rica	Nassau, Bahamas
Ottawa, Canada	Beijing, China	La Paz, Bolivia	San Salvador, El Salvador	Bridgetown, Barbados
Nicosia, Cyprus	Hong Kong, China	Santa Cruz, Bolivia	Guatemala City, Guatemala	Santa Domingo, Dominican Republic
Copenhagen, Denmark	Tokyo, Japan	Trinidad, Bolivia	Tegucigalpa, Honduras	Port-au-Prince, Haiti
Cairo, Egypt	Seoul, South Korea	Brasília, Brazil	Ciudad Juarez, Mexico	Curaçao, Netherlands Antilles
London, England	Vientiane, Laos	Santiago, Chile	Hermosillo, Mexico	Port of Spain, Trinidad and Tobago
Paris, France	Kuala Lumpur, Malaysia	Barranquilla, Colombia	Mazatlán, Mexico	
Berlin, Germany	Manila, Philippines	Bogotá, Colombia	Mérida, Mexico	
Frankfurt, Germany	Singapore, Singapore	Guayaquil, Ecuador	Mexico City, Mexico	
Athens, Greece	Bangkok, Thailand	Quito, Ecuador	Monterrey, Mexico	
New Delhi, India	Chiang Mai, Thailand	Asunción, Paraguay	Tijuana, Mexico	
Milan, Italy	Songkhla, Thailand	Lima, Peru	Managua, Nicaragua	
Rome, Italy	Udorn, Thailand	Caracas, Venezuela		
The Hague, Netherlands	Hanoi, Vietnam			
Lagos, Nigeria				
Islamabad, Pakistan				
Peshawar, Pakistan				
Moscow, Russia				
Pretoria, South Africa				
Madrid, Spain				
Bern, Switzerland				
Ankara, Turkey				
Istanbul, Turkey				
Tashkent, Uzbekistan *				

*Office scheduled to open in 2002.

Source: U.S. Drug Enforcement Administration (www.dea.gov) February 2002.

TABLE 6.5   Drug Abuse Trends (Selected Drugs) among Eighth Graders, Tenth Graders, and High School Seniors (1997 and 2001)

	8TH GRADERS		10TH GRADERS		H.S. SENIORS	
	1997 %	*2001* %	*1997* %	*2001* %	*1997* %	*2001* %
ANY ILLICIT DRUG USE						
Lifetime	29.4	26.8	47.3	45.6	54.3	53.9
Annual	22.1	19.5	38.5	37.2	42.4	41.4
30-day	14.6	11.7	23.0	22.7	26.2	25.7
MARIJUANA/HASHISH						
Lifetime	22.6	20.4	42.3	40.1	49.6	49.0
Annual	17.7	15.4	34.8	32.7	38.5	37.0
30-day	10.2	9.2	20.5	19.8	23.7	22.4
Daily	1.1	1.3	3.7	4.5	5.8	5.8
INHALANTS						
Lifetime	21.0	17.1	18.3	15.2	16.1	13.0
Annual	11.8	9.1	8.7	6.6	6.7	4.5
30-day	5.6	4.0	3.0	2.4	2.5	1.7
HALLUCINOGENS						
Lifetime	5.4	4.0	10.5	7.8	15.1	12.8
Annual	3.7	2.5	7.6	5.2	9.8	8.4
30-day	1.8	1.2	3.3	2.1	3.9	3.2
COCAINE						
Lifetime	4.4	4.3	7.1	5.7	8.7	8.2
Annual	2.8	2.5	4.7	3.6	5.5	4.8
30-day	1.1	1.2	2.0	1.3	2.3	2.1
CRACK COCAINE						
Lifetime	2.7	3.0	3.6	3.1	3.9	3.7
Annual	1.7	1.7	2.2	1.8	2.4	2.1
30-day	0.7	0.8	0.9	0.7	0.9	1.1
HEROIN						
Lifetime	2.1	1.7	2.1	1.7	2.1	1.8
Annual	1.3	1.0	1.4	0.9	1.2	0.9
30-day	0.6	0.6	0.6	0.3	0.5	0.4
TRANQUILIZERS						
Lifetime	4.8	4.7	7.3	8.1	7.8	9.2
Annual	2.9	3.0	4.9	5.9	4.7	6.5
30-day	1.2	1.6	2.2	2.9	1.8	3.0
ALCOHOL						
Lifetime	53.8	50.5	72.0	70.1	81.7	79.7
Annual	45.5	41.9	65.2	63.5	74.8	73.3
30-day	24.5	21.5	40.1	39.0	52.7	49.8
Daily	0.8	0.9	1.7	1.9	3.9	3.6

(continued)

TABLE 6.5 CONTINUED

	8TH GRADERS		10TH GRADERS		H.S. SENIORS	
	1997 %	2001 %	1997 %	2001 %	1997 %	2001 %
CIGARETTES						
Lifetime	47.3	36.6	60.2	52.8	65.4	61.0
30 day	19.4	12.2	29.8	21.3	36.5	29.5
½ pack per day	3.5	2.3	8.6	5.5	14.3	10.3
STEROIDS						
Lifetime	1.8	2.8	2.0	3.5	2.4	3.7
Annual	1.0	1.6	1.2	2.1	1.4	2.4
30-day	0.5	0.7	0.7	0.9	1.0	1.3
MDMA (ECSTACY)						
Lifetime	3.2	5.2	5.7	8.0	6.9	11.7
Annual	2.3	3.5	3.9	6.2	4.0	9.2
30-day	1.0	1.8	1.3	2.6	1.6	2.8

it worth it? After careful analysis of the data provided in Table 6.5, one might question the sanity of such a large budget, as well as the fiscal responsibility of government for the continuation or existence of a drug enforcement agency. Given this agency's mission statement, DEA has had little if any impact on drug use/abuse by eighth graders, tenth graders, or high school seniors. Of course the criminal justice system in general, and law enforcement specifically, argue that any decline reflects progress in the drug war and any increase in illegal drug use justifies more resources. Thus, a built-in rationale for the continuation of increased resources escapes logic and reason. We suggest that perhaps it might be useful to consider the enormous amount of money spent in the name of the drug war, and we dare suggest that $82 billion is perhaps too much money for such meager results.

During fiscal year 2001 there were 9,209 DEA employees; 4,601 of these were special agent officers authorized to carry a firearm and make arrests.[103] In 1997 there were 2,946 DEA officers who were authorized to carry a firearm and make arrests.[104] The 4,601 special agents in 2001 represent a more than 70 percent increase over 1997. In 2000, less than 18 percent of all DEA officers authorized to carry a weapon and make arrests were ethnic minorities, and only 8.4 percent were women—the lowest representation of women in all federal law enforcement agencies.[105]

Immigration and Naturalization Service. With the exception of four brief years under federal authority through an 1864 law intended to increase immigration, early control of immigration was a responsibility of the states. During this period there were many problems and inconsistencies associated with immigration to the United States resulting from the divided authority of control by individual states. The Immigration Act of 1891 brought immigration back under the control of the federal government. During the early 1900s, the Bureau of Immigration was under the control of the Department of Commerce and Labor. Later, immigration and naturalization were separated into two departments with separate functions—immigration and naturalization—until 1933, when these functions were combined in the **Immigration and Naturalization Service (INS)** in 1933. In 1940, the INS was transferred to the Department of Justice, where it remains today.[106]

The Immigration and Naturalization Service employs the largest number of federal officers authorized to carry a firearm and make arrests. In 2000, the INS enforcement budget was approximately $2.8 billion. In 1993, the INS budget was about $1.5 billion. In

2000, INS had 17,654 officers with arrest power. This reflects an increase of nearly 30 percent over 1996 figures (12,403).[107] Women and ethnic minorities in 2000 composed 11.3 percent and almost 40 percent respectively of those INS officers authorized to make arrests. Compared to 1996 official data, the representation of women officers declined. In 1996, women accounted for 12.7 percent of INS employees authorized to carry firearms and make arrests.[108] In addition, in 2000 there were 11,377 support personnel.[109] Nearly half of INS officers who are authorized to make arrests work for the U.S. Border Patrol. Operating through three regional offices, under the direction of this agency's headquarters in Washington, D.C., the INS directs the activities of more than thirty districts and over twenty Border Patrol sectors in the United States and three district offices (with thirty-nine area offices) outside the United States. Offices outside U.S. boundaries are used as conduits between various U.S. and foreign service offices around the world.[110]

In 1998, data show that 172,547 aliens were removed from U.S. soil. This figure was up dramatically from 1991, when 33,389 aliens were deported. Even more dramatic is the fact that in 1991, almost 44 percent of those deported were deported for criminal involvement. In 1998, however, less than 21 percent were deported because of criminal behavior. In 1999, INS boasted that it had removed more than 176,990 "criminal and other aliens." Interestingly, INS claims that in 1999, 62,359 aliens were linked to criminal behavior.[111] The INS has one problem with criminal classifications. On February 17, 2000, it was reported that INS had worked with Los Angeles Rampart Division in questionable deportation processes.[112] Such reports raise the issue of INS classification processes. Another issue raised is the dramatic increase in deported aliens involved in criminal activity between 1998 and 1999. To illustrate, in 1998, 35,783 were deported because of criminal behavior.[113] As previously noted, in 1999, there were 62,359 aliens deported for criminal involvement. This represents an increase of more than 57 percent in one year. We can't help but wonder what Native Americans think as they review the "Scalp List" composed of "illegal" aliens by the INS.

Federal Bureau of Investigation.   The Bureau of Investigation emerged in 1908. In the 1920s, this agency was the target of congressional criticism for questionable surveillance methods directed at U.S. Congress members.[114] The agency acquired its current name, **Federal Bureau of Investigation,** in 1935 and became the first full-time federal investigative agency. The FBI is not a police agency; it is an investigative agency with broad jurisdiction extending to all areas and concerns relevant to U.S. interests. The FBI is particularly active in investigations pertaining to sabotage, treason, civil rights violations, robbery (federally insured banks), and other violations of federal law.

Until recently, there was no uniform definition of domestic terrorism and no specific legislative provisions that addressed domestic terrorism. However, given that the FBI is responsible for the investigation of domestic terrorism, the Bureau created its own definition. This definition was grounded on the premise that domestic terrorism is the unlawful or threatened use of violence by individuals, or groups, within the boundaries of the United States or Puerto Rico against individuals or property for the purpose of coercing individuals, groups, or the government for political or social objectives.[115] Of course, after the events of September 11, 2001, in New York City and Washington, D.C., no one can trivialize the importance and existence of terrorism. In decades past, however, the definition formulated by the FBI was used in quite a different way. For example, it was employed, at least in part, against a variety of Americans in World Wars I and II, throughout the 1950s (the McCarthy communist witch-hunts), and during the 1960s and 1970s against civil rights advocates and anti–Vietnam War protesters.

The Federal Bureau of Investigation is the third largest Department of Justice employer. In 2000, with a budget of $3.3 billion, the FBI had 11,523 officers with authorization to carry a firearm and make arrests. Recently, we visited the Federal Bureau of Investigation Employment Web page (http://www.fbi.gov/employment/employ.htm) and discovered a glaring contradiction. At the top of the page is a photograph that includes two males and two females (a demonstration of gender equality) and two whites and two ethnic minorities (an example of racial equality). As we observed this picture a question surfaced: *What is wrong with this picture?* It fails to reflect the true demographics of the FBI. In reality, almost 83 percent of the FBI officers who have arrest powers are men, and more than 83 percent are white.

Department of the Treasury. The Department of the Treasury is home to four federal government agencies that have more than 19,254 personnel authorized to carry weapons and make arrests and 12,979 support personnel.[116] The Department of the Treasury has two principal components: department offices and treasury bureaus. *Departmental offices* are largely responsible for policy formulation and management. Department offices are headed by assistant secretaries and are directly responsible for reporting to the secretary of the treasury, who is the primary economic adviser to the president. *Treasury bureaus* include the various agencies of the Treasury Department. Each bureau is headed by an assistant secretary who reports to the under secretary of the treasury. The basic functions of the Department of Treasury include

1. Managing federal finances
2. Collecting taxes, duties, and monies paid to and due to the United States and paying all bills of the United States
3. Producing all postage stamps, currency, and coinage
4. Managing government accounts and the public debt
5. Supervising national banks and thrift institutions
6. Advising on domestic and international finances
7. Enforcing federal finance and tax laws
8. Investigating and prosecuting tax evaders, counterfeiters, forgers, smugglers, illicit spirits distillers, and gun-law violators
9. Protecting the president, vice president, their families, candidates for those offices, foreign missions resident in Washington, and visiting foreign dignitaries[117]

The four federal law enforcement agencies within the Department of the Treasury that we discuss here are the U.S. Customs Service, the U.S. Secret Service, the Internal Revenue Service, and the Bureau of Alcohol, Tobacco, and Firearms.

U.S. Customs Service. The U.S. Congress authorized the creation of the **U.S. Customs Service** in 1789. The principal functions of this agency are (1) enforcing import and export laws and regulation of U.S. ports of entry, (2) assessing and collecting duties on imported merchandise, (3) functioning as the first line of defense in the nation's war on narcotics at ports of entry, and (4) combating smuggling and related fraud.[118]

Operating with a $2.2 billion budget in 2000, the U.S. Customs Service employed 10,522 officers with arrest power during that year. This figure includes 7,729 inspectors and 2,779 criminal investigators. Processing more than a million people per day, this agency is responsible for enforcing in excess of 400 laws pertaining to drugs, customs, export, and revenue fraud.[119] More than 80 percent of all the customs officers authorized to carry weapons and make arrests are male, and 64.5 percent are white.

U.S. Secret Service. Authorized under Title 18, United States Code, Section 3056, the **U.S. Secret Service** was created in 1865. It was established as a law enforcement agency for the purpose of curtailing the counterfeiting operations that emerged with the introduction of paper currency during the Civil War.[120] In the aftermath of the assassination of President William McKinley in 1901, the Secret Service was given another function— protecting the president, vice president, and their families, presidential and vice-presidential candidates, foreign missions residing in Washington, and visiting foreign dignitaries. Other responsibilities include the investigation of credit-card fraud and computer fraud and providing physical security for the White House, the main treasury building, and foreign embassies and missions in Washington, D.C.[121] The Secret Service also plays a role in the so-called drug war.[122]

As the second largest U.S. Treasury Department employer, the Secret Service operated on a 2000 budget of $762 million and employed 2,710 agents authorized to carry firearms and make arrests. Males accounted for 90.9 percent of all Secret Service agents (women accounted for 9.1 percent), and 79.5 percent of agents were white.[123]

Internal Revenue Service. Starting in 1862, the **Internal Revenue Service (IRS)** now has three principal divisions: (1) the Investigative Intelligence Division, responsible for investigating tax-law violations and various automatic weapons registration laws, (2) the Audit Division, which is often a component of federal coordinated drug interdiction programs, and (3) the collections division, which has the responsibility to act on court orders to collect revenues due to the U.S. government.

The Internal Revenue Service had a 2000 budget of almost $438 million and within the Criminal Investigation Division employed 2,726 special agents who have authorization to carry firearms and make arrests. Women accounted for 27.3 percent of these agents, and 21 percent of the agents were ethnic minorities.[124]

Bureau of Alcohol, Tobacco, and Firearms. In addition to being another tax-collecting agency under the direction of the Department of the Treasury, the **Bureau of Alcohol, Tobacco, and Firearms (ATF)** is also an enforcement and regulatory extension of the parent department. In 1862, Congress established the office of Internal Revenue within the Department of the Treasury. The Volstead Act in 1919 (Prohibition) paved the way for the eventual conception and implementation of the Bureau. The passage of the National Firearms Act (1934) and the Federal Firearms Act (1938), in response to the proliferation of weaponry by organized crime during Prohibition, also played a role in the shaping of the future Bureau of Alcohol, Tobacco, and Firearms. In 1972, through Treasury Department order no. 221, the Bureau of Alcohol, Tobacco, and Firearms became a bonafide bureau within the Treasury Department.[125] And then there is Waco, Texas, where in 1993, seventy-six people died, including twenty-seven children, as a result of an ATF raid on the Branch Dividian compound.

The Bureau of Alcohol, Tobacco, and Firearms currently has eighteen field division offices throughout the United States. From these sites, the ATF operates four ongoing programs. The *alcohol program* regulates the qualification and operations of distilleries, wineries, and breweries operating in the United States, as well as importers and wholesalers in the alcohol industry. The *tobacco program* inspects manufacturer applications and qualifications and investigates contraband tobacco products. Both programs enforce the appropriate taxation requirements relevant to alcohol and tobacco. The *arson and explosive program* provides resources to local communities for the investigation of incidents involving explosives and in cases of arson-for-profit. The ATF has National Response Teams, International Response Teams, and Arson Task Forces, which can be dispatched with minimal notification. The ATF maintains the Explosive Incident System, a computerized collection of data on national explosives. The *firearms program* brings ATF agents into the realm of violent offenders, career criminals, and narcotics traffickers. To monitor and control the illegal use of firearms, the ATF enforces federal firearms laws, issues firearms licenses, and conducts compliance inspections.[126]

In 2000, the ATF was the fourth largest enforcement agency with the Treasury Department and operated with a budget of $644 million. There were 1,967 officers with arrest power and authority to carry firearms. Of these officers, 88 percent were males, and 19.7 percent were ethnic minorities.[127]

SUMMARY

Policing has experienced significant changes in the past few decades. In the aftermath of recent legislation following the events of September 11, 2001, policing during the first decade of the twenty-first century is likely to continue undergoing significant changes. In the midst of all these changes the police institution has been engaged in promoting the fear of crime (by greatly exaggerating the extent of crime), while at the same time "selling" the illusion that the public needs the police to protect them and, moreover, that the police really can protect them.

Developing along with dramatic changes in our social institutions and severe economic problems has been the expansion of police powers unknown in previous eras. We noted in this chapter the close parallel between the urban police and the military, with the police copying much of the technology and even terminology and hierarchy from the military. Further, a wide variety of police agencies operate at every level of government, from the federal to the local. We noted the increasing number of women and minorities within the police institution, although each still constitutes a very small segment of this traditionally white male institution—particularly women. Especially noteworthy is the extent to which law enforcement has become global, with the DEA spreading all over the globe in search of drug dealers.

KEY TERMS

Alcohol, Tobacco,
    and Firearms (ATF)   165
broken-windows theory   143
county law enforcement   152
Department of Justice   157
Drug Enforcement
    Administration (DEA)   159
Federal Bureau
    of Investigation (FBI)   163

federal law enforcement   157
fifth armed force   147
Immigration and Naturalization
    Service (INS)   162
Internal Revenue
    Service (IRS)   165
jurisdiction   147
local law enforcement   150

state law enforcement   154
U.S. Customs Service   164
U.S. Marshals Service   158
U.S. Secret Service   164

NOTES

1. Miller R. L. *Drug Warriors and Their Prey: From Police Power to Police State*. Westport CT: Praeger, 1996.

2. Shirer, W. L. *The Rise and Fall of the Third Reich*. New York: Simon & Schuster, 1960; Aycoberry, P. *The Social History of the Third Reich, 1933–1945*. New York: New Press, 1999.

3. Weinreich, M. *Hitler's Professors: The Part of Scholarship in Germany's Crimes against the Jewish People*. New Haven: Yale University Press, 1999.

4. Dulffer, J. *Nazi Germany 1933–1945: Faith and Annihilation*. London: Arnold, 1996.

5. Walker, S., and C. M. Katz. *The Police in America: An Introduction* (4th ed.). New York: McGraw-Hill, 2002.

6. Manning, P. "The Police: Mandate, Strategies, and Appearances." In L. Gaines and T. Ricks (eds.), *Managing the Police Organization*. St. Paul, MN: West, 1978.

7. Bercal, T. "Calls for Police Assistance." *American Behavioral Scientist* 13: 681–691 (1970); Myer, J., and W. Taylor. "Analyzing the Nature of Police Involvement: A Research Note Concerning the Effects of Forms of Police Mobilization." *Journal of Criminal Justice* 3: 141–146 (1975); Mastrofski, S. "Community Policing as Reform: A Cautionary Tale." In J. Greene and S. Mastrofski (eds.), *Community Policing*. New York: Praeger, 1988; Walker and Katz, *The Police in America*.

8. Nelsen, J. (ed). *Police Brutality: An Anthology*. New York: Norton, 2000.

9. Duneier, M. *Sidewalk*. New York: Farrar, Straus and Giroux, 1999; Parenti, C. *Lockdown America: Police and Prisons in the Age of Crisis*. New York: Verso, 1999.

10. Wilson, J. Q., and G. Kelling. "Broken Windows." *Atlantic Monthly* (March 1982). A study of foot patrol by the Police Foundation (*The Newark Foot Patrol Experiment*. Washington, D.C. The Police Foundation, 1981) found little evidence in support of this theory, although it did conclude that the police could reduce citizen fears of crime. For a thorough critique of broken windows, see Karmen, A., "Smarter Policing and Stepped-Up Imprisonment as the Primary Causes of Falling Crime Rates in New York City: The Emergence of an Urban Legend?" *The Justice Policy Journal* (2001, online at: http://www.cjcj.org/journal/volno1/karmen/) and Karmen, A., *New York Murder Mystery: The Story Behind the Crime Crash of the 1990s*. New York: New York University Press, 2000.

11. Miller, J. G. *Search and Destroy: African American Males in the Criminal Justice System*. Cambridge: Cambridge University Press, 1996.

12. Shirer, *The Rise and Fall of the Third Reich*; Aycoberry, *The Social History of the Third Reich*.

13. Giddens, A., and D. Held (eds.). *Classes, Power, and Conflict: Classical and Contemporary Debates*. Berkeley:

University of California Press, 1982; Giddens, A. *The Global Third Way Debate.* Cambridge: Polity Press, 2001; Domhoff, W. G. *The Powers That Be.* New York: Vintage, 1979; Domhoff, W. G. *Who Rules America Now? Power and Politics in the Year 2000.* Mountain View, CA: Mayfield, 1998; Chomsky, N. *World Orders Old and New.* New York: Columbia University Press, 1996; Chomsky, N. *Class Warfare.* Monroe, ME: Common Courage Press, 1996; Chomsky, N. *Secrets, Lies and Democracy.* Tucson, AZ: Odonian Press, 1994.

14. Chomsky, *Secrets, Lies and Democracy;* Schlesinger, P., and H. Tumber. *Reporting Crime: The Media Politics of Criminal Justice.* Oxford: Clarendon Press. 1994; Parenti, *Lockdown America.*

15. Schlesinger and Tumber, *Reporting Crime;* Chomsky, *Secrets, Lies and Democracy.*

16. Miller, *Drug Warriors and Their Prey.*

17. Ibid.

18. Graber, D. *Crime News and the Public.* New York: Praeger, 1980.

19. Schlesinger and Tumber, *Reporting Crime.*

20. Males, M. A. *Framing Youth: 10 Myths about the Next Generation.* Monroe, ME: Common Courage Press, 1999.

21. Cited in Miller, *Drug Warriors and Their Prey,* p. 29.

22. Los Angeles Police Department, 2000; Columbus, Ohio Police Department, 1998; Pittsburgh Police Department, 1997.

23. See *United States v. New Jersey* (1999); *United States v. City of Pittsburgh* (1999); *United States v. City of Steubenville, Ohio* (1997).

24. Source: Gallup Poll [Online]. http://www.gallup.com/poll/releases/pr001127as [January 21, 2002].

25. Source: Gallup Poll [Online]. http://www.gallup.com/poll/releases/pr001127asp 2000 in *Sourcebook of Criminal Justice Statistics, 2000,* table 2.25, 2001.

26. *Sourcebook of Criminal Justice Statistics, 2000,* table 2.27, p. 117, 2001.

27. Samaha, J. *Criminal Justice* (5th ed.). Belmont, CA: Wadsworth, 2000; Miller, L. S., and K. M. Hess. *The Police in the Community: Strategies for the 21st Century* (2nd ed.). Belmont, CA: Wadsworth, 1998; LaGrange, R. L. *Policing American Society* (2nd ed.). Chicago: Nelson-Hall, 1998; Roberg, R. R., and J. Kuykendall. *Police in Society.* Belmont, CA: Wadsworth, 1993; Walker, S. *The Police in America: An Introduction* (2nd ed.). New York: McGraw-Hill, 1992.

28. Levine, M. *Deep Cover.* New York: Delacorte, 1990; Levine, M. *Big White Lie: The CIA and the Cocaine Crack Epidemic.* New York: Thunder's Mouth, 1994; Scott, P. D., and J. Marshall. *Cocaine Politics: Drugs, Armies and the CIA in Central America.* Berkeley: University of California Press, 1998.

29. Tabb, W. *The Amoral Elephant: Globalization and the Struggle for Social Justice in the Twenty-First Century.* New York: Monthly Review Press, 2001.

30. Chomsky, N. *Profit over People: Neoliberalism and Global Order.* New York: Seven Stories Press, 1999.

31. Parenti, *Lockdown America.*

32. Walker and Katz, *The Police in America.*

33. Samaha, *Criminal Justice;* Miller and Hess, *The Police in the Community;* LaGrange, *Policing American Society;* Roberg and Kuykendall, *Police in Society;* Walker, *The Police in America.*

34. Scheb, J. M., and J. M. Scheb II. *Criminal Law and Procedure* (4th ed.). Belmont, CA: Wadsworth, 2002.

35. Shelden, R. G., and W. B. Brown. "Correlates of Jail Overcrowding: A Case Study of a County Detention Center." *Crime and Delinquency* 37(3): 347–362 (1991); Walker, *The Police in America.*

36. Shelden, R. G., S. Tracy, and W. B. Brown. *Youth Gangs in American Society* (2nd ed.). Belmont, CA: Wadsworth, 2001.

37. Bartollas, C., and L. Hahn. *Policing in America.* Boston: Allyn and Bacon, 1999, pp. 38–39.

38. Fairchild, E., and H. R. Dammer. *Comparative Criminal Justice Systems* (2nd ed.). Belmont, CA: Wadsworth, 2001; Reichel, P. L. *Comparative Criminal Justice Systems: A Topical Approach* (3rd ed.). Upper Saddle River, NJ: Prentice-Hall, 2002.

39. U.S. Department of Justice, Bureau of Justice Statistics. *Federal Law Enforcement Officers, 2000.* NCJ 187231. Washington, DC: U.S. Department of Justice, July 2001; 1999 Sourcebook, table 1.23 [Online] 2001.

40. U.S. Department of Justice, Office of Justice Programs. *Local Police Departments 1999.* Washington, DC: NCJ, 2001.

41. Bureau of Justice Statistics, *Federal Law Enforcement Officers, 2000.*

42. Hoffmann, J. "Washington, D.C.: America's Most Policed City." *Law and Order* (February 1992), pp. 56–60.

43. U.S. Department of Justice, Bureau of Justice Statistics. *Local Police Departments 1997.* NCJ 173429. Washington, DC: U.S. Department of Justice, 2000, p. 1.

44. Shelden and Brown, "Correlates of Jail Overcrowding."

45. U.S. Department of Justice, Bureau of Justice Statistics. *Local Police Departments 1999.* NCJ 186478. Washington, DC: U.S. Department of Justice, 2000, p. 1.

46. Office of Justice Programs, *Local Police Departments 1999.*

47. Bureau of Justice Statistics, *Local Police Departments 1997,* p. 6.

48. U.S. Department of Justice Statistics. *Trends in Justice Expenditures and Employment.* NCJ 178271, table 4 [Online]. http://www.usdoj.gov/bjs/data/eetrnd04.wk1 [May 21, 2001].

49. Office of Justice Programs, *Local Police Departments 1999.*

50. Pate, A., and E. H. Hamilton. *The Big Six: Policing America's Largest Cities.* Washington, DC: Police Foundation, 1991.

51. Bureau of Justice Statistics, *Local Police Departments 1997,* p. 3, table 5.

52. Ibid.

53. Ibid., p. 5, table 7.

54. Walker and Katz, *The Police in America.*

55. Ibid.

56. Bureau of Justice Statistics, *Local Police Departments 1997,* p. 5, table 8.

57. U.S. Department of Justice, Bureau of Justice Statistics. *Law Enforcement Management and Administrative Statistics.* Washington, DC: Government Printing Office, 1998, p. vii.

58. Folley, V. I. *American Law Enforcement.* Boston: Allyn and Bacon, 1980, p. 228.

59. U.S. Department of Justice, Bureau of Justice Statistics. *Sheriff's Departments 1997.* NCJ 173428. Washington, DC: U.S. Department of Justice, 2000, p. 6, table 9.

60. U.S. Department of Justice Statistics. *Trends in Justice Expenditures and Employment.* NCJ 178271, table 4 [Online]. http://www.usdoj.gov/bjs/data/eetrnd04.wk1 [May 21, 2001].

61. Thompson, J. A., and G. L. Mays. *American Jails: Public Policy Issues.* Chicago: Nelson-Hall, 1998.

62. *Sourcebook of Criminal Justice Statistics, 2000,* table 6.22.

63. Bureau of Justice Statistics, *Sheriff's Departments 1997,* p. 3, table 5.

64. Ibid., p. 5, table 7.

65. Ibid., p. 5, table 8.

66. Gaines, L. K., V. E. Kappeler, and J. B. Vaughn. *Policing in America.* Cincinnati: Anderson, 1994.

67. Berg, *Law Enforcement;* LaGrange, *Policing American Society.*

68. Wiebe, R. H. "The Anthracite Strike of 1902: A Record of Confusion." *The Mississippi Valley Historical Review* 48(2): 229–251 (September 1961).

69. Johnson, D. R. *American Law Enforcement: A History.* St. Louis: Forum Press, 1981; Berg, *Law Enforcement;* Roberg and Kuykendall, *Police and Society;* LaGrange, *Policing American Society.*

70. U.S. Department of Justice Statistics. *Trends in Justice Expenditures and Employment.* NCJ 178271, table 9 [Online]. http://www.usdoj.gov/bjs/data/eetrnd04.wk1 [May 21, 2001].

71. Ibid.

72. U.S. Department of Justice, Bureau of Justice Statistics. *Law Enforcement Management and Administrative Statistics, 1999: Data for Individual State and Local Agencies with 100 or More Officers.* NCJ 184481. Washington, DC: U.S. Department of Justice, 2000, p. 229.

73. Balkin, J. "Why Policemen Don't Like Police Women." *Journal of Police Science and Administration.* 30: 16 (1988).

74. Grennan, S. A. "Findings on the Role of Officer Gender in Violent Encounters with Citizens." *Journal of Police Science and Administration* 15(1):78–85 (1987).

75. Scharfman, S. "America's Invisible Veterans." *Veterans of Foreign Wars of the United States Magazine* 77(3): 26–28 (November 1989); Mithers, C. L. "Missing in Action: Women Warriors in Vietnam, Culture Critique." *Telos* 3: 70–90 (Spring 1986).

76. Van Devaner, L. *Home before Morning.* New York: Beaufort Books, 1983; Norman, E. "Post Traumatic Stress Disorder in Military Nurses Who Served in Vietnam during the War Years 1965–1973." *Military Medicine* 153: 238–242 (1988).

77. Van Devaner, L. *Home before Morning.* Meshad, S. *Captain for Dark Mornings.* Playa Del Rey, CA: Creative Image Associates, 1982.

78. U.S. Department of Justice, Bureau of Justice Statistics, *Federal Law Enforcement Officers, 2000,* p. 1.

79. Ibid., p. 7.

80. U.S. Department of Justice, Bureau of Justice Statistics. *Federal Law Enforcement Officers 1996.* NCJ 164617. Washington, DC: U.S. Department of Justice, December 1997, p. 6.

81. U.S. Department of Justice, Bureau of Justice Statistics. *Federal Law Enforcement Officers 1993.* NCJ 151166. Washington, DC: U.S. Department of Justice, December 1994, p. 2.

82. Bureau of Justice Statistics, *Federal Law Enforcement Officers 2000,* p. 2.

83. U.S. Department of Justice. http://www.usdoj.gov/02organizations [February 2002].

84. Ibid.

85. Human Rights News. www.hrw.org/2002/02/ins0208.htm [February 8, 2002].

86. Zinn, H. *You Can't Be Neutral on a Moving Train.* Boston: Beacon Press, 1994; Isserman, M., and M. Kazin. *America Divided.* New York: Oxford University Press, 2000.

87. Halberstam, D. *The Best and the Brightest.* New York: Ballantine Books, 1992.

88. Nicosia, G. *Home to War: A History of the Vietnam Veteran's Movement.* New York: Crown, 2001.

89. Zinn, H. *A People's History of the United States, 1492–Present.* New York: HarperCollins, 1999.

90. Gaines, Kappeler, and Vaughn, *Policing in America.*

91. Berg, *Law Enforcement.*

92. Ibid.

93. Friedman, L. M. *Crime and Punishment in American History.* New York: Basic Books, 1993; Zinn, *A People's History of the United States.*

94. U.S. Marshals Service Missions. http://usdoj.gov/marshals/missions.html [February 2002].

95. Berg, *Law Enforcement;* Gaines, Kappeler, and Vaughn, *Policing in America.*

96. Levine, *Deep Cover* and *Big White Lie: The CIA and the Cocaine Crack Epidemic;* Miller, *Drug Warriors and Their Prey.*

97. DEA Mission Statement. U.S. Drug Enforcement Administration (www.dea.gov), February 2002.

98. U.S. Drug Enforcement Administration (www.dea.gov), February 2002.

99. National Institute on Drug Abuse, National Institute of Health. http://www.drugabuse.gov/ [February 2002].

100. Maguire, K., and A. Pastore (eds.). *Sourcebook of Criminal Justice Statistics—1997.* Washington, DC: U.S. Department of Justice, Bureau of Justice Statistics, 1998.

101. National Drug Control Strategy: FY 2001 Budget Summary, p. 13; Summary: FY 2002 National Drug Control Budget, p. 13. *Sourcebook of Criminal Justice Statistics, 2000,* 2001; U.S. Drug Enforcement Administration (www.dea.gov), February 2002.

102. National Drug Control Strategy: FY 2001 Budget Summary, p. 13; Summary: FY 2002 National Drug Control Budget, p. 13; *Sourcebook of Criminal Justice Statistics, 2000.* 2001.

103. U.S. Drug Enforcement Administration (www.dea.gov), February 2002.

104. Maguire and Pastore, *Sourcebook of Criminal Justice Statistics—1997.*

105. Office of Justice Programs. *Federal Law Enforcement Officers, 2000,* p. 7.

106. Franklin, F. G. *The Legislative History of Naturalization in the United States.* New York: Arno Press, 1969; LeMay, M., and E. R. Barkan. *U.S. Immigration and Naturalization Laws and History: A Documentary History.* Westport, CT: Greenwood Press, 1999.

107. Maguire and Pastore, *Sourcebook of Criminal Justice Statistics—1997.*

108. Ibid.

109. Office of Justice Programs, *Federal Law Enforcement Officers, 2000,* p. 2.

110. Immigration and Naturalization Service: Overview. http://www.ins.usdoj.gov/graphics/aboutins/thisisins/overview.htm [February 2002].

111. Ibid.

112. *Los Angeles Times,* February 17, 2000.

113. *Sourcebook of Criminal Justice Statistics, 2000* [Online], table 4.47.

114. Demaris, O. *The Director: An Oral Biography of J. Edgar Hoover.* New York: Harper's Magazine Press, 1975; Gentry, C. *J. Edgar Hoover: The Man and the Secrets.* New York: Norton, 1991.

115. Federal Bureau of Investigation. *Terrorism in the United States, 1998.* Washington, DC: Federal Bureau of Investigation, 1999.

116. Office of Justice Programs, *Federal Law Enforcement Officers, 2000,* p. 2.

117. Department of the Treasury. http://www.ustreas. gov/opc/opc0042html#dep [February 2002].

118. Ibid.

119. Office of Justice Programs, *Federal Law Enforcement Officers, 2000,* p. 3.

120. Berg, *Law Enforcement.*

121. Department of the Treasury. http://www.ustreas. gov/opc/opc0042html#dep [February 2002].

122. Berg, *Law Enforcement.*

123. Office of Justice Programs, *Federal Law Enforcement Officers, 2000,* p. 6.

124. Ibid.

125. Bureau of Alcohol, Tobacco, and Firearms. http://www.atf.treas.gov/about/history.htm.

126. Bureau of Alcohol, Tobacco, and Firearms. http://www.atf.treas.gov/about/programs/profire.htm.

127. Office of Justice Programs, *Federal Law Enforcement Officers, 2000,* p. 6.

CHAPTER SEVEN

POLICE FUNCTIONS
AND PROBLEMS

On Feb. 4, four white officers of the NYPD shot and killed Amadou Diallo, a 22-year-old street merchant from Guinea. The officers riddled Diallo and the vestibule of his Bronx apartment with 41 bullets from their Glock 9 mm semiautomatic pistols. The police struck Diallo 19 times from a distance of only 2 feet. Diallo was unarmed.[1]

It is after midnight and the suspect enters a local strip bar. Three patrol cars race up the street and jump the curb to block the entrance.... Three patrol cars surround the front of the establishment. The arrest team charges in the front door with their weapons drawn. The officers retrieve the suspect and drag him out to the hood of the patrol car.... The suspect denies any wrongdoing and becomes upset and confused by the arrest. He appears to be slightly intoxicated or high on drugs. He is forced to sit down on his handcuffed hands with his legs crossed.

The suspect says, "What is this shit? This is all a bunch of bullshit, man. You guys don't got shit on me, man. Kiss my ass."

One of the officers responds by forcefully shoving the suspect against the grill of the car. The officer places his flashlight against the side of the suspect's face and presses it hard into the suspect's cheek [and says], "Listen shorty, you say one more word and that's your hospital word. I will lay you out in a heartbeat so shut your damn mouth."

A drug bust in Washington, D.C.[2]

What is expected of American policing is largely interest based. The state wants police to maintain social control through law enforcement or order maintenance methods. Powerful interest groups want the police to protect their property and enforce laws that favor businesses and corporations. The public wants the police to provide security, prevent crimes, and respond to their calls and complaints on demand.

There is another element linked to democratic society that the general public has integrated into its expectations of policing—the notion of personal liberties, or respecting the public's constitutional rights. This expectation, however, seems to have diminished since September 11, 2001. The general public has barely protested the policy makers who have authorized the police to invade citizen privacy, and this lawmaking body has weakened the Fourth Amendment restrictions previously placed on American law enforcement in the area of search and seizure. One explanation for this absence of protest is probably linked to the notion that to complain about the loss of rights is unpatriotic—which seems exactly the opposite of the intentions of many of America's founders. Much of today's policing apparatus centers its attention on **proactive policing.** Many believe this strategy actually works to prevent crime—perhaps it does have such an impact—but it is intrusive on the lives of Americans. **Reactive policing,** in contrast, responds to criminal behavior after it has occurred. American policing is characterized by the dichotomy of law enforcement versus order maintenance.

ENFORCING THE LAW OR ORDER MAINTENANCE?

Police operations typically consist of patrol, investigation, traffic control, and special unit activities. As a rule, there are two principal rationales behind police operations: (1) law enforcement and (2) service. The rationale adopted by police administrators, and adapted to by police officers, influences the way in which police operations are organized and conducted.

The law enforcement rationale is, simply stated, the enforcement of the laws germane to a given jurisdiction. In the case of local law enforcement, police enforce laws relative to their local jurisdiction. Of course, they are responsible for the enforcement of county, state, and federal laws that also apply to their jurisdiction. The enforcement of laws is also contingent upon priorities and resources available to a law enforcement agency. For example, a local newspaper in Flint, Michigan, recently reported that local law enforcement must readjust its priorities for making arrests because the Genesee County sheriff's office says the county jail is operating above capacity and that if nothing is done to expand incarceration space there will be no place to lock up those arrested.[3]

At the center of law enforcement in recent years lies the war against crime. The war against crime has many **fronts.** For example, there is the war against *drugs,* the war against *gangs,* the war against *drunk drivers,* the war against *child abuse.* Today, we now have the war against *terrorism.* There has not been a war against white-collar crime, or a war against corporate crime, or a war against state crime announced in recent years. The wars that have been declared, however, have had brutal consequences over the past few decades. If we look carefully at the wars related to state-defined crimes during the 1960s and 1970s, we are likely to run across documents exposing fire hoses and dogs used against civil rights marchers in Alabama. We may also become confronted with events at the 1968 Democratic Convention in Chicago, where the law enforcers brutalized, in front of television cameras, hundreds of antiwar demonstrators. We can also find documentation that reveals massive beatings and arrests of members of Vietnam Veterans against the War at the 1972 Republican Convention in Miami, or we might run across articles and films reflecting the brutalization and murder of unarmed university students at Kent State University in 1970. All of these events have been called battles in the war against crime. Some have suggested that one of the primary roles of law enforcement in the war against crime is to simply maintain order.

Order maintenance is a function of policing that operates to keep things controllable. In other words, police who practice order maintenance see no advantage in disturbing the normal routine of an area or community as long as the ongoing questionable or illegal behavior in that area or community is discreetly conducted. If that behavior threatens to expand beyond its geographical confines, or is conducted in less discreet ways, the police will generally take action. Police who practice order maintenance more or less allow various questionable or illegal behaviors to continue without interference as long as those behaviors are discreet and do not run the risk of extending to the larger population.

POLICING STYLES

American law enforcement has embraced three **policing styles** to fulfill the expectations of the interest groups they choose to serve: legalistic, watchman, and service.[4]

The *legalistic style* of policing emphasizes law enforcement. Instead of relying on informal methods of social control, the police set about to strictly enforce the law without consideration of the seriousness of the offense. This style of policing is often associated with those agencies that pride themselves on being strictly professional, but it can thrive only during periods of prosperity and plentiful resources. Jails tend to fill rather quickly in geographic areas where the legalistic style of policing is emphasized. If there is no additional money for jail construction, or expansion of the court system, law enforcement administrators are forced to ratchet-down the legalistic methods practiced by their officers.

The *watchman style* of policing gives highest priority to order maintenance. Order maintenance, simply stated, reflects the notion that it is important to allow society to operate rather smoothly and police intervention is necessary only when order is clearly threatened. This approach is conducive to the practice of allowing behavior, legal or illegal, to go unchecked until that behavior threatens to contaminate larger portions of society. Such behavior may also draw police intervention if it poses political embarrassment to political leaders in power. This style of policing is germane to geographic regions with small police agencies and in areas where people live in relatively homogeneous communities.

The *service style* of policing is germane to departments that take all situations seriously but acknowledge that all situations do not require or necessitate arrest. Problem-solving takes precedence over catching criminals. This style of policing attempts to extract the positive elements of the legalistic and watchman styles and provide services and protection to communities. It is most common in small or affluent communities.

In most instances, police departments have aspects of all three styles in operation, although from time to time one style may receive more emphasis.[5] The personality of an individual officer may also dictate the style of policing he or she practices on a day-to-day basis. Some officers consider themselves crime-fighters. These officers may lean toward the legalistic style. Officers who are looking forward to retirement may subscribe to the watchman style of policing—stay back unless something very serious presents itself. Certain officers see their role as helping citizens, and these officers are likely to prefer service-oriented policing.

There are many activities associated with the function of American policing. Patrol is the duty that most police are currently assigned to.[6] There are many types of police patrol. Automobiles, motorcycles, bicycles, boats, fixed-wing aircraft, and helicopters are all patrol vehicles. There also are foot patrols and patrols that require officers to develop equestrian skills—horse patrol. However, most departments rely on the automobile patrol. The automobile patrol seems to be the preferred method of maintaining order and enforcing laws in nearly all jurisdictions. Police drive through their assigned sectors looking for the usual and the unusual. The unusual is not defined as a criminal act, but "not fitting in" can draw the attention of police officers. In addition, automobile patrol is usually limited to behavior in the "open." Some people, generally economically disadvantaged people, spend more time in open view than people who are not economically disadvantaged.[7]

Generally speaking, officers assigned to patrols are responsible for maintaining order or preserving the peace, enforcing laws, traffic control, investigating crimes, and answering calls from citizens. To a large degree, these responsibilities are prioritized by administrators or supervisors. For example, it is not uncommon for a shift supervisor to announce that "Officers A and B have not written very many tickets this month. Is there a problem, officers?" In response to being singled out in that way, Officers A and B might spend their entire shift writing tickets, perhaps even issuing a ticket to a driver whose front bumper extends two inches over the white line at a crosswalk. Often, however, patrolling responsibilities and prioritizing have a more profound impact on communities and in some instances on entire cities.

In the early 1990s New York City greeted William Bratton as new commissioner of the New York Police Department. Bratton centered his attention on the New York subways and reinvigorated the subway police. He was able to acquire new equipment and weapons for officers working below the streets. In an all-out war against fare evasion and the homeless people who live in the New York subway tunnels, he authorized sweeps of the subway trains and eventually claimed that the subway system had been recaptured for citizens.

His justification for such action stemmed from the *broken-windows theory,* which posits that more serious crimes evolve from minor infractions.[8] Mayor Rudolph Giuliani came to power in New York City also during the 1990s. The Giuliani-Bratton team moved the war on crime from the subways to the streets. War was declared on window washers (the unemployed individuals who washed car windshields for tips at city intersections), prostitutes, truant children (many of whom were truant because they had problems coping with inner-city school violence), and homeless people living under bridges. The people of New York rejoiced. After all, it is unsettling to be employed and have to contend with, or see, the dangerous population of homeless and unemployed people on a daily basis in the streets—it gives capitalism a bad name.[9]

Giuliani and Bratton may have cleaned up New York City, but where did they put the rubbish? Did the homeless and the unemployed simply disappear or vanish from the face of the earth? Should this be of concern to us? During the Giuliani-Bratton war against the poor, little mention was made of policing insider-trading violations, fraud, or other white-collar crimes occurring in New York at the time. Police patrol operations of the variety just discussed demonstrate what is commonly referred to as *selective law enforcement,* whereby administrative policies prioritize the types of laws to be enforced. Selective law enforcement is also linked to police discretionary power and practices—who will be arrested and who will simply receive a warning.

SPECIAL UNITS

Another function of law enforcement has been the creation of specialty units to combat specific types of crimes and respond to specific circumstances. Some special units have been components of law enforcement for many years. Vice and narcotics units/squads are employed to combat offenses such as pickpocket activities, prostitution, and illegal drug activities. Some of the special units that have been created over the past few years include SWAT (special weapons and tactics) teams—"Ninja Turtle units," which sport the latest in high-tech military attire. It is difficult to determine what impact special units have on the war against crime. Their performance is generally evaluated by police administrators or by the media, which generally provide police with good press as previously noted. It is difficult to evaluate SWAT team–like units because there is no way to compare these units with the proficiency levels of line officers. There are also gang units. The creation of SWAT and gang units was thought to be necessary for responding to special situations that patrol officers were not equipped to handle for a variety of reasons—training, physical and psychological conditions, and so on. In addition, law enforcement agencies have specialized investigative units. Often these units employ detectives, generally selected based on experience, expertise, and in some cases political connections with administrators.

Investigative units center their attention on robberies, burglaries, auto theft, and murder/homicide. Policing agencies generally support the existence of their special-unit programs. We simply state for the record the fact that crime rates have been consistent over the past several decades and, beyond large prison populations, there seems to be little evidence indicating that any special unit has made a major impact on its particular area of expertise. Youngsters today and members of that age group at the start of the drug war seem to be using illegal substances at a similar rate. Homicide detectives can do little to stop homicide; they are usually brought into a case when someone is reported missing or there is a body. Vice-squad detectives try in vain to control the world's "oldest profession": prostitution. Gang activities do seem to have declined in recent years, and we are certain that gang units around the country are taking credit. However, we contend that any decline is more likely a result of increases in employment and age/demographic changes rather than of gang-squad activity.[10]

THE POLICE SUBCULTURE

Subcultures are "various groups within the society who share elements of the basic culture but who also possess some distinctive folkways and mores."[11] The **police subculture** has been described by Manning and Van Maanen as follows:

> The occupational culture [subculture] constructed by the police consists of long-standing rules of thumb, a somewhat special language and ideology that help edit a member's everyday experiences, shared standards of relevance, matter-of-fact prejudices, models for street-level etiquette and demeanor, certain customs and rituals suggestive of how members are to relate not only to each other but to outsiders, and a sort of residual category consisting of the assorted miscellany of some rather plain police horse sense. All of these cultural modes of thinking, knowing, and doing are, of course, so rooted in the recurrent problems and common experiences of the police that they are regarded by insiders as perfectly natural responses to the world they inhabit. Indeed, cultures arise as a way of coping with, and making sense of, a given environment. That this occupational culture has displayed such remarkable stability through time is itself testimony to the persistence of the problematic habitat within which police work takes place.[12]

Like every subculture, the police subculture nestles within the broader social culture. Subcultures are small composites of the larger society; the members of a subculture have a vested interest in the subculture's interests, concerns, and values. For example, members of a sorority or fraternity are often most comfortable with members of their own house. Occupational distinctions also contribute to the gravitation to subculture groups by members of a given occupation. Military personnel are more comfortable with other military personnel than they are with civilians not subjected to, or familiar with, military regimentation. Some civilians discuss passive resistance, opposition to war, and other concerns at odds with the worldview of career military personnel, for whom war is often the key to promotion. Similarly, police officers are most comfortable with other police officers.

Socialization into the police subculture generally occurs in three stages. The police academy is the scene of the introductory stage. A civilian applicant is transformed into a police officer recruit and then into a bona fide police officer and member of the police subculture. The application process and oral examination begin to weed out individuals who will not fit into the police subculture. One of our former students confided that he had "blown" the oral exam in his application to become a police officer:

> I was asked what I would do if I saw a fellow police officer being attacked by someone in the street. My response was that first I would sort out the situation in my mind, and then call for backup and then proceed to help the officer. The answer they wanted was to not think about the situation—just go and help the officer immediately. I guess that means that because I would think first then I wouldn't be a good cop. Maybe they are right, but I do not believe that thinking first should disqualify me—but it did.

Oral exams are subjective exams. The outcome of an oral exam may hinge on a recent directive to the board or on an applicant's lack of eye-to-eye contact with the interviewer. Applicants typically come from working-class families. They are not preoccupied with becoming authoritarians. More often than not, they are seeking employment, and most have an idealistic notion that as police officers they will be able to help people.[13] The police academy stresses technical training—firearms training, arrest procedures, legal statutes, and survival skills—and subscription to values embraced by the occupation. Survival skills training emphasizes the notion that police officers must rely on other police officers.

The second stage of the socialization process occurs after graduation from the academy. The recruit is now a rookie police officer. Most recent graduates are assigned to a field training officer (FTO). The FTO is often a seasoned veteran who has the responsibility to familiarize the recruit with life on the streets. The FTO might be a *progressive* police officer who stresses protection of civil liberties, or he or she may subscribe to the *civilians-as-scumbags* view, which stresses the notion that it is "us against them." The recruit has very little if anything to do with the selection of an FTO. In many cases, the new recruit is not aware that he or she is being brought under the influence of the subculture.[14] In many instances, recruits do not realize that their previous social networks are being altered. Their former friends are now being replaced with relationships developed during their academy experience and their early field experiences with their FTO.[15]

The third stage, which tends to solidify the commitment to policing, occurs when the individual makes the transition from rookie to police officer—becomes one of the "guys" (whether the individual is female or male). The relatively new police officer may be assigned to a partner, has passed the often required probationary period, and believes she or he deserves the title *officer.* Of course, more seasoned officers may continue to view her or him as a rookie. The relationships developed in the academy and during the rookie period have matured and solidified. The new officer may still cling to previous relationships, but the commitment to those relationships often diminishes. At this juncture the person begins to develop a police officer style.

The search for a style or niche in policing is not an easy task.

> I maintain that the work group molds the officer's personality. I call it street survival. Rookies find themselves under tremendous pressure and tend to gravitate from one end of the pendulum to the other in their search to find a comfortable style of policing. Every rookie knows his or her reputation needs to be established before fully being accepted as a fellow officer. Hence, rookies tend to be impetuous, aggressive, and very rough around the edges. They need to learn when and how to bullshit in the street, how to finesse the person they are confronting, and how to read the interactional cues and body language that dictate appropriate courses of action and impending danger.[16]

The typology of modern policing styles was developed by John Broderick. He identified four styles: enforcer, idealist, realist, and optimist:

1. The *enforcer* focuses on clearing the streets of criminals. Individual rights or constitutional safeguards are not high priorities for officers subscribing to this style.
2. The *idealist* is the opposite of the enforcer. Officers subscribing to this style have faith in the law and procedures intended to protect citizens' rights.

3. The *realist* is a cynic. Officers subscribing to this style have little faith in the criminal justice system. Often they become alienated from other officers, in part because of their belief that cleaning the streets or preserving individual rights is not going to make much of a difference.
4. The *optimist* embraces the notion that police can make a significant difference in society. Rather than placing crime fighting at the top of their list of priorities, these officers see their role as being service providers.[17]

In their efforts to "enforce the law" and especially to "maintain order," the police continuously create many problems for themselves. In the name of enforcing the law, they actively participate in the violation of the law. Cases of what is commonly known as *police corruption* have been a mainstay of American policing since the nineteenth century. It is to this problem that we now turn.

POLICE CORRUPTION

One of the difficulties limiting any discussion of police corruption is that of obtaining accurate data. The fact that the police are highly secretive about their activities no doubt contributes to this problem. Also, more often than not, investigations of police corruption are in-house investigations conducted by the internal affairs division. A related problem is that citizens' complaints often become so entangled in bureaucratic red tape that most citizens give up or bring no charges at all. When police corruption is exposed, it is usually when an individual police officer or a small number of officers blow the whistle or investigative reporters dig a little deeper than usual and uncover and then expose police corruption. One common source of exposure over the years has been the work of special crime commissions.

Since the Wickersham Commission in 1931, various governmental commissions have found corruption within police departments to be common.[18] The most thorough investigations into this problem were made by the **Knapp Commission** in New York City in 1973. The Knapp investigation stemmed from allegations brought forth by the plainclothes patrolman Frank Serpico, who became a celebrity (his story was made into a book, a movie, and a TV series). In the words of the Commission's final report: "We found corruption to be widespread."[19]

The Commission found that plainclothesmen were involved in a "pad," or collections of payments (up to $3,000 per month), from several gambling establishments. The share per month per officer ranged from $300 to $400 in midtown Manhattan to $1,500 in Harlem. Officer Frank Serpico charged that nineteen Bronx plainclothesmen received an average monthly share (called the "nut" by the police) of $800. The Commission found that Brooklyn plainclothesmen brought in an average "nut" of $1,200.[20]

Payoffs in narcotics enforcement (known as "scores") were common. The Commission found a pattern "whereby corrupt officers customarily collected scores in substantial amounts from narcotics violators. These scores were either kept by individual officers or shared with a partner and, perhaps, a superior officer. They ranged from minor shakedowns to payments of many thousands of dollars." The largest payoff discovered was $80,000.[21]

The Commission found that there were regular payoffs from construction sites, bars, grocery stores, and other business establishments, mostly for around $20 but so numerous as to add substantially to an officer's take-home pay. After-hours bars, prostitutes, and individuals wanting their court cases fixed also paid officers on a regular basis. Even superior officers were not immune. Quite often they had patrolmen serve as "bagmen" who collected "fees" (bribes) for their superiors in return for a percentage of the "take."

The Commission distinguished between two categories of corrupt policemen: meat-eaters and grass-eaters. **Meat-eaters** were those heavily involved in receiving payoffs. **Grass-eaters** accepted payoffs only if they happened to come their way. The Commission believed that the grass-eaters were the heart of the problem:

> Their great numbers tend to make *corruption* "respectable." They also tend to encourage the code of silence that brands anyone who exposes corruption a traitor. At the time our

investigation began, any policeman violating the code did so at his peril. The result was described in our interim report: "The rookie who comes into the department is faced with the situation where it is easier for him to become corrupt than to remain honest."[22]

As the Knapp Commission suggested, officers tend to be socialized into a police subculture that supports various forms of deviant activities. The Commission distinguished between the *bad-apple theory* and the *group support theory* of police corruption. Stoddard, in another study (of a police department in the southwestern part of the country), found widespread support for certain forms of deviance among officers. Specifically, Stoddard found an informal code that supported deviancy. Rookies were pressured to go along with this code, and failure to do so resulted in group ostracism. "Lack of acceptance not only bars the neophyte from the inner secrets of the profession but may isolate him socially and professionally from his colleagues and even his superiors."[23] The **bad-apple theory** suggests that police corruption stems only from a few bad apples in an otherwise clean barrel. The **group support theory** suggests that the barrel is not so clean after all and that deviancy, though not indulged in by all police officers within a department, is condoned by most officers.

Both the bad-apple and the group support theories fail to adequately explain police corruption as a persistent phenomenon. Both imply that a new kind of police officer (perhaps of the Serpico variety) is all that is needed. But the persistence of corruption and the social, political, economic, and legal contexts of it suggest that this type of reform would not solve the problem. One reason is the fact that so much money is involved and there are very powerful interests (usually on the part of "respectable" people) enmeshed in police corruption. In other words, evidence suggests that police corruption is not the problem; the problem appears to be that the economic and political structure of American society breeds corruption. A study by Chambliss of corruption in Seattle lends support to this view.

Chambliss found corruption to be widespread in Seattle as he studied the problem through personal observation over a period of several years. This corruption involved not only police officers but also members of organized crime and key political and business figures, as well as high-ranking police officials. Chambliss discovered that all of these individuals participated in such illegal activities as gambling, prostitution, and loan-sharking, and individual police officers took bribes of substantial amounts. Most of these activities were restricted to the fringes of slum communities, where "respectable" citizens could participate but not be seen by their fellow citizens. The police made a few token arrests and even some "well publicized raids" but avoided involving influential citizens.

Chambliss suggests that there existed a symbiotic relationship between the law enforcement bureaucracy and the major suppliers of vice in Seattle:

> The gambling, prostitution, drug distribution, pornography, and usury which flourish in the lower-class center of the city do so with the compliance, encouragement, and cooperation of the major political and law enforcement officials in the city. There is in fact a symbiotic relationship between the law enforcement–political organizations of the city and a group of *local,* as distinct from national, men who control the distribution of vices.[24]

He says that in the study of organized crime there has been an overemphasis on the *criminal* and "a corresponding de-emphasis on *corruption* as an institutional component of America's legal–political system. Concomitantly, it has obscured perception of the degree to which the structure of America's law and politics creates and perpetuates syndicates that supply the vices in our major cities."[25] Chambliss concludes:

> Organized crime becomes not something that exists outside law and government but is instead a creation of them, or perhaps more accurately a hidden but nonetheless integral part of the governmental structure. The people most likely to be exposed by public inquiries (whether conducted by the FBI, a grand jury, or the Internal Revenue Service) may officially be outside of government, but the cabal of which they are a part is organized around, run by, and created in the interests of economic, legal, and political elites.[26]

Another implication of Chambliss's study is that law enforcement is a form of class domination, especially in the case of vice laws. As Chambliss found out (and as most observers have noted), those who were arrested were mainly small-time, lower-class people. The well-to-do who actively participated in these vices were rarely if ever arrested. From this perspective, the police serve to perpetuate profit-seeking ventures of the "private enterprise system" (i.e., privately run by a small minority).

Seattle is only one of several other cities across the nation that have experienced this type of corruption. In each case, the law enforcement bureaucracy was deeply enmeshed in the corruption.[27]

Lest you think that police corruption is a problem of the past, consider a recent scandal in Los Angeles, centering on a special antigang unit called **CRASH** (Community Resources against Street Hoodlums). The unit was originally called TRASH (the "T" stood for Total); the name was changed for obvious reasons. Under this program the police engaged in "surveillance and harassment." Their explicit purpose was, to use one officer's words, to "jam" suspected gang members—to harass and then move on, making no arrest in most cases. Officers were rotated out of the unit after two or three years and thus never had a real opportunity to develop detailed knowledge about the communities.[28]

During one five-week period in 1995, gang-squad officers were accused of brutalizing and violating the rights of two families in their homes. These cases cost taxpayers about $1 million to settle the family claims. In one case, a 15-year-old was hit in the mouth with a shotgun butt, and his father was suffocated until he passed out and was later taken to the hospital. According to police records, there was not even an internal investigation conducted of these incidents. The department appears to have ignored the claims. It has been reported that at least twelve officers were relieved of duty for illegally shooting suspects, planting evidence, beating one man, falsifying evidence, and many other crimes. All twelve belonged to the LAPD's elite CRASH antigang unit. But that was the least of their troubles, as it turned out.

Public Servants or Public Thugs? The Rampart Scandal in Los Angeles

There are those who suggest that American law enforcement has overstepped its boundaries. Those boundaries are defined by the U.S. Constitution and the Bill of Rights. In some cases, those boundaries are defined through criminal statutes.[29] Time and time again, law enforcement has been confronted with acts of brutality and abuse of authority. Rodney King (Los Angeles, 1992), Malice Green (Detroit, 1992), Waco, Texas (1993), and the **Rampart scandal** (Los Angeles, 1999). Time and time again, the explanation has been directed to the bad-apple theory. The problem may not be the apples at all. The problem may be the barrel.

By late October 1999, the Los Angeles Police Department (LAPD) recognized the dilemma they were in. A LAPD lieutenant revealed that the Rampart investigation had revealed that a sergeant in the antigang unit had given officers instructions to plant guns on suspects, and that evidence of stealing drugs and using prostitutes to sell drugs was part of the routine by some LAPD police officers. The investigation into the LAPD Rampart station became significantly larger than police officials had early revealed publicly. In fact, as the investigation continued, it was revealed that the sergeant had done more than simply give orders to plant weapons on suspects. He also helped to create fictitious crime scenes such as the one where one 19 year old, Francisco Ovando, was shot in 1996, framed, and falsely imprisoned. There was hard evidence that members of the CRASH unit stole drugs from dealers and then employed street prostitutes to sell the drugs for their own profit. One officer indicated that the CRASH unit officers behaved like the gangs they were supposed to police.[30]

In mid-November it was revealed that Rampart police officers conducted random stops and confrontations involving minor offenses that resulted in beatings and detention of citizens. Although 40 percent of the Rampart officers were Latinos, residents indicate that those officers were among the worst. Some people indicated that even the Latino officers would refer to them as "wetbacks" and often asked them why they did not go back to Mexico. Some people indicated that Rampart officers set them up so they could not acquire legal residency status. One area resident, Al Pina, 36, who moved to the area to take a job as vice president of the local community development corporation, stated that he was surprised to see the number of random stops conducted by Rampart police. In fact, Pina was also stopped by three officers, restrained, and searched, as another officer held a gun on him. When the officers released him, he asked why he had been singled out for such treatment. Officer David Solis told him he "fit the profile of a drug dealer." Pina, a clean-cut former Air Force sergeant, said he had never felt so humiliated in his life. In another case, Juan Jimenez, 20, a United Parcel Service stock clerk, indicated he had been detained and handcuffed by police at least twelve times in 1999. He was en route to night school or to his volunteer job where he tutored children. On one occasion, Jimenez had been mugged, and he called the police. When the police responded, they handcuffed and searched him. In poor neighborhoods, everyone becomes a target for police abuse of power.[31]

In 1998, Walter Rivas was arrested and framed by Officer Michael Buchanan. Buchanan asked Rivas, "Who do you think they are going to believe, are they going to believe you or me?" The focus on Buchanan placed the arrest and conviction of hundreds into question. Buchanan was relieved of duty in October 1999 in connection with another case, in which he and officer Perez had framed a suspect.[32] By mid-December, it was projected that as many as three thousand criminal cases may have been affected by questionable police tactics including perjury and planting evidence on suspects.[33]

POLICE ABUSE OF POWER

It is safe to say that the police have the kind of power reserved for a select few in any society: the power not only to deprive a person of liberty (via arrest) but also to take someone's life. One of the most controversial issues in policing has been the use of violence against citizens. And the ultimate occurs when a police officer kills a citizen. This issue arouses the most controversy because it inevitably involves the killing of a minority citizen, especially African Americans.

The case of Amadou Diallo illustrates this issue better than any other. Diallo, a 22-year-old man from Guinea living in New York City, was shot no less than 19 times (police fired 41 times) by four white New York City police officers who were involved in some "aggressive patrol." The four officers were part of an elite, 380-member Street Crime Unit unleashed on the streets of New York to "get tough" on crime.[34] The officers claimed that Diallo acted "suspicious" while starting to enter his apartment building and, when asked to "freeze," brought out his wallet to show his ID. Apparently he was a bit confused about what the police wanted him to do, having received contradictory orders to show some ID yet "not move." The officers say they thought his wallet was a gun. A subsequent trial resulted in an acquittal for all four.[35]

This police action was part of Mayor Rudolph Giuliani's "crackdown" on crime in New York City. Previous to this case was that of a Haitian immigrant, Abner Louima, who was sodomized with a toilet plunger while in police custody.[36] Once again, the police were engaged in "aggressive" police work, this being part of the mayor's "zero tolerance" policy on crime in New York City, which resulted in numerous lawsuits and charges of police harassment (police misconduct charges went up 45% between 1993 and 1997).

It was constantly claimed by Giuliani and law enforcement officials that the "zero tolerance" policy was responsible for a 50 percent drop in index crimes in New York City from 1990 to 1996. Yet the crime rate had already begun to drop long before this so-called quality-of-life policing was initiated. In fact, crime rates dropped all over the country, with or without such police tactics.[37] Examples of such tough police tactics abound, ranging from normal everyday methods of harassment in minority communities—a long tradition documented in numerous studies—to physical brutality and murder.[38]

The Rodney King beating—documented by accident when a citizen with a camcorder happened to be near the scene and taped almost the entire incident—resulted in nationwide publicity and a highly emotional trial, resulting in an acquittal of all the officers involved, although three were subsequently convicted on federal civil rights violations. To most minority citizens—especially those living in inner-city ghettos—this police behavior was "business as usual." In 1994, the Mollen Commission on police corruption in New York City noted widespread police brutality in the Bronx, discovered that one officer in particular was known as "the Mechanic" for his tendency to "tune people up"—police jargon for a beating. In Los Angeles it was recently observed that whenever African Americans encounter a police officer, "They don't know whether justice will be meted out or whether judge, jury and executioner is pulling up behind them."[39]

There is plenty of evidence that police brutality and police killings have historically been aimed at racial minorities. For example, until recent years the ratio of African Americans to whites who were shot and killed by the police went as high as 8 to 1. In recent years, after a multitude of complaints resulting in police departments changing their policies, the ratio has declined to a still-unacceptable 3 to 1.[40]

Then there's the problem of **racial profiling** and the numerous instances in which African Americans are pulled over for **DWB (driving while black).** Chambliss reports that a special unit of the Washington, D.C., police known as the Rapid Deployment Unit (RDU) patrols certain areas in the ghetto "continuously looking for cars with young black men in them." Vehicular stops for DWB, says Congressman John Conyers (D-Michigan), are "well-known to African-American males across the country."[41] A recent study found that between 1995 and 1997, 70 percent of the drivers stopped on Interstate 95 in Maryland were black, even though black and Hispanic motorists constituted only about 17.5 percent of those speeding.[42]

This type of behavior by the police is typical of "policing the ghetto" in American society. This stems from the idea that the ghetto is like an "internal colony." The ghettos within most inner cities of America are almost totally separated from the rest of society (both literally and figuratively speaking). Part of this separation can be seen in some of the most common problems that plague these areas: poverty, unemployment and underemployment, substandard housing, inadequate social services, high crime rates, and high rates of alcohol and drug abuse. In a real sense, these ghettos are so separated from the rest of society that they can be likened to colonies. In a recent study Massey and Denton illustrate that what this problem boils down to is specific patterns of *segregation:*

> residential segregation has been instrumental in creating a structural niche within which a deleterious set of attitudes and behaviors—a culture of segregation—has arisen and flourished. Segregation created the structural conditions for the emergence of an oppositional culture that devalues work, schooling, and marriage and that stresses attitudes and behaviors that are antithetical and often hostile to success in the larger economy.[43]

Because of segregation (especially within the housing market), African Americans have been far less able than other minorities (e.g., Mexican Americans, Jews, Italians, Poles) to escape. Historically, note Massey and Denton, until about 1900 most African Americans lived in areas that were largely white. Massey and Denton document the changes through the use of an "isolation index"—the percentage of African Americans who live in black-only neighborhoods dominated by African Americans. In 1930 the isolation index stood at 31.7 in northern cities (data for southern cities are unavailable); by 1970 this percentage had increased to 73.5.[44]

Massey and Denton note that about one-third of all African Americans presently live in areas characterized by what they say is **hypersegregation,** conditions of "intense racial segregation." These areas are *highly segregated* in at least four of the five dimensions of segregation identified by Massey and Denton: unevenness, isolation, clustering, concentration, and centralization. By *unevenness* they mean that within an urban area African Americans may be overrepresented in some areas and underrepresented in others. *Isolation* is in reference to African Americans and whites rarely living in the same neighborhoods. *Clustering* occurs when African American neighborhoods constitute a continuous enclave occupying a large area of land instead of being scattered about the city. *Concentration* occurs when they are concentrated in one small area instead of being sparsely distributed throughout a city. *Centralization* is high when most African Americans live in the central core of a city instead of being spread out along the periphery. According to Massey and Denton,

> A high score on any single dimension is serious because it removes blacks from full participation in urban society and limits their access to its benefits…[B]lacks…are more segregated than other groups on any single dimension of segregation, but they are also more segregated on all dimensions simultaneously; and in an important subset of U.S. metropolitan areas, they are very highly segregated on at least four of the five dimensions at once, a pattern we call hypersegregation.[45]

The police can be likened to an "alien force" in "enemy" territory. Several surveys on police attitude toward ghetto residents and comparisons between ghetto police and ghetto residents in terms of socioeconomic characteristics provide evidence of this.[46] Besides, policing the ghetto is beneficial to the police bureaucracy in that arrests of urban, lower-class minorities are much easier to make because these citizens are so powerless. In contrast, arrests of "white middle-class offenders (on college campuses, for example, or in the law offices of Wall Street) are guaranteed to cause the organization and the arresting officers strain because people with political influence or money hire attorneys to defend them." Thus, in a class-stratified society "the powerless, the poor, and those who fit the public stereotype of 'the criminal' are the human resources needed by law enforcement agencies to maximize gains and minimize strains."[47]

One of the most persistent problems facing the American police and helping to create social contexts within which corruption and the abuse of power take place is the enforcement of laws that have no "complaining victim," otherwise known as *victimless crimes*. Indeed, just about every case of police corruption and most cases in which the police are involved in the abuse of power occur within such a context. Prostitution, gambling, and drugs provide the most common contexts for these problems. The next section focuses on how the police engage in the "war on drugs."

THE POLICE AND THE WAR ON DRUGS[48]

The "war on drugs" targets minority groups, especially African Americans. Indeed, there is abundant evidence that the "war on drugs" has been in reality a "war on African Americans" on a scale that is unprecedented in American history. As the research by Jerome Miller has shown, young African American males have received the brunt of law enforcement efforts to "crack down on drugs." He notes that in Baltimore, for example, African Americans were being arrested at a rate six times that of whites, and more than 90 percent of the arrests were for possession.[49] Although the arrest rate for both races among juveniles for heroin and cocaine possession was virtually the same in 1965, by the 1970s the gap began to widen, and by 1990 the arrest rate for African Americans stood at 766, compared to only 68 for whites. Overall, in 1980 the national rate of all drug arrests was about the same for black and white juveniles; during the early 1980s the arrest rate for whites dropped by one-third, while the rate for blacks remained about the same. But as the "war on drugs" expanded, the arrest rate for black youths went from 683 in 1985 to 1,200 in 1989, which was five times the rate for whites. By 1991 it went to 1,415! Nationally, between 1987 and 1988 the number of whites brought into the juvenile court remained virtually the same (up 1%), but the number of minorities referred to the court increased by 42 percent. In Miller's own study of Baltimore, he found that during 1981 only 15 white juveniles were arrested on drug charges, compared to

86 African Americans; in 1991, however, the number of whites arrested dropped to a mere 13, while the number of African Americans skyrocketed to 1,304, or an increase of 1,416 percent! The ratio of African American youths to whites went from about 6 to 1 to 100 to 1![50]

Another study found that "black youths are more often charged with the felony when [the] offense could be considered a misdemeanor." Also, those cases referred to court "are judged as in need of formal processing more often when minority youths are involved." When white youths received placements, such "placements" are more often than not "group home settings or drug treatment while placements for minorities more typically are public residential facilities, including those in the state which provide the most restrictive confinement."[51] A study by Edmund McGarrell found evidence of substantial increases in minority youths being referred to juvenile court, thus increasing the likelihood of being detained. But cases of the detention, petition, and placement of minorities nevertheless exceeded what would have been expected given the increases in referrals. There has been an increase in the formal handling of drug cases, which has become a disadvantage to minorities. "Given the proactive nature of drug enforcement, these findings raise fundamental questions about the targets of investigation and apprehension under the recent war on drugs."[52] As noted in a study of Georgia's crackdown on drugs, the higher arrest rate for African Americans was attributed to one single factor:

> it is easier to make drug arrests in low-income neighborhoods.... Most drug arrests in Georgia are of lower-level dealers and buyers and occur in low-income minority areas. Retail drug sales in these neighborhoods frequently occur on the streets and between sellers and buyers who do not know each other. Most of these sellers are black. In contrast, white drug sellers tend to sell indoors, in bars and clubs and within private homes, and to more affluent purchasers, also primarily white."[53]

Not surprisingly this has had the same impact when considering adult minorities, as they have been systematically singled out in this "war." Although we cover imprisonment rates in Chapter 11, we must mention here that drug offenses account for most of the increase in prison populations in recent years, and it not surprising to find that the prison and jail populations are increasingly dominated by minorities, especially African Americans. Between 1960 and 1992, the percentage of nonwhite inmates rose from around one-third to over half, and the proportion of inmates convicted of drug offenses rose from a mere 5 percent to almost 30 percent. More alarmingly, from 1986 to 1991, right in the middle of the crackdown on drugs, the proportion of African Americans incarcerated for drug offenses went up an incredible 465.5 percent!

Not surprisingly, the overall arrest rate on drug charges has zoomed upward since the early 1980s, especially for African Americans. For instance, the arrest rate for white juveniles on drug charges was greater than the rate for African American juveniles in the early 1970s, but the most recent data (1995) show that the arrest rate for African American juveniles is about four times greater than the rate for whites! Clearly, the police are continuing to carry out their historical mandate to control the "dangerous classes," which today means African Americans and other minorities, in addition to the poor in general.

The police also are involved in another "war" that targets these same "dangerous classes"—namely, the "war on gangs." Indeed, controlling gangs has become one of the major roles of the police institution and in fact the entire criminal justice system. This is our subject in the next section.

THE POLICE AND THE WAR ON GANGS[54]

Because the police are often viewed as society's "first line of defense" against crime, it obviously follows that they are the first segment of the criminal justice system that responds to the youth gang dilemma. The police have responded to gangs with a multitude of ma-neuvers. California's State Task Force offered a number of policy (and legislative) sugges-tions to combat youth gangs: (1) design and develop statewide gang information systems; (2) launch school-based gang and narcotics prevention programs; (3) provide technical as-sistance to local law enforcement agencies in gang analysis; (4) identify gang members under the supervision of the Department of Youth Authority, and intensify parole supervi-sion; (5) establish and expand special units in probation to supervise gang members; (6) create a Southeast Asian youth-gang prevention and intervention program; (7) establish standards throughout the correctional system to discourage gang membership; and (8) using ex-gang members and community street workers, establish a model gang inter-vention program. Although many of these suggestions do not affect law enforcement *directly,* they all have an impact on law enforcement's role in "policing" youth gangs.[55]

In a desperate attempt to find solutions to the problem of youth gangs, violence, and drugs, law enforcement embarked on a voyage that started with proactive approaches such as creating and sponsoring new programs with catchy acronyms—D.A.R.E. (Drug Aware-ness Resistance Education) and S.A.N.E. (Substance Abuse Narcotics Education)—and paying gang members to "fight crime." Some researchers promote the notion that "foot pa-trols" should be a major tactic used against gangs; others like Boyle and Gonzales embrace police programs that target schools and neighborhoods and provide instruction on develop-ing self-esteem, dealing with peer-group pressure, decision making, and so on.[56]

Many police officers in a major midwestern police department agree that a dual-strategy approach is crucial, but both dimensions must be implemented simultaneously: (1) an immediate response that requires interdiction (monitor or arrest) to preserve the peace and save lives and (2) implementation of long-range plans that include "realistic" options from which youth may choose (preventive measures such as job training and cre-ation, recreation facilities that provide supervised activities for youth, etc.). One officer who had worked with gang members for nearly eight years, in the course of his regular patrol duties, stated, "Many of these kids have zero options. They live in a shit hole. I can arrest them. They may, in rare instances, actually do some time. When they get out, they are dumped back into the same shit hole."[57] Another officer pointed out that "These kids have no place to play. They find some structure (e.g., a street-light pole) to nail a back-board and hoop, and play basketball in the middle of the street. They disrupt traffic and make drivers mad. Pretty soon the kids just say fuck it and go find something else to do—they go banging."[58] Most interesting is the reference to "kids," suggesting an acknowledg-ment by these officers that these youths are not "necessarily" gangsters or criminals; rather, many of them are "children." This language is qualitatively different from the rhetoric used by those who have bastardized the term "kids" (a term frequently associated with a stage of human development) to less flattering abstractions like "scavengers," which is used by Taylor.[59] Of course, in a broader sense, these officers are drawing attention to structural issues germane to many neighborhoods in the inner city.

The interdiction dimension of law enforcement's response to youth gangs is a reflec-tion of the tremendous pressure placed on police to produce results. Many law enforce-ment agencies have come to rely on special units. Several scholars have pointed out advantages from the creation of these units.[60] Others are less than enthusiastic about the special-unit approach.[61] With a nearly impossible mandate (to eradicate or at least control youth gangs), many law enforcement administrators and local governments often find themselves financially driven to replenish insufficient resources. Many have had to tap into funding sources that contribute to the continued "exploitation" of America's youth gangs.

During the past few years the federal government has provided funding assistance through block grants designated for youth-gang interdiction. Most often, these grants are used to create and support social control strategies rather than solution-oriented approaches. We found one law enforcement agency that formed a special "gang unit" in order to com-pete for a piece of the block-grant "pie." This particular jurisdiction did not have a youth-gang problem at the time of application, nor does this jurisdiction have a gang problem now.

During an interview, the detective in charge of the newly formed "gang unit" revealed that "The mayor wanted a gang unit because he had heard that federal grant money was available for police departments that had adopted this sort of special unit." When asked what his gang unit did, he responded, "Nothing. We don't have any gangs in this community. We have some kids who play with spray paint. At best, we have a few gang 'wanna-bees.'"[62]

In another instance, one major midwestern urban police department has a gang squad consisting of more than sixty officers and five units: administrative, enforcement, investigation, intelligence, and surveillance.[63] The general responsibilities of the squad include

1. Identification and patrol of high youth-group activity, and "shooting scenes" that do not result in death and are not dealt with by other special units.
2. Identification of active criminal youth and their leaders.
3. Collection, analysis, and dissemination of all information related to youth-group problems.
4. Investigation, enforcement, and intelligence gathering related to all youth-group criminal activities.
5. Deploying both uniformed and plainclothes officers as required to respond to scenes of youth-group criminal problems. This includes planned youth events that have the potential for youth criminal problems and violence (e.g., rock concerts, rap concerts, high school sporting events, ethnic festival events).
6. Surveillance of youth-oriented activities.
7. Handling, investigating, and securing warrants in probate and recorder's court for all arrests and detentions stemming from firearms offenses occurring in and around public and private schools in the city.

Specific enforcement unit duties include "aggressive enforcement" that targets areas that have a *potential* for youth-crime activity (e.g., schools, gatherings of youth for social functions, and neighborhoods experiencing high incidents of street shootings and gang activity) and aggressive techniques (traffic stops, stop-and-frisk, etc.). The duties of the investigative unit include conducting live "show-ups" and preparing warrant requests for the prosecution of gang members and their associates. The surveillance unit targets individuals, vehicles, groups, or locations on the basis of information provided by the investigation and intelligence units.

The intelligence unit is responsible for such things as preparing profiles on perpetrators of criminal acts who are involved with various gangs and maintaining files with information relevant to gangs (nickname file, vehicle file, gang membership, affiliation with other gangs, etc.). This special unit uses the following criteria (similar to those used by many other jurisdictions) to identify gang members: (1) an individual admits membership in a gang; (2) a reliable informant identifies an individual as a gang member; (3) a reliable informant identifies an individual as a gang member, and this information is corroborated by independent information; (4) an individual resides in or frequents a particular gang area, adopts a gang's style of dress, use of hand signs, symbols, and tattoos, and associates with known gang members; (5) an individual has been arrested several times in the company of identified gang members for offenses consistent with usual gang activity. When there are strong indications that an individual has a "close relationship" (how this is to be determined is not specified) with a gang but does not fit the above criteria, he or she is identified as a "gang associate."

An obvious paradox exists for this gang squad when one considers the specific duties of each unit in the context of what the squad calls its underlying philosophy. The squad is essentially a *proactive* group that curtails the activity of youthful offenders through *proactive enforcement in areas that are heavily concentrated with gang members.* What should also be obvious is that such a philosophy results in concerted efforts to maintain control and surveillance in mostly minority and lower-class communities, because individuals living there have the greatest probability of being identified as "gang members."[64]

On any given day, rarely are more than four or five officers actually working on gang-specific cases within their jurisdiction. Typically, "working gangs" for this squad is limited to conducting investigations when alleged gang members are "possible" suspects in a crime. Moreover, it is common knowledge among police officers throughout this department that assignment to the gang squad provides strong credentials for promotion; thus, membership in the gang squad in this jurisdiction is little more than a "political" position. Several officers agreed with one officer's perception, "Members of the gang unit profile around and play cowboy. When they do make contact with gang members they do little more than harass them." Another officer stated, "We (patrol officers) are the ones who work the gangs. We deal with them on a daily basis. The gang squad is too busy dealing with the media, and kissing the Chief's ass." Suggesting that this perception may extend beyond this midwestern jurisdiction, a San Jose police veteran of twenty-two years remarked, "Gang units are like every other special unit in policing—full of bullshit and totally political."[65]

Conducting "sweeps" or "rousts" of targeted areas is another strategy employed by police: many police officers converge on a target area for the purpose of eradicating (or relocating) specific forms of criminal or undesirable behavior. Similar methods were employed by the SS to "relocate" the Jewish population in Nazi Germany; however, we suspect that the American public, including political officials, is not willing to go quite that far to provide a "solution" to the youth-gang problem. Following public outcries to local officials about prostitution, police have had some success in "relocating" prostitutes using sweeps and rousts. In the case of youth-gang interdiction, this tactic is analogous to an attempt to put out a forest fire with a water bucket. It is possible to remove prostitutes from a particular neighborhood (at least for a while). It is more difficult, and legally and morally questionable, to remove youth-gang members from their neighborhoods, homes, or families. Often this tactic does more harm than good, particularly when local citizens view this approach as an example of racism (e.g., Watts, Newark, and Detroit during the 1960s; instrumental in events leading to riots in South Central Los Angeles in 1992).

An example of suppression tactics can be seen in **Operation Hammer** and similar police suppression tactics in Los Angeles during the late 1980s. This was a major police response to gangs in South Central Los Angeles under the administration of Police Chief Daryl Gates. The crackdown began in April 1988 and focused on ten square miles in the South Central area. It was like a "search and destroy" mission in Vietnam.[66] A total of 1,453 arrests were made, mostly for minor offenses—curfew violation, disturbing the peace, and the like. Hundreds more had their names and addresses inserted into an "electronic gang roster" for "future intelligence."[67] To aid in this repressive activity, the police used a special "mobile booking" operation next to the Los Angeles Coliseum. The overall purpose was social control (of African American youth) rather than a serious attempt at reducing crime. Proof of this is the fact that out of the 1,453 arrests, 1,350 persons (93%) were released without any charges filed. More interesting is that half of them turned out *not* to be gang members. Only 60 felony arrests were made, and charges were filed on only 32 of these. Around 200 police officers were used, while during the same period there were two gang-related homicides.[68]

Suppression efforts in the "war on gangs" and "war on drugs" in Los Angeles have met with similar results. For instance, Chief Gates launched **GRATS** (Gang Related Active Trafficker Suppression program) in February and March of 1988, just before Operation Hammer took place. GRATS targeted "drug neighborhoods" for raids by 200 or 300 police officers, who stopped and interrogated anyone suspected of being a gang member, based on how a person dressed and the use of "gang hand signals." Nine sweeps took place, resulting in 500 cars being impounded and around 1,500 arrests. Gates wanted to "get the message out to the cowards out there…that we're going to come and get them." Apparently the message didn't get through, for after the chief gave a speech praising his sweeps, a few members of the Crips gang fired on a crowd on a street corner in South Central, killing a 19-year-old woman.[69]

This crackdown was supported by many conservative leaders, including County Supervisor Kenneth Hahn, who asked for the use of the National Guard, suggesting that Los

Angeles was "fighting the war on gang violence…that's worse than Beirut." A state senator's press secretary argued that "when you have a state of war, civil rights are suspended for the duration of the conflict." Meanwhile, the NAACP reported that during these events there were hundreds of complaints about unlawful police conduct and charges that the police were in effect contributing to gang violence by leaving suspects stranded on enemy turf and even going so far as to write over Crip graffiti with Blood graffiti and vice versa.[70]

Moore notes a similar crackdown on gangs in Los Angeles that took place on four consecutive weekends in the late 1980s, which netted 563 arrests (mostly on outstanding warrants), three ounces of cocaine, and $9,000 in cash related to the drug trade.[71] In San Diego a similar sweep resulted in 146 arrests during a one-week period (mostly for minor offenses, as usual), and only 17 individuals were still in custody at the end of the week. Similar suppression efforts have been tried, with the same results, in Chicago, Milwaukee, Baltimore, and Boston.[72]

In still another crackdown, Chief Gates ordered a raid that turned into what some called an "orgy of violence" as police punched and kicked residents, threw washing machines into bathtubs, smashed walls and furniture with sledge hammers and axes, and even spray-painted slogans on walls, including "LAPD Rules." The result: two minor drug arrests. The police took disciplinary action against thirty-eight officers, including a captain who ordered his officers to "level" and "make uninhabitable" the apartments that were targeted: another Vietnam-style "search and destroy" activity.[73]

Operation Hammer and other suppression efforts resulted in the arrests of an estimated fifty thousand African American youth, as many as 90 percent of whom were never formally charged. Nevertheless, Chief Gates continued such sweeps as a sort of "semi-permanent community occupation" and created "narcotic enforcement zones"—one was known as Operation Cul-de-Sac. These zones—sort of like the Berlin Wall—extended from South Central to the San Fernando Valley to the north.[74]

Behind such crackdowns—and the "war on gangs" in general—is a widespread racist belief system. Typical of such racist beliefs is a comment made by Chief Daryl Gates, chief architect of gang suppression efforts in Los Angeles. Concerning a scandal involving the deaths of African American men because of the police use of the chokehold he remarked: "We may be finding that in some Blacks when [the carotid chokehold] is applied the veins or arteries do not open up as fast as they do on normal [sic] people."[75]

Ironically, one of America's gross social injustices (also believed to be a contributing factor to the proliferation of youth gangs) may actually assist law enforcement in their quest for "victory" over youth gangs—racial segregation. There are social control advantages resulting from segregation. Jackson writes, "Segregation may reduce the pressure on authorities to police minority populations, since segregation reduces interracial crime, the phenomenon most likely to result in pressure on crime control authorities." Moreover, she adds, "Fear of crime, coupled with fear of loss of dominance, provides fertile ground for a mobilization of policing resources."[76]

CAN THE POLICE PREVENT CRIME?

In a seminal study of the police, David Bayley begins with the statement: "The police do not prevent crime. This is one of the best kept secrets of modern life. Experts know it, the police know it, but the public does not know it. Yet the police pretend that they are society's best defense against crime and continually argue that if they are given more resources, especially personnel, they will be able to protect communities against crime."[77]

As shown in the two previous sections, the addition of more officers and special units within police departments for the infamous "war on drugs" and "war on gangs" has failed to significantly reduce either of these two social problems. So it is with the problem of crime in general. As dozens of studies have demonstrated, adding more cops bears little or no relationship to actual levels of crime (the yearly mantra of police departments is "we need more police officers," always claiming it will help keep citizens safe). In general, cities with the highest crime rates have the most police per capita.[78]

When more police are added, the usual result is that there is more reported crime, although in some instances there is little or no change in overall crime rates. Much ado is often made about the ratio of police to citizens. This ratio varies considerably, from a high 6.7 officers per 1,000 citizens in Washington, D.C. (which has consistently had one of the highest crime rates in the country), to a low 1.6 officers per 1,000 citizens in San Jose.[79]

Some might argue that it is not so much the number of officers in a department, but rather how they are used that impacts crime rates. Three key areas of policing strategies have been investigated to test this idea: the level of street patrols, rapid response to emergency calls for service, and expert investigations by detectives. Research has found that increasing the response time to a crime, expert investigations by detectives, nor changing the number of patrols in a particular area have any appreciable effect on crime rates.[80]

Regarding changes in response time, we can simply say this: the vast majority of crimes are "cold" by the time, the police are notified (i.e., well before the police know about a crime, the offender is gone). If the police arrive within one minute of a crime being committed, they are more likely to make an arrest; as the time increases, the chances become correspondingly remote.

Similarly, expert investigations by detectives do little to solve crimes unless there is a specifically named suspect. When there is a named suspect, there is about an 86 percent chance of clearing the crime by an arrest. When there is no named suspect, the chances are reduced to 12 percent.[81] The majority of cases have no named suspect. Moreover, as noted in Chapter 2, the percentage of crimes cleared by an arrest has not changed much over the past thirty years.

Altering the level of police patrols in an attempt to lower crime has been subjected to some important empirical investigations. The first and most famous of these experiments was held in Kansas City. The next section explores this experiment in more detail.

The Kansas City Experiment

It was always assumed—without question and without supporting evidence—that adding more cops, especially in high-crime areas, would result in a lower crime rate, mostly because a greater police presence would deter would-be criminals. In 1972 the Kansas City police department decided to test this idea. In the southern part of the city (a high-crime area) fifteen police beats were divided into five groups of three matched beats each. Each group had similar beats in terms of population characteristics, crime levels, and calls for police service. Three different patrol strategies were used for a period of one year. One beat (chosen at random) was patrolled in the normal manner. The second beat increased patrol levels (often called *saturation patrol*); In the third beat, the police came to the area only when there was a complaint.[82]

Before and after the experiment, people in each beat were interviewed to find out how they felt about police services, if they had been victimized by a crime, and to what extent they were fearful of crime. To the surprise of many, by the end of the year there had been no significant differences among the three beats in terms of criminal activity, the amount of reported crime, and victimization rates. Interestingly, citizens in the areas where patrols were increased felt more apprehensive about the likelihood of being the victim of a crime, and respect for the police had actually decreased.

The results do not suggest that police have absolutely no effect on crime. They do suggest, however, that adding police patrols does not reduce crime. In any given area, the number of police patrols is rather small to being with. Thus, additions still leave few officers patrolling an area. Also, many offenders or potential offenders are not concerned about the level of police patrol. In fact, because most crimes are not planned in advance, whether police are around is irrelevant. In the case of violent crimes, most are committed between people who are at least casually acquainted and most are committed indoors (robbery excepted).

Another study of foot patrol in Newark arrived at similar results. In this case, although the crime rate was not affected by increasing foot patrols, citizens' fear of crime was reduced.[83]

Before concluding this section of the chapter, we should point out that there are some things the police can do that have a positive impact on crime. Certain types of crackdowns, in which a specific type of crime or a particular area of a city is targeted with a special police effort, have been shown to be somewhat effective. Also, what has come to be known as *problem-oriented policing* in which certain hot spots are targeted, has helped. The key here is not a mere addition of police officers, but an emphasis on what the officers actually do. Examples include the SMART program in Oakland, California, which targeted drug hot spots by mobilizing not only the police but other agencies (housing, etc.). With these types of programs, however, there is always the danger criminal activities will be displaced to other locations, or that once the heat is off the criminal activities will return. After all, this is an example of reacting after the fact, with no concern for rooting out the *causes* of the problem.[84]

SUMMARY

The police in modern American society function mainly to maintain order. This function all too often leads to significant problems, not the least of which occurs when the police violate the laws they are supposed to enforce. Further, they are socialized into a special subculture that often leads them to abuse their awesome power. Whether through harassment ("driving while black"), the enforcement of drug laws, or the war on gangs, the police too often abuse and sometimes kill citizens, especially the poor and racial minorities. The police institution can be viewed as an "army of occupation" in the inner-city ghettos of this country, which in turn are little more than "internal colonies" isolated or segregated from mainstream society.

KEY TERMS

bad-apple theory 177	hypersegregation 180	proactive policing 171
CRASH 178	meat-eaters 176	racial profiling 180
driving while black (DWB) 180	Operation Hammer 185	Rampart scandal 178
grass-eaters 176	order maintenance 172	reactive policing 171
GRATS 185	police subculture 174	Knapp Commission 176
group support theory 177	policing styles 172	

NOTES

1. Love, D. A. "Justice Department Must Take Over NYPD." *Las Vegas Review-Journal,* February 19, 1999.

2. Chambliss, W. J. *Power, Politics and Crime.* Boulder, CO: Westview Press, 1999, pp. 66–67.

3. "Solutions Scarce for Jail Too Small for County Needs." *Flint Journal,* February 13, 2002.

4. Wilson, J. Q. *Varieties of Police Behavior.* Cambridge, MA: Harvard University Press, 1968.

5. Senna, J. J., and L. J. Siegel. *Introduction to Criminal Justice* (9th ed.). Belmont, CA: Wadsworth, 2002.

6. Bayley, D. H. *Police for the Future.* New York: Oxford University Press, 1994.

7. Klockars, C. B. *The Idea of Police.* Newbury Park, CA: Sage, 1985.

8. Wilson, J. Q., and G. Kelling. "Broken Windows." *Atlantic Monthly* (March 1982).

9. Parenti, *Lockdown America,* 1999; Duneier, *Sidewalk.*

10. Shelden, Tracy, and Brown, *Youth Gangs in American Society.*

11. Weston, L. *The Study of Society* (2nd ed.). Guilford, CT: Dushkin, 1977, p. 562.

12. Manning, P. K., and J. Van Maanen (eds.). *Policing: A View from the Streets.* Santa Monica, CA: Goodyear, 1978, p. 267.

13. Van Maanen, J. *Tales of the Field: On Writing Ethnography.* Chicago: University of Chicago Press, 1988.

14. Berg, *Law Enforcement.*

15. Scheingold, S. A. *The Politics of Law and Order: Street Crime and Public Policy.* New York: Longman, 1984.

16. Doerner, W. C. "I'm Not the Man I Used to Be: Reflections on the Transition from Professor to Cop." In A. S. Blumberg and E. Niederhoffer (eds.), *The Ambivalent Force.* New York: Holt, Rinehart and Winston, 1985, pp. 394–399.

17. Broderick, J. *Police in a Time of Change* (2nd ed.). Prospect Heights, IL: Waveland Press, 1987.

18. U.S. National Commission on Law Observance and Enforcement (Wickersham Commission). *Reports.* Washington, DC: U.S. Government Printing Office, 1931.

19. Knapp Commission. "Police Corruption in New York." In J. Skolnick and T. C. Gray (eds.), *Police in America.* Boston: Little, Brown, 1975, p. 235.

20. Mass, P. "Serpico: The Cop Who Defied the System," ibid.

21. Knapp Commission, "Political Corruption in New York," p. 235.

22. Ibid., p. 237.

23. Stoddard, E. R. "The Informal 'Code' of Police Deviancy." In Skolnick and Gray, *Police in America,* p. 262.

24. Chambliss, W. J. "Vice, Corruption, Bureaucracy and Power." In W. J. Chambliss (ed.), *Criminal Law in Action.* New York: Wiley, 1975, p. 150.

25. Ibid., p. 144.

26. Ibid.

27. For another example see Gardiner, J. "Wincanton: The Politics of Corruption." In W. J. Chambliss (ed.), *Crime and the Legal Process.* New York: McGraw-Hill, 1969.

28. Klein, M. *The American Street Gang.* New York: Oxford University Press, 1995, pp. 164–165.

29. Miller, *Drug Warriors and Their Prey;* Miller, *Search and Destroy;* Parenti, *Lockdown America;* Cole, D. *No Equal Justice: Race and Class in the Criminal Justice System.* New York: New Press, 1999.

30. "LAPD Corruption Probe Grows to 7 Shootings." *Los Angeles Times,* October 22, 1999.

31. "Crime, Poverty Test Rampart Officers' Skill." *Los Angeles Times,* November 10, 1999.

32. "Latest Rampart Case Focuses on Third Officer." *Los Angeles Times,* December 2, 1999.

33. "Rampart Probe May Now Affect over 3,000 Cases." *Los Angeles Times,* December 15, 1999.

34. "Police Shooting Deepens Racial Tension." *Los Angeles Times,* February 15, 1999.

35. Ibid.; see also Love, "Justice Department Must Take Over NYPD"; "The Message of the Diallo Protests." *New York Times,* February 29, 2000.

36. Beals, G., and M. Bai. "The Thin Blue Line." *Newsweek,* September 1, 1997.

37. Cole, *No Equal Justice,* pp. 45–46.

38. See Cole's book for a summary. There also are numerous studies dating back to the 1930s that can be cited: the Wickersham Commission reports (see note 18); the Kerner Commission report (U.S. Riot Commission. *Report of the National Advisory Commission on Civil Disorders.* New York: Bantam Books, 1967); the Christopher Commission report on the Rodney King incident (Christopher Commission. *Report of the Independent Commission on the Los Angeles Police Department.* Los Angeles: The Commission, 1991).

39. Cole, *No Equal Justice,* p. 23, quoting California Assemblyman Curtis Tucker.

40. Walker and Katz, *Police in America,* p. 290.

41. Chambliss, *Power, Politics and Crime,* pp. 64–68.

42. Cole, D. "Take the Unnecessary Force out of Law Enforcement." *Las Vegas Review-Journal,* May 21, 1999.

43. Massey, D. S., and N. A. Denton. *American Apartheid: Segregation and the Making of the Underclass.* Cambridge, MA: Harvard University Press, 1993, p. 8.

44. Ibid., p. 48.

45. Ibid., p. 74.

46. For a review of this evidence from surveys from the 1960s and 1970s see Shelden, R. G. *Criminal Justice in America: A Sociological Approach.* Boston: Little, Brown 1982, ch. 5; more recent evidence is reviewed in Lynch, M., and R. Michalowski. *The New Primer in Radical Criminology.* Monsey, NY: Criminal Justice Press, 2000, pp. 160–162.

47. Chambliss, *Power, Politics and Crime,* p. 77.

48. This section is taken from Sheldon, R. G. *Controlling the Dangerous Classes: A Critical Introduction to the History of Criminal Justice.* Boston: Allyn and Bacon, 2001, ch. 2.

49. Miller, *Search and Destroy,* p. 8; see also Currie, E. *Reckoning: Drugs, the Cities, and the American Future.* New York: Hill and Wang, 1993; Tonry, M. *Malign Neglect: Race, Crime, and Punishment in America.* New York: Oxford University Press, 1995.

50. Miller, *Search and Destroy,* pp. 84–86.

51. Ibid., p. 257, citing Kempf, K., *The Role of Race in Juvenile Justice Processing in Pennsylvania.* Study Grant #89-90/J/01/3615, Pennsylvania Commission on Crime and Delinquency (August 1992).

52. McGarrell, E. 1993. "Trends in Racial Disproportionality in Juvenile Court Processing: 1985–1989." *Crime and Delinquency* 39: 29–48 (1993).

53. Fellner, J. "Stark Racial Disparities Found in Georgia Drug Law Enforcement." *Overcrowded Times* 7(5): 11 (October 1996).

54. This section is taken from Shelden, *Controlling the Dangerous Classes,* ch. 2.

55. State Task Force on Youth Gang Violence. *Final Report.* Sacramento: California Council on Criminal Justice, 1986, p. 37.

56. Wilson, J. Q., and G. L. Kelling. "Making Neighborhoods Safe." *Atlantic Monthly* (February 1989), pp. 46–52; Boyle, J., and A. Gonzales. "Using Proactive Programs to Impact Gangs and Drugs." *Law and Order* 37: 62–64 (1989).

57. Shelden, Tracy, and Brown, *Youth Gangs in American Society,* p. 209.

58. Ibid.

59. Taylor, C. S. *Dangerous Society.* East Lansing: Michigan State University Press, 1990, p. 105.

60. Skolnick, J. *Justice without Trial* (3rd ed.). New York: Macmillan, 1994; Skolnick, J., and H. Bayley. *The New Blue Line: Police Innovation in Six American Cities.* New York: Free Press, 1986.

61. Walker, S. *Sense and Nonsense about Crime and Drugs* (5th ed.). Belmont, CA: Wadsworth, 2001; Goldstein, H. *Problem Oriented Policing.* New York: McGraw-Hill, 1990.

62. Shelden, Tracy, and Brown, *Youth Gangs in American Society,* p. 209.

63. Ibid., pp. 210–211.

64. Ibid., p. 211.

65. Ibid., p. 212.

66. Miller, *Search and Destroy.*

67. Davis, M. *City of Quartz.* New York: Vintage Books, 1992, p. 268.

68. Klein, M. *The American Street Gang.* New York: Oxford University Press, 1995, p. 162.

69. Davis, *City of Quartz,* pp. 268–274.

70. Ibid., p. 274.

71. Moore, J. *Going down to the Barrio.* Philadelphia: Temple University Press, 1991, pp. 3–4.

72. Klein, *The American Street Gang,* pp. 162, 166.

73. Davis, *City of Quartz,* p. 276.

74. Ibid., p. 277.

75. Ibid., p. 272.

76. Jackson, P. "Minority Group Threat, Social Context, and Policing." In A. E. Liska (ed.), *Social Threat and Social Control.* Albany: State University of New York Press, 1992, p. 90.

77. Bayley, *Police for the Future,* p. 3.

78. Ibid., pp. 4–5.

79. Walker, *Sense and Nonsense,* pp. 78–79.

80. Bayley, *Police for the Future,* pp. 5–7; Walker, *Sense and Nonsense,* pp. 85–88.

81. Walker, *Sense and Nonsense,* p. 87.

82. Kelling, G. L., T. Pate, D. Diekman, and C. E. Brown. *The Kansas City Preventive Patrol Experiment: A Summary Report.* Washington, D.C.: The Police Foundation, 1974.

83. The Police Foundation. *The Newark Foot Patrol Experiment.* Washington, D.C.: The Police Foundation, 1981.

84. Green, L. "Cleaning Up Drug Hot Spots in Oakland, California: The Displacement and Diffusion Effects." *Justice Quarterly* 12: 737–754.

CHAPTER EIGHT

CRIMINAL COURTS
The System and Participants

In the spring of 1999, in a Michigan court, a young African American male was sentenced to prison. An observer wrote the following account:

> In the spring of 1999, a young African American male was sentenced to prison for the crime of burglary in a Michigan court. Sitting behind the young man was an older woman who wept and an older man who simply placed his head in his hands and just sat there. The couple appeared to be the young man's parents. After informing the young man of his sentence, the judge made a profound, concluding statement that "justice had been served." After the judge left the courtroom, two officers of the court walked over to the young man—one on each side—and instructed him to "come with us." The defense attorney patted the young man's shoulder, turned, and walked away. There was no exchange of words between this young man and his white attorney. The older couple stood up. The woman reached out to her son, but the officers would not allow the young man to take her hand. He was quickly ushered out of the courtroom. The older man put his arm around the woman and they walked out of the courtroom. The woman was crying profusely. He tried to comfort her. Following them out of the courtroom, they got into a very old vehicle and drove off. Exhaust fumes could be seen for nearly a block before they turned at an intersection and disappeared. This observation is not an isolated event in the annals of American jurisprudence.

It is jurisprudence history, and it is repeatedly enacted in criminal courtrooms across America. Some form of "justice" may have been served in the courtroom episode noted above, but it was not *social* justice.[1]

The American criminal courts stand between the police and the prison system. The judicial system is a major institution in American society. You cannot travel very far in America without seeing a reminder of the central role of the courts. Pass through any town of any size, and the local courthouse is likely to stand out among all of the buildings you will see. In fact, in many towns the courthouse stands in the center of town. Often many other important government offices are found within (or in close proximity to) this building (local police or sheriff's department, jail, city hall, post office, etc.). In many small towns the courthouse is surrounded by several small businesses. The courthouse grounds are often neatly landscaped, with park benches and picnic tables. And invariably you will find, in huge letters, the slogan "Justice for All" or something similar, along with perhaps the symbol of the "blind lady of justice" nearby plus the American and state flags.

The courts are certainly among the busiest of all government institutions, and they differ from most other institutions in at least two important ways.[2] First, the courts are places where citizens most directly interact on an individual basis, rather than in groups (with some exceptions, to be sure). Second, the courts are places where people go to "get what is their due" or "have their day in court," whether in a small-claims case or a traffic case or as victims in a criminal case. Yet at the same time the courts are perhaps one of the least understood institutions—at least by the general public. Opinion polls consistently find that the public is more ignorant of the court system than of any other institution. Also, surveys consistently show that the public often feels mistreated by the courts and dealt with in a disrespectful way. People come to the court system wanting some resolution, either protection or punishment; too often, they get neither and their claims are treated as "trivial" or "frivolous."[3] This is especially the case among ordinary, working-class citizens.[4] As this suggests, social class plays a key role here. Are the courts really the "people's courts," or are they just another arm of the rich and powerful, a locus of class domination where one class stands in judgment of another? In this chapter we explore these and other issues.

The court has been defined as "an agency or unit of the judicial branch of government …which has the authority to decide upon cases, controversies in law, and disputed matters of fact brought before it."[5] Such a definition is frequently associated with justice, fairness, impartiality, objectivity, and other lofty concepts. Actually, the court is not an agency or a component of any agency but is more like an independent branch of government "stipulated in both the Constitution of the United States and in state constitutions."[6] On the surface, this statement suggests that the court is autonomous of other branches of government and other institutions, but the court is simply another government institution—often with an agenda far removed from any notions of justice and impartiality.

Criminal courts have been described as "marketplaces in which the only commodity traded seriously is time."[7] Civil courts can be viewed in a similar light, except that the commodities traded are power and privilege. Power and privilege allow corporations to do pretty much as they will—removing people from their homes (relocation of Native Americans), deciding which parent receives custody of children in divorce cases, controlling women's bodies (abortion issues), deciding who can work and who cannot (labor issues), keeping people living in poverty (welfare issues). Power and privilege control and impact many other social issues that face contemporary society. Obviously this view implies, at the very least, that the court is not justice oriented, objective, or impartial. In fact, this view suggests that the court operates in a stock-market atmosphere in which justice exists in the "eyes of the beholder" and fairness is replaced by the whims of the powerful. Such an outlook also considers the ideology of the court to be interest serving. And the function of the court is limited to efficiency. This is not any different than many other institutions within capitalist society.

Most people do not think of the court as a self-serving institution that conceals its true identity behind a cloak of justice, fairness, impartiality, and so on. Rather, most people choose to view the court as simply a guardian of justice. Of course, justice is whatever you want it to be at a given time. It is typically said that "justice" is served if a court decision favors us or our ideas about the disposition of a case in which we are familiar. We tend to turn on that definition when a court decision is against us, or against what we think the court ought to have done, resulting in the charge of "injustice." Thus, when a defendant stands before the sentencing judge, after being found guilty of a crime, and is informed that he or she is sentenced to a term in prison, many applaud the decision and say that "justice" has been served. Few consider another form of justice that is relevant to most criminal cases—*social justice,* which necessitates consideration of concepts such as race/ethnicity, sex/gender, and social class. When the topic of social justice is brought up, it is generally rejected with contempt or, at the very least, dismissed as simply another example of liberal thought that fails to recognize that all poor or disadvantaged people do not commit crimes.

But more than this, *the American criminal court system is almost by definition class biased.* Why? Simply because what is defined as "criminal" usually applies to behaviors that are typically committed by those of lower social standing, and various administrative and civil laws (or in some cases no laws at all) are reserved for processing cases involving those of higher social standing, charged with "crimes" not covered by the "criminal law." A good example is described by Lynch and Michalowski:

> consider a poor woman prosecuted for selling crack, and a rich doctor administratively sanctioned for illegally prescribing Viagra to men who have no medical problem. Even if both were prosecuted according to legal procedures that were absolutely flawless, the difference in the systems that would judge them, and the resources each could muster in their defense, guarantee that the outcomes will be far removed from any standard of equality before the law. However, in a male- and white-centered society such as America, the legal system finds little reason to concern itself with a product that is promoted by white, male drug company executives and distributed by affluent white, male doctors to a clientele consisting primarily of white men who want to increase their sexual pleasure. In contrast, when poor people, particularly poor people of color, sell or use "illegal" drugs as part of a street-level system of self-medication, political leaders react with outrage, the legal system responds with drug wars and the courts lock up thousands of poor drug dealers and users behind bars. In the American way of doing justice, the sexual pleasure of white men is far more important than the lives of poor people of color.[8]

What the previous example suggests is that in the American system of justice there is a belief that as long as certain legal principles ("procedural law") are followed, then "equal justice" will be the result. Nothing could be further from the truth, and as we proceed to examine the criminal court system, the class and racial biases will become more obvious. But you should note that we are, after all, talking about the *criminal* court system. For the $500 billion to $1 trillion corporate and white-collar crime business, there are numerous administrative and regulatory procedures available. This might lead you to believe that a "higher class" of criminals requires a "higher class" of courts! Examples of such agencies abound; some of them are the Federal Deposit Insurance Corporation (FDIC; dealing with crimes committed by large commercial banks), Securities and Exchange Commission (dealing with crimes in the stock-market industry), Food and Drug Administration (responding to crimes committed within the food and drug industry), Federal Trade Commission (dealing with unfair, deceptive practices and antitrust violations), and Occupational Safety and Health Administration (OSHA; dealing with workplace safety and health).[9] Few corporate and white-collar defendants find themselves in crowded jails waiting to make bail or hoping for a decent lawyer (or *any* lawyer for that matter), and few have been followed by uniformed city police officers, handcuffed, and taken to jail. Review the account of the crimes committed by these corporate thugs and white-collar frauds in Chapter 2 to see the extent of the harm leveled against the American people, in comparison with the relatively harmless actions of drug users and their small-time distributors! We do indeed have a dual system of justice: one for the rich and famous and another for the poor.

In the remainder of this chapter we introduce you to the criminal court system. First we give a brief survey of the development of the American court system. A review of the history of the courts demonstrates that although "justice" has often been served, "social justice" has not. This problem can be traced back to the beginning of the American court system during colonial times. We present a broad overview of the system itself, comparing the federal and state systems. We also consider in some detail the major actors who play the most important roles in the court system: prosecutors, defense attorneys, and judges.

A BRIEF HISTORY

Modern American courts have their roots within colonial society. Throughout the seventeenth century, colonial courts began their ascension to a three-tiered court system (very much as state courts are arranged today). Below the legislature, there were high courts (superior courts) where governors or their designates presided over criminal trials as well as civil trials that were previously heard in lower courts. The lower courts handled most of the trials and levied and collected taxes. These lower courts also provided residents with socializing opportunities and a place to conduct business and engage in lively political discussions.[10] "Ordinary people *used* the courts to get justice for themselves, vindication, restitution; and in criminal as well as civil matters."[11] The courts were also used as places to vent frustration and anger, thus fostering the stability of colonial society.[12]

The original charter of Massachusetts Bay Colony created two types of courts: a "general court" and a "court of assistants." The former acted as a legislative body and as the highest court; the latter (which consisted of the governor, deputy governor, and magistrates) was in charge of appeals from the lower courts, which came to be known as county courts. County courts were the heart of the local system of criminal justice—the same kinds of courts are found in most cities and towns today. What is perhaps most interesting about these courts is the fact that they performed so many different functions: probate, spending money on road and bridge repairs, various forms of licensing, providing the maintenance of the local ministry, regulation of wages, and of course all matter of criminal cases.[13]

Within these county courts the person who performed most of the day-to-day duties was the **justice of the peace.** This individual was appointed by the governor (who was himself an appointee of the English king) and was controlled, for all practical purposes, by the local elites. Actually this office took the place of the local magistrate in the 1860s.[14]

As the legal profession grew during colonial times, it became more and more specialized as increasing numbers of lawyers participated in formal training. Most lawyers learned the trade through apprenticeships with older lawyers. In fact, some of the most famous lawyers of the eighteenth century, many of whom directly participated in the writing of the Constitution, received their training this way. Among the notables included Thomas Jefferson and James Wilson (both signed the Declaration of Independence). The legal profession, then as now, soon began to be dominated by an upper crust of wealthy and powerful lawyers.

Perhaps the central figure of the colonial court system was the justice of the peace. As is typical of today, most of the cases brought into this court were quite minor offenses; the crime called "breach of peace" was the most common. Religious influences are reflected in the fact that three offenses constituted a large proportion of all cases (in one court almost one-third of the cases): "profane swearing," "profane cursing" (it is not clear what the difference was), and "profaning the Sabbath." Theft cases were about 10 percent of the total.[15] Indeed, religion and sex influenced early American courts and processes. Religion was woven into codes throughout the colonies but was most evident in the northern colonies as reflected in Massachusetts Bay Colony. "In one part of the *Laws and Liberties of Massachusetts*...[t]he code contained a list of 'capital laws.' Each one came equipped with citations from the Bible."[16] If there was one area where there was evidence of the occasional repressive features of colonial, especially Puritan, law, it was in the case of the famous witch trials in Salem, Massachusetts.[17]

After the American Revolution a "federal" court system emerged, complete with appellate courts and, of course, the United States Supreme Court. This was an important development in the history of criminal justice. Following the American Revolution there was quite a debate between those ("Federalists") who believed that there should be a federal court system and those ("Anti-Federalists") who did not. This debate was actually part of the much larger debate concerning whether there should be a strong central government. In time, the "Federalists" won out, though with some compromises, such as the establishing of district courts. This was facilitated through the **Judiciary Act of 1789** and the **Reorganization Act of 1801.** The district courts were empowered to enforce federal laws but structured along state lines, and judges had to be residents of that state. Various state courts were soon established by state legislative bodies.[18] By the end of the eighteenth century there was very little distinction between trial and appellate courts. In many instances, "High-court judges often doubled as trial or circuit judges."[19] As America entered the nineteenth century, state courts, unlike the federal courts, began to specialize in the adjudication of various types of cases (probate, wills, etc.).

Of major importance was the creation of the highest court of the country, the Supreme Court, established in 1789 with the passage of the Judiciary Act. If there was ever an instance where evidence of the upper-class bias of the legal system was the clearest, the composition of the United States Supreme Court is just such an instance. It was created by a special Senate committee headed by Oliver Ellsworth, who wrote the bill and would become the third chief justice. Throughout the history of the Supreme Court, its members have been drawn overwhelmingly from the upper crust of society. This was especially the case in the nineteenth century, as almost all of the justices came from the "landed gentry" and were schooled in the most prestigious, mostly Ivy League, universities. The makeup of very first court (1790–1801) reflects this class bias, as does that of the second court, the Marshall Court (1801–1836), one of the most influential in the early years.[20]

The biggest changes in the American court system came after the Civil War, largely because of the huge growth in population, especially the emergence of large cities. The old agrarian court system of small-town America could not handle the changes. New courts emerged, including small-claims courts, so-called lower courts (often called municipal courts or justice of the peace courts, which handle misdemeanors, including traffic citations), felony courts (often called superior courts, district courts, and the like), and juvenile courts (begun in 1899).

We now turn to an examination of the current criminal court system. As in earlier days, most of the cases are relatively minor, and the overwhelming majority of the people brought into these courts come from the ranks of the urban poor and especially racial minorities.

THE CRIMINAL COURT SYSTEM: AN OVERVIEW

When we examine the criminal court system, we once again see that social class, race, and sex play a major role. Most of the cases coming before these courts, in sharp contrast to those coming before the civil courts, involve defendants from relatively poor and low-income backgrounds. Like the society that surrounds it, the American bar system is highly stratified, and the majority of criminal lawyers occupy the lowest rung of this hierarchy. Thus, low-status lawyers defend and prosecute the low-status violators of the law, and low-status members of the judiciary judge the proceedings. However, even the lowliest of these lawyers and judges have enjoyed advantages stemming from levels of income and education far removed from the experience of most of the individuals caught up in the criminal justice system.

In the United States there are two major court systems: federal and state. Within each system there are two general types of courts: trial and appellate. This is what is known as the **dual court system.** Trial courts (such as the U.S. district courts) hear cases and decide on guilt or innocence. Appellate courts (such as the U.S. courts of appeals) hear appeals from trial courts.[21] Let us briefly review the federal and state court systems.

Federal Courts

The federal court system consists of: (1) district courts, which are the trial courts for violations of federal laws (there are eighty-nine districts in 50 states, plus one in the District of Columbia and four in U.S. territories, such as Puerto Rico); (2) administrative courts or agencies, which include such regulatory agencies as the Federal Trade Commission, Securities and Exchange Commission, and National Labor Relations Board; (3) U.S. circuit courts of appeals, twelve in all, each representing a particular district; and (4) the U.S. Supreme Court, the court of last resort on the appeals route.

There is at least one **U.S. district court** in each state (California, New York, and Texas have four each). There are more than six-hundred district court judges (they serve for life after being nominated by the president and confirmed by the Senate). These judges have complete judicial powers as they conduct trials, accept guilty pleas, and impose sentences. There are about five-hundred U.S. magistrates, who hear minor offenses and conduct preliminary hearings. District courts have jurisdiction over both criminal and civil matters. The total number of cases handled in these courts rose by almost 50 percent between 1980 and 1996, while the number of judges during this period increased by about 25 percent and the average number of cases per judgeship went up by almost 20 percent. Drug cases accounted for most of the increase, going from just over 4,000 cases to a little over 12,000 (a 187 percent increase); drug cases went from 13 percent of the total to 25 percent of the cases during this period.[22]

The **U.S. courts of appeals** were created in 1891 to relieve the Supreme Court of the growing number of appeals. These courts are the intermediate appellate courts of the federal system. Twelve of these courts represent specific geographical regions (see Figure 8.1). A thirteenth is the U.S. court of appeals for the federal court system.[23]

The total number of appeals has increased significantly in recent years, going up by 120 percent between 1980 and 1996. Most of these appeals have to do with civil cases. The largest proportion have to do with cases filed by private persons (58% of the total); the next largest category is devoted to petitions by prisoners (about 27% of the total appeals cases in 1996).

Federal appeals court judges are appointed by the president and serve for life. These judges represent the upper crust of society. Consider the appointments made between 1963 and 2000. The percentage of appointees who were minorities ranged from a high of 26.2 percent during the Clinton administration (1992–2000) to none in either the Ford years

FIGURE 8.1   United States Courts of Appeals

Circuit 1	Maine, New Hampshire, Massachusetts, Rhode Island, Puerto Rico
Circuit 2	Vermont, New York, Connecticut
Circuit 3	Pennsylvania, New Jersey, Delaware
Circuit 4	Maryland, West Virginia, Virginia, North Carolina, South Carolina
Circuit 5	Texas, Louisiana, Mississippi
Circuit 6	Michigan, Ohio, Kentucky, Tennessee
Circuit 7	Indiana, Illinois, Wisconsin
Circuit 8	North Dakota, South Dakota, Minnesota, Iowa, Nebraska, Missouri, Arkansas
Circuit 9	Montana, Idaho, Washington, Oregon, Nevada, California, Arizona, Alaska, Hawaii, Guam, N. Mariana Island
Circuit 10	Wyoming, Utah, Colorado, New Mexico, Oklahoma, Kansas
Circuit 11	Alabama, Georgia, Florida
Circuit 12	District of Columbia

(1974–1976) or the second of Reagan's two terms (1984–1988). The proportion who received their undergraduate education at either private or Ivy League schools ranged from a low of 50 percent during the Ford years to a high of 75.7 percent during the Reagan administration (1980–1988). Most of the appointees received their law degrees from private or Ivy League schools. Clearly, women have been in the minority with respect to appellate court appointments, ranging from none during the Nixon and Ford years (1968–1976) to 19.6 percent during the Carter administration (1977–1981) and 32.8 percent during the Clinton administration.[24]

The **U.S. Supreme Court** is the highest court in the country. It consists of nine justices: eight associate justices and a chief justice, who are nominated by the president, confirmed by the Senate, and serve for life. Through a **writ of certiorari** a lower court is ordered to produce the records of a trial for the Supreme Court for review, and the final appeal begins. In some cases, the Supreme Court may receive an *in forma pauperis* **request** from a prisoner—a request to file an appeal with the Supreme Court for the payment of legal fees.[25] Despite the increase in the number of appeals filed in district courts, the number of cases heard by the U.S. Supreme Court has decreased during the past twenty years, going from 176 cases heard in 1976 to 90 heard in 1995.[26]

It is important to note the significance of the U.S. Supreme Court justices. As previously noted, they are nominated by the president. A president is able to influence judicial proceedings for decades through the nomination of Supreme Court justices. Nominees for the U.S. Supreme Court are typically selected on the basis of their political views, which are generally determined by their previous judicial views and decisions. Voters may vote a president out of office, but they are not able to rid themselves of U.S. Supreme Court justices at the polls. Supreme Court justices often continue to propagate the views of their nominating administration well into the tenure of another administration.[27]

State Courts

Most criminal and civil cases in the United States come before the state court system. Most criminal cases are heard in **trial courts of limited jurisdiction,** known collectively as *lower* or *inferior* courts. These courts have different names in different places—such as municipal, justice of the peace, city, magistrate, and county courts. They are usually created by local governments (cities or counties). Within these courts are heard misdemeanors, traffic cases, city ordinance cases, minor civil disputes, and the like. They are also responsible for initial appearances and preliminary hearings for felony cases. They are certainly the most numerous of the courts, as they number almost 14,000 and collectively represent 84 percent of all state judicial bodies. The number of judges serving in these courts, according to the most recent count, is 18,272. They dispose of about 71 million cases each year![28]

Trial courts of limited jurisdiction are the courts most citizens come in contact with if they violate some law. Such courts can also be viewed as "poor people's courts," for the vast majority who parade through them are drawn from the ranks of the poor and working class. We know this from studies of jail populations and bail procedures and studies of lower courts' processing of cases.[29] One study found that three-fourths of defendants were too poor to hire their own attorneys and thus had to be provided one by the court.[30]

Appeals from lower courts are heard in **trial courts of general jurisdiction.** These are the major trial courts and are known as district, circuit, superior, and common pleas courts (in New York they are called supreme courts and county courts). These courts adjudicate primarily felony cases (and some serious misdemeanors).

Appeals from these courts go either to *intermediate courts of appeals* or to *state supreme courts.* Intermediate courts are found in thirty-eight states, mainly the most populous states, and are known as appeals courts, courts of civil appeals, superior courts, commonwealth courts, courts of criminal appeals, courts of appeals, appellate courts, and courts of special appeals. The number of judges within each appellate court varies from only three in Alaska to eighty-eight in California.

Within the state court system, the "court of last resort" is the *state supreme court.* These courts are found in each state, and they go by different names. Most are called the Supreme Court. Others are called Court of Appeals (e.g., New York), Supreme Judicial Court (e.g., Massachusetts), Court of Criminal Appeals (e.g., Texas), and Supreme Court of Appeals (West Virginia). At the state level, these courts are the equivalent of the U.S. Supreme Court.[31]

PARTICIPANTS IN THE COURT SYSTEM

The criminal court system is a bureaucracy. As in other bureaucracies there are a number of actors who play certain roles in the daily functioning of the system. What should be emphasized is the fact that the key participants engage in daily interaction with each other. The popular image of the courts as "adversarial" places where the two major combatants— the prosecutor and the defense—"duke it out" while the judge sits above the fray as a "neutral" observer or referee is not accurate. There is a great deal of cooperation among all of the principal courtroom participants. It should be noted that their salaries come out of the same general fund and the same signature appears on their paychecks. One of the best ways of describing this cooperation is to refer to these actors as a courtroom workgroup.

The Courtroom Workgroup

The **courtroom workgroup** comprises the officials of the court whom you are likely to see on any given day should you walk into a courthouse anywhere in the country.[32] These officials include the three major actors—the judge, prosecutors, and defense attorneys— along with a host of other important players, such as the court clerk, court reporter, bailiff, police officers, and interpreters. These "courthouse regulars" interact with each other inside and outside the courtroom. Their interactions essentially determine the ebb and flow of court cases. They may be seen with one another at lunch and sometimes after hours (if you are curious, check out bars and restaurants in close proximity to courthouses between roughly 5 and 7 P.M. on any given day and see how many of these individuals are socializing). Detailed studies of this group have discovered that the majority of members' interactions are friendly. One study found that more than 80 percent of both public defenders and district attorneys believe they cooperate with each other "always" or "often" in their daily interactions.[33]

Unlike workgroups in other organizations, within the modern court system most of the key players work for some other institution. The judge is an elected official and is accountable to the general public. The prosecuting attorneys generally work under another publicly elected official, the district attorney. The public defender works for a separate organization. Bailiffs may work for the local police department or sheriff, and court clerks work for the county or city. Ideally, private defense attorneys work for their clients; however, one might make the argument that they actually work for themselves and their own interests.

Like members of other workgroups, members of the courtroom workgroup interact with one another each working day, and as a result certain personal ties or bonds are created (on a local golf course over the weekend you might observe a judge playing a round with a prosecutor or a defense attorney). They also share a mutual interdependence or cooperative relationship as they come to share common interests in the disposition of cases. The bottom line is that they come to be more concerned with the maintenance of a smoothly running court system than with seeing that "justice" is done (although "justice" may be served in this way). They also share in the decision making, often engaging in various forms of informal norms that guide decision making. Studies consistently show that there is a great amount of agreement on such issues as bail, adjudicating guilt, and imposing sentences.[34]

The Prosecutor: Gatekeeper of the Court System

The **prosecutor** is most commonly referred to as the *district attorney* (other job titles include county attorney, state's attorney, and prosecuting attorney). This person occupies one of the most powerful positions in the entire criminal justice system, because he or she is the gatekeeper for the court system. As Chambliss and Seidman remark: "The prosecutor stands astride the criminal process, controlling the gates that lead to the trial court.... [T]he prosecutor's decision to initiate a prosecution, and the degree to be charged, lies entirely in his discretion. That discretion is, for all practical purposes, unreviewable."[35]

The prosecution of criminal cases is assuming a high priority within the criminal justice system, if increased funding is any indication. U.S. Department of Justice figures reveal that whereas in 1979 prosecutorial expenditures were $1.7 billion, in 1990 they stood at $5.5 billion, an increase of 230 percent. During this same period, the number of *federal* prosecutors went from 1,621 to 3,883, an increase that was ten times more than the population increase.[36]

Historical Development of the Office of Prosecutor. Historically, the functions, roles, duties, and jurisdiction of the prosecutor have changed drastically. In colonial times the victim had a much larger role. Usually, the victim hired a private prosecutor (usually a privately retained lawyer) for the case. Judges and juries had a more influential role during this period. Trials were the order of the day, and they were very swift. Following conviction the convicted person was "hanged, banished, lashed, or given in servitude to the victim until he made good his debt."[37] At this time, there were no prisons as such, no officially authorized police force, and no public prosecutor. In other words, the *state* had not yet stepped in to dominate the criminal justice process. In a small, relatively homogeneous, and agriculturally based society, there was little need for a centralized state apparatus. All of this changed during the nineteenth century as the Industrial Revolution progressed.

In the nineteenth century the entire criminal justice system underwent some noteworthy changes. By the end of the eighteenth century, shortly after the American Revolution, the states had begun to enact legislation creating "public" prosecutors and state prisons. The result was that the "domain of the victim of crime in the criminal justice system was greatly reduced. He no longer played a correctional role; and his role in the investigation and apprehension of criminals was minimized."[38]

Recall from Chapter 5 that policing emerged as a distinct occupation in the nineteenth century. The use of the grand jury began to diminish as the states, in their constitutions, "either did not provide for a grand jury system or provided for one but also allowed for the option of proceeding by way of information filed by the prosecutor." An information is an instrument filed with the court by the prosecutor which simply provides relevant demographic data, charges, and the name(s) of victims. "The prosecutor's domain expanded considerably. The victim of a crime was beginning to be largely ignored, while the criminal justice process was placed into the hands of 'experts,' a group of trained 'professionals' who ostensibly would have the knowledge and motivation to 'serve the public'."[39]

Also in the nineteenth century there was an increase in the police's authority in the charging decision. In fact, until the present century the police had almost total control of this crucial decision. Today, however, the functions of the police, the prosecutor, judges, and juries, as well as the penal system, are fairly distinct, with some exceptions to be sure.

The Prosecutor Today. Four characteristics of the office of district attorney reflect the power of this office.[40] First, the office has extremely broad discretion in the handling of cases, because the prosecutor is part of the executive branch of government and thus separate from the judiciary. Second, the office is decentralized. There are more than eight thousand state, county, city, and township district attorney offices in the country, and they are often huge bureaucracies, ranging from staffs of one or two staff in small towns to more than five hundred (in Los Angeles, for instance). Third, the office of prosecutor has local autonomy; it is practically unsupervised, except by local voters. (In our opinion, however, voting for the local district attorney reflects true "democracy" in theory only. Few voters have any real knowledge of this particular branch of local government, and the voting is like any other voting, subject to the usual political fraud that plagues elections in general.) Fourth, and related to the issue of voting, is the fact the district attorney is generally, at least in theory, a "public" official, subject to election by the people in the district. What this means is that the office of prosecutor is inherently political. This is *not* the case in Alaska, Connecticut, Delaware, the District of Columbia, New Jersey, and Rhode Island, where the chief prosecutors are appointed or are members of the state attorney general's office. And in the federal system, all U.S. attorneys are appointed by the president and confirmed by the Senate.

Much of the work within the prosecutor's office is done by assistant district attorneys (also known as deputy district attorneys), who are usually hired immediately after law school or after a brief period as solo practitioners. Not surprisingly, the turnover is quite high, because the job is not very glamorous and the caseload can get high (as many as a hundred cases). As Neubauer notes, given the kinds of cases that are handled, "the criminal courthouse can become a depressing place to work. Moreover, regular trial creates numerous physical and psychological pressures."[41]

Prosecutors, like most criminal lawyers, tend to come from middle-class backgrounds. In contrast to their counterparts in civil and corporate law, prosecutors tend to be products of less prestigious law schools, and they typically graduated in the middle of their class, as several studies covering four decades have shown.[42] There is an interesting stratification system within the legal profession. As one writer puts it: "The legal profession, like other occupations, is rigidly stratified. Entry into the profession, mobility within it and the status level in the profession which a lawyer eventually achieves are all strongly influenced by class origins, education, and job experience."[43]

Fishman's data on New York City prosecutors confirm what the literature has found with regard to criminal lawyers in general. Most of those in Fishman's sample came from middle-class backgrounds, although half had working-class or lower-middle-class backgrounds. Most attended local public schools, private four-year colleges, and local law schools. Indeed, the lack of status accorded to the practice of criminal law reveals the stratification within the legal profession.[44] This process tends to "channel minority and lower class lawyers into less prestigious positions."[45] This is especially the case with public defenders, whom we discuss in the next section.

The prosecutor's office is indeed a sort of "launching pad" for a political career.[46] Many a judge, legislator, governor, congressional representative, and senator began his or her career in the prosecutor's office. But, as some studies suggest, this is not always the case. Many individuals use this job as a way of gaining experience before entering private practice.[47] What is perhaps most important to note is the fact that prosecutors are typically reelected or promoted on the basis of conviction rates, or a good "batting average." This "batting average" is based on the misleading statistic of "cases won" or "successful convictions," which usually is a measure not of "justice" but of the rate of successful "negotiations." Moreover, as observers of the courts are aware, the conviction rate is *not* based on the percentage of the *total* number of cases referred to the prosecutor's office, but rather is based on the number of cases "accepted for prosecution." Thus, the conviction rate does not include all of the cases that are "denied." This is like computing one's batting average in baseball by leaving out all the times a batter gets on base because of a "fielder's choice" (and in effect counting a "fielder's choice" like a sacrifice fly or a walk).

The discretion inherent in this office is revealed by the fact that as cases proceed through the judicial system, between one-third and one-half are screened out by the prosecutor's office. This fact was demonstrated in studies conducted as far back as the 1920s; several state crime surveys (e.g., in Missouri, Illinois, and Ohio) noted that almost half of all police cases presented to the prosecutor's office were rejected.[48] A study in Washington, D.C., in the mid-1970s found that out of every 100 felony cases submitted to the prosecutor, 50 were either rejected at an initial screening stage or dropped at a later stage, another 19 were reduced to misdemeanors (3 of which were acquitted), and several more were dismissed by the judge, acquitted by juries, and so on, so that at the end there were only 16 guilty pleas or verdicts.[49]

The prosecutor does more than screen criminal cases. Prosecutors perform five major activities:

1. *Fighting.* The prosecutor is supposed to "fight for justice" on behalf of "the people," especially if the case goes to trial.
2. *Negotiating.* Few cases go to trial, so the prosecutor spends much time negotiating with the defense attorney, in a manner not unlike negotiations between a car sales-person and a customer.
3. *Drafting.* Much of a prosecutor's time is spent in drafting documents such as search warrants, preparing motions, filing informations charging defendants with crimes, filing "briefs," and handling similar bureaucratic chores.
4. *Counseling.* This role involves dealing with the major "clients" of the court system—the victims of crimes—by "coaching" witnesses, arranging restitution, and fulfilling similar duties.
5. *Administering.* Large numbers of cases mean doing a lot of routine administrative work such as getting trial dates set, deciding what cases to plea-bargain, hiring new assistants, and preparing budgets.[50]

The prosecutor has also been described as the chief *law enforcement officer* in the district, a *bureaucrat* responsible for the supervision of what in many jurisdictions is a vast bureau-cracy employing hundreds of people, and a politician because, after all, he or she is an elected official.[51]

It should also be noted that the decisions made by the prosecutor are largely hidden from public view, as are the decisions made by most other criminal justice officials. Only rarely, in a high-profile or celebrity case, are such decisions made public. But even then many of the day-to-day decisions are kept away from public view. Even in the O. J. Simp-son case, Marcia Clark, Christopher Darden, and the rest of the prosecution team made many decisions that the public was never aware of.

The Defense Attorney

The Right to Counsel.   In a 1932 decision the U.S. Supreme Court ruled that defendants had a right to counsel in cases in which the death penalty might be imposed (*Powell v. Al-abama,* 287 U.S. 45, 1932). This case left unresolved the problem of providing counsel when the defendant is too poor to afford a lawyer in noncapital cases. Then in *Betts v. Brady* (316 U.S. 455, 1942) the Court ruled that there is no such guarantee in state courts unless the defendant could show that to be deprived of counsel would result in a denial of due process. This decision was overturned in a landmark decision (*Gideon v. Wainwright,* 372 U.S. 335, 1963) in which the Court ruled that a defendant accused of a felony even in a noncapital case should be provided counsel.

In *Gideon* the Court faced an ideological challenge to the myth of "equal justice for all." It was shown that Clarence Earl Gideon, who had asked for counsel but was denied, had acted as his own lawyer but was no match for an experienced prosecutor. It was found that any lawyer would have been able to prove Gideon innocent (as a subsequent trial was to show). This was a clear case in which the fact of being poor (which Gideon was) led to a denial of due process.[52] The Supreme Court stated the obvious (372 U.S. at 344):

> Reason and reflection require us to recognize that in our adversary system of criminal jus-tice, any person hauled into court who is too poor to hire a lawyer, cannot be assured a fair trial unless counsel is provided for him. This seems to us an obvious truth. Governments, both state and federal, quite properly spend vast sums of money to try defendants accused

of crime. Lawyers to prosecute are everywhere deemed essential to protect the public's interest in an orderly society. Similarly, there are a few defendants charged with a crime, few indeed, who fail to hire the best lawyer they can get to prepare and present their defense. That government hires lawyers to prosecute and defendants who have the money hire lawyers to defend are the strongest indications of a widespread belief that lawyers in criminal courts are necessities, not luxuries.... From the very beginning, our state and national constitutions and laws have laid great emphasis on procedural and substantive safeguards designed to assure fair trials before impartial tribunals in which every defendant stands equal before the law. This noble ideal cannot be realized if the poor man charged with crime has to face his accusers without a lawyer to assist him.

Several years later (1972) the Supreme Court ruled that indigents accused of misdemeanors must also be provided with counsel in cases that could lead to imprisonment (*Argersinger v. Hamlin,* 407 U.S. 25, 1972). The right to counsel was eventually extended to various "critical stages" of the criminal justice process, starting with custodial interrogation (*Miranda v. Arizona*) and continuing through subsequent hearings, such as the preliminary hearing (*Coleman v. Alabama,* 399 U.S. 1, 1970) and police lineups (*United States v. Wade,* 406 U.S. 25, 1972).

In theory, all defendants, rich and poor alike, have a guarantee of counsel. But the real issue is the quality of counsel and the question of whether "justice" is being served. Can the average defendant receive the best counsel, given the bureaucratic nature of the court system? Can every defendant get the kind of counsel that celebrity defendants receive? Obviously not, given the degree of inequality existing in our society. Do public defenders and other lawyers for the poor provide the same kind of defense that a rich man would receive from a retained lawyer? Given the fact that the majority of those in prison come from poor backgrounds, had public defenders, and had to await their trial in jail, the answer to these questions has to be no. Why is this so?

Types of Defense Attorneys. Today there are generally four types of defense attorneys: (1) privately retained, (2) court-appointed or *assigned counsel,* (3) the contract attorney, and (4) public defenders. In some areas legal aid services (such as storefront law offices in poor communities) are provided.

Even though defense counsel is a right at each stage of the criminal justice process, most defendants do not have attorneys to call upon immediately following arrest. What happens in the majority of cases is that counsel is assigned by the court (or the case is assigned to the public defender's office) during the initial court appearance.[53] It is important to note that the average defendant is allowed only *one* lawyer, rather than an entire legal *team* as is the case during many celebrity cases—not to mention dozens of investigators, expert witnesses, and so on.

Under the *assigned-counsel system* a court appoints a specific attorney to handle a case. This is common throughout America, especially in large urban courts, where about three out of every four defendants are "indigent"—too poor to hire their own attorney.[54] In some areas the percentage is even higher, such as in Seattle, where the proportion of felony defendants who were indigent in a recent year was 88 percent, and in Monterey, California, where 92 percent of felony defendants were indigent.[55] The judge usually has a list of lawyers in private practice in a particular county or a list of those who have volunteered to serve as counsel for indigents. Often, these lawyers are inexperienced and many take the cases simply because they need the money or the experience or both. And the money won't make them rich, as their hourly fees generally range from $25 to $40. This system resembles managed care in the health system, where in cases of psychotherapy, therapists are hired by insurance companies to see ten or more clients each day for about the same amount of money as assigned counsel. Not surprisingly, the "care" received by clients in each case suffers. Here is another instance of "money talks." Thus, "justice" is itself a "commodity" and fits in nicely within the overall capitalist framework of "commodity production."

A more recent system that has emerged is the *contract system,* used in a few but a growing number of counties. As the term implies, local governments sign contracts with local attorneys to handle indigent cases. This represents a sort of "privatization" of due process, as one study concluded.[56] It is a process in which a system of "competitive bidding" is often done, with the result being that the lowest bidder, not necessarily the best bidder, often "wins" the contract. It should come as no surprise that several states have filed suits against this practice. In one case the practice was ruled unconstitutional. This was in Arizona, where the state supreme court held that the Mohave County contract system used the lowest bidder in violation of the Fifth and Sixth Amendments.[57]

It is apparent that providing attorneys for indigent defendants is not a high priority. To begin with, among the three major components of the criminal justice system, the *least* amount of annual expenditures goes to the general category of "judicial and legal." In 1996, this segment received around $26 billion, compared to $53 billion for police and just under $41 billion for corrections.[58] Expenditures on counsel for the indigent represent a very small percentage of this total. According to most recent data (1990), just over $1 billion went toward public defenders' offices. This represented an increase from only $200 million in 1976, prompting some critics to complain about the "rising costs"![59]

The *retained-counsel system* is generally far superior, especially if a defendant can afford the fees. With enough money, private attorneys can hire investigators and spend more time collecting evidence, finding witnesses, and taking other measures to ensure an adequate defense. This is particularly true if the attorney works for a law firm and the defendant is out on bail to assist in his or her own defense.

The *public defender system* is the most common and the one most criminal defendants have to rely on. Because this system is so common, we devote a separate "case study" section to it.

Case Study: The Public Defender. The public defender system has existed for centuries. It was found in ancient Rome, fifteenth-century Spain, and many other European countries prior to this century. In the United States the first public defender program was instituted in Los Angeles in 1913. It replaced the assigned-counsel system that had been common in the nineteenth century in large American cities.

The move away from assigned counsel and toward **public defenders** was merely part of a broader attempt to make the criminal justice system more efficient. Indeed, under the assigned-counsel system there were more trials, and an adversarial system prevailed. The public defender system was intended to reduce delays and promote "a situation conducive to cooperation" between defense and prosecution:

> The design and organization of the public defender system was to be consistent with and reflective of the modern system emphasizing a division of labor; through specialization and cooperation, the public defender and the district attorney were to omit the cumbersome technicalities, safeguards, and loopholes employed by private counsel on behalf of rich defendants.[60]

A letter by a public defender in Portland, Oregon, appearing in 1914, indicates the aims of this system:

> As the work was new here there was some question as to how far the public defender should go, how energetic he should be in defense of those he represents. For that reason it was thought best…that the public defender should limit his defense to assisting court in bringing out the prisoner's side of the case, rather than making a vigorous fight on technical grounds necessary to secure an acquittal.[61]

In other words, the public defender system was a system for the poor. The rich, of course, could afford to pay the high fees charged by private counsel, who would then present a "vigorous" defense. Hence, the loopholes in the law, the delays, the dismissals on technicalities, and other legal maneuvers were to become the province of the rich.

There were ideological reasons for adopting the public defender system. This system emerged in America during a period of large-scale immigration and communist revolution

(1910–1920). Many believed that it was necessary to provide defense counsel to the poor so that our system of justice would not engender a sense of injustice. Chief Justice Charles Evans Hughes said in 1920 (emphasis added): "There is no more serious menace than the discontent fostered by a belief that one cannot enforce his legal rights because of poverty. *To spread that notion is to open a broad road to Bolshevism.*"[62] Thus, it is clear that the establishment of public defender systems would at least give the outward appearance that justice was equal in the United States.

The public defender is encouraged to "cooperate" and take the perspective of the prosecutor. There are few rewards for noncooperation, so public defenders learn to adopt a bureaucratic (or magisterial) model of defense. If the public defender were to choose to adopt an adversarial stance, he or she would interrupt the normal bureaucratic processes. Chambliss and Seidman describe the following case to illustrate this problem:

> The lawyer author remembers a young and relatively inexperienced public defender who took his position seriously. Instead of pleading practically everybody guilty (as his predecessor had done), he began to try a relatively high proportion of his cases. The docket in the local trial court immediately slowed up. Out of three judges assigned to that particular bench, one began to spend all his time on criminal trials instead of a third of that time.... After some six months, this young public defender received a peremptory order to come to the state capitol to see the Chief Justice. The Chief Justice read him the riot act in terms of the need to avoid "frivolous" trials and the like, warning him of the necessity of "co-operating" with the prosecution and the judges. The Chief Justice was successful; the public defender resigned.[63]

There is really little comparison between the private counsel system and the public defender system. Public defenders become very closely tied to the court bureaucracy and, like other criminal justice workers, depend on the court system for their livelihoods. Whereas the average defendant confronts the court system only once or twice, the public defender comes in contact with it daily. Thus, cooperating with prosecutors and judges becomes an absolute necessity if one is to continue working in the field. In many ways prosecutors and public defenders are like professional wrestlers who fight in a different town each night and make sure they don't hurt each other.[64]

One study found that public defenders are assigned to certain courtrooms and handle all the cases within those courtrooms instead of handling one particular case from beginning to end. Thus, one defender handles the preliminary hearing, another handles the arraignment, and still another goes to trial, if it comes to that.[65] One might call this the "Henry Ford" approach to defending a client. And when a public defender does handle a case, chances are that the defendant will plead guilty. Public defenders often have extremely large caseloads—350 cases or more. In Connecticut, the public defender's office handles around 75 percent of all felony cases in the state, and each lawyer in that office represents, on average, more than 1,000 people each year.[66]

Most public defenders pursue their cases vigorously and at the same time process their cases expeditiously, obtaining just as many favorable outcomes for their clients as retained counsel.[67] They do so in spite of extremely low funding. In 1990 public defenders received just over 2 percent of the total expenditures on the criminal justice system. The resources made available to these lawyers are woefully inadequate.[68] It seems obvious to us that providing adequate counsel for poor people is not a high priority; after all, poor defendants represent the "surplus population" of American society. However, given the heavy caseloads of many public defenders, we certainly commend those who do actively defend their assigned clients.

The Practice of Criminal Law.   Criminal defense lawyers have been portrayed in many TV shows and motion pictures. The all-time favorite is probably Perry Mason, but more recently lawyers have been portrayed in movies based on John Grisham books, such as *The Firm* and *The Rainmaker,* plus the award-winning television show *The Practice.* In reality, there are few Perry Masons (or real-life counterparts such as Edward Bennett Williams,

Johnnie Cochran, F. Lee Bailey, and Robert Bennett). These people portray aggressive, knowledgeable, witty, smooth-talking defense attorneys who are no friends to the prosecutors, who vigorously defend each client, who own expensive cars and private jets, wear fashionable clothes, and live in beautiful homes in Beverly Hills.

Criminal lawyers constitute a minority in the legal profession, and defense attorneys are a minority within that small group. The exact number of criminal lawyers is not known, but according to one source out of 800,000 lawyers in the United States, only 10,000 to 20,000 focus on criminal matters (no more than 2.5% of the total), and the majority of these are public defenders.[69] This is not much of an improvement from figures given as of 1973, when there were about 20,000 criminal lawyers out of about 350,000 practicing attorneys (6%), and only about 6,000 (2%) confined their practice to criminal law on a full-time basis.[70]

According to one study, most lawyers never practice criminal law.[71] There are essentially two major kinds of lawyers, or what Heinz and Laumann call the *two hemispheres of the profession,* based on the kinds of clients served. One "hemisphere" is the *corporate client sector* (lawyers in this sector work in large law firms and handle regular clients and make large sums of money). The other "hemisphere" is the *personal client sector* (lawyers in this sector are often referred to as *solo practitioners*). Criminal lawyers that fit into the latter category are a dying breed, as more and more are found within public defender or district attorney offices.[72]

The practice of criminal law undeniably has the lowest status in the legal field, not surprisingly because these lawyers represent mostly "garden variety" and low-status criminals—burglars, rapists, drug dealers, and so on. With the exception of public defenders (who work in an office with other public defenders and have a steady supply of clients), most spent the bulk of their time "hustling clients" by hanging around courthouses or hoping to get referrals from other lawyers in the area who do not specialize in criminal law. (The difference between a solo practitioner and a public defender or some other lawyer working in a firm is like the difference between a psychotherapist or physician in a solo practice with his or her own office and personal secretary—or no secretary at all—and a psychotherapist or physician in a group practice with one or more secretaries.)

The lawyer–client relationship (i.e., private lawyers) begins with the collection of fees. Indeed, before anything of substance transpires between a lawyer and client, the payment of fees must be taken care of. Most lawyers ask for some or all of the money "up front."[73] In setting the amount, the seriousness of the offense is the most important factor, followed by the length of time it will take to handle the case and the client's ability to pay. An important factor is whether the case goes to trial. Lawyers charge more if a case goes to trial, so most clients are willing to plea-bargain—cop a plea—and save money. Although his study is dated, Wice found the average fee for misdemeanors to range from $500 to $1,000; for felonies, from $1,000 to $2,500 (nontrial); and for felonies that go to trial, $2,000 or more.[74] Analysis of fees in the assigned-counsel system in Colorado reveals the standard hourly fee is only about $25 to $30; if the case goes to trial, the fees are considerably more, ranging from $250 to $5,000.[75] No matter what figure is used, the typical criminal lawyer in the personal client sector does not earn very much and has to work very hard to get what money he or she does earn. Compare this with what some of the top defense lawyers in the corporate client sector get, which may be in excess of $500 *per hour!*

Blumberg argues that the practice of criminal law is in many respects a "confidence game." He suggests that in order to collect fees, lawyers have to convince the client that a "service" has been or will be rendered. Because most clients plead guilty and much of the legal work is done behind the scenes (negotiation over the telephone, letters typed, forms filled out, conversations with colleagues) and away from clients' views, there are often few visible results (compared with, for instance, the work of a plumber, shoe repairer, roofer, etc.). Thus, much of the behavior of the lawyer consists of giving at least the appearance that help and service will be forthcoming as soon as the fee payment is settled. (In most cases, secretaries collect a minimum fee, often $15, before the lawyer and client ever meet face to face. This is especially true for legal offices that advertise their fees in newspapers.

After the fee has been collected and the case has ended, the lawyer then prepares and, if necessary, tries to "cool out" the client if he is defeated (especially if the client goes to prison).[76] Cool out is slang for counseling someone after he has been conned, had, or taken advantage of. In this case, the defendant who has hired a lawyer has been led to believe that there will be a favorable outcome in his case. When the outcome is not favorable, the lawyer "cools out" the defendant's anger in a way that makes it seem like it could have been worse or it was not that bad.

In addition to collecting fees, there is the problem of convincing the client to cop a plea. In a sense, says Blumberg, the defense lawyer acts as a "double agent." He or she is seemingly defending the client's interest and playing an adversary role against the prosecutor yet in reality is doing the opposite. The lawyer is cooperating with the prosecutor and tries to convince the client that he or she should plead guilty for "considerations," such as a reduced sentence or dropped charges.

Obviously, the practice of criminal law is not as glamorous as TV shows and motion pictures try to portray it. For most (except public defenders), it is a constant, daily struggle to obtain clients and collect fees while hanging around courthouses, bail bond companies, and jails hoping to pick up clients or seeking information on an existing client. A perceptive study by Wice confirms this seamy view. Here's his overview of the world of the criminal lawyer:

> The average criminal lawyer would work a six-day week with twelve-hour days. A typical day would begin at 8:00 A.M., as the lawyer tried to take care of personal business and prepare for that day's court appearances. Since court usually began at 9:00 A.M., this left only one hour to straighten out his affairs. Once at the courthouse, the lawyer was rarely able to return to his office until the late afternoon (4:30 to 5:30) when the court was adjourned. The early evening (5:00 to 8:00) was then reserved for seeing clients and then preparation of the next day's cases. Many of the younger criminal lawyers appeared to be the most driven and put in the longest hours. They would often come into the office for six to eight hours on Saturday, seeing clients and researching cases, and a few would even venture in on Sunday mornings if extra work was needed on a complex case.[77]

Wice found that most criminal lawyers obtain their clients through referrals from other lawyers (usually civil lawyers), friends, or family of former clients. Bail bondsmen, police officers, jailhouse runners, and others associated with the justice system also refer clients. Some clients are assigned by judges as part of the assigned-counsel system.

The Judge

Neubauer writes of the symbol of the judge as follows:

> For most Americans, the judge is the symbol of justice. Of all the actors in the criminal justice process, the public holds the judge most responsible for ensuring that the system operates fairly and impartially. Thus, the quality of justice is commonly equated with the quality of the judge. The judge's standing as the symbol of justice is reinforced by the mystique surrounding the position—the flowing black robes, the gavel, and the honorific "all rise" when the judge enters the courtroom.[78]

There are several myths associated with judges, some of them previously mentioned. Judges are supposed to be neutral arbitrators and committed to the ideals of equal justice for all; and they are supposed to interpret *existing* laws. In fact, judges may be highly prejudiced and committed to the maintenance of the status quo; and they may actually be creators of law.

Judges engage in five key tasks. First, they serve as umpires or referees during a trial, roles with which you probably are familiar. Judges must constantly interpret the law and use a great deal of discretion. Quite often judges create new laws or at least new interpretations of old laws. Second, they participate in plea negotiations to one extent or another. Some judges participate openly in court or in their chambers. Others will have nothing to do with plea negotiations, (plea bargaining is discussed in Chapter 9). Third, judges make rulings (usually in writing) on legal motions made by lawyers. Here is where they are most likely to create new laws by setting new precedents. They also spend some of their time reviewing and signing search warrants and arrest warrants and authorizing wiretaps. Fourth, judges engage in various forms of counseling—of witnesses, lawyers, police officers, and other criminal justice workers. Fifth, judges are administrators. Often a particular judge is in charge of a particular court, so much so that the judge considers it to be his or her court. Thus, judges must spend a great deal of time keeping court *dockets* (a calendar showing court cases) current.[79]

Judicial Selection and Judicial Careers

There are generally three ways of selecting judges. The first is by *election,* which may be either partisan (e.g., Republicans v. Democrats) or nonpartisan. The second, used in sixteen states, is *merit selection* (commonly referred to as the *Missouri Plan*). The third is by *appointment* (either legislative or gubernatorial).

Popular elections are usually low-key affairs in which there is little controversy. Most of the time the incumbent wins. The average citizen knows little or nothing about the judges running for office. Many people don't even care. In Memphis, Tennessee, in 1970 a judge who won election had actually died a few months earlier. Because of some bureaucratic rule, his name appeared on the ballot. Whether the voters simply did not know that the judge had died or they felt that, even dead, he was better than any of the other candidates is not known.

The *Missouri Plan* of merit selection was established in 1940 in Missouri in order to get politics out of the courthouse. Today, sixteen states use this method, which works as follows. When a vacancy occurs, a special committee of citizens and lawyers sends a list of recommendations to the governor. The governor then makes an appointment from this list. One year later there is a special election in which the voters are asked whether this judge should remain in office. If the voters say yes, then the judge serves a full term of office. Understandably, few judges have been defeated. One study found that over a twenty-year period in Illinois, only 22 judges were removed in 1,864 retention elections.[80]

Unfortunately, politics is not removed through the Missouri Plan. One study showed that it results in the selection of judges who are essentially similar in class, political affiliation, and legal experience to those already in power in a given state.[81] But this is to be expected, given the nature of the electoral system in this country. As in most elections, the voters are presented with a list of candidates from which to choose. Little wonder that voter turnout for judicial elections is so small. Also, it is not surprising that most judges are and have been white, male, Protestant, and upper middle class.[82]

Judges do, of course, vary in their training and status in the legal profession. The status of judges reflects the duties they perform and the level of the court in which they preside. Appellate court judges are highest in status and salary, and lower court judges are lowest. The most famous judges have been U.S. Supreme Court justices. Names such as Holmes, Cardoza, Frankfurter, Brandeis, Douglas, and Warren come to mind. The chief justice attains the highest status. State supreme court justices and other appellate judges are next in status, followed by trial court judges.

The appellate system (including the Supreme Court) ultimately rules the entire criminal court system, and judges who serve within this system are drawn almost solely from the ranks of the upper class. This fact has been noted by several scholars spanning many years.[83] These judges are not "instruments of ruling class domination" as some Marxists assert; they do have some degree of autonomy and do occasionally make rulings in favor of disadvantaged groups; but they are hardly revolutionaries bent on creating lasting and radical social changes. Thus, the criminal court system, like the entire criminal justice system, remains largely a system of *class justice.* It reinforces and perpetuates the system of class inequality that surrounds it.[84]

Lower court judges earn the lowest salary and are the least qualified. In most states the qualifications for justices of the peace and other kinds of lower court judges do not include the possession of a law degree. A rather notorious municipal court judge in North Las Vegas not only lacked a law degree but did not even have an undergraduate degree. Yet he served several years as the only judge of that court, before being driven out by the state ethics commission. The low status of lower court judges parallels the low status of lawyers practicing in the lower courts and the low status of most of the defendants.

The careers of judges also vary according to level of legal education and social class background. Federal judges, appellate judges, and many trial court judges serve for life; most lower court judges serve for only a few years. However, many lower court judges do move on to higher posts, but rarely higher than trial courts. Some judges are political appointees and leave their posts when there is a change in administration. For the most part, the career of a judge is a long and fruitful one.

SUMMARY

The majority of all criminal cases in America are processed through the lower courts. These courts handle virtually all of the misdemeanors, initial appearances, and preliminary hearings. Trial courts, the next most dominant type of court, handle primarily felony cases and conduct trials. Appellate courts, such as the state supreme courts and the U.S. Supreme Court, focus solely on appeals.

Attorneys practicing criminal law are a small minority in the field of law. Both prosecutors and defense lawyers stand at the bottom of the status hierarchy of their professions, as do most of the judges they face. Furthermore, because they all depend on one another for their livelihoods (forming a courtroom workgroup) and owe their livelihoods to the court bureaucracy (particularly public defenders and prosecutors), the ideal adversarial relationship rarely exists. Instead, "justice"—quality defense for all and the protection of the public—often becomes secondary to organizational goals and personal careers. Most who practice law at this level (especially public defenders and prosecutors) eventually move on to private practice, judgeships, politics, or some other legal careers.

Providing counsel for indigents has long been a practice, but the right to counsel at every stage of the criminal justice process is a recent development. Three methods of criminal defense are common: the public defender system, the assigned-counsel system, and the retained-counsel system. Although the retained-counsel system is far superior to the other systems, there are more advantages in having public defenders than in having assigned counsel. No matter what type of attorney a person has, pleading guilty for "considerations" becomes part of the routine.

KEY TERMS

Betts v. Brady   201
courtroom workgroup   198
dual court system   195
Gideon v. Wainwright   201
in forma pauperis request   197
Judiciary Act of 1789   195
justice of the peace   194

Powell v. Alabama   201
prosecutor   199
public defender   203
Reorganization Act of 1801   195
trial courts of general
   jurisdiction   197

trial courts of limited
   jurisdiction   196
U.S. courts of appeals   196
U.S. district courts   196
U.S. Supreme Court   197
writ of certiorari   197

NOTES

1. These observations of a Detroit courtroom were made in February 1999 by William B. Brown, coauthor of this book.

2. Zemans, F. K. "In the Eye of the Beholder: The Relationship between the Public and the Courts." In G. L. Mays and P. R. Gregware (eds.), *Courts and Jus-*

tice: A Reader. Prospect Heights, IL: Waveland Press, 1995, p. 9.

3. Ibid., pp. 15–16.

4. Merry, S. E. *Getting Justice and Getting Even: Legal Consciousness among Working-Class Americans.* Chicago: University of Chicago Press, 1990.

5. Rush, G. E. *Dictionary of Criminal Justice.* Boston: Holbrook Press, 1977, p. 78.

6. Turkel, G. *Law and Society: Critical Approaches.* Boston: Allyn and Bacon, 1996, p. 139.

7. Jackson, B. (ed.). *Law and Order: Criminal Justice in America.* Chicago: University of Illinois Press, 1984, p. 77.

8. Lynch, M. J., and R. Michalowski. *The New Primer in Radical Criminology: Critical Perspectives on Crime, Power and Identity* (3rd ed.). Monsey, NY: Criminal Justice Press, 2000, p. 169.

9. Ibid., pp. 156–157.

10. Knappman, E. W. *Great American Trials: From Salem Witchcraft to Rodney King.* Detroit: Visible Ink Press, 1994.

11. Friedman, L. M. *Crime and Punishment in American History.* New York: Basic Books, 1993, p. 31.

12. Chapin, B. *Criminal Justice in Colonial America: 1600–1660.* Athens: University of Georgia Press, 1983, and *Provincial America: 1600–1763.* New York: Free Press, 1996.

13. Friedman, L. M. *A History of American Law.* New York: Simon & Schuster, 1973, p. 35.

14. Ibid. For a more detailed look at the justice of the peace see Shelden, *Controlling the Dangerous Classes,* ch. 3.

15. Shelden, ibid.

16. Friedman, *A History of American Law,* p. 34.

17. For a more complete treatment of this topic see Shelden, *Controlling the Dangerous Classes,* ch. 3. See also Knappman, *Great American Trials.*

18. Neubauer, D. *America's Courts and the Criminal Justice System* (5th ed.). Belmont, CA: Wadsworth, 1996, pp. 41–42.

19. Friedman, *A History of American Law,* p. 140.

20. Shelden, *Controlling the Dangerous Classes,* ch. 3.

21. Neubauer, *America's Courts and the Criminal Justice System,* p. 45. For a fascinating look at the work of the U.S. court of appeals in a book of fiction see Patterson, R. N. *Protect and Defend.* New York: Ballantine Books, 2000.

22. Neubauer, ibid., p. 47; Maguire K., and A. L. Pastore (eds.), *Sourcebook of Criminal Justice Statistics—1996.* Washington, DC: U.S. Department of Justice, Bureau of Justice Statistics, 1997, p. 422.

23. Neubauer, *America's Courts and the Criminal Justice Systems,* p. 48.

24. *Sourcebook of Criminal Justice Statistics, 2000,* online, table 1.67.

25. Rush, G. E. *Dictionary of Criminal Justice.* Boston: Holbrook Press, 1977, p.184.

26. Maguire and Pastore, *Sourcebook of Criminal Justice Statistics—1996,* p. 483.

27. Dean, J. *The Rehnquist Choice.* New York: Free Press. 2001.

28. Neubauer, *America's Courts and the Criminal Justice Systems,* p. 51.

29. Reiman, *The Rich Get Richer and the Poor Get Prison;* Chiricos, T. G., and W. Bales. "Unemployment and Punishment: An Empirical Analysis." *Criminology* 29 (November 1991).

30. Wice, P. B. *Chaos in the Courthouse: The Inner Workings of the Urban Criminal Courts.* New York: Praeger, 1985.

31. Neubauer, *America's Courts and Criminal Justice System,* pp. 52–53.

32. Ibid., pp. 70–77; Walker, S. *Sense and Nonsense about Crime and Drugs* (5th ed.). Belmont, CA: Wadsworth, 2001, pp. 52–54.

33. Lichtenstein, M. "Public Defenders: Dimensions of Cooperation." *The Justice System Journal* 9: 102–110, (1984).

34. Walker, *Sense and Nonsense about Crime and Drugs,* pp. 52–54.

35. Chambliss and Seidman, *Law, Order and Power,* pp. 396–397. The wide discretion granted to the prosecutor has been recognized by many experts for years. For instance, the American Bar Association's *Standards Relating to the Prosecution and Defense Function* merely "admonishes" prosecutors not to be unduly influenced by personal or political motivations and not to charge more than can be "reasonably supported at trial" (Scheb and Scheb, *Criminal Law and Procedure,* p. 437). Gottfredson and Gottfredson, in their comprehensive review of decision making in the criminal justice system, observe that "the decision whether or not to charge is the single most unreviewed exercise of the power of criminal law available to an individual in the American system of justice" (Gottfredson, M. R., and D. M. Gottfredson. *Decision Making in Criminal Justice: Toward the Rational Exercise of Discretion.* New York: Plenum Press, 1988, p. 114).

36. Donziger, S. *The Real War on Crime.* New York: HarperCollins, 1996, p. 186.

37. McDonald, W. F. (ed.). *The Prosecutor.* Beverly Hills, CA: Sage, 1979, p. 22.

38. Ibid., p. 24.

39. Ibid.

40. Neubauer, *America's Courts and the Criminal Justice System,* pp. 80–82.

41. Ibid., p. 84.

42. Schur, E. *Law and Society: A Sociological View.* New York: Random House, 1968; Neubauer, *America's Courts and the Criminal Justice System,* p. 84.

43. Fishman, J. J. "The Social and Occupational Mobility of Prosecutors: New York City," in McDonald, *The Prosecutor,* p. 239.

44. Ibid.; see also Wice, P. B. "The Private Practice of Criminal Law: Life in the Real World." *Criminal Law Bulletin* 14(5): 381–409 (September–October 1978), and *Chaos in the Courthouse.*

45. Lynch, M. J., and W. B. Groves. *A Primer in Radical Criminology* (2nd ed.). New York: Harrow and Heston, 1989, p. 102.

46. Flemming, R., P. Nardulli, and J. Eisenstein. *The Craft of Justice: Politics and Work in Criminal Court Communities.* Philadelphia: University of Pennsylvania Press, 1992.

47. Neubauer, *America's Courts and the Criminal Justice System,* p. 82.

48. McDonald, *The Prosecutor,* p. 33.

49. Gottfredson and Gottfredson, *Decision Making in Criminal Justice,* p. 116.

50. Neubauer, *America's Courts and the Criminal Justice System,* pp. 82–84.

51. Jacoby, J. E. "Pushing the Envelope: Leadership in Prosecution." *Justice System Journal* 17: 291–307 (1995).

52. For a fuller treatment of this case see Lewis, A. *Gideon's Trumpet.* New York: Harper & Row, 1964.

53. Benner, L. A., B. Neary, and R. M. Gutman. *The Other Face of Justice: A Report of the National Defender Survey.* Chicago: National Legal Aid and Defender Association, 1973; Neubauer, *America's Courts and the Criminal Justice System,* pp. 111–114.

54. Wice, *Chaos in the Courthouse.*

55. Hanson, R., and J. Chapper. *Indigent Defense Systems: Report to the State Justice Institute.* Williamsburg, VA: National Center for State Courts, 1991.

56. Worden, A. P. "Privatizing Due Process: Issues in the Comparison of Assigned Counsel, Public Defender, and Contracted Indigent Defense System." *Justice System Journal* 14: 390–419 (1991), and "Counsel for the Poor: An Evaluation of Contracting for Indigent Criminal Defense." *Justice Quarterly* 10: 613–637 (1993); Spangenberg Group. *Contracting for Indigent Defense Services: A Special Report.* Washington, DC: Bureau of Justice Statistics, 2000.

57. *Smith v. State,* 140 Arizona 355, 1984.

58. Maguire K., and Pastore, A. L. (eds.). *Sourcebook of Criminal Justice Statistics—1999* (Washington DC: U.S. Department of Justice, Bureau of Justice Statistics, 2000), table 1.2.

59. Smith, S. K., and C. J. De Francis. *Indigent Defense.* Washington, DC: U.S. Department of Justice, 1996, p. 17; Neubauer, *America's Courts and the Criminal Justice System,* p. 114.

60. Barak, "In Defense of the Rich," p. 8.

61. Ibid., p. 10.

62. Ibid.

63. Chambliss and Seidman, *Law, Order and Power,* p. 402.

64. Neubauer, *America's Courts and the Criminal Justice System,* pp. 112–113.

65. Rosett, A., and D. R. Cressey. *Justice by Content: Plea Bargains in the American Courthouse.* Philadelphia: Lippincott, 1976, p. 120.

66. Donziger, *The Real War on Crime,* p. 188.

67. Hanson, R., W. Hewitt, and B. Ostrom. "Are the Critics of Indigent Defense Counsel Correct?" *State Court Journal* (Summer 1992), pp. 20–29; McIntyre, L. *The Public Defender: The Practice of Law in the Shadows of Repute.* Chicago: University of Chicago Press, 1987.

68. Donziger, *The Real War on Crime,* p. 189.

69. Cole, G. F., and C. E. Smith. *The American System of Criminal Justice* (8th ed.). Belmont, CA: Wadsworth, 1998, p. 134.

70. Shelden, R. G. *Criminal Justice in America: A Sociological Approach.* Boston: Little, Brown, 1982, p. 219.

71. Heinz, J., and E. Laumann. *Chicago Lawyers: The Social Structure of the Bar.* New York: Russell Sage Foundation, 1982.

72. Neubauer, *America's Courts and the Criminal Justice System,* p. 107.

73. Wice, "The Private Practice of Criminal Law," p. 391; Lushing, P. "The Fall and Rise of the Criminal Contingent Fee." *Journal of Criminal Law and Criminology* 82: 498–568 (1992).

74. Wice, ibid., p. 394.

75. Cole and Smith, *The American System of Criminal Justice,* p. 319.

76. Blumberg, A. "The Practice of Law as a Confidence Game." In W. J. Chambliss (ed.), *Criminal Law in Action.* New York: Wiley. 1975.

77. Wice, "The Private Practice of Criminal Law," p. 383.

78. Neubauer, *America's Courts and the Criminal Justice System,* p. 119.

79. Ibid., pp. 120–121.

80. Hall, W., and L. Aspin. "What Twenty Years of Judicial Retention Elections Have Told Us." *Judicature* 70: 340–347 (1987).

81. Watson, R., and R. Downing. *The Politics of the Bench and Bar.* New York: Wiley, 1969.

82. Hogarth, J. *Sentencing as a Human Process.* Toronto: University of Toronto Press, 1971; Bottomley, A. K. *Decisions in the Penal Process.* South Hackensack, NJ: Fred B. Rothman, 1973; Neubauer, *America's Courts and the Criminal Justice System.*

83. Beard, C. *An Economic Interpretation of the Constitution.* New York: Macmillan, 1935; Domhoff, G. W. *Who Rules America? Power and Politics in the Year 2000.* Mountain View, CA: Mayfield, 1998; Chambliss and Seidman, *Law, Order and Power.*

84. Lynch and Groves, *A Primer on Radical Criminology,* p. 105; this theme is discussed in more detail in Shelden, *Controlling the Dangerous Classes.*

CHAPTER NINE

CRIMINAL COURTS

The Process

Well, Metro picked up this girl, right? And she was busted for solicitation. Actually, she probably wasn't soliciting at all, but she was wearing these kinds of clothes where her tits are hanging out. She really looked good though. She is checked out and we find she is a school teacher in _____ County in _____. *(Laughter.)* So we tell her that if she cooperates, she will be on her way back home in no time. Otherwise we will be forced to notify her school board. She gets really scared, you know? Well, the dumb bitch pleads guilty, pays the fine, and then she is on her way.... Do you want another beer?[1]

If I have done my homework, which I always do, I have a good idea if someone deserves to be allowed bail. The crime they are charged with is the first consideration, and then, well of course, their criminal record has revealing qualities also.... Yes, I consider the whole criminal record, all arrests and convictions.... You have to understand these people; just because they evade conviction does not, by any stretch of the imagination, mean they were innocent.[2]

PRETRIAL COURT PROCESSES

Before a case can proceed into formal court processing, the person who was arrested by the police has to be charged by the prosecutor with a specific crime or crimes. Many cases brought to the prosecutor's office by the police following an arrest are not accepted—that is, not formally charged. Because the prosecutor can be viewed as the gatekeeper of the court system, the decision to prosecute a case becomes one of the most critical decisions in the entire court process. Given the obvious impact on the lives of people who go through any court process, the decisions made by the prosecutor in the screening process have a profound impact on the lives of both victims and defendants. Let us examine this decision.

Deciding Whether to Prosecute

As many as half of all cases submitted to the prosecutor's office are not accepted for prosecution. In court jargon, the case is "nollied," "nolled," or "nol-prossed"—the allusion is to *nolle prosequi,* a Latin expression meaning "unwilling to prosecute." But many times the police, sometimes in cooperation with the prosecutor, engage in *overcharging*—charging the defendant with the most serious counts of a crime. These "inflated" counts often extend beyond the boundary of what the prosecutor actually believes the defendant can be convicted of (e.g., charging possession of drugs with the intent to sell when simple possession would be the most realistic charge). Overcharging also includes adding superimposed charges (e.g., in addition to possession with intent, charge possession of drug paraphernalia, resisting arrest, and perhaps multiple charges for possessing more than one drug), which tend to "soften" the defendant to the prospects of pleading to a single count. In many instances, the prosecutor "denies" all but one of the charges.[3]

To give you an idea of what happens to felony cases that are referred to the prosecutor's office, a U.S. Department of Justice survey is revealing. Comparing two cities—Golden, Colorado, and Salt Lake City, Utah—the survey found significant variation, but on the whole prosecutors eliminated many cases by reducing charges to misdemeanors. In Salt Lake City, out of every 100 arrests, 74 were accepted for prosecution; of these, 32 (43%) were reduced to misdemeanors and referred to a misdemeanor court (i.e., a lower court); of the remaining 42 felonies, 1 was referred elsewhere, and the remainder proceeded to court for final plea; of the remaining 41 cases, 29 pleaded guilty, 4 went to trial, and 8 were dismissed. In Golden, a larger percentage was accepted for prosecution (81%), and a higher proportion was reduced to misdemeanors (53%); however, about the same number ended up going to court (33 out of 38 cases), with 23 guilty pleas, 2 going to trial, and 8 being dismissed. It is interesting to note that in both cities about the same overall percentage of the 100 cases ended up with guilty pleas (29% in Salt Lake City and 23% in Golden).[4]

The actual decision to accept or deny a case is typically based on several interrelated factors. In the survey noted above, researchers found, after looking at case attrition in four large cities (New York, San Diego, Salt Lake City, and New Orleans), that the most common reason given for denying a case for prosecution was problems with evidence: the prosecution determined that there was either insufficient evidence or no evidence at all. This was the major factor in 62 percent of the cases in New York, 54 percent of the cases in San Diego, 58 percent of the cases in Salt Lake City, and 38 percent of the cases in New Orleans (which leads us to wonder why these defendants were arrested in the first place). The second major factor (found in 23% of the cases in New York, 15% in San Diego, 12% in Salt Lake City, and 30% in New Orleans) was "witness problems" (which arise in most personal crimes, such as assault and rape). Together evidence problems and witness problems accounted for the vast majority of denials. Further analysis found that these factors were almost as important in determining dismissal of cases after the filing of an information or an indictment. Unfortunately, the study did not examine such variables as race and class. Is there a selection bias at this stage? The evidence available suggests that the answer to this question is yes.

Class and Racial Bias in Charging Decisions.   We have already noted that various police decisions are often biased against racial minorities and lower-class citizens. This bias extends, at least indirectly, to the prosecutor's office. A 1970s study found that the race of the victim and the race of the defendant play a key role in the decision to prosecute. Specifically, when the defendant is African American and the victim is white, and when both the offender and the victim are white, chances are greater for the case to be accepted for prosecution. Chances for denial are greater if both the victim and the offender are African American. Also, in situations where the victims are white and employed, the cases are far more likely to be accepted and processed into the judicial system.[5] A more recent study in Florida of 1,017 homicide defendants came up with identical findings. In this case, when there was a white victim and an African American offender, the charge was upgraded to something more serious.[6]

A recent study in Los Angeles County found clear evidence of racial bias in prosecutors' charging decisions. Specifically, after controlling for current offense, prior record, whether a weapon was used, and other variables, researchers found that African Americans and Hispanics were the least likely to have their cases rejected by the prosecutor. Another study found evidence that in the instance of murder, those cases involving a white victim were far more likely to be fully prosecuted than were cases with African American victims. Another study found that white suspects were actually *more* likely to have their cases dismissed by the prosecutor, but this was because of the fact that racial minorities are far more likely than whites to be arrested on rather questionable evidence to begin with.[7]

Social class differences in prosecutors' charging decisions have been found in several recent studies. These differences are especially evident in comparisons of ordinary street crimes with white-collar and corporate crimes.[8]

The Initial Appearance

According to the Sixth Amendment to the Constitution, a defendant cannot be held for an indefinite period of time without a court appearance. In **Mallory v. United States** (354 U.S. 455, 1957) the Supreme Court ruled that a suspect must come before a judge "as soon as possible" following an arrest. In practice this usually means the next working day (or if the arrest was made on the weekend, the following Monday morning). This first appearance in court is usually known as the **initial appearance.** The main purpose of this hearing is to arrange for some form of **pretrial release,** usually through **bail.** During this hearing the judge has three important duties to perform. First, the judge informs the defendant of the charge(s) against him or her (often the defendant is given a copy of the information or complaint), so that there is no misunderstanding of what is going on. Second, the defendant is informed of his or her constitutional rights, including the right to counsel and the right to remain silent. Third, there is a determination of whether to release the defendant pending subsequent hearings, including a trial, and the amount of bail if the individual is to be set free.[9]

Social class and race are obvious factors affecting defendants' prospects for pretrial release. First, people with little or no money frequently have a difficult time paying bail. Second, race becomes a proxy indicator of social class; this is particularly true in the case of African Americans and Latinos, who are disproportionately overrepresented among the social class that has little or no money to pay bail. The quality of defense counsel is another variable that must be factored into the pretrial release process. Indigent defendants or defendants without the means to pay bail also cannot afford to pay an attorney to represent them in the initial appearance. Before we proceed to the topic of defense attorneys, however, it is necessary to take a closer look at pretrial detention and bail.

Pretrial Detention and Bail. *Pretrial detention* is the remedy used by the judicial system to determine which defendants can get out of jail before trial and which defendants are not released before trial. The Fifth Amendment stipulates that no person can be held, "nor deprived of life, liberty or property, without due process of law." Thus far, it appears that the Supreme Court has not seriously considered at what point pretrial detention becomes excessive or in violation of due process. Instead, the Supreme Court has directed courts to deal with the due process issue on a case-by-case basis.[10] Also, according to legal principles, a person is presumed innocent until proved guilty "beyond a reasonable doubt," and there can be no punishment without conviction, nor can anyone be detained for the purposes of punishment. On the surface, these are certainly ideal principles; however, the reality of criminal justice is often the opposite. On any given day, tens of thousands of people are held in jail awaiting court appearances (sometimes for many months). They have not been proved guilty; many are there simply because they cannot afford bail. Some defendants are detained because the court has ruled that they are dangerous to society or pose a flight-from-prosecution risk. Well before the Bail Reform Act of 1984, the Supreme Court had sustained the constitutionality of detention if it could be argued successfully that the defendant was a flight risk.[11]

There are several legally prescribed factors associated with the decision to deny pretrial release. The Seventh Circuit Court ruled that the trial court judge must consider all of these factors.[12] First, the nature of the offense charged is considered, including whether the offense is of a violent nature or involves narcotics. Second, the strength of the evidence against the defendant is considered. The Ninth Circuit Court ruled that the strength of evidence against the defendant is *least* important.[13] Third, the history and characteristics of the defendant are scrutinized. The defendant's character, physical and mental condition, employment status and history, family and community ties, drug and alcohol abuse history, and criminal record are examined. The legal status (e.g., probation, parole, release on bail) of the defendant at the time the alleged offense occurred is another element considered in the scrutiny of the defendant's history and characteristics. Finally, the nature and level of danger that the release of the defendant would present to the community are taken into account.[14] Additional considerations are contingent upon the situation in which pretrial release is sought—for example, release pending trial, release pending sentencing or appeal, release of a material witness, or release following a violation of conditions of a previous pretrial release.[15]

The issue of dangerousness has been visited extensively by the U.S. circuit courts. For instance, the Third Circuit Court upheld pretrial detentions on the grounds that a defendant is *likely* to commit one of a number of previously designated offenses that are considered dangerous to the community.[16] The Second Circuit Court concurred with the ruling of the Third Circuit Court but rejected the notion that evidence must demonstrate the relationship between future dangerousness and the present offense.[17] Finally, and in accordance with the position of the 98th Congress, the Ninth Circuit Court considered potential economic danger to the community as grounds to support pretrial detention.[18]

If no other court remedy will reasonably ensure both the defendant's appearance in court and the safety of the community, the judge must remand the defendant to detention to await trial.[19] Most courts subscribe to the assumption that if a defendant is a flight-from-prosecution risk, or the defendant poses a danger to society, then the defendant must be detained.[20] According to 18 U.S.C. 3142(e), however, all reasonable less restrictive alternatives to detention must be explored. But the Eighth Circuit Court pointed out that reasonable assurance does not mean guarantee.[21]

Bail is a form of "security" that a defendant puts forth that guarantees that he or she will appear in court when required. It is a form of release for the defendant. In most jurisdictions a defendant can, in effect, *buy* his or her freedom. In most jurisdictions bail is set on misdemeanor charges by a police official, usually a desk sergeant at the station house where the defendant was booked. For felonies, bail is typically set by a judge in a courthouse during the initial appearance, although legislative bodies often establish minimum and maximum parameters from which judges can assign bail.

In most courts there are clearly established procedures for releasing a defendant. If the charge is a minor misdemeanor, the individual is usually released almost immediately by posting bail at the police station according to a predetermined *bail schedule,* which specifies a monetary amount needed to secure one's release—in a word, the "price" the accused can pay to "purchase" his or her freedom, much like shopping for an item at a retail store. The spirit of capitalism is alive and well in this system! There also is a bail schedule for more serious misdemeanors and felonies, except in felonies what usually happens is that the accused stands before a judge during the initial appearance. Usually, the judge merely refers to the bail schedule and sets bail accordingly. In more serious cases, the defendant along with his or her attorney and the prosecutor argue whether the individual should be released on bail.

There are four ways to secure one's release following an arrest:

1. Posting a cash bond. The defendant posts the full amount of the bond with the court.
2. Posting a property bond. A piece of property (e.g., a home) is used as collateral.
3. Being released on personal recognizance without having to post bond. This is usually reserved for persons charged with minor crimes or for prominent citizens of a community.
4. Using the services of a bail bondsman. The defendant pays the bondsman a certain percentage (typically 10%) of the bond (which is usually not refundable) and is allowed to go free.

Most defendants use bail bondsmen because cash bonds and property bonds require a sizable amount of cash or property, which most defendants do not have.

Bail dates back to early English society and was originally established to ensure that an accused appeared for trial.[22] Today that is still one of the major justifications for having some form of bail. Other justifications include the need to protect society from criminal acts. The amount of bail is supposed to reflect the likelihood of the defendant's appearing in court or the "seriousness" of the crime. In most states maximum and minimum amounts of bail are set by law for each type of crime (e.g., not less than $5,000 nor more than $15,000 for robbery). Sometimes judges develop their own criteria for determining the amount of bail. The result is often a great deal of variation from one judge to another.

Some may argue that in addition to the seriousness of the offense, factors such as prior records, the strength of the case, and an individual's ties to the community (job, how long in residence, etc.) are considered when judges set bail. But in the majority of cases the real reason people are held in jail awaiting trial is not that they are "dangerous" or are likely to commit further crimes but that they simply cannot afford to post the bond. Numerous studies, covering more than forty years, consistently demonstrate two major points.[23] First, whether a person is released from jail pending the final disposition of the case is strongly dependent on his or her class and race. Minorities and the poor are far more likely to remain in jail. Second, comparisons of those who remain in jail and those released show that those released fare much better in terms of the likelihood of being convicted and if convicted the likelihood of being sentenced to a term of imprisonment.

One of the most convincing studies was conducted by Patterson and Lynch, who focused attention on compliance with a bail schedule. The study examined whether the amount of bail required was below, above, or within the amount in the schedule. The researchers discovered significant differences based on both race and gender. Specifically, they found that whites and females were far more likely than minorities and males to receive bail that was below the schedule amount. Just over one-fifth of the whites (21.3%), compared to only 12.5 percent of the minorities, received bail below the schedule (minorities were slightly more likely to receive bail in an amount above the bail schedule); more than one-fourth of the females (26.9%) had bail below the schedule amount, compared to only 15.5 percent of the males. This relationship remained regardless of other factors, such as the seriousness of the offense and prior criminal record. In a comparison of defendants brought to court on violent felonies in Detroit, it was found that 71 percent of the African Americans, but only 53 percent of the whites, were detained. The final outcome: 88 percent of those detained were sent to prison, compared to only 45 percent of those not detained.[24]

Race may at times interact with other variables that are themselves directly related to the amount of bail imposed. Farnworh and Horan discovered when comparing African

Americans and whites who had private attorneys that the amount of bail was greater for African Americans.[25] Many studies have shown that employment status is directly related to being out on bail—employed defendants are far more likely to be granted low bail or released on their own recognizance. A class action lawsuit filed in New York City in the 1960s resulted in a detailed study of the granting of release, either on bail or on personal recognizance. Among other findings of this study, almost half (46%) of the employed defendants were released pending the outcomes of their cases, compared to just over one-fourth (26%) of the unemployed. This study, incidentally, also showed that regardless of the variable controlled for, those released had much better outcomes of their cases (e.g., degree of punishment) than those who remained in jail.[26] Still another study found that African Americans who were unemployed were the most likely to be detained.[27] Similarly, another study found that having a prior felony conviction more adversely affected African Americans than whites and that having more education and a higher income had a more positive effect for whites than for African Americans.[28]

As this research clearly shows—and we return to this subject in Chapter 11—jails (which hold mostly pretrial detainees who have not been convicted of any crime) are little more than modern-day poorhouses fostering a form of apartheid.

Bail Bondsmen.   Around most courthouses and jails you undoubtedly have seen what often appear to be rather sleazy storefront offices with huge letters out front proclaiming "Bail Bonds, 24-Hour Service" or some catchy phrase like "Freedom for Sale." The sign displayed by a bail bondsman in Southern California promised "I'll Get You Out If It Takes 20 Years." Welcome to the world of the bail bondsman, a very shrewd businessperson who is one among many who make a profit out of crime.

In most criminal cases the decision of whether a defendant goes free is made by a bail bondsman. The bail bondsman has enormous power, for he or she (men have no monopoly on this line of work) decides whether a suspect is a "good risk" to "do business with." The bail bondsman is usually backed up by large insurance companies. A handful of companies control almost all corporate bail bonds in the country. The bail bondsman must contribute to a reserve fund 10 percent of the premiums he or she collects, and the company levies another 20 percent for posting the bond. That leaves the bondsman with a 70 percent profit on all premiums collected from defendants.

Over the years many critics have complained about the often shady practices of bail bondsmen, especially when they hire bounty hunters to track down individuals who skip town. There have been many cases of bounty hunters breaking into the homes of suspected bail-jumpers, only to discover that they had the wrong address. In some notorious cases the occupants of the house have been killed. Bail bondsmen also have been linked to many corrupt practices. Such practices have resulted in at least five states abolishing bail bonding for profit (Kentucky, Oregon, Wisconsin, Nebraska, and Illinois).[29]

Bail bondsmen have a close working relationship with others in the criminal justice system. Bondsmen can help the courts by "managing the population of arrested persons." They do this by careful screening of defendants, releasing those they consider to be "good risks" and thereby reducing congestion in the jails and the courts. This relationship appears to be reciprocal, for judges routinely do not pressure bondsmen to make good on bonds that are forfeited because the defendants did not show up for court. (The entire bond is forfeited and owed to the court if a defendant fails to appear for trial or other court appearance.) Bondsmen also have become part of the courtroom workgroup and are on a first-name basis with many of the court actors. They are sometimes financial contributors to judges' reelection campaigns.[30]

Some Effects of the Bail System.   One of the most controversial features of the criminal justice system is **pretrial preventive detention.** This is the practice of refusing to grant bail to defendants who are declared "dangerous" and who present a "clear danger" to the community. This measure was part of the 1970 District of Columbia Crime bill, pushed through Congress by the Nixon administration.

Preventive detention is based on the unproved assumption that there is a way to predict who will commit a crime if released. Perhaps the most controversial part of this practice surrounds the term *dangerous*. We must ask, Who is dangerous and how do you determine this? In one of the earliest critiques of preventive detention, the American Friends Service Committee asserted in the early 1970s that *dangerous* has historically been reserved for those who in some way challenge existing power relationships. In *Struggle for Justice* the Committee wrote:

> Those persons or groups that threaten the existing power structure are dangerous. In any historical period, to identify an individual whose status is that of a member of the "dangerous classes," the label "criminal" has been handy. The construct, criminal, is not used to classify the performers of all legally defined delicts [offenses against the law], only those whose position in the social structure qualifies them for membership in the dangerous classes.[31]

Are those currently locked up in jail awaiting trial "dangerous"? How many, when released, commit new offenses, and how many fail to appear in court? In Washington, D.C., during the first ten months of the original Preventive Detention Law, only 20 of 6,000 felony defendants had bail revoked, and only 4 of the 20 were eventually detained.[32] Let's review additional data in pursuit of answers to these questions.

One of the first surveys to assess this problem examined 1972 data on jail inmates across the nation. Of those awaiting trial, 32 percent were charged with index crimes against a person, and 23.3 percent were charged with index crimes against property. However, 67 percent of those charged with personal crimes (those offenses, such as murder, rape, and robbery, that are most often considered "serious" crimes) *had bail set* but could not afford to pay it. If these "serious" offenders constituted a threat to the community, why was bail set in the majority of cases? Subsequent surveys discovered the same thing.[33]

We conducted a study of jail inmates in Las Vegas. We found that the majority were awaiting the final disposition of their cases and were eligible for some form of bail *but could not afford to pay it*. Relatively few could be characterized as "dangerous." The most common charges pending were probation/parole violations (24%—by statute these individuals were not eligible for bail), drugs (15%), "all other offenses" (13%), larceny (8%), burglary (8%), fraud or forgery (7%), and traffic violations (6%). These together constituted 81 percent of the cases, hardly qualifying as "dangerous."[34]

The same kind of distribution has been found whenever any researchers examine, in detail, jail populations. For instance, Irwin's study of the San Francisco jail came up with almost identical findings (1985), as did Miller in Jacksonville, Florida (1996).[35] In Irwin's sample, among the felonies, 30 percent were charged with drug offenses, 14 percent were charged with burglary, and another 12 percent were charged with assault (and most of the "assault" cases did not involve any injuries to the victims and were subsequently reduced to misdemeanors—a common occurrence all over the country and supported by Miller's data).[35] Miller's data show that among the more than 13,000 charges against those booked into jail during a two-month period, the most common were, in rank order: "all other offenses" (19%), traffic, except DUI (18%), petty theft (mostly shoplifting, 11%), drugs (8%), aggravated assault (5%), and simple assault (5%). Together these accounted for 66 percent of the cases. As already noted, most of the "aggravated" assaults did not involve an injury and were reduced to a misdemeanor.[36]

National data on felony defendants from the seventy-five largest counties in 1994 (keep in mind that a significant proportion, sometimes as many as half, of jail inmates are charged with misdemeanors) provide additional support for the view that most jail inmates are not truly dangerous. According to this study, 35 percent were charged with drug offenses, and 31 percent were charged with property offenses. As shown in Table 9.1, among the 25 percent charged with violent offenses, the bulk were charged with assault. It should

TABLE 9.1   A Profile of Felony Defendants Booked into Jail, 1994

MOST SERIOUS CHARGE	NUMBER	PERCENTAGE	MOST SERIOUS CHARGE	NUMBER	PERCENTAGE
All offenses	52,610	100.0	Theft	5,893	11.2
Violent offenses	13,512	25.7	Other property	5,824	11.1
Murder	521	1.0	Drug offenses	18,182	34.6
Rape	543	1.0	Trafficking	7,672	14.6
Robbery	4,081	7.8	Other drug	10,510	20.0
Assault	6,128	11.6	Public-order offenses	4,570	8.7
Other violent	2,239	4.3	Weapons	2,021	3.8
Property offenses	16,346	31.1	Driving-related	1,281	2.4
Burglary	4,629	8.8	Other public-order	1,267	2.4

Source: Reaves, B. A. *Felony Defendants in Large Urban Counties, 1994.* Washington, DC: U.S. Department of Justice, Bureau of Justice Statistics, 1998, p. 2.

be noted that these were the defendants' "most serious" charges and that most (57%) had other charges, predominantly other felonies. What is perhaps most interesting about this study is the fact that *the majority were released before the final disposition of their cases.* This includes just over half of all violent offenders (55%), including two-thirds of those charged with assault and almost two-thirds (64%) of those charged with property crimes and roughly the same percentage of those charged with drug offenses (66%) and public-order offenses (64%).[37]

What happens to individuals who are released? Numerous studies conducted during the past thirty or forty years have shown that most of those released on their own recognizance show up for court. What is important is that the defendants with "roots in the community" (are employed there, have family or relatives living in the area, lived there for several years, etc.) are released, meaning that they are not at all "dangerous."[38] Recent data confirm older studies. For instance, in 1994, of those defendants who were released, three-fourths (76%) made all of their court appearances, and bench warrants were issued for the remainder. A higher percentage of those charged with drug offenses failed to appear (29%), and one-fourth of the property offenders failed to appear. A total of 15 percent were rearrested for a new offense, mostly the same type of offense as the original charge. Thus, drug offenders who were rearrested were rearrested on another drug charge, burglary offenders were rearrested on another burglary charge, and so on. Interestingly, violent offenders who were released were the least likely to re-offend.[39]

Some Effects of Awaiting Trial in Jail.   Awaiting trial in jail has proved to have many disadvantages. Defendants cannot spend time on the defense of their cases, attorneys are limited in the amount of time they can spend with their clients, and defendants are separated from their families and their jobs (if they have jobs, they may lose them). In addition, the inability to make bail is a form of sentence, or "punishment without conviction," and there is no guarantee that the time spent in jail will be counted as time served toward the sentence. There is also a qualitative effect of not making bail, especially the image the defendant makes in court. Though written more than thirty years ago, Skolnick's observation is still relevant today:

> The man in jail enters the courtroom under guard, from the jail entrance. His hair has been cut by the jail barber, he often wears the clothes he was arrested in. By contrast, the civilian defendant usually makes a neat appearance, and enters the courtroom from the spectators' seats, emerging from the ranks of the public.[40]

A more important disadvantage of awaiting trial in jail involves the sentence. Several studies, spanning four decades, have shown that those awaiting trial in jail receive longer sentences than those out on bail. (Remember, making bail has little relationship to the seriousness of the offense. It depends almost entirely on the defendant's economic resources and race.)[41] More recent studies have arrived at almost identical conclusions. A study in Detroit found that the incarceration rate for those detained was 88 percent, compared to only 45 percent of those released.[42] A study in Connecticut arrived at similar conclusions.[43] Although the U.S. appellate courts have engaged in a smoke-and-mirrors approach to pretrial detention, supporting the general view that pretrial detention is custody rather than punishment,[44] we argue that anyone who makes such a claim, as well as those who accept those claims, knows very little about life inside America's jails. Jail confinement is punishment.

It should be obvious that the "blind lady of justice" that graces most courthouses is not so blind after all, for class and race enter into the picture quite frequently. By the time we arrive at the next critical stages of the criminal justice process, we are left with mostly lower-class and minority defendants, most of whom will spend a considerable amount of time behind bars awaiting their fate in court. In the remainder of this chapter we explore what happens during subsequent stages within the court system, beginning with the preliminary hearing, plea bargaining, and that rare occurrence, the criminal trial.

The initial appearance is technically the first stage in the criminal justice process following an arrest and the defendant's first exposure to the court system. Yet at this juncture the case may not have even been reviewed in any detail by the district attorney's office (in fact, a member of the district attorney's office may not be assigned at this time), and the defendant may not even have an attorney. The real "action" does not begin, for the most part, until the preliminary hearing, which can be viewed as a mini-trial.

The Preliminary Hearing

The **preliminary hearing** is often referred to as the *probable-cause hearing,* for one of its major aims is to determine whether there is probable cause to believe that a crime was committed and the defendant committed it. The state does not have to prove its case "beyond a reasonable doubt." Rather, the state has to present a *prima facie* case (Latin for "at first sight" or "on the face of it") that the defendant committed the crime. It should be noted that, legally speaking, at this stage there may be a "reasonable doubt" about the defendant's guilt, but this is not at issue at this time.

The preliminary hearing is usually required when a felony is charged by an *information* (a formal complaint filed by the prosecutor's office). In jurisdictions where the charge is filed with a grand jury, the preliminary hearing is often not used. In federal courts it is rarely used at all. It is currently used in about half of the states.[45]

The hearing process begins with the defendant presenting himself or herself before the court. The defendant is brought in by the bailiff (if held in jail) or emerges from the spectator's section (if at liberty through bail). Also appearing are the arresting or investigating officer, witnesses (if any), the prosecuting attorney, and defense counsel (if the defendant has one).

The hearing formally begins when the prosecuting attorney asks the arresting or investigating officer to give his or her account of the case. Other witnesses, usually victims, are then asked to do the same. The defense attorney, if assigned or present, calls witnesses (if any) and may ask the defendant to give his or her version. Cross-examination of witnesses is done by both sides. Most of what takes place is routine and takes no more than ten minutes. The defendant does not have to enter a plea at this stage.

During the preliminary hearing the judge often considers the social context of the offense to see whether prosecution is really justified or whether the defendant is a genuine threat to the community. For instance, the conduct in question may be normal in a particular community (e.g., in accordance with subculture norms), or the complainant and the defendant know one another and by the time the preliminary hearing is held the problems that produced the offense have been settled. In many cases, class, racial, and sex biases enter into the defense-making process as, for example, when both victim and offender are members of minority groups and in cases of rape in which it is alleged that the victim may have "led on" the defendant. Some cases are dismissed because the complainants fail to show up.

There are two additional functions of the preliminary hearing. One is that of **discovery.** The preliminary hearing may give the defense some idea of the strength of the state's case, although the prosecutor does not have to show his or her entire hand. The preliminary hearing also gives the defense some extra time to prepare the case.

The second function involves testimony. The defense may want to obtain exact testimony from the state's witnesses (the entire preliminary hearing is usually recorded). In Los Angeles, for instance, the state tends to bring forth a fairly complete case, for most cases are ultimately settled in a "trial on the transcript" in which a judge makes a final disposition based on the transcript from the preliminary hearing.[46] The defendant has the right to waive the preliminary hearing, which most defendants do, often pleading guilty merely to shorten their stay in jail. Indeed, for many defendants, jail itself is a strong inducement to plead guilty.

The Grand Jury.   The *grand jury* is a group of citizens (from twelve to twenty-three) who have the duty of hearing complaints in criminal cases and deciding whether the evidence presented by the prosecutor warrants handing down an *indictment* (or a *true bill*) charging a defendant with a crime. Grand juries are also authorized to carry out investigations of various problems existing (or alleged to exist) in a community, such as the conditions of public facilities (e.g., jails and hospitals) and alleged misconduct of public officials. The grand jury can only make recommendations to the prosecuting attorney; it is not authorized to determine guilt or innocence. (In reality, some of the findings of a grand jury may be so stacked against a defendant that, for all intents and purposes, the defendant has been proved guilty.) Grand jury sessions are not open to the public. Only the prosecutor, witnesses, court reporters, and other officials are allowed to be present. Lawyers representing defendants and witnesses are not allowed, although they can be in the doorways of the hearing room.

Grand juries can examine criminal-law violations *prior* to an arrest. If they find probable cause, then a warrant is issued, and the criminal justice process begins. This often happens in drug cases and in government corruption and white-collar offenses. In most areas prosecutors use the grand jury only in important felony cases. Grand juries are always used in federal cases because they are guaranteed under the Fifth Amendment. Some states require that the grand jury review all felonies. Defendants may (and usually do) waive a grand jury review.

The grand jury originated in about the twelfth century as a result of a struggle between England's King Henry II and the Catholic Church. Henry wanted to end the jurisdiction of the church in cases in which church members were charged with a crime and received the "benefit of clergy" (see Chapter 10 for a more detailed discussion of benefit of clergy). The church was generally more lenient than the king would be and gained money through the collection of fines. The grand jury consisted of a panel of sixteen men assembled by the king to investigate and bring charges against people who were suspected of law violations. The king "created a citizens' police force as a means of ensuring central control over criminal prosecution."[47] In time, an accusation by a grand jury became the equivalent of a guilty verdict because the king had so much control over it.

By the seventeenth century two changes in criminal justice had altered the role of the grand jury. First, petit juries (trial juries) began to replace "trial by ordeal" (e.g., placing an accused's hand in boiling water). Second, Parliament emerged, and its taxing power replaced the grand jury's function of levying fines. However, during the seventeenth century the grand jury continued to be used as a means of political control and repression, such as when King Charles II used it to attempt a Catholic control of the Protestants by seeking indictments against the Duke of York.[48]

The first grand jury in America was instituted in Massachusetts in 1635. By 1683 all of Britain's North American colonies had them. During the colonial period grand juries initiated investigations frequently because there were no police forces and no office of public prosecutor as we know them today. Grand juries were quite independent at this time.

After the American Revolution the grand jury was included in many state constitutions and was included in the Fifth Amendment ("No person shall be held to answer for a capital or otherwise infamous crime, unless on a presentment or indictment of a Grand Jury"). The purpose of a grand jury was to shield citizens against abuse by the state. In reality, however, it tended to be more protective of the privileged and powerful than of the average citizen. For instance, when the Federalists were in power (e.g., John Adams), the grand jury was used to indict the Republicans (Anti-Federalists), especially for charges of treason under the sedition laws. However, even the Republicans, when they came to power, used the grand jury against their political enemies (e.g., Thomas Jefferson's indicting of Aaron Burr).[49]

Later, white-controlled grand juries indicted blacks for violating slave codes and other antiblack laws but failed to indict the Ku Klux Klan. In 1948 a grand jury in New York indicted Communist Party members for violating the Smith Act (prohibiting the teaching and advocation of the overthrow of the government). Grand juries were also used in the 1950s during the McCarthy era.

The Nixon administration had the Justice Department assemble various elements to form a "political grand jury network." The Internal Security Division (inactive since the McCarthy era) was reactivated under the leadership of Robert Mardian (later involved in the Watergate scandal). Guy Goodwin, a prosecutor, was appointed as the head of a special litigation section. Goodwin organized a network of grand juries all over the country to locate "enemies" of the Nixon administration for prosecution. Among the targets of Goodwin's crew were the Black Panther Party, Vietnam Veterans against the War, Daniel Ellsberg (the man behind the "Pentagon Papers" controversy), the Los Angeles antidraft movement, and the American Indian Movement. Between 1970 and 1973, Goodwin supervised over 100 grand juries, which returned about 400 indictments. But only 15 percent ended in convictions.[50]

More often than not, a felony case proceeds through the system via an information filed by the prosecutor's office rather than a grand jury indictment. After the preliminary hearing the defendant is brought into the trial court for the arraignment.

The Arraignment

The defendant first enters a plea during the **arraignment.** Typically, the arraignment is a ritual in which all participants take part. The court scene is usually as follows. The state is represented by one or two deputy district attorneys who sit at a table with large stacks of files in front of them, each file representing a case on the court docket. As the judge calls out the case number and the defendant's name, the defense counsel approaches a table opposite that of the state. In the district court of Las Vegas, Nevada, the following typically takes place (much of what the judge says is taken from a prepared form that all judges use).[51]

The judge asks whether the defendant wants the information or indictment read in open court by the clerk. The defendant answers (or the attorney answers for the defendant) no. The judge then asks the following questions: "What is your age?" "What is the extent of your formal education?" "Do you understand, read, and write the English language?" After these questions are answered, the judge then asks "Is the defendant ready to enter a plea?" and "What is your plea to the information?" If the defendant pleads not guilty, the judge sets a date for the trial. Most of the time, however, the defendant enters a guilty plea. After this is done, the judge then asks the following questions: "Is your plea of guilty freely and voluntarily made? Without threat or fear to yourself or anyone closely related to or associated with you?" The defendant (or the defense attorney) answers yes and no respectively to these questions. Then the judge asks the defense attorney: "Did you advise the defendant of the elements of the crime with which he (she) is charged, the burden of proof required by the state in the prosecution of this matter, and the defense, if any, available to him (her)?" The defense attorney answers yes. The judge then asks the defendant the following series of questions:

> "You heard these questions Mr. (Ms.) (defendant's name)?"
>
> "Did you understand them?"
>
> "Did you have discussions with (defense attorney or deputies defender's office) on these matters?"
>
> "Did you understand what you and he (she) were talking about?"

All of these questions are answered yes. The judge then asks the defense attorney: "Was he (she) also advised of the penalty?" ("Yes, your honor.") "What was he (she) advised?" (The defense attorney states the penalties for the crime.) Turning to the defendant, the judge then asks the following questions:

> "Do you understand that the court could impose such a sentence by reason of your plea of guilty?"
>
> "Do you understand also that you have the right to a speedy and public trial by an impartial jury, free of prejudicial publicity?"
>
> "Do you understand you have the right to be confronted with the witnesses against you and to have an opportunity to cross-examine them?"
>
> "Do you understand that you have the right to have compulsory process for obtaining witnesses in your favor?"
>
> "Do you understand that you may refuse to testify or make any statement on your own behalf and the prosecution may not comment on your failure to testify at the trial?"
>
> "Do you understand that you have the right to the assistance of counsel at all stages of these proceedings?"
>
> "Knowing these rights are available to you, do you ask this court to accept your plea of guilty?"
>
> "Is this a negotiated plea?"

All of these questions are answered yes by the defendant, after which the judge asks: "What is the extent of these negotiations?" The defense attorney then explains what the negotiations were. The judge also asks the representative from the district attorney's office if this is what the agreement was, to which the representative answers yes. After this, the judge once again turns to the defendant and asks a series of questions as follows:

> "Mr. (Ms.) (defendant's name), you heard the representations of counsel. Is that your understanding of the negotiations undertaken in your behalf by the public defender with the district attorney?"
>
> "Aside from this, has anyone made any promise of lesser sentence, probation, reward, immunity, or anything else in order to induce you to plead guilty?" (The defendant answers no when in reality he (she) should be saying yes, because plea bargaining, as we discuss later in this chapter, almost always implies the promise of a lesser sentence or some other kind of reward.)
>
> "Do you understand that the matter of probation and sentence is to be determined solely by this court and no one else?"
>
> "Are you pleading guilty because in truth and in fact you are guilty, and for no other reason?" (Again, the defendant answers yes when in fact he (she) should be saying no.)
>
> "What happened on (gives the date of the crime) that causes you to enter a plea of guilty?" (Defendant briefly describes the crime.)

"Do you have a copy of the information before you?"

"Are all the statements in that information true?"

"And you admit your guilt to this offense?"

After the defendant answers yes to the final questions, the judge then states: "The court accepts the defendant's plea of guilty. This matter is referred to the Department of Parole and Probation for presentence investigation and report. Entry of judgment and imposition of sentence is set over to (day, month, and time).[11] And the ritual of the arraignment comes to a close.

All of the preceding takes no more than about ten minutes. Each year, all around the country, this scene (or something very similar to it) is repeated for thousands of cases. Members of the district attorney's office play a small role in the proceedings. At times it appears they are performing routine clerical duties that someone with very little legal training could perform. However, every once in a while—about 5 to 10 percent of the cases—the defendant pleads not guilty, and a date is set for trial. We discuss the criminal trial shortly, but first we need to consider what took place behind the scenes—namely, plea bargaining.

The bargaining and exchange that takes place is the rule rather than the exception. In the next section we explore this facet of the court system. Plea bargaining is the reality of criminal justice today. Instead of being handed down by judges and juries, sentences are negotiated in judges' chambers, courtroom hallways, restaurants, and bars, during telephone conversations, and through other means *outside the courtroom.*

PLEA BARGAINING: MAINTAINING BUREAUCRATIC EFFICIENCY

In the early 1960s TV series *Rawhide,* starring, among others, a young Clint Eastwood, at the end of each show the "trail boss" always called out "Head 'em up, move 'em out." This statement, in our view, is an appropriate summary of the modern court system, for it often resembles a cattle drive on the open range where the goal is to move cattle, a valuable commodity, as quickly as possible toward their destination so as to make a quick sale and large profit. "Justice," whatever this may mean, often takes a back seat to the goals of "bureaucratic justice" as cases need to be moved along as swiftly as possible; otherwise, the system would soon collapse. Not surprisingly, approximately 90 percent of all criminal cases never come to trial.[52] These cases are settled through guilty pleas; the outcome of the case has been negotiated (in a manner not unlike ordinary business deals or transactions) between the prosecuting attorney and the defense attorney. This negotiation is what is commonly referred to as **plea bargaining.**

The public and many in law enforcement do not like plea bargaining because it seems that the offender "gets off easy." What is not understood is that very few really "get off easy" because of this practice. Most defendants, by the time they get to this stage, are guilty of some offense—usually something less serious than the original charge. A guilty plea simply saves the state—and taxpayers—a lot of money.[53]

In the plea-bargaining process the defendant, the defense attorney, and the prosecutor engage in negotiations during which the defendant pleads guilty in return for certain concessions. This procedure is used mainly to expedite cases, even though many within the system might deny this reality. The reality is that if one goes to trial and is convicted, the sentence is almost always more severe. But if the defendant "strikes a deal," he or she receives a benefit. This was admitted by the U.S. Supreme Court in *Brady v. United States* in 1970 when it ruled that the state can constitutionally "extend a benefit to a defendant who in turn extends a substantial benefit to the state" (397 U.S. 742, 90 S. Ct. 1463, 1471, 25 L. Ed. 2d 747, 1970). Thus, plea bargaining is the classic quid pro quo—"You scratch my back and I'll scratch yours."

There are three types of bargaining.[54] A *bargain concerning the charges* may take one of two forms. First, the charge is reduced in terms of the severity of the corresponding penalty (e.g., grand larceny reduced to petty larceny). A common example of this type of bargaining involves reducing the *level* of the offense. For instance, a felony may be reduced to a misdemeanor. Second, the defendant pleads to the most serious of several charges, and the remainder of the charges are dropped (pleading guilty to burglary and dropping possession of burglary tools, trespassing, etc.).

A *bargain to reduce the sentence to a lighter sentence, such as probation,* occurs in many cases because so many sentencing structures offer probation as an option. A defendant can plead guilty, and the "concession" is that the defendant is granted probation instead of going to prison. A *bargain for concurrent charges* lets the defendant plead guilty to several charges and agree to serve one sentence for all charges. This is called a *concurrent sentence.*

At this point it is necessary to ask why and when plea bargaining got started.

Historical Development of Plea Bargaining

Plea bargaining, as we know it today, did not become a dominant method of disposing of cases until the early part of the twentieth century. Prior to this time, courts in both Europe and the United States either did not allow plea bargaining or strongly discouraged it. Most defendants pleaded not guilty and appeared before a judge or a judge and jury.[55] In 1824 only 11 percent of all defendants in Boston pleaded guilty. In 1839 in New York state only 25 percent of all felony convictions were from guilty pleas. Compare these rates with those of today and you get an idea of how plea bargaining has changed.[56]

Trials before the nineteenth century were conducted at a swift pace (about ten or twenty per day), mainly because there were so few cases, defendants had no lawyers, cases were not very complex, and the victims usually served as the prosecutors (or hired private counsel to prosecute the cases). There were few motions, no long speeches, no *voir dire* of jurors, and no other delaying tactics. Also, there were few rules of evidence or other procedural rules that would prolong trials. Furthermore, there was no professional police force to screen cases early, and judges and juries pretty much dominated the judicial system.[57]

The appellate courts, when they heard such cases (which was rarely), were very unfavorable toward plea bargaining. There were several cases in the nineteenth century in which the courts reversed the lower-court decisions because there were guilty pleas. The first case in which the Supreme Court approved a guilty plea was in 1892 (*Hallinger v. Davis,* 146 U.S. 314), but there was no apparent "bargain," only a plea of guilty.[58]

Guilty pleas in return for certain concessions began to appear with more and more regularity after the turn of the twentieth century. Most of the bargaining that began to take place was part of the more widespread corruption within the criminal justice system. Both lawyers and the police, for instance, engaged in plea negotiations in return for specific fees from defendants. In one case a New York attorney made financial arrangements with a judge that enabled the attorney to "stand out on the street of the Night Court and dicker away sentences in this form: $300 for ten days, $200 for twenty days, $150 for thirty days."[59]

By the 1920s, as several state crime surveys around the country found, the majority of all felony cases were disposed of by pleas of guilty. According to these surveys, the most noteworthy increase in guilty pleas came between 1910 and 1920. The majority involved rewards in the form of reduced charges, the most common of which was from a felony to a misdemeanor. Another common reward was that a guilty plea reduced one's chances of a prison sentence by about one-half.[60]

Several reasons are cited in the literature as to why plea bargaining was so common by the turn of the twentieth century. One of the principal reasons was that during the last half of the nineteenth century criminal justice was taken over by professionals. There was also a growing belief that through guilty pleas such methods as probation could be used to "cure" the "deviants" of society. This belief was part of a change in perspective on punishment, a shift toward "treatment" in penological circles. Friedman also argues that there began to be a widespread assumption that the defendant had already been "tried," in effect, by the police and prosecutors. With the rise of "professional" police and "public" prosecutors, it was assumed that screening of cases had become more efficient.[61]

At that time the courts (i.e., judges and juries) were losing their dominant position as a result of the increase in screening by the police and prosecutors. Another factor, already suggested, was the corrupt nature of the criminal justice system—not surprising given the widespread influence of political machines. In fact, many positions within the criminal justice system were "rewards" given to people for "service" to these machines.[62] Offenders viewed the system as a place where bargaining and manipulation could take place, and so began the practice of bribery and the "fix."[63]

Aschuler cites as a major cause of the growth of plea bargaining the increase in the volume of cases, in part because of the increase in the number of laws passed during the late nineteenth and early twentieth centuries. Roscoe Pound noted that over half of those arrested in Chicago in 1912 violated laws that had not existed twenty-five years earlier. As a result of this increase there was tremendous pressure to expedite cases.[64]

We must also take into consideration the widespread changes in the political economy. As Barak notes, plea bargaining emerged as part of a much larger regulative movement both within and outside the criminal justice system.[65] Indeed, the late nineteenth century witnessed some rather drastic changes, the most important of which was the shift from laissez faire to corporate capitalism. According to the historian William A. Williams, the new corporate leaders feared social upheaval and revolution and thus instigated widespread reforms in order to aid in the development of the new economic order. The result was the adaptation of all major social institutions (including the criminal justice system) to the needs of corporate capitalism and the new types of social relationships within the society as a whole. Put differently, and quoting from Theodore Roosevelt, "The interest of the public is inextricably bound up in the welfare of our business."[66]

Williams further noted that there were two activities required for corporate capitalism to maintain control and dominance of the social system. First, it had to maintain internal stability. Second, it had to coordinate and control the interrelationships of America's social institutions. The criminal justice system began to function more and more as a repressive state apparatus in order to maintain social stability (we need only cite the repression of workers' movements and the Palmer Raids during and after World War I).[67] It is not coincidence that the majority of cases during this period involved poor people or immigrants. Typically, these people had no counsel, and plea bargaining became an efficient method of convicting and hence controlling them.[68]

Another related factor was the more widespread movement among business leaders to make social institutions (e.g., education, city government), including the criminal justice and juvenile justice systems, more efficient (following some of the basic principles of American business). Indeed, "expediency, efficiency, and economy" were the watchwords of criminal justice and other reforms of the period.[69]

An example of the prevailing attitude toward criminal justice is expressed in this quotation from a 1912 article: "the duties of the judicial office…can be directed toward increased *efficiency in the administration of justice* [emphasis in the original] and this, after all, is the only justifiable reform, change, modification or revolution which we ought to take with the courts."[70] In short, plea bargaining meant that criminal cases could be efficiently, expediently, and economically disposed of. Plea bargaining reflected such business practices as cooperation (which is the hallmark of the negotiation between prosecutor and defense counsel), coordination, and centralization.

Plea bargaining became standard practice within the criminal justice system in the early part of the twentieth century. It continues to be condemned by the appellate courts, but this is irrelevant because so few cases are appealed. Finally, it was legitimated by the Supreme Court in *Santobello v. New York* (404 U.S. 257) in 1971 when the Court ruled that plea bargaining is "an essential component of the administration of justice."[71]

The Plea-Bargaining Process

The plea-bargaining process actually may begin at the arresting stage. The police, fully aware of the reality of plea bargaining, often overcharge (if they don't, then the prosecutor does). The police either throw in several charges growing out of a single incident (e.g., in addition to simple assault, they might add resisting arrest, disturbing the peace, and other charges if the scene was a tavern), or they charge a more serious offense than the existing evidence would support (e.g., first-degree or second-degree murder when the case is an obvious manslaughter). Also, the police may overcharge in order to develop informants. For instance, they might apprehend a known addict and tell him that they will charge him with possession of drugs, attempting to sell drugs, or other offenses unless he "cooperates" with them in locating big-time drug dealers. Moreover, in their attempts to "clear" a number of unsolved crimes, the police may agree not to charge the offender at all or to "go easy" on him if he confesses to these crimes.[72]

Obtaining guilty pleas saves the prosecutors time and money, and it increases the prosecutor's "batting average" of convictions. The prosecutor, as well as other actors in the court system, know full well that the system would break down completely if more than 10 or 15 percent of the cases went to trial. Prosecutors often deliberately overcharge (if the police have not already done so) because they believe that overcharging is a "lever" to get a guilty decision.[73] Bureaucratic efficiency rather than "justice" seems to be the basic goal here. Moreover, seeking guilty pleas in order to increase the conviction rates of prosecutors is consistent with a capitalist ethic of producing "commodities"; in this case the commodity is humans who are prosecuted.

Ironically, in most cases it is not the prosecutor who puts pressure on defendants to plead guilty; it is the defense attorney. Studies dating back several years note that defense attorneys seek guilty pleas from their clients instead of trying to have their cases dismissed.[74] Blumberg goes so far as to suggest that defense attorneys play the role of "double agent": they appear to be seeking acquittals for their clients but in reality are cooperating with the prosecutors to obtain guilty pleas. Blumberg further suggests that lawyers have a vested interest in maintaining good relations with the court if they want to have a steady caseload and a successful career. The client becomes a "secondary figure in the court system," and the defense attorney "has far greater professional, economic, intellectual and other ties to the various elements of the court system than he does to his client."[75] However, since by the time the defendant arrives at this stage there is sufficient evidence to convict on *some* charge, the defense attorney may really be acting in the defendant's best interest by avoiding a trial. But this assumes that the defendant can be proved, in a trial, to be "legally guilty," which may not be the case.

In most cases there is a great deal of cooperation between the defense counsel and the prosecutor, because both are members of the courtroom workgroup (see Chapter 8). Indeed, the defense attorney may see a particular defendant once in a lifetime but may face the prosecutors, judges, and other members of the court staff daily. It is obvious where the loyalties of defense attorneys (in particular public defenders) fall.

Most of the plea-bargaining sessions are routine. There is a great deal of agreement among the participants, and often there are unspoken assumptions about what everyone expects. That most cases are routine is common knowledge among experienced court personnel. As in many other bureaucratic settings, court lawyers (after becoming enmeshed in the subculture norms of the court) develop a sense of "typical" cases, which Sudnow has called **normal crimes.** This means that lawyers learn to *typify* certain *categories* of crime. For each crime, they believe that there are typical (i.e., normally occurring) offender characteristics, situations, or circumstances and certain types of sentences that are usually handed down. The novice lawyer learns from more experienced personnel that, for instance, "in cases such as this one, the defendant is usually an amateur, so we go easy the first time around. And the judge is usually willing to grant probation or a suspended sentence."[76] Comments by Mather almost thirty years ago still ring true today:

> the P.D. refers to offenses in terms of their social reality rather than their legal definition. That is, *legally* the case may be a burglary, but "really" it is just a petty theft. Likewise, Grand Theft Auto may be a serious crime according to the Penal Code, but because of the circumstances which typically surround it, everyone knows it's usually "nothing serious."[77]

Judges, too, go along with this procedure and deal with "typical" cases in rather routine ways. Often they engage in "pre-plea bargains" in their chambers with the district attorney and the defense attorney. One judge made the following comment:

> On a three count forgery case, the defense attorney asks the D.A., "Can I have one count?" The D.A. says, "Yes, which one?" The defense attorney says, "Count 2." And that's it. No bargain has been made. No promise that counts 1 and 3 will be dismissed in exchange for the plea to count 2. *It's simply that everyone knows what the standard practice is.* Or here's another example. The defense attorney comes into court and asks the D.A., "What does Judge Hall give on bookmaking cases?" The D.A. says, "He usually gives $150 fine on the first offense." The attorney says, "Fine. We'll enter a plea to count 1." Again no promise was made by anybody. *It's just that everyone know what customarily will happen* [emphasis in the original].[78]

As implied in the preceding discussion, plea bargaining is typically done not in open court but behind closed doors and, in some cases, as the following quotation illustrates, in the halls of the courthouse:

> The elevator doors opened into a smoky, crowded corridor at the Hall of Justice. Stepping out, a deputy public defender encounters a deputy district attorney.
> "Hey," said the defender hurriedly. "How about Alvarado? We plead and you recommend 45 days."
> "No way," replied the D. A.'s man. "Gotta have at least 90."
> "Oh," said the defender, moving on down the corridor. "We'll think about 60."[79]

It is often suggested that plea bargaining takes place because the courts simply have too many cases. Yet plea bargaining is just as likely to take place in courts with small caseloads. And the extent of plea bargaining does not correlate with the overall crime rate of a jurisdiction or with the extent of court resources.[80]

Plea bargaining can better be explained by the fact that by the time the case gets to this stage it may be what is commonly known as a "dead bang case"—one in which there is overwhelming evidence that the defendant is in fact guilty. Another factor is the fact that trials are expensive and time-consuming. If every offender (not to mention every victim) demanded "justice" or a "day in court," the system would completely break down.

Much ado has been made about plea bargaining, with many claiming that it allows the "guilty to go free" or otherwise "beat the system." Plea bargaining survives largely because the criminal courts are little more than "supermarkets" that "handle a high volume of business with fixed prices." Once the courtroom workgroup agrees about the "going rate" for different crimes, not too much actual bargaining takes place. Studies show that there is a high degree of regularity and predictability in how cases are disposed of in the court system. You can usually predict the outcome if you know the seriousness of the top charge in addition to the defendant's prior record.[81]

The Consequences of Plea Bargaining

One of the most common results of plea bargaining is that those who insist on a trial by jury typically receive harsher sentences than those who plead guilty. The negative consequences of going to trial are readily acknowledged by members of the court system. Mather quotes a district attorney who said:

> What often happens, though, is that by going to trial he [the defendant] gets convicted of a lot more serious charge than if he had taken a disposition to a lesser charge. Like we told them in that case…this morning robbery conviction with a finding of "armed" would mean state prison. In (nontrial) dispositions, the judge is saying the defendant will get something less for pleading guilty. But if the case goes to trial, then the judge is no longer bound by

any earlier conditions…A plea bargain may involve a different charge than the charge at the trial, that's why the sentence would be different.[82]

Research shows that the seriousness of the offense plays a key role in determining whether a case will go to trial. Violent crimes (murder, rape, and manslaughter) are the most likely to go before a jury; most property crimes and especially drug offenses are settled by a guilty plea. However, even when controlling for the seriousness of the crime and even for the severity of the charge (e.g., first degree versus second degree, etc.), those who plead guilty and those who choose a bench trial are less likely to go to jail than those who go before a jury. Factors such as age, sex, race, jail status (at liberty or in jail), and type of counsel (public defender versus retained) did not have a great bearing when controlled for. In other words, the key factor was whether a person went before a jury. Going before a judge on a bench trial (this procedure is similar to what normally happens in misdemeanor cases in lower courts) or pleading guilty was the most important factor.[83]

Another consequence of plea bargaining is that the defendants who have been arrested and charged on several occasions "learn the ropes" and are thus able to take advantage of the bargaining system.

Race is also an important factor. An analysis of almost 700,000 cases in California from 1981 to 1990 discovered that plea bargaining favored whites over minorities. Regardless of other factors (e.g., offense charged), whites did better than minorities at "getting charges dropped, getting cases dismissed, avoiding harsher punishment, avoiding extra charges, and having their criminal records wiped clean." This study further found that out of 71,668 defendants with no prior record who were charged with a felony, one-third of the whites, compared to one-fourth of minorities, received a charge reduction; minorities were much more likely than whites to receive prison or jail sentences; for the sale of drugs, minorities were twice as likely to go to prison as whites.[84] This same study quoted a public defender and a judge who both admitted that such treatment stemmed from a combination of "unconscious stereotyping and deliberate discrimination." A public defender stated as follows:

> If a white person can put together a halfway plausible excuse, people will bend over backward to accommodate that person. It's a feeling, "You've got a nice person screwing up," as opposed to the feeling that "This minority person is on a track and eventually they're going to end up in state prison."[85]

Here we have a classic case of racial stereotypes guiding the actions of those involved in decisions that affect lives. As the previous quotation suggests, if the perception of the defendant is that he or she is someone who is basically a good person who "made a mistake," then the final disposition is likely to be lenient; but if the defendant is perceived to be a "criminal" or someone likely to be "heading down the wrong path" (or, in the words of the public defender quoted above, is "on track") then the final disposition is likely to be more severe. A close look at sentencing practices and the composition of today's prison system is solid proof of a systematic class and racial bias (see Chapter 10).

TRIAL JURIES

Most criminal cases are settled through a guilty plea. A few cases, however, do end up before a jury. The jury trial is supposed to be one of the cornerstones of the American criminal justice system. Indeed, the right to a trial by a jury of one's peers is written in several parts of the U.S. Constitution, especially in the Sixth Amendment, which states that "in all criminal prosecutions, the accused shall enjoy the right to a speedy and public trial, by an impartial jury."

The modern jury system can be traced back as far as Roman civilization before Christ. The most common means of settling criminal disputes in England prior to the

Norman invasion were trial by ordeal and trial by compurgation. In the case of the former, the accused was subjected to some form of torture (usually fire or water). If the accused survived, he or she was deemed truthful because God ordained survival. In the case of the latter, a defendant who could muster together thirty men to testify on his or her behalf was considered truthful.[86]

With the signing of Magna Carta in 1215, protection of a trial by a jury of one's "peers" was given to noblemen (those persons with property). Several centuries later this protection was given to the common people. However, such "protection" was often illusory, because juries in England during the seventeenth and eighteenth centuries were composed primarily of men of property. Thus, guarantee of a trial by jury may be more ideology than fact, for the trial puts forth the image to others that there is "equal justice for all."[87]

Today in America an accused person has the right to a trial if the offense is punishable with more than six months' imprisonment (in either state or federal court). Of course, states and localities may, at their discretion, extend this guarantee to those accused of lesser offenses (*Baldwin v. New York,* 399 U.S. 66, 1970).

The size of the trial jury has traditionally been twelve people, but in recent years the courts have ruled that this does not have to be the case. In fact, the U.S. Supreme Court ruled in **Williams v. Florida** (399 U.S. 78, 1970) that a jury of six was constitutional.

Another traditional practice has been that a jury verdict must be unanimous. In 1972, however, the Supreme Court ruled in two decisions (*Johnson v. Louisiana,* 406 U.S. 356, and *Apodaca v. Oregon,* 406 U.S. 404) that unanimity is not always required. In federal trials, however, jury verdicts must be unanimous.

Jury Selection

Ideally juries are representative of the community or a cross-section of the community. This is not often the case, especially when we consider the methods by which juries have been selected. Until recently, in most jurisdictions the *master jury list* was made up from voter registration lists, which left out large numbers of people, especially the poor and nonwhites, in addition to young people.

When it comes time to select members of a jury (i.e., when a trial is scheduled), a jury pool, or **venire,** is selected. This is a list of people from whom a trial jury will be chosen. Those on this list will be summoned to appear for jury duty. Not all of those on the list will actually serve. Several kinds of people are automatically disqualified: ex-felons, individuals below a certain age, those who are not residents of the United States, those unable to understand English, those who have personal connections with the case (e.g., relatives of the defendant), and those connected with the legal system (judges, lawyers, police officers, etc.).

Jury selection is one of those points within the criminal justice process at which racial bias is perhaps most evident. Over the years, the jury has been viewed as a "bulwark against government tyranny, a repository of democratic deliberation, and a stirring example of representative government in action." The U.S. Supreme Court has ruled that it is "an inestimable safeguard against the corrupt or overzealous prosecutor" and a defendant's "fundamental protection of life and liberty against race or color prejudice." In fact, the first law the Supreme Court ever struck down as racially discriminatory was one that restricted jury service to white men only.[88]

Despite what the Supreme Court says, racial discrimination in the jury selection process continues to be a problem. In fact, as several studies have found, the typical case involving a black defendant, especially in the South, is one in which the defendant faces an almost all-white jury because most blacks were excluded for one reason or another.[89] The main reason is that jury lists are most commonly based on voter registration lists. Many African Americans in recent years have been deprived of the right to vote because they have been convicted of a felony—mostly drug offenses. In fact, about 13 percent of all black males have been disenfranchised because of a felony conviction. No wonder they rarely appear on juries, especially in the South. Southern states have the highest percentage of blacks ineligible to vote because of felony convictions. Florida and Alabama lead the way with 30 percent.[90] Moreover, many jury lists are based on motor vehicle registration records and driver's license lists, where poor and racial minorities also are underrepresented. Another reason why minorities and the poor are not likely to serve on juries is that they move more often than better-off individuals and are therefore less likely to receive a jury summons. Finally, even if they receive a summons, they are less likely—for many different reasons, not the least of which is their general distrust of the criminal justice system—to respond to it.[91]

You might think that the Supreme Court would intervene more often to eliminate such obvious biases. Not so. The Court refused to review a case in New York City in which less than 2 percent of blacks and Puerto Ricans were summoned for jury duty, even though these two groups constituted about 36 percent of the residents.[92] An important issue here is the fact that poor people and racial minorities would bring into the courtroom a much different perspective than whites and the well-to-do. The Rodney King case illustrates this problem well; the original trial of the police officers was held not in South Central Los Angeles but in an almost all-white community, suburban Simi Valley, northwest of Los Angeles.

Perhaps the most critical point in the selection of the jury is the *voir dire* ("look-speak" in French), the examination of a potential juror in order to decide whether he or she is suitable for a particular case. Defense attorneys and prosecutors question prospective jurors about their biases and preconceived notions about the case. If the attorney for either side believes that a prospective juror would not decide the case in a fair manner, the attorney can issue a *challenge for cause* and prevent that person from serving on that particular jury for a specific reason. A more important type of challenge (and one more often used) is the **peremptory challenge,** which both the prosecutor and the defense may use to dismiss a potential juror without giving a reason. A limited number of challenges can be made. Attorneys' reasons for dismissing jurors may be based on hunches or on scientific criteria. The use of social scientists and "jury consultants" to create juror profiles has increased in recent years.

It is during the peremptory challenge that racial bias often plays a key role. The Supreme Court has ruled that race-based peremptory challenges are unconstitutional, but no mechanisms have been established to prevent them. A study in Dallas, Texas, for instance, found that the peremptory challenge was used to eliminate almost 90 percent of the eligible black jurors. A study of several counties in Georgia found that during a seven-year period one prosecutor in death penalty cases used about 90 percent of his challenges to eliminate black jurors.[93] The Supreme Court tried to correct these and other obvious problems in the case of *Batson v. Kentucky* in 1986, but this decision has had little effect in practice.[94]

A review of published decisions between 1986 and 1992 involving *Batson* challenges found that "in almost any situation a prosecutor can readily craft an acceptable neutral explanation to justify striking black jurors because of their race." They are "too old," "too young," employed as a teacher, "did not make eye contact," "made too much eye contact," lived or worked in the same neighborhood as the defendant, or "had previously been involved in the criminal justice system."[95] These "neutral" excuses are generally accepted by judges and fellow prosecutors and even some defense attorneys. After all, in most courts they are all part of the same courtroom workgroup, and they "travel in the same social circles, may well have contributed to the judge's election campaign, and may be personal friends with the judge," so the judge accepts such excuses as "genuine and rarely overturns them."[96]

Obviously race matters, and the foregoing problems in jury selection support our contention that in the American criminal court system, the poor and racial minorities are generally processed and judged by mostly white and well-to-do people. It is a system of class and racial justice.

Jury Decisions

Can juries render impartial verdicts? This question is often fiercely debated by those involved in studying the criminal court system. To us, however, it seems largely irrelevant in the grand scheme of things, because less than 10 percent of all criminal cases ever reach a jury. Nevertheless, a discussion of jury decision making should be undertaken.

Studies show that jurors are usually able to render impartial verdicts. Rita Simon[97] found that juries rely very heavily on evidence presented during a trial, more so than on procedural comments of attorneys, personal opinion, and other factors. Other studies have found that juries have been able to understand judges' instructions and to understand the evidence presented. Research has also found that pretrial publicity often biases juries. One study by Padawer-Singer and Barton found that (in an experiment) in a case in which the defendant was in fact guilty, 78 percent of the "prejudiced" jurors voted for conviction, compared to 55 percent of the "nonprejudiced" jurors.[98]

Recognizing this problem, judges have tried several strategies to eliminate it. They may issue *gag orders* to limit the amount of information given to the media. They may authorize a *change of venue*—the transfer of a case to another location because of local pretrial publicity. Finally, a judge may *sequester a jury.* When the court session is over for the day, sequestered jurors are tightly regulated. They stay in a hotel, eat together, are not allowed access to television, radio, or newspapers, and have limited contact with the outside world.

More often than not, the decision of the jury corresponds to what the judge would decide. In one study (Kalven and Zeisel) it was found that the judge and the jury agreed in 75 percent of the cases. The most common reasons for disagreement were "issues of evidence." Personal feelings about the defendant accounted for only 11 percent of the disagreement.[99]

Above and beyond these issues is a much more important one concerning the overall function of the jury trial in the administration of justice. Although it is true that juries are capable of rendering relatively impartial judgments, the total effect on the system of justice may be minimal, at least in a direct sense. A trial by jury mostly serves a legitimating function. The existence of the jury system (even if most cases never go this far) legitimates the entire criminal justice system and reinforces the ideology of "equal justice for all." As Chambliss and Seidman remark: "The existence of the jury makes it possible for the judge and the whole judicial system to appear to be above the [class] struggle, making judgments fairly in the event of conflicts between the State and its subjects."[100] For instance, even in some of the political trials of the 1960s (especially the Chicago 7 case), jury verdicts of not guilty often resulted in claims that the "System works" or "There *is* justice in America," even though the length and cost of these trials were usually enough to break up or otherwise thwart a radical movement and injustices continued to exist both inside and outside the judicial system.

The criminal justice system is further legitimated by the mere fact that in the trial system both "adversaries" can be made to be equal in resources and rules of evidence are strictly observed to ensure a "fair" trial. This further reinforces the notion that this is a society run by the "rule of law" rather than the rule of powerful men.

STAGES IN THE CRIMINAL TRIAL

The criminal trial, though a rare event, is clearly one of the most visible aspects of the entire criminal justice system. Given the publicity of the O. J. Simpson case, it is easy to see why. It is also an important event because it involves a jury of rather ordinary men and women, drawn from the outside community. Also, a trial can have far-reaching effects on the administration of justice, at least in terms of public perceptions of how the system works. Unfortunately, citizens often get the wrong impression about the system of criminal justice as a result of following a jury trial.

There are several stages in a typical trial: (1) *voir dire* and jury selection, (2) opening statements by prosecutor and defense, (3) prosecutor's presentation of evidence, (4) defense pretrial motions and hearings on motions, (5) presentation of defense evidence, (6) rebuttal by the state, (7) prosecutor's closing arguments, (8) defense's closing arguments, (9) prosecutor's reply arguments, (10) judge's instructions to the jury, (11) jury deliberation and verdict.[101]

PRETRIAL MOTIONS

Pretrial motions are written requests to the court by either the prosecutor or the defense attorney seeking certain objectives prior to trial. There are eight major types of pretrial motions. Typically there are separate hearings where evidence is brought to bear on these motions. These motions are:

1. *Motion to dismiss.* Most commonly filed by the defense, this motion generally claims that there is not sufficient evidence to bring this case to court in the first place (President Clinton's lawyer did this, successfully, in the Paula Jones case in 1998.)

2. *Motion to determine the competency of the accused to stand trial.* This is where the defense is claiming that the defendant is for various reasons incompetent to stand trial, because of some form of "mental illness."

3. *Motion to suppress evidence obtained through unlawful search or seizure.* A very common motion, this is filed by the defense attorney. The court is asked to "suppress" evidence because it was taken in violation of the Fourth Amendment. Thus, the defense is requesting that such evidence not be used during the trial, which could have an important bearing on the case, even causing the case to be dismissed.

4. *Motion to suppress confessions, admissions, or other statements made to the police.* Like the previous example, this motion seeks to suppress various statements made to the police that may be in violation of the *Miranda* rule.

5. *Motion to suppress pretrial identification of the accused.* This relates to eyewitness identification that may violate due process standards.

6. *Motion to require the prosecution to disclose the identity of a confidential informant.* Unless the informant was an "active participant" in the offense, the prosecution is not usually required to release such information. Often used in drug cases.

7. *Motion for change of venue.* Either the defendant or the prosecutor may move to have the trial moved to another location. This is most often done in cases where there has been extensive media coverage. One of the most famous cases was that of Sam Shepherd, the Cleveland doctor accused of killing his wife (the television series and movie *The Fugitive* were based on this case). The attorney who made a name for himself in this case was F. Lee Bailey, an instrumental figure in the O. J. Simpson case, a case involving huge pretrial and during-the-trial publicity and a change of venue from Santa Monica to downtown Los Angeles. The issue here is whether the defendant can get a fair trial in the location where the crime was committed. (The case of the Oklahoma bombing is another recent example.)

8. *Motion for a continuance.* On a variety of grounds, either the prosecutor or the defense may request either a continuance or a postponement of the trial. Sometimes this is for normal human matters (sickness, etc.), and sometimes it involves locating important witnesses or evidence. Often it is made by the defense when a new attorney is assigned to the case and needs more time to prepare the case. This is probably one of the most common motions.[102]

Two of the most common and most important pretrial defense motions are attempts to suppress illegally seized evidence and motions for continuances. The defense attorney, for instance, might try to show that some (or all) of the state's evidence (e.g., drugs seized in a possession or sale-of-drugs case) was obtained in violation of the exclusionary rule. The defense might also try to obtain a change of venue if there has been a great deal of pretrial publicity. Another important motion is for a continuance of the trial. Continuances usually aid defense counsel in the preparation of the case and give defense counsel more time to become more acquainted with the case. Continuances are often used in cases in which defendants are able to make bond.[103] One advantage of having retained counsel at this stage is shown with data from a study by Banfield and Anderson, which found that those with retained counsel were more likely to have more continuances than those with other types of counsel. It was also found that the greater the number of court appearances, the greater was the likelihood of dismissal or acquittal, usually because of the fact that witnesses (and often even the victims) disappear, give up and stop coming, or tend to become less certain of some facts, such as the identity of the offender.[104]

In a criminal trial the accused has raised an "issue of fact"—that is, the accused has challenged the allegations made by the state. The basic issue is whether the defendant committed the alleged offense. Larger moral or social–political issues are usually ignored. Motives are rarely explored (except in rare instances of insanity defenses). The question becomes a rather simple one: Is the defendant guilty or innocent?[105]

In a criminal trial, as in other courtroom procedures, there are many rituals, some of which are symbolic and reinforce dominant American values (e.g., respect for the law, equal justice for all, the rule of law). Whether "justice" is really administered may be an open question. The criminal trial, perhaps more than anything else, may simply be an attempt to legitimate the judicial system and the political economy that surrounds and supports it. The trial, moreover, is supposed to be "above politics" and "neutral." But during the late 1960s and early 1970s this perspective on the trial and, for that matter, the entire judicial system was called into question by the many radical-criminal trials that made the headlines.

THE TRADITIONAL CRIMINAL TRIAL

In the **traditional trial** of a criminal case there are a number of roles, each with its own behavior expectations. We can conceive of the trial as analogous to a theater production. The major roles are those of judge, prosecutor, defense attorney, bailiff, marshal, defendant, member of the jury, spectator, and member of the press.

The judge's role is that of a "neutral" arbitrator. The defense attorney's role is that of a person speaking out "on behalf" of the client. The prosecutor represents "the people" or the "state" (which are supposed to be synonymous). The defendant is supposed to be passive and is not expected to want (or have the ability) to defend himself or herself. The spectator is supposed to be passive, sit quietly, and observe (as do all others) "proper" courtroom demeanor.

The judge is perhaps the most interesting actor and the most symbolic. He or she sits high above the action, with the American flag on one side and the state flag on the other side. The judge dresses in a black robe and is addressed as "your honor." All are supposed to rise when the judge walks in. The traditional symbol of justice, a woman with a blindfold, is prominently displayed either inside the courtroom or near the main entrance outside the building.

Adherence to these symbols and the formalities and power relations within the courtroom processes themselves serve to legitimate (if not to mystify) the existing judicial system and the law. The judge, the court, and the law often become synonymous with or symbolic of God and country. Failure to adhere to these symbols can result in a "contempt of court" citation or removal from the courtroom.

Until the late 1960s and early 1970s the social, political, and economic context within which justice was meted out rarely entered into the courts (notable exceptions include the trials of the International Workers of the World and Sacco and Vanzetti during the early part of the twentieth century[106]). Usually the issues focused on the narrow concerns of individual criminal acts and the guilt or innocence of individuals. This, of course, has corresponded with the traditional legal notions of *mens rea* (individual guilt) begun around the eleventh century in England. Since then, however, several radical-criminal trials have raised questions about the legitimacy of the judicial system.

CHALLENGING THE SYSTEM: RADICAL-CRIMINAL TRIALS

During the late 1960s and early 1970s several trials sent shock waves through the legal establishment. The defendants in these **radical-criminal trials,** or political trials, already held in contempt society's traditional economic and political institutions and desired to create very fundamental changes. Eventually, as Sternberg notes, "It dawned upon these defendants that far from being 'agents' of the other institutions of power, the courts themselves were another creator and center of the very status quo they were determined to change." These defendants viewed the criminal courts as agents of powerful interests or, more specifically, as representatives of a ruling class and constituting an oppressive institution.[107]

Many defendants sought to raise what they believed to be important moral and political issues "in an effort to generate jury sympathy for the defendants and the cause they represented."[108] Indeed, many did not attempt to deny that they had committed the alleged "criminal" act. What they often did was deny that the act was, or should be, in itself "criminal." Thus, to them "real" guilt or innocence was not the issue. A defendant in the 1969 Milwaukee Twelve draft-card burning case said: "I'm not saying the jury should find us innocent. I'm simply hoping that the court will allow us to demonstrate the reasonableness of our belief and to (let the jurors) decide for themselves whether, in fact, it was reasonable."[109]

Phillip Berrigan, one of the Baltimore Four accused of draft-card burning and sentenced in April 1968, tried, in his remarks to the court, to place this conviction in a larger perspective. He wrote:

> But whatever work is useful to describe our nation's plight, we ask today in this court: What is lawful about a foreign policy which allows economic control of whole continents, which tells the Third World, as it tells our black people, "You'll make it sometime, but only under our system, at the pace we decide, by dole, by handout, by seamy charity, by delayed justice. Don't try it any other way!" What is lawful about peace under a nuclear blanket, the possible penetration of which impels our leaders to warn us of one hundred million American casualties?…What is lawful about the rich becoming richer, and the poor poorer, in this country or abroad?… [T]hese are not times for building justice; these are times for confronting injustice. This, we feel, is the number-one item of national business—to confront the entrenched, massive, and complex injustice of our country. And to confront it justly, nonviolently, and with maximum exposure of oneself and one's future.[110]

For Berrigan, then, the burning of draft cards was an act of civil disobedience, and the fact that it was "unlawful" was irrelevant. What was relevant was the war in Vietnam, racism abroad and at home, the discrepancy between the rich and the poor. However, the court, ostensibly being "above politics," could decide only the "issue" of guilt or innocence and as a result sentenced the Baltimore Four to prison.

In some cases the defendants sought to show the jury that the federal government itself was involved, in the sense that FBI agents (agents provocateurs) were responsible for the alleged crimes or in some cases even "set up" the defendants. This was especially true in the Gainesville Eight trial against the Vietnam Veterans against the War. The government charged them with conspiring to disrupt the Republican National Convention in 1972. However, the government itself ended up on trial. In this case, as Fred Cook states, "The government, in effect, was found guilty."[111]

In some radical-criminal trials the tactics used by the defendants challenged the authority of the court and court officials, to the utter disbelief of the latter. The large number of contempt citations, the "gagging and shackling" of Black Panther Bobby Seale during the Chicago Seven trial, and other forms of punishment demonstrate "the depth and breadth of a culture shock experienced by officers of the criminal court."[112] The Chicago Seven trial perhaps best illustrates these points and exposes the often farcical nature of court proceedings. The defendants used several tactics to challenge the legitimacy of the court:

1. Direct and verbal attacks on judges and other officials or on the judicial process itself. The defendants often insisted that they be allowed to speak for themselves.
2. Ignoring the proceedings, such as by refusing to stand when the judge entered the courtroom or reading books or magazines during the proceedings.
3. Mocking legal procedures, such as when Jerry Rubin appeared in a black robe, or unresponsive answers were given to what court officials thought were straightforward questions, such as when Abbie Hoffman gave "Woodstock Nation" as his address.

4. Refusing to limit interactions to traditional actors inside the courtroom. The defendants in the Chicago Seven trial often argued with prosecution staff in the hallways, and many gave speeches attacking the proceedings and gave them to large audiences, often in front of the courthouse.
5. Attempts to restructure and even reverse traditional roles, as when Bobby Seale charged the judge with "contempt of the American people."
6. Defendants planning and standing together in solidarity in their challenges to the court (with shouts of "Right On!").

Defendants in radical-criminal trials often helped their lawyers with defense strategy and discussed moral and political issues while on the witness stand (often bringing charges of "immaterial" and "irrelevant" from prosecutors and judges, who would warn them to "stick to the issues"). Many defendants chose to represent themselves because of certain restrictions placed on lawyers. A lawyer, having been socialized into courtroom procedures, typically seeks a purely *legal* remedy (e.g., acquittal, shortened sentences), which often involves compromises and accommodations. A lawyer who behaves otherwise is likely to be disbarred. Defendants in the White House Seven trial (1973), charged with praying for peace on the White House lawn, stated:

> We could not bring ourselves to be represented by counsel, feeling that to do so would be participating in a kind of cat-and-mouse game with the government. We felt that rather than seeking to support our legal innocence in court, it was our simple duty to speak the truth of how we were led to that place.[113]

Defendants who act as their own lawyers are often given some latitude by judges because such defendants are considered ignorant of "traditional rules of evidence and proper courtroom procedure." However, defendants' ignorance of "proper" courtroom procedures can be turned to their own advantage, enabling them "to inject political or moral issues into the proceedings."[114]

The role of spectator underwent rather drastic changes and, in fact, changed from one of mere "spectator" to one of active "participant" in delegitimating the court. Audience participation was almost a daily event at most trials. Attempts to control spectators were largely unsuccessful. Most of them had ideologies very similar, if not identical, to those of the defendants. Defendants, then, viewed audiences as "their people" and their interventions as "the will of the people." Sternberg comments as follows:

> It follows that the intervening audience in the radical trial was invariably on the side of the defendants and hostile to the institutionalized judiciary. In the progressive and interactive dialogue among and between defendants and members of the audience…an increasingly strengthened structure of "resonating sentiments" emerged. At the same time, the dissonance of sentiments between the court on the one hand and the defendants and the audience on the other became magnified. Examples were the massive support the audience gave to Bobby Seale in the courtroom, time after time answering his defiant raised and clenched fist with cries of "Right On"; the solidarity the New York Panther defendants displayed with a spectator whom Judge Murtaugh ordered removed for interrupting the proceedings, one defendant saying, "If she goes out, we go out!"; the concerted outrage of the entire audience when Judge Hoffman bound and gagged Seale; the continuous open as well as sub rosa exchange between defendants and audiences in New York and Chicago, as if the official court personnel were either absent or simply did not count. In all these instances, audience and defendants constructed a mutually supportive and subversive social reality under the very gavel and noses of the judge, prosecutors and marshals.[115]

From the perspective of judges and other court officials, nothing like this had ever happened. So entrenched were they in the formal rules and regulations that they utterly failed to comprehend the radical position. Moreover, the trials themselves raised some important constitutional issues, such as the Sixth Amendment guarantee of the right to confront witnesses *directly,* and both the Sixth and Fourteenth Amendments, which guarantee a "public" trial. In 1970 the Supreme Court ruled that defendants waived the right to confront their accusers by "disorderly behavior" and that they could be bound and gagged or even expelled. The Court did not rule on the other issue. From the defendants' perspective in these cases, a "public" trial meant just that—a truly *public* hearing with active participation by members of the audience.[116]

These trials did, however, reveal the court system for what it is: a system in which dissent is stifled, in which the "rule of law" and corresponding ideologies are legitimated, and in which larger issues of social, economic, and political justice are ignored. In short, the court system merely processes defendants and does nothing about the causes of crime. It is a court system resembling a microcosm of a capitalist society in which "exchange" and "bargaining" between unequals goes on, all in the name of "justice."

This is quite typical in a capitalist society, where "commodities" are *produced socially but owned privately.* In other words, commodities are produced mainly for *private profit* rather than for *social good.* Within the justice system, "justice will be pursued socially, but the benefits of justice will accrue to particular individuals," especially those with power. The courts are agencies that attempt to rectify problems caused by the capitalist system itself, such as gross social inequalities. As such, the courts are attempting to solve a *social problem* by merely *punishing individuals.* By focusing almost exclusive attention on individual offenders, the courts merely reinforce the myth that individuals, rather than the surrounding social system, need correcting. This ideology is further reinforced by the mystique of the "law" displayed every day in every court—the extreme formalism of the court process, with the swearing on the bible, the robes of the judges, the ubiquitous "scales of justice" signified by the "blind lady"—which masks what is really occurring in the outside world.[117] The various radical-criminal trials of the 1960s and 1970s, along with the system's response to mass civil disobedience during the riots of the 1960s and more recently the riots following the Rodney King decision, demonstrated clearly how the courts are unable to deal with these outside issues.[118]

SUMMARY

As cases proceed through the court system, there are several distinct stages in which cases are sifted and sorted, with some disappearing and others moving forward. The most important decision is made by the prosecutor, in whose hands is placed the critical decision of whether to accept a case presented by the police. About 75 percent of cases are either dismissed or reduced down to a misdemeanor. Class and race tend to play an important role in a prosecutor's decision.

As the processing continues, bail and pretrial detention become critical issues. Here we see quite easily the effects of both class and race on decision making. Minorities and lower-class citizens are at a decided disadvantage when they are brought into the court system during these early stages.

Once the prosecutor accepts a case, several stages follow. The first is the initial appearance. The defendant comes before a judge of a lower court and is given his or her rights; the charges are read; bail is set. If the defendant has no attorney, one is usually appointed or the public defender's office is notified. In the next stage, the preliminary hearing, the defendant comes before the same judge (usually), along with his or her lawyer, and hears some (or all) of the evidence that the state has. The prosecutor has to establish that there is probable cause that the defendant committed the crime. On some occasions a grand jury is used.

The next stage is the arraignment, which is normally a rather formal procedure. If the defendant's attorney has engaged in plea negotiations with the prosecutor, the judge asks some routine questions and sets a sentencing date. If not, then a trial date is set.

Plea bargaining is the most common form of judicial disposition in the modern criminal court system. Plea bargaining did not come to dominate the process until the end of the nineteenth century. Such negotiations take place mostly outside of the courtroom between the defense and prosecuting attorneys. Individuals who plead guilty (regardless of the offense) tend to receive lighter sentences than those who go to trial. Individuals who choose to exercise their rights and demand a jury trial are more likely to receive harsher penalties in the event they are found guilty. Trial juries are rarely used.

In this chapter we distinguished between the traditional criminal trials and the radical-criminal trials of the late 1960s and early 1970s.

KEY TERMS

arraignment 221	normal crimes 226	pretrial release 213
bail 213	peremptory challenge 230	radical-criminal trials 233
discovery 220	plea bargaining 223	traditional trials 233
initial appearance 213	preliminary hearing 219	*venire* 229
Mallory v. United States 213	pretrial motions 232	*voir dire* 230
nolle prosequi 212	pretrial preventive detention 216	*Williams v. Florida* 229

NOTES

1. From a 1990 interview with assistant prosecutors in a jurisdiction in the southwestern United States.

2. From a 1990 interview with a midwestern trial judge that focused on pretrial detention.

3. Filing multiple charges often has the effect of increasing the likelihood of a defendant's being unable to make bail, because for each charge an additional monetary amount is needed to secure bail, which in turn contributes to jail overcrowding because too many defendants cannot pay the additional fees. See Shelden, R. G., and W. B. Brown. "Correlates of Jail Overcrowding: A Case Study of a County Detention Center." *Crime and Delinquency* 37 (July 1991).

4. Bureau of Justice Statistics. *The Prosecution of Felony Arrests, 1988.* Washington, DC: U.S. Department of Justice, 1992.

5. Myers, M. A., and J. Hagan. "Private and Public Trouble: Prosecutors and the Allocation of Court Resources." *Social Problems* 26(4): 439–451 (April 1979).

6. Donziger, *The Real War on Crime,* p. 110.

7. Walker, Spohn, and DeLone, *The Color of Justice,* pp. 133–134.

8. Reiman, *The Rich Get Richer and the Poor Get Prison,* pp. 118–119.

9. In most minor misdemeanor offenses, especially traffic cases, this is the only appearance in court, and the case is usually disposed of at this time, as the accused enters a plea of guilty, not guilty, or no contest. Typically no lawyers are involved, and the defendant pleads guilty and pays a fine. In some cases, of course, a simple citation is given, and the accused sends a check to the court and that ends it. The stages discussed in this chapter usually occur with serious misdemeanors or felonies.

10. 48r U.S. 739 (1987).

11. *Bell v. Wolfish,* 441 U.S. 520, 533–534 (1979).

12. *United States v. Torres,* 929 F. 2d 291–292 (7th Cir. 1991).

13. *United States v. Winsor,* 785 F. 2d 755, 757 (9th Cir. 1986).

14. 18 U.S.C. 3142 (g).

15. S. Rep. No. 225, 98th Congress, 1st Sess. 23 (1983), reprinted 1984, U.S.C.C.A.N. 3182, 3206.

16. *United States v. Himler,* 797 F. 2d 156, 160 (3rd Cir. 1986).

17. *United States v. Friedman,* 837 F. 2d 48, 49 (2nd Cir 1988).

18. *United States v. Reynolds,* 956 F. 2d 192 (9th Cir. 1992).

19. 18 U.S.C. 3142(e).

20. *United States v. Fortna,* 769 F. 2nd 243, 249 (5th Cir. 1985); *United States v. Ramirez,* 843 F. 2nd 256, 257 (7th Cir. 1988).

21. *United States v. Orta,* 760 F. 2nd 887–92 (8th Cir. 1985).

22. Goldfarb, R. *Ransom: A Critique of the American Bail System.* New York: Harper & Row, 1965.

23. Among the most important of these studies are Foote, C. "Compelling Appearance in Court: Administration of Bail in Philadelphia." *University of Pennsylvania Law Review* 102: 1031–1079 (1954); Rankin, A. "The Effect of Pretrial Detention." *New York University Law Review* 39: 641–655 (June 1964); Suffet, F. "Bail Setting: A Study of Courtroom Interaction." *Crime and Delinquency* 12: 318–331 (October 1966); Farrell, R., and V. L. Swigert. "Prior Offense Record as a Self-Fulfilling Prophecy." *Law and Society Review* 12: 437–453 (1978); Bynum, T. "Release on Recognizance: Substantive or Superficial Reform?" *Criminology* 20: 67–82 (1982); Patterson, E. B., and M. J. Lynch. "Biases in Formalized Bail Procedures." In M. J. Lynch and E. B. Patterson (eds.), *Race and Criminal Justice.* New York: Harrow and Heston, 1991.

24. Patterson and Lynch, "Biases in Formalized Bail Procedures"; Walker, S., C. Spohn, and M. De Lone. *The Color of Justice: Race, Ethnicity, and Crime in America.* (2nd ed.) Belmont, CA: Wadsworth, 2000, p. 130.

25. Farnworth, M., and P. Horan. "Separate Justice: An Analysis of Race Differences in Court Processes." *Social Science Research* 9: 381–399 (1980).

26. Single, E. "The Unconstitutional Administration of Bail: Bellamy v. the Judges of New York City." *Criminal Law Bulletin* 8(6): 459–513 (July–August 1972).

27. Chiricos and Bales, "Unemployment and Punishment."

28. Albonetti, C. A., R. M. Hauser, J. Hagan, and I. H. Nagel. "Criminal Justice Decision Making as a Stratification Process: The Role of Race and Stratification Resources in Pretrial Release." *Journal of Quantitative Criminology* 5: 57–82 (1989).

29. Neubauer, *America's Courts and the Criminal Justice System*, pp. 185–186.

30. Ibid., p. 187.

31. American Friends Service Committee. *Struggle for Justice*. New York: Hill & Wang, 1971, pp. 77–78.

32. Shelden, R. G. *Criminal Justice in America: A Sociological Approach*. Boston: Little, Brown, 1982, p. 192.

33. Ibid.

34. Shelden and Brown, "Correlates of Jail Overcrowding."

35. Irwin, J. *The Jail*. Berkeley: University of California Press, 1985.

36. Miller, J. *Search and Destroy: African-American Males in the Criminal Justice System*. New York: Cambridge University Press, 1996.

37. Reaves, B. A. *Felony Defendants in Large Urban Counties, 1994*. Washington, DC: U.S. Department of Justice, Bureau of Justice Statistics, 1998.

38. Shelden, *Criminal Justice in America*, pp. 193–194.

39. Reaves, *Felony Defendants in Large Urban Counties*.

40. Skolnick, J. "Social Control in the Adversary System." *Journal of Conflict Resolution* 11: 263 (1967).

41. For a review of earlier studies see Shelden, *Criminal Justice in America*, ch. 7.

42. Walker, Spohn, and DeLone, *The Color of Justice*, pp. 130–131.

43. Donziger, *The Real War on Crime*, p. 111.

44. Jackson, P. G. *Competing Ideologies of Jail Confinement*. In J. A. Thompson and G. L. Mays (eds.), *American Jails: Public Policy Issues*. Chicago: Nelson-Hall, 1991.

45. Scheb, J. M., and J. M. Scheb II. *Criminal Law and Procedure*. St. Paul, MN: West, 1989, p. 439.

46. Ibid.

47. Clark, L. D. *The Grand Jury: The Use and Abuse of Political Power*. New York: Quadrangle/New York Times, 1975, p. 9.

48. Ibid., pp. 9–10.

49. Ibid., pp. 20–21.

50. Ibid., p. 213.

51. Based on observations of R. G. Shelden, the senior author.

52. Neubauer, *America's Courts and the Criminal Justice System*, p. 228; Reaves, *Felony Defendants in Large Urban Counties*, p. 28.

53. Fuller, J. R. *Criminal Justice: A Peacemaking Perspective*. Boston: Allyn and Bacon, 1998, pp. 109, 114–115.

54. Neubauer, *America's Courts and the Criminal Justice System*, pp. 217–218.

55. Alschuler, A. W. "Plea Bargaining and Its History." *Law and Society Review* 13(2): 211–245 (Winter, 1979).

56. Ibid., p. 216.

57. Langbein, J. H. "Understanding the Short History of Plea Bargaining." *Law and Society Review* 13: 261–272 (Winter, 1979).

58. Alschuler, "Plea Bargaining and Its History."

59. Ibid., p. 228.

60. Ibid., pp. 229–231.

61. Friedman, "Plea Bargaining in Historical Perspective"; Mather, L. M. "Comments on the History of Plea Bargaining." *Law and Society Review* 13: 281–285 (Winter 1979).

62. Haller, M. H. "Plea Bargaining: The 19th Century Context." *Law and Society Review* 13: 273–279 (Winter 1979).

63. For a good historical account of machine politics and other forms of government corruption around the turn of the twentieth century see Steffens, L. *The Shame of the Cities*. New York: McClure, Phillips, 1904.

64. Aschuler, "Plea Bargaining and Its History," p. 234.

65. Barak, G. "In Defense of the Rich; The Emergency of the Public Defender." *Crime and Social Justice* 3: 2 (Summer 1975).

66. Williams, W. A. *The Contours of American History*. New York: Franklin Watts, 1973, p. 392. See also Shelden, *Controlling the Dangerous Classes*.

67. Wolfe, A. *The Seamy Side of Democracy*. New York: McKay, 1973, ch. 2.

68. Barak, "In Defense of the Rich"; Harring, S. "Class Conflict and the Suppression of Tramps in Buffalo, 1892–1894." *Law and Society Review* 11: 873–911 (Summer 1977).

69. Barak, ibid., p. 6. We encourage you to consult several excellent books covering the Progressive era that document the adaptation of the social order to the needs of American business. Some historians give specific examples of how certain business practices were copied in nonbusiness areas, such as in the public school system. For a review of this literature see Shelden, *Controlling the Dangerous Classes*.

70. Quoted in Barak, "In Defense of the Rich," p. 7.

71. Langbein, "Understanding the Short History of Plea Bargaining," p. 262.

72. Chambliss, W. J., and R. Seidman. *Law, Order and Power* (2nd ed.). Reading, MA: Addison-Wesley, 1982, pp. 404–405.

73. Neubauer, *America's Courts and the Criminal Justice System*, p. 223.

74. Newman, D. J. "Pleading Guilty for Considerations: A Study of Bargain Justice." *Journal of Criminal Law, Criminology and Police Science* 46: 780–790 (1954); Neubauer, D. W. *Criminal Justice in Middle America*. Morristown, NJ: General Learning Press, 1974; Blumberg, A. "The Practice of Law as a Confidence Game: Organization Co-optation of a Profession." In W. J. Chambliss (ed.), *Criminal Law in Action*. New York: Wiley, 1975. Further confirmed by recent studies, summarized by Neubauer, *America's Courts and the Criminal Justice System*, ch. 12.

75. Blumberg, "The Practice of Law as a Confidence Game," p. 264.

76. Sudnow, D. "Normal Crimes: Sociological Features of the Penal Code in a Public Defender's Office." *Social Problems* 12: 255–276 (Winter 1965).

77. Mather, L. M. "Some Determinants of the Method of Case Disposition: Decisionmaking by Public Defenders in Los Angeles." *Law and Society Review* 8: 200 (Winter 1973).

78. Ibid., p. 199.

79. Neubauer, *America's Criminal Courts and the Criminal Justice System*, p. 218.

80. Ibid., p. 219; see also Boland, B., and B. Forst. "Prosecutors Don't Always Aim to Please." *Federal Probation* 49: 10–15 (1985); Holmes, M., H. Daudistel, and

W. Taggart. "Plea Bargaining and State District Court Caseloads: An Interrupted Time Series Analysis." *Law and Society Review* 26: 139–160 (1992).

81. Walker, S. *Sense and Nonsense about Crime and Drugs* (5th ed.). Belmont, CA: Wadsworth, 2001, pp. 156–160.

82. Mather, "Some Determinants of the Method of Case Disposition," p. 206.

83. Eisenstein, J., and H. Jacob. *Felony Justice.* Boston: Little, Brown, 1977; Nardulli, P. F., R. B. Fleming, and J. Eisenstein. *The Tenor of Justice.* Urbana: University of Illinois Press, 1988; Ulmer, J. T. *Social Worlds of Sentencing.* Albany: State University of New York Press, 1997.

84. Donziger, *The Real War on Crime,* p. 112.

85. Ibid., p. 113.

86. McCart, S. W. *Trial by Jury: A Complete Guide to the Jury System.* Radnor, PA: Chilton, 1964; Barnes, H. E. *The Story of Punishment.* Montclair, NJ: Patterson Smith, 1972, pp. 25–37 (originally published in 1930).

87. Hay, D. "Property, Authority and the Criminal Law." In D. Hay, P. Linebaugh, J. G. Rule, E. P. Thompson, and C. Winslow (eds.), *Albion's Fatal Tree: Crime and Society in 18th Century England.* New York: Pantheon, 1975.

88. Cole, D. *No Equal Justice: Race and Class in the American Criminal Justice System.* New York: New Press, 1999, p. 101.

89. Stevenson, B. A., and R. E. Friedman. "Deliberate Indifference: Judicial Tolerance of Racial Bias in Criminal Justice." *Washington and Lee Law Review* 51: 519–524 (1994).

90. Fellner, J., and M. Mauer. "Nearly 4 Million Americans Denied Vote Because of Felony Convictions." *Overcrowded Times* 9(5) (October 1998).

91. Cole, *No Equal Justice,* p. 104.

92. Ibid., p. 112.

93. Ibid., p. 117.

94. 476 U.S. 79 (1986).

95. Raphael, M. J., and E. J. Ungvarsky. "Excuses, Excuses: Neutral Explanations under *Batson v. Kentucky.*" *University of Michigan Judicial Law Reform* 229 (1993), cited in Cole, *No Equal Justice,* p. 120.

96. Cole, ibid., pp. 122–123.

97. Simon, R. "Murder, Juries, and the Press," *Trans-Action* 3 (May–June, 1966), pp. 52–70.

98. Padawer-Singer, A. M., and A. H. Barton. "The Impact of Pretrial Publicity on Jurors' Verdicts," in R. J. Simon (ed.), *The Jury System in America: A Critical Overview.* Beverly Hills, CA: Sage, 1975.

99. Kalven, H., and H. Zeisel. *The American Jury.* Boston: Little, Brown, 1966; see also Simon, R. (ed.). *The American Jury System: A Critical Overview.* Beverly Hills, CA: Sage, 1975.

100. Chambliss and Seidman, *Law, Order and Power,* p. 443.

101. Neubauer, *America's Criminal Courts,* 1996, pp. 354–355.

102. Scheb and Scheb, *Criminal Law and Procedure,* pp. 444–446.

103. McIntyre, D. M., "A Study of Judicial Dominance of the Charging Process," *Journal of Criminal Law, Criminology and Police Science* 59 (December, 1968), p. 472.

104. Banfield, L. and C. D. Anderson. "Continuances in Cook County Courts," *University of Chicago Law Review* 35 (1968), pp. 259–316.

105. Chambliss and Seidman, *Law, Order and Power.*

106. For a more complete discussion of these cases see the following works by Howard Zinn: "Upton Sinclair and Sacco and Vanzetti." In *The Zinn Reader: Writings on Disobedience and Democracy.* New York: Seven Stories Press, 1997, and *People's History of the United States,* pp. 322–331 (discussion of the International Workers of the World).

107. Sternberg, D. "The New Radical-Criminal Trials: A Step toward a Class-for-Itself in the American Proletariat." In R. Quinney (ed.), *Criminal Justice in America: A Critical Understanding.* Boston: Little, Brown, 1974, p. 279.

108. Barkan, S. E. "Political Trials and the Pro Se Defendant in the Adversary System." *Social Problems* 24: 325 (February 1977).

109. Ibid., p. 324.

110. Berrigan, P. *Prison Journals of a Priest Revolutionary.* New York: Holt, Rinehart and Winston, 1970, pp. 11–12.

111. Cook, F. "Setting Up the Vets." In S. Weissman (ed.), *Big Brother and Holding Company: The World behind Watergate.* Palo Alto, CA: Ramparts Press, 1974, p. 75.

112. Sternberg, "The New Radical-Criminal Trials," p. 280.

113. Barkan, "Political Trials and the Pro Se Defendant in the Adversary System," p. 328.

114. Ibid., pp. 329–330.

115. Sternberg, "The New Radical-Criminal Trials," pp. 285–286.

116. *Illinois v. Allen,* 397 U.S. 337 (1970).

117. Lynch and Groves, *A Primer on Radical Criminology,* pp. 98–99.

118. Feagin, J. R., and H. Vera. *White Racism.* New York: Routledge, 1995, pp. 83–108; Balbus, I. *The Dialectics of Legal Repression.* New York: Russell Sage Foundation, 1973.

CHAPTER TEN

SENTENCING

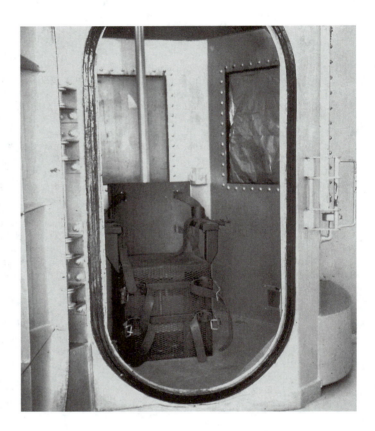

How often do you read about a case in the newspapers or learn about one on television in which the defendant receives a sentence that, to you at least, makes no sense whatsoever? More often than not it is a sentence that you (and many others) believe is too lenient. Also, you may notice some disparities in sentences in cases that appear to be identical—one person gets life in prison and another gets five to ten years. And, of course, you constantly read about offenders "getting off" because of "loopholes" in the law or "technicalities." You probably conclude that there is little rhyme or reason to the sentencing practices in the courts today.

In reality your conclusions would be incorrect, largely because they are based on the unusual cases (the "celebrated" cases noted in the wedding cake model of criminal justice) that make the headlines, not on the thousands of cases that are routinely processed day in and day out in the nation's courts. Upon closer inspection there are many consistent patterns in the sentencing practices within the court system, and it is possible to predict what an actual sentence will be in the vast majority of cases.

In this chapter we review some of the kinds of sentences handed out in today's criminal justice system. We examine the various justifications or rationales for punishment. We examine the different types of sentences that are available, ranging from various forms of probation to the ultimate punishment, the death penalty. Finally, we examine in some detail the various factors that influence the actual sentence, including race, gender, and social class. We discuss discrepancies in sentences, especially when comparing white-collar/corporate crimes with ordinary crimes.

JUSTIFICATIONS FOR PUNISHMENT

Why do we punish those who violate the law? Throughout history many different methods have been used to punish people, and various justifications for their use have been offered. We deal with the various *methods* of punishment in the next chapter. Here we review four justifications for punishing law violators: (1) retribution, (2) isolation/incapacitation, (3) deterrence, (4) rehabilitation.

Retribution

Retribution (or revenge/retaliation) is one of the most popular and oldest justifications for punishment. It is based on *lex talionis* (the law of retaliation)—the "eye-for-an-eye and tooth-for-a-tooth" principle. In some societies this principle was adhered to literally. In tribal societies in which the basis of social solidarity was blood ties (of a family or clan), offenses were settled by either a feud or clan punishment. For instance, if a member of clan A injured a member of clan B, clan B felt justified (or duty bound) to retaliate against clan A, rather than just against the individual member who committed the offense. In more advanced tribal societies (and other types of societies) retaliation meant **restitution,** or to return *in kind* (through fines or payments in kind). In this form of punishment, known as *wergeld* (literally, "man-money"), the victim was compensated either with money or with something else deemed valuable. In earlier societies the amount of compensation varied according to the crime and the victim's social rank (the higher the rank, the greater the compensation). Today retribution exists in some form, but when restitution is the punishment (e.g., fines), the state rather than the victim is compensated.[1]

Isolation/Incapacitation

Isolation/incapacitation means that an offender should be isolated from society or otherwise prevented from committing additional crimes. According to this view, isolating offenders is the only purpose of punishment.[2] In other words, regardless of what others may do as a result of the offender's punishment, at least the offender cannot further victimize society *while incarcerated.* The practice of isolating offenders dates back many centuries and includes such forms of punishment as banishment, exile, transportation, and the castration of rapists. Imprisonment is the modern version of isolation.

Deterrence

Many believe that the purpose of punishment is **deterrence**—preventing or discouraging the commission of crimes. There are two versions of the deterrence argument. **Special deterrence** is based on the assumption that by punishing an offender we deter him or her from committing crimes in the future. **General deterrence** rests on the assumption that by punishing individual offenders we set an example for others and deter them from committing crimes.

Rehabilitation

Rehabilitation is often cited as a justification for punishment because it is believed that someone who commits a crime has some kind of problem and the punishment should be geared toward correcting this problem. The individual's values, attitudes, work skills, education, or other characteristics are in some way deficient and should be improved upon through the use of various kinds of punishments. Thus, the judge may sentence an individual to a period of probation because this person needs drug counseling for an addiction and he or she can get the most help if placed on probation with the stipulation that he or she attend a drug treatment program.

Keep in mind that rehabilitation, deterrence, and so on, are rationalizations, not explanations, for punishment. They do not explain why certain forms of punishment are used and why certain forms of punishment are predominant during certain periods of history and then disappear or are used less often as other forms of punishment appear.[3]

THE SENTENCING PROCESS

The Sentencing Authority

The ultimate authority on sentencing lies with state legislatures, although the *sentencing structure* lies within all three branches of government. The legislative branch, however, has been largely responsible for the passage of laws and the establishment of sentences for each law. For most offenses, the legislatures give the courts several alternatives and a wide amount of discretion. For instance, first-degree burglary may call for a term of from one to five years in the state prison, or two years of probation, or a fine of $10,000.

Traditionally, the judicial branch (not only judges but the probation department as well) has had primary authority over who actually ends up in prison. An executive agency—the parole board—has had control over the actual length of time a person remains in prison. More recently the legislative branch has increased its control over sentencing, and the judiciary and parole boards have become more formalized in their decisions.[4] Some recent legislative decisions have resulted in very drastic changes in the other two branches, especially with so-called mandatory sentencing structures, such as "three strikes and you're out" legislation in California and other states. More about this shortly.

Given that judges and juries have a wide variation of penalties to impose on an offender, how do we account for the patterns of sentencing we observe? There are a number of different inputs that enter into the sentencing process.[5] These include the offender's status and race, gender, the offense, outside pressures (public, police, prosecutors), the relative ability and status of the defense attorney, and personal relationships between defense counsel and the court. One of the keys to understanding the different types of sentences meted out in court is the presentence investigation report.

The Presentence Investigation Report

The **presentence investigation (PSI) report** comes from the probation department of a court. This report is usually completed after the offender is convicted (through a plea or a jury trial) and focuses on several areas. The two major areas that the report focuses on are the legal and the social aspects of the case. In the case of the former, the report contains such information as the offender's prior record and the circumstances surrounding the crime for which the offender was convicted. The offender's past employment record, age, marital status, education, and many other nonlegal variables also are discussed in some detail. The report closes with a specific sentence recommendation.[6] Several studies show that around 90 percent of the time judges go along with what probation departments recommend. Thus, a sentence is determined by the probation department, although its recommendation is likely to conform to whatever it believes a particular judge is likely to do.[7]

In theory, one of the most important facts about an offender that is taken into account is the amenability of the accused to be "rehabilitated." Often, a probation officer's report that a defendant is "sorry" or "repentant" can mean probation. The defense counsel tries to persuade the judge that the defendant is a "respectable" person, one who is not really a "criminal," and one whose reputation, family, and friends will suffer if a harsh (or any) sentence is imposed. It is important to note that if in fact the accused *is* a "respectable" member of the community, at least from the standpoint of the judge (e.g., a white-collar offender, an upper-middle-class person who committed a felony), the sentence will be light in most instances, because judges normally consider the prior record of the offender as a major determining factor.

Ostensibly, the PSI report is supposed to be based on purely "objective" factors, so that stereotypes do not enter into the picture. Some critics charge that this report perpetuates the myth of "individualized justice" in that probation officers place the offender within predetermined sentencing categories. The probation officers doing the "investigation" (which itself is often perfunctory, routine, and filled with numerous inaccuracies, hearsay, rumors, and downright lies) have a gut feeling about a certain defendant and the kind of sentence he or she "deserves." With this prejudgment built in, the probation officers adjust the report accordingly. So, for instance, in most jurisdictions there is a point system whereby a certain score, based on such factors as prior record, employment and educational history, and family background, results in a certain sentence recommendation. There is enough ambiguity among the variables being considered to adjust the scores accordingly.

A study by Brown strongly supports this notion. Employing a quasi-experimental method, whereby several case scenarios were given to randomly selected presentence investigators, Brown found very little sentence-recommendation consistency. In fact, the participants (all veteran presentence investigators), using the same guidelines prescribed by their agency, rarely agreed on an appropriate recommendation. The only discernible consistency to surface was inconsistency in the decision-making process of recommending sentences.[8]

SENTENCES IN FELONY CASES

There are four major sentences in felony cases—imprisonment, probation, fines, and capital punishment—plus several variations.

Imprisonment: Types of Sentences

For those who are sentenced to a term of imprisonment, there are several alternatives. Generally, there are six major types of sentences.[9]

Concurrent and Consecutive Sentences. These sentences are handed down in cases in which the defendant is convicted of more than one crime or more than one count of the same crime (e.g., three separate burglaries, five burglaries, and two drug possession charges). A **concurrent sentence** combines the charges in one sentence. For instance, a defendant who is convicted of three counts of burglary, each carrying a maximum of five years, might be sentenced to one five-year term. A defendant who received a **consecutive sentence** would serve time on each of the charges. A person convicted of three counts of burglary might be sentenced to fifteen years in prison—three terms of five years.

Suspended Sentences. In many instances the court is allowed to place an individual on probation and, in effect, "suspend" the sentence pending good behavior. If the individual does not violate any of the various "conditions of probation," then he or she will be released from the sentence without serving any time in prison. However, if any of the conditions are violated or if a new crime is committed, the offender may be placed in prison and begin serving the original sentence.

Indefinite Sentences. An **indefinite sentence** specifies a minimum and maximum penalty for certain offenders, such as one to five years or ten to twenty years. In most states an inmate is eligible for *good-time credit* on the original sentence because of favorable behavior while in prison. This can reduce the actual time served on a sentence.

Definite and Determinate Sentences.   A **definite sentence** is a specific sentence set by the legislature, which allows the sentencing judge or corrections officials no discretion. In some states there is **determinate sentencing,** which allows the judge to set a fixed term within certain statutory parameters. Under this scheme an offender is required to serve a particular sentence with the possibility of early release. Another variation is a sentence of life *with* the possibility of parole and life *without* the possibility of parole. In Nevada, for instance, a person who is sentenced to life *with* the possibility of parole is eligible for parole consideration after five years (good-time credit is not counted). A person who is sentenced to life *without* the possibility of parole is eligible to go before a pardons board (similar to a parole board), after serving ten years. The pardons board can recommend that the inmate become eligible for consideration of parole. Thus, "life *without* the possibility of parole" does not really mean what it says.

Mandatory Sentences.   These types of sentences result from mandates by state legislatures (almost always resulting from local or even national political moods, frequently during election years) requiring certain kinds of offenders who commit certain types of crimes to be sentenced to a term in prison for a set minimum amount of time. In some states (Arizona is one), "use a gun, go to prison" laws give neither judges nor prosecutors any discretion. Similarly, *habitual offender laws* stipulate that after an offender is convicted of so many serious crimes (usually two or three major felony convictions), the individual is to be sentenced to a very lengthy term in prison, often for life (sometimes without the possibility of parole). Perhaps the most famous of these laws are "three strikes and you're out" laws, which began in California in the early 1990s.

A Special Example: Three Strikes and You're Out!   A product of political posturing and the cynical desire among politicians to get votes by playing on public fears of crime, legislators in California and elsewhere used the popular baseball phrase to obtain the needed support. Almost instantly, the catchy phrase became part of American popular culture. This would be the ultimate get-tough stance on crime, showing little regard for the consequences. Originally passed in 1993 in California, three-strikes legislation was supposed to impose extremely harsh sentences after a conviction for a third felony. In California the "third strike" would result in a sentence of twenty-five years to life or in some cases even more time. In theory, the law was aimed at the "toughest criminals"—mostly repeat, serious, especially violent offenders. Unfortunately, it was based on the erroneous assumption that the criminal justice system is "too lenient" on criminals (when in fact the opposite is true); it also was based on a few celebrated cases, especially the kidnapping and murder of Polly Klass.[10] It has also been described as "politicized crime control policy."

To be certain, three-strikes legislation had the support of the U.S. Supreme Court—a judicial body which has been transformed from a guardian of the U.S. Constitution to an entity preoccupied with politics. In 1980, only three states had nonviolent statutes similar to the three strikes made popular in California (Texas, Washington, and West Virginia). The principal issues associated with three-strikes policies are judicial discretion and the proportionality of punishment, which is linked to the Eighth Amendment's addressing the issue of cruel and unusual punishment. The U.S. Supreme Court paved the way for three-strikes legislation in its decision in *Rummel v. Estelle* (1980), in which the Court distanced itself from the precedent of proportionality established in *Weems v. United States* (1910).[11] In 1973, William Rummel received his third felony conviction in Texas, which resulted in the application of a mandatory life sentence. Rummel had been convicted of three property offenses resulting in a total monetary crime value of less than $230. In 1978 the Fifth Circuit Court overturned the conviction in rehearing, based on the argument that the penalty was in violation of the precedence of proportionality;[12] then the court overturned its own position later that year.[13] In 1980, on appeal to the U.S. Supreme Court, Chief Justice William Rehnquist took the position that Texas was not in violation for imposing such a sentence for three nonviolent offenses.[14] Thus, the Court agreed that mandatory life in prison was an acceptable punishment for three nonviolent offenses committed over about a nine-year period and totaling less than $230.

Currently at least twenty-four states have enacted some form of "three strikes and you're out" legislation. What has been the result? To extend the baseball metaphor, this law *has struck out looking* in terms of its impact on the crime problem! First of all, it has had little if any impact on the overall crime picture. Supporters claimed that this law was responsible for the drop in crime in California during the 1990s. California Secretary of State Bill Jones, who wrote the original law while he was a state assemblyman, is one of those making such a claim. However, he and other supporters fail to recognize that virtually all states experienced a drop in crime during the 1990s, and most of them had no three-strikes laws.

Second, there have been hundreds of examples of relatively minor offenders sentenced to long prison terms under this legislation. For instance, a Kansas mother of two was sentenced to life for possessing $40 worth of cocaine; a man in Southern California was sentenced to twenty-five years for stealing a couple slices of pizza; a man received a fifty-year sentence for stealing some videos worth about $150 from two Kmart stores in San Bernardino, California. This last example resulted in a recent federal appeals court decision that ruled that the three-strikes law constituted cruel and unusual punishment.[15] This was a petty theft, normally considered a misdemeanor in California and carrying a sentence of no more than six months in jail. Because the defendant had been previously convicted of several offenses (all were nonviolent crimes), under the law the video thefts were enhanced to felonies.

As several studies have noted, most of the defendants sentenced under the three-strikes law have been nonviolent offenders and older offenders (those with low recidivism rates to begin with). The application of this law also has resulted in more jury trials, further clogging the system and costing taxpayers more. And the law has resulted in a large increase in the number of individuals going to prison (mostly small-time offenders), has had little impact on the crime problem, but has been used as a plea-bargaining tool.[16]

In ruling on the theft-of-videos case, the federal appeals court judges said that their ruling suggested that the law was cruel and unusual in this specific case only. However, several legal experts immediately noted that this ruling might have broader appeal, because several other people had been sentenced to unusually long prison terms for similar crimes. In fact, the lawyer for the defendant in the video-theft case said there were 350 people serving a sentence of twenty-five years to life for petty theft. The appeals court noted that as of May 2001, more than 6,700 offenders had received a 25-to-life sentence and more than 43,000 had been sentenced to significantly longer terms for only their "second strike." In such cases, the legislation deviates from the baseball metaphor, for in baseball it takes three strikes to get a batter out!

Third, detailed research on the impact of the three-strikes law shows that it targets mostly racial minorities. For instance, data collected in Los Angeles County found that black offenders were targeted in 57 percent of the cases and were being charged with three-strike offenses at a rate 13 to 17 times greater than white offenders. Analysis of statewide data in California discovered that, as of 1997, while blacks constituted about 7 percent of the total population, they accounted for 20 percent of all felony arrests, 31 percent of the state prisoners, and a whopping 43 percent of those locked up under the three-strikes provisions; further, blacks constituted 37 percent of those convicted of a "second strike" and 44 percent of those convicted of a "third strike."[17]

In short, analysis of actual data (as opposed to the rhetoric of politicians) shows what a monumental failure this piece of legislation has been. However, we can certainly conclude that it has had a positive effect on all of those who benefit from the prison-industrial complex, because it has expanded the size of the prison population in California and elsewhere.

Sentencing Guidelines

There is a tendency within any capitalist society to make things efficient, streamlined, systematized, or just plain bureaucratized so as to make outcomes more predictable. This was clearly seen around the turn of the twentieth century with the rise of what came to be called *scientific management.* This was a system devised by Frederick Taylor in an attempt to increase factory production by getting the most work out of each worker and to do so with some scientific rationale. The more general aim was not to increase production but rather to figure out a method of making a profit in the most systematic way. In time this need for efficiency and predictability had a spillover effect, as it impacted many other areas of social life, including the criminal justice system.[18]

So it is with *sentencing guidelines.* These guidelines came about mostly because of dissatisfaction with the sentencing practices of certain judges in certain parts of the country. Part of this stemmed from a general feeling, especially among the public, that the court system was too lenient (a rather ironic charge since our system metes out the most severe sentences of any democratic society in the world). Another complaint was that there were too many disparities in sentencing (again somewhat ironic because no two cases are exactly alike and each crime has its own unique context). Critics wanted to take some of the discretion away from judges, ostensibly to eliminate these discrepancies. In short, sentencing guidelines were established mainly to lend a certain predictability to the sentences handed down for certain crimes. Scientific management was applied to the American court system. However, politics played a key role in the crafting of sentencing guidelines as well.

In 1986, Len Bias, a University of Maryland basketball star, was drafted by the Boston Celtics. Shortly after the announcement of his soon-to-be professional basketball career, Bias died. The cause was crack cocaine—at least that was the *published* cause of death. Some suggest it was simply cocaine. The U.S. Congress, with support from then President Reagan, used the Bias incident to push through Congress legislation that increased sentences for drug offenders. Millions of African Americans were living in poverty, and all of a sudden Len Bias's death drew attention to the African American community. Of course, nothing was accomplished to alleviate the pains of poverty, but legislators discovered a way to ensure that more African Americans would be sent to prison, and for much longer periods of time, through the Anti–Drug Abuse Act of 1986. In 1980, African Americans made up 23 percent of all those arrested for drugs. Now, nearly 60 percent of all narcotics convictions involve African Americans.[19]

Guidelines started to be developed within the federal system and within some state court systems during the 1980s. In theory, each sentence would be based on a certain *score* reflecting the seriousness of the crime, the offender's prior criminal history, and the offender's "social stability" (education, employment history, marital history, etc.). Certain *points* would be assigned to each factor that went into the total "equation," so in the end there would be *uniformity* in sentencing. Just as in businesses following scientific management principles, a certain series of steps would produce a certain, predictable number of criminal justice outcomes.

The Minnesota Sentencing Guidelines, devised in the state of Minnesota, served as a model for other states. A judge needed only to look at a chart in order to determine what the sentence would be for an offender convicted in court. The chart showed a specific range for each offense (e.g., 30–36 months).[20]

The problem with this approach is clear: we are dealing with human beings, and a person's liberty is at stake, not a certain quota of hamburgers made! Moreover, as some research made clear, the various factors that determined the length of a sentence tended to mask racial criteria and produce an increase in discrepancies based on race. Many have criticized the use of special "sentencing commissions" within some states, because they result in the kinds of discrepancies such guidelines were suppose to reduce. One report noted that in New York there were so many different political philosophies on the state commission that there was little agreement on the guidelines. Another report compared sentencing guidelines in Minnesota and Pennsylvania and found that sentences in Minnesota were much less punitive than sentences in Pennsylvania, in part because so many commission members in Pennsylvania had close ties to the political establishment.[21]

We have served on various state and local "commissions," "task forces," and the like, and it has been our experience that they are largely an exercise in futility. Most members act in their own self-interest (e.g., to please their employers or pad their résumés) and in general put forth merely an image that something is being done to solve a particular problem. Hence, it is not too surprising to find sentencing guidelines serving little or no purpose in the grand scheme of things, and there is abundant evidence that disparities based on race and class have become worse in the past twenty years, especially when we consider the results of the "war on drugs" (which we do later in this chapter).

Actual Sentences in Felony Cases

In the final stage of the criminal court process, the actual sentencing of the guilty defendant, what sorts of sentences are "typical"? More than thirty years ago the sociologist David Sudnow observed that courtroom workgroups have a tendency to develop norms for "typical" crimes that carry "typical" sentences. These "typical" (or "normal") crimes are actually a form of stereotypes describing the "typical" defendant, the "typical" circumstances surrounding the offense and, of course, the "typical" sentence that is imposed. Over the years, defense attorneys, prosecutors, and judges develop shared ideas about what is an "appropriate" sentence for a particular offense and offender. The appropriate sentence usually takes into consideration the seriousness of the crime, the prior record of the defendant, and any aggravating or mitigating circumstances (which can vary considerably). However, lurking in the background of these cases are the various prejudices of the individual actors within the court system. Why else do we find the vast majority of those sentenced to prison from very poor backgrounds and racial minorities? One particular study not only documents the obvious racial bias within the system but also shows how such a bias is so often obscured by the methods in studies that claim no bias is present.

The criminologist Margaret Farnworth and her colleagues examined a sample of cases in which defendants were sentenced for possession of marijuana with the intent to sell.[22] They first examined the data on these sentences in a manner that has become very traditional among social scientists. They operationalized "race" as "white" and "nonwhite." When they did this, they found no significant differences between the two groups as far as the sentence was concerned: whites were just as severely treated as nonwhites. However, as is usually the case, Hispanics have "disappeared" from these kinds of studies by being lumped together with whites (they are also treated this way in the annual FBI crime report). When Farnworth and her colleagues separated out Hispanics and controlled for a number of other factors, they found that whites received the least severe sentences, Hispanics received the most severe sentences, and blacks fell somewhere in between.

It should be noted that sentences do in fact vary considerably according to conviction offense. For instance, a study of a sample of sentences in state courts around the country in 1996 found that, overall, 38 percent of offenders were sent to prison, 31 percent were sent to jail, and 31 percent were given probation.[23] However, when looking at the specific offense a person was convicted of, researchers noticed some interesting variations. For example, 92 percent of those convicted of murder were sent to prison, but only 42 percent of those convicted of aggravated assault were sent to prison (28% of them were granted probation). Property offenses varied considerably, with 45 percent of the burglary convictions receiving a prison sentence, compared to only 26 percent of the fraud cases. This particular example is noteworthy, for fraud is typically associated with a higher class of offender and usually treated as a white-collar offense. For property offenders combined, 34 percent were sent to prison, 28 percent were sent to jail, and 38 percent were granted probation. Drug offenders were highly likely to receive a prison sentence. Thirty-five percent of all drug offenders were sent to prison; another 37 percent were sentenced to jail. Thus, drug offenders were about as likely as property offenders to go to prison or jail but less likely to be granted probation.

Both class and racial biases begin to appear very early in the criminal justice process: technically, when laws are first made; but within the actual system at the stage of police processing and then, more critical for the court system, of the setting of bail. Thus, by the sentencing stage, the majority of those left are racial minorities and the poor. If you doubt the charge of racial and class bias in criminal court processing, take a look at some of the many studies that document it.[24] A Florida study found that although the poor were no more likely to receive harsher sentences than the nonpoor for property crimes, they were in the case of violent crimes and drug violations. A study of drunk driving convictions found that those with the highest level of education (a measure of social class) received the most favorable treatment from charging through sentencing. Another study found that among members of a group convicted of similar crimes who had similar prior records, unemployed people were more likely than those who were employed to be awaiting trial in jail (and for longer periods of time) and were twice as likely to be sent to prison. Also, several studies have found that those with public defenders (an indication of lower status, because they have to be "indigent" in order to qualify) are treated more harshly than those with private attorneys.

As for race, some studies have come up with very mixed conclusions, but most research reveals a racial bias at all stages of court processing, including sentencing. For instance, in the state of New York, minorities were more likely to be incarcerated even when other factors (like offense and prior record) were taken into consideration. A study in Florida found that black defendants were far more likely to be sentenced under habitual offender laws and thus get stiffer penalties than their white counterparts, especially for drug and property crimes. Racial and class bias is most flagrant when it comes to drug offenses (more about this later in the chapter). It should be noted that some studies in the past that found no evidence of racial bias indicate that "prior record" and "seriousness of the offense" predict actual sentence better than race does. What these studies ignore, however, is the fact that in most instances race is closely related to the offense charged and also to prior record. As has been noted by many researchers, blacks and other minorities living in inner-city ghettos (especially in housing projects and "gang" territories) are practically guaranteed to have some contact with the police (if for no other reason than "driving while black" or "standing while black") and hence have a "prior record" (mostly minor offenses).[25]

Some studies have found some evidence of more lenient treatment being given to blacks. Much of this "leniency" stems from the relationship between the victim and the offender. Generally speaking, when both the victim and the offender are black, the sentence will be much less severe than in cases where the victim is white and the offender is black. This is especially true for capital crimes, to which we now turn.

CAPITAL PUNISHMENT: LEGALIZED HOMICIDE

A Brief History

Capital punishment is one of the oldest forms of punishment, dating back several thousands of years. It has had a long and turbulent history in America. It has gone through periods in which most states either abolished it altogether or didn't use it and periods in which it was commonly used. Two landmark Supreme Court decisions have rekindled the controversy surrounding the death penalty: *Furman v. Georgia* (408 U.S. 238, 1972) and *Gregg v. Georgia* (428 U.S. 153, 1976). After these two decisions were handed down, the use of death penalty sentences increased dramatically. Between 1976 and November 2001, more than 5,000 people were sentenced to death, and 745 of them were executed. During this period, the racial breakdown of those executed was 55 percent white, 36 percent black, and the remainder other races. Since 1608, there have been an estimated 19,300 people executed in this country, mostly from hanging (electrocution began in the 1890s, and today the preferred method is lethal injection). As of November 2001, there were 3,709 on death row, with about 1,200 added just since 1990. California leads the way as far as the total number of death row inmates (602); Texas is second (454). Texas leads the country in executions (238 since 1976).[26]

In *Furman v. Georgia* there were nine separate opinions, one from each of the justices. Overall the Court ruled that the death penalty *as it was administered* constituted cruel and unusual punishment, in violation of the Eighth and Fourteenth Amendments of the Constitution. The Court did not rule that the death penalty *in and of itself* constitutes cruel and unusual punishment. The response by the states was almost immediate. Appeals began flowing into the court system, and within four years of *Furman* the Supreme Court made perhaps its most significant ruling on the matter.

In the case of *Gregg v. Georgia* the Court upheld the Georgia statute calling for the death penalty for murder. The Court ruled: "A punishment must not be excessive, but this does not mean that the states must seek the minimal standards available. The imposition of the death penalty for the crime of murder does not violate the Constitution." In two other decisions the Court ruled similarly (*Proffit v. Florida,* 1976 and *Jurek v. Texas,* 1976). However, in *Coker v. Georgia* (1977) the Court ruled that the death penalty for rape constituted cruel and unusual punishment.

After a de facto abolition of the death penalty, it was reactivated in 1977 with the execution of Gary Gilmore by a firing squad in Utah (this state is the only one that allows the prisoner a choice between a firing squad or hanging). As of the end of 1995, 38 states plus the federal government had the death penalty. As of October 1999, there were about 3,600 under the penalty of death, awaiting their appeals; 83 had been executed in 1999 by October.[27] During 1995, 56 were executed; Texas led the way with 19. Three states—California, Texas, and Florida—together accounted for almost 40 percent of those on death row (38.8%). Since it resumed executions in 1982, Texas leads the nation with more than 100, far ahead of the state ranked second (Florida, with 36). Virtually all of those on death row today have been convicted of murder.[28] A total of 358 were executed between 1977 and 1995.[29]

The Race Factor

Race figures prominently in the imposition of the death penalty. For instance, of the 4,172 prisoners executed between 1930 and 1995, over half (52%) were African Americans. Between 1930 and 1972, a total of 455 people were executed for rape, 89 percent of them African Americans. When researchers consider the race of the victims, race once again enters into the picture. For instance, 82 percent of the victims of those executed were white, whereas about 50 percent of the victims of *all* homicides were African American. Several studies have noted that there are vast discrepancies in the application of the death penalty according to the race of the victim and the race of the offender. When the victim is white and the offender is African American, the death penalty is given about 35 percent of the time, compared to only 14 percent when the victim is African American and the offender is white. The death penalty is given in 22 percent of the cases in which whites kill whites and in only 6 percent of the cases where African Americans kill African Americans. The study by Balbus and his associates also found that the race of the victim plays a key role in a prosecutor's decision to seek the death penalty and a jury's decision to impose it. Even after controlling for an astounding 200 variables, the Baldus group still found race to be the most significant variable! Other recent studies have arrived at identical results. These studies, by the way, examined data from several different states.[30]

It is obvious that the death penalty, as it has been applied through the years, discriminates against blacks, the poor, and the uneducated. Evidence of racial discrimination in the imposition of the death penalty has been documented in several studies, dating back more than seventy years. Guy B. Johnson studied homicide cases in Richmond, Virginia, and in five counties in North Carolina during the 1930s. He found that the death penalty was most often applied when the victim was white and the offender was black, and least likely when both the offender and the victim were black.[31] Wolfgang, Kelly, and Nolde studied 439 cases of men sentenced to death in Pennsylvania for murder between 1914 and 1958. They found that 20 percent of the whites had their sentences commuted to life imprisonment, whereas only 11 percent of the blacks did, a statistically significant relationship.[32]

Studies of rape have also found a strong relationship between the race of the victim and the imposition of the death penalty. Elmer Johnson, in a study of rape cases resulting in the imposition of the death penalty in North Carolina between 1909 and 1954, found that blacks were more likely than whites to be executed. A study of Florida cases found that blacks who raped whites were much more likely to receive the death penalty than whites who raped blacks.[33] Wolfgang and Reidel studied 3,000 rape convictions in eleven southern states between 1945 and 1965. They found that "Among 1,265 cases in which the race of the defendant and the sentence are known, nearly seven times as many Blacks were sentenced to death as whites."[34] They also found that 36 percent of the blacks who raped whites were sentenced to death, while all other racial combinations resulted in only 2 percent being sentenced to death. These relationships held true even when the researchers held constant such other factors as prior record and contemporaneous offenses (e.g., murder while committing robbery).

Research documenting racial bias in the death penalty continues to the present, with the consistent finding that African Americans are more likely than whites to be charged with capital crimes and then to be sentenced to death if so charged.[35] There is evidence that juries are often prejudiced against minorities and are more likely to convict (in capital cases) minorities than they are to convict whites.[36] Finally, research has found that of the more than 15,000 executions between 1608 and 1986, a mere 30 cases were found (about 0.2%) in which a white person was executed for killing a black.[37]

The Controversy Continues: *McCleskey v. Kemp*

Many of those studies gained some prominence in one of the most significant Supreme Court cases concerning the death penalty: ***McCleskey v. Kemp*** in 1987. It was here that research concerning the race of the victim was cited. Not surprisingly the case originated in Georgia, just like the *Furman* and *Gregg* cases. The defendant, Warren McCleskey, an African American, was convicted of killing a white police officer. Part of the defense strategy was to use the study by Balbus (see note 30). Despite the overwhelming evidence in support of the importance of the race of the victim, the Supreme Court rejected the appeal. While accepting the validity of the Balbus study, the Court nevertheless ruled that, regardless of statistical correlations, in the case of McCleskey there was no evidence that "*any of the decisionmakers in McCleskey's case acted with discriminatory purpose*" (emphasis added). The Court also suggested that *at best,* all that could be shown was a "discrepancy that appears to correlate with race."

What is perhaps most interesting about this ruling is that the Court appeared to be afraid of what the "logical conclusions" of such evidence might be. Justice Lewis Powell, writing for the majority, noted that such evidence "throws into serious question the principles that underlie our entire criminal justice system.... [I]f we accepted McCleskey's claim that racial bias impermissibly tainted the capital sentencing decision, we would soon be faced with similar claims as to other types of penalty." Not surprisingly, the ruling came in for immediate attack, including four dissenting justices (Blackmun, Marshall, Brennan, and Stevens). Heaven forbid, they suggested, that others might challenge such obvious biases, "even women" (wrote one justice). One scholar noted sarcastically that concluding that "at most" there appears to be a "discrepancy" is like saying that "at most" the many studies on lung cancer "indicate a discrepancy that appears to correlate with smoking."[38] Most of the critics voiced the opinion that this ruling sent a message that racial bias is perfectly constitutional. McCleskey was eventually executed in the electric chair on September 26, 1991.

Justice Thurgood Marshall, who joined two other justices in a dissent for a stay of execution, stated that it appears that "the court values expediency over human life."[39]

David Cole has argued that it would be nearly impossible to prove that a prosecutor and a jury have imposed the death penalty in a particular case because of the defendant's race. He notes that there are "long-standing rules" that prohibit defendants from obtaining discovery from the prosecution and therefore "unless the prosecutor admits to acting for racially biased reasons, it will be difficult to pin discrimination on the prosecutor." Similarly in the case of jurors. In short, says Cole, "defendants are precluded from discovering evidence of intent from the two actors whose discriminatory intent the *McCleskey* Court required them to establish."[40]

Subsequent cases on this issue had almost identical results. In one such case, *Dobbs v. Zant* (a 1989 case in, naturally, Georgia!), the Court rejected the appeal even though several jurors referred to African Americans as "coloreds" and two admitted using "nigger" in their conversations. Even the defense attorney (a court-appointed attorney) admitted using "nigger" and believed that African Americans make good basketball players but not teachers![41]

In other words, the Supreme Court has concluded that "discrimination is inevitable," a "natural by-product of discretion" and hence "constitutionally acceptable."[42] So there you have it, the highest court in the country that espouses "equal justice for all" telling us, in effect, that racial bias is supported by the U.S. Constitution! Some members of Congress responded to the *McCleskey* decision by adding a "Racial Justice Act" to the Omnibus Crime Bill of 1994. By a slim majority, the House voted for this provision, which would have allowed those on death row to challenge their sentence based on statistical evidence of race discrimination in capital cases, as had McCleskey. But it was defeated in the Senate and dropped from the 1994 bill. Senator Orin Hatch (R-Utah) remarked, quite candidly, that this "so-called Racial Justice Act has nothing to do with racial justice and everything to do with abolishing the death penalty.... It would convert every death penalty case into a massive sideshow of statistical squabbles and quota quarrels."[43] What more can be said, given this kind of "worse-case scenario" logic!

One issue that is often overlooked (but fortunately not forgotten by critics of the death penalty) is that of those wrongly convicted. One detailed study found evidence of some 400 defendants sentenced to death who turned out to be innocent. An estimated two dozen were actually executed, and many more spent years in prison. Not surprisingly, a disproportionate number have been African Americans.[44] During the past decade more attention has been focused on the possibility that people could be sentenced to death when there may be some question about their guilt. A Columbia University study of 4,578 cases between 1973 and 1995 found that there were serious "reversible errors" in almost 70 percent of capital cases that were reviewed. Death sentences were overturned in two-thirds of the appeals, with ninety-five death row prisoners having been completely exonerated. The use of DNA testing has resulted in 107 persons being released between 1989 and 2002, twelve of whom were on death row. Total error rates have reached as high as 70 percent in some courts.[45]

Meanwhile, the use of the death penalty has increased as appeals have declined and the process from conviction to execution has been stepped up. More are being executed every day. A few states, such as Texas, have turned executions into a "sideshow" (to use Senator Hatch's terminology) with crowds of people outside applauding as soon as a defendant is executed. African Americans and other minorities continue to receive the death penalty in numbers far greater than their proportion in the general population. Almost without exception, the executed are drawn from the ranks of the "dangerous classes." Indeed, the death penalty is the ultimate penalty for this class.[46]

What is even more crucial is that actual sentencing practices contain rampant racial and class biases. This is especially true when we consider the impact of the "war on drugs." Here we see clear evidence of racial bias—in fact, evidence that suggests that the aim of this "war" was not the eradication of drugs but the containment of the minority population.[47] This problem is the subject of the next section.

CLASS AND RACIAL DIFFERENCES IN SENTENCING: THE IMPACT OF THE "WAR ON DRUGS"

More than any other public policy in the past hundred years, the "war on drugs" has had a huge impact on the criminal justice system. With the emphasis placed almost totally on a legalistic response to the "drug problem," the police have responded with literally millions of arrests for drug possession and sales during the past two decades. Not surprisingly there has been a predictable impact on the criminal courts and the rest of the criminal justice system.

Data on court commitments to state prisons during the 1980s and early 1990s clearly show the dramatic changes for drug offenses. Between 1980 and 1992, sentences on drug charges increased by more than 1,000 percent. In contrast, there was a more modest increase of 51 percent for violent offenses. Race played a key role in these increases, especially during the late 1980s and early 1990s. The number of African Americans sentenced to prison for drug charges increased by over 90 percent, almost three times greater than white offenders.[48] Currie noted that between 1985 and 1995 the number of African American inmates sentenced for drug crimes increased by 700 percent.[49] Tables 10.1 and 10.2 illustrate these figures.

Not only were more African Americans sentenced for drug crimes, but the *severity* of their sentences increased compared to whites'. In 1992, in the federal system, the aver-

TABLE 10.1   Court Commitments to State Prison, by Crime Type, 1980–1992

OFFENSE	1980	1992	PERCENTAGE INCREASE
Total	131,215	334,301	155
Violent	63,200	95,300	51
Property	53,900	104,300	94
Drugs	8,900	192,000	1,046
Public order	5,200	29,400	465

Source: Mauer, M. *Americans behind Bars: The International Use of Incarceration, 1992–1993.* Washington, DC: Sentencing Project, 1994; Gilliard, D. K., and A. J. Beck. *Prisoners in 1993.* Washington, DC: Bureau of Justice Statistics, 1994.

TABLE 10.2   Court Commitments to State Prison, 1988–1992

OFFENSE	1988	1992	PERCENTAGE INCREASE
VIOLENT			
White	26,299	33,376	26.9
Black	30,677	40,803	33.0
PROPERTY			
White	37,978	44,344	16.8
Black	33,901	39,085	15.3
DRUGS			
White	18,851	25,474	35.1
Black	26,769	51,970	94.1

Source: Maguire, K., and A. L. Pastore (eds.). *Sourcebook of Criminal Justice Statistics—1995.* Washington, DC: Department of Justice, Bureau of Justice Statistics, 1996, p. 550.

age sentence length for African American drug offenders was about 107 months, compared to 74 months for white drug offenders (see Table 10.3). There has been a huge discrepancy when comparing powder and crack cocaine sentences in the federal system. In 1995, for instance, African Americans constituted a phenomenal 88 percent of those sentenced for crack cocaine, compared to less than 30 percent of those sentenced for powder cocaine (see Table 10.4).

Sentencing in the federal system for drug offenses shows some startling changes during the past half-century. As shown in Table 10.5, between 1945 and 1995 the proportion of those going to prison for all offenses rose from 47 percent to 69 percent, compared to a decrease of those granted probation (from 40% to 24%), while the average sentence has risen by over 300 percent. The changes in the sentences for drug-law violations are

TABLE 10.3 Average Sentence Length for Offenders Convicted of Various Crimes in U.S. District Courts, by Race, 1992 (sentences in months)

	WHITES	BLACKS	OTHER
All offenses	56.8	84.1	60.8
Violent offenses	92.4	103.9	76.1
Drug offenses	73.6	106.9	77.2

Source: Maguire and Pastore (1996), p. 474.

TABLE 10.4 Drug Offenders Sentenced Under the U.S. Sentencing Commission Guidelines, by Race, Powder Cocaine, and Crack, 1995

	POWDER COCAINE		CRACK COCAINE	
RACE	*N*	%	*N*	%
White	977	22.0	168	4.5
Black	1,274	28.6	3,330	88.4
Hispanic	2,166	48.7	245	6.5
Other	33	0.7	23	0.6

Source: Maguire and Pastore (1996), p. 492.

TABLE 10.5 Getting Tough on Crime in the Federal System, 1945–1995

YEAR	PROBATION (%)	PRISON (%)	AVERAGE SENTENCE (MONTHS)
1945	39.8	47.3	16.5
1955	41.6	50.0	21.9
1965	37.5	47.5	33.5
1975	47.9	46.2	45.5
1985	37.4	48.5	60.2
1995	24.4	69.1	66.4
Percentage change (1945–1995)	−15.4	+21.8	+302.0

Source: Maguire and Pastore (1996), p. 477.

most dramatic. As noted in Table 10.6, whereas in 1945 the percentage of drug offenders going to prison was high enough at 73 percent, by 1995 fully 90 percent were going to prison! And the average sentence for drug cases went from only 22 months in 1945 to almost 90 months in 1995, an increase of 300 percent! Finally, while in 1980 the most serious offense for those admitted to federal prison was a violent crime in about 13 percent of the cases and a drug offense in just over one-fourth of the cases, by 1992 in almost half of the cases (48.8%) the most serious offense was drugs, compared to a violent crime in less than 8 percent of the cases. In the meantime, the average maximum sentence *declined for violent crimes (from 125 months to 88 months) and almost doubled for drug offenses (from 47 months to 82 months)*! (See Table 10.7.)

More detailed data from U.S. district courts (federal system) show that whereas in 1982 about 20 percent of all convictions were for drugs, by 1994 this percentage had increased to about 36. During this same period, the proportion of those convicted on drug charges who were sentenced to prison increased from 74 percent in 1982 to 84 percent in 1994, and their actual sentences increased from an average of 55 months in 1982 to 80 months in 1994; the average sentences for murder during this period actually *decreased* from 162 months to 117 months, while for all violent offenses the average sentence declined from 133 months to 88 months. Incidentally, on any given day, almost 60 percent (58.6%) of all federal prisoners are serving time for drug offenses; of these, 40 percent are African American.[50]

TABLE 10.6 Sentences in Federal Courts for Drug Law Violations, 1945–1995

YEAR	PROBATION (%)	PRISON (%)	AVERAGE SENTENCE (MONTHS)
1945	24.2	72.7	22.2
1955	18.2	80.8	43.5
1965	27.4	71.6	60.3
1975	39.4	60.0	45.3
1985	23.7	75.1	64.8
1995	9.3	90.1	88.7
Percentage change (1945–1995)	–14.9	+17.4	+300.0

Source: Maguire and Pastore (1996), p. 491.

TABLE 10.7 Federal Prison Admissions, 1980–1992

	1980	1986	1990	1992
NUMBER ADMITTED	13,766	23,058	28,659	33,622
MOST SERIOUS OFFENSE				
Violent	12.9%	7.9%	7.1%	7.8%
Drug	26.7%	40.2%	49.2%	48.8%
MAXIMUM SENTENCES (MEAN)				
Violent	125	132	89	88
Drug	47	58	81	82

Source: Beck, A. J., and P. M. Brien. "Trends in the U.S. Correctional Populations: Recent Findings from the Bureau of Justice Statistics." In K. C. Haas and G. P. Alpert (eds.), *The Dilemmas of Corrections* (3rd ed.). Project Heights, IL: Waveland Press, 1995, p. 59.

The trend in getting tougher on drugs is further illustrated by the proportion of sentences relative to arrests. For instance, as indicated in Table 10.8, between 1980 and 1992 the number sentenced to state prisons for murder per 1,000 arrests *decreased* from 621 to 521— that is, in 1980, 62.1 percent of those arrested for murder went to prison compared to 52.1 percent in 1992. For drug offenses, the number going to prison per 1,000 arrests was only 19 in 1980 but 104 in 1992 (from 1.9% to 10%)! In other words, *it has become progressively more serious to have been caught with drugs than to have killed someone!*[51]

One of the most recent sources of data on court cases is a U.S. Department of Justice report that examined felony defendants in the largest seventy-five counties in 1994.[52] Here we can see the effects of the "war on drugs" and its impact on the nation's court system; we also can clearly see the effects of race. The most serious charge in just over one-third (34.6%) of the cases was a drug offense (with nontrafficking drug offenses being the most common—58% of all drug charges), followed closely by a property crime (31.1%), with about one-fourth (25.7%) being violent offenses, mostly assaults (constituting 45% of all the violent crimes).

Not surprisingly, race figured prominently in these cases. African Americans constituted over half (56%) of all defendants and 62 percent of those charged with drug offenses. Another study noted that almost *all* (99%) drug-trafficking defendants between 1985 and 1987 were African Americans![53] In some cities, the proportion of felony defendants who were African American was quite high. For example, African Americans constituted 93 percent of all felony defendants in Wayne County (Detroit), 90 percent in Baltimore, and 85 percent in Cook County (Chicago) and Kings County (Seattle), but only 14 percent in Maricopa County (Phoenix) and 9 percent in Honolulu.[54]

Many of these defendants had prior experiences with the justice system. For example, about one-fourth (24%) were on probation or on parole, and another 12 percent were on pretrial release status at the time of their most recent arrest. These figures varied by offense, with 39 percent of the drug defendants having an active status within the criminal

TABLE 10.8   Court Commitments to State Prisons Relative to Adult Arrests, 1980 and 1992

	1980	1992	PERCENTAGE CHANGE	NUMBER PER 1,000 ARRESTS	
				1980	*1992*
VIOLENT OFFENSES					
Murder	11,300	10,000	–12	621	521
Rape	4,900	7,400	51	182	224
Other sexual assault	3,400	11,700	244	61	132
Robbery	25,000	33,400	34	245	262
Aggravated assault	10,600	25,100	137	45	58
PROPERTY OFFENSES					
Burglary	30,200	44,500	47	107	159
Larceny/theft	10,100	30,100	198	14	29
Motor vehicle theft	3,000	9,400	213	40	85
Fraud	6,800	12,400	82	19	24
DRUG OFFENSES	8,900	102,000	1,046	19	104
WEAPONS	1,600	8,000	400	11	43

Source: Beck and Brien (1995), p. 55.

justice system at the time of their arrest, while 45 percent of those were charged with public-order offenses. Also, about two-thirds (68%) had at least one prior arrest, with 23 percent having had ten or more prior arrests. The most likely persons to have had prior arrests were drug offenders and public-order offenders (72%). Just over half (56%) had at least one prior felony arrest, with about one-fifth (22%) having had five or more prior felony arrests. Moreover, over half (55%) had had at least one prior conviction, with 38 percent having prior felony convictions (mostly of a nonviolent nature). Clearly these defendants were no strangers to the criminal justice system.[55]

The majority of these defendants (62%) were released pending the final disposition of their cases. Of these, the most common form of release was on their own recognizance and through some form of financial release (surety bond, etc.). The median bail amount for those released was $5,000; the median for those detained was $15,000. Most of the defendants who were released were set free within twenty-four hours (51%), with more than three-fourths (79%) being released within one week. Most (76%) of those released made all of their court appearances. Those charged with violent crimes were the *most likely* to make all of their court appearances (85%); drug defendants were the *least likely* (71%). Of those who were rearrested while on release status, only 15 percent were rearrested for a new offense.[56]

A total of 72 percent of these defendants were ultimately convicted—61 percent on a felony charge and 11 percent on a misdemeanor charge. Not surprisingly, few of those convicted ever went to trial (4% of those convicted of a felony and none of those convicted of a misdemeanor). Of those not convicted, most had their cases dismissed. It is interesting to note that those *charged with violent offenses were the most likely to have their cases dismissed* (36%). Also not surprisingly, more than three-fourths (79%) of those who were detained were convicted, compared to only 67 percent of those released; 84 percent of the drug defendants who were detained were convicted, compared to 69 percent of the violent offenders.[57]

The largest percentage of convictions were for drug offenses (31%); property crimes ranked second (accounting for 29% of the total); violent crimes ranked third (16%). In terms of sentencing (more on sentencing below), those convicted of violent crime were the most likely to be sent to prison (76%), with public-order offenders a close second (71%) and drug offenders third (68%, with 75% of those convicted of trafficking sent to prison). All together, two-thirds (67%) of those convicted were sentenced to prison. Not surprisingly, violent offenders received the harshest sentences (median of 72 months); the median sentence for drug offenders was 36 months (48 months for traffickers). Unfortunately, no cross-tabulations are provided for race and sentencing in this study, but given data presented in other tables in this chapter, we know that race is crucial.[58]

If this is not enough evidence of racial bias, consider the following data. Surveys of illegal drug use have consistently shown that there are few if any differences between blacks and whites. In fact, one of the most recent surveys found that the greatest usage is among whites.[59] Nevertheless, African Americans are about eight times more likely to be sentenced for a drug crime than whites![60]

From this discussion we can conclude that social class and race do play important roles in the processing of criminal cases, at the sentencing stage and at all other stages. Sometimes, as these studies show, the importance of social class and race is not always obvious to the ordinary observer, but in the case of white-collar and corporate crimes it is more obvious.

The next topic to be considered is alternatives to a sentence to prison or jail.

ALTERNATIVES TO INCARCERATION

There are a number of alternatives to incarceration that are available to the courts. The most popular is probation. Keep in mind the fact that the purpose of these alternatives is diversion. **Diversion** is "an attempt to divert, or channel out" offenders from the criminal or juvenile justice system—in other words, to get offenders out of the system as early as possible.[61] This strategy is based on the belief that justice system processing often does more harm than good. The basis of the argument is that courts may inadvertently stigmatize some offenders (especially young offenders) for relatively petty acts that are best handled outside the court system or ignored entirely. Diversion programs are designed, in part, to deal with the problem of overcrowded juvenile detention centers, jails, and prisons, so that greater attention can be devoted to more serious offenders.

Diversion has been practiced since the beginning of the criminal justice system, in that most of the cases processed never make it to jail or prison. Some alternative sentence is usually imposed. The most common alternative has always been probation.

Probation

A sentence of probation suspends an offender's sentence to prison or jail and permits the offender to spend a certain amount of time in the community "under supervision" of the department of probation. If probation is granted, the defendant must meet certain conditions, such as keeping a job and reporting periodically to a probation officer. The term of probation varies and depends on several factors, but after this term has ended, the defendant is discharged and is considered to have "done his time." But if at any time during the probationary period the defendant violates a law or the conditions of probation, the defendant can be sentenced to the original term in prison.

Suppose the sentence is from one to five years in prison, but that sentence is suspended and the offender is given two years on probation. If the offender successfully completes the two years without committing new crimes and without violating any of the conditions of probation, then the overall sentence is completed and the person is free.

Among the most controversial conditions of probation is urine testing. A national survey found that 27 percent of the motions to revoke probation brought to the court by a probation offender were for failing a drug test; 20 percent were for not participating in a required treatment program; 18.5 percent for "absconding" (e.g., leaving the state or county without permission); 12 percent for committing a new felony and another 4 percent for committing a misdemeanor; 10 percent for "failure to report"; and 8.5 percent for other technical violations.[62] It should be noted that probation officers have a great deal of discretion as to whether to report violations if they are known. Probation officers range from relatively lenient "social worker" types who go out of their way to help an offender to "law and order" types who see themselves as cops and like to brag about the weapons they carry and the number of probation violators they have "nabbed."

Probation has its origins in English common law and is related to the practice known as *benefit of clergy,* which originated in the twelfth century (as noted in Chapter 9). Under this system, a clergyman convicted of a crime could be released under the supervision of the church. Later this practice included those who were literate (a small minority at first).

The origins of probation can be traced to the efforts of a man named John Augustus, a Boston shoemaker. During the 1840s he volunteered to take on the responsibility of supervising offenders in the community as an alternative to sending them to prison or jail. In 1878 Massachusetts passed a law authorizing the use of probation, and by 1917 the probation system was used in twenty-one states. By 1925 probation for juvenile offenders was available in every state, but it was not available to adults until 1956.

The practice of placing offenders on probation ostensibly arose for purely humanitarian reasons. However, the continued growth of the use of probation, especially in recent years, can be attributed to factors other than humanitarian reasons. Much has to do with monetary concerns. It costs far less to supervise an offender on probation than in jail or prison. For instance, the average cost of probation is around $850 per year per offender, versus between $20,000 and $40,000 to house someone in prison for one year.[63]

In recent years the number of offenders placed on probation has soared. For example, in 1980 the number on probation at year-end reached 1,118,097; in 1998 that number had increased by 206 percent to about 3.4 million.[64] A detailed look at those on probation in 1997 shows a much larger percentage of white offenders than black offenders on probation. Out of a total of 2,149,900 blacks in jail, in prison, on parole, or on probation, about 48 percent were on probation; the comparable percentage for whites was 63. Also, probation is more often the sentence given to female offenders—in this survey, 76 percent compared to 54 percent for males.[65]

No state allows probation as an alternative sentence for first-degree murder, but most states allow probation for almost all other crimes. Several states, however, have a list of crimes for which probation cannot be granted (e.g., Illinois, New York, and California have such lists for several crimes). In 1997, out of 3.2 million offenders placed on probation, almost half (45%) had felony convictions; another 24 percent were convicted of misdemeanors. What is perhaps most noteworthy about this survey is the fact that for 514,082 offenders the offense was either unknown or not reported by the agencies participating in the survey.[66]

Probation officers are often seen as performing the duties of social worker—they become a "broker" of services. An officer might help an offender get a job, find housing, and obtain various treatment services (e.g., drug treatment). What usually happens is that some sort of "risk classification" scheme is devised in order to assess the needs of the client, in addition to the degree of risk he or she poses to the community at large. In some communities wracked by violence, gangs, drugs, and general urban decay, the probation officer is tempted to remain in his or her office instead of making "house calls." This reluctance may be understandable given the sometimes dangerous conditions, but very often the probation officer is the only person standing between an offender and the temptations to return to crime.

Probation has become highly bureaucratized. Nearly every court system—both adult and juvenile—has a probation department connected to it in some way. Caseloads are large. The average probation officer supervises between 50 and 100 offenders, but sometimes the number reaches 300 or more.[67] Many who engage in this line of work are overwhelmed by the responsibilities and care little about the persons they supervise. In fact, the "supervision" is often little more than surveillance consisting of a few phone calls. In many instances probation officers follow this motto: "Trail 'em, Surveil 'em, Nail 'em, and Jail 'em."[68] This approach leads to a high rate of *revocation* and a return to the original sentence to prison or jail. Given that there are so many conditions of probation, this outcome is not surprising.

One of the most popular variations of probation is *intensive supervision probation*. It differs from regular probation in the intensity of the supervision. During normal probation, the probation officer sees the offender perhaps once a month, if at all. Most of the time the offender merely has to report in once a month or more, depending on the conditions of probation. Intensive supervision probation places several restrictions on the offender, such as curfews, "house arrest" (staying at home unless going to work or school), electronic monitoring, frequent drug testing, and frequent visits by the probation officer.[69]

There is a higher failure rate among offenders placed on intensive supervision, but not because these offenders are more dangerous or more prone to commit crime. The main reason for the higher rate is that with more frequent contact between the probationer and the probation officer and more frequent drug testing and more rules and regulations, the likelihood of "detecting" a violation increases. And that is exactly what happens.[70]

Fines

Fines have been one of the most common forms of punishment throughout history. Fines are usually levied in misdemeanor cases (especially traffic cases) and for white-collar and corporate crimes. Rarely is fining used in felony cases, although the statutes often allow for it as an alternative. Crimes committed by individuals from class backgrounds similar to legislators' and judges' are the most likely to have fines levied as punishment; crimes ("felonies") committed by individuals of other class backgrounds rarely are fineable offenses and usually result in the incarceration of the offender.[71]

It is not known exactly how much money is collected in fines during the course of a year, but an early-1980s study estimated that more than $1 billion in fines are levied in any given year, so this has become big business for the courts.[72] Fines are used in virtually every country as the preferred sentence. Given the punitive nature of the United States, it is not surprising that the United States almost stands alone in demanding some sort of prison or jail sentence along with a fine and is the least likely to hand out fines as a percentage of all convictions. Scandinavian countries and Germany levy fines in as much as 90 percent of all cases.[73]

Restitution and Community Service

Restitution and community service are among the oldest sentences in the history of the criminal justice system. They date as far back as the Code of Hammurabi (around 1760 B.C.) and are mentioned in the Roman Law of the Twelve Tables.[74] The idea is rather simple: such sentences require the offender to do something *for the community*—in many cases this includes for the victims—rather than the community or state doing something *to the offender.* Restitution could be in the form of direct payment to persons victimized by the crime (e.g., the theft of money) or direct service to the community. Community service usually consists of some type of work, such as cutting and pruning trees, painting park benches, removing graffiti, and picking up trash. Sometimes offenders with special skills—carpentry, electrical, and so on—are used for special projects. Evaluations claim a great deal of success and a high rate of compliance among offenders.[75]

Community service is related to *restorative justice,* an attempt to *restore* that which was taken away by the criminal act. The goal is to restore the well-being of the victim and of the larger community while simultaneously seeing that the offender takes responsibility for his or her actions. Sometimes this is done through face-to-face meetings between offenders and their victims. Such a meeting, even one between someone who murdered a loved one and a member of the victim's family, often serves to bring closure.

Home Confinement/House Arrest

Another alternative to incarceration that shows much promise is **home confinement,** more popularly known as *house arrest* (the popularity of this term reflects the punitive nature of American society). Under this plan, an offender sentenced to a certain period of probation must remain at home unless he or she is going to work or school or somewhere very specific. Usually some sort of *electronic surveillance* is used. Some means of surveillance, such as an ankle bracelet, are literally attached to the offender. In other instances, the probation officer activates a special telephone that automatically dials the offender's number at certain times, and the offender has to pick up the phone after so many rings.

Some question the constitutionality of home confinement, saying that it may violate the Fourth Amendment's protection against unreasonable searches and seizures. At the very least it is at odds with the expectation that a person's home is private. One critic wonders whether we are moving toward a "maximum-security society."[76] Some serious problems are associated with the monitoring devices themselves. Some report that an offender is at home when he or she really is away, and vice versa. Also, what is to prevent acquaintances (including other offenders) from visiting the person's home, and what is to prevent the offender from committing a crime while in the home (spouse and child abuse)? Not surprisingly, the failure rate has been high for this program.[77]

Drug and Alcohol Treatment

Because so many offenders have serious drug or alcohol problems that bring them into contact with the criminal justice system, one popular alternative sentence is ordering the offender to get treatment. As a condition of probation, for instance, an offender may be ordered to attend AA or NA meetings, in addition to enrollment in special drug or alcohol treatment programs within the community.

A recent trend involves *drug courts,* which oversee court-ordered treatment in a community drug treatment program. The offender is assigned a primary counselor, a specific treatment plan is developed, and frequent appearances in drug court are required to help monitor the offender's progress. Whether this will be successful remains to be seen, especially in light of some research that questions claims of success.

Initial reports about the much-heralded Dade County Circuit Court (Miami) claimed success. It was said that offenders sentenced to this drug court were less likely to be rearrested (or, if rearrested, had longer times between court appearances and rearrest) and were less likely to be incarcerated. Similar findings were reported for the Broward County (Florida) drug court.[78] However, more sophisticated analyses produced different results. Actual participation in drug courts has been rather poor. For instance, only 41 percent of those eligible for a Washington, D.C., program attended. Completion of the program takes much longer than originally anticipated (cases were left open for eleven months, rather than the original goal of six). Further, many people drop out of the program.[79]

The jury is still out on drug courts. Any type of program that keeps offenders with drug problems out of prison is a necessary step, given the almost total lack of drug treatment programs in prison. Recently, California voters passed Proposition 36, which mandates that in certain instances drug offenders be sentenced to drug treatment rather than prison.

Boot Camps

Given the punitive nature of American society and the attractiveness of military-style discipline, it is not surprising that boot camps were seen as an attractive alternative to incarceration in prison or jail.

They emerged in the 1980s with much hype and fanfare. Both law enforcement officials and politicians jumped on the bandwagon, viewing boot camps as a "magic bullet" that would "shape up" young offenders. By 1996 there were boot camps in thirty-two states plus the federal prison system.[80]

Boot camps were designed for short periods of incarceration, around six months, in a facility separate from a regular prison. The inmates were relatively young and inexperienced minor offenders. They participated in intense physical, educational, and drug abuse programs, followed by a period of intense supervision within the community. Most of these programs included military drill, as in regular military boot camps.[81]

The image was a popular one: inmates forced to rise early in the morning and to adhere to a rigid military-type training regimen led by a stereotypical mean-faced drill instructor who was to instill discipline and respect for authority. The image reflected society's need to inflict some degree of pain while at the same time developing character and discipline.[82]

The research on boot camps is clear: they are almost total failures when it comes to reducing crime. There is evidence that offenders do make some improvements *while in the program* (more favorable attitudes compared to those in prisons).[83] But in general, the research concludes that most boot camps "have no discernible effect on subsequent reoffending."[84] Among the reasons for this lack of success is the fact that up to one-third of offenders never complete the program. Another reason is the tendency of judges to engage in **net widening**—putting in the program extremely low-risk offenders who could just as easily benefit from other, less dramatic programs.

The most important reason why this type of program fails is that it ignores one of the leading principles behind real military boot camps: the promise of a reward at the end. Military boot camps hold out the promise of a career in the military, opportunities to advance in rank, education and training, and other benefits. In contrast, most boot camp graduates are simply released back into the community with few or no employment or educational prospects.

Another problem is the tendency of some drill instructors to go overboard in their treatment of inmates. There have been numerous incidents of verbal and physical abuse within boot camps. Physical abuse has led to inmates' deaths. In one instance the FBI was called in to investigate.[85] A case in Arizona involved a boot camp director who was arrested on murder and child abuse charges following the death of a 14-year-old who collapsed and died in 116-degree heat. Two other boot camp workers were arrested, one charged with "spanking, stomping, beating and whipping more than 14 children."[86]

SUMMARY

In this chapter we considered the final act in the formal criminal justice process—sentencing. We described various justifications for punishment (retribution, incapacitation, deterrence, and rehabilitation) and explained several sentencing options. The most repressive of these is the death penalty, which, like all other aspects of the criminal justice system, is tinged with racism. The impact of race on sentencing is seen most clearly in the "war on drugs," which most often targets African Americans and other minorities.

KEY TERMS

boot camp   260
concurrent sentence   243
consecutive sentence   243
definite sentence   244
determinate sentencing   244
deterrence   241
diversion   256
Furman v. Georgia   249

general deterrence   241
Gregg v. Georgia   249
home confinement   259
indefinite sentence   243
isolation/incapacitation   241
lex talionis   241
McClaskey v. Kemp   250
net widening   260

presentence investigation (PSI)
   report   242
rehabilitation   241
restitution   241
special deterrence   241
wergeld   241

NOTES

1. Barnes, H. E. *The Story of Punishment.* Montclair, NJ: Patterson Smith, 1972, ch. 2 (originally published in 1930); Barnes, H. E., and N. K. Teeters. *New Horizons in Criminology.* Englewood Cliffs, NJ: Prentice-Hall, 1951, pp. 287–288.

2. Wilson, J. Q. *Thinking about Crime.* New York: Vintage Books, 1975; van Den Haag, E. *Punishing Criminals.* New York: Basic Books, 1975; Bennett, W. J., J. J. DiIulio Jr., and J. P. Walters. *Body Count.* New York: Simon & Schuster, 1996.

3. For a discussion of this and related questions see Shelden, R. G. *Controlling the Dangerous Classes: A Critical Introduction to the History of Criminal Justice.* Boston: Allyn and Bacon, 2001.

4. Neubauer, D. *America's Courts and the Criminal Justice System* (7th ed.). Belmont, CA: Wadsworth, 2002, pp. 390–392.

5. Chambliss, W. J., and R. Seidman. *Law, Order and Power* (2nd ed.). Reading, MA: Addison-Wesley, 1982, pp. 447–472.

6. Neubauer, *America's Courts and the Criminal Justice System,* pp. 417–418.

7. These studies cover more than thirty years. See, for instance, Carter, R. M., and L. T. Wilkins. "Some Factors in Sentencing Policy." In R. M. Carter and L. T. Wilkins (eds.), *Probation, Parole and Community Corrections* (2nd ed.). New York: Wiley, 1976; Campbell, C., C. McCoy, and C. Osigweh. "The Influence of Probation Recommendations on Sentencing Decisions and Their Predictive Accuracy." *Federal Probation* 54:13–21 (1990).

8. Brown, W. B. "The Subjective Nature of Decision Makers in the Domain of Objective Sentence Processing." Unpublished doctoral diss., University of Nevada–Las Vegas, 1992; see also Rosencrance, J. "Maintaining the Myth of Individualized Justice: Probation Presentence Reports." *Justice Quarterly* 5:235 (1988).

9. Scheb, J. M., and J. M. Scheb II. *Criminal Law and Procedure.* St. Paul, MN: West, 1989, pp. 544–545.

10. Walker, S. *Sense and Nonsense about Crime and Drugs* (5th ed.). Belmont, CA: Wadsworth, 2001. The father of Polly Klass, Marc Klass, publicly criticized this type of legislation. He formed the nonprofit KlassKids Foundation, which, among other goals, seeks means of prevention rather than merely harsh reaction. He wrote the foreword to Peter Elikann's critique of the current "demonization" of children as "superpredators" (Elikann, P. *Superpredators: The Demonization of Our Children by the Law.* Reading, MA: Perseus, 1999).

11. *Weems v. United States,* 217 U.S. 349 (1910).

12. *Rummel v. Estelle,* 568 F. 2d 1193 (5th Cir. 1978).

13. Ibid.

14. Ibid.

15. Weinstein, H. "3-Strikes Sentence Is Ruled Cruel." *Los Angeles Times,* November 4, 2001.

16. Stolzenberg, L., and S. J. D'Alessio. "Three Strikes and You're Out: The Impact of California's New Mandatory Sentencing Law on Serious Crime Rates." *Crime and Delinquency* 43:4 (1997); Turner, M. G., J. L. Sundt, B. K. Applegate, and F. T. Cullen. "Three Strikes and You're Out Legislation: A National Assessment." *Federal Probation* 59:16–35 (1995); W. Dickey. "The Impact of 'Three Strikes and You're Out' Laws: What Have We Learned." *Overcrowded Times* 7(5) (October 1996).

17. Schiraldi, V., and T. Ambrosio. "Striking Out: the Crime Control Impact of Three Strikes Laws." *Justice Policy Institute* (March 1997); Dickey, W., and P. S. Hollenhorst. "Three-Strikes Laws: Massive Impact in California and Georgia, Little Elsewhere." *Overcrowded Times* 9(6) (December 1998); Males, M., D. Macallair, and K. Taqi-Eddin. "California's Three-Strikes Law Ineffective." *Overcrowded Times* 10(4) (August 1999).

18. One example is in the field of education. See Spring, J., *Education and the Rise of the Corporate State.* Boston: Beacon Press, 1972, esp. pp. 95–96. As this relates to the modern police, see Shelden, *Controlling the Dangerous Classes,* ch. 2.

19. Cole, D. *No Equal Justice: Race and Class in the American Criminal Justice System.* New York: New Press, 1999; Parenti, C. *Lockdown America: Police and Prisons in the Age of Crisis.* New York: Verso, 1999; Miller, J. G. *Search and Destroy: African-American Males in the Criminal Justice System.* Cambridge: Cambridge University Press, 1996.

20. Wilkins, L. T., J. M. Kress, D. M. Gottfredson, J. C. Calpin, and A. M. Gelman. Sentencing Guidelines: Structuring Judicial Discretion. Washington, DC: U.S. Government Printing Office, 1978; Bureau of Justice Assistance. National Assessment of Structured Sentencing. Washington, DC: U.S. Department of Justice, 1996.

21. Petersilia, J., and S. Turner. "Guideline-Based Justice Prediction and Racial Minorities." In N. Morris and M. Tonry (eds.), *Crime and Justice* (vol. 15). Chicago: University of Chicago Press, 1987; Kramer, J. H., and R. L. Lubitz. "Pennsylvania's Sentencing Reforms: The Impact of Commission-Established Guidelines." *Crime and Delinquency* 31:481–500 (1985); Tonry, M. "Sentencing Commissions and Their Guidelines." in M. Tonry (ed.), *Crime and Justice: A Review of Research* (vol. 17). Chicago: University of Chicago Press, 1993; Martin, S. E., "The Politics of Sentencing Reform: Sentencing Guidelines in Pennsylvania and Minnesota." In A. Blumstein, J. Cohen, S. Martin, and M. Tonry (eds.), *Research and Sentencing: The Search for Reform* (vol. 2). Washington, DC: National Academy Press, 1983.

22. Farnworth, M., R. Teske, and G. Thurman. "Ethnic, Racial and Minority Disparity in Felony Court Processing." In M. J. Lynch and E. B. Patterson (eds.), *Race and Criminal Justice.* Albany, NY: Harrow and Heston, 1991.

23. Levin, D., P. Langan, and J. Brown. *State Court Sentencing of Convicted Felons, 1996.* Washington, DC: U.S. Department of Justice, Bureau of Justice Statistics, 2000.

24. The following sources are used in the following discussion: Hawkins, D. F. "Which Way toward Equality? Dilemmas and Paradoxes in Public Policies Affecting Crime and Punishment." In C. Herring (ed.), *African Americans and the Public Agenda.* Thousand Oaks, CA: Sage, 1997; Radelet, M., and G. Pierce. "Race and Prosecutorial Discretion in Homicide Cases." *Law and Society Review* 19:587–621 (1985); Chiricos, T. G., and W. D. Bales. "Unemployment and Punishment: An Empirical Assessment." *Criminology* 29:701–724 (1991); La Free, G. *Rape and Criminal Justice: The Social Construction of Sexual Assault.* Belmont, CA: Wadsworth, 1989; Spohn, C., J. Gruhl, and S. Welch. "The Impact of Ethnicity and Gender of Defendant on the Decision to Reject or Dismiss Felony Charges." *Criminology* 25: 175–191 (1987); D'Alession, S. J. and L. Stolzenberg. "Socioeconomic Status and Sentencing of the Traditional Offender." *Journal of Criminal Justice* 21: 71–74 (1993); Nienstedt, B. C., M. Zatz, and T. Epperlein. "Court Processing and Sentencing of Drunk Drivers." *Journal of Quantitative Criminology* 4: 39–59 (1988); Nelson, J. F. "Hidden Disparities in Case Processing: New York State, 1985–1986." *Journal of Criminal Justice* 20: 181–200 (1992); Crawford, C., T. Chiricos, and G. Kleck. "Race, Racial Threat, and Sentencing of Habitual Offenders." *Criminology* 36: 481–511 (1998); Lauritsen, J. L., and R. J. Sampson. "Minorities, Crime and Criminal Justice." In M. Tonry (ed.), *The Handbook of Crime and Punishment.* New York: Oxford University Press, 1998; Peterson, R. D., and J.

Hagan. "Changing Conceptions of Race: Towards an Account of Anomalous Findings of Sentencing Research." *American Sociological Review* 49: 56–70 (1984).

25. See Chambliss, W. J. "Crime Control and Ethnic Minorities: Legitimizing Racial Oppression by Creating Moral Panics." In D. F. Hawkins (ed.), *Ethnicity, Race, and Crime.* Albany: State University of New York Press, 1995; and Chambliss, W. J. *Power, Politics and Crime.* Boulder, CO: Westview Press, 1999, for discussion of this problem.

26. The following discussion and all statistics cited are drawn from the following sources: Sellin, T. "Executions in the U.S." In J. T. Sellin (ed.), *Capital Punishment.* New York: Harper & Row, 1967; Bedau, H. A. (ed.). *The Death Penalty in America* (4th ed.). Garden City, NY: Doubleday, 1996; Haas, K., and J. Inciardi (eds.). *Challenging Capital Punishment: Legal and Social Science Approaches.* Newbury Park, CA: Sage, 1988; Radlett, M. (ed.). *Facing the Death Penalty: Essays on a Cruel and Unusual Punishment.* Philadelphia: Temple University Press, 1989; "Capital Punishment USA—An Overview" (online: www. geocities.com/trctlll/overview); "Death Row Inmates by State" (online: www.deathpenalty-info.org/DRowInfo); "Execution Update" and "Death Row Statistics" (online: www.deathpenaltyinfo.org).

27. This is according to an Associated Press story dated October 30, 1999. This story also indicated that the Supreme Court was to hear arguments concerning four death penalty cases, including one claiming that death by the electric chair constitutes cruel and unusual punishment, in violation of the Eighth Amendment. The eighty-three who had been executed as of this date marked the highest ever for one year since 1954.

28. Mays, G. L., and L. T. Winfree Jr. *Contemporary Corrections.* Belmont, CA: Wadsworth, 1998, pp. 80–81.

29. Walker, S., C. Spohn, and M. DeLone. *The Color of Justice: Race, Ethnicity, and Crime in America* (2nd ed.). Belmont, CA: Wadsworth, 2000, p. 232.

30. Balbus, D. C., G. Woodworth, and C. A. Pulaski. *Equal Justice and the Death Penalty: A Legal and Empirical Analysis.* Boston: Northeastern University Press, 1990; Gross, S. R., and R. Mauro. *Death and Discrimination: Racial Disparities in Capital Sentencing.* Boston: Northeastern University Press, 1989.

31. Johnson, G. B. "The Negro and Crime." *The Annals* 217: 93–104 (1941); see also Garfinkel, H. "Research Note on Inter- and Intra-Racial Homicides." *Social Forces* 27: 369–381 (1949).

32. Wolfgang, M. E., A. Kelly, and H. C. Nolde. "Comparisons of the Executed and the Commuted among Admissions to Death Row." In M. E. Wolfgang, L. Savitz, and N. Johnston (eds.), *The Sociology of Punishment and Correction.* New York: Wiley, 1962.

33. Johnson, E. H. "Selective Factors in Capital Punishment." *Social Forces* 36: 165–169 (1957).

34. Wolfgang, M., and M. Riedel. "Race, Judicial Discretion, and the Death Penalty." In W. J. Chambliss (ed.), *Criminal Law in Action.* New York: Wiley, 1975, pp. 371–372.

35. Harries, K., and D. Cheatwood. *The Geography of Execution: The Capital Punishment Quagmire in America.* Lanham, MD: Rowman and Littlefield, 1997; International Commission of Jurists. "Administration of the Death Penalty in the United States." *Human Rights Quarterly* 19: 165–213 (1997).

36. Barkan, S. B., and S. F. Cohen. "Racial Prejudice and Support for the Death Penalty by Whites." *Journal of Research in Crime and Delinquency* 31: 202–209 (1994).

37. Radelet, M. L. "Executions of Whites for Crimes against Blacks: Exceptions to the Rule?" *The Sociological Quarterly* 30: 529–544 (1989).

38. Kennedy, R. *Race, Crime and the Law.* New York: Vintage, 1997, p. 336.

39. Walker et al., *The Color of Justice,* p. 252.

40. Cole, *No Equal Justice,* p. 135.

41. Ibid.

42. Ibid., p. 137.

43. Quoted in Kennedy, *Race, Crime and the Law,* p. 346.

44. Radelet, M. L., H. A. Bedau, and C. E. Putnam. *In Spite of Innocence.* Boston: Northeastern University Press, 1992.

45. Liebman, J. S., J. Fagan, S. Rifkind, and V. West. "A Broken System: Error Rates in Capital Cases, 1973–1995." *The Justice Project.* New York: Columbia University (online: www.TheJusticeProject.org); Weinstein, H. "Inmate Seeks to Halt Execution for DNA Tests." *Los Angeles Times,* April 28, 2002; Weinstein, H. "Md. Governor Calls Halt to Executions." *Los Angeles Times,* May 10, 2002.

46. Frazier, C. E., and E. W. Bock. "Effects of Court Officials on Sentence Severity." *Criminology* 20: 257–272 (1982).

47. Baum, *Smoke and Mirrors;* Shelden, *Controlling the Dangerous Classes;* Shelden, R. G., and W. B. Brown. "The Crime Control Industry and the Management of the Surplus Population." *Critical Criminology* 8 (Autumn 2000).

48. Maguire, K., and A. L. Pastore (eds.). *Sourcebook of Criminal Justice Statistics—1995.* Washington, DC: U.S. Department of Justice, Bureau of Justice Statistics, 1996, p. 550.

49. Currie, E. *Crime and Punishment in America.* New York: Metropolitan Books, 1998, pp. 12–13.

50. Maguire and Pastore, *Sourcebook of Criminal Justice Statistics—1995,* pp. 468, 472, 576.

51. Beck, A. J., and P. M. Brien. "Trends in the U.S. Correctional Populations: Recent Findings from the Bureau of Justice Statistics." In K. C. Haas and G. P. Alpert (eds.), *The Dilemmas of Corrections* (3rd ed.). Project Heights, IL: Waveland Press, 1995, p. 55.

52. Reaves, B. A. *Felony Defendants in Large Urban Counties, 1994.* Washington, DC: U.S. Department of Justice, Bureau of Justice Statistics, 1998.

53. Baum, *Smoke and Mirrors,* p. 249.

54. Reaves, *Felony Defendants in Large Urban Counties, 1994,* p. 43.

55. Ibid., pp. 8–14.

56. Ibid., p. 19.

57. Ibid., p. 24.

58. Ibid.

59. Donziger, S. *The Real War on Crime.* New York: HarperCollins, 1996, p. 118. In the June 6, 2000, edition of the *International Herald Tribune,* it was reported that whites are five times more likely than blacks to use drugs (cited in *Index on Censorship,* October 2000, p. 114).

60. Further detail is provided in Shelden, R. G., W. B. Brown, and S. Listwan. "The New American Apartheid: The Incarceration of African-Americans." In S. L. Browning, R. R. Miller, and R. D. Coates (eds.), *The Common Good: A Critical Examination of Law and Social Control.* Charlotte, NC: Carolina Academic Press, 2002.

61. Bynum, J. E., and W. E. Thompson. *Juvenile Delinquency: A Sociological Approach* (3rd ed.). Boston: Allyn and Bacon, 1996, p. 430; Walker, *Sense and Nonsense about Crime and Drugs,* p. 213.

62. Burke, P. *Policy-Driven Responses to Probation and Parole Violations.* Washington, DC: National Institute of Corrections, 1997.

63. Donziger, *The Real War on Crime,* p. 190; Austin and Irwin, *It's about Time,* p. 223.

64. Austin and Irwin, ibid., p. 4.

65. U.S. Department of Justice, Bureau of Justice Statistics. *Correctional Populations in the United States, 1997.* Washington, DC: U.S. Department of Justice, November 2000, p. 2.

66. Ibid., p. 36.

67. Donziger, *The Real War on Crime,* p. 191; Petersilia, J. "Probation and Parole." In M. Tonry (ed.), *Handbook of Crime and Punishment.* New York: Oxford University Press.

68. Miller, J. G. *Search and Destroy: African-American Males in the Criminal Justice System.* Cambridge: Cambridge University Press, 1996, p. 131.

69. Gendreau, P., F. T. Cullen, and J. Bonta. "Intensive Rehabilitation Supervision: The Next Generation in Community Corrections?" *Federal Probation* 58: 72–78 (1994).

70. Petersilia, J., and S. Turner. *Intensive Supervision for High Risk Probationers: Findings From Three California Experiments.* Santa Monica, CA: Rand Corporation, 1990.

71. Shelden, *Controlling the Dangerous Classes.*

72. Quoted in Cole, G., and C. Smith. *The American System of Criminal Justice* (9th ed.). Belmont, CA: Wadsworth, 2001, p. 471.

73. Tonry, M. "Intermediate Sanctions." In M. Tonry (ed.), *Crime and Justice* (vol. 20). Chicago: University of Chicago Press, 1996.

74. Shelden, *Controlling the Dangerous Classes,* ch. 1.

75. Tonry, M. *Sentencing Matters.* New York: Oxford University Press, 1996.

76. Corbett, R., and G. Marx. "Critique: No Soul in the New Machine: Technofallacies in the Electronic Monitoring Movement." *Justice Quarterly* 8: 399–414 (1991).

77. Clear, T., and A. Braga. "Community Corrections." In J. Q. Wilson and J. Petersilia (eds.), *Crime.* San Francisco: ICS Press, 1995, pp. 421–444. For a more general critique of surveillance see Staples, W. G. *The Culture of Surveillance: Discipline and Social Control in the United States.* New York: St. Martin's Press, 1997.

78. Goldkamp, J., and D. Weiland. "Assessing the Impact of Dade County's Felony Drug Court." *National Institute of Justice Research in Brief.* Washington, DC: U.S. Department of Justice, December 1993; Terry, W. C. "Felony and Misdemeanor Rearrests of the First Year Cohort of the Drug Court in Broward County, Florida." Paper presented at the American Academy of Criminal Justice Sciences, Las Vegas, 1996.

79. Harrell, A., S. Cavanagh, and J. Roman. "Evaluation of the D.C. Superior Court Drug Intervention Program." Washington, DC: National Institute of Justice, 2000.

80. Walker, *Sense and Nonsense about Crime and Drugs,* pp. 222–224.

81. Ibid.

82. Austin and Irwin, *It's about Time,* p. 167.

83. Mackenzie, D. L., and J. W. Shaw. "Inmate Adjustment and Change during Shock Incarceration: The Impact of Correctional Boot Camp Programs." *Justice Quarterly* 7: 125–150 (1990).

84. Walker, *Sense and Nonsense about Crime and Drugs,* p. 224,

85. Austin and Irwin, *It's about Time,* p. 168.

86. "Boot Camp Chief Held in Boy's Death." *Los Angeles Times,* February 16, 2002.

CHAPTER ELEVEN

THE MODERN PRISON SYSTEM

Pelican Bay State Prison

When you journey across the American landscape, you cannot help but see prisons and jails just about everywhere. Because these institutions are seemingly everywhere, you might take for granted that they are inevitable, a natural by-product of the existence of crime in American society. However, this is not the case. The prison as we know it today is of recent origin, taking root after the American Revolution but growing at a very slow pace. Before we explore the modern American prison system, a brief look at history is in order.[1] We trace the development of the American prison system through six periods: (1) 1790–1830: early American prisons; (2) 1830–1870: the Pennsylvania and Auburn systems; (3) 1870–1900: reformatories; (4) 1900–1946: the "Big House"; (5) 1946–1980: the "correctional institution"; (6) since 1980: "warehousing."[2]

EARLY AMERICAN PRISONS, 1790–1830

The use of imprisonment as punishment did not occur until the late eighteenth century in America. Throughout colonial America the most common form of punishment was a combination of banishment and various forms of public punishments, such as the stocks, the pillory, and branding. The primary method of social control in such a society was rather informal, with local families, the community, and the church providing most forms of punishment.

Shortly after the end of the American Revolution a group of prominent citizens, such as Benjamin Franklin, Benjamin Rush, and William Bradford, came together to update the criminal code of 1718. The new law, passed in 1786, authorized a penalty of "hard labor, publicly and disgracefully imposed" for certain crimes.[3] Prisoners were sentenced to perform hard labor in the city streets. However, convicts began to draw crowds of sympathetic people. Shortly thereafter, a group calling itself the Philadelphia Society for Alleviating the Miseries of Public Prisons amended the law and in 1788 suggested that sentences be more private and even called for *solitary confinement* within the confines of the old Walnut Street Jail.[4]

The **Walnut Street Jail** became the first *state* prison in America, and it was part of a much larger effort to create a powerful and centralized state apparatus. This state apparatus not only helped secure the new order but also helped perpetuate the existing class divisions. Takagi states that "The success of the Revolution at home was brought about by the creation of a class divided society based upon private property and the ratification of the new Constitution was to guarantee the privileges and power of the bourgeoisie."[5] In fact, James Madison made it quite clear when he wrote in *The Federalist* that "The diversity in the faculties of men, from which the rights of property flow, is not less an insuperable obstacle to a uniformity of interests. The protection of these faculties is the first object of government." Continuing, Madison argues that one of the duties of a government or state is to regulate various interests, including "a landed interest, a manufacturing interest, a mercantile interest, a moneyed interest, with many lesser interests."[6]

There were, indeed, class divisions at the end of the eighteenth century. And there was a great deal of disorder, stemming mainly from economic crises and general uncertainty over the future of American society. Shays's Rebellion was one among several popular revolts of the time against the existing form of government and economy.[7] It also marked the beginning of the newly emerging ruling class of businesspeople who would eventually become the "tools and tyrants" of the government, "overwhelming it with their force and benefitting from its gifts."[8]

Prominent Americans were concerned about maintaining social order. As Rothman writes: "What in their day was to prevent society from bursting apart? From where would the elements of cohesion come?" The major worry, as Rothman suggests, was whether the poor would "corrupt society" and criminals would "roam out of control." Thus, continues Rothman, comprehension and control of deviance "promised to be the first step in establishing a new system for stabilizing the community, for binding citizens together.... And here one also finds the crucial elements that led to the discovery of the asylum." In the end, the prison system became one among several methods of reforming and controlling the "dangerous classes."[9]

While imprisonment slowly became a dominant method of punishing offenders, methods of "penal discipline" began to change. There were for a time two contrasting methods, which came to be known as the Pennsylvania and Auburn systems.

THE PENNSYLVANIA AND AUBURN SYSTEMS OF PENAL DISCIPLINE, 1830–1870

Many reformers believed that criminals lacked respect for authority and proper work habits and that changing these criminals could be accomplished only through a system of penal discipline emphasizing hard labor. Other reformers believed that criminals were "sinners" and needed to "repent" for their crimes. The idea of penance is said to have originated in the medieval monasteries of Europe for monks who had sinned or committed crimes (hence the term *penitentiary*).[10] Penance could be accomplished only through the use of solitary confinement and no contact with other prisoners or with the outside world. These two views came to be known respectively as the Auburn and Pennsylvania plans of penal discipline and prison construction.

Under the **Pennsylvania plan** two prisons were constructed during the early nineteenth century in Pennsylvania. The first (known as the Western Penitentiary) was opened in 1826 in Pittsburgh. The other (known as the Eastern Penitentiary) was opened in 1829 in Philadelphia, in a location known as Cherry Hill. The architecture of these prisons reflected the basic plan for solitary confinement. The cells were arranged like spokes on a wheel, all radiating from a common central area. Each cell had an outside exercise yard. Each prisoner was allowed short periods in this yard for daily exercise but spent most of the time inside the cell working at some menial task or individual craft. Each prisoner was blindfolded as he entered the prison to begin his sentence and was prohibited from contact with other prisoners. Only approved visitors from the outside were allowed to visit the prisoner.[11]

The **Auburn plan,** which emphasized work in association with other prisoners, began in New York and was supported by prominent citizens of the state, including political leader and former governor De Witt Clinton and former governor and former U.S. Supreme Court Chief Justice John Jay. The first prison modeled after this plan was called the Newgate Prison, which opened in New York in 1797. In 1821 the second prison was opened in Auburn.[12]

The Pennsylvania plan soon came into disfavor because so many prisoners died or became insane, and there was a significant rise in the number of suicides as well (the English novelist Charles Dickens visited the Eastern Penitentiary and called the conditions horrible). It should be noted that in a sense this system is alive and well in present-day America, at the Pelican Bay State Prison, located in remote Crescent City, California (just south of the Oregon border). At this prison there is a security housing unit (SHU). Prisoners in this unit are not allowed to congregate with one another or work at any time during the day or night. They are locked up in windowless cells for twenty-three hours a day. Many prisoners reportedly go insane, and suicide is a constant problem.[13]

Prison administrators following the Auburn plan developed the **congregate system** and the **silent system.** Prisoners worked together during the day but were not allowed to speak to one another, and they were kept in solitary confinement at night. The Auburn plan was used by prisons throughout the nation during the nineteenth century. It became the dominant form because it was so profitable.

Prison administrators at Auburn called their system "humanitarian," but the system they created was almost as repressive as methods used in previous years. Elan Lynds, the first warden at Auburn, introduced the "lock-step" (prisoners marched single file, shuffling their feet and keeping their eyes right) and was a strong advocate of whipping, including the use of the cat-o'-nine-tails. Two Frenchmen, Gustave de Beaumont and Alexis de Tocqueville, who toured American prisons in 1831, noted that the Pennsylvania system produced "more honest men" and the Auburn system produced "more obedient citizens."[14] They also could have added that the Auburn system attempted to produce an ideal worker for the factory system, a worker who was obedient, passive, and silent and who would not complain about the grueling working conditions.[15]

The Auburn system fit nicely within the larger structure of capitalism, characterized as it was by the need for cheap labor. Early prison factories resembled factories on the outside, and for a time prisoners produced goods that were sold in the free market on the outside. As a method of punishment the Auburn system was ideally suited for an emerging capitalist society, because it attempted to inculcate habits of hard work, punctuality, and obedience.

THE REFORMATORY, 1870–1900

By midcentury several reformers and students of the prison system noted with dismay the brutality that existed within these institutions. Beaumont and Tocqueville had commented that while American society provided the most extended liberty, the prisons offered the spectacle of the most complete despotism.[16] As crime and disorder continued to rise in America, reformers searched for some alternative to the prevalent regimes of custody. Some began to believe that prisoners should be "rehabilitated" and "reeducated" and should be allowed to earn their freedom while learning a specific trade. These beliefs led to the introduction of the indeterminate sentence, parole, and vocational and educational training. All of these programs emerged with the rise of a new type of prison—the **reformatory.**[17]

The reformatory idea received its impetus from Captain Alexander Maconochie, who headed the penal colony on Norfolk Island in Australia. Maconochie introduced the **mark system** whereby a prisoner's sentence would be reduced if he obeyed prison rules (the modern version is known as *good time*).[18] About the same time, in England, Sir Walter Crofton introduced the **Irish system,** which used indeterminate sentences and parole. If a prisoner proved he was "reformed" (a term that has never been precisely defined), he was given a pardon, or **ticket-of-leave.** The prisoner was still under some sort of supervision by the state until the expiration of his sentence. In the reformatory system in America the ideas of Crofton and Maconochie were combined with such innovations as classification of inmates according to offense, personality, and other characteristics. In America, the ticket-of-leave came to be known as **parole.**[19]

The reformatories were designed to transform the "dangerous criminal classes" into "Christian gentlemen and prepare them to assume their 'proper place' in society as hard-working, law-abiding lower class citizens." These institutions would also inculcate into them good old-fashioned "American values" such as "habits of order, discipline, self-control, cheerful submission to authority, as well as respect for God, law, country, and the principles of capitalism and democracy."[20]

All of these programs were put into practice in a new prison at Elmira, New York. The Elmira Reformatory was opened in 1877 and still stands today. Under the administration of Zebulon Brockway (a popular prison reformer and administrator and also the author of several books), a wide variety of programs were introduced, including industrial and academic education, religious services, library facilities, an institutional newspaper, and a gymnasium. The development of the reformatory came at a time of new hope among penologists, exemplified by the first annual meeting of the National Congress of Penitentiary and Reformatory Discipline, in Cincinnati in 1870 (this organization is today known as the American Correctional Association). It was here that Brockway "electrified" the audience with his presentation on "The Ideal of a True Prison for a State," which came to be called the "new penology."[21]

Brockway's proposal was influenced by a study done by two penologists of the period, Enoch Cobb Wines and Theodore Dwight, who published *Report on the Prisons and Reformatories of the United States and Canada* in 1867.[22] Wines and Dwight urged the development of a "new" type of institution in order to separate veteran and younger criminals. Their "adult reformatory," they said, would "teach and train the prisoner in such a manner that, on his discharge, he may be able to resist temptation and [be] inclined to lead an upright, worthy life."[23]

The recommendation was taken up by New York in an 1870 law that created the Elmira Reformatory with the aim of housing "male first-time offenders between the ages of sixteen and thirty" and providing "agricultural labor" and "mechanical industry." Following the "Declaration of Principles" issued by the 1870 National Congress of Penitentiary and Reformatory Discipline, this institution would specifically provide "treatment" based on a new "medical model" using the "indeterminate sentence," along with a very carefully calculated system of classification, "intensive academic and vocational instruction, constructive labor, and humane disciplinary methods." An intensive period of parole would follow, intended to extend treatment into the community.[24]

Brockway was the first and most popular administrator of the Elmira Reformatory. He called his new institution a "reformatory hospital" and the "college on the hill." However, the Elmira Reformatory under Brockway was a military-like fortress that emphasized "coercion and restraint" and ushered in a new era of "treatment." Brockway defined "reformation" as the "socialization of the anti-social by scientific training while under complete governmental control." The Elmira Reformatory "became like a garrison of a thousand prisoner soldiers.... By means mainly of the military organization...[t]he general tone...gradually changed from that of a convict prison to the tone of a conscript fortress."[25] In reality, it became "benevolent repression" under a strict military form of discipline, rather than reform.[26]

The Elmira Reformatory and other reformatories failed to live up to the promise of reforming criminals, and it "failed signally to provide the right sort of psychological surroundings to expedite this process [of reformation]. The whole system of discipline was repressive, and varied from benevolent despotism, in the best instances, to tyrannical cruelty in the worst."[27] Elmira was originally built to house five hundred inmates, but by 1899 it housed around fifteen hundred. This prompted one writer of the period to state: "What had begun as a bold experiment lost the inspiring impulse of its first promoters, and became routine work and mass treatment."[28] Beatings were routine, often done in the bathroom (called the "slaughterhouse" by inmates). Brockway himself administered some of the punishment. He was described by inmates as a "different man" at these times, as if he enjoyed the beatings. Brockway rationalized this by calling it part of his "scientific criminology" and renaming corporal punishment "positive extraneous assistance." Solitary confinement was dubbed "rest cure cells."[29]

Elmira and many other "asylums," however, were never specifically designed for any purpose other than custody and control. More than this, it was a system of *class* control, for the prisons (then and now) were populated by the poor, the powerless, and (especially during the nineteenth century) immigrants.

During the nineteenth century, American prisons gradually took on the appearance of huge granite and stone fortresses. These "edifices" eventually were called the "Big House" (and would become the setting of gangster movies in the 1930s and 1940s starring such famous actors as James Cagney and Humphrey Bogart).

THE "BIG HOUSE," 1900–1946

The **"Big House"** became the dominant type of prison until the late 1940s and early 1950s. This prison was typically a huge granite structure capable of housing two thousand or more prisoners, with some housing more than four thousand. These institutions were supposed to eliminate the most abusive forms of punitiveness and prison labor within existing prisons.[30] Most had large cell blocks with three or more floors, or tiers, of cells, usually housing one or two men in each cell. Many were built in the late nineteenth century, such as Jackson (Michigan), San Quentin (California), Joliet (Illinois), and Sing Sing (New York), but most were built in the twentieth century, such as Stateville (Illinois) and Attica (New York).[31] Although the "Big House" was, in a sense, an "industrial" prison, with factories producing various goods, most prisoners spent their time in relative idleness toward the end of the 1930s. When they did work, one of the major products was license plates.

The reform agenda as practiced within reformatories during the late nineteenth and early part of the twentieth century ran up against the hard realities of the prison. The twentieth-century prison, mostly in the form of "the Big House," was this reality. Rothman concludes his analysis of prison reforms during this period with the observation that the reality of the prison "is not one of the inmates exercising in the yard or attending classes or taking psychometric tests, but of the physical presence of the walls."[32] It was these high walls (some as high as 30 feet above the ground) that helped wardens and guards keep their jobs, for legislatures and the general public seemed to be content with one thing: maintaining a "quiet joint" (i.e., no riots, no escapes, a smooth running institution). The high walls gave the public the illusion that "hardened criminals" were safely behind bars so they could no longer prey on innocent citizens.

Until 1895 prisoners convicted of federal crimes were housed in state prisons. The number of prisoners housed in state prisons more than doubled from 1,027 in 1885 to 2,516 in 1895. During this period federal prisoners were used as contract labor. But in 1897 Congress outlawed this practice, and eventually it was decided that federal prisoners should be transferred to a separate institution.[33] Thus, federal prisoners began to be housed at Fort Leavenworth, an old military prison in the eastern part of Kansas. Eventually a new prison was built nearby; it opened in 1928. In the meantime two federal prisons had been built by the federal government, one in Atlanta and the other on McNeil Island, Washington. Atlanta was opened in 1899, and McNeil Island was opened in 1907.[34]

The passage of several federal laws (e.g., Mann Act in 1910, Harrison Narcotic Act in 1914, Volstead Act in 1918, Dyer Act in 1919) resulted in an increase in federal prisoners. Subsequently, in 1925 Congress authorized the construction of a federal reformatory at Chillicothe, Ohio, and the construction of the first federal prison for women, which was opened in 1927 at Alderson, West Virginia.[35]

With the creation of the federal prison system and the passage of new federal laws (especially the Volstead Act, which brought into being organized crime), new federal prisons were constructed. The most famous is Alcatraz, which was opened in 1934. It is located on an island in San Francisco Bay, directly across from Fisherman's Wharf.

THE "CORRECTIONAL INSTITUTION," 1946–1980

The federal Bureau of Prisons helped develop a new system of classification, new prison industries, a federal system of probation and parole, and new educational and vocational training programs. Perhaps most important was the new system of classification. First, there was a classification system according to types of prisons. Five types of facilities were developed: penitentiaries, reformatories, prison camps, hospitals, and drug treatment facilities. Second, within each facility, classification was done according to age, offense, sex, and other criteria. In the 1970s the federal system established a classification system based on security level. Five levels were identified:

1. *Minimum:* mostly federal prison "camps." Many are next to military bases, and inmates provide additional labor for the base.
2. *Low:* double-fenced perimeters and mostly dormitory-style living arrangements.
3. *Medium:* cell-type living arrangements and double-fenced perimeters with electronic detection systems.
4. *High:* most commonly known as U.S. penitentiaries, with high-security perimeter double fences or walls, along with very close supervision of inmates in cell-type housing.
5. *Administrative:* special-needs institutions housing pretrial defendants, noncitizen detainees, and "extremely dangerous, violent, or escape-prone inmates."[36]

With the federal government leading the way, a new era of penology began to emerge, especially after World War II. This "new penology" ushered in a new type of prison system and new terminology. Thus began the age of the "correctional system" and a host of new prison workers, whom Irwin has called **correctionalists.** These individuals were a "growing body of college-educated employees and administrators of prisons, parole, and probation and a few academic penologists." They "were convinced and were able to convince many state governments and interested segments of the general population that they could reduce crime by curing criminals of their criminality."[37] Instead of a prison there was to be a "correctional system"; instead of prisoners or convicts, there would be "inmates"; and guards would be "correctional officers."[38] The prison system remained a system to house the "dangerous classes," but the new terminology seemed to be an attempt to mask its true functions and create the false impression that something positive was being accomplished within the walls.

Many of the "Big Houses" were replaced by shiny new "correctional centers." In line with a "new" era of "treatment," there also emerged a new three-level security classification for these new prisons. Thus, we find *maximum-, medium-,* and *minimum-*security "correctional institutions." Examples of minimum-security prisons (most have no walls) include the California Institution for Men at Chino (a state institution), a federal institution at Seagoville, Texas, and another at Wallkill, New York.

Part of the "corrections" system included the emergence of what many have called the "rehabilitative ideal" or the emphasis on "treatment" (a term that was changed to "rehabilitation"). During the 1940s and 1950s "correctionalists" implemented this "new penology" according to three essential procedures: the indeterminate sentence, classification, and specific treatment programs.[39] Classification was to be done by a "team" of psychologists, social workers, counselors, and other professionals who would form a special "classification committee" to determine the proper course of "treatment" for the prisoner. Advocates of this "new penology" even went so far as to create a name change for the American Prison Association (formerly the Congress of Penitentiary and Reformatory Discipline), calling it the American Correctional Association in 1954—a name that exists to the present day. New names were invented to replace old, punitive practices. The "hole" (locus of solitary confinement) was renamed the "adjustment center." Soledad Prison in California was renamed the "California Treatment Facility." And in place of granite walls, new "correctional institutions" were surrounded by tall fences (today reinforced with razor wire, some charged with electricity) and guard towers.[40] Nevertheless, for all practical purposes, they remained essentially *prisons.*

The indeterminate sentence was implemented in most states. While some reformers advocated a sentence of zero to life for all offenders (in other words, literally a sentence of indeterminate length), most state legislatures implemented a modified version, such as one to ten years for larceny, passed in California. More power was granted to parole boards as a result of indeterminate sentencing laws. Ideally, parole boards would release an offender only when they felt he or she was "rehabilitated." But this assumed that those in charge of the prisons "had procedures for identifying and changing criminal characteristics, which they did not, and that parole boards had procedures for determining when these changes had occurred, which they did not."[41]

The belief in rehabilitation was based on the *medical model* of treatment for criminals. Based largely on psychological theories of crime (see Chapter 4), this model believed that criminals were "sick" and needed to be diagnosed and treated accordingly.

Although classification was supposed to be improved so that criminal behavior could be cured, the procedures adopted never attained this ideal. On the one hand, theories of criminal behavior were never developed sufficiently to effect an adequate "cure" for criminality, and treatment programs were never fully implemented in most prisons. On the other hand, classification (and most other prison procedures) continued to be determined by concerns over custody and security. Thus, the classification procedures tended to ignore a prisoner's treatment needs, however ill defined.

For the most part, prisons in the post–World War II era continued pretty much the way they had before. Rotman's assessment captures the basic problems of rehabilitation within these prisons:

> despite the rhetoric of rehabilitation, this new wave of treatment euphoria shared with previous efforts the same paucity of practical realizations. Because of the limited professional possibilities offered by the penitentiary setting, the treatment staff was still generally composed of less qualified individuals. In addition, there was a permanent conflict, ideological and professional, between the custody and the treatment staffs regarding issues of discipline and security.[42]

Irwin's comments echo those of Rotman:

> The public and most government policy makers continued to demand that prisons first accomplish their other assigned tasks: punishment, control, and restraint of prisoners. In addi-

tion, the new correctional institutions were not created in a vacuum but planned in ongoing prison systems which had long traditions, administrative hierarchies, divisions, informal social worlds, and special subcultures among the old staff. The new correctionalists were never able to rid the prison systems of the old regime, though often they tried; and the old timers, many of whom were highly antagonistic to the new routine, resisted change, struggled to maintain as much control as possible, and were always successful in forcing an accommodation between old and new patterns. So correctional institutions were never totally, or even mainly, organized to rehabilitate prisoners.[43]

THE MODERN ERA AND INTO
THE TWENTY-FIRST CENTURY

Prisons as a Growth Industry

It is no exaggeration to say that during the past two decades the American prison system has been a growth industry. There are now more than 2 million people behind bars in America, with an incarceration rate above 700 per 100,000 population (if we include jails), triple what it was twenty years ago.[44] We are way ahead of other industrial democracies, whose incarceration rates tend to cluster in a range from around 55 to 120 per 100,000 population. Some countries have incarceration rates well below that range, like Japan's rate of 37. The average incarceration rate of all countries of the world is around 80. Canada has a rate of only 115. America's incarceration rate is almost nine times greater than the international average.[45]

Table 11.1 shows the growth of America's prison system during the past seventy-plus years. Notice that the most significant increases occurred after 1975, roughly coinciding with the onset of the "war on drugs."

How do we explain this phenomenal growth? Part of this growth can be attributed to the "war on drugs," which took off during the mid-1980s and began to have its effects on jail and prison populations by the late 1980s and early 1990s.[46] Indeed, a recent estimate is that convictions for drugs accounted for almost *half* of the increase in state prison inmates during the 1980s and early 1990s.[47] As noted in Table 11.2, between 1988 and 1994 the number of prisoners convicted of drug offenses went up by 155.5 percent. By comparison, only modest increases were seen for violent and property offenders. Between 1980 and 1992, court commitments to state prisons on drug charges alone increased by more than 1,000 percent. Figures from U.S. district courts (federal system) show that whereas in 1982 about 20 percent of all convictions were for drugs, by 1994 this percentage had increased to about 36. During this same period the proportion of those convicted on drug charges who were sentenced to prison increased from 74 percent in 1982 to 84 percent in 1994, and their actual sentences increased from an average of 55 months in 1982 to 80 months in

TABLE 11.1   The Growing Prison Population, 1925–1999 (rates per 100,000 in state and federal prison)

YEAR	NUMBER	RATE PER 100,000	YEAR	NUMBER	RATE PER 100,000
1925	91,669	79	1975	240,593	111
1935	144,180	113	1985	480,568	202
1945	133,649	98	1995	1,085,363	411
1955	185,780	112	1999	1,366,721	476
1965	210,895	108			

Source: Maguire, K., and A. Pastore (eds.). *Sourcebook of Criminal Justice Statistics—1995.* Washington, DC: U.S. Department of Justice, Bureau of Justice Statistics, 1996, p. 518; Austin, J. and J. Irwin. *It's about Time: America's Imprisonment Binge* (3rd ed.). Belmont, CA: Wadsworth, 2001, pp. 2–4; Beck, A. J. "Prisoners in 1999." Washington, DC: U.S. Department of Justice, Bureau of Justice Statistics, August 2000, p. 3.

TABLE 11.2   State Prison Inmates, by Offense, 1988–1994

OFFENSE	1988	1994	PERCENTAGE INCREASE
Violent	282,700	429,400	51.9
Property	161,600	209,800	29.8
Drugs	79,100	202,100	155.5

Source: Mauer, M. "Racial Disparities in Prison Getting Worse in the 1990s." *Overcrowded Times* 8(1): 11 (February 1997).

1994. The average sentences for murder during this time period actually *decreased* from 162 months to 117 months, while for all violent offenses the average sentence declined from 133 months to 88 months. Incidentally, on any given day, almost 60 percent (58.6%) of all federal prisoners are serving time for drug offenses; of these 40 percent are African American.[48]

Prisons seem to be everywhere. You can hardly drive anywhere in the country without passing one, especially in rural areas. If one were to place a black dot denoting the location of every prison on a map of the United States, you would probably not be able to see the map for the dots!

As we noted in Chapter 1, the modern American prison system can be described as a **prison-industrial complex.** This is part of a much larger *criminal justice–industrial complex.* You can clearly see the size of this complex by first noting the annual expenditures of the three main components of the criminal justice–industrial complex—law enforcement, courts, corrections. During the 1980s and early 1990s, total expenditures increased by almost 200 percent; the largest increase, for corrections, was more than 250 percent. The most recent estimates indicate that the total expenditures are in the neighborhood of $150 billion annually. One writer recently estimated that if recent trends continue, then by the year 2005 annual expenditures will be around $200 billion; another estimates that this figure will be reached by 2002. Incidentally, in 1996 the defense budget was $296 billion.[49]

The boom in criminal justice expenditures can also be expressed in terms of per capita growth. In 1982, the per capita expenditure on the entire criminal justice system was $158: $82 for the police, $37 for the courts and $39 for corrections. In 1993, the total per capita expenditure was $370 (up 144%): $162 for the police (an increase of 97%), $84 for the courts (up 149%), and $124 for corrections (up by 217%).

Capital expenditures within the criminal justice system also underwent dramatic increases during this period. For instance, money spent on construction went from $544 million in 1982 to a whopping $1.5 billion in 1993, an increase of 172 percent. Not surprisingly, payrolls experienced tremendous increases. For the entire criminal justice system, a total of $2 billion was spent in fiscal year 1982; in fiscal 1993 a total of just under $5 billion was spent (up 142%). At the federal level payrolls went up by 183 percent during this time, while they increased by 137 percent at the state and local level.

The amount of money that flows into the coffers of the prison-industrial complex from tax dollars alone is quite substantial. The total operating budget for both state and federal correctional institutions came to almost $30 billion in fiscal 1996 (the most recent year for which data are available). It costs between $20,000 and 40,000 per year to house one inmate in the U.S. prison system! And remember, this does not count the costs of building prisons. A detailed summary is provided in the most recent Bureau of Justice Statistics study on expenditures at the state level alone. State expenditures in constant dollars tripled from 1984 to 1996, from just under $7 billion to more than $22 billion. Expenditures on medical care average around $6.54 per inmate per day (around $2 million total). Not surprisingly, the bulk of the budget goes toward salaries and benefits (94%). This same report noted that expenditures for prisons increased more than any other category of state spending. For comparison, between 1985 and 1996 prison expenditures increased by 7.3 percent, compared to only 3.6 percent for education and 6.6 percent for health.

Prison construction has become a booming business. During the past decade about 92,000 new beds were added each year. And the beds are very expensive, ranging from $70,000 in a maximum-security prison to $29,000 in a minimum-security prison. As of 1998, the total cost of new prison construction was $3.88 billion—and this is just for the cells! For every 92,000 beds added, there is an estimated cost of $1.3 billion per year. The construction of new prisons has become such a big business that there is a special newsletter called *Construction Report* to keep vendors up-to-date on new prison projects. Recent issues reported the simultaneous construction of dozens of new prisons; in 1996 alone construction was begun on 27 federal prisons and 96 state prisons.

Such growth is not uniform throughout the country. Some states have experienced a far greater growth in imprisonment. In Texas, for example, the number of prisoners increased by more than 100,000 during the 1990s. This number (100,000) is much larger than the *total* prison population of France or Great Britain and roughly equal to Germany's prison population.[50] For comparison it should be noted that the number of persons on probation and parole went up by 206 percent and 220 percent respectively between 1980 and 1998; today there are more than 6 million within the criminal justice system on any given day, up from less than 2 million in 1980.[51]

In addition, the actual *number of prisons* has increased along with, in some cases, the *capacity within* the prison—some "megaprisons" can hold from 5,000 to 10,000 inmates.[52] In 1990 there were a total of 1,287 prisons (80 federal and 1,207 state prisons); by 1995 there were a total of 1,500 prisons (125 federal and 1,375 state prisons), representing an increase of about 17 percent. The federal system experienced the largest increase, going up by 56 percent. During this five-year period, prison construction varied widely by state and region. The largest increases occurred in the South, adding 95 prisons for an increase of 18 percent. The state of Texas leads the way, adding 49 new prisons for an increase of 114 percent. Oklahoma added 17 new prisons for an increase of 74 percent.[53] Texas currently leads the nation with 102 prisons, an increase of 155 percent from 1991.[54] As of December 31, 2000, Texas had 163,190 prisoners: one out of every twenty state residents was behind bars, up from one out of every twenty-five in 1996. During the 1990s almost one out of every five new prisoners added in the United States was in Texas (18%). The Texas prison population tripled during this decade.[55]

But there is more to this system than merely prisons. According to the American Correctional Association's *1997 Directory,* there are many different kinds of facilities that house those sentenced by the courts. There are "Diagnostic/Reception Centers," "Work Release Centers," and "Boot Camps," to name just a few. As of fiscal year 1996, there were 2,499 state facilities and 385 federal, for a total of 2,884. For juveniles, there were a total of 2,297 state facilities and 98 federal facilities, for a total of 2,395. All together there were 5,278 correctional facilities. And this number does not include local jails.[56]

Jails: Temporary Housing for the Poor

During the course of a year, around 20 million people are arrested and taken to jail. This is a characteristic American practice, as there is such a strong belief in using "edifices" such as jails to enforce the law through coercion. The vast majority of those who end up in a local jail do not get a "get-out-of-jail-free card" as in Monopoly. Most have little or no capital with which to secure their release. An old saying applies here: "Those without capital, get punishment."

Virtually every large city and small town has at least one jail. Jails are ubiquitous features of modern life. Many old jails—some dating back to colonial times—remain standing as tourist attractions. The modern jail is a purely local institution (mostly city or county operated) that in effect provides temporary housing for the poor. Usually you find four types of prisoners in jails: (1) persons serving short sentences for misdemeanor convictions (normally public-order crimes such as disturbing the peace, drunkenness, vagrancy, and loitering, along with petty theft, and "contempt of court"—often for failure to pay traffic fines); (2) persons convicted of a felony and awaiting transfer to a prison; (3) persons on hold temporarily for other jurisdictions (including federal offenders); and (4) persons awaiting their final court disposition. Those waiting for their final court disposition constitute the largest category. These jail prisoners have not been found guilty (although most will eventually plead guilty). Most are in jail because they cannot afford bail, usually a relatively small amount ($500 or so). Jails are the modern-day equivalent of eighteenth- and nineteenth-century poorhouses or, as one writer suggests, "the ultimate ghetto of the criminal justice system."[57]

The modern jail originated in England with the Norman Conquest in the eleventh century. Under King Henry II the jail (or *gaol*) began to take on the characteristics and functions known today. Henry II sought to establish at least one jail in each county, under the control of a local sheriff. By the thirteenth century all but five counties had a jail. The county sheriff was a royal appointee, "a functionary who upheld his master's interests against local powers."[58] Social control by the king was thus delegated to the local level, thereby masking the true source of control.

From the beginning, jails were used almost exclusively to house the poor, and a term often used interchangeably with *jail* was **debtor's prison.** It was ironic that on the one hand, the financing of local jails depended on user fees paid to jailers, yet on the other hand, the majority of jail prisoners were drawn from the poorest classes. One eighteenth-century reformer noted that such fees were extracted "from misery."[59]

Not surprisingly, corruption was rampant yet little was done to correct the problem—probably because, then as now, much profit was to be made from the existence of crime. The jails of London functioned as "brothels, taps, criminal clubs, and asylums for thieves, robbers, and fraudsmen, and when their raw material—prisoners—threatened to run out, minions would bring false charges to replenish the supply." Also not surprisingly, the well-being of the prisoners was virtually ignored. As a result of their poverty, many either starved to death or died from some disease.[60]

By the middle of the fourteenth century the threat of incarceration in London jails was used to extract payment from those in debt—hence the term *debtor's prison.* The debts of many people who ended up in jail for nonpayment could never be paid, for the means to do so were taken away by the mere fact of being in jail. Some debtors elected to remain in jail until their death, because death would cancel their debts and save their families from being charged. Even though technically the jailing of people because of their debts ceased by the nineteenth century, many still went to jail on the charge of "contempt of court," usually for failure to pay a fine, which essentially served the same purpose then and still does today.[61]

Jails in the American colonies served similar functions but eventually became temporary holding facilities for individuals awaiting court appearances or those serving short sentences. Most of those who could secure their release pending their day in court did so through the system of *bail.* The use of bail dates back to early English society (at least as early as A.D. 1000) and was originally established to ensure that an accused appeared for trial.[62] Groups of ten families under the control of the tythingman in effect "pledged" to ensure that a defendant would appear in court. Crime prevention in those early small, agrarian communities was a collective responsibility. It no longer is. In modern societies, characterized by mobility and anonymity, bail stands for a different sort of pledge—a pledge of money or property, often provided by the defendant's family, relatives, or friends. The problem today is that most accused people come from the poorest sectors of society, and they and their families, relatives, and friends have little or no property.[63]

Jails also served another function. For years, starting at least as far back as the mid-fourteenth century, jails amounted to **workhouses.** This function of the jail can be traced to the **Statutes of Labourers,** passed in England in 1349 (in part because of labor shortages caused by death from the Black Death), which forced "vagabonds" and other undesirables to accept work at the prevailing wage or go to the workhouse. The Elizabethan Poor Law of 1572 further stigmatized the poor. It distinguished between the common criminal and the "unworthy poor." "Hard labor" became a standard form of punishment for those "guilty" of nothing more than poverty. In time it became difficult to distinguish between a "pauper" (a person living in poverty) and a "vagabond" (a person who wandered about the country without working). Eventually, in the United States, these two terms were replaced by "welfare dependent" and "petty persistent offender," and in time "mentally ill."[64]

Who's in Jail?   According to the most recent data, as of June 30, 1996, there were 518,492 inmates held in local jails.[65] More detailed data from 1995 show that the overall jail incarceration rate in the United States stood at 257 per 100,000. Racial differences were significant: for whites the rate was 122; for African Americans it was 700, almost seven times greater. These rates represent a rather dramatic increase over the mid-1980s. In 1985, the overall rate was 145 for whites and 368 for African Americans. Thus, in ten years the overall rate increased by 77 percent; the rate for whites showed an increase of 67 percent, while the rate for African Americans increased by 90 percent. The exact racial breakdown in 1996 was 42 percent white, 41 percent African American, and 17 percent other races, mostly Hispanic.[66] What is important to note is that the preceding data are based on "one-day counts" of inmates in randomly selected jails around the country. Considerably more individuals see the inside of a jail during the course of a given year. More than 20 million persons are arrested each year, and it is reasonable to assume that the majority of these individuals find themselves spending at least a few hours inside a jail. The fact that around half are released within twenty-four hours does not diminish this statistic. In fact, it would be safe to conclude that close to 10 percent of the adult population spends some time in jail during the course of a year; more significantly, a third or more of all African American males spend some time in jail during the course of a year.[67]

Conditions of Local Jails.   The words used to describe contemporary American jails include *degrading, filthy, inhumane,* and *human jungles*—to mention only a few. Many blue-ribbon commissions have documented these conditions over the years (such as the Wickersham Commission of the 1930s and the President's Commission of 1967), and there have been journalistic exposés in newspapers and other media.[68] But conditions today are little better than conditions in earlier years, and as proof we can merely cite the number of lawsuits filed on behalf of jail inmates for various unconstitutional conditions, including overcrowding, plus the large number of suicides and assaults that occur in local jails. As of 1996, thirty-six states plus the District of Columbia, Puerto Rico, and the Virgin Islands were under some form of court orders or consent decrees to either limit the population or improve conditions of jails and prisons. Suits have been filed charging inadequate medical care, mental health care, and legal access, as well as sexual harassment and abuse. Inadequate medical care is the most common complaint. Conditions have been so bad that some states that hold prisoners of other states in local jails have been sued and ordered to return the prisoners to their original states. As of 1995 an estimated 320 jails, including more than one-fourth of the nation's largest jails, were operating under a court order or consent decree.[69] In fact, a growing number of jail inmates have been convicted but are serving their time in jail because of prison overcrowding!

In many jails (such as Cook County Jail in Chicago, the Tombs in New York City, and the jail system in Los Angeles, which houses more than 20,000 inmates on any given day) gang rapes, suicide, and many other forms of violence are common, as are poor food and generally unsanitary living conditions. Adequate medical facilities are almost nonexistent. Studies of the effects of jail overcrowding document several adverse effects and note some of the still-existing horrible conditions in many jails. Among the physiological effects are elevated blood pressure and coronary problems. Behavioral problems are numerous, including assaults. More general problems include lack of recreational and educational opportunities, poor food service, lack of treatment programs (especially for drugs and alcohol), inhumane disciplinary practices (e.g., placement in solitary confinement for minor violations), and abuse from guards and other inmates.[70]

Almost thirty years ago Jessica Mitford reported on an experiment involving judges, prosecutors, police, lawyers, and others who volunteered to spend a day and a night in

Washington, D.C.'s Lorton Jail. Mitford did her "time" in the Women's Detention Center. She found that the usual procedure during what is known as "reception" included vaginal checks (to look for contraband drugs), head checks for lice, spraying with Lysol, and other degrading ceremonies. There were many petty rules and regulations (including one against talking "too loud"), and there were bed checks at odd hours. Infractions of rules resulted in disciplinary measures imposed by what could only be described as a kangaroo court; violators often were sent to "adjustment" (a euphemism for "the hole" or "solitary").

Mitford concluded that jails such as Lorton offer a "life of planned, unrelieved inactivity and boredom…no overt brutality but plenty of random, largely unintentional cruelty …a pervasive sense of helplessness and frustration engulfing not only the inmates but their keepers, themselves trapped in the weird complex of paradoxes that is the prison world."[71] Mitford discovered that few of the *women* at Lorton had been charged with serious crimes, the majority having been accused of prostitution and drug offenses. She asked: "Is this not the essence of women's prisons, the punishment of unchaste, unwomanly behavior, a grotesque bow to long-outmoded nineteenth century notions of feminine morality?" One of the judges who participated in the experiment declared: "We wouldn't stand for having the bears in the zoo treated as we treat the men in Lorton."[72] But we do, because this class of inmates is typically perceived as "animals" or worse.

It should be noted that, perhaps as a result of the deinstitutionalization of mental patients in the 1970s and 1980s, a large proportion of those in jail have serious mental and behavioral problems, prompting many to characterize modern jails as "contemporary society's mental health clinic."[73] In effect, deinstitutionalization has been replaced by the "criminalization of mental illness," and these inmates receive little or no treatment. What is especially important is the issue of HIV and AIDS. Growing numbers of jail inmates have AIDS. The most recent estimates indicate that as many as 6,700 prisoners have some type of HIV infection, with almost 2,000 confirmed cases, as of June 30, 1993.[74] For the prison population as a whole, the number of prisoners known to be HIV-positive was 24,226 as of 1995, up from 20,651 in 1992; the total number of confirmed AIDS cases in 1995 was 5,099.[75]

The Functions of Jails: Managing the "Rabble" Class.   The typical jail population has been called "social refuse," "social junk," "riffraff," "social trash," "dregs," and many other degrading names. After a detailed study of the San Francisco City Jail, John Irwin concluded that most jail prisoners have two essential characteristics, which he calls "detachment" and "disrepute." He suggests that they are detached in the sense that they are not very well integrated into mainstream society; they have few ties to "conventional social networks," perhaps because they have rather "unconventional values and beliefs" (which came first, few ties or "unconventional values and beliefs" is an excellent question, which is beyond the present text). By "disrepute" Irwin means that they are "offensive," "irksome," and often threatening. They may even be described as "dirty" and "smelly" and lacking in social graces. They are "bothersome" and may even be "eyesores." They are, to Irwin, part of what he terms the **rabble,** meaning the "disorganized" and "disorderly," the "lowest class of people."[76]

Irwin concluded that detachment and disrepute, more than any crimes they may commit, lead to their arrest. Thus, in his view, jail serves the function of "managing" this rabble class. In this sense, jail is a sort of "subsidiary" of a much larger "welfare system" that serves to "regulate the poor."[77] Individuals who commit serious violent and property crimes are eventually sent to prison, so obviously not everyone sitting in jail is *only* detached and disreputable. But the jail still serves the overall purpose of "managing" the "rabble."

Irwin's study parallels nicely the more recent study by Miller in Jacksonville, Florida.[78] The majority of the offenses committed by jail prisoners in both locations were rather petty. Irwin conducted extensive interviews with many prisoners and was able to classify them according to the degree of seriousness of the charges against them and the degree of "offensiveness" they displayed. In general, using a seriousness scale devised by several prominent criminologists,[79] Irwin determined that only a very small percentage of crimes could be categorized as "serious" (around 4 percent); the vast majority he classified as "petty" (scoring from 0 to 5 on a seriousness scale that goes as high as 35.7). The average seriousness score from Irwin's sample was around 3.[80]

Irwin then classified the prisoners by type. The most common type was what he termed "petty hustlers," which constituted 29 percent of his felony sample. This type was followed in frequency by "derelicts" and "corner boys" (each at 14%, for a total of 28%), followed by "aliens" (9%), "junkies," "gays" and "square johns" (each constituting 6%) and "outlaws" (really serious types, 4%), "lowriders" (4%), and "crazies" (4%). Most of these individuals (57%) represented a mild degree of offensiveness and committed mostly petty crimes.

Clearly, most jail prisoners do not fit the popular image of the "dangerous felon" so often portrayed in the media and by politicians. We have observed local campaigns to expand jail capacities and to build more jails based on such misconceptions, put forth by those with vested interests in building new jails. Our research clearly dispels these myths. In one of our studies, focusing on an attempt to build a new jail in Las Vegas, Nevada, data supplied by local jail officials revealed that most of those brought to the jail would be released within two to three days, including many charged with serious crimes, such as homicide, rape, robbery, and assault.[81]

Modern prisons (along with local jails) constitute a sort of *ghetto* or *poorhouse*[82] reserved primarily for the unskilled, the uneducated, the powerless, and, in increasing numbers, racial minorities, especially African Americans. That is why we call this system the *New American Apartheid.* This is the same segment of American society that has seen their incomes drastically reduced and has become more involved in drugs and the subsequent violence that extends from the lack of legitimate means of goal attainment.[83] That is why we call this system the **new American apartheid.**

The New American Apartheid: The Incarceration of African Americans

Apartheid is a policy that produces systematic racial segregation or discrimination and is usually associated with pre-Mandela South Africa. The word *apartheid* was introduced to the world by South Africa in 1948.[84] This term stems from the Dutch *apart* (which means the same as the English word), and *heid* (which translates as the suffix "hood"). The term was adopted to soften the image of the harsh racial segregation policies practiced by the South African government. World attention was focused on South Africa's segregation practices, and the government thought that the substitution of the word *apartheid* for *segregation* would divert world attention away from its discriminatory practices. Very soon, however, the world realized that nothing had actually changed with respect to the treatment of blacks in South Africa. Thus, that exercise in semantics failed. South Africa made one more attempt to fool world opinion and introduced the concept *autogenous development.* But the world quickly recognized this new attempt to divert attention from the government's segregation policies. It made no difference whether extreme discriminatory practices were called *segregation, apartheid,* or *autogenous development;* the result was still racial isolation.

There seems to be a pattern of contradictions by the United States between what is professed to be policy direction and what is actually supported by the U.S. government. America has always been a country that professes to place high value on children. However, in 1989, the United States refused to support the United Nations' General Assembly Resolution 44/25, which was a product of the Convention on the Rights of the Child. This resolution was for the adoption of basic rights of children, such as the right to life.[85] There is further evidence of differences between the United States' public posture and its global voting record. The United States claims to be in favor of policing international criminals, yet in 1998 America refused to ratify the United Nations' attempt to create an International Criminal Court in Rome.[86] Prior to the call for votes, the United States requested a nonrecorded vote on the matter of adopting the statute establishing an international criminal court. Speaking to the issue of apartheid in 1973, the International Convention on the Suppression and Punishment of the Crime of Apartheid declared apartheid a crime against humanity and argued that apartheid should be treated as a crime against humanity—an international crime. To date, the United States has not yet ratified this resolution.[87]

Racial segregation is now a characteristic of many of America's inner cities. Central cities now contain 80 percent of the urban nonwhite population, and one-third of the African American urban population resides in the nation's ten largest central cities.[88] There have been symbolic attempts to reduce racial segregation in American cities. We use the term *symbolic* because these attempts have often been politicized and skewed to serve the interests of the elite or they have been grossly underfunded to ensure their failure.[89] To illustrate, the Housing Acts of 1949, 1954, and 1965 provided federal funding to local authorities to acquire slum property and begin redevelopment of that property. In order to qualify for federal funds, local governments had to ensure that affordable living accommodation would be provided for displaced families living in the redevelopment zones. The process used was commonly known as urban renewal and sometimes referred to as "negro removal." The solution was high-density public housing. Today, these public housing projects are often referred to as the "projects." Razing slum areas and the construction of public housing often resulted in an overall reduction in living accommodations.[90] In a study of African American youth gangs in Detroit, it was noted that for that city there was a net loss of 31,500 homes between 1980 and 1987. Today, many African Americans find themselves once again involved in a "negro removal" program—but instead of being removed from one inner-city slum area to a more high-density slum area, they find themselves removed from the inner cities entirely and compartmentalized in America's prison industry.[91]

It is obvious from the examination of arrest and prison data that the groups being targeted by the criminal justice system are disproportionately drawn from the most marginalized populations. African Americans, particularly males, are especially vulnerable. For example, in 1995, according to the Sentencing Project in Washington, D.C., about one-third of all African American males between the ages of 20 and 29 were, on any given day, in jail, in prison, on probation, or on parole, a percentage that was up from 25 percent in 1990. In some cities these percentages were even higher, such as in Washington, D.C., where the figure was about 60 percent.[92] For comparison purposes, on any given day, more African American males are likely to be in prison or jail than in college! In California African Americans are imprisoned at a rate of 1,951 per 100,000, compared to only 215 for whites. Stated somewhat differently, although African Americans constitute less than 7 percent of California's population, they compose about one-third of the prison population; Hispanics make up 24 percent of the state's population yet constitute 34 percent of the prison population.[93]

Methods of controlling the surplus population include legislation that defines what is a "crime" and sentencing structures that define what crimes are "serious." Many sentencing structures have a built-in class and racial bias. Consider the drug laws, especially those pertaining to crack cocaine. The penalty for possession or sale of crack cocaine is far greater than for similar quantities of the powder cocaine. It just so happens that crack is far more likely to be used by African Americans. Little wonder that the enforcement of drug laws has been one of the major reasons the prison population has increased so rapidly in recent years. According to Austin and Irwin, the proportion of admissions to prisons that were racial minorities increased from 42 percent to 51 percent between 1981 and 1991, while the proportion sentenced because of drug-law violations increased from 9 percent to 25 percent.[94]

Indeed, a most persuasive argument can be made suggesting a close correlation between the "wars" on drugs and on gangs and the growth of the prison-industrial complex. This "war on drugs" was launched by President Reagan in the mid-1980s. He promised that the police would attack the drug problem "with more ferocity than ever before." What he did *not* say, however, was that the enforcement of the new drug laws "would focus almost exclusively on low-level dealers in minority neighborhoods." Indeed, the police found such dealers in these areas mainly because *that is precisely where they looked for them*, rather than, say, on college campuses.[95] The results were immediate: the arrest rates for African Americans on drug charges shot dramatically upward in the late 1980s and well into the 1990s. In fact, although African Americans constitute only around 12 percent of the U.S. population and about 13 percent of all monthly drug users (and their rate of illegal drug use is roughly the same as whites'), they represent 35 percent of those arrested for drug possession and 74 percent of those sentenced to prison on drug charges. The evidence of racial disproportionality in the drug war is overwhelming. For instance, drug arrest rates for minorities went from under 600 per 100,000 in 1980 to over 1,500 in 1990, while for whites they essentially remained the same. As far as prison sentences go, studies of individual states are telling. For instance, in North Carolina between 1980 and 1990, the rate of admissions to prison for non-whites jumped from around 500 per 100,000 to almost 1,000, while in Pennsylvania, non-white males and females sentenced on drug offenses increased by 1,613 percent and 1,750 percent respectively. In Virginia the percentage of commitments for drug offenses for minorities went from just under 40 in 1983 to about 65 in 1989, while for whites the percentage actually *decreased* from just over 60 percent in 1983 to about 30 percent in 1989.[96]

The rate of incarceration for African Americans exceeds that for whites by a ratio of 8 to 1. Moreover, a recent study found that while 2 percent of *all* adults have been disenfranchised because of a felony conviction (mostly drug convictions), *about 13 percent of all black men have been!* In six states the percentage of black men disenfranchised is 25 percent or more, *going higher than 30 percent in Alabama and Florida.*[97]

We need not elaborate the obvious any further, for the fact remains that the "war on crime" and the "war on drugs" disproportionately target racial minorities (especially women, a topic discussed in Chapter 14), who find themselves in alarmingly increasing numbers behind bars and generally subjected to the efforts of the criminal justice system. The situation is not likely to improve, especially as long as federal, state, and local governments continue to increase the money used for crime control instead of for prevention. With increasing attention given to the public's *reaction* to crime, the attention given to the ultimate *sources* of crime will decrease, exacerbating the problem.

As already noted, drug offenses have accounted for most of the increases in prison populations in recent years. However, the prison and jail populations have become increasingly dominated by minorities. For African Americans in particular, we find that their presence within the nation's prison system to be directly linked to the "war on drugs." From 1986 to 1991, right in the middle of the crackdown on drugs, the proportion of African Americans incarcerated for drug offenses went up an incredible 465.5 percent! The imprisonment rate as of December 31, 1999, was almost 3,408 for African American males, compared to a rate of 417 for white males; for African American females the rate was 212, versus 27 for white females.[98]

The racial differences are perhaps more dramatically underscored when we consider the percentage of each racial group as a percentage of their numbers in the total population. For 1995, almost 10 percent (9.3%) of *all* African Americans were in jail, in prison, on probation, or on parole, up from only 5.2 percent in 1985 (an increase of almost 80%). In contrast, the comparable figures for whites were 2.0 percent in 1995 and 1.2 percent in 1985 (an increase of 67%).[99]

The most dramatic representation of the racist nature of the criminal justice system can be seen in Table 11.3. Here we can see that the odds of an African American male going to prison are more than one in four (28.5%), compared to about one in twenty-five for white males.[100] Put somewhat differently, an African American male child's chances of going to prison were more than six times greater than his white counterpart's! And such odds do not diminish until age 40.

Many African Americans have been unjustly subjected to some of the most repressive types of legislation passed in recent years, such as three-strikes and habitual offender laws. A study by the National Council on Crime and Delinquency found evidence of systematic racial bias in Florida's habitual criminal law: African American offenders were about twice as likely to receive this type of sentence, even when researchers controlled for the current offense and prior record.[101]

Finally, we should note the well-publicized statistic that in 1995 around one-third of all African American males in their 20s were in jail, in prison, on probation, or on parole,

TABLE 11.3   Percentage of Persons Not Previously Incarcerated Who Are Expected to Go to State or Federal Prison Later in Life (by age, as of 1991)

	BIRTH	20	25	30	35	40
TOTAL	5.1	4.5	3.1	2.1	1.4	.9
SEX						
Male	9.0	7.9	5.5	3.7	2.5	1.6
Female	1.1	1.0	.8	.6	.3	.2
RACE						
White	2.5	2.3	1.7	1.2	.9	.6
Male	4.4	4.1	3.0	2.1	1.5	1.1
Female	.5	.5	.4	.3	.2	.1
Black	16.2	14.1	9.6	6.0	3.6	2.0
Male	28.5	25.3	17.3	10.8	6.5	3.6
Female	3.6	3.5	2.8	1.9	1.1	.6
Hispanic	9.4	8.7	6.4	4.9	3.8	2.3
Male	16.0	14.8	11.1	8.6	6.8	4.3
Female	1.5	1.5	1.2	.9	.6	.4

Source: Proband, S. C. "Black Men Face 29 Percent Lifetime Chance of Prison." *Overcrowded Times* 8(1): 22 (February 1997).

a figure that stood at one-fourth around 1990.[102] More recent figures are not available. Given recent trends in the coming years we may see an even greater percentage.

One often overlooked effect of the booming imprisonment rate is the impact on minority communities. Recent research by the criminologist Todd Clear finds a negative impact in a number of areas. For instance, there has been a displacement of economic assets from minority communities to rural, white communities. "Each prisoner represents an economic asset that has been removed from that community and placed elsewhere." By this Clear means that the prisoner would normally spend money in and around his or her own community. But once in prison, the person spends money at the prison commissary. Clear estimates that each prisoner accounts for around $25,000 in income for the community where the prison is located. Thus, instead of providing some support for his or her children and local purchases in his or her own community, it is transferred to a rural, almost all-white community.[103]

The modern American prison system is beginning to resemble the gulags of the Soviet Union. We explore this topic next.

The American "Gulag"

One of the earliest exposures of **gulags**—forced-labor camps—in the West occurred with the publication of the Russian author Alexander Solzhenitsyn's *The Gulag Archipelago*.[104] This book described life in thousands of Soviet prison camps, located mostly in isolated areas like Siberia. These camps originally were set up in the 1920s under Joseph Stalin. The number of camps grew from around 350,000 in 1929 to more than 1.5 million by 1931. These labor camps were set up ostensibly to help the growth of industrialization following the 1917 Russian Revolution.[105]

Gulags persist to the present day, not only in Russia but in such countries as China, North Korea, and Sudan. A recent report even noted the existence of gulags in Canada during the 1930s, known as "project 51" in Lac Seul, Northern Ontario.[106]

You might be tempted to think that the gulag phenomenon is either an aberration (such as Canada's "project 51") or something restricted to third-world or totalitarian societies. However, a close look at the modern American prison system might suggest otherwise. Indeed, at least three authors have suggested as much. In the early 1990s the Norwegian criminologist Nils Christie suggested that the "crime control industry" in America was beginning to look like the equivalent of the Russian gulag.[107] In a 1996 paper, Stephen Richards also used the term *gulag* to describe the modern prison system.[108] A 1999 commentary by the syndicated columnist Alexander Cockburn referred to the American prison system as a "gulag."[109] We don't have to look very far back in history to find an almost exact equivalent of gulags in this country—the so-called relocation centers used to house Japanese Americans during World War II.

Today the American prison system has many of the characteristics of gulags. Prisons are found in nearly every part of the country, most of them (especially those built during the past twenty years) in rural areas. There is a great deal of human rights abuse in American prisons (and also in jails and juvenile correctional facilities), such as cruel and unusual punishment (e.g., long periods in solitary confinement) and extreme brutality and violence. An excellent example comes from a case in Corcoran State Prison, about 170 miles northwest of Los Angeles (built at a cost of $289 million). Four prison guards went on trial for forcing gang fights that turned fatal. The guards were charged with staging "gladiatorial combats" between rival gangs. The guards were eventually acquitted in a manner that raises serious questions about the influence of one of the most powerful guard unions in the country, the California Correctional Peace Officers Association (with a budget of $17 million and 17 staff attorneys—more later about this union).[110] Moreover, there is a great deal of forced (and cheap) labor, which produces great profits for corporations.

An Example: The Texas, Michigan, and California Gulags.[111]   To get an idea of the "gulag" look of the American prison system, consider what is happening in Texas, Michigan, and California, three states that have obviously found building prisons a lucrative business to be in. One of the most interesting things about the American prison system is that most prisons are located in rural areas.

Texas is a classic example, now boasting over 100 prisons (most built since 1980). A sense of the rural location of most of these facilities emerges from population statistics for some of the towns in which they were built (population according to the 1990 census): Iowa Park (pop. 6,072), Teague (3,268), Dilley (2,632), Brazoria (2,717), Kennedy (3,763), Dalhart (6,246), Marlin (6,386), Rusk (4,366), Richmond (9,801), Woodville (2,636), Navasota (6,296), Fort Stockton (8,524), Childress (5,055), and Cuero (6,700). A check of the 1998 Rand McNally road atlas reveals that several Texas prisons and other facilities are located in towns not even found on the map—places such as Lovelady, Midway, Tennessee Colony (with three separate prisons each housing over 3,000 inmates), Rosharon (with four prisons housing over 6,000 inmates), and Venus (with a privately run prison 1,000 inmates). Such institutions are found in every part of the state, from the far eastern part (Woodville, located a few miles north of Beaumont along U.S. Route 190) to Lamesa (in the Texas Panhandle about 30 miles south of Lubbock where U.S. 180 meets U.S. 87) and Fort Stockton (about 100 miles southwest of Odessa along Interstate 10). The town of Beeville, located between Corpus Christie and San Antonio along U.S. 181, has a population of just over 13,000 and two prisons with about 7,200 prisoners! The journalist Joseph Hallinan appropriately describes this little town as a sort of "prison hub" not unlike what Detroit was to cars.[112]

The Texas prison system has more than 42,000 employees, operates its own heath services system (with more than 8,000 personnel, including 200 doctors), and has 35 lawyers working for it. Farming is big business. The system controls more than 134,000 acres (about 200 square miles), operating the largest horse and cattle herds in the state (more than 10,000 head of cattle and around 1,500 horses). The system operates 42 factories within 32 prisons under its own "Texas Correctional Industries." As of December 31,

1999, 706,600 people were under some form of supervision in the Texas criminal justice system, and the total prison and jail population was 207,526—which translates to a rate of 1,035 (second only to Louisiana's). This is higher than the overall U.S. rate of 682 and Russia's rate of 685. The total prison population was 149,684, up from 92,669 in 1994.[113]

As of 1996, Michigan had 39 prisons and 15 prison camps, the majority of which were built in the 1980s and are in rural areas. Towns hosting prisons include Munising (pop. 2,783), Baraga (1,231), Carson City (1,158), Grass Lake (903), Coldwater (9,607), Ionia (5,935), New Haven (2,331), St. Louis (3,828), Newberry (1,873), Eastlake (473), Freeland (1,421), Plymouth (9,560), Standish (1,377), and Lapeer (7,759). Kinchebe is not on the map; the nearest town to it is Rudyard (pop. 900). There are at least eight prisons located in the Northern Peninsula—Munising, Baraga, Newberry, Kinchebe, and Marquette (pop. 21,900)—housing more than 5,000 inmates. There are four facilities in Kinchebe alone, one of which is located on an abandoned Air Force base purchased by the state in 1978. The facility at Newberry was opened in 1995 on the site of a former state mental institution.[114] As of December 31, 1997, there were 44,771 inmates and an incarceration rate of 457 (ninth in the nation, excluding the District of Columbia).[115]

California also exemplifies the gulag mentality. As of the spring of 1996, there were 32 state prisons (in 1980 there were 12), plus 38 forestry camps and a multitude of community facilities. Largely as a result of the recent three-strikes laws, it was expected that by 2001 the state would have around 250,000 inmates (it had 157,547 as of December 31, 1997) an incarceration rate of 475 (tenth in the nation, excluding the District of Columbia), and around 50 prisons. Some of the rural towns hosting California's prisons are Avenal (pop. 9,770), Susanville (7,279), Techachapi (5,791), Calipatria (2,690), Baker (650), Imperial (4,113), Chowchilla (5,930), Blythe (8,428), Soledad (7,146), Ione (6,516), Crescent City (4,380), Coalinga (8,212), Jamestown (2,178), and Adelanto (8,517).

Other Examples of Gulags.   There are numerous additional examples that can be taken from any other state in the country. For instance, there is the Limestone Correctional Center in a town called Capshaw, Alabama, near the Tennessee line. Not only is Capshaw not on the Rand McNally map, but there is no official population, except for the 1,700 prisoners. Then there is the Clinton Correctional Facility in Dannemora, a town of around 4,500 in upstate New York near Plattsburgh (appropriately known as Little Siberia). Then there is Tamms, Illinois (pop. 742), located in the extreme southern part of the state, along state route 127. This is another "supermax" prison—each cell cost $120,000 to build and $35,000 per year to operate. A sign outside of town proudly says "Welcome to Tamms, the home of Supermax," and a local fast-food restaurant, Burger Shack 2, sells a "Supermax burger." There's a long waiting list for employment; $25,000 per year to start is not bad in a rural area where higher-paying jobs are lacking.[116]

Finally, it should be noted that these rural prisons represent, in effect, a return to the days of slavery. Black men and women are segregated from their own communities and placed in remote areas that may seem like the old southern plantations to those locked up. At a prison in Angola, Louisiana, you can see prisoners coming in from the fields at the end of each day.[117] After years of struggle for various civil rights (e.g., the end of segregated drinking fountains, the right to vote, the right to schooling) since the days of slavery, millions of the great-great grandchildren of former slaves find themselves in almost identical situations. It is curious to note that blacks are imprisoned at a rate almost eight times greater than whites, despite the fact that, as research has recently noted, whites use illegal drugs at a rate five times greater than blacks.[118]

A recent development in the prison system is the movement toward privatization. This movement encompasses not just the prison system but the criminal justice system in general, plus many other government-operated systems (including the public schools and even the Social Security retirement system). Some comments on this phenomenon seem warranted, especially since proponents of privatization claim that private industry can do a better job building and operating prisons and save taxpayers money in the process.

The Privatization of Prisons: More Profits
for Private Industry

Privatization occurs when a private corporation takes over the operation of a jail or prison or builds and operates one (usually contracting directly with the state). Several years ago researchers warned about the tremendous growth in privatization in general, especially the private police industry. They quoted a source who called this phenomenon "creeping capitalism" or the transfer of "services and responsibilities that were once monopolized by the state" to "profit-making agencies and organizations."[119] It should be noted that privatization is a trend affecting more than the criminal justice system. This "contracting out," as it is often termed, involves a number of services formerly provided by state and local governments, such as public education, health care, and waste collection. There are "at least 18 categories of government services" that saw an increase in private-sector involvement between 1987 and 1995.[120]

Privatization has become, in the words of Edward Herman, "one of the mantras of the New World Order. Economic, political and media elites assume that privatization provides undeniable benefits and moves us toward a good society." The movement toward privatization stems from recent trends toward greater and greater corporate power. This increased power has contributed to the emergence of neoliberal ideology. Among the core beliefs of this ideology are "the efficiency of the private market, the inefficiency of government, and the dual menaces of inflation and budget deficits." Herman also notes that "Part of the design of neoliberal politicians and intellectuals has been to weaken the state as a power center that might serve ordinary citizens and challenge the rule of the market." Contributing to this trend is the increase in capital flow away from urban centers, leaving them in dire financial straits, as governments "have had to limit business taxes and spending on social benefits in order to provide a 'favorable investment climate,' leaving them under financial stress."[121]

Through privatization, states can get around voter resistance to prison construction bonds by having private corporations build the prison. Those corporations then turn around and send huge bills to the state and thus taxpayers. This is a classic case of "socializing the costs and privatizing the benefits."[122]

As of December 31, 1998, there were approximately 132,000 prisoners in privately operated prisons and jails, up from only 3,100 in 1987 (an increase of more than 4,000 percent). At that time the largest proportion were under control of two companies, Corrections Corporation of America and Wackenhut Corrections (over 90,000 prisoners), with facilities in the United States and abroad.[123]

The 1995 annual report of Corrections Corporation of America (CCA) is quite revealing. CCA says that it is the "leading private sector provider of detention and corrections services to federal, state and local governments." A subsidiary, CCA International, provides similar "services" in foreign countries. Another subsidiary, TransCor America, "is the nation's largest and most experienced prisoner extradition company." CCA is a big corporation; its stock trades on the New York Stock Exchange. It presently operates forty-six correctional facilities, including one in England, two in Australia, and two in Puerto Rico. It is a growth corporation, indicating an obvious vested interest in a relatively high rate of incarceration. From 1986 to 1995, revenues went from $13 million to $207 million (an increase of 1,492%), assets increased from $8 million to almost $47 million (an increase of 488%), and stockholders' equity went from $24 million to $96 million (up 300%). (Corrections Corporation of America has recently fallen on bad times, as we note below.)

A number of serious problems have occurred with respect to the privatization of prisons and jails. Perhaps the most serious issue is the fact that private profit is the driving force in the privatization of the correctional system. "Crime Can Pay," a March 1996 report by Equitable Securities included a "strong buy" recommendation for investors. The report concluded: "We consider the industry very attractive. There is substantial room for continued private-prison growth." The potential for profits did not escape Wall Street. Ted Goins, of

Branch, Cabell and Co., Richmond, Virginia, compiled a list of "theme stocks" for the 1990s. His highest recommendation went to Corrections Corporation of America. A Prudential Securities vice president who is part of a "prison-financing team" is quoted as saying, "We try to keep a close eye on all the crime bills." Wall Street is indeed eager to back the growth in "crime control stocks." Such companies as Merrill Lynch, Prudential Securities, Smith Barney Shearson, and Goldman Sachs are leaders in support of privatization. One writer noted: "Between 1982 and 1990 California voters approved bonds for prison construction totaling $2.4 billion. After interest is paid to lenders, the total cost will be $4.1 billion. Now the big investors are bullish on private prisons." The firm of Raucher, Pierce and Refsnes of Dallas, Texas, are the underwriters and investment bankers for Wackenhut Corrections. This company is reportedly doing from $5 million to $7 million worth of business each year, mostly "buying bonds and securities from the private prison companies or the state entities which issue them and reselling them to investors. That securities market is now a 2–3-billion dollar industry, up from nothing eight years ago." Enthralled about the profits, securities firms have launched the "next phase" of such development. During this phase, private companies will finance their own construction, with help from securities firms. Such an industry obviously depends on a steady supply of prisoners and just as obviously does not have a vested interest in reducing crime and protecting victims.[124] One interesting example of the profit-seeking frenzy appears in a 1996 World Research Group conference brochures. The investment firm noted, "While arrests and convictions are steadily on the rise, profits are to be made—profits from crime. Get in on the ground floor of this booming industry now!"[125]

As noted in a *Wall Street Journal* story, some of the companies that produced the technology used in the Vietnam War are manufacturing and selling high-tech weaponry to fight the "war on crime." A new "iron triangle" (consisting of politicians, small communities, and businesses) has been forged, and businesses, large and small, are lining up to reap the enormous profits. Wall Street financial giants such as Goldman Sachs, Merrill Lynch, and Prudential are competing to underwrite prison construction with private, tax-exempt bonds that require no voter approval. Such defense industries as Westinghouse Electric, Minnesota Mining and Manufacturing, and GDE Systems (a division of the old General Dynamics) are among those competing for a piece of the action.[126]

One of the problems of privatization, especially when it comes to health care, is that profits are placed well above the needs of the people. A recent issue of Ralph Nader's *Health Letter* reveals some of the problems. In an article called "Milton, Matthew and Managed Care," Nobel Prize–winning economist Milton Friedman is quoted saying, "Few trends could so thoroughly undermine the very foundation of our free society as the acceptance by corporate officials of a social responsibility other than to make as much money as possible." The writer also quotes Saint Matthew, who said that "No man can serve two masters...you cannot serve God and mammon." In this article it is noted that one of the recent trends in managed care is the phenomenon of "unprofitable patients" who were "dumped by HMO's because, as a result of their age and attendant medical problems, they were not profitable enough." The writer then noted the irony that "what is bad news for the dumped patients is obviously good news for Wall Street and the insurance company owners."[127] The article concludes with a quote from an editorial in the *New England Journal of Medicine,* which stated:

> The most serious objection to such [investor-owned] care is that it embodies a new value system that severs the communal roots and samaritan traditions of hospitals, makes doctors and nurses the instruments of investors, and views patients as commodities.... In our society, some aspects of life are off-limits to commerce. We prohibit the selling of children and the buying of wives, juries and kidneys.... [H]ealth care is too precious, intimate, and corruptible to entrust to the market.[128]

Likewise with the privatization of prisons.

We have seen numerous instances of serious problems with the privatization of prisons and other components of the criminal justice system. Not that the prison system has been all that successful in reducing crime, but at least prison administrators, and in fact the entire criminal justice system, are at least theoretically accountable to the public, because tax dollars support them. With privatization, there is no accountability. Numerous scandals demonstrate this—escapes, cost overruns, and so on. Russell Clemens, an economist with the Department of Research for the American Federation of State, County, and Federal Employees, put the problem in perspective when he noted that the various "problems regarding security, staffing, and quality of services have plagued prison privatization from its inception." He pointed out that in addition to numerous escapes there have been problems pertaining to health care and food service—"the low quality of service in privately operated prisons." The riots at a private prison in New Jersey operated by Esmor Corrections Corporation are illustrative. After this riot there was a lot of media coverage, and Esmor's stock went from $20 per share to $7. Since this riot, numerous private-prison corporations have been caught failing to report problems within their prisons. The reason is simple: such secrecy protects shareholders "from adverse market reactions that would likely occur if a problem were to be reported."[129]

As already suggested, profits from prisons are dependent on the continued increase in prison admissions. What if prison admissions begin to decline? There is already some evidence of this. For instance, in New York state a recent downward trend in the number of prisoners is resulting in the reduction of prison staff at many prisons. The New York Department of Corrections froze hiring at thirty-six of the state's prisons, with the expectation that just over 600 jobs will be eliminated. One facility in upstate New York is illustrative.[130]

In 1998 a $90 million jail was built in tiny (pop. 2,400) Cape Vincent, near the St. Lawrence River. Now with recent downward trends in prison populations residents are worried. One prison worker said, "Who ever thought crime would go down? Who ever thought we would run out of inmates?" And worry they should, for about $2.4 billion per year goes into the state prison system, and millions of dollars flow into the upstate economy each year. Salaries for correctional officers start at around $33,000, with raises to $44,000 after twenty years. Not bad in a rural area, where the cost of living is so much lower than in the cities.

A recent analysis of the impact of the privatization of prisons comes from a report by a group known as "Good Jobs First." In a detailed study of sixty private prisons (constituting half of the privatized prisons in the country), Good Jobs First found that the benefits promised to state and local governments failed to materialize. More important, however, they found that at least 73 percent of the prisons had received a development subsidy from local, state, or federal government sources, over one-third (37%) had received low-cost construction via tax-free bonds or other government-issued debt securities, 38 percent had received property-tax abatements, and another 23 percent had gotten subsidies for water, sewer or utility hookups, access roads, and so on. The two largest private companies involved in prison building, Corrections Corporation of America and Wackenhut, were heavily subsidized (78% of CCA prisons and 69% of Wackenhut's prisons were subsidized). The study could find no evidence that prison privatization had the desired effects on local communities.[131] Whether privatization of prisons continues (there are serious doubts that it will), prisons and jails will continue to operate and will provide steady employment for a large workforce, plus continuous profits for those businesses that provide various goods and services (security devices, food, linen, etc.).

In the next chapter we take a much closer look at the modern prison system. Specifically we provide a detailed profile of the typical prisoner and a look at life inside a prison. Prisons bear no resemblance to the "country clubs" alluded to by uninformed politicians trying to get elected on a "get tough on crime" platform. Sadly, such get-tough sentiments only contribute to the problem of crime.

SUMMARY

Prisons are a relatively recent invention in America, having their start in the early years of the republic. Of the two contrasting models of prisons, the Auburn plan eventually became the dominant one after the Pennsylvania plan developed severe problems. But, as noted, some of the ideas embedded within the Pennsylvania plan are alive and well in modern "supermax" prisons. The growth of the prison population in this country began in the late 1970s, and the building frenzy began in earnest in the middle of the "war on drugs" during the late 1980s. The current prison population approaches 2 million.

The effects of the drug war and the prison-building frenzy have been most negatively felt in minority communities. The prison system exemplifies a "new American apartheid," existing alongside residential apartheid. At the close of the twentieth century, African Americans were imprisoned at a rate almost eight times that for whites. Most of the growth has come not from convictions for traditional crimes such as murder, robbery, and burglary but from convictions for drug-related crimes.

As part of the overall prison system, jails represent yet another illustration of the effects of both race and class. They are the "ultimate ghetto" of the criminal justice system. Housing mostly minor offenders and overwhelmingly members of the lower class and racial minorities, jails function chiefly to "manage" the "rabble" or "dangerous classes."

Most of the recently built prisons have been placed in remote rural areas of the country. Because of innumerable human rights abuses, these new prisons bring to mind the Russian gulags. Local communities seem to want prisons built, for they bring jobs and economic uplift.

This chapter described the modern prison system as fostering a form of apartheid as those incarcerated are now mostly racial minorities, especially African Americans. This type of apartheid is similar to residential segregation but perhaps more pernicious.

Finally, we discussed the growing trend toward privatization of prisons. Although big business has been heavily involved in seeking profits from building and managing prisons, the promises that were made turned out to be true. More and more communities and states are finding that the alleged benefits were mostly empty promises.

KEY TERMS

Auburn plan 266	Irish system 267	rabble 276
"Big House" 268	mark system 267	reformatory 267
congregate system 266	new American apartheid 277	silent system 266
correctionalists 269	parole 267	Statutes of Labourers 274
debtor's prison 274	Pennsylvania plan 266	ticket-of-leave 267
Elizabethan Poor Law 274	privatization 283	Walnut Street Jail 265
gulags 280	prison-industrial complex 272	workhouses 274

NOTES

1. Most of the information on pp. 264–271 is from Shelden, R. G. *Controlling the Dangerous Classes: A Critical Introduction to the History of Criminal Justice.* Boston: Allyn and Bacon, 2001, ch. 4.

2. The first five periods were suggested by John Irwin in his *Prisons in Turmoil.* Boston: Little, Brown, 1980. The last period (covering the years since Irwin's book) was suggested by Robert Weiss (personal communication).

3. Takagi, P. "The Walnut Street Jail: A Penal Reform to Centralize the Powers of the State." *Federal Probation* (December 1975), p. 20; see also Barnes, H. E. *The Story of Punishment.* Montclair, NJ: Patterson Smith, 1972, p. 81 (originally published in 1930).

4. Takagi, ibid., p. 23.

5. Ibid., pp. 22–23.

6. Madison, J. "No. 10: Madison." In A. Hamilton, J. Madison, and J. Jay (eds.), *The Federalist Papers.* New York: Mentor, 1961, pp. 78–79.

7. Zinn, H. *A People's History of the United States* (2nd ed.). New York: HarperCollins, 1995, pp. 90–96.

8. Chomsky, N. *Powers and Prospects.* Boston: South End Press, 1996, pp. 123–125, 154.

9. Rothman, D. J. *The Discovery of the Asylum.* Boston: Little, Brown, 1971, pp. 58–59. It should be noted that Rothman (using a consensus argument) continually suggests that "Americans" wanted social order, and so on, never mentioning the fact that it was a relatively small ruling elite that wanted a *certain kind of order,* one that would primarily benefit members of their own class. See Chomsky, ibid., for further elaboration of this theme.

10. Mellosi, D., and M. Lettiere. "Punishment in the American Democracy: The Paradoxes of Good Intentions." In R. P. Weiss and N. South (eds.), *Comparing Prison Systems: Toward a Comparative and International Penology.* Australia: Gordon and Breach, 1998, p. 22.

11. Barnes, H. E., and N. Teeters. *New Horizons in Criminology.* Englewood Cliffs, NJ: Prentice-Hall, 1959, pp. 338–339.

12. Barnes, *The Story of Punishment,* p. 132.

13. Austin, J., and J. Irwin. *It's about Time: America's Incarceration Binge* (3rd ed.). Belmont, CA: Wadsworth, 2001, pp. 127–128; J. Hallinan, *Going up the River: Travels in a Prison Nation.* New York: Random House, 2001, pp. 117–118.

14. de Beaumont, G., and A. de Tocqueville. 1964. *On the Penitentiary System in the United States and Its Application in France.* Carbondale, IL: Southern Illinois University Press (originally published 1833).

15. Mellosi, D., and M. Lettiere. "Punishment in the American Democracy"; Foucault, M. *Discipline and Punish: The Birth of the Prison.* New York: Vintage Books, 1979.

16. de Beaumont and de Tocqueville, *On the Penitentiary System.*

17. Barnes and Teeters, *New Horizons in Criminology,* p. 417ff; Barnes, *The Story of Punishment,* p. 144ff.

18. Barnes, ibid. p. 145.

19. Simon, J. *Poor Discipline: Parole and the Social Control of the Underclass, 1890–1990.* Chicago: University of Chicago Press, 1993.

20. Pisciotta, A. *Benevolent Repression: Social Control and the American Reformatory-Prison Movement.* New York: New York University Press, 1994, p. 4.

21. Walker, S. *Popular Justice: A History of American Criminal Justice* (2nd ed.). New York: Oxford University Press, 1998, p. 95.

22. Wines, E. C., and T. Dwight. *Report on the Prisons and Reformatories of the United States and Canada.* New York: AMS Press, 1973 (originally published in 1867).

23. Pisciotta, *Benevolent Repression,* p. 11.

24. Ibid., pp. 12–13.

25. Platt, A. *The Child Savers* (rev. ed.). Chicago: University of Chicago Press, 1977, pp. 67–68.

26. Pisciotta, *Benevolent Repression,* p. 22.

27. Barnes, *The Story of Punishment,* p. 147.

28. Platt, *The Child Savers,* p. 68.

29. Walker, *Popular Justice,* pp. 97–98.

30. Rotman, D. "The Failure of Reform: United States, 1865–1965." In N. Morris and D. Rothman (eds.), *The Oxford History of the Prison.* New York: Oxford University Press, 1998, p. 165.

31. Irwin, *Prisons in Turmoil,* p. 3; G. F. Killinger and P. Cromwell (eds.). *Penology.* St. Paul, MN: West, 1973, p. 47.

32. Rothman, D. *Conscience and Convenience: The Asylum and Its Alternatives in Progressive America.* Boston: Little, Brown, 1980, pp. 157–158.

33. Rotman, "The Failure of Reform," p. 166.

34. Allen, H. E., and C. E. Simonsen. 1998. *Corrections in America* (8th ed.). Upper Saddle River, NJ: Prentice-Hall, 1998, pp. 538–539.

35. Ibid., pp. 538–539; Rotman, "The Failure of Reform," p. 167.

36. Allen and Simonsen, *Corrections in America,* pp. 540–546.

37. Irwin, *Prisons in Turmoil,* pp. 38–39; Rotman, "The Failure of Reform," pp. 169–171.

38. Barnes and Teeters, *New Horizons in Criminology,* p. 440.

39. Irwin, *Prisons in Turmoil,* p. 40; Rotman, "The Failure of Reform," pp. 169–170.

40. Rotman, ibid., p. 170.

41. Irwin, *Prisons in Turmoil,* pp. 41–42.

42. Rotman, "The Failure of Reform," p. 169.

43. Irwin, *Prisons in Turmoil,* pp. 46–47.

44. Ziedenberg, J., and V. Schiraldi. "Poor Prescription: The Costs of Imprisoning Drug Offenders in the United States." Washington, DC: Justice Policy Institute (www.cjcj.org/drug), 2000, and "Texas Tough? An Analysis of Incarceration and Crime Trends in the Lone Star State." Washington, DC: Justice Policy Institute, 2000; *The Punishing Decade: Prison and Jail Estimates at the Millennium.* Washington, DC: Justice Policy Institute, 1999.

45. Currie, E. *Crime and Punishment in America.* New York: Metropolitan Books, 1998, p. 15; Mauer, M. *Race to Incarcerate.* New York: New Press, 1999, p. 25.

46. Baum, D. *Smoke and Mirrors: The War on Drugs and the Politics of Failure.* Boston: Little, Brown/Back Bay Books, 1997; Miller, J. *Search and Destroy: African Americans Males in the Criminal Justice System.* New York: Cambridge University Press, 1996; Reinarman, C., and H. G. Levine. *Crack in America.* Berkeley: University of California Press, 1997; and Currie, E. *Reckoning: Drugs, the Cities, and the American Future.* New York: Hill and Wang, 1993.

47. Beck, A. J., and P. M. Brien. "Trends in the U.S. Correctional Populations: Recent Findings from the Bureau of Justice Statistics." In K. C. Haas and G. P. Alpert (eds.), *The Dilemmas of Corrections* (3rd ed.). Project Heights, IL: Waveland Press, 1995, p. 54.

48. Maguire, K., and A. L. Pastore (eds.). *Sourcebook of Criminal Justice Statistics—1995.* Washington, DC: U.S. Department of Justice, Bureau of Justice Statistics, 1996, pp. 468, 472, 576.

49. In the next several paragraphs numerous statistics are cited, all of which are drawn from the following sources: Chambliss, W. J. *Power, Politics and Crime.* Boulder, CO: Westview Press, 1999; Dyer, J. *The Perpetual Prisoner Machine: How America Profits from Crime.* Boulder, CO: Westview Press, 2000, p. 11; McGarrell, E., and T. J. Flanagan. *Sourcebook of Criminal Justice Statistics—1985.* Washington, DC: U.S. Department of Justice, 1986, p. 2; Maguire, K., and A. Pastore (eds.). *Sourcebook of Criminal Justice Statistics—1994.* Washington, DC: U.S. Department of Justice, 1995, p. 4; Donziger, *The Real War on Crime,* p. 85; Dyer, ibid., pp. 11–13; Bureau of Justice Statistics. "State Prison Expenditures, 1996." Washington, DC: U.S. Department of Justice, August 1999.

50. Currie, *Crime and Punishment in America,* p. 13; Ziedenberg and Schiraldi, "Texas Tough."

51. Austin and Irwin, *It's about Time,* p. 4.

52. Ibid., pp. 125–131.

53. Mays, G. L., and L. T. Winfree Jr., *Contemporary Corrections.* Belmont, CA: Wadsworth, 1998, p. 171.

54. Rush, G. *Inside American Prisons and Jails.* Incline Village, NV: Copperhouse, 1997, p. 157.

55. Ziedenberg and Schiraldi, "Texas Tough," pp. 1–2. In Louisiana, almost half of the state prisoners are housed in local detention facilities known as parish (county) prisons. The parish sheriffs make contracts with the state before they build these facilities in order to ensure a sufficient number of prisoners to maintain the facility. Personal communication from Professor Marianne Fisher-Giorlando, Grambling State University.

56. American Correctional Association. *1997 Directory.* Lanham, MD: American Correctional Association, 1997, pp. xxii–xxiv.

57. Goldfarb, R. *Ransom: A Critique of the American Bail System.* New York: Harper & Row, 1965, and *Jails: The Ultimate Ghetto of the Criminal Justice System.* New York: Doubleday, 1975.

58. McConville, S. "Local Justice: The Jail." In Morris and Rothman, *The Oxford History of the Prison,* p. 268.

59. Ibid.

60. Ibid., pp. 269–270.

61. Ibid., pp. 271–272.

62. Goldfarb, *Jails.*

63. McConville, "Local Justice," p. 279; see also Shelden, *Controlling the Dangerous Classes.* A recent study found that nationwide about 80 percent of felony defendants in the 70 largest counties were indigent (Cole, D. *No Equal Justice: Race and Class in the American Criminal Justice System.* New York: New Press, 1999, p. 66).

64. McConville, "Local Justice," pp. 282–284; for a more detailed discussion of the law of vagrancy, see Shelden, *Controlling the Dangerous Classes,* pp. 34–38.

65. Proband, S. C. "Jail and Prison Populations Continue to Grow in 1996." *Overcrowded Times* 8(4) (1997).

66. Maguire and Pastore, *Sourcebook of Criminal Justice Statistics—1995,* pp. 511–513.

67. Miller, *Search and Destroy;* Mauer, *Race to Incarcerate.*

68. President's Commission on Law and Administration of Justice. *The Challenge of Crime in a Free Society.* Washington, DC: U.S. Government Printing Office, 1967; U.S. National Commission on Law Observance and Enforcement (Wickersham Commission). *Reports.* Washington, DC: U.S. Government Printing Office (1931).

69. Bronstein, A. J., and J. Gainsborough. "Prison Litigation: Past, Present, and Future." *Overcrowded Times* 7: 3 (June 1996); Mays and Winfree, *Contemporary Corrections,* p. 358; Stojkovic, S., and J. Klofas. "Crowding and Correctional Change." In T. Alleman and R. L. Gido (eds.), *Turnstile Justice: Issues in American Corrections.* Upper Saddle River, NJ: Prentice-Hall, 1998.

70. Mays and Winfree, ibid., p. 358; Stojkovic and Klofas, ibid., pp. 98–99.

71. Mitford, J. *Kind and Usual Punishment.* New York: Vintage Books, 1974, p. 30.

72. Ibid., pp. 29–30.

73. Mays and Winfree, *Contemporary Corrections,* p. 125.

74. Ibid., pp. 125–126.

75. Maguire and Pastore, *Sourcebook of Criminal Justice Statistics—1997,* p. 552.

76. Irwin, J. *The Jail.* Berkeley: University of California Press, 1985, pp. 1–2.

77. Piven, F. F., and R. Cloward. *Regulating the Poor: The Functions of Social Welfare.* New York: Vintage Books, 1972.

78. Miller, *Search and Destroy.*

79. See, for example, Wolfgang, M., P. Figlio, and P. Tracy. "The Seriousness of Crime: The Results of a National Survey." Final Report to the Bureau of Justice Statistics. Washington, DC: Department of Justice, 1981.

80. Irwin, *The Jail,* pp. 20–22.

81. Shelden, R. G., and W. B. Brown. "Correlates of Jail Overcrowding: A Case Study of a County Detention Center." *Crime and Delinquency* 37 (July 1991).

82. For more detailed treatment of the notion of jails and prisons as poorhouses see Morris and Rothman, *The Oxford History of the Prison.*

83. Fowles, R., and M. Merva. "Wage Inequality and Criminal Activity: An Extreme Bounds Analysis for the United States." *Criminology* 34: 163–182.

84. In 1948, the year the Nationalist Party came to power in South Africa and instituted apartheid, the Mississippi Supreme Court, in *Murray v. State,* decided that segregated seating in courtrooms was not a constitutional

violation. The court argued that such seating arrangements were grounded firmly in community custom. It was not until 1963, in *Johnson v. Virginia,* that the U.S. Supreme Court ruled that segregated seating in a courtroom constituted a denial of equal protection (Higginbotham Jr., A. L. *Shades of Freedom: Racial Politics and Presumptions of the American Legal Process.* New York: Oxford University Press, 1996).

85. Henkin, L., R. C. Pugh, O. Schachter, and H. Smit. *International Law: Cases and Materials* (3rd ed.). St. Paul, MN: West, 1993.

86. United Nations Press Release. "UN Diplomatic Conference Concludes in Rome with Decision to Establish Permanent International Criminal Court." July 17, 1998.

87. Lillich, R. B., and H. Hannum. *International Human Rights: Problems of Law, Policy, and Practice.* New York: Little, Brown, 1995.

88. Piven, F. F., and R. A. Cloward. *The Breaking of the American Social Compact.* New York: New Press, 1997.

89. Handler, J. F., and Y. Hasenfeld. *We the Poor People: Work, Poverty, and Welfare.* New Haven: Yale University Press, 1997; Wilson, W. J. *When Work Disappears: The World of the New Urban Poor.* New York: Vintage Books, 1997; Massey, D. and N. Denton. *The American Apartheid: Segregation and the Making of the Underclass.* Cambridge, MA: Harvard University Press, 1993; Harrington, M. *The Other America.* New York: Macmillan, 1962, and *The New American Poverty.* New York: Penguin Books, 1984.

90. Massey and Denton, *The American Apartheid.*

91. Brown, W. B., "The Fight for Survival: African American Gang Members and Their Families in a Segregated Society." *Juvenile and Family Court Journal* 49(2): 1–14 (1998).

92. Donziger, S. *The Real War on Crime: The Report of the National Criminal Justice Commission.* New York: Harper Perennial, 1996; Miller, *Search and Destroy.*

93. Koetting, M., and V. Schiraldi. *Singapore West: The Incarceration of 200,000 Californians.* San Francisco: Center on Juvenile and Criminal Justice, July 1994.

94. Austin and Irwin, *It's about Time.*

95. A Delaware prosecutor is quoted as follows: "Sure, it's true we prosecute a high percentage of minorities for drugs. The simple fact is, if you have a population, minority or not, that is conducting most of their illegal business on the street, those cases are easy pickings for the police." (Mauer, *Race to Incarcerate,* p. 142).

96. Donziger, *The Real War on Crime,* p. 115; Tonry, M. *Malign Neglect: Race, Crime, and Punishment in America.* New York: Oxford University Press, 1995; Mauer, *Race to Incarcerate;* Cole, *No Equal Justice.*

97. Fellner, J., and M. Mauer. "Nearly 4 Million Americans Denied Vote because of Felony Convictions." *Overcrowded Times* 9(5) (October 1998).

98. Beck, A. J. "Prisoners in 1999." Washington, DC: Bureau of Justice Statistics, August 2000.

99. Maguire and Pastore, *Sourcebook of Criminal Justice Statistics—1997,* p. 464.

100. Ibid., p. 480.

101. Austin and Irwin, *It's about Time,* pp. 38–41.

102. Mauer, *Race to Incarcerate.*

103. Clear's study cited in Street, P. "Race, Prison, and Poverty." *Z Magazine* (May 2001), pp. 25–31.

104. Solzhenitsyn, A. *The Gulag Archipelago.* New York: Bantam Books, 1970.

105. Conquest, R. "Playing Down the Gulag." *Times Literary Supplement* (February 24, 1995); Harris, J. R. "The Growth of the Gulag: Forced Labor in the Urals Region, 1929–1931." *The Russian Review* 56: 265–281 (1997).

106. Collins, C., and J. L. Askin-Steve. "The Islamic Gulag: Slavery Makes a Comeback in Sudan." *Utne Reader* (March–April, 1996); Lilly, J. "Great Leader's Gulag: Siberian Timber Camps Are Relics of the Cold War." *Far Eastern Economic Review* (September 9, 1993), pp. 21–22; Pasqualini, J. "Glimpses inside China's Gulag." *The China Quarterly* 134: 352–358 (1993); Tracey, D. "Inside North Korea's Gulag." *Reader's Digest* 143: 149–155 (1993); Wu, H. "The Need to Restrain China." *Journal of International Affairs* 49: 355–360 (1996).

107. Christie, N. *Crime Control as Industry: Towards Gulags, Western Style* (3rd ed.). New York: Routledge, 2000. Christie's original observations came with the first edition of this book in 1993.

108. Richards, S. "Commentary: Sociological Penetration of the American Gulag." *Wisconsin Sociologist* 27: 18–28 (1996).

109. Cockburn, A. "With 'Gladiator Days,' Prisons Adopt the Gulag Paradigm." *Las Vegas Review-Journal,* November 12, 1999, p. 11B.

110. Ibid.

111. Information about these prison systems is from American Correctional Association, *1997 Directory*; and Rush, *Inside American Prisons and Jails.*

112. Hallinan, *Going up the River,* pp. 3–4.

113. Zeidenberg, J., and V. Schiraldi. "Texas Leads U.S. in Incarceration Growth." Washington, DC: Justice Policy Institute, 2000.

114. Many state mental institutions were closed in the 1960s and 1970s as part of a "deinstitutionalization" movement. Today, ironically, many of the same buildings house prison inmates. It has been estimated that as many as 70 percent of prison inmates suffer severe mental problems. Schlosser, E. "The Prison Industrial Complex." *Atlantic Monthly* (December 1998).

115. Proband, S. C. "Prison Populations Up 5.2 Percent in U.S. in 1997." *Overcrowded Times* 9(4) (1998).

116. Hallinan, *Going Up the River,* pp. 101, 111, 126.

117. Personal communication from Professor Marianne Fisher-Giorlando, Grambling State University.

118. *International Herald Tribune,* June 6, 2000, cited in *Index on Censorship* 29: 114 (September/October 2000).

119. Spitzer, S., and A. T. Scull. "Privatization and Capitalist Development: The Case of Private Police." *Social Problems* 25: 18–29 (1977).

120. Laursen, E. "A Tale of Two Communities." *Z Magazine* (October 1996), pp. 45–50.

121. Herman, E. "Privatization: Downsizing Government for Principle and Profit." *Dollars and Sense* (March/April 1997), pp. 10–12.

122. Dyer, *The Perpetual Prisoner Machine,* p. 245.

123. Austin and Irwin, *It's about Time,* p. 66.

124. Brayson, C. "Crime Pays for Those in the Prison Business." *The National Times (September 1996),* pp. 28–35; Thomas, P. "Making Crime Pay: Triangle of Interests Creates Infrastructure to Fight Lawlessness." *Wall Street Journal,* May 12, 1994, pp. A1, A6.

125. Pens, D., and P. Wright (eds.). *The Celling of America: An Inside Look at the U.S. Prison Industry.* Monroe, ME: Common Courage Press, 1998, p. 156.

126. Thomas, "Making Crime Pay."

127. Wolfe, S. M. "Milton, Matthew and Managed Care." *Health Letter* 15 Washington, DC: Public Citizen Health Research Group, 1999, p. 12.

128. Ibid., p. 11.

129. Dyer, *The Perpetual Prisoner Machine,* pp. 203–204.

130. Rohde, D. "A Growth Industry Cools as New York Prisons Thin." *New York Times,* August 21, 2001.

131. Mattera, P., and M. Khan. *Jail Breaks: Economic Development Subsidies Given to Private Prisons.* Washington, DC: Good Jobs First, October 2001.

CHAPTER TWELVE

DOING TIME IN
AMERICAN PRISONS

THE PRISON WORLD

Who Goes to Prison and for What Crimes?

The typical prisoner incarcerated in the state prison system (where most prisoners are found) is an African American male between 18 and 29 with less than a high school diploma who was convicted for either a property or a drug offense. The majority of prisoners were sentenced as a result of a new court conviction (67%). More than one-fourth were on parole at the time they were arrested (29%). Around 16 percent of the parole violators were sent to prison for a technical violation of parole guidelines (mostly for flunking urine tests). About one-fourth have no prior felony convictions.[1]

These figures are telling and roughly correspond with Bureau of Justice Statistics data on prison populations, which show that in 1992 about 30 percent of all admissions to state prisons were parole or probation violators. In 1991 a survey of all state prisoners found that 45 percent had been on probation or parole at the time of their most recent conviction. The differences in these two statistics can be attributable to the fact that many in the latter group had committed a new crime. In the federal system only 24 percent were on probation or parole at the time of their convictions, no doubt because so many were arrested on drug charges and many of these had no prior convictions. This is supported by data showing that for federal cases, the proportion sentenced on drug charges went from just over one-fourth (26.7%) in 1980 to almost half (48.8%) in 1992, compared to a drop in the proportion sentenced for violent crimes, which went from about 13 percent in 1980 to around 8 percent in 1992. Incidentally, the maximum average sentence in the federal system for violent crimes *decreased* during this period (from 125 months to 62 months), while for drug offenses there was an *increase* from 47 months to 82 months.[2]

Austin and Irwin examined a sample of prisoners in three states: Nevada, Illinois, and Washington. They first examined the crimes that the prisoners were convicted of and sent to prison for. They looked at the level of seriousness of these crimes.[3] The crimes fit into four general categories, ranging from most serious to least serious. The most common category, contrary to popular belief, was what Austin and Irwin considered as "petty crimes," representing just over half (52.6%) of all the inmates. These the researchers describe as "crimes with no aggravating features"—that is, no large amount of money was involved, no one was injured, and so on. They included shoplifting and smoking a marijuana cigarette (possession of marijuana is a felony in Nevada).

An example of a "petty crime" is provided by Austin and Irwin in the following story:

> Edmond is a 50-year-old white carpenter who works in Florida in the winter and Seattle in the summer. He had been arrested once 22 years ago for receiving stolen property. He was passing through Las Vegas on his way to Seattle and says he found a billfold with $100 on a bar where he was drinking and gambling. The owner, who suspected him of taking it, turned him in. He was charged with grand larceny and received three years.[4]

Almost 30 percent (29.3%) of the inmates had been convicted of "moderate crimes." These included acts that resulted in minor injury, use of heroin, selling marijuana, use of a weapon, and theft of more than $1,000. The next most common category was "serious crimes," which constituted 13.2 percent of the inmates. These crimes included theft of more than $10,000, attempted murder, and sale of heroin. Finally, almost five percent (4.8%) were "very serious crimes." These included rape, manslaughter, homicide, and kidnapping.

Austin and Irwin also examined the "criminal careers" of these offenders, taking into account not only the current offense but offenses committed in the past. As they properly note, the notion that the "career criminal" is a crazed person who commits one felony after another is not accurate. What Austin and Irwin found was quite the opposite. They identified five distinct patterns of crime among these offenders: (1) "into crime" (43%), (2) "crime episode" (19%), (3) "being around crime" (18%), (4) "one-shot crime" (14%), and (5) "derelicts" (6%). These patterns are remarkably similar to those identified by Irwin and others in studies conducted around thirty years ago.[5]

Individuals in the "into crime" category were heavily involved in a wide variety of criminal behaviors, almost on a daily basis. They are described and describe themselves as "dope fiends," "hustlers," "gang bangers," and the like. More than half of these individuals were in prison before, and about a third of them served time as juvenile offenders. Yet most of these very active criminals were convicted of "petty crimes" and did not fit the popular image of the "vicious predator." Rather, in the words of Austin and Irwin, they were "disorganized, unskilled, undisciplined petty criminals who very seldom engaged in violence or made any significant amounts of money from their criminal acts."[6] This category is similar to the "disorganized criminal" described by Irwin in an earlier study (see note 5).

Individuals in the "crime episode" category were much less involved in a criminal lifestyle than were members of the "into crime" group. Rather, most of these individuals had lived a relatively conventional life free of crime—although most were not exactly strangers to the world of crime, most had been arrested a few times, and a few had served time. They got involved in some sort of "crime spree" (a drinking "binge," a party where things got "out of hand," etc.) and landed in prison.

Individuals in the "being around crime" category were what some researchers have called "corner boys."[7] These are mostly young males who "hang out" in lower-class neighborhoods where crime is a fact of life. The individuals within this category generally are not regular members of gangs or other groups involved in crime, but they are acquaintances and can be seen with such individuals from time to time. Occasionally they are confronted by the police and feel the need to exhibit some form of macho behavior in order to conform to the "code of the streets." This behavior can easily lead to an arrest. Or they are witnesses to a crime by simply being present or are drawn into a crime because they see an opportunity to make some easy money (without any careful planning).[8]

Individuals in the "one-shot crime" category had no prior serious involvement in crime. The seriousness of the offense or the fact that the crime was associated with some mandatory sentencing law landed them in prison. Austin and Irwin describe a middle-aged man who was out of work and was lured into buying some cocaine by an undercover drug agent. Recent trends in prison populations suggest that more and more prisoners are serving their first prison sentence and growing numbers have little if any prior involvement in serious crime. Data from the Bureau of Justice Statistics show that from 1979 to 1991 the proportion of state prisoners with no previous sentence went from 17.1 percent to 19.3 percent. In the federal system the proportion with no prior prison experience stood at 43.3 percent in 1991.[9]

Individuals in the "derelicts" category had, in Austin and Irwin's words, "lost the capacity to live in organized society." Most had extensive records, mostly for petty crimes. Thus, they had the highest rate of imprisonment (91% had a prior prison record), including doing time as a juvenile (71%). Most used drugs and alcohol rather extensively.

A Look inside the Prison World

What happens inside a prison? How do people survive such confinement? Austin and Irwin give a rather vivid description of the current "warehousing" of prisoners:

> Convicted primarily of property and drug crimes, hundreds of thousands of prisoners are being crowded into human (or inhuman) warehouses where they are increasingly deprived, restricted, isolated, and consequently embittered and alienated from conventional worlds and where less and less is being done to prepare them for their eventual release. As a result, most of them are rendered incapable of returning to even a meager conventional life after prison. Because most will be released within two years, we should be deeply concerned about what happens to them during their incarceration.[10]

If you spend any time examining the daily activities of a prison (whether as a prisoner, a member of the staff, or an outside observer), you are confronted with the fact that the emphasis at all times is on custody. At various times during a twenty-four-hour period, all activities cease, and "counts" are made (at least four times daily and sometimes as often as every two hours). There are also periodic searches of cells, special passes permitting movement about the institution, and myriad rules and regulations governing just about every behavior imaginable. The "count" is "the most important task for which the custody staff is responsible." It is a reflection of what Allen and Simonsen call the **lock psychosis**—an "unreasonable fear by prison administrators that leads them to lock prisoners behind several layers of barred doors and other barricades." This exaggerated fear of inmates or ex-inmates is "usually far out of proportion to the real danger they present."[11]

Prison Security Levels.   The degree of restriction depends on whether a prison is a maximum-, medium-, or minimum-security prison. These three types of prisons are found in nearly every state and in the federal prison system. A **Maximum-security prison** is typically a large fortress-like prison. Old maximum-security prisons (the classic "Big House," described in Chapter 11) have high, concrete walls. Newer models have chain-link fences topped with razor wire, along with strategically placed towers where guards with an assortment of firearms stand watch. One type of maximum-security prison has been dubbed the **super-max prison.** It is reserved for the "baddest of the bad." Examples are the Federal Penitentiary at Marion, Illinois, the Federal Correctional Complex in Florence, Colorado, and Pelican Bay State Prison in Crescent City, California.

Opened in 1989 and reserved for the "most disruptive offenders" (all male), Pelican Bay was built at an estimated cost of $278 million. It was designed to hold 2,080 prisoners but at the end of 1994 held 3,759 prisoners. Within this, the ultimate in super-max prisons, there is a special section known as the Security Housing Unit (SHU) for the "worst of the worst"! Intended to hold 1,056, as of December 1994 the SHU held 1,504 prisoners. This unit is completely segregated from the main prison. SHU prisoners spend 22½ hours per day in their cells. They are permitted only an hour and a half for exercise in small yards connected to their cells, which are all concrete with 20-foot-high cement walls. They eat all their meals in their cells. The SHU even has its own infirmary, law library, and room for parole hearings.[12]

A similar unit is the Inmate Management Unit at the Oregon State Prison. Chuck Terry, a product of both the California and the Oregon prison systems, quoted a prisoner who described this place as follows:

> Most of the people in here are dings, cell warriors, shit slingers, and PC [protective custody] cases. They call this the Thunderdome because of the way sound is intensified and echoes. The cell warriors and dings never seem to sleep. They make noise constantly; hollering, whistling, kicking the doors, jumping on the metal bunks, arguing, etc. IT'S LOUD.... We're trapped in a little cell 24 hours a day (or 23½ hours 5 days, and 24 hours two days) and subjected to this psychotic noise and sleep deprivation. Then there's the design of the place. We're watched 24 hours a day. Try to take a shit and wipe your ass with a female cop watching you. Degradation![13]

Medium-security prisons are somewhat less restrictive. In fact, they are often called "correctional institutions" or "correctional facilities." However, most have guard towers and chain-link fences topped with razor wire. Many have *congregate housing,* or dormitory-style living arrangements. One of the first prisons to use this design was the Norfolk Prison Colony in Massachusetts (later renamed Massachusetts Correctional Institution at Norfolk), opened in 1931. This prison resembles a college campus.[14] Some medium-security prisons have a "podular" design with different areas or "pods" with a congregate living area, with common toilet and shower areas, and each inmate having his own cell. Each cell had a solid-core door with a lock controlled by the prisoner. Entry to the pod is controlled from the outside. These pods resemble college dormitories. There are fewer rules, and inmates in some areas may be allowed to wear civilian clothes when not working. Movement about the prison is not as restricted as in maximum-security prisons.[15]

Minimum-security prisons often have the appearance of college campuses (many prisons for women are like this). Some are called "ranches" or "farms." Most prisoners housed in these kinds of institutions pose little security threat, and most are nonviolent offenders (many are white-collar offenders). Although some of these institutions may be considered "country clubs," inmates *are* confined and cannot leave.

The Daily Routine.   Most of the work in a prison is done to keep the institution running smoothly. Most jobs performed by prisoners, if they work at all (many are idle or work only a few hours each day), consist of sweeping, cooking and serving meals, washing clothes and other prison articles, filing and typing and other administrative duties, library work, running errands, and the like.

The jobs performed by the staff help maintain the prison and also reflect the overwhelming concern with custody instead of with "treatment" (however this is defined). For instance, as of January 1, 1996, there were 213,370 correctional officers and only 11,298 employees categorized as part of the "treatment staff" (psychiatrists, psychologists, social workers, caseworkers, recreation therapists, and counselors), or 5 percent of the total. Also, there was a ratio of 5.3 line correctional officers for every inmate, up from 4.9 in 1990.[16]

What is a typical day like in a prison? Although the daily routine may vary from one institution to another, several accounts from different sources at different periods of time give a fairly accurate picture of this routine. We begin by quoting a former inmate's description of what occurred during his first few weeks in the Nevada State Prison in Carson City in 1978:

> For the first thirty days, all new inmates are held in the "fish tank." This is a portion of the prison where the incoming are initially diagnosed. Each inmate is given a cell which is actually like a small room with a heavy metal door, and for most of the day that is where he stays. It is a time for prison officials to observe the inmates (like in a fish bowl), to administer medical and psychological tests, to have the inmate speak with the chaplain, and with the counselor, and to ascertain if there are any enemies in the general population who might cause the inmate harm (or find out if the inmate might have the idea of harming someone else). Haircuts are given (boot camp style), and showers are allowed once a day, and three meals are delivered to each cell by cart. Advice is given as to how to behave on the yard, and everyone is drilled on the rules and regulations and how the administration and guard staff operate. Inmate programs are explained, and the inmates are cautioned as to what type of activities to avoid (especially the "gang" related type).
>
> A good portion of my days were spent in isolation and I thought a great deal about "doing" my time. I wasn't exactly sure what to expect out there "on the yard," but I realized I would have to be very careful with whom I associated, with what I said and what I did. I would have to be very cautious with all aspects of my behavior staying alert to both the inmates and the guards around me. I would have to pace myself as I got integrating into this community, a community where I would be spending a great deal of monotonous time; day to day, week to week, month to month, year to year.[17]

Another description is given of the routine in a maximum-security prison in Massachusetts:[18]

7:00 A.M.	Rise for the count. Wash and clean cell, making sure your bed is made. Also, stand at the door for the count.
7:20 A.M.	Breakfast.
8:00 A.M.	Work call. If you are unassigned, you go to the TV block or stay in your room.
11:35 A.M.	Work for the morning is complete and the men come in from the shop, returning to their rooms to wash up for dinner and to stand at the door for the count. This is the time to let the guard know if you do not want to go to the meal. This is so for each meal.
1:00 P.M.	Dinner over and this is the time for any announcements to be called, so listen for your name. You may be wanted to go to a hospital visit or the dentist. After any announcements, work call is again called and if and when you are assigned to a job you are to go to it.
3:45 P.M.	The men return from the shops at this time. This begins your free time. On clear days, the yard is open and you can go out until yard time is called. At this time the library is open to take books out and return them.
4:20 P.M.	Count time is called again, this time for supper. When count is called, return to your room and stand at the door.
5:45 P.M.	Another count is called at this time, and this is when the mail is given out, plus any receipt for money, etc.

6:00 P.M.   Count is called complete and the evening activities are announced: gym, avocation and discussion groups, etc.

10:00 P.M.   Count is again called to return to your room for the night, so stand at your door until the guard passes it.

11:00 P.M.   Lights out.

In the early 1980s, the senior author of this book spent two years observing life at the Southern Nevada Correctional Center in Jean, Nevada (a medium-security prison forty miles south of Las Vegas). At that time, most of the inmates had job assignments, at least this is what was indicated on the daily roster. In reality, most work lasted no more than two or three hours, if that much. Observations of this prison revealed a great deal of idleness. Men spent most of the day (in warm months) in the yard getting a tan, listening to radio, playing cards, or engaging in other activities. Others spent the bulk of their time in the housing units either playing cards or watching television (there were televisions in each dormitory-type unit, and they were turned on during most of the day). One of the major complaints heard was that of boredom. Numerous present-day accounts reveal that little has changed over the years.[19]

All of these activities take place within what Goffman calls a **total institution.** Everything that a prisoner does (eat, sleep, work, play, etc.) takes place within the confines of one physical space, whereas in the free world these activities take place in separate locations. In the ideal total institution "all phases of the day's activities are tightly scheduled, with one activity leading at a prearranged time into the next, the whole sequence of activities being imposed from above by a system of explicit formal rulings and a body of officials."[20] Even in such an institution, however, those confined do have some leeway in the kinds of activities they can engage in. The total institution in the sense that Goffman describes probably does not exist. Nevertheless, prisoners can (and many do) become totally dependent on those who rule. It is almost as if the prisoners return to the days of their childhood, for they can have all their basic needs provided for by the prison, and they do not have to assume any responsibility for providing these needs. Watterson, in her study of women's prisons, describes this situation as analogous to a "concrete womb" (more is said about her study in Chapter 14).[21]

The fact that prisoners do not have to make any important decisions about their lives is a crucial point. Most of us make many decisions throughout the course of our lives, decisions about meeting our most basic needs. We also are responsible for taking care of personal matters, some of which we do almost without thinking about it. For instance, we open checking or savings accounts, we pay our monthly bills, we get up in the morning and drive to work, we shop for our food and decide what will be on the menu each night, and we make hundreds of other decisions that are part of everyday living. In a prison (or in other total institutions such as mental hospitals, army boot camps, and boarding schools), most of these decisions are made for those confined. The longer a person spends within such an institution, the greater is the chance of becoming totally dependent and not learning how to meet these normal responsibilities. Little wonder that many prisoners find it so difficult to readjust to outside life, where they must be solely responsible for making decisions and meeting their own needs. In some cases, dependency becomes almost total.

It is appropriate at this time to consider some of the effects of being in prison, of being locked up and shut away from the outside world. For most of us this is hard to imagine. Try to imagine what life would be like if you were confined to the physical space of your campus, even if within this space you could do just about anything you wanted to do. No matter how many things you could do here, no matter how comfortable it was, and no matter how many of your basic physical needs were met (food, shelter, clothing, etc.), you would soon long to escape because one of your most basic needs would not be met—namely, the freedom to move about and go where you want to go and to associate with whomever you want to. Let us now discuss the pains of imprisonment and the inmate social system.

The Pains of Imprisonment. More than forty years ago Gresham Sykes conducted a study of the New Jersey State Prison in which he noted several different effects of incarceration on those confined. These are what he termed the **pains of imprisonment,** and they are as true today as ever.[22]

The first of these pains is the *deprivation of liberty,* the most obvious and immediate deprivation. It is a double form of deprivation, because the prisoner may be confined *within* the prison (placed in segregation, placed in solitary confinement, locked in his or her own cell, etc.). Imprisonment signifies the "moral rejection" by society and often results in what Goffman has called the *mortification of the self.*[23] The prisoner is stripped (both literally and figuratively) of his or her "self," most personal possessions are taken away, and a number is assigned to replace one's personal name. The new prisoner (of course, the more often a person has been to prison, the less painful all of this is) goes through various "status degradation ceremonies."[24] The "fish" (prison argot for newly arrived prisoner; appropriately the new prisoner is usually placed in what is popularly known as the "fish tank") is told in no uncertain terms that he or she is a lowly creature, even in the prison world. For many, it is a sort of "time out from personal identity" as one must separate his "private world" from his "public world."[25]

Second, the prisoner suffers the *deprivation of goods and services.* What a person would normally have access to in the outside world is prohibited in prison—a car, money, clothes, adequate medical services, and so on. Of course, for some, there is not much of a loss because they had nothing on the outside. But some actually desire to go to prison (especially if they have been in before) because at least in prison they get "three squares a day."

Third, there is the *deprivation of heterosexual relationships.* Indeed, a few prisons allow conjugal visits, but these visits are usually restricted to married couples and to only a few hours at a time, and often there is some form of supervision by officials. Homosexuality is common. Undoubtedly, some of these relationships are voluntary, but forced homosexuality is common, including homosexual rapes. The most common form of homosexuality occurring on a regular basis is between aggressive males (known variously as "wolves" or "jockers") and passive males (often called "punks"). What often occurs is that an experienced convict (the "wolf" or "jocker") entices a young "fish" into a relationship by seemingly offering friendship and "protection" from other "wolves" and by showing affection with the presentation of various gifts (cigarettes, a "cushy" job, etc.). After a while, the wolf demands sex in return (usually threatening to "turn him loose" on other "wolves").

The fourth is the *deprivation of autonomy.* One's freedom of movement and opportunity to be creative and independent are severely thwarted in prison. Also, one's privacy is reduced considerably, especially in prisons that are overcrowded and where there are two or more prisoners to a room.

Finally, there is the *deprivation of security.* In the outside world a person is relatively free from personal victimization; in prison it is a constant threat. As Sykes suggests: "Rubbed raw by the irritants of custodial life, and frequently marked by long histories of aggressive behavior, inmates are likely to explode into violence or take what they want from other inmates with the threat of force." The prison world is a violent world, rife with many of the same kinds of aggression and exploitation found in the outside world, only more directly visible.[26]

More recent studies suggest that doing time in today's prisons has even more negative consequences. Austin and Irwin's study documents that more and more prisoners are becoming withdrawn and many have become what Austin and Irwin term "crippled." Today more and more prisons are built in remote areas of society (see Chapter 11) where the only thing on the minds of the administration is security and reduced contacts with the outside. "These practices, along with greatly diminished rehabilitative resources, are producing prisoners who have deteriorated in prison and return to the outside much less well equipped to live a conventional life than they were when they entered."[27] Many prisoners are transformed into individuals who are alienated from the rest of the world. This alienation has five dimensions. First, they experience a sense of *powerlessness,* expecting that one cannot bring about changes they seek. Second, there is *meaninglessness* in the sense that they do not know what to believe. Third, there is *normlessness,* meaning that deviant behaviors are necessary to achieve success. Fourth, there is *detachment* in that the prisoner becomes disassociated from core beliefs and values of society. Fifth, there is *self-estrangement* in that one experiences oneself as "alien and unworthy."[28]

The prison is a society within a society. Those who inhabit its world create a world with its own culture, its own rules, and its own statuses. It is a society with relatively scarce goods and resources. A power structure often emerges as prisoners compete for a share of the goods and services that are available.

The Inmate Social System.   Like any other organization or institution, the prison contains a cultural system complete with its own norms and corresponding social roles. This is not difficult to understand, because those in prison (both the "keepers" and the "kept") must somehow learn to adapt to an unusual situation. Indeed, the prison is an enclosed structure where a large number of people live under often extreme conditions in a high-density area. Human beings being adaptable creatures, it is no surprise that they develop methods of adapting. Years ago, McCorkle and Korn observed that an **inmate social system** provides "a way of life which enables the inmate to avoid the devastating psychological effects of internalizing and converting social rejection into self-rejection. In effect, it permits the inmate to reject his rejectors rather than himself."[29]

The inmate social system is a system that exists in every institution in the country. There is a set of social roles and cultural norms that existed long before the prisoner arrived, and it will exist long after the prisoner's departure. It is a subculture that experienced inmates learn to adapt to, so much so that even if transferred from one prison to another, from one jail to another, an inmate immediately is able to make adjustments and often feel "at home." (Because of the large number of interinstitutional transfers and the general mobility of people in society today, it is not unusual for a prisoner recently released from, say, Attica, to commit a crime in California and meet up with old friends in San Quentin, or vice versa.)

In addition, there is what is known as the **inmate code,** a set of norms that describes how prisoners should behave. This code "provides a philosophy of doing time, includes ways of implementing the maxims of the code, includes rationalizations for criminal behavior, and satisfactory solutions for obtaining illegal goods and services to mitigate the prison poverty imposed upon the inmates."[30] Such a code is quite similar to the "code of the streets" and is "imported" into the prison environment.[31] This code contains several rules. The following five are most important:[32]

1. Don't interfere with inmate interests; this also includes more specific injunctions, such as never rat on a con (to "rat" is to "snitch" or to be a "stool pigeon").
2. Don't lose your head; do your own time.
3. Don't exploit inmates—that is, don't steal from fellow prisoners, share goods and services with others, and so on.
4. Don't weaken—in other words, one should be able to "take it," to "be tough," and, above all else, "be a man."
5. Don't be a sucker; don't trust guards or other staff; don't work too hard, and so on.

Another important part of the inmate social system are distinct roles or social types, often referred to as *argot roles.* These roles include the following:[33]

1. *Rat,* otherwise known as the "squealer." This individual betrays others and is one of the most despised of all inmates in the prison world.
2. *Center man,* also known as the "square John." This individual tends to take on the perspectives and values of persons in charge of the institution, rather than those of the inmate culture; he usually comes from a relatively stable working-class background and does not have a long history of criminal offenses.

3. *Gorilla.* This individual uses violence as a means to gain specific ends; he often preys on weaker inmates to get what he wants. A variation is characterized as "tough."

4. *Weaklings,* the opposite of "gorillas" and "toughs." These individuals find it difficult to adapt to prison life. A variation is the "rapo," the inmate who constantly maintains his innocence, which is a constant irritation to other inmates (who say "stop complaining" and "do your own time.")

5. *Merchant,* also known as the "peddler" and "entrepreneur." This individual engages in a wide variety of economic activities (cigarettes, drugs, alcohol, etc.); also known as the "racketeer."

6. *Wolves, punks, fags.* These are homosexual roles. "Wolves" play the aggressive male role, "punks" are those who are "made" (victimized), and "fags" were homosexual prior to coming to prison.

7. *Ball buster.* This person is always giving prison staff a hard time and, from the inmate culture's view, makes things worse for others by always "fouling things up" and acting the "fool."

8. *Right guy.* In contrast to the "ball buster," the "right guy" can "take it" and "dish it out." He is the most loyal of inmates. He never "rats" and "does his own time."

9. *Tough guy* and *hipster.* The "tough guy," in contrast to the "ball buster," "is regarded by other inmates with a curious mixture of fear and respect"; this person "represents the deference of terror" and does not act "wild" but rather is cold and calculating and "won't take anything from anybody." The "hipster" puts up a false front, acts tough but really isn't, and tries too hard to belong.[34]

Concerning the "right guy" a former inmate described this role as follows:

> Being "one of the boys" carried with it a certain set of responsibilities. These responsibilities centered on being a "right guy" and this meant that one would not walk away from confrontation, nor "let out" any information on what others might be doing. It also meant, at times, knowing about and even participating in behavior that could lead to serious problems.
>
> With these kinds of responsibilities one is forced to stay keenly aware of the surrounding circumstances, to stay on top of their game in order that the "right guy" reputation stay intact. It's a difficult and wearing activity, and you have little room to escape its pressures. And I could not forget that I had an additional sentence hanging over my head should I get into trouble. Despite my outward "coolness" and my being in with the right crowd, I recognized that I was in a precarious situation. I hoped, and sometimes prayed, that I could manage to keep everything going as smoothly as it had.[35]

These roles are not rigid, and they are not found in every prison. There are many variations, and not every prisoner fits into a particular category. Moreover, the inmate code is more of an ideal than a reality, for it is violated on a more or less daily basis. If these codes were adhered to (or even believed in) by all prisoners, the prison would be a utopian community, a socialist commonwealth. Unfortunately, this is not the case, given the number of assaults, rapes, knifings, and even killings that take place within many prisons. In fact, violence is so ever-present that we devote a special section to the subject later in this chapter.

Adapting to life behind bars often takes several forms. Researchers have called these forms of adaptation "doing time" and a fascinating process known as *prisonization.*

Doing Time and Prisonization

In a classic study undertaken over forty years ago, Donald Clemmer first used the term **prisonization** to refer to the process in which a person takes on "the folkways, mores, customs and general culture of the penitentiary."[36] The extent to which one becomes enmeshed in the prison culture—that is, becomes prisonized—depends on factors such as age, previous prison experiences, length of sentence, relations with people on the outside, and type of crime committed. All prisoners, to some extent, become prisonized. Perhaps the ultimate indication of prisonization is the belief that life inside prison is better (or at least no worse) than life outside, which leads a released prisoner to commit crimes in such a way that apprehension is almost a certainty.

Research subsequent to Clemmer's pioneering work has continued to document this process. For example, Wheeler found that the extent of prisonization (measured in terms of prisoners' lack of commitment to staff role expectations and degree of commitment to the inmate social system) varied according to the length of time served. He found that the percentage of those exhibiting a high degree of conformity to staff role expectations *decreased* with the length of time served. The degree of prisonization corresponded to three phases of the prisoner's institutional career. During the early and late stages (the first and last six months of the sentence), there was a high degree of conformity. During the middle phase, there was a low degree of conformity. It should be noted, however, that less than half of the prisoners exhibited a high degree of conformity at any time. Also, many prisoners adhere to staff expectations only to the extent necessary to present a favorable image so as to increase the likelihood of being released. No doubt many are simply playing a "con" (or game) in order to present a favorable image.[37]

Researchers have found that adherence to prison norms is partly the result of adherence to similar norms on the streets (the prison "code" is in part "imported" into the prison system). In fact, certain norms and values included within the inmate code are also found in certain segments of the population on the outside, especially in the lower-class world where most offenders reside. Irwin's study of inmates in the 1960s found that the degree of prisonization depends mainly on the type of criminal experiences a person has had and the degree to which one develops a criminal identity.[38]

Irwin identified three modes of adaptation to imprisonment: jailing, doing one's own time, and gleaning. *Jailing* is full participation in the prison world. Inmates who adopt this mode become highly prisonized. For those with a lot of prior experience in jails and prisons, the prison may become "reality" and the world outside an "illusion."[39] Prisoners who *do their own time* either plan to "go straight" and commit no more crimes or plan to return to a life of crime upon release; they undergo no significant change of attitude or worldview while in prison. Inmates who engage in what Irwin calls *gleaning* look ahead to the time when they will be released and try to change their life patterns and self-concepts in a significant way, such as by returning to school or changing work careers.[40]

In Irwin's sample of 116 felons, 15 percent were *jailers* who "tend to make a world out of prison."[41] This role is especially characteristic of persons whom Irwin calls *state-raised youth*. These are offenders who "grew up" within various institutions—foster care, group homes, and the like, in addition to juvenile detention centers and correctional facilities— rarely spending any significant amounts of time in free society. Irwin describes their worldview as distorted, stunted, and incoherent. The prison world becomes their only meaningful world.

Most of those who "do their own time" (they are often "right guys") are part of the "thief subculture." They stay out of trouble, they don't "rat," and they participate in a wide variety of officially supported programs. This type of participation is known as *programming*. It is a method used by many inmates (not just thieves) to get out as soon as possible. They participate, superficially, in many different "treatment" programs to "look good" to the parole board. Many prison administrators and various education, vocational, and psychological staff members actively encourage inmates to "program."

Gleaning, according to Irwin, is becoming more common. Many prisoners become self-educated, learn a new trade, and in general attempt to "improve their mind" or "find themselves."[42] It is not known for sure how many honestly pursue these activities. Some may be playing a "con" game to help themselves get out of prison, which is, after all, the major goal of most prisoners. The experiences of one prisoner, Jim Palombo, demonstrates the importance of seeking self-improvement through the educational process. Completing his undergraduate degree while still in prison was Palombo's method of turning his life

around. Even while still in jail waiting for his prison sentence to begin, Palombo was formulating his plan:

> But I knew that I was fortunate. I still had possession of the abilities I had, until now, abused;
> abilities given to me by another source that I had wrongly credited to my own being. I was
> now hoping, no I was making a pact with myself, that through whatever lie ahead, I would
> make my "time" payoff. I would put my abilities to proper use, I would somehow get a col-
> lege education and I would redeem myself with it. It was time to move on, and, as the ironies
> of life often are, it was in this kind of place, in jail, that I felt the spirit to make it happen.[43]

After arriving at the main prison (Nevada State Prison in Carson City), Palombo kept
thinking about his plan:

> I was trying to numb myself to the surroundings, and at the same time I kept thinking about
> my parents and my family and myself. Education kept popping into my head.... I'll get into
> it, I'll learn, I'll get my degree, I'll not waste the years in here, I'll turn this all around and
> become something...something more than what this place was suggesting...something
> more than what that little boy at the airport had seen. I must do it.[44]

The Sub-Rosa Economy

Gang activity in prisons has increased tremendously in recent years. Many prison gangs
(discussed in detail later in this chapter) are extensions of street gangs in most large cities.
In many cases, street-gang members who are sent to prison are offered immediate protection and membership in their own gang upon their arrival. They have little trouble adjusting to prison life, and their arrival is like a homecoming—they meet old friends from the
streets. Aside from protection, gangs provide many services to their members. For instance, the relative poverty of prison inmates is partially offset by the various rackets and
economic activities controlled by the gangs on the inside. Such activities involve cigarettes, food, clothing, and drugs. But the most important role these gangs play is that of
providers of psychological support.

Almost thirty years ago three researchers documented the existence of a **sub-rosa
economy** within the prison system. Williams and Fish studied Menard State Prison in Illinois, and Davidson studied San Quentin in California.[45] In Menard, Williams and Fish
found several "routes" or highly organized and systematic theft of, among other items, food
from the kitchen and cigarettes. In San Quentin the smuggling of drugs was at this time one
of the most lucrative activities, with a possible profit in excess of $100,000 per year.

These activities illustrate how resourceful prison inmates (or anyone confined) can
be, primarily because of the need to improve the deprived conditions within the prison system, a system of forced poverty. Williams and Fish describe the use of waste materials that
to the ordinary observer might seem of no use to anyone. One example is potato peelings,
which the inmates used to make beer. The production and distribution of homemade beer
(often called "pruno") was a lucrative activity.

Many goods and services that are forbidden inside prison but are taken for granted in
the outside world become symbols of prestige and status within the prison world. Williams
and Fish describe one example:

> If a free world citizen pays a laundry worker to place an extra crease in his shirt, it is an act
> hardly worthy of note, as it is assumed to be a small matter of personal preference. When the
> convict pays a laundry worker [payment usually comes in the form of a pack of cigarettes or
> some other medium of exchange] to place a crease in his shirt it is significant, for he may be
> demonstrating to the convict world his power and economic acumen. He is expressing a
> modest version of the Veblenian "conspicuous consumption." In the free world, the inmate
> would attempt to excel in the standard American way of acquiring material goods coveted by
> others, especially material goods easily displayed to strangers as well as to friends. On the
> streets the inmate might drive the flashiest automobile on the block and wear dapper clothes.

In prison, since he is required to be uniformly drab and poverty stricken, small adjustments to his uniform are his way of displaying success to friends and strangers alike—his mode of conspicuous consumption. Small uniform adjustments, a crease here and a tuck there, are no less significant on the inside than big automobiles on the outside.[46]

The prison world is in many ways a microcosm of the outside society, especially when it comes to economic activities and "conspicuous consumption." Examples that we have seen within the Nevada prison system include personal coffee cups (in the chow hall prisoners have to drink coffee out of plastic drinking glasses), personal televisions, radios, and stereos in one's cell (which inmates call their "house"), personally decorated "houses,"and personalized clothing (especially shirts and shoes, for all prisoners are required to wear blue jeans) sent in from friends and family on the streets. In short, inmates do just about anything to make prison life more bearable. Perhaps these activities, including the making of pruno and the various sub-rosa economic activities, are a positive sign of mental health, indicating that at least prisoners are active and creative rather than dull and robot-like.

Inmate Views of the "Outside"

Life in prison is not always pleasant. Not only can it be dangerous at times, but it can also be boring and it can have a negative effect on one's personality and worldview. One effect, pointed out by Irwin, is that being in prison produces a very disjointed and often unrealistic view of the outside world. Because most prisoners will return to the outside world eventually, while in prison they make plans about what they will do after they are released. Conversation about these plans often takes up most of their waking hours.

Prisoners learn a convict's perspective of "the streets," a perspective that plays an important role in shaping their behavior when they are released.[47] While in prison they learn from others what is likely to happen following their release. Often they hear stories (some true, some false, but most of them exaggerated) about a particular individual and what he did when he got out, or they learn directly from those who return to prison on new charges. Irwin suggests that prisoners develop three perspectives on the degree of success following release: "making it," avoiding the "old bag," and "doing all right."

"Making It" and Avoiding the "Old Bag." "Making it" simply refers to staying out of prison. Much of this involves keeping financially viable, coping with the parole system (e.g., avoiding being harassed by the parole agent and getting sent back for technical violations, or "some chicken-shit beef," as some cons refer to it), and avoiding the "old bag"— that is, the deviant ways that resulted in the prison sentence the first place. Avoiding the "old bag" does not always mean staying perfectly "clean," for some do commit crimes. Staying out of the "old bag" more often means avoiding certain types of crimes or simply avoiding getting apprehended.

"Doing All Right." "Doing all right" means making up for pleasures missed while in prison. Irwin identifies three styles of "doing all right" (remember, this is from a perspective shaped while the person is still in prison).

Conventional Styles. There are several. The "settling down" style means getting a job, getting married, and so on. The "transformation" style means seeking a new career, enrolling in college, and altering one's former lifestyle and work habits considerably. The "swinger" style means involvement in action-seeking activities such as nights on the town, parties, sports, picking up women, and trips to Las Vegas or other resort towns. The "playboy" style entails making plenty of money, leading the "good" life, driving fancy cars, and wearing good clothes. What prisoners see as the "good" life is shaped by what they see on television (they spend many hours watching television) and what they read in magazines. Thus, it is a very exaggerated vision that leads to many problems of adjustment following release. A variation is the "rich old lady" scheme, which means finding a wealthy woman and leading the playboy life or, more realistically, finding and marrying a career woman.

Marginal Styles.   These styles include getting involved in what Irwin calls "kinky occupations." He means occupations on the margin between legality and illegality, such as those that may open up opportunities for illegal activities—bellboys, cab drivers, bartenders, working at casinos in Las Vegas or Atlantic City, and so on. There are also "artist styles" (writers, painters, musicians, etc.) and "student intellectual" styles. A recently emerging style is that of the "revolutionary" or "radical"—politically aware prisoners join organizations (e.g., Black Panthers, Muslims, Socialists) in an attempt to make radical kinds of changes or adopt radically different lifestyles.

Criminal Styles.   These styles include the "big score" (one more major crime that, it is hoped, will result in a large monetary gain), drug deals, "hustles" (e.g., numbers, bookmaking, pool playing, gambling), and "escapades" (most common among state-raised youth)—going on a rampage and committing several crimes.

The plans of many prisoners go awry because their perceptions of life on the outside (from inside the prison) are distorted and exaggerated. The outside world, they soon learn, is more complicated then it seems on television and in magazines.

Prison life is not at all like what most of the public imagines—a sort of country club where inmates loaf and watch their own televisions, work out with weights, enroll in education programs, eat good food, and generally have a great time at public expense. If prisons are so comfortable, why aren't there long lines of people waiting to get inside? With few exceptions prisons today are dangerous places. Although there are few deaths, the threat of injury through some kind of attack is constant, especially given the number of gangs in prison. In the next section we explore the problem of violence.

PRISON VIOLENCE

In the modern prison, a new inmate often faces some difficult decisions. In the words of an inmate at the maximum-security prison at Leavenworth, Kansas: "Every convict has three choices. He can fight [kill someone], he can hit the fence [escape], or he can fuck [submit]."[48] That inmate may be exaggerating the need to kill someone; what he is referring to is the need to be ready to "get physical" with those who may prey on you.

Data collected by Austin and Irwin on violence in California's prisons demonstrate the extent of the problem. They note that the total number of violent incidents grew from 365 in 1970 to 9,769 in 1998 and the *rate* (per 100 prisoners) increased from 1.4 to 6.6. Generally, the most common type of violent incident was an assault without a weapon; a close second for most of those years was an assault *with* a weapon. In 1998, about 43 percent of the violent incidents did not involve a weapon, while 23 percent did.[49]

Austin and Irwin explored some of the reasons for the increase in violence inside prisons. One reason is the reduction of resources—educational, recreational, vocational—available to prisoners. The get-tough policies of the past couple of decades have resulted in more money being spent on security. Another reason is that there are fewer contacts with loved ones, because more and more prisons are built in remote rural areas (e.g., the prisons in extreme northern Michigan are at least a full day's drive for inmates' relatives living in Detroit, which most of the inmates call home). This remoteness has also contributed to an overall decline in local services and support (e.g., churches).[50]

Other reasons for the increase in violence noted by Austin and Irwin include the often arbitrary forms of punishment meted out by the prison staff and a growing number of what inmates refer to as "chickenshit rules." Also, increasingly, there has developed a sort of "gulag mentality" as the amenities enjoyed by earlier generations of prisoners (freedom to decorate their walls with pictures, to alter prison clothing, to keep birds and other small pets in their cells, etc.) have been slowly taken away. The warden at the federal prison at Lompoc, California, destroyed a row of beautiful old eucalyptus trees that had surrounded the prison for fifty years or so and then poisoned the squirrels that had lived in those trees and had provided enjoyment for the inmates (feeding them, watching them play, etc.) Then the Lompoc warden "mounted a genocidal war against the cats and raccoons that roamed the prison grounds." No wonder the inmates called him "Defoliating Bob"![51] Such "amenities" may seem trivial to outsiders and evidence that prisons are "country clubs," but to prisoners they make a world of difference and their removal generates anger and resentment of those in authority.

Prison Riots

In February 1980, a riot at the New Mexico State Prison left thirty-three inmates dead and more than eighty people injured. Most of the inmates who were killed were prison "snitches" or "rats." This was one of the most brutal prison riots in history. Ironically, several of the snitches who were killed had warned officials about a possible riot. The prison was severely overcrowded—at 150 percent over its capacity. Prior to the rioting, a group of inmates had filed a lawsuit citing, among other things, corruption and nepotism. Officials failed to act. After the riot, the federal district court was empowered to oversee the operation of the prison.[52]

The New Mexico riot was not the first. Several noteworthy prison riots preceded it, especially during the 1960s and early 1970s, when there were politically motivated rebellions that culminated in the tragedy at Attica in 1971, where several inmates and guards were killed in an unprecedented attack by the state police.

Early Prison Riots. Prior to the 1960s, inmates inside the nation's prison system rarely united behind common ideologies and goals that went beyond the prison system itself. Most riots were a form of protest about prison conditions. Rather than challenging the prison system itself as part of a much larger system of control or various social issues outside the prison system, prisoners protested over bad food, treatment by the guards, work, job training, and so on.[53] Riots of this kind have been termed **frustration riots** because they vent inmates' frustration over the lack of decent conditions and successful treatment programs. Between 1950 and 1953 alone there were more than fifty such riots.[54] One of the most famous, however, the so-called Battle of Alcatraz, occurred in 1946. A group of inmates tried to take over the prison and escape. In a scene similar to events portrayed in the movie *The Rock,* prison guards, Marines, the Coast Guard, the harbor police, and the Army became involved in protecting "the rock."

One reason why such relatively narrow concerns prevailed was that those in power within the inmate social system (e.g., "gorillas" and "racketeers") had a vested interest in maintaining the status quo. Another reason was that few inmates had developed any kind of political or social consciousness.

Another form of rioting—**race riots**—emerged in the 1960s as more and more racial minorities began to be sentenced to prison. These riots were mostly apolitical uprisings. During 1969 and 1970 there were a reported ninety-eight of them.[55] However, these disturbances were just a hint to what was to come.

The Politicalization of Prison Riots: 1960s and 1970s. As the civil rights movement grew during the early 1960s, a number of factions developed within it. One faction was the Black Muslims, a movement that found its way into the prison system (with the help of Malcolm X, an ex-con himself). The Black Muslims' insistence that African Americans were victims of white racism rather than personal inadequacies was especially relevant to African American inmates, who for so many years had accepted the notion that they were "sick" or just plain "criminals." The Muslims "introduced the notion of collective oppression to black prisoners, which counteracted the prison ideology of individual pathology."[56]

Their advocacy of organization, self-discipline, and collective unity presented definite threats to prison authority. Two tactics advocated by the Muslims were strikes and lawsuits. These tactics were subsequently picked up and were frequently used by inmates to protest prison conditions and to extend their constitutional rights inside the prison walls. The Muslims influenced African American prisoners in another, more significant way—namely, by helping them see that they were part of a larger oppressed class and were prisoners both inside and outside the prison walls.

During the 1960s the prison was becoming less isolated from the outside world. One result of the many changes during this period (such as the civil rights movement) was that the prison became a center for radical activity. This was facilitated by the qualitative changes in prison populations, specifically the influx of relatively more educated and politically sophisticated young whites and African Americans convicted for drug-law violations and protest activities. Also, there was an increase in books and articles written by inmates and ex-inmates, and these writings were to have a significant impact on militant inmates, fostering their belief that they were part of an oppressed class.[57]

A growing number of prisoners were becoming "politicized." Instead of protesting against prison conditions per se, they brought inside the prison gates the broader political protest of the outside world. The prison was viewed as more than a building filled with "criminals." Critics said that it was just one aspect of a much larger network of economic and political oppression in American society as a whole.

One result was **political riots,** or rebellions. A number of these incidents occurred during the late 1960s, culminating in the rebellion in 1971 at Attica, one of the most violent in prison history. In California prisons there were strikes and revolts at San Quentin in 1967, 1968, and 1970, and at Soledad and Folsom prisons in 1970. Each of these revolts showed evidence of tremendous unity and a breakdown of racial animosities.[58] In 1970 inmates at the Tombs jail in Manhattan revolted and presented a list of demands that went beyond the prison itself; many of these demands were identical to those that would be made at Attica a year later.[59] Finally, the revolt at Attica showed even more unity and lack of racial animosities. Tragically, ten hostages and twenty-nine inmates were killed in the unprecedented attack by the New York State Police, ordered by the governor of New York. An additional eighty-five inmates, three hostages, and one state police officer were wounded.[60]

Recent Prison Riots: The Rage Riot.   Following the 1970s rebellions, prisons seemed to go back to a somewhat normal existence. It became obvious that prisoners were not as solidified as before and became quite fragmented. There are many reasons for this. One reason was the transferring of several thousand "troublemakers" to other institutions. Another reason was the end of the Vietnam War and the end of antiwar protests. Still another reason was the growing conservative backlash against social protest and social reform of the 1960s. Indeed, by the middle of the 1970s the conservative view on crime was becoming more and more dominant. There is a suspicion that one method of controlling popular protests was the classic divide-and-rule strategy where fears and insecurities were manipulated by the "powers that be" and stereotypes about crime and criminals were perpetuated.[61] Then, too, the 1980s was a period marked by extensive greed and selfishness, which no doubt has spilled over into the prisons where it is almost literally "every man for himself."

What emerged in the late 1970s and beyond was a disturbance known as **rage riots.**[62] These kinds of riots were often very spontaneous and expressive, as most of the violence was directed at fellow inmates, rather than prison officials or the "system" itself. Often they were the result of racial conflicts, especially between rival gangs. Often they were a sort of payback against specific inmates or types of inmates, as what occurred in the New Mexico riots in 1980. This behavior is typical in the prison world of today, filled as it is with hopelessness and alienation, where any notion of rehabilitation has been thrown in the trash basket of history.

It remains to be seen what sorts of disturbances are on the horizon. Given the explosive mixture of severe overcrowding, budget cutbacks on prison rehabilitation programs, gangs, and deteriorating social conditions on the outside, we may see newer forms of prison rioting—perhaps even a return to the political riots of the late 1960s and early 1970s.

One cannot discuss prison violence without reference to the growing problem of gangs in the prison system. As many researchers have noted, the gang problem has emerged as one of the key issues confronting our society. Yet, the emergence of gangs cannot be understood apart from the deteriorating social conditions facing millions of inner-city people, especially African Americans and Hispanics.[63] With the growth of these urban gangs, it is not surprising that the criminal justice system has responded in its typical get-tough fashion, and that has resulted in a phenomenal increase in the number of gang members receiving prison sentences—some excessively long.[64]

Prison Gangs

There has been little research directed toward gangs in the prison system; therefore, we do not have a great deal of information about those who belong to **prison gangs.** There are only a handful of systematic studies of the problem, and the most up-to-date research is found in a special edition of *The Prison Journal,* which contains seven articles reporting original research.[65]

The Extent and Nature of the Gang Problem in the Prison System.   Gangs can be found today in virtually every adult and juvenile correctional institution. A survey by Buentello, Fong, and Vogel found that within the Texas prison system there were a total of eight gangs with a total membership of 1,174.[66] A study by Ralph and Marquart noted that in Texas there were nine gangs with almost 2,500 members. (We do not know which set of data is the correct one.) Ralph and Marquart further note that among the gangs found within this prison system are the Mexican Mafia (with almost 1,000 members), the Texas Syndicate, the Aryan Brotherhood, the Hermanos de Pistoleros Latinos, and the Texas Mafia.[67] A survey by Knox and Tromanhauser of juvenile facilities found that almost half of the juveniles incarcerated had been in a gang at some point in time. In their survey of adult institutions, Knox and Tromanhauser found that just over one-fourth (27.7%) of the prison administrators surveyed said that gangs "significantly affected their correctional environment," while almost half (45.4%) said that their staff had had some training in dealing with the gang problem. Also, about 70 percent said that the gang problem had existed for less than five years, while about one-third said that the problem had existed for more than five years. These authors also report that where gangs control much of the illicit drug importation into the prison, there is a significantly higher threat of violence to staff.[68]

In their survey of juvenile correctional facilities, Knox and Tromanhauser reported that the majority of gang members, not surprisingly, were either Hispanic or African American and the vast majority were male. Another noteworthy characteristic of gang members, in contrast to nongang juveniles, was the extent of time spent incarcerated: gang members had more experience with incarceration than nongang juveniles. Other significant differences between the two groups include the following: gang members started drinking and using drugs at an earlier age; they spent more time drinking and using drugs, and their level of consumption was significantly higher.[69]

An interesting finding from the Knox and Tromanhauser juvenile correctional survey was that gang members were far more sexually active than nongang juveniles (and began having sex earlier) and were more likely to have caused a pregnancy (or become pregnant) and were more likely to be diagnosed with a sexually transmitted disease. Also, gang members were far more likely to engage in fights, use weapons, attempt suicide, and smoke cigarettes. Such behaviors and general lifestyles, say the authors, result in greater health risks that confront correctional administrators.[70]

The Relationship between Street Gangs and Prison Gangs.   There are three perspectives that attempt to explain prison-gang development. One argues that prison gangs are imported street gangs. The second argues that prison gangs are indigenous, arising within the prison itself partly as a means of belonging and protection. The third perspective explains prison gangs as emulating gangs in other prisons or gangs on the outside.[71]

The first perspective is the most common explanation for the emergence of prison gangs. We do know that there is a close relationship between youth street gangs and the prison system. Largely in response to the rising arrest rate for violent crimes and drug possession/sales in the 1960s and 1970s, the population of today's prison system has reached an all-time high. Recent observers have noted that in many respects the gangs on the streets have been imported into the prison system. As Jacobs, Moore, and Hagedorn have documented, most of the gangs within any given urban area have their direct counterparts within the state prison system. In Jacob's study of Stateville (one of the major prisons in Illinois), it was found that the inmate system was organized in ways almost identical with the gangs on the streets of Chicago.[72] In a nationwide survey, Camp and Camp found that of thirty-three state prison officials who indicated they had gangs, a total of twenty-one said that these gangs had their counterparts in the cities of these states.[73]

Information from the streets is relayed to prison-gang members by visits from friends and relatives and by new prison inmates as well. As Jacobs notes: "the influx of gang members has been so great that a communication link between street and prison has been established merely through the steady commitment of members."[74]

According to Jacobs, prison gangs first emerged in the West, in the state of Washington in 1950 and in California in 1957. Twelve years later, in 1969, prison gangs began in Illinois. During the 1970s, states adjacent to California and bordering Mexico, as well as two states to the north of Illinois, had gangs develop inside their prison systems. In the 1980s, development continued in Missouri and Kentucky. Prison gangs spread by transfers or rearrests of gang members in another jurisdiction. In these cases the inmate in a new prison setting sometimes tried to reproduce the organization that gave him an identity in the prior prison setting. In other cases, charismatic leaders imitated what they had heard about other gangs. Many even adopted the name of a gang from another jurisdiction but had no affiliation or communication with it. Contributing to the growth of gangs has been the problem of racism within prison walls, with gangs usually being organized along fairly strict racial lines.

Buentello, Fong, and Vogel attribute the recent growth of prison gangs to judicial intervention into the area of prisoner's rights, which, they claim, weakened the authority of prison officials, especially in the area of providing protection for inmates. As a result many inmates began to organize themselves for self-protection. Yet at the same time prison violence increased. In Texas, for example, homicides increased from twelve in 1982 to twenty-seven in 1985. Gangs are reportedly responsible for half of all prison management problems in the country as a whole.[75]

Prison gangs, not unlike many on the streets, adhere to a code of secrecy and emphasize power and prestige, measured in terms of the ability to control other inmates and specific activities within the institution. Money and drugs in particular represent tangible symbols of a gang's ability to control and dominate others, and of its ability to provide essential protection, goods, and services for its members. The gang's ability to bring status and prestige for the members reinforces gang commitment and solidarity.[76]

Jacobs also found that one of the distinguishing characteristics of the prison gang, unlike most gangs on the streets, is the virtual absence of any noncriminal, nondeviant activities. Activities are usually criminal or deviant in nature. The gang member is completely immersed in being a career prison gangster, leaving little time and less inclination for other than asocial behavior.[77] A study by Shelden found that, compared to nongang inmates, gang members tend not to participate in legitimate activities within the prison, especially rehabilitation programs.[78]

Prison gangs have several additional characteristics. They are organized along racial and ethnic lines and have a well-defined hierarchical structure. They recruit based on "homeboy" preprison experiences. They adhere to a very strict code of silence and are committed to the gang for life. This loyalty is reflected in the common expression "Blood in, blood out."[79]

Hagedorn found that, among the gang members he interviewed, most believed that "prison strengthens gang involvement," which is exactly the opposite of the intended effect of incarcerating gang members.[80] Spergel notes that the prison "may be regarded both as facilitating and responding to gang problems."[81] Further, incarceration may be a short-term solution to the problem, but in the long run it "has led to increased gang cohesion and membership recruitment in many institutions, and may have indirectly worsened the problem in the streets," because some gangs are formed in the prison and are transferred out into the streets. In other words, gangs inside the prison system often have their own unique histories and distinct origins. Therefore, we need to be cautious about the common view that gangs are "mere extensions" of street gangs, for that is clearly not always the case.[82]

Moore goes even further and argues that the prison system, at least for Chicanos in the Los Angeles area, is only one of several institutions they normally come into contact with (other institutions include the welfare system and the police). She observed that there exists among many Chicano youth a sort of "anticipatory socialization" to prison. She also notes that "Prison is an omnipresent reality in barrio life, and contact with it is continuous and drastic, affecting nearly everybody in the barrio.... Prison adaptations are seen by convicts themselves as variants of adaptations to street life."[83] Further, the prison

> is experienced as a climax institution of the Anglo world as it impinges upon the barrio. Prison exaggerates many of the familiar features of outside Anglo institutions. Even more important, social relationships in prison are familiar because the Chicano's fellows in prison are the same people he sees on the streets of Los Angeles.... [I]n exaggerated form, the prison is a climax institution representing the same forces that the Chicanos of Los Angeles have felt all their lives.[84]

In short, Moore finds that inside the prison the gangs are alive and well. They provide many things to Chicano convicts. There is a strong emphasis on family-like relationships. One routine among Chicano prisoners is to watch the bus bring in new prisoners and look for "homeboys." They offer them immediate assistance and welcome them to the prison. Also, these gangs are very active participants in the sub-rosa prison economy of drug smuggling.[85] Moore notes that within the prison system of California during the 1970s the so-called Mexican Mafia reportedly began to get involved in an illegal drug market outside the prison. In 1977 there was an indictment of thirty men who were involved in a $50 million a year heroin operation that was run from inside the prison.[86]

According to Camp and Camp, gangs are the most significant reality behind prison walls. The unaffiliated convict enters the prison fearing that his life may be in danger from gangs. Even if he is not immediately concerned with survival, he will face the prospect of being "shaken down" for commissary items or sex. The guards can be of little help in protecting him. In one way or another, the convict must find a strategy for dealing with the gang situation.[87]

In contrast to the recruitment pressures experienced by the unaffiliated convict, the gang member from the street has no trouble whatsoever in adjusting to the new environment. Besides offering physical security, the gang in the prison, as on the street, serves important material and psychological functions for its members. The gang functions as a communication network, as well as a convenient distribution network for contraband goods. It also provides a source of identification and a feeling of belonging. Other gang members become one's family and are often referred to "my homes" or just "homes" (short for "homeboy"). Members live for, and die for, the gang. The organizations, with their insignias, colors, salutes, titles, and legendary histories, often provide the only meaningful reference group for their members.[88]

Gang members remain oriented toward the same membership group and leadership hierarchy as they did before coming to prison. Rather than experiencing a collapse upon passing through the gates, they maintain the same self-identity as they held on the streets. The prison gang helps them in their transition to prison life.

Some valuable insights about prisons and gangs were provided by the popular rapper Ice T in an interview in *Playboy* magazine. He began by stating that "Most gang members aren't afraid of getting thrown into jail. What do they have to lose? To most of them, jail is no different from home. They ain't going to do nothing but kick it with the homies in jail." Continuing, he said that the "gang mentality is pounded into your head in prison." Further:

> There is drama in jail. By the time you come home, you're really banging. When the police take a gangster off the street and put him in jail, his criminal side is totally reemphasized. ...My hope is that the gang truce can reach into the prisons, because the prisons really run the streets. In the joint you get favors by seeing what you can do for somebody on the outside.... A lot of the guys who are getting killed on the streets are being reached by people in the joint.... All these shots are being called by people in the joint, and if they decide the war is over in there, then it will be over outside, too."[89]

A somewhat different perspective on prison gangs is provided in Reiner, who notes that prison gangs

> are more akin to organized crime networks than to street gangs.... [F]ears of a prison/street gang nexus seem to be overblown. No law enforcement authority interviewed for this report saw any trend toward prison gang control over street gangs. Individuals often belong to both types of gangs, and may move back and forth between them.... But apart from producing a pool of recruits for the business, street gangs rarely play any direct role in such [prison gang operated] enterprises."[90]

A perspective similar to Reiner's is offered by Buentello, Fong, and Vogel in their study of Texas prison gangs.[91] They argue that these gangs are not merely extensions of street gangs. They state that eight prison gangs developed in the 1980s *within* the Texas prison system.

According to Buentello, Fong, and Vogel, the prison gang develops in five stages. The first stage begins with the new inmate entering the prison system with feelings of isolation, fear, and loneliness. The inmate begins the *prisonization* process, described earlier in this chapter. To overcome his fears and sense of isolation, the inmate moves into the second stage when he begins to get involved in a small, informal "clique" of inmates with whom he feels comfortable and shares some common interests. Some of these informal groups get disbanded as a result of transfers or release.

The third stage involves the development of "self-protection" groups. In a process similar to group formation on the outside, during this stage the clique either becomes large or some members perceive hostility from other groups in the prison. The authors cite the examples of the Black Muslims and the formation of the Texas Syndicate, formed by Texas-born inmates in the California prison system during the 1970s. Both provided protection. Leadership in the group is still rather informal, and there is no formal code of conduct as yet. Leaders are usually selected based on the charisma of an individual. They do not generally participate in criminal activities and do not engage in violent behavior unless provoked. Eventually some of the members of these kinds of groups move on to the fourth stage.[92]

The fourth stage is reached when "certain members begin to exert stronger influence over other members and over events of the group." Eventually these individuals become leaders and begin to transform the group into a "predator group."[93] It is at this stage that members begin to discuss having formal rules. They also begin to organize certain criminal activities, such as extortion, prostitution, gambling, and violence against other inmates, as they begin to enjoy more power over other inmates. In time, some of these groups evolve to the fifth stage, in which they become prison gangs.

During this final stage, the group members begin to see themselves as "part of an established organized crime syndicate. Involvement in contract murder, drug trafficking, extortion, gambling, and homosexual prostitution is required of gang members."[94] The group has formal rules and a constitution; there is a hierarchy of leadership; and inmates are members for life, which means that they continue their criminal activities for the gang after they are released.

At first, gang members wore gang tattoos. Recently gangs changed the rule and no longer require members to do so. This makes it more difficult for officials to identify individuals as gang members. Gangs also now use "associates/sympathizers" and "wannabes" to help them in some of their criminal activities.

There may be one additional reason behind riots and disturbances within the prison system, along with the development of prison gangs, and that is the lack of genuine rights accorded to prisoners.

PRISONERS' RIGHTS

As a result of the prison revolts of the 1960s and the civil rights movement, the courts abandoned their traditional **hands-off doctrine** toward prisons. This policy had been affirmed in an 1871 case (*Ruffin v. Commonwealth*) in which the Supreme Court ruled that, in effect, a person convicted of a crime and sent to prison becomes a "slave of the state" and forfeits all rights. This view was to change dramatically, beginning in the mid-1960s. Since then there has been a tremendous increase in prison-related litigation. Between 1966 and 1994 the number of *habeas corpus* lawsuits filed by inmates in state prisons went from 5,830 to 11,918 (an increase of 104%), while the number of civil rights lawsuits went from a mere trickle of 281 to an astounding 37,925 during the same period (a 135-fold increase).[95] The most important Supreme Court decisions have centered on four fundamental constitutional rights: (1) First Amendment rights concerning free speech and religious practice, (2) Fourth Amendment rights concerning unreasonable searches and seizures, (3) Eighth Amendment rights concerning cruel and unusual punishment, and (4) Fourteenth Amendment rights concerning due process.

One of the first of these cases was that of ***Cooper v. Pate*** (378 U.S. 546, 1964). The Court ruled that prisoners were entitled to protection under the 1871 Civil Rights Act and thus may challenge the conditions of their confinement in the courts. In other words, prisoners may sue for such things as inadequate medical care, brutality by guards, theft of personal property, and other civil rights violations.

Among the most important First Amendment cases was a decision that arose from a suit filed by prisoners practicing the Black Muslim religion. In ***Fulwood v. Clemmer*** (206 F. Supp. 370, 1962) the Court ruled that the Black Muslim religion was a bona fide religion and that prison administrators cannot deny inmates the right to practice it. A similar case involved a Buddhist prisoner (*Cruz v. Beto*, 92 S. Ct. 1079, 1972).

The Fourth Amendment prohibition of "unreasonable" searches and seizures has not resulted in many noteworthy cases. In ***Bell v. Wolfish*** (441 U.S. 520, 1979), the Supreme Court ruled in favor of traditional "strip searches" (including searches of body cavities following a visit from someone from the outside), as long as the reasons for the search "outweigh" the inmate's personal rights. In ***Hudson v. Palmer*** (468 U.S. 517, 1984), the Court upheld the right of prison officials to search inmate cells and to take any personal property found. However, courts also ruled that such searches cannot by done merely to "harass or humiliate" inmates and that inmates do in fact have some degree of privacy (*U.S. v. Lilly*, 576 F. 2d 1240, 5th Cir., 1978; *Block v. Rutherford*, 104 S. Ct. 3227, 1984).

Bell v. Wolfish is also an important Eighth Amendment case. Some consider it one of the most important cases the Supreme Court has ever decided because it represented a "return to the hands-off approach to prisoners' rights."[96] This case determined that "double-bunking" did not constitute "cruel and unusual punishment." This was further reinforced in ***Rhodes v. Chapman*** (452 U.S. 337, 1981), an Ohio case involving a prison designed to hold one inmate per cell (cells with only 63 square feet—8-by-8 feet), in which fourteen hundred inmates were double-bunked. In a curious bit of logic the Supreme Court ruled that overcrowding is not necessarily dangerous if prison services are available, and that living conditions may be "restrictive and harsh" because such conditions are part of the punishment prisoners receive as a result of being convicted. Further, in order to be unconstitutional, the conditions must demonstrate almost deliberate attempts to inflict "wanton and unnecessary infliction of pain." It is interesting to note that the suit was supported by the American Medical Association and the American Public Health Association!

Many other cases have centered on Eighth Amendment rights. Perhaps the most famous grew out of the Cummins Farm Unit of the Arkansas State Penitentiary, where Tom Murton (appointed warden by then-governor Winthrop Rockefeller) uncovered bodies of inmates who had been killed and buried on prison grounds. It was also discovered that prison administrators used a number of cruel methods of punishment, including the "Tucker telephone" (attaching electrical wires to an inmate's testicles and administering a shock), whippings, beatings, and even killings.[97] A federal court ruled in **Holt v. Sarver** (300 F. Supp. 825, 1969) that such punishment constituted cruel and unusual punishment. (This case was popularized in the film *Brubaker,* starring Robert Redford.) In a related case, **Pugh v. Locke** (406 F. Supp. 318, 1976), federal judge Frank Johnson ruled that the Alabama prison system itself constituted cruel and unusual punishment and ordered prison officials to bring the prisons up to minimal standards or close down the entire system.

One of the most controversial issues has been due process rights and prison disciplinary procedures. Certain disciplinary measures deprive inmates of certain liberties and privileges, such as good-time credits and access to the general population. One of the first issues addressed by the courts was solitary confinement (or the "hole"). Although the courts have not ruled that solitary confinement per se constitutes cruel and unusual punishment, it has been ruled that in some instances it does and that procedures culminating in a sentence to solitary confinement require certain due process safeguards. In a 1966 case a federal district court ruled that the confinement to a "strip" cell at the California Correctional Training Center at Soledad constituted cruel and unusual punishment (*Jordan v. Fitzharris,* 257 F. Supp. 674).

The key to this issue is the **disciplinary hearing.** Whenever an inmate is charged with an infraction of prison rules, he or she is granted a hearing before a disciplinary committee. It should be noted that within the prison system an inmate can be written up for the violation of some of the most petty and vague rules, such as being "disrespectful toward an officer," the definition of which is left entirely in the hands of prison guards. In **Wolff v. McDonnell** (418 U.S. 539, 1974) the Supreme Court ruled that minimal due process safeguards should be observed because such procedures could result in the loss of good-time credit. The Court specifically ruled that a written notice of all charges must be given at least twenty-four hours before the hearing, that the inmate must be given a hearing before an "impartial tribunal or fact-finder," and that a written statement noting the evidence relied upon and the reasons for the disciplinary action must be given. The Court also said that the inmate does not have the right to counsel but left the door open concerning the issue of the right to counsel, saying that the decision "Is not graven in stone." The inmate, however, may act in his or her own defense.

In a later decision, **Meachum v. Fano** (965 S. Ct. 2532, 1976), the Court ruled on a case involving the transfer of inmates to a more secure facility (from a medium- to a maximum-security prison). The Court noted that the Fourteenth Amendment applies when the extant liberty interest of a prisoner is threatened by the action of prison officials. This principle involves the prisoner's remaining in the general prison population. In other words, once a prisoner has been granted something that has a significant liberty value (e.g., probation, parole, good-time credit, placement in the general population), then the taking away of this liberty cannot be done without the benefit of due process.

Most of the Eighth Amendment cases have centered on the **conditions of confinement** within prisons. In several cases spanning around fifteen years (1976–1991) the Supreme Court ruled that those in charge of prisons must end brutality, unsanitary conditions, and inadequate food and follow specific guidelines. In **Ruiz v. Estelle** (679 F. 2d 1115, 5th

Cir., 1982), a federal judge in eastern Texas issued a far-reaching decree against the Texas Department of Corrections. The judge ordered the department to change what were unconstitutional conditions, such as overcrowding, unnecessary use of force by guards, poor health care practices, and the so-called **building-tender system,** which allowed some inmates to control others. Building-tenders (BTs) were "snitches" bribed by the prison (with special privileges) to report "troublemakers" (both inmates and guards) to prison authorities. Some have argued that one outcome of *Ruiz v. Estelle* was the disruption of the traditional social system based on an informal system of control ("divide and rule") and the creation of a new bureaucratic order. Since *Ruiz v. Estelle,* levels of violence have risen as inmate gangs have emerged to provide security and stability.[98]

Unfortunately, there is a "fly in the ointment" concerning the few rights that prisoners have been granted. Because of the many vague rules and regulations, the tremendous discretionary power exercised by prison officials, and the fact that months or even years may pass before the courts hear about abuses, prison inmates' constitutional rights may still be violated. One common method of violating these rights (and a very convenient method of control) is *administrative segregation.* In most prisons, prison officials can place an inmate in "close custody" or in solitary confinement in order to protect the inmate either from himself or herself or from others. The phrase "for his own protection," however, is open to abuse. Obviously, there is little argument in cases involving physical threats to inmates (e.g., rape) and the threat of suicide or escape. But in some cases, "for his own protection" can mean anything.

That the recent Supreme Court rulings have signaled a return to the hands-off doctrine is not surprising given the conservative makeup of the justices. In ***Wilson v. Seiter*** (501 U.S. 294, 1991) the Court ruled that, even though the inmates (in Ohio) experienced a number of horrible conditions (overcrowding, excessive noise, inadequate heating and cooling, improper ventilation, unsanitary dining facilities and food, etc.), these conditions were not the result of "deliberate indifference" by administrators. This had been the ruling in an earlier case (*Estelle v. Gamble,* 429 U.S. 97, 106, 1976) involving poor medical treatment in which the Court ruled that future cases concerning the Eighth Amendment must demonstrate "deliberate indifference." What constitutes "deliberate indifference" and how one proves it is unclear. In the *Wilson* case, Justices White, Marshall, Blackmun, and Stevens, though concurring with the ruling, warned that this decision may result in "serious deprivations of basic human needs" and will not be rectified because of "an unnecessary and meaningless search for 'deliberate indifference.'"

Some have suggested that the modern era is a period of "one-hand-on, one-hand off" or "hands semi-off." One interpretation of recent Supreme Court rulings is that "prisoners have constitutional rights but that those rights are not unrestricted."[99] Prisoners' rights are indeed not unconditional.

One final comment is in order. Perhaps you are wondering whether giving prisoners "too many" rights results in "frivolous lawsuits" filed by prisoners seeking personal notoriety or "taking advantage of the system." Taking this attitude to the extreme logical conclusion would be like saying that all American citizens (including the rich) have too many rights and this overabundance results in "frivolous lawsuits" that tie up the courts. Perhaps these lawsuits are the price we pay when we grant rights to *all* people.

GETTING OUT OF PRISON ON PAROLE

Parole is the release of an offender from prison prior to the expiration of the original sentence. The majority of those released from prison each year are paroled. In 1998 more than 600,000 prisoners were released from prison, the majority under some form of community supervision, typically a department of parole.[100] The number of people on parole has risen rapidly in recent years. In 1980 there were 220,438 on parole; by 1998 this number had risen by 220 percent to 704,964.[101]

Parole has its origins at the Elmira Reformatory in 1876. Another kind of parole, known as *aftercare,* actually began with juveniles sentenced to houses of refuge during the early nineteenth century.[102] It can be argued that parole was originally established as a "politically expedient method of controlling inmate resentment over disparate sentences." Prior to the establishment of parole, the only way to get an early release was through executive clemency by the governor, which during the nineteenth century was a process that took far too much time for governors and often proved to be politically embarrassing in negative cases (as when someone granted clemency committed a crime).[103] Hardly anyone seems to like the parole system. Conservatives often argue that parole lets "dangerous offenders" loose in the community (a gross exaggeration). Liberals argue that the decisions to release are too often arbitrary and without scientific foundation.[104]

Granting Parole

There are several "release mechanisms" whereby a prisoner is let out of prison. First, there is *discretionary release,* where the prisoner is released by a *parole board* prior to the expiration of his or her sentence. This is done by releasing the offender to the supervision of a *parole agent* employed by the department of parole within a state. Of all of the inmates released during a given year, about 36 percent are released through this method.

The most common method of release (about 37% of the cases) comes through *mandatory release.* The prisoner has served his or her entire sentence, minus what is known as "good time." The prisoner is still under the supervision of a parole department, however.

A third method is known as *unconditional release.* The prisoner has served his or her entire sentence and will have no supervision. The prisoner has, in common parlance, "done his time." This occurs in about 20 percent of the cases.[105]

The decision to release a prisoner on parole is left entirely up to a parole board. This is a group of individuals who usually are appointed by the governor of a state. In California the parole hoard is known as the California Adult Authority (for juveniles it is called the California Youth Authority). Most boards are autonomous units—that is, they are not situated within a department of corrections, and they have no direct institutional ties. Nevertheless, parole boards work very closely with institutional officials in making their decisions. They rely very heavily on the information and recommendations of prison staff, and they place a heavy emphasis on an inmate's performance while in prison.

The decision to grant parole is made during a parole hearing. At the hearing are the offender, the parole board, and, in many cases, prison officials and interested citizens. (Most state laws stipulate that any citizen may attend a parole hearing. This law is not well known, however, which probably keeps the hearings hidden from the view of the average citizen.) During the hearing the parole board reviews the prisoner's case and asks a series of questions. Stanley describes the typical hearing as follows:

> The prisoner is greeted by name—usually his first name—and an effort is made to put him at ease. The tone adopted is normally friendly, but in a majority of hearings observed in the present study it became patronizing and sometimes demeaning: "Well, John, have you been behaving yourself lately?" "What can we do with you now, Bill?" (In fairness to parole board members it must be acknowledged that the stakes in this proceeding are very high, that the situation is tense, and that anything the member says can be objected to by a rubbed-raw prisoner or critical observer.) The conversation usually centers on one or more of three subjects: the inmate's prison record, his parole plans, and the circumstances of his crime.[106]

Some boards require an inmate to have either a specific job awaiting him or her following release or other resources (family, friends, etc.) that would keep him or her financially viable until a job is found.

What factors weigh most heavily in the decision to parole? A recent survey by the Association of Paroling Authorities found nine factors considered important. A close look at these factors reveals that the prisoner's behavior *prior* to going to prison looms large, meaning that the person is was still being judged long after conviction and sentencing. The most important factor is the nature of the most recent offense, followed closely by "history of prior violence" and "prior felony convictions." Other factors, in order of importance, are: possession of a firearm, previous incarceration, prior parole adjustment, prison disciplinary record, psychological reports, and victim input.[107] In short, whether the offender has been "rehabilitated" (however this is defined) is irrelevant.

Several attempts have been made to identify factors that will enable one to predict the probability of success upon release on parole, but without much success. Generally, clinical judgments about a parolee's chance of success are not very good. Certain statistical predictors of recidivism, such as the U.S. Parole Commission's Salient Factor Score (SFS), are often much better. This is based on a summary of points assessed for various background variables, not limited to prior record and the like. One study looked at parole outcome in Texas, California, and Michigan and found the best predictors of recidivism were the following factors: prior criminality, young age (at start of offense career), drug abuse, and poor employment history. Yet even these factors failed to predict more than 10 percent of the variance. Other studies have arrived at similar conclusions.[108]

In reality, it appears members of parole boards base their decisions on intuition or hunches. They tend to develop, with experience, a "feeling" of whether a particular inmate is ready for release. More often than not, this "feeling" is based on possible negative reactions on the outside—either by influential members of a community or by someone higher up in the governmental hierarchy (whether in the corrections department or elsewhere).

In recent years a good percentage of the increase in parole populations reflects the fact that prisons are perpetually overcrowded. Indeed, the number of persons arrested and convicted has been consistently on the increase over the years, and parole boards may be under intense pressure to release prisoners if for no other reason than to make room for more.[109]

Success on Parole

How successful is parole? A great deal of research has been undertaken to determine the relative success of parole. The basic question is, What percentage of parolees commit additional crimes and are reincarcerated? That actually is two separate questions, for one of the problems concerning recidivism is how we define it and how we measure it. It is often said (usually with little supportive evidence) that prisons are "schools of crime" and that about 50 to 75 percent of those released from prison return once again.

This contention was borne out by recent studies conducted by the U.S. Department of Justice and the Rand Corporation. In the Department of Justice study, a follow-up of 108,580 prisoners released in 1980 in eleven states found that 63 percent were rearrested within three years at least once for either a felony or a misdemeanor offense. The majority (80%) were arrested for property, drugs, or public-order crimes. Rand Corporation researchers looked at prisoners released from Illinois and California prisons. They discovered that from 40 to 45 percent were rearrested with the first year and from 60 to 70 percent were rearrested for felonies and serious misdemeanors within three years. What is interesting about the Rand study is the fact that a comparable group never sent to prison but instead placed on probation had a much lower rate of recidivism. Further, among those who were rearrested, the rate of offending was much less than it had been prior to their going to prison. So at least there was a "suppression effect"—in other words, they're still doing it, but not quite as often. That may be small consolation for some victims. It would be like saying "He's still battering his wife, but not quite as often as before." At the same time, however, the Rand study demonstrated the overall impact of those rearrested was negligible: an impact on the overall crime rate in Illinois and California of around 2 percent or less. It also was found that reductions in arrest rates were mostly because of simple maturation: as prisoners got older, their crime rates dropped considerably. Most prisoners have peak ages of criminality between 15 and 24. The typical prisoner is 30 or older when released—well beyond his or her "prime" as far as crime is concerned.[110]

The Increase of Parole Failures: Why?

There is a growing trend toward parole failures and rising recidivism rates, although not a rising trend in serious crime committed by parolees. Between 1980 and 1996 the number of parole violations increased by 508 percent (from 28,817 to 175,305). However, fully two-thirds (68.5%) of parole violations were "technical" violations—no new crime was committed. Austin and Irwin, after an exhaustive investigation into the prison and parole system, arrived at the following conclusion:

> This trend is attributable in large part to dramatic changes in the nature of parole supervision and the imposition of increasingly more severe conditions of supervision on parolees. Instead of a system designed to help prisoners re-adjust to a rapidly changing and more competitive economic system, the current parole system has been designed to catch and punish inmates for petty and nuisance-type behaviors that do not in themselves draw a prison term.[111]

What are "technical violations"? Every parole department has a number of rules and regulations that parolees must follow. They range from the obvious ("obey all federal, state, and local laws") to rather vague stipulations ("meet family responsibilities and support dependents"). They also relate to situations that may be largely out of the control of the parolee, such as "maintain gainful employment." The parolee is also generally required to "report to the parole officer as directed" and to "notify the parole officer of any change in residence."

Parole revocation is a serious matter, and the U.S. Supreme Court has ruled on how this should be handled. In 1972, the Supreme Court case of *Morrissey v. Brewer* (408 U.S. 471, 1972) opened the door to granting due process rights to parolees. Prior to this case, the courts had taken a hands-off position, concluding that parole boards are "administrative" in function and that to interfere would damage their role as *parens patriae* (substitute guardian or parent) and hence interfere with rehabilitative efforts. It was commonly held that parole was a "privilege" rather than a "right" and that a "contract" existed between the parolee and the parole board; thus, violating a parole condition constituted a violation of this contract. Moreover, it was believed that parole was still a form of custody, albeit outside prison walls. Revocation was not thought to be part of normal "criminal" prosecution and hence due process rights were not applicable. The Court ruled that

> Whether parole is a right or a privilege is not the crucial question. The issue is the extent to which an individual would be "condemned to suffer grievous loss." The liberty enjoyed by a parolee is important: if terminated, some elements of due process must be involved. The state's interest in protecting society does not preclude or hinder an informal hearing at parole revocation.

In a later case, *Gagnon v. Scarpelli* (411 U.S. 778, 782, 1973), the Court ruled that a parolee "is entitled to two hearings," one at the time of arrest and detention and another when the final decision is made. Yet despite this ruling, parolees are still not given such rights as the right to counsel, the right to call witnesses, or the right to an impartial judge and jury. Furthermore, parole can be revoked "if the board feels there is a preponderance of evidence that the parolee was not meeting parole obligations."[112] Parole hearings are often pro forma ceremonies, lasting perhaps a few minutes before a board hearing officer.

Parole violations accounts for a sizable proportion of the recent increases in prison populations. In Texas, for instance, in 1998 more than one-third (36%) of prison admissions were parole violations, and another 40 percent were for probation violations. What sorts of "crimes" did they commit? A study by the National Council on Crime and Delinquency examined the state of Nevada and found that more than 1,000 of the 6,200 prisoners as of 1993 were parole or probation violators. A typical case was a convicted burglar who had his parole revoked for "failure to maintain verifiable residence" and "failure to pay supervision fees" (yes, in some jurisdictions the parolee is required to pay to be "supervised" by a parole agent). Another case involved a parolee who failed to participate in drug testing and out-patient drug abuse counseling, two common requirements for many parolees.[113]

What should be underscored here—and we cannot emphasize this too strongly—is that the vast majority of parolees are extremely poor, lack a high school degree, and have few job skills and little in the way of employment history. They are, in short, members of the growing *underclass* in American society, part of the "surplus population" eliminated from the primary labor market through changes in the American economic system. In short, they are "superfluous" as far as profits are concerned. One of the goals of the parole system is to "manage" this class.[114] Simon describes the plight of these mostly urban parolees as follows: "For far too many of those not in custody life consists of forced idleness, deprivation, and exposure to criminal violence (conditions experienced by many *in* custody as well). The resulting sense of despair leaves many vulnerable to the attraction of drugs, unsafe sex, and involvement in criminal lifestyles."[115]

Simon's own study of 265 parolees in California found plenty of evidence to back up the claim that they are among the urban underclass. The majority of those living in the inner-city areas had no work, and the only means available to earn income was through various forms of welfare or illegal means.

It is any wonder that most parolees, with little going for them prior to their most recent prison sentence, find it almost impossible to survive legitimately after release? In the next section we provide a summary of the interviews conducted by James Austin and John Irwin in their analysis of the parole system in California. Some of the information provided below comes from Irwin's original study conducted in the late 1960s, but the analysis is as current as ever.[116]

Being on Parole

The problem of reentry into society—or, as many inmates express it, "hitting the streets"— is an acute one for the majority. The problem is not unlike the problems confronted by soldiers returning from war. John Irwin describes the problem in the following way:

> The impact of release is often dramatic. After months of anticipation, planning, and dreaming, the felon leaves the confined, routinized, slow-paced setting of the prison and steps into the "streets" as an adult-citizen. The problems of the first weeks are usually staggering and sometimes insurmountable. Becoming accustomed to the outside world, coping with parole, finding a good job—perhaps finding any job—and getting started toward a gratifying life style are at least difficult and for many impossible.
>
> When released, the convict can be seen to be proceeding along a narrow and precarious route, beset with difficult obstacles. If the obstacles are too difficult, if satisfaction and fulfillment are not forthcoming, and/or his commitment to straightening up his hand is too weak, he will be diverted from the straight path toward systematic deviance. He himself believes in the route's precariousness and the high probability of his failure, and this intensifies its precariousness. Many of the obstacles are, however, both very real and very difficult.[117]

In their latest study, Austin and Irwin note that parolees must immediately struggle to achieve some degree of financial support, affordable housing, clothes, and so on, just in order to apply for a job. They receive little in the form of financial assistance. In Nevada, for instance, they receive only $21 to help in the "transition" to normal life. Some have help from their families and friends, but too often this is not much, as they are almost invariably poor themselves. Speaking of employment, in the state of California, in the 1960s when Irwin first reported these problems, parolees had an unemployment rate of around 50 percent. If this seems high, compare it to 1991 figures in the same state, showing a 70 percent unemployment rate.[118]

Irwin delineates three major obstacles the parolee faces: (1) "getting settled down" and "getting on your feet"; (2) "doing good"; (3) coping with the parole system. The parole agent is often unable to empathize with the parolee and understand these problems. Part of this stems from the contradictory roles of the parole officer: he or she is both a police officer and a social worker or "friend." The average parole officer comes from a stable middle- or working-class background and usually fails to understand the client's lower-class background. The parole officer often does not have the time to help the parolee and has difficulty helping the parolee find work, a place to stay, clothes, money, and other necessities of life. Let us examine in more detail some of the problems facing parolees.

Getting Settled Down and Getting on Your Feet.   Most parolees are very optimistic when they get out. For months they have been planning what they will do and how they will do it. Unfortunately, most of these plans are too optimistic, possibly because their assumptions, a highly idealized set of assumptions, have been shaped from within the prison system. The most immediate concern is to "get their feet on the ground" or "get into a groove of some kind." This desire is often thwarted in the first few days or weeks by what Irwin calls "disorganizing events," which contribute to a disequilibrium. There is the impact of moving from one world (the prison) to another (the "streets"). Parolees are faced with many demands for which they are not prepared. Quite often parolees are lonely, for most of their former friends have little or nothing in common with them, and their best friends may still be back in prison. What parolees perhaps first notice is the pace of the outside world. Indeed, prison was very slow and routinized, and the outside world seems too fast and chaotic by comparison. One inmate told Irwin: "I mean, I was shook, baby. Things were moving too fast, everybody rushing somewhere. And they all seemed so cold, they had this up tight look." Another inmate said: "The first thing I noticed was how fast everything moves outside. In prison everybody walks slow. Outside everyone's in a hurry."[119]

Some parolees have a less difficult time readjusting. Returning to a familiar area, returning to one's family, and having a steady job waiting help one readjust. The majority of parolees are faced with rather severe handicaps when it comes to obtaining employment. Most of them have no job when they are released, few have any marketable skills, and few had any steady work experience prior to incarceration. Few are able to learn marketable skills while in prison.

Doing Good.   After "settling down" following the initial impact, those who have made it this far still face several obstacles to their goal of "doing good." These obstacles include becoming involved in what Irwin calls a "new meaning world." The parolee must find a group of people with whom he or she shares a "meaning of the world," or individuals with whom he or she has something in common. The parolee often runs into difficulty. Friends he or she knew and had something in common with prior to incarceration have had different experiences, and they may no longer have anything in common. When most people meet people they haven't seen in years, they find it a bit uncomfortable after they have exchanged formal pleasantries and exchanged old stories. They soon discover that they no longer have anything in common. Parolees who face this problem may eventually long for old prison buddies and old activities, Many end up spending a great deal of time around former "hangouts," such as bars and poolrooms.[120]

Many parolees do not "do good" when they get out. Many never get beyond "making it" or "settling down." Others are unable to find work, or if they find work, it is seasonal or otherwise dependent on market fluctuations. Some realize that the dreams they had in prison have vanished or were perhaps too unrealistic. When the ex-con fails to reach the level of what he considers "doing good," he is at a critical turning point. The first critical point comes after he has been successful at "making it" but sees that he is not going to go beyond this point.

Coping with the Parole System

If those problems are not enough, the parolee also confronts problems with the parole system itself. He is first faced with the conditions of parole, a set of rules that the parolee is supposed to follow. The parolee must deal with a parole system that is too often designed to "trail 'em, nail 'em, and jail 'em." While conducting a study of jail overcrowding in Las Vegas in the late 1980s, we were told by the director of the State of Nevada Department of Parole and Probation that "we train our agents to catch violators." In other words, the current system of parole has been transformed from its original aim of assisting parolees (playing the role of "social worker") to a system that is strictly law enforcement. One Las Vegas parole officer continually bragged about the absconders he had gone after and captured. In one case he traveled all the way to New Orleans to catch one of his parolees who had committed a couple of technical violations. He was, in common parlance, a gung-ho type of agent who could not wait to catch someone violating a rule.

During the first few weeks on parole the parolee becomes aware that there is an important distinction between the formal expectations of the parole system itself and the informal expectations of the parole officer to whom the parolee is assigned. The parolee soon learns that the parole officer has a great deal of discretion. Furthermore, the parolee learns that some of the conditions of parole are so vague and comprehensive that it is almost impossible not to violate some of them. Indeed, in order to meet certain conditions of everyday living, some rules must be broken. For instance, in some jurisdictions one condition is that the parolee must obtain permission in order to drive a car and must also have a driver's license. To register a car, one must have insurance (which is not stated in the conditions). But before the parolee can afford insurance (and thus drive), the parolee must find a job and often must drive to where he or she works.

Another rule specifies that the parolee must not associate with ex-inmates and with people with "bad reputations." For most parolees, this is virtually impossible. In the lower-class milieu it is common to know many people with some form of arrest record (if for nothing else than being arrested on "suspicion"). Also, the parolee must not drink alcoholic beverages "in excess." Here, too, we find that in their environment drinking is an acceptable pastime. (It is interesting to note that drinking "in excess" apparently has no class boundaries, for drinking is acceptable among all classes.) These two restrictions, especially the latter, are indicative of the puritanical and conservative elements of society who originally made up these rules. What this segment of society considers as "proper" may be at odds with working- and lower-class lifestyles. It is surely a convenient method that the powerful use to control the powerless. This is especially apparent when we consider the amount of discretion the parole officer has.

To repeat, the parole officer occupies the contradictory positions of friend and police officer. The parole officer is supposed to "work with" the parolee, yet how he or she is supposed to do this is rarely made explicit. In addition, the parole officer is supposed to enforce the rules. The manner in which this is done, and the degree to which the rules and regulations are enforced, varies from one parole officer to another and from one parole office to another. Some spend much of their time acting as vigilantes and go out of their way to catch their parolees committing infractions. Others (probably the majority) fall somewhere between the extremes of "law enforcement officer" and "social worker."

The parole officer, it must be remembered, works within the parole system and is under constant pressure to be "on top" of a case. The parole officer must be constantly aware of what each parolee is doing. If there is a "blow up"—if the parolee commits a new crime—the parole officer must be prepared to answer to higher-ups. In order to do this, he or she must maintain a readiness to strictly enforce the rules. The parole officer has a strong desire to please the parole board, and in many cases the parole board is reluctant to return a parolee to prison on one minor technical violation (although this does happen). Irwin found that parole officers tend to "bank" incidents of violations of parole rules. The parole officer is preparing for the possibility of having to build a strong case. He or she may make a mental note or record in the log every minor violation committed by the parolee.[121]

Drug Testing

Ostensibly designed to help people cope with drug problems, drug testing has become a huge business. Over 15 million Americans were tested in 1996, double what the number was five years earlier, at a cost of $600 million. Drug testing in the private sector increased by 305 percent between 1987 and 1994. About 80 percent of all large corporations test their employees. One method of drug testing is the "Drug Alert" tester, made by SherTest Corporation. It targets family members. This device, the company claims, can be used to increase love and care between parents and children by "breaking down the barriers of denial between parent and child." Another company, Barringer Technologies, Inc., makes "particle detection devices" for the police, claiming it has sold "thousands" of $35 "testing kits." Psychometrics Corporation introduced a new kit, selling for $75, and the day after this product hit the market, the value of the company's stock tripled![122]

Drug testing has become a convenient "management" tool for the parole system. Given that so many parolees had serious drug problems in the past, many fail the drug test. And thousands find themselves heading back to prison, largely because of doing so.[123]

SUMMARY

Prison populations are at an all-time high and have increased in recent years in unprecedented numbers, largely as a result of the "war on drugs." Most of those currently incarcerated are drawn from the ranks of the unskilled and uneducated. The majority are nonwhite, especially African Americans.

One of the most important features of the prison system is the inmate social system, which has probably existed in some form since prisons were first built. Although many of the norms and values of the inmate social systems were brought into the prison from the culture of the streets, they nevertheless take on exaggerated importance inside the walls. One indication of this is the existence of a sub-rosa economy in which just about everything becomes a commodity to be bartered and exchanged. This economy and the inmate social system as a whole help mitigate the pains of imprisonment.

We discussed extreme responses to imprisonment, prison violence in general, and prison riots as a particular form of violence. Special attention was paid to the emerging importance of the existence of gangs within prisons. Gangs are a reflection of conditions existing on the outside and account for much of the violence inside prisons today.

We discussed the issue of prisoners' rights. Technically prisoners have been granted many rights denied to them in the past, but these rights are far short of being unconditional.

The state's control over those who deviate from the norms extends beyond the prison system. The most common form this control takes is the parole system. Parole decisions are often capricious and dependent on the attitudes and values of parole board members. Inmates denied parole are usually informed indirectly, often several days following the hearing. Success on parole depends on such factors as work history, drug or alcohol use, previous criminal offenses, and previous prison terms, and it is measured solely in terms of recidivism. Being on parole presents the ex-offender with several problems of adjustment. Parole violations have been on the rise in recent years, no doubt because of social factors outside the control of both parolees and parole agents (e.g., economic conditions) and the tendency for the parole system to emphasize the law enforcement goals of "catching violators."

KEY TERMS

Bell v. Wolfish   309
building-tender system   311
conditions of confinement   310
Cooper v. Pate   309
disciplinary hearing   310
frustration riot   303
Fulwood v. Clemmer   309
gleaning   299
hands-off doctrine   309
Holt v. Sarver   310
Hudson v. Palmer   309

inmate code   297
inmate social system   297
lock psychosis   292
maximum-security prison   292
Meachum v. Fano   310
medium-security prison   293
minimum-security prison   293
pains of imprisonment   296
political riot   304
prison gang   305
prisonization   298

Pugh v. Locke   310
race riot   303
rage riot   304
Rhodes v. Chapman   309
Ruiz v. Estelle   310
sub-rosa economy   300
super-max prisons   293
total institution   295
Wilson v. Seiter   311
Wolff v. McDonnell   310

NOTES

1. Austin, J., and J. Irwin. *It's about Time: America's Incarceration Binge* (3rd ed.). Belmont, CA: Wadsworth, 2001.

2. Beck, A. J., and P. M. Brien. "Trends in the U.S. Correctional Populations: Recent Findings from the Bureau of Justice Statistics." In K. C. Haas, and G. P. Alpert (eds.), *The Dilemmas of Corrections* (3rd ed.), Project Heights, IL: Waveland Press, 1995, pp. 56–59.

3. Austin and Irwin based the "seriousness" of crime on that of the general public, which was measured by the Center for Studies in Criminology and Criminal Law at the University of Pennsylvania.

4. Austin and Irwin, *It's about Time,* p. 27. In this specific example, it is important to note that this incident occurred in Nevada, where just about any offense committed within a gaming establishment is treated much more harshly than would otherwise be the case. One reason is that the state of Nevada wants to maintain an image suggesting that it is not only "tough on crime" but, more important, casinos are legitimate enterprises where people can come and have fun while feeling safe (see Farrell, R., and C. Case. *The Black Book and the Mob.* Madison: University of Wisconsin Press, 1995).

5. Irwin, in his earlier research on a sample of offenders in California, found eight criminal identities (see our discussion of typologies of criminal behavior in Chapter 2): (1) the *thief* (8% of his sample); (2) the *hustler* (7%), (3) the *dope fiend* (a term used by many drug users; 13%), (4) the *head* (user of psychedelic drugs, such as marijuana and LSD; 8%); (5) the *disorganized criminal* (one who pursues "a chaotic, purposeless life, filled with unskilled, careless, and variegated criminal activity"; they "make up the bulk of convicted felons"; 27%); (6) the *state-raised youth* (the young offender who has served one or more terms in youth institutions and, in a sense, has been reared, during the formative years, in various kinds of state institutions; 15%); (7) the *lower-class man* (the man from a lower-class background who has not had a long criminal career but who just happened to have committed a felony; 6%); (8) the *square John* (the conventional person from a stable working-class background who simply made a mistake and ended in prison; 16%). See Irwin, J. *The Felon.* Englewood Cliffs, NJ: Prentice-Hall, 1970.

6. Austin and Irwin, *It's about Time,* p. 41.

7. For a classic case study see Whyte, W. F. *Street Corner Society.* Chicago: University of Chicago Press, 1943; see also Hagedorn, J. *People and Folks* (2nd ed.). Chicago: Lakeview Press, 1998.

8. Shelden, R. G., S. Tracy, and W. B. Brown, *Youth Gangs in American Society* (2nd ed.). Belmont, CA: Wadsworth, 2001, pp. 78–82.

9. Beck and Brien, "Trends in U.S. Correctional Populations," p. 53.

10. Austin and Irwin, *It's about Time,* p. 90.

11. Allen, H. E., and C. E. Simonsen. *Corrections in America* (8th ed.). Upper Saddle River, NJ: Prentice-Hall, 1998, pp. 457, 460.

12. Austin and Irwin, *It's about Time,* pp. 117–129; Rush, G. *Inside American Prisons and Jails.* Incline Village, NV: Copperhouse, 1997, pp. 44–45; Mays, G. L., and L. T. Winfree Jr. *Contemporary Corrections.* Belmont, CA: Wadsworth, 1998, p.155; Tracy, C. "Beyond the Veil: The Changing Nature of the Prison Experience from a Convict Perspective." Paper presented at the Annual Meeting of the Justice Studies Association, Norton, MA, May 30–June 1, 2001. An Associated Press story ("Death Toll in California's Prisons Highest in More Than a Decade. *Las Vegas Review Journal,* February 22, 1998) noted that a record number of 16 prisoners died in 1997 as a result of fights between prisoners, the highest since 1987, when 19 died. A total of 13 of these deaths occurred within the highest-security prisons housing the "most dangerous." The most deaths occurred at Pelican Bay, all resulting from clashes between inmates. The story also noted that there are almost 156,000 prisoners in California and prisons are at 193 percent of designed capacity—meaning they are severely overcrowded.

13. Terry, C. "Beyond Punishment: Perpetuating Difference from the Prison Experience." *Humanity and Society* 24: 111 (May 2000).

14. Larson, C., and G. Garrett. *Crime, Justice and Society* (2nd ed.). Dix Hills, NY: General Hall, 1996, p. 338.

15. Mays and Winfree, *Contemporary Corrections,* pp. 156–157.

16. Allen and Simonsen, *Corrections in America,* p. 481.

17. Palombo, J. *From Heroin to Heresy.* Binghamton, NY: William Neil, 2000, p. 30.

18. Larson and Garrett, *Crime, Justice, and Society,* pp. 336–337.

19. See citations above and also Silberman, M. *A World of Violence: Corrections in America.* Belmont, CA: Wadsworth, 1995.

20. Goffman, E. *Asylums.* New York: Doubleday, 1961, p. 6.

21. Watterson, K. *Women in Prison: Inside the Concrete Womb.* Boston: Northeastern University Press, 1996.

22. Sykes, G. *Society of Captives.* Princeton, NJ: Princeton University Press, 1958.

23. Goffman, *Asylums,* p. 14.

24. Garfinkel, H. "Conditions of Successful Degradation Ceremonies." *American Journal of Sociology* 61: 420–424 (March 1956).

25. Silberman, *A World of Violence,* p. 17.

26. Sykes, G. *Criminology.* New York: Harcourt Brace Jovanovich, 1978, p. 525.

27. Austin and Irwin, *It's about Time,* p. 110.

28. Ibid., p. 112.

29. McCorkle, L., and R. Korn. "Resocialization within Walls." In N. Johnston, L. Savitz, and M. E. Wolfgang (eds.), *The Sociology of Punishment and Corrections.* New York: Wiley, 1962, p. 99.

30. Williams, V., and M. Fish. *Convicts, Codes and Contraband.* Cambridge, MA: Ballinger, 1974, p. 41.

31. Irwin, J., and D. Cressey. "Thieves, Convicts, and the Inmate Culture." *Social Problems* 10: 142–155 (Fall 1962).

32. Sykes, G., and S. L. Messinger. "The Innate Social Code and Its Functions." In M. E. Wolfgang, L. Savitz, and N. Johnston (eds.), *The Sociology of Crime and Delinquency.* New York: Wiley, 1962, pp. 92–94. Although this article is quite dated, more recent research suggests that inmate codes are still very much part of the prison social system. See Mays and Winfree, *Contemporary Corrections,* pp. 199–200.

33. Sykes, *Society of Captives;* Irwin and Cressey, "Thieves, Convicts, and the Inmate Culture; Schrag, C. "Some Foundations for a Theory of Corrections." In D. R. Cressey (ed.), *The Prison.* New York: Holt, Rinehart and Winston, 1966; Irwin, *The Felon;* Austin and Irwin, *It's about Time;* Terry, "Beyond Punishment."

34. Sykes, *Society of Captives,* p. 103.

35. Palombo, J. E. *From Heroin to Heresy: The Making of An American Social Thinker.* New York: William Neal Co., 2000, p. 37.

36. Clemmer, D. *The Prison Community.* New York: Holt, Rinehart and Winston, 1958, p. 299.

37. Wheeler, S. "A Study of Prisonization," in Johnston, Savitz, and Wolfgang, *Sociology of Punishment and Corrections.* A cross-cultural study on prisons in five countries confirmed Wheeler's findings. Akers, R. L., N. S. Hayner, and W. Grunninger. "Time Served, Career Phase and Prisonization: Findings from Five Countries." In R. C. Leger and J. R. Stratton (eds.), *The Sociology of Corrections.* New York: Wiley, 1977; Austin and Irwin, *It's about Time,* p. 110.

38. Irwin, *The Felon;* Irwin, J., and D. Cressey. "Thieves, Convicts, and the Inmate Culture." *Social Problems* 10 (Fall, 1962), pp. 142–155.

39. Silberman, *A World of Violence,* p. 15.

40. Irwin, *The Felon,* p. 68.

41. Ibid., p. 74.

42. Ibid., pp. 76–78.

43. Palombo, *From Heroin to Heresy,* p. 20.

44. Ibid., p. 23.

45. Williams and Fish, *Convicts, Codes and Contraband;* Davidson, R. T. *Chicano Prisoners: The Keg to San Quentin.* New York: Holt, Rinehart and Winston, 1974.

46. Williams and Fish, *Convicts, Codes and Contraband,* p. 51.

47. Irwin, *The Felon,* ch. 4.

48. Quoted in Silberman, *A World of Violence,* p. 15.

49. Austin and Irwin, *It's about Time,* pp. 101–102.

50. Speaking of remoteness, journalist Joseph Hallinan visited one such remote prison in the extreme northwest part of Virginia, in a small area known as Wallens Ridge (in Wise County). He noted that visits by family and friends are rare, because there are no airports or train stations and not even Greyhound buses come there. He says this inaccessibility is intentional, for the designers wanted this to be a place of exile. At the grand opening in April 1999 a large banner hung over the entrance read: "Future Destination of Virginia Exile." See Hallinan, J. *Going down the River: Travels in a Prison Nation.* New York: Random House, 2001, pp. 206–208.

51. Austin and Irwin, *It's about Time,* p. 107.

52. Colvin, M. "The 1980 New Mexico Prison Riot." *Social Problems* 29: 449–463 (1982).

53. Fox, V. *Violence behind Bars.* Westport, CT: Greenwood Press, 1974 (originally published in 1956); Pallas, J., and R. Barber. "From Riot to Revolution." In R. Quinney (ed.), *Criminal Justice in America: A Critical Understanding.* Boston: Little, Brown, 1974.

54. Mays and Winfree, *Contemporary Corrections,* pp. 210–211.

55. Ibid.; Jacobs, J. B. *Stateville.* Chicago: University of Chicago Press, 1977.

56. Pallas and Barber, "From Riot to Revolution," p. 345.

57. See Fanon, F. *The Wretched of the Earth.* New York; Grove Press, 1963; Malcolm X. *The Autobiography of Malcolm X.* New York: Grove Press, 1966; Cleaver, E. *Soul on Ice.* New York: Dell, 1968; Jackson, G. *Soledad Brother.* New York: Bantam, 1970; Berrigan, D. *America Is Hard to Find.* Garden City, NY: Doubleday, 1972.

58. Pallas and Barber, "From Riot to Revolution"; Atkins, B. M., and H. R. Glick (eds.). *Prisons, Protest and Politics.* Englewood Cliffs, NJ: Prentice-Hall, 1972, pp. 99–140; Pell, E. *Maximum Security.* New York: Dutton, 1972, pp. 141–210; Mattick, H. "The Prosaic Sources of Prison Violence." *Society* (November–December, 1973); Yee, M. S. *The Melancholy History of Soledad Prison.* New York: Harper & Row, 1973.

59. Badillo, H., and M. Haynes. *A Bill of No Rights: Attica and the American Prison System.* New York: Outbridge and Lazard, 1972, pp. 13–34; Pallas and Barber, "From Riot to Revolution," pp. 349–350.

60. Wicker, T. *A Time to Die.* New York: Quadrangle/New York Times, 1975; Badillo and Haynes, ibid.

61. Such fear and the use of various racial stereotypes have been documented by Mann, C. R. *Unequal Justice: A Question of Color.* Bloomington: Indiana University Press, 1995; Baum, D. *Smoke and Mirrors: The War on Drugs and the Politics of Failure.* Boston: Little, Brown/Back Bay Books, 1997; and Chambliss, W. J. "Crime Control and Ethnic Minorities: Legitimizing Racial Oppression by Creating Moral Panics." In D. F. Hawkins (ed.), *Ethnicity, Race, and Crime.* Albany: State University of New York Press, 1995.

62. Mays and Winfree, *Contemporary Corrections,* pp. 211–212.

63. Shelden, Tracy, and Brown, *Youth Gangs in American Society.*

64. For a review of these policies, see ibid., ch. 9.

65. Camp, G., and C. Camp. *Prison Gangs: Their Extent, Nature, and Impact on Prisons.* Washington, DC: U.S. Department of Justice, 1985; Jacobs, J. B. "Street Gangs behind Bars." *Social Problems* 21: 395–408 (1974), and Jacobs, *Stateville;* Buentello, S. R., S. Fong, and R. E. Vogel. "Prison Gang Development: A Theoretical Model." *The Prison Journal* 121: 3–14 (1991); Knox, G. W., and E. D. Tromanhauser. "Gangs and Their Control in Adult Correctional Institutions." *The Prison Journal* 121: 15–22 (1991).

66. Buentello, Fong, and Vogel, "Prison Gang Development."

67. Ralph, P. H., and J. W. Marquart. "Gang Violence in Texas Prisons." *The Prison Journal* 121: 38–49 (1991).

68. Knox and Tromanhauser, "Gangs and Their Control," pp. 16–18.

69. Knox, G. W., and E. D. Tromanhauser. "Gang Members as a Distinct Health Risk Group in Juvenile Correctional Facilities." *The Prison Journal* 121: 61 (1991).

70. Ibid., pp. 64–65.

71. Knox and Tromanhauser, "Gangs and Their Control," p.16.

72. Jacobs, "Street Gangs behind Bars"; Moore, J. W. *Homeboys: Gangs, Drugs, and Prisons in the Barrio of Los Angeles.* Philadelphia: Temple University Press, 1978; Hagedorn, *People and Folks.*

73. Camp and Camp, *Prison Gangs.*

74. Jacobs, "Street Gangs behind Bars," p. 398.

75. Buentello, Fong, and Vogel, "Prison Gang Development."

76. Jacobs, *Stateville.*

77. Ibid.

78. Shelden, R. G. "A Comparison of Gang Members and Non-Gang Members in a Prison Setting." *The Prison Journal* 121: 50–60 (1991).

79. Buentello, Fong, and Vogel. "Prison Gang Development," p. 3.

80. Hagedorn, *People and Folks,* p. 161.

81. Spergel, I., *Youth Gangs: Problems and Response.* Chicago: School of Social Work Administration, University of Chicago, 1990, p. 6.

82. Hagedorn, J. "Back in the Field Again: Gang Research in the Nineties." In C. R. Huff (ed.), *Gangs in America.* Newbury Park, CA: Sage, 1990, p. 248.

83. Moore, *Homeboys,* pp. 40, 98.

84. Ibid., pp. 94–95, 102.

85. Ibid., pp. 99–102.

86. Ibid., p. 218.

87. Camp and Camp, *Prison Gangs.*

88. Ibid.

89. Ice T. Interview. *Playboy Magazine* (November 1994), pp. 64–65.

90. Reiner, I. *Gangs, Crime and Violence in Los Angeles: Findings and Proposals from the District Attorney's Office.* Arlington, VA: National Youth Gang Information Center, 1992, pp. 50–51.

91. Buentello, Fong, and Vogel. "Prison Gang Development."

92. Ibid., p. 5.

93. Ibid., p. 8.

94. Ibid.

95. Ibid., p. 348.

96. Ibid., p. 356.

97. Murton, T., and J. Hyams. *Accomplices to the Crime: The Arkansas Prison Scandal.* New York: Grove Press, 1969.

98. Marquart, J. W., and B. M. Crouch. "Judicial Reform and Prison Control: The Impact of *Ruiz v. Estelle* on a Texas Penitentiary." *Law and Society Review* 19: 557–586 (1985).

99. Mays and Winfree, *Contemporary Corrections,* p. 368.

100. Austin and Irwin, *It's about Time,* p. 139; Stanley, D. T. *Prisoners among Us: The Problem of Parole.* Washington, D.C.: Brookings Institution, 1976.

101. Ibid., p. 4.

102. Pickett, R. *House of Refuge: Origins of Juvenile Reform in New York State, 1815–1857.* Syracuse: Syracuse University Press, 1969.

103. Simon, J. *Poor Discipline: Parole and the Social Control of the Underclass, 1890–1990.* Chicago: University of Chicago Press, 1993, p. 34.

104. Walker, S. *Sense and Nonsense about Crime and Drugs* (5th ed.). Belmont, CA: Wadsworth, 2001, p. 219.

105. Petersilia, J. "Probation and Parole." In M. Tonry (ed.), *The Handbook of Crime and Punishment.* New York: Oxford University Press, 1998, pp. 568–569.

106. Stanley, *Prisoners Among Us,* p. 35.

107. Runda, J., E. Rhine, and R. Wetter. *The Practice of Parole Boards.* Lexington, KY: Association of Paroling Authorities, 1994.

108. See Petersilia, "Probation and Parole," for summaries of these studies.

109. Ibid.

110. Austin and Irwin, *It's about Time,* pp. 142–143.

111. Ibid., p. 144. The figures on parole failures are also from this source.

112. Ibid.

113. Austin, J., A. McVey, and F. Richer. *Correctional Options for the State of Nevada to Constrain Prison Population Growth.* San Francisco: National Council on Crime and Delinquency, 1993. Quoted in Austin and Irwin, *It's about Time,* pp. 145–146.

114. For fuller treatment of this issue, see Shelden, *Controlling the Dangerous Classes.* More specific treatment of this subject as it applies to the parole system can be seen in Simon, *Poor Discipline,* esp. Ch. 5.

115. Simon, ibid., pp. 141–142.

116. Austin and Irwin, *It's about Time,* pp. 146–157. See also Irwin, *The Felon.*

117. Irwin, ibid., p. 107.

118. Austin and Irwin, *It's about Time,* p. 148.

119. Quotes from Irwin, *The Felon,* pp. 112–114.

120. Ibid., pp. 131–134.

121. Ibid., p. 162.

122. Staples, W. G. *The Culture of Surveillance: Discipline and Social Control in the United States.* New York: St. Martin's Press, 1997.

123. Austin and Irwin, *It's about Time,* p. 150.

CHAPTER THIRTEEN

THE JUVENILE JUSTICE SYSTEM

YOUTH CRIME IN AMERICA

Juveniles commit a wide variety of offenses, ranging from murder and assault to curfew violation and loitering. Self-report studies indicate that practically every youth at some point in his or her teenage years does something that could result in an arrest. Most are never arrested, and only a very small percentage end up in the juvenile justice system. What about those who are arrested? What are they arrested for? What is the distribution of arrests in terms of race and gender? Table 13.1 shows the total numbers and percentage distribution of juvenile arrests, based on the FBI crime categories, for 1998. Tables 13.2 shows some recent trends for juvenile arrests, expressed in *rates* per 100,000 population (ages 5 to 17).

These figures indicate that the majority of juveniles who are arrested are charged with property offenses, some serious but most minor, along with drug offenses and a variety of rather petty crimes (disorderly conduct, liquor laws, etc.). More specifically, as shown in Table 13.1, the majority of juvenile arrests are for Part II offenses. "All other offenses" constitute the largest chunk of these arrests, followed by "other assaults," with drug offenses, curfew and loitering, and disorderly conduct not far behind. Not surpris-

TABLE 13.1   Total Arrests of Youths under Age 18, 1998

	NUMBER	PERCENTAGE
TOTAL ARRESTS	1,855,002	100.0
INDEX CRIMES		
Murder	1,470	0.07
Rape	3,769	0.02
Robbery	23,400	1.3
Aggravated assault	51,360	2.8
Burglary	81,894	4.4
Larceny–theft	300,033	16.2
Motor-vehicle theft	38,386	2.1
Arson	6,324	0.3
Violent-crime totals	79,999	4.2
Property-crime totals	426,637	23.0
Total index crime	506,636	27.2
PART II OFFENSES		
Other assaults	168,240	9.1
Forgery and counterfeiting	5,006	0.3
Fraud	7,689	0.4
Embezzlement	1,108	0.06
Stolen property	24,159	1.3
Vandalism	90,156	4.9
Weapons	32,232	1.7
Prostitution	1,019	0.05
Sex offenses	11,208	0.6
Drugs	146,394	7.9
Gambling	1,149	0.06
Offenses against the family and children	6,945	0.4
Driving under the influence	14,501	0.8
Liquor laws	111,838	6.0
Drunkenness	17,648	1.0
Disorderly conduct	132,410	7.1
Vagrancy	2,110	0.1
Curfew and loitering	136,293	7.3
Runaways	117,089	6.3
All other offenses	320,207	17.3

Source: Federal Bureau of Investigation. *Crime in the United States, 1998.* Washington, DC: U.S. Government Printing Office, 1999, p. 220.

ingly, among the Part I offenses, larceny–theft constitutes the largest category. It should be noted that the most common of these offenses is shoplifting.

Table 13.2 shows some trends from 1989 to 1998. Total arrests went up slightly (+9.4%), but there was a noteworthy drop in index crimes, especially murder, rape, and motor-vehicle theft. Noteworthy changes in the Part II category occurred in "other assaults." These are mostly minor personal crimes resulting in few injuries. The bulk of these offenses occur near or around schools. A significant increase, almost 64 percent, occurred in drug offenses. This stems directly from the infamous "war on drugs." Finally, curfew and loitering offenses increased the most, going up by 145.5 percent. This increase can be attributed mostly to the increasing attention to both gangs and drugs, as police all over the country engage in crackdowns on places where teenagers congregate, in the hopes that

TABLE 13.2   **Juvenile Arrest Rates (per 100,000 ages 5 to 17), 1989–1998**

	NUMBER		
	1989	*1998*	**PERCENTAGE CHANGE**
TOTAL	2,888.7	3,159.8	+9.4
INDEX CRIMES	1,092.5	878.4	–19.6
Murder	3.9	2.7	–30.1
Rape	7.7	6.6	–14.3
Robbery	43.6	42.0	–3.7
Aggravated assault	82.5	88.4	+7.2
Burglary	204.6	140.7	–31.2
Larceny–theft	611.9	519.2	–15.1
Motor-vehicle theft	127.4	68.2	–46.5
Arson	11.1	10.8	–2.7
SELECTED PART II OFFENSES			
Other assaults	191.9	285.6	+48.8
Fraud	10.2	13.0	+27.5
Stolen property	63.0	40.9	–35.1
Vandalism	160.9	154.4	–4.0
Weapons	55.2	56.2	+1.8
Drugs	155.8	255.4	+63.9
Driving under the influence	26.2	23.9	–8.8
Liquor laws	176.1	187.2	+6.3
Drunkenness	34.4	30.8	–10.5
Disorderly conduct	149.6	212.7	+42.2
All other offenses	400.7	541.2	+35.1
Curfew and loitering	99.1	243.3	+145.5
Runaways	227.3	190.9	–16.0

Source: Federal Bureau of Investigation. *Crime in the United States, 1998.* Washington, DC: U.S. Government Printing Office, 1999, p. 214.

they will be able to deter teenage drug use and gang participation. This zeal has resulted in higher arrest rates for relatively minor offenses—but not much more.[1]

Table 13.3 shows a slightly different perspective on recent trends. Here we show the rank order of juvenile arrests for 1989 and 1998. Note that in both years "all other offenses" and "larceny–theft" ranked number one or number two, together constituting around one-third of all arrests. "Other assaults" appeared in the top five in both years. Drugs and curfew and loitering jumped into the top five in 1998 (the latter was not even ranked in the top ten in 1989). In both years, the top five categories constituted more than half of all arrests, and all ten categories accounted for over 80 percent.

There are noteworthy differences according to both race and gender. Table 13.4 shows some trends in the arrest rates for white and African American youths, for selected offense categories. As noted here, the arrest rates for African Americans exceed the rates for whites by around a 4-to-1 ratio in 1998, yet this is a significant drop from 1980, when the ratio was about 6-to-1. But note that these differences are more than offset by the arrest rates for drugs. Thus, while in 1980 the arrest rate for whites was *higher* than the rate for African Americans, by 1989 the rate for African Americans far exceeded that for whites, with a ratio of almost 6 to 1. Yet between 1989 and 1998, the differences dropped significantly, so that the African American arrest rate exceeded the white rate by about 2.5 to 1. Thus, as so many have noted, the "war on drugs" targeted African Americans at an alarming rate during the

TABLE 13.3 Rank Order of Juvenile Arrests in 1989 and 1998 (percentage distribution)

1989	1998
1. Larceny–theft (21.2)	**1.** All other offenses (17.1)
2. All other offenses (13.9)	**2.** Larceny–theft (16.4)
3. Runaways (7.9)	**3.** Other assaults (9.0)
4. Burglary (7.1)	**4.** Drugs (8.1)
5. Other assaults (6.6)	**5.** Curfew and loitering (7.7)
Sub-total 56.7	58.3
6. Liquor laws (6.1)	**6.** Disorderly conduct (6.7)
7. Vandalism (5.6)	**7.** Runaways (6.0)
8. Drugs (5.3)	**8.** Liquor laws (5.9)
9. Disorderly conduct (5.2)	**9.** Vandalism (4.9)
10. Motor-vehicle theft (4.4)	**10.** Burglary (4.5)
Total 83.3	86.3

Source: Federal Bureau of Investigation. *Crime in the United States, 1998.* Washington, DC: U.S. Government Printing Office, 1999, p. 214.

1980s, but the targets became increasingly white youths in the 1990s. Still, the drug arrest rate for African Americans remains considerably higher than for whites.

Table 13.5 shows comparisons are based on gender. Contrary to popular opinion and media accounts, there has been no "wave of violence" among girls.[2] Juvenile arrests are far higher for males in virtually every category of offenses. However, note that among the most significant trends are the arrests for drugs. Clearly, girls have been targeted almost as often as boys, as the drug arrest rate increased by almost 90 percent for girls during the 1990s, compared to only about 63 percent for boys.

You probably have serious questions about these data, seeing as how they are based on police reports. More important, what needs to be asked is what happens *after* an arrest by the police? What about the charges? How many are dismissed? How many are reduced to lesser offenses? How many result in a petition to juvenile court? How many result in some form of incarceration? We address these and related questions later in this chapter. But first let us briefly review the history of the juvenile justice system.

A BRIEF HISTORY OF THE JUVENILE JUSTICE SYSTEM IN AMERICA[3]

The appearance of adolescence as a social category in the nineteenth century coincided with increasing concern for the regulation of the "moral behavior" of young people.[4] Although entirely separate systems to monitor and control the behavior of young people began to appear during the early part of the nineteenth century, differential treatment based on age did not come about overnight. The roots of the juvenile justice system can be traced to much earlier legal and social perspectives on childhood and youth. One of the most important of these was the legal doctrine known as *parens patriae* (literally "parent of the country").

Parens patriae originated in medieval England's chancery courts and referred to the power of the ruler to administer the estates of landed orphans. *Parens patriae* established that a king or queen, acting as "parent of the country," had the legal authority to take care of his or her people, especially those who were unable, for various reasons (including age), to take care of themselves. The ruler or authorized royal agents could assume the role of

TABLE 13.4   Juvenile Arrest Rates (per 100,000, ages 5–17), for Selected Offenses, by Race, 1980–1998

	1980		1989		1998	
	White	*Black*	*White*	*Black*	*White*	*Black*
INDEX CRIMES						
Violent	105	632	105	656	110	423
Property	1,290	2,679	1,070	2,169	738	1,411
Total	1,395	3,311	1,175	2,825	848	1,834
DRUGS	219	196	125	632	238	594
TOTAL (ALL ARRESTS)	3,980	6,300	3,339	7,088	3,268	6,005

PERCENTAGE CHANGE	1980–1989	1989–1998	1980–1998
TOTAL INDEX			
White	–15.8	–27.8	–39.2
Black	–14.7	–35.1	–44.6
VIOLENT			
White	0.0	+4.8	+4.8
Black	+3.8	–35.5	–33.1
PROPERTY			
White	–17.1	–31.0	–42.8
Black	–19.0	–34.9	–47.3
DRUGS			
White	–42.9	+90.4	+8.7
Black	+222.4	–6.0	+203.0
ALL OFFENSES			
White	–16.1	–2.1	–17.9
Black	+12.5	–15.3	–4.7

Source: Federal Bureau of Investigation. *Uniform Crime Reports, 1980,* p. 205, *Uniform Crime Reports, 1989,* p. 191, *Uniform Crime Reports, 1998,* p. 229. Washington, DC: U.S. Government Printing Office.

guardian and administer the property of orphaned children. By the nineteenth century interpretation this legal doctrine had evolved to the point where the state assumed wardship over a minor child and, in effect, played the role of parent if the child had no parents or if the existing parents were declared unfit.[5]

In the American colonies, officials could "bind out" as apprentices the "children of parents who were poor, not providing good breeding, neglecting their formal education, not teaching a trade, or were idle, dissolute, unchristian or incapable."[6] Later, during the nineteenth century, *parens patriae* supplied (as it still does to some extent) the legal basis for court intervention into the relationship between children and their families.[7]

In the United States, interest in the state regulation of youth was directly tied to explosive immigration and population growth. Between 1750 and 1850 the population of the United States went from 1.25 million to 23 million. The population of some states, such as Massachusetts, doubled; New York's population increased fivefold between 1790 and 1830.[8]

TABLE 13.5 Juvenile Arrest Rates (per 100,000, ages 5–17), for Selected Offenses, by Gender, 1980–1998

	1980		1989		1998	
	Male	*Female*	*Male*	*Female*	*Male*	*Female*
INDEX CRIMES						
Violent	232	27	254	34	227	48
Property	1,644	396	1,458	403	1,033	428
Total	1,876	423	1,712	437	1,260	476
DRUGS	246	52	265	37	431	70
TOTAL (ALL ARRESTS)	4,637	1,234	4,437	1,314	4,525	1,724

PERCENTAGE CHANGE	**1980–1989**	**1989–1998**	**1980–1998**
TOTAL INDEX			
Male	−8.7	−26.4	−32.8
Female	+3.3	+8.9	+12.5
Violent			
Male	+9.5	−10.6	−2.2
Female	+25.9	+41.2	+77.8
Property			
Male	−11.3	−29.1	−37.2
Female	+1.8	+6.2	+8.0
Drugs			
Male	+7.7	+62.6	+75.2
Female	−28.8	+89.2	+34.6
All offenses			
Male	−4.3	+2.0	−2.4
Female	+6.5	+31.2	+39.7

Source: Federal Bureau of Investigation. *Uniform Crime Reports, 1989,* p. 177, *Uniform Crime Reports, 1999,* p. 215. Washington, DC: U.S. Government Printing Office.

Many people coming into the United States during the middle of the nineteenth century were of Irish or German background; the fourfold increase in immigrants between 1830 and 1840 was in large part a product of the economic hardships faced by the Irish during the potato famine. The social controls in small communities were overwhelmed by an influx of new-comers, many of whom were either foreign born or of foreign parentage. The problem of "juvenile delinquency" emerged as one among many social problems urban dwellers faced.[9]

This is an important development that needs further comment. The term *juvenile delinquent* originated early in the 1800s and referred to two different qualities: (1) *delinquent,* which means "failing to do something that is required" (as in a person being "delinquent" in paying taxes), and (2) *juvenile,* meaning "malleable," not yet fixed in one's ways, and subject to change and to being molded (i.e., "redeemable"). By the 1700s, with colleges and private boarding schools developing, various "informal" methods of social control of privileged youth emerged (this paralleled the emergence of capitalism and the need to reproduce the next generation of capitalist rulers). Eventually, more formal systems of control emerged to control working and lower-class "delinquents" around the early 1800s, including the juvenile justice system and uniformed police.[10] In other words, the attitude that even working- and lower-class offenders could be "redeemed" developed.[11]

Throughout the nineteenth century, social reformers (starting with New York City's Society for the Reformation of Juvenile Delinquents, which helped found the first house of refuge in 1824, and ending with Child Savers of Illinois, which helped establish the first juvenile court) constantly called attention to the fact that young children, some as young as 6 or 7, were locked up with adult criminals in jails and prisons and were also appearing with increasing regularity in criminal courts. It was believed that such practices not only were inhumane but also would lead inevitably to the corruption of the young and the perpetuation of youthful deviance or perhaps a full-time career in more serious criminality.[12]

One view of the history of juvenile justice policies in the United States is that they tend to go in cycles, fluctuating from an emphasis on acting in the "best interest of the child," or rehabilitation (based on the *parens patriae* doctrine), to an emphasis on upholding certain rights that also apply to adults, along with their corresponding punishments. In recent years the cycle has shifted toward the latter view—that is, an emphasis on due process rights and punishment.[13]

This cycle begins with the case of *Ex Parte Crouse* in 1838. (This case is reviewed in more detail in Chapter 14.)[14] In this case the Pennsylvania Supreme Court ruled that the Bill of Rights did not apply to juveniles. The justices asked, "May not the natural parents, when unequal to the task of education, or unworthy of it, be superseded by the *parens patriae* or common guardian of the community?" Further, the Court observed that: "The infant [Mary Ann Crouse] has been snatched from a course which must have ended in confirmed depravity"[15]

The ruling assumed that the Philadelphia House of Refuge (and presumably all other **houses of refuge**) had a beneficial effect on its residents. It "is not a prison, but a school," the Court said, and because of this is not subject to procedural constraints. Further, the aims of such an institution were to reform the youngsters within them "by training…[them] to industry; by imbuing their minds with the principles of morality and religion; by furnishing them with means to earn a living; and above all, by separating them from the corrupting influences of improper associates."[16]

About thirty years later, in Illinois, a case arose that challenged the *Crouse* case. This was the case of *People v. Turner* (1870), concerning a boy named Daniel O'Connell. Young Daniel was incarcerated in the Chicago House of Refuge, not because of a criminal offense, but because he was "in danger of growing up to become a pauper." His parents, like Mary Ann Crouse's father, filed a writ of *habeas corpus,* charging that his incarceration was illegal. What is most intriguing about this case is that although the facts were almost identical to the *Crouse* case, the outcome was the exact opposite.

The case went to the Illinois Supreme Court. This court concluded that Daniel was being *punished,* not treated or helped by being in the house of refuge. The Illinois court based its ruling on the *realities* or *actual practices* of the institution, rather than merely on "good intentions" as in the *Crouse* case. The Illinois court rejected the *parens patriae* doctrine. The judges concluded that Daniel was being "imprisoned," and thus they based their reasoning on traditional legal doctrines of the criminal law. They therefore emphasized the importance of *due process* safeguards. The Pennsylvania court in the *Crouse* case viewed the house of refuge in a very favorable light, praising it uncritically. But the Illinois court in the *O'Connell* case viewed the house of refuge in a negative light, addressing its cruelty and harshness of treatment.[17]

The *O'Connell* decision was to have far-reaching effects in the development of the movement to establish the juvenile court in Chicago in 1899. (The child saving movement is covered in more detail in Chapter 14.) However, it needs to be mentioned that the founders of the juvenile court established this institution in part to get around the argument in the *O'Connell* case. In *Commonwealth v. Fisher* (1905), the Pennsylvania Supreme Court returned to the logic of the *Crouse* case. Eventually, this case would be overturned when the U.S. Supreme Court ruled that certain constitutional rights should be accorded to children.

A new cycle has evolved into the recent get-tough on juvenile crime movement. It seems as though certain politicians and criminal justice officials have decided that if children are to be accorded the same rights as adults, then children should be ready to assume adult responsibilities and receive adult-type punishments for their crimes.

THE RIGHTS OF JUVENILES

The distinguishing characteristic of juvenile law is that youths under a certain age may be arrested and processed for behavior for which adults would not be penalized. Such offenses are referred to as **status offenses.** Many of these offenses originally applied mainly to children of immigrant parents. The vagueness of these statutes was noted in previous chapters. Yet after more than 150 years these laws are still being applied vigorously against the children of the poor, and they are just as vague as they have always been. A close look at modern juvenile laws demonstrates this fact.

The juvenile court today has jurisdiction over youths under a certain age who (1) violate laws applicable to adults, (2) commit what are known as *status offenses,* and, (3) are dependent or neglected. The upper age limit of juvenile court jurisdiction in most states is 17. In eight states, however, the upper age limit is 16, and in three states it is 15.[18] In a growing number of states youths who commit certain offenses are turned over to the adult system. This process, known as *certification* or *waiver,* is discussed later in this chapter.

Status offenses have become one of the most controversial aspects of juvenile law. Most of this controversy stems from the vagueness of the statutes; some of it no doubt stems from the *parens patriae* justification for state intervention; much of it stems from the differential application of such offenses, especially the use of a double standard of treatment for males and females brought within the juvenile court jurisdiction.[19] Status offenses involve such behaviors as truancy, violating curfew, running away from home, "ungovernable," "incorrigibility," "wayward," and "unruly." Many states use such acronyms as *CHINS* (children in need of supervision), *MINS* (minors in need of supervision), *PINS* (persons in need of supervision), and *FINS* (families in need of supervision).

The juvenile code of Michigan gives the court jurisdiction if the child "has run away without sufficient cause; is disobedient; associates with immoral persons or is leading an immoral life," or if the child "habitually idles away time."[20] The ambiguity of such statutes gives those in authority a tremendous amount of discretionary power and often leads to arbitrary decisions based on subjective value judgments often imbued with class, race, and sexual biases.[21] These laws also tend to reinforce the dependent status of youth; indeed, one gets the impression that youth are little more than slaves who must remain in their "place." One text on juvenile law noted that "The relationship between the child, his parents and society is fundamentally a property relationship. Most of the laws relating to children reflect the prevailing attitude that they are the possessions of their parents and/or the state and not very valuable possessions at that."[22]

During the past three decades there has been an increase in the use of attorneys in juvenile court cases and a greater emphasis on procedural rights, at least in the courts in major metropolitan areas. This change can be attributed to four important U.S. Supreme Court decisions.

In *Kent v. United States* (383 U.S. 541, 1966), the Supreme Court reviewed a minor's waiver from the jurisdiction of a juvenile court to that of an adult court. The procedure reflects a desire to deal more severely with juveniles who are charged with serious crimes, such as rape and murder. A youth who is waived to an adult court is considered an adult and is treated as such.

This case involved 16-year-old Morris Kent, who in September 1961 raped a woman and stole her wallet. The juvenile court judge waived Kent to the jurisdiction of an adult court, but without a hearing, without having talked with Kent's lawyer, and without having released a copy of the information contained in Kent's social service file, on which the waiver decision was partly based. Kent was convicted and sentenced in adult court to a term of thirty to ninety years in prison.

On appeal, the case came before the U.S. Supreme Court in 1966. The Court ruled that when a case is to be transferred from the juvenile court to an adult court, the youth has a right to defense counsel and a right to have a hearing and that counsel must be given access to the youth's social history file. Also, the lower court must provide a written statement giving the reasons for the waiver, and the defense counsel must be given access to all records and reports used in reaching the decision to waive. In this case Justice Abe Fortas issued one of the strongest indictments of the juvenile court: "There is evidence, in fact, that there may be grounds for concern that the child receives the worst of both worlds; that he gets neither the protection accorded to adults nor the solicitous care and regenerative treatment postulated for children."[23]

Perhaps the most significant case regarding juvenile court procedures was **In re Gault** (387 U.S. 1, 1967). Gerald Gault, age 15, was taken into custody, without notification of his parents, by the sheriff, and brought to the juvenile court of Gila County, Arizona, on the complaint of a neighbor about a telephone call that included lewd remarks that she believed Gault had made. At the time, Gault was on six months' probation after having been found delinquent for stealing a wallet. He was not given adequate notification of the charges and not advised that he could be represented by counsel, nor did his accuser appear in court. He was convicted of this offense and sentenced to the State Industrial School until the age of 23. Had Gault been an adult, the longest sentence he would have received would have been six months in a local jail. Gault's attorneys filed a writ of *habeas corpus* in the Superior Court of Arizona, and its denial was subsequently affirmed by the Arizona Supreme Court.

On appeal to the U.S. Supreme Court, Gault's attorneys argued that the juvenile code of Arizona was unconstitutional. Reversing the lower-court decision, the justices flatly declared that "the condition of being a boy does not justify a kangaroo court."[24] The Court held that at the adjudicatory hearing, juvenile court procedures must include (1) adequate written notice of charges, (2) the right to counsel, (3) privilege against self-incrimination, (4) the right to cross-examine accusers, (5) a transcript of the proceedings, and (6) the right to appellate review. The *Gault* decision began what many have referred to as a "revolution in juvenile court practices." (Unfortunately, neither *Gault* nor subsequent Court cases have considered a juvenile's rights prior to the adjudicatory hearing, such as intake and detention decisions.)

Another significant case was **In re Winship** (397 U.S. 358, 1970), which addressed how much proof is necessary to support a finding of delinquency. At the time, the standard was "a preponderance of the evidence." Rejecting the idea that the juvenile justice system was a civil system, the Supreme Court held that the due process clause of the Fourteenth Amendment required that delinquency charges in the juvenile system have to be proved "beyond a reasonable doubt," like charges in the adult system.

In **McKeiver v. Pennsylvania** (403 U.S. 528, 1971) the Court dealt with the right to trial by jury, normally guaranteed to adults but traditionally denied to juveniles. Indeed, this issue had been part of *Ex Parte Crouse*. However, in *McKeiver,* the Court did not deviate from the traditional view with regard to juveniles, as it had in previous cases. It ruled that jury trials were admissible but not mandatory within the juvenile court. (Ten states currently allow jury trials for juveniles.) In this decision the Court reasoned that a number of problems might arise if jury trials were mandatory, among them publicity, which would be contrary to the confidentiality characteristic of juvenile justice.

JUVENILE COURT: THE STRUCTURE

The centerpiece of the juvenile justice system is the juvenile court. Juvenile courts vary from one jurisdiction to another in size and functions. Some jurisdictions do not have a juvenile court as such and hear cases on special days in other courts. Those areas that have juvenile courts may have anywhere from a small courthouse with a skeleton staff to a large, bureaucratic complex with many separate divisions (often occupying different buildings over several acres of land) and employing over a hundred people. Some juvenile courts (e.g., Honolulu, New York City, Las Vegas) are called *family courts* and handle a wide variety of family-related problems (child custody, child support, etc.).

Typically, juvenile courts are part of county or city district courts, municipal courts, county courts, and other types of court systems found within a county or city governmental structure. Most juvenile courts have at least the following divisions: (1) intake and detention, (2) probation, (3) records, (4) psychological services, (5) judges and personnel staff, (6) medical services (doctor and nurses), and (7) volunteer services.

Among the most important juvenile court personnel are the judges, referees, probation and parole officers, and the defense and prosecuting attorneys. Judges are usually elected officials and have a wide variety of duties, not unlike more traditional judges. Referees (sometimes called "masters") are typically lawyers who perform some of the same functions as do regular judges and are used to supplement the job of the juvenile court judge.

Defense attorneys have become a regular fixture of the court since the *Gault* decision in 1967 ruled that every youth has the right to an attorney. More often than not this attorney is part of the public defender system. However, many youths who appear in juvenile court are still not represented by an attorney.

The prosecutor is generally a member of the local district attorney's office who has been assigned to the juvenile court (just as other district attorneys may be assigned to areas such as domestic violence, gang prosecution, appeals, etc.). Like their criminal court counterparts, these prosecutors are involved in every stage of the process, including such important decisions as whether to charge, what to charge, whether to detain, and whether to certify a youth as an adult.

There are several other personnel within a juvenile court; many of them make some very important decisions. These include intake workers (who are generally the first personnel a youth actually sees when taken into custody and who often decide whether to detain), detention workers (who supervise youths who are detained), and probation and parole officers (who supervise youth placed on probation and those released from institutional care, respectively).

Although the juvenile court differs in many significant ways from the adult system, there are numerous similarities. For instance, in both, cases proceed generally from arrest, through pretrial hearings, through the actual court process, to disposition, and finally to some form of punishment or treatment in a "correctional institution." Juvenile court terminology, however, differs significantly. In juvenile court, a *petition* is the equivalent of an indictment, a trial is called an *adjudicatory hearing,* which is often followed by a *disposition hearing,* roughly the equivalent of a sentencing hearing in the adult system. Parole is known as *aftercare,* and a sentence is called a *commitment.* The term *detention* denotes a form of jailing, and being *taken into custody* is the same as being arrested.[25]

Next we discuss in some detail how a youth comes to the attention of the juvenile court and is processed within it.

JUVENILE COURT: THE PROCESS

In the typical case, a juvenile is referred to the juvenile (or family) court as a result of a contact with the police. In the case of status offenders, the referral often comes from either a parent or a school official. There are eight major stages that the majority of cases proceed through. These stages are described in Figure 13.1.

Who Is Referred to Juvenile Court and for What?

Obtaining accurate data on juvenile court processing is difficult, for several reasons. First, the most common source of national figures has been the Office of Juvenile Justice and Delinquency Prevention (OJJDP), which publishes surveys of juvenile court cases based on the voluntary submission of data from the National Juvenile Court Data Archive by

FIGURE 13.1   The Juvenile Court Process

ARREST

When a juvenile is arrested by the police, one of three options is usually available: they can release the youth with a simple warning, issue a misdemeanor citation (sort of like a traffic ticket, ordering the youth to appear in court at a certain date), or physically take the youth to the juvenile court and the intake division, where he or she is booked.

INTAKE

This is the first step following the police decision to take the youth to the court. The intake process is a sort of initial screening of the case by staff members. Normally there are also probation officers (sometimes called "intake officers") who review the forms filled out by a staff member who collects some preliminary information (e.g., alleged offense, various personal information about the youth, including name, address, phone number, parents' names, etc.). During this stage, a decision is made as to whether to file a *petition* to appear in court on the charges, to drop the charges altogether (e.g., for lack of evidence), or to handle informally.

DIVERSION

In the event that the intake decision is to handle informally, probation staff, usually in cooperation with the prosecutor's office, will either release the youth without any further action or propose a diversion alternative. Diversion entails having the youth and his or her parent or guardian agree to complete certain requirements instead of going to court. This may include supervision by the probation department, plus satisfying various requirements: a curfew, restitution, community service, substance-abuse treatment, and so on. After a certain length of time, if the youth successfully completes the program, charges are usually dropped; if not, the youth is brought back into court via a formal petition.

DETENTION

If the case is petitioned to court, the next major decision is whether to detain the youth or release him or her to a parent or guardian, pending a court appearance. The reasons for detaining a youth usually include (1) safety (does the youth pose a danger to himself or herself or to others) or (2) flight risk (does he or she pose a risk to flee or not appear in court). If the youth is detained, then a hearing must be held within 24 to 72 hours, in order for a judge to hear arguments as to whether the youth should be detained any longer. Bail is not generally guaranteed.

TRANSFER/WAIVER

In rare cases, a youth may be transferred or "waived" to the adult system. This is usually (but not always) done only in the case of extremely serious crimes or when the youth is a "chronic" offender.

ADJUDICATION

This is the juvenile court equivalent of a trial in the adult system. Rather than a jury hearing the case, the final decision rests with a judge or referee. Both defense and prosecuting attorneys present their cases if a youth denies the petition. If the youth admits to the charges, the case proceeds directly to the next stage.

DISPOSITION

This is the equivalent of the sentencing stage of the adult system, known as the *disposition hearing*. Numerous alternatives are available at this stage, including outright dismissal, probation, placement in a community-based program ("boot camp," wilderness training, group home, substance-abuse treatment facility, etc.), or incarceration in a secure facility (e.g., "training school").

AFTERCARE

This stage occurs after a youth has served his or her sentence. It is roughly the equivalent of "parole" in the adult system.

both state and local agencies.[26] Such information is not uniform and not derived from any probability sampling procedure. Moreover, not all states are included. In the most recent year available at the time of this writing (1997), only 1,317 juvenile court jurisdictions in 26 states (containing 52% of the juvenile population in the country) were provided to the national archive.

Second, and perhaps most important, the statistics group cases referred to court according to the usual FBI offense categories (index and Part II crimes). As noted in Table 13.6,

TABLE 13.6   Delinquency Cases in Juvenile Court, 1997

MOST SERIOUS OFFENSE	NUMBER OF CASES	PERCENTAGE	PERCENTAGE CHANGE, 1988–1997
DELINQUENCY CASES			
TOTAL	1,755,100	100.0	48
PERSON OFFENSE	390,800	22.2	97
Homicide	2,000	0.1	31
Rape	6,500	0.4	48
Robbery	33,400	1.9	55
Aggravated assault	67,900	3.9	66
Simple assault	248,800	14.2	124
Other violent sex offense	10,200	0.6	59
Other person offense	22,000	1.3	72
PROPERTY OFFENSE	841,800	48.0	19
Burglary	135,900	7.7	2
Larceny–theft	401,300	22.9	23
Motor-vehicle theft	48,800	2.8	−11
Arson	9,300	0.5	44
Vandalism	114,800	6.5	41
Trespassing	65,100	3.7	28
Stolen property	33,800	1.9	5
Other property	32,800	1.9	60
DRUG-LAW VIOLATION	182,400	10.4	125
PUBLIC-ORDER OFFENSE	340,100	19.4	67
Obstruction of justice	132,600	7.6	78
Disorderly conduct	92,300	5.2	107
Weapons offense	38,500	2.2	74
Liquor-law violation	11,100	0.6	−31
Nonviolent sex offense	11,100	0.6	−4
Other public order	54,600	3.1	56
STATUS OFFENSES	158,500	100.0	101
Running away	24,000	15.1	93
Truancy	40,500	25.6	96
Ungovernability	21,300	13.4	65
Liquor-law violation	40,700	25.7	56
Miscellaneous	32,100	18.2	367

Source: U.S. Department of Justice. *Juvenile Court Statistics, 1997.* Washington, DC: Office of Juvenile Justice and Delinquency Prevention, May 2000. Online (www.ncjrs.org/html/ojjdp/jcs_1997).

the offenses are grouped into five major categories: person, property, drugs, public order, and status offenses. Note that this categorization is based on the *most serious offense charged*. If a juvenile has multiple charges of a less serious nature, these offenses are not included in the totals. Thus, a very incomplete picture is presented from these data.

In 1997 an estimated 1,755,100 delinquency and 158,000 status-offense cases were processed within the juvenile court across the nation. Of the delinquency cases, the majority were either property offenses (48%) or public-order offenses (19.4%). Relatively few were serious violent offenses (homicide, rape, robbery, and aggravated assault, constituting only 6.3% of all cases). The most common offense against the person was "simple assault" (totaling 14.2% of all delinquency cases). Drugs accounted for about 10 percent of the total. What is perhaps most noteworthy is that between 1988 and 1997 the number of drug cases referred to juvenile courts increased by 125 percent, more than any other offense category. What is clear from this picture is the relatively minor nature of most juvenile crime. Thus, within the property-offense category, larceny–theft (chiefly shoplifting) leads the way, accounting for almost half of the total (48%). Vandalism, trespassing, and "other property" together constitute another 12 percent. Combining the larceny–theft category with vandalism, trespassing, "other property," simple assault, and public-order offenses, the total comes to about two-thirds of all offenses (68.6%). Not exactly a picture of wild juvenile predators running amok![27]

As for status offenses, the only data available from the OJJDP report are those cases that are actually petitioned to court, rather than all status offense referrals. In 1997, a total of 158,500 cases were petitioned, representing a 101 percent increase over 1987. As noted in Table 13.6, the most common status offense is liquor-law violations (25.7%), with truancy ranked a close second (25.6%). The miscellaneous category accounted for just under one-fifth of the total (18.2%). Note that this category jumped up by 367 percent over 1988. Among the most common miscellaneous status offenses are curfew violations, tobacco, and violations of court orders. The rise in this particular offense may stem mostly from greater law enforcement attention devoted to gang-related behavior over the past several years.[28]

As for the actual processing of cases through the juvenile court, just over half (57%) of all delinquency referrals were petitioned to court. Of those petitioned to court, 58 percent were adjudicated, with the remainder handled informally (the majority of these cases—59%—were dismissed). Of those adjudicated, a slight majority (55%) were placed on probation. Of those not petitioned, almost half (44%) were dismissed outright, with no further handling, while almost one-third (32%) were placed on informal probation. The most severe disposition, an out-of-home placement, occurred in 28 percent of the petitioned cases.[29]

The disposition of these cases did not vary too much according to the offense charged, although some noteworthy differences can be found. Thus, while 58 percent of all personal offenses were petitioned, so were 53 percent of property offenses, 63 percent of drug offenses, and 61 percent of public-order offenses. Of those petitioned to court, 30 percent of the person-offense cases were placed (meaning an out-of-home placement, ranging from a community-based program to a training school), but so were 26 percent of the property offense cases, 24 percent of the drug cases, and fully one-third of the public-order cases.

During the period 1988–1997, the number of cases petitioned to court increased by 75 percent, the most notable of which were drug cases, with an increase of 144 percent, much greater than the increase in person offenses (up 116%), public-order offenses (up 115%), and property offenses (up 39%).

As for status offenses, just over half were adjudicated, with the majority (59%) placed on probation. Among those not adjudicated, the majority (62%) were dismissed. For both delinquency and status offenses, relatively few ended up being placed in some kind of institution. For delinquency cases, just under 10 percent (9.8%) were placed; for status offenders, 7.3 percent were placed.

Race and Juvenile Court Processing

Race figures prominently in the processing of cases through the juvenile court system. To begin with, as noted in Table 13.7, the referral rates for African American youths are significantly higher than for both whites and other races. Thus, the overall rate for African American youths was more than double the rate for whites and about three times greater than the rate for other races. When comparing according to offense charged, for crimes against the person, African Americans had a rate three times higher than whites and more than four times higher than other races. As for the changes over time, from 1988 to 1997, the rate of referral for public-order offenses increased by 87 percent for African Americans, compared to a more modest 35 percent increase for whites. White youths, however, saw their rate for drug offenses shoot up by 119 percent, compared to a 70 percent increase for African Americans. Still, rates for drugs remained much higher for African Americans.

Given the fact that the police make so many arrests of persons under the age of 18, it should come as no surprise that the largest percentage of referrals to the juvenile court come from the police (over 80%). Thus, it is safe to conclude that the first stage of the juvenile justice system begins when the police apprehend a youngster for an alleged offense. We now turn to a more detailed look at the police response to juvenile crime.

The Police Response

The police, of course, have a great deal of discretion as to what courses of action to take when dealing with juveniles, or any other member of the public for that matter. Once the police have apprehended a youth, several alternatives are available:

1. They can release with a warning.
2. They can release after filling out an interview card or some other official report that does not constitute an arrest but nevertheless is an official record of a youth's deviant behavior. This information may be used against a youth at a later date, but the youth is not given the opportunity to answer the charges, a problem that has yet to be dealt with by the courts.
3. They may make a "station adjustment," in which the youth is brought to the police station and is (a) released to a parent or guardian with an official reprimand, (b) released with a referral to a community agency that deals with youth problems, or (c) released with a referral to a public or private mental health or social welfare agency.
4. They may take the youth to the intake division of the juvenile court.[30]

TABLE 13.7   Percentage Change in Delinquency Cases (per 1,000 juveniles), by Race, 1988–1997

	CASE RATES				CASE RATES		
	1988	*1997*	PERCENTAGE CHANGE		*1988*	*1997*	PERCENTAGE CHANGE
WHITE	**39.6**	**50.8**	**28**	**OTHER RACE**	**33.3**	**37.7**	**13**
Person	5.4	10.3	89	Person	4.8	6.9	46
Property	24.6	25.7	4	Property	21.7	21.6	0
Drugs	2.4	5.3	119	Drugs	1.4	2.5	71
Public order	7.1	9.6	35	Public order	5.4	6.7	25
BLACK	**89.6**	**123.7**	**38**				
Person	21.5	33.3	55				
Property	46.5	51.3	10				
Drugs	7.9	13.4	70				
Public order	13.7	25.7	87				

Source: U.S. Department of Justice. *Juvenile Court Statistics, 1997.* Washington, DC: Office of Juvenile Justice and Delinquency Prevention, May 2000. Online (www.ncjrs.org/html/ojjdp/jcs_1997).

The police are provided with few guidelines about how to determine what action to take in the case of a juvenile. In most states the police are empowered to arrest juveniles without a warrant if there is "reasonable grounds" to believe that the child (1) committed a delinquent act, (2) is "unruly," (3) is in "immediate danger from his or her surroundings," or (4) has run away from home. In California the officer is given the following standard: "In determining which adoption of the minor he will make, the officer shall prefer the alternative which least restricts the minor's freedom of movement, provided such alternative is compatible with the best interests of the minor and the community."[31]

As numerous studies have shown, the race, class, and demeanor of a youth often play a crucial role in police decision making, especially when there are no complainants and for misdemeanor offenses.[32] A study by Bishop and Frazier is instructive because they followed a cohort of more than 54,000 youths from arrest to adjudication in the juvenile court. While holding constant such factors as seriousness of offense and prior record, they concluded that "race is a far more pervasive influence in processing than much previous literature has indicated."[33]

The Effect of the "War on Drugs" on Referrals to Juvenile Court

Race may actually play an indirect role, in that race relates to offense, which in turn affects the police decision to arrest. Race may also relate to the *visibility* of the offense. This is especially the case with regard to drugs. There is abundant evidence that the "war on drugs" has, in effect, resulted in a targeting of African Americans on a scale that is unprecedented in American history. As the research by Jerome Miller has shown, young African American males have received the brunt of law enforcement efforts to "crack down on drugs."[34] He notes that in Baltimore, for example, African Americans were being arrested at a rate six times that of whites, and more than 90 percent were for possession.[35] While the arrest rate for both races among juveniles for heroin and cocaine possession was virtually the same in 1965, by the 1970s the gap began to widen, and by 1990 the arrest rate for African Americans stood at 766, compared to only 68 for whites. Overall, in 1980 the national rate of all drug arrests was about the same for African American and white juveniles; during the early 1980s the arrest rate for whites dropped by one-third, while the rate for African Americans remained about the same.

But as the "war on drugs" expanded, the arrest rate for African American youths went from 683 in 1985 to 1,200 in 1989, which was five times the rate for whites; by 1991 it went to 1,415! An even more alarming study in Baltimore found that total arrests for African American youths were around 86 in 1981 (versus 15 for whites); by 1991 that number had increased to 1,304 for African Americans, compared to a mere 13 for white youths! Nationally, between 1987 and 1988 the number of whites brought into the juvenile court remained virtually the same (up 1%), but the number of minorities referred to the court increased by 42 percent. In Miller's own study of Baltimore, he found that during 1981 only 15 white juveniles were arrested on drug charges, compared to 86 African Americans; in 1991, however, the number of whites arrested dropped to a mere 13, while the number of African Americans skyrocketed to 1,304, an increase of 1,416 percent! The ratio of African American youths to whites went from about 6 to 1 to 100 to 1![36]

Juvenile court cases reflect the role of race in drug cases. According to 1997 data (see discussion above), the rate (per 1,000) of African American youths referred to court on drug charges was 13.4, compared to a rate of only 5.3 for white youths.[37]

Another study found that "black youths are more often charged with the felony when [the] offense could be considered a misdemeanor." Also, those cases referred to court "are judged as in need of formal processing more often when minority youths are involved." When white youths received placements, such "placements" are more often than not "group home settings or drug treatment while placements for minorities more typically are public residential facilities, including those in the state which provide the most restrictive confinement." It is true that there have been significant increases in minority youths being referred to juvenile court, which increases the likelihood of being detained. But cases of the detention, petition, and placement of minorities nevertheless exceeded what would have been expected given the increases in referrals. There has been an increase in the formal handling of drug cases, which has become a disadvantage to minorities. "Given the proactive nature of drug enforcement, these findings raise fundamental questions about the targets of investigation and apprehension under the recent war on drugs."[38] As noted in a study of Georgia's crackdown on drugs, the higher arrest rate for African Americans was attributed to one single factor:

> it is easier to make drug arrests in low-income neighborhoods.... Most drug arrests in Georgia are of lower-level dealers and buyers and occur in low-income minority areas. Retail drug sales in these neighborhoods frequently occur on the streets and between sellers and buyers who do not know each other. Most of these sellers are black. In contrast, white drug sellers tend to sell indoors, in bars and clubs and within private homes, and to more affluent purchasers, also primarily white.[39]

Some studies have suggested that social class, rather than race per se, best predicted police decisions. For instance, research by Sampson found that the overall socioeconomic status of a community was more important than other variables, although race figured prominently. In general, the lower the socioeconomic standing of the community as a whole, the greater will be the tendency for the police to formally process youth they encounter. Of course we must remember that minorities, especially African Americans, are far more likely than whites to be found within the lower class and living in poverty.[40]

Demeanor has always played a significant role in police decision making, especially when it comes to juveniles. Youths who "smart off" or otherwise do not display the "proper" deference are usually the most likely to be formally processed, for, in police parlance, they "flunked the attitude test." This is especially the case with minor offenses and even when there is little or no evidence that a crime has been committed.[41] Like social class, race figures into this equation because so many African American youth are angry at the white establishment, especially at representatives like the police, and express their anger during their contacts with the police. Many display a "defiant air" that challenges the police.[42]

Regardless of whether race, class, or demeanor is statistically more relevant, one fact remains: growing numbers of African American youths are finding themselves within the juvenile justice system. They are more likely than their white counterparts to be detained, more likely to have their cases petitioned to go before a judge, more likely to be waived to the adult system, and more likely to be institutionalized.[43] While some of this relates to the nature of the offense, as we have shown, the likelihood of one race being associated with a particular offense, especially drugs, cannot be denied.

Case Study: The "Saints" and the "Roughnecks"

In this section we provide a summary of what we believe is one of the most interesting studies of delinquency ever conducted. It reveals the often subtle, and not so subtle, class bias in the definition of and response to "delinquency." The study, conducted by William Chambliss about twenty-five years ago, remains relevant today. One of the important aspects of this study is that it underscores the importance of social definitions of what constitutes "delinquency" and what is considered to be "normal" youthful behavior, part of "growing up," "sowing wild oats," and "boys will be boys." Such definitions are very much influenced by social class position.[44]

Chambliss's study consisted of observations made over several years of two groups of teenagers, which he called the "Saints" and the "Roughnecks," and of how the police, the school system, and the community in general responded to their deviant activities. The Saints were eight white boys from upper-middle-class backgrounds, and the Roughnecks were six white boys from lower-class backgrounds. Both groups engaged in a wide variety of delinquent behavior.

The Saints developed an ingenious scheme for cutting school and did so successfully almost every day. They had access to cars and made a habit of traveling to a nearby town (where they were not known and would not be seen by members of their own community) and engaging in a variety of activities. On weekends especially they were far from being "saints," for they would travel to a town about twenty-five miles away and "raise hell." Such acts as vandalism, drinking and driving, shouting obscenities to girls and police, and committing various "pranks" (such as removing danger signs from areas where the road was being repaired or where it was washed out) were committed regularly.

The Saints were viewed by teachers and local community members as "good kids" and "promising young men" with a "bright future." Teachers and police regarded their activities (when they were caught, which was rare) as "pranks" or "kid's stuff" or part of "growing up" or "sowing wild oats." In short, this was behavior that would not lead to more serious problems or criminal activity. Most of the boys were A and B students (despite their frequent absences from school).

The Roughnecks engaged in activities very similar to those of the Saints, but their activities were more visible to the local community. From the perspective of the police, teachers, and the local community, the Roughnecks were "bad kids," and their acts "proved" they were "headed for trouble." Local residents would say, "Too bad that these boys couldn't behave like the other kids in town; stay out of trouble, be polite to adults, and look to their future."[45] They were more often picked up by the police and harassed by the police, both of which resulted in a strong dislike for the police by the Roughnecks, and vice versa. To the police, teachers, and the community they were "troublemakers." In school they were noted as "poor students," although they did manage to keep a C average.

The differential treatment, suggests Chambliss, stemmed in part from the greater visibility of the Roughnecks:

> This differential visibility was a direct function of the economic standing of the families. The Saints had access to automobiles and were able to remove themselves from the sight of the community. In as routine a decision as to where to go to have a milkshake after school, the Saints stayed away from the mainstream of community life. Lacking transportation, the Roughnecks could not make it to the edge of town, The center of town was the only practical place for them to meet since their homes were scattered throughout the town and any noncentral meeting place put an undue hardship on some members. Through necessity the Roughnecks congregated in a crowded area where everyone in the community passed frequently, including teachers and law enforcement officers.[46]

Moreover, since the Roughnecks were from the lower class, they fit the stereotype of "criminal" or those "headed for trouble," and police and others acted accordingly. The demeanor of the two groups, as expected, differed a great deal, The Saints were "respectful" and "deferential" toward those in authority; the Roughnecks acted "disrespectful" and failed to defer to authority.

Not only did the Roughnecks have police records (the Saints did not), but they also had rather predictable adult careers. One ended up serving a life sentence for murder, another became a small-time gambler, another was sentenced to a thirty-year sentence for murder, and a fourth was last known to be a truck driver. Two were athletes while in school and obtained scholarships to colleges from which they were eventually graduated. They were last reported as being coaches on the high school level. In contrast, only one of the Saints failed to finish college; when last seen he had been unemployed for over a year. One became a doctor, another became a lawyer, and still another was working on a Ph.D. The rest held high-ranking positions in the business world.

How can we explain the difference between these two groups? If we assume that these two groups are typical of other American youths, then we can conclude the following: The criminal justice system and other control/processing institutions (e.g., schools) help maintain the class structure by channeling youth in directions appropriate to their class background. The criminal justice system (at least in effect), by defining certain acts as "delinquent" or "criminal," helps prevent upward mobility for the majority of lower-class youths. It is noteworthy that the two Roughnecks who "made it" did so through their athletic abilities, one of the few means of upward mobility for lower-class youths. Chambliss makes the following observation:

> The answer lies in the class structure of American society and the control of legal institutions by those at the top of the class structure. Obviously, no representative of the upper class drew up the operational chart for the police which led them to look in the ghettoes and on street-corners—which led them to see the demeanor of lower-class youth as troublesome and that of upper-middle-class youth as tolerable. Rather, the procedures simply developed from experience—experience with irate and influential upper-middle-class parents insisting that their son's vandalism was simply a prank and his drunkenness only a momentary "sowing of wild oats," experience with cooperative or indifferent, powerless, lower-class parents who acquiesced to the law's definition of their son's behavior.[47]

The Intake Process and the Decision to Detain

When youths are referred to juvenile court, they come in contact with the **intake division** (in most metropolitan courts). This division is staffed by full-time employees of the court who are usually college graduates in such subjects as social work, sociology, or criminal justice. One of the first decisions these employees have to make is whether the case falls within the jurisdiction of the court. Also, they need to determine whether a youth needs to be placed in detention. This decision is usually based on certain specified criteria that are measured through the use of a risk assessment instrument, such as the one shown in Figure 13.2. A risk assessment instrument is an "objective" method of determining whether a youth is a "danger to himself or others," is unlikely to appear in court, or has no place to go (e.g., he or she is abandoned). Available data indicate that the majority of youths referred to court are placed in detention at least for a few hours, with an average length of stay about fifteen days.[48]

It could be argued that detention should be reserved for youths who are charged with serious crimes. This is not the case, however. The most recent survey, from 1997, shows that juveniles who are detained are charged with a variety of offenses—the largest proportion are relatively minor offenses. For example, those charged with "technical violations" (mostly probation or parole violations, but no criminal charges) constituted just over 22 percent, while drug offenders were 8 percent of the total and public-order offenders another 9 percent of the detainees. Violent index crimes constituted about 21 percent of the total, and index property crimes accounted for another 22 percent. Contrary to the adult system, in the majority of states juveniles are not permitted bail.[49]

The decision to detain a youth is marked by significant racial differences. As shown in Table 13.8, no matter what the most serious offense charged happens to be, African American youths have dramatically higher rates of detention than both whites and Hispanics. For all offenses, the detention rate for African Americans if five times that of whites. For crimes against the person, the difference is even greater (a 7-to-1 ratio). African Americans are *ten times more likely to be detained for a drug offense.* Studies show that those who are detained are far more likely to be treated with the most severe final disposition.[50]

We can see a sort of *cumulative racial bias* that begins with arrest patterns. A detailed look at arrest patterns comes from a study of California cases in 1989.[51] After examining over 3 million cases statewide, Krisberg and Austin found that while African American youths constituted just under 9 percent of the total population, they were about 20 percent of those arrested, and their arrest *rate* was more than double the rate for whites. Consistent with our *criminalization model,* as we go further into the system, we find that African American youths are far more likely to begin to receive the most severe disposition. Thus, African American youths are detained at a rate almost *five times greater than* whites. The rate differentials remain higher for African American youths even when other variables are considered, such as the type of offense charged and whether individuals were on probation at the time of the arrest.

FIGURE 13.2   Los Angeles County Detention/Release Scale

1. Most Serious Present Offense   _____

    Serious/Violent Offense
        WIC 707 (b) offense   10
        Other violent (battery, assault)   7

    Serious Property/Drug Offenses
        Burglary, Grand theft, MV theft, Sale of narcotics   5

    All Other Crimes   3

    Status Offenses, Noncriminal Violations   0

2. Number Sustained Petitions, Last 12 Months   _____

    Two or more   5
    One   3
    None   0

3. Youth Residing With: _____

    Out of home (institutions, group home, etc.)   2
    In home (parent, guardian, relative)   0

4. Under Influence of Drugs/Alcohol at Time of Arrest?   _____

    Yes   2
    No   0

5. Probation Status   _____

    Active probation, new criminal offense alleged   4
    Active probation, no criminal allegation   2
    Not on active probation   0

6. Warrant Status   _____

    Minor is subject of active bench warrant   10

Total Score   _____

Detain/Release Scale

    0–9 = Release
    10+ = Consider for Home Detention, DAAP, or
    Secure Detention

Source: Wiebush, R. G., C. Baird, B. Krisberg, and D. Onek. "Risk Assessment and Classification for Serious, Violent, and Chronic Juvenile Offenders." In J. Howell, B. Krisberg, J. D. Hawkins, and J. Wilson (eds.), *Serious, Violent, and Chronic Juvenile Offenders.* Thousand Oaks, CA: Sage, 1995, p. 193.

In most states there is a requirement that within a certain period of time (usually between 48 and 72 hours) some form of judicial review of the decision to detain must be undertaken. A formal *detention hearing* is set up to make this determination, presided over by a judge or referee.

A controversial issue related to detention is *preventive detention,* which is a practice of placing a youth in secure confinement mostly because of what he or she *might* do in the future. It is, in effect, a form of "punishment without trial." The case of *Schall v. Martin* (467 U.S. 253, 1984) raised this question. The plaintiffs charged that the New York Family Court Act was unconstitutional because the practice of preventive detention amounted to punishment without due process. The U.S. district court ruled in favor of the plaintiffs and struck down the New York law, and the case was affirmed by the U.S. court of appeals. However, the U.S. Supreme Court reversed the decision, claiming that the practice of pre-

TABLE 13.8   Offense Profile of Detained Juveniles by Race (per 100,000 juveniles), 1997

MOST SERIOUS OFFENSE	TOTAL	WHITE	BLACK	HISPANIC
TOTAL	96	54	273	130
Delinquency	91	49	263	127
PERSON	29	14	88	42
Violent index crime	20	8	67	33
Other person crime	9	6	22	9
PROPERTY	25	16	64	30
Property index crime	21	13	53	25
Other property crime	4	2	11	5
DRUG	8	3	31	10
PUBLIC ORDER	9	5	26	12
TECHNICAL VIOLATION	21	12	54	33
STATUS OFFENSE	5	4	10	3

Source: Sickmund, M., and Y. Wan. "Census of Juveniles in Residential Placement Data Book." Online (www.ojjdp.ncjrs.org/ojstatbb/cjrp/index.asp).

ventive detention protects both juveniles and society from criminal activity while on release status.

However, the theory behind that ruling is seriously flawed, for it assumes that there is a valid method of predicting who is most likely to commit a crime while released. Indeed, risk assessment instruments can be misused or err in their predictive accuracy. For example, one study determined that the risk assessment score assigned to youths placed in detention was a poor predictor of recidivism.[52] Another study found that probation officers often use risk assessment instruments to "certify" what they have already decided based on their "gut feelings" and prejudices.[53] Also, the theory ignores the fact that even among those detained, the majority either have their cases dismissed or receive some form of probation. Moreover, as already noted, the majority who are detained did not commit a serious crime.

After the decision to detain has been made, the intake officer has several options. These include (1) counsel, warn, and release, sometimes called *informal adjustment;* (2) *informal probation* (release under certain conditions, with supervision by a volunteer or a regular probation officer, and after a certain period of time if no new offense is committed, the case is dismissed); (3) referral to another agency; (4) outright dismissal; (5) filing a *consent decree* (somewhat more restrictive than informal probation); and (6) filing a petition to have the youth appear in court for a formal *adjudicatory hearing.*[54]

What are the final decisions at this stage? Nationwide, only a slight majority (56%) of intake cases end up with a petition to court. Most of those that are not petitioned are either dismissed outright or placed on informal probation. In many of these cases the youth, in effect, engages in some form of "plea bargaining," because in order to avoid a formal petition the youth usually has to admit guilt. In other words, a youth is "sentenced" to some form of probation, community service, house detention, and so on, in return for an admission of guilt.

Class and race have been found to be at least indirectly related to decision making at the intake stage. Many studies beginning in the 1950s have demonstrated the influence of class and race. A review of the evidence by Krisberg and Austin led to the conclusion that "nonwhite youth experience significantly higher rates of detention, petition filing, and placements than do white youth."[55]

We are not suggesting that everyone connected with the juvenile justice system is a racist and practices discrimination, although to be sure many hold typical stereotypes about youths from certain race or class backgrounds. Part of the problem is institutional: such negative stereotypes are deeply imbedded in our culture; staffing of juvenile courts and police departments is largely white dominated; there is widespread poverty and joblessness affecting minority communities, which in turn results in the lack of available resources (e.g., alternatives to formal court processing) to deal with crime-related issues and the general failure of schools.

Adjudication

Adjudication is the juvenile court counterpart of trial in adult court, but in many respects it has been very different over the years. Often the hearings are rather informal (sometimes they are merely conversations between a judge, parents, and the child), and they are closed to the public and to reporters. In recent years the procedures have become more formal, especially in large metropolitan courts—in many cases, nearly as formal as in adult court.

There are two types of hearings. The *adjudicatory hearing* is the fact-finding stage of the juvenile court process. After this stage is the *disposition hearing,* in which the final disposition is determined (roughly equivalent to the sentencing stage in the adult system). In most urban courts both the defense and the prosecutor present the evidence of the case. As in the adult court counterpart, hearsay evidence is inadmissible, the defendant has the right to cross-examine a witness, the defendant is protected against self-incrimination, and a youth's guilt must be proved beyond a reasonable doubt.

In the majority of juvenile courts, the disposition hearing is a separate hearing altogether. During this hearing, the judge relies heavily on two important court documents, usually prepared by the probation department of the court: the legal file and the social file. The *legal* file contains a complete referral history, including the nature of all the offenses that brought the youth into court prior to the current offense, along with prior dispositions. The *social* file is probably more important, for it contains a wide range of personal information about the juvenile—family background, school records, psychological profile, and the like. Together these two documents aid the probation department in preparing the *presentence report* (or *predisposition report*), roughly the equivalent of the one prepared in the adult system.

Perhaps the most important part of the presentence report is the recommendation as to the course of action taken by the court. Typically some sort of a "treatment plan" is prepared for the case, along with the actual sentence. More often than not, the judge agrees with the recommendation.[56]

Several dispositions are available to juvenile court judges. These alternatives can be grouped into three categories: (1) dismissal, (2) probation, (3) commitment to some type of institution (with levels of security ranging from group homes to training schools). It should be noted that a fourth alternative is waiver to an adult court, and we review this option later in the chapter.

As many studies have shown, the youth's prior record, current offense, and previous sentences are among the most important factors in determining the final disposition.[57] But, several studies have noted the importance of race and other social factors in determining the final disposition.[58] Minorities, especially African Americans, do not fare well throughout the court process. Even if the effects of race may disappear by the time the final disposition is made, race has already shaped previous processing decisions, such as the decision on what offense to charge and the decision to detain. More important, what many prior studies fail to mention is that even "prior record" and other "legal" variables are closely related to race and class, for racial minorities are far more likely than their white counterparts to be stopped and questioned by the police, to be viewed as potential "gang" members, to be picked up and charged with minor offenses during police sweeps (especially crackdowns on "gang" activity), and to be stopped for simply being black or "driving while black" (DWB) or "standing while black" (SWB).[59] The effects are obvious: African American youths and other minorities are far more likely than whites to be placed in some form of institution.

Viewing these dispositions from the perspective of the philosophy of the juvenile court (i.e., *parens patriae*), we see an interesting irony. The court philosophy and theoretical perspective on delinquency assume that delinquency is a symptom of some sort of problem and that the court should "protect" or "look after" children who come to its attention or otherwise "treat" these problems. Yet the court either dismisses outright or gives minimal or no supervision to over two-thirds of all who come through its doors. This is especially true when we consider that those who are placed on probation get very little supervision, as so many studies have shown. Although quite dated, a survey of juvenile courts in 1976 by Sarri and Hasenfeld noted that probation officers saw their clients about an average of once a month for an average of 30 minutes and that overall they spent about 40 percent of their time in direct contact with clients, mostly in the office. They further note:

> Observation of 78 probation interviews in the field sample revealed that very little counseling occurred, most of the interviews (68 percent) involved surveillance—either general checks on youth's current conditions (e.g., at home or school) or specific discussions of probation rules. Very few interviews (14 percent) involved actual problem solving. In 70 percent of the probation interviews observed, no services were requested, and in 54 percent no services were suggested by the worker. Services were requested and offered for interpersonal problems in only 2 percent and 3 percent, respectively, of the interviews.[60]

Sarri and Hasenfeld reached the following conclusion, with which we concur:

> Throughout this study one is repeatedly confronted with inescapable ambiguities and contradictions in the goals, ideology, structure, and operations of juvenile courts. Thus, for example, courts profess to pursue both a "crime control" and a "youth concern" goal. Courts operate under the assumption that they must protect the community, yet the bulk of the cases referred to them are in fact "juvenile nuisances." Courts profess to assist troubled youth to receive needed services and yet they tend to be quite isolated from the community network of youth serving agencies. Courts develop complex and elaborate decision-making structures, presumably to identify the needs of the child and determine the best approaches to meet them. Yet over half of all the children referred to the courts are sent away with little more than a friendly warning, and most of the rest are put on probation, which is little more than surveillance. Courts establish formal procedures to maintain due process, but, in practice, adhere to few of them.[61]

It appears that not too much has changed since the time those observations were made by Sarri and Hasenfeld. Writing almost twenty years later, Krisberg and Austin observed:

> Our analysis paints a discouraging picture. Juvenile laws are vaguely worded and inconsistently applied, permitting extensive abuses in the handling of children by social control agencies whose discretion is largely unchecked. Instead of protecting children from injustices and unwarranted state intervention, the opposite effect frequently occurs. The practices and procedures of juvenile justice mirror our society's class and racial prejudices and fall disporportionately on African-American, Latino, and poor people.[62]

Jerome Miller, reflecting on his own thirty-plus years of working with youthful offenders, notes that one of the problems within the modern juvenile justice system is the method of diagnosing youth and recommending appropriate dispositions. He notes that the "treatment options" that the diagnostician has in mind help to determine the actual diagnosis of the youth, rather than the other way around, as we generally assume. In reality, he notes, "the theory-diagnosis-treatment flow runs backward. The diagnostician looks first to the means available for handling the client, then labels the client, and finally justifies the label with psychiatric or sociological theory. Diagnosis virtually never determines treatment; treatment dictates diagnosis."[63]

Within the formal juvenile justice system the most severe disposition alternative has always been and continues to be commitment to some form of secure facility, commonly known as juvenile institutions.

JUVENILE INSTITUTIONS

Commitment to a juvenile correctional institution often represents the "end of the line" for some youthful offenders. These institutions, starting with houses of refuge, do not have a very positive history. Conditions in **training schools** (the direct heirs of houses of refuge) have not improved that much over the years. Any "treatment" that goes on in these institutions is a rare event.

There are several different correctional institutions to which a youth can be committed. Some of these institutions are public (i.e., run by state or local government), and others are privately funded. Correctional institutions can be further subdivided into those providing short-term confinement (usually ranging from a few days to a couple of months) and those providing long-term confinement (ranging from three or four months to one or two years). Among the former are:

1. Adult jails (most often used where separate juvenile facilities are lacking, such as in small rural communities)
2. Detention centers (typically found within the local juvenile court complex)
3. Shelter care facilities (usually local facilities reserved for status offenders and dependent, neglected, and abused children)

Facilities offering long-term confinement include:

1. Reception and diagnostic centers. Usually attached to a training school, this is a place where offenders, prior to starting their sentence, are evaluated by a psychologist or social worker to determine what sort of treatment will be required; usually the stay is no more than a month.
2. Ranches and forestry camps. Usually located near state parks or in rural areas, these are small facilities where the residents do conservation work or various sorts of farm/ranching type work.
3. Boot camps. A recent phenomenon, these are operated somewhat like their military counterparts. Confinement lasts anywhere from 30 to 120 days. As of 1994 there were only nine such programs in the country.
4. Training schools. By far the largest and most popular, these institutions are a carry-over from nineteenth-century houses of refuge and reform schools and in many respects represent a juvenile version of adult prisons.[64]

As of October 29, 1997, there were 76,503 committed juveniles in correctional institutions; of this number a total of 51,136 were in public facilities and 25,367 in private institutions.[65] According to the 1997 census, although in both types of institutions delinquent offenses constitute the majority of the major charge against the offenders, a significant percentage of those committed to private facilities were in for status offenses (15.2%).

Of the delinquency offenses, the most common in public facilities were violent index crimes (32%), followed closely by property index crimes (28%). A total of 9 percent were charged with drug offenses in public facilities. The offense profile for those in private facilities is somewhat different: 21 percent charged with violent index crimes, 32 percent charged with index property crimes, 15 percent charged with status offenses, and 11 percent charged with drug offenses.

Racial Composition of Juvenile Institutions

Incarceration is a fate that awaits many minority youths. The percentage of incarcerated youths who are racial minorities has risen steadily over the years. National figures show that in 1950 only 23 percent of those in training schools were minorities, in 1960 this figure was 32 percent; in 1970 it was up to 40 percent; in 1989 minorities constituted 60 percent of those in public training schools; in 1997 the percentage stood at 66 percent. The majority of youths confined in *private* facilities are white, no doubt because most of the costs are paid for by family members, usually through their insurance.[66]

Not surprisingly, the overall *rate* of incarceration was considerably higher for minorities. The 1997 census of committed juveniles (see Table 13.9) reveals stark contrasts:

1. The overall rate for African American youths stood at 737, compared to a rate of 377 for Hispanics and only 146 for whites.
2. Even considering the most serious offense charged, commitment rates for minorities far exceeded those of whites: for personal crimes, the African American rate was 279 compared to only 42 for whites and 152 for Hispanics; for drug offenses, the African American rate stood at 94 and the Hispanic rate was 35, compared to merely 8 for whites. In other words, for drug offenders, *the African American incarceration rate was more than ten times greater than for whites.*
3. In every other offense category, whites had the lowest rate and African Americans had the highest, with Hispanics in the middle.[67]

The distribution of these rates—African Americans first, Hispanics second, whites third—reminds us of a phrase we heard repeatedly during the civil rights movement: "If you're white, you're all right; if you're brown, stick around; if you're black, stay back."

Studies in individual states are often even more revealing. Take California, for example, which currently ranks among the top five states in its rate of incarceration for juveniles.[68]

TABLE 13.9   Offense Profile of Committed Juveniles by Race (per 100,000 juveniles), 1997

MOST SERIOUS OFFENSE	TOTAL	WHITE	BLACK	HISPANIC
TOTAL	266	146	737	377
Delinquency	249	132	701	367
PERSON	93	42	279	152
Violent index crime	71	29	219	125
Other person crime	22	13	60	27
PROPERTY	86	55	207	114
Property crime index	73	47	175	99
Other property	12	8	32	15
DRUG	24	8	94	35
PUBLIC ORDER	24	14	63	39
TECHNICAL VIOLATION	22	13	58	28
STATUS OFFENSE	17	14	36	9

Source: Sickmund, M., and Y. Wan. "Census of Juveniles in Residential Placement Data Book." Online (www.ojjdp.ncjrs.org/ojstatbb/cjrp/index.asp).

Krisberg and Austin's study of California found that the rate of commitment to a private facility was 467 for African Americans, compared to only 153 for whites; the rate of commitment to secure county facilities was 1,114 for African Americans compared to only 294 for whites; the rate of commitment to the California Youth Authority (CYA), the most secure institutions in the state (tantamount to "junior prisons") was 529, compared to only 47 for whites. The figures on commitments to the CYA reveal that even when considering the nature of the offense, current probation status, sex, age, and the number of offenses, African Americans were far more likely than whites to be committed. Like the figures for detention, sentences for drug offenses were dramatic: for felony drug offenses, African Americans were *seven times more likely than whites to be committed.*[69] More recent figures on the racial distribution of the California Youth Authority show that as of the year 2,000 minority youths constituted the overwhelming majority, with Hispanics accounting for almost half (48%) and African Americans constituting 29 percent. Whites were only 16 percent of the total.[70]

Commitment rates in Nevada are far higher for African Americans than for whites (a rate of 936 for African Americans and 383 for whites).[71] In 1999 a new super-max youth prison was opened in North Las Vegas to house offenders classified as "Level IV"—the highest classification in the state, based on alleged degree of "dangerousness." This was a new category, mostly reflecting a youth's prior record and based on a point system—the more points, the more dangerous the person. There was literally no scientific rationale for the point system, and no research was cited that would warrant such a point system. Curiously, the higher the level of classification, the greater was the percentage of minorities. This institution, Summit View Correctional Center, was built and operated by Correctional Services Corporation, a private company. Within one year of opening, the prison was beset by a number of problems, not the least of which was too many empty beds (a certain number of residents were needed in order to make a profit). The state could not find enough "dangerous" youth to qualify for Level IV (in fact, for a time the prison "borrowed" a few Level III youths from the detention center at the juvenile court in Las Vegas). The state, however, did find a large number of minority youths to house in this prison; a recent census revealed that about 80 percent of the youths were minorities.[72]

Some Effects of Incarceration

Why are we so critical of these institutions? The reasons are many and varied, and should be obvious as soon as institutional atmospheres are closely examined. What is life like in secure training schools today? Sadly, not much different from what it has always been. Several studies covering a period of around thirty years document the continuation of horror stories within these institutions.[73]

In a survey of forty-two juvenile correctional facilities conducted in the 1970s by the National Assessment of Juvenile Corrections the focus was on, among other things, some of the effects of being institutionalized on the youths themselves. The study distinguished between "newcomers," those who had been at the facility two months or less, and "veterans," those who had been incarcerated nine months or more. The survey found some rather significant differences between programs having large proportions of veterans and those having relatively few veterans.[74]

Generally, it was found that the veterans were significantly more likely than the newcomers to (1) commit more offenses and have friends who committed offenses while incarcerated; (2) have learned more ways to break the law while incarcerated (46 percent of the veterans, compared to 20 percent of the newcomers); and (3) become more "hardened" over time (being "hardened" was measured in several ways, such as being critical of the staff, previous encounters with institutions, and number and seriousness of offenses while incarcerated). It was also found that the longer a youth remained in the institution, the more the youth would (1) fight with other youths, (2) use drugs, (3) steal something, (4) run away, and (5) hit a staff member. These problems become most acute when, as the researchers put it, there is a "critical mass" of veterans within a program (most often a training school).

It was found that these problems are more apparent in larger institutions (i.e., training schools).

That the strong prey on the weak in these institutions is nothing new, as numerous studies, some dating back to the 1950s, indicate. These studies also found that there exists in these institutions a very potent inmate subculture, not unlike the subcultures found in adult prisons.[75] In most of the larger institutions there is a hierarchy within a strongly defined *peer subculture*. The most commonly found social roles are those of the "toughs" or "dukes" and the "punks"; the "punks" are the lowest in social status (they are the youths who have been victimized sexually or "punked out").

Another study noted how youths entering the institution quickly earn reputations, either as strong boys or as weak ones:

> Once boys were in the intake cottage, the other boys immediately subjected them to tests designed to ascertain whether they could be exploited for food, clothes, cigarettes, and sex. Sexual exploitation was found to be severe, with blacks pressuring whites in most of the encounters. If the new boy looked and acted tough, exploitation was minimized; if any weaknesses were shown, he was immediately misused by the others.... Nearly all of the most seriously exploited were white, and most of the exploiter boys were black. As in many adult prisons, the whites were disorganized and the blacks stuck together. Boys were acquainted with the local version of the convict code shortly after arrival. This code had standards for all prisoners but also some that were specific to blacks or Caucasians. The general code items were "exploit whomever you can," "Don't kiss ass," "don't rat on your peers," "don't give up your ass," "be cool," "don't get involved in inmate affairs," "don't steal squares (cigarettes)," and "don't buy the mind fucking thing." Additional norms for blacks were "exploit whites," "no forcing sex on blacks," "defend your brother," and "staff favor whites." For whites, the additional norms were "don't trust anyone" and "everybody for himself."[76]

A very detailed study of an institution in Columbus, Ohio, focused on the extent of victimization within these institutions and describes a rather brutal social system. Within the "jungle" (the term the inmates themselves use) the powerful prey on the weak (not surprising, for this is what they learned from our culture long before they arrived at this institution). The overwhelming majority engage in some form of exploitation.[77] What is most interesting about this study is that the authors returned fifteen years later for a follow-up. What they found was not encouraging. They discovered that the youth culture still exists and victimizes the weak, though less for sex than for food, clothing, and toiletries. Consensual sexual behavior seems to be more prevalent; the proportion who are violent are in the minority; the majority are minor drug dealers, addicts, and users of drugs. Gangs do not dominate within the institution, as popularly believed. Most discouraging is the fact that treatment has "all but disappeared," with the lone exception of a drug-abuse program. The authors quoted one social worker who said that "We don't do anything in here for kids." Another member of the staff added that "This place is a warehouse for children."[78] Is this surprising, given how the surrounding society has given up on these kinds of youth, the majority of whom are African Americans?

Increasingly, the juvenile courts, perhaps giving in to the law-and-order rhetoric of the past two decades, have begun to rely on one of the most extreme dispositions within the juvenile justice system—namely, certifying a youth as an adult. It is as if they have said: "We give up! We have done everything we can think of to help you." Yet, as we show in the next section, the individuals the court has given up on are disporportionately African American youths. They are, in effect, disposable children.

GIVING UP ON DELINQUENT YOUTH: TRANSFER TO THE ADULT SYSTEM

One of the fastest growing changes within the juvenile justice system is known as *waiver* or *certification*. If a juvenile court believes that an offender is too "dangerous" or is "not amenable to treatment," the court transfers its jurisdiction (i.e., "waives") to the adult system by, legally speaking, making the youth an adult.[79] Generally, juvenile courts either lower the age of jurisdiction (*judical waiver*) or exclude certain offenses (legislative waiver)—in most jurisdictions, homicide. Every state presently has some provisions for transferring offenders to adult courts. In some states, only the age provisions are used. Growing numbers of states are making the age lower and lower (e.g., in Vermont it is age 10; in Montana, 12; in Georgia, Illinois, and Mississippi, 13). Most states, however, do not go below age 14.[80]

Despite the hoopla surrounding this issue—politicians all over the country claim there are "dangerous" youths everywhere who need to be certified—during 1998 (the latest year for which figures are available), only 8,100 were transferred to the adult system, down from 12,100 in 1994. In 1989, only 8,000 were transferred. Also, most of those transferred have been charged with property crimes or with drug and public-order crimes (64%) rather than personal crimes (36%). African Americans remain the most likely to be transferred, receiving this disposition in numbers far greater than their numbers in the general population (42% of those transferred compared with 55% of whites). It is interesting to note, however, that the percentage of those transferred who were African Americans has declined from 50 percent.[81]

The movement to transfer youth seems more a political issue than a public safety issue. Many local politicians gain votes for their get-tough stance on juvenile crime, using mostly anecdotal evidence to support their cause.[82] In other cases it is merely an attempt to get rid of "troublesome cases."[83] In fact, transferring juveniles to adult court *does not result in a reduction of crime and may even contribute to at least a short-term increase in crime.*[84]

Judicial waivers and prosecutorial discretion are often arbitrary, fluctuate from judge to judge and jurisdiction to jurisdiction, and form no consistent pattern.[85] For instance, a study in Florida found that juvenile waivers to adult court between 1981 and 1984 were predominately low-risk juveniles and property offenders. These juveniles were not accused of committing a violent crime.[86] The examination of legislative waivers, particularly changes, is a reflection of perceived public opinion, changing values and norms, and a response to the get-tough stance on juvenile crime. Legislative waiver strategies attempt to reconcile the cultural conceptions of youth and choose between the boundaries of criminal activities and criminal responsibility of youth.[87]

Although the minimum age varies across states, three states—Indiana, South Dakota, and Vermont—allow the certification of a juvenile as young as 10 years old. Although state laws differ, most state laws have a variation or combination of requirements from *Kent v. United States* (383 U.S. 541, 566–567, 1966) that meet specific age and serious-crime criteria. The crime must be serious, aggressive, violent, premeditated, and done in a willful manner. Further, the crime must be against persons and result in a serious personal injury. Juveniles are evaluated on their sophistication or maturity, indicated by external factors such as emotional attitude and the juvenile's record and history. And the evaluation must conclude that the public is adequately protected, in that if the juvenile is not treated and punished as an adult, the public would not be protected from future victimizations. All of these transfer processes authorize juvenile courts to waive juvenile delinquency cases to adult criminal proceedings.

There are three types of legislative waivers: discretionary, mandatory, and presumptive. All waivers must meet some criterion in any given case: a minimum age, a specified type or level of offense, serious record of previous delinquency, or a combination of these three criteria. Waivers may be initiated by prosecutors' filing a motion or by the juvenile court.

Discretionary waivers (found in forty-six states) specify broad standards to be applied for consideration of a waiver. Most common is when the court exercises its discretion to waive jurisdiction when the interests of the juvenile would be served. Further, some state legislation call on waivers when public safety or interest requires it or when the juvenile does not seem responsive to rehabilitation. Many states combine these standards. For instance, a waiver in the District of Columbia requires adult prosecution of a juvenile if doing so is in the interest of the public welfare and security and there are no prospects for rehabilitation. In contrast, Kansas allows waivers whenever the court finds "good cause" and Missouri and Virginia allow waivers when the juvenile is not a "proper subject" for treatment.[88] In 1997, Hawaii lowered the age limit for discretionary waivers, adding language that allows a waiver of a minor at any age (previously age 16) if charged with first- or second-degree murder (or attempts) and there is no evidence that the person is committable to an institution for the mentally defective or mentally ill.[89]

The statutes of fourteen states provide *mandatory waivers* in cases that meet certain age, offense, or other criteria. In these states, the proceedings are initiated in juvenile court, sending the case to the adult criminal court. All states with mandatory waivers specify age and offense requirements. Ohio requires that a juvenile who commits any criminal offense at the age of 14 or higher and meets certain legislative requirements must be waived to criminal court. West Virginia requires that a juvenile must be 14 and have committed specific felonies before his or her case is waived to criminal court. Delaware and Indiana do not specify an age. In Connecticut, the law stipulates that where the mandatory waiver provision applies, the juvenile's counsel is not permitted to make any argument or file a motion to oppose transfer, arguably a due process violation. In fact, mandatory waiver occurs where a probable-cause finding is necessary; the court makes it without notice, a hearing, or any participation by the juvenile or his or her attorney.

Presumptive waivers (found in fifteen states) place the burden of proof on the juvenile. If a juvenile meets a specific age, offense, or other statutory criterion and fails to make an adequate argument against transfer, the juvenile court must send the case to criminal court. In some states, older juveniles are singled out even when the offense they are accused of would not otherwise trigger a waiver. For example, in New Hampshire crimes that would merely authorize consideration of a waiver in the case of a 13 year old, require one for a 15 year old.

Although these provisions of juvenile transfer to criminal court are generally believed to be responses to the increase in juvenile violence, a large number of laws also include prosecution for nonviolent offenses. Most often arson and burglary (in twenty-one states) and drug offenses (in nineteen states) committed by a juvenile may be prosecuted in criminal court. Nine states authorize or mandate prosecution for escape (Arkansas, Illinois, Michigan, Oregon), soliciting a minor to join a street gang (Arkansas), "aggravated driving under the influence" (Arizona), auto theft (New Jersey), perjury (Texas), and treason (West Virginia). Further, many states allow or require transfers for misdemeanors, ordinance violations, and summary statute violations, such as fish and game violations.[90]

JUVENILES INCARCERATED IN ADULT PRISONS

The trend to waive youths to criminal court coincides with the increased willingness of criminal courts and juries to sentence adult offenders to death.[91] According to the Office of Juvenile Justice and Delinquency Prevention, 7 percent of all juvenile admissions to custody in 1998 were referred directly to criminal court. The average daily juvenile population held in adult jails in 1992 was 2,527, an increase of 62 percent since 1983.[92] In 1996, the one-day count of juvenile offenders held in local adult jails was 8,100, an increase of 20 percent from 1994.[93] The average prison sentence for juvenile offenders convicted as an adult averaged about nine years; for violent offenses the average was almost eleven years.[94]

Get-tough policies for juvenile offenders are viewed as a deterrent for "out of control" juveniles and to protect society, yet in reality incarcerating juveniles in adult facilities has proved to be detrimental. Failure to separate juveniles from adults leads to exposure to people with extensive criminal records, and juveniles are an easy target for sexual or physical assault.[95] Juveniles housed in adult penitentiaries and jails commit suicide at a far higher rate, and this applies to juveniles as young as 12 and to relatively minor, nonviolent offenders. Studies have found that juveniles who are prosecuted and punished as adults are more likely to re-offend and to do so more quickly, compared to juveniles who are dealt with by the juvenile justice system.[96]

Federal and state governments and correctional authorities have recognized the inherent dangers in housing juveniles with adults, yet their responses to the need to protect incarcerated children from adult inmates are inconsistent. In 1974, the U.S. Congress passed legislation to provide a strong financial incentive for states to separate adult and juvenile offenders. In 1980, Congress reviewed the evidence of the detrimental effects of housing juveniles with adults and passed legislation requiring the complete removal of juveniles from adult jails and police lockups. However, the protection offered by the federal legislation applies to only some juveniles. States are not required to separate juveniles from adults if a juvenile is prosecuted as an adult for violating a state criminal law. In some jurisdictions, a juvenile who commits even a relatively minor, nonviolent offense may be imprisoned in the general population. For instance, in 1977, Native American Yazi Plentywounds (age 16) was convicted for shoplifting two bottles of beer. He was sentenced to two years at the adult state prison in Cottonwood, Idaho, because he had a prior conviction for "grand theft"— breaking a shop window worth $300 in order to steal some cases of beer.[97]

APPLYING THE DEATH PENALTY TO JUVENILES

The death penalty is an inappropriate penalty for individuals who have not attained full physical or emotional maturity at the time of their actions. Currently, thirty-eight states and the federal government have statutes authorizing the death penalty for certain forms of homicide. Of these thirty-eight states, four use age 17 and twenty use age 16 as the minimum age a person must be in order to receive the death penalty. About one in every fifty individuals on death row is a juvenile offender. Almost 3 percent of all new court commitments to death row are persons who committed their crimes while a juvenile.[98] Imposing sentences of "life without parole" on waived youth for crimes they committed at age 13 or 14 and executing them for crimes they committed at age 16 or 17 challenges the social construction of adolescence and the idea that juveniles are less criminally responsible than adults.[99] Strieb found that executions for crimes committed by youths under age 18 account for 1.8 percent (357) of all confirmed legal executions carried out since 1642.[100]

As of June 1999, there were seventy persons (twenty-four in Texas) on death row who were juvenile offenders when they committed their crime. Between 1973 and June 1999, thirteen juvenile offender executions were carried out in the United States. Three juvenile offenders were executed in the United States in January 2000.[101] The United States accounts for the majority of known juvenile offender executions (ten since 1990). More than seventy-two countries that retain the death penalty in law have abolished it for juvenile offenders. The United States stands with five other countries in which such executions are reported to have been carried out in the 1990s: Iran, Pakistan, Saudi Arabia, Yemen, and Nigeria. The United States is the only Western democratic nation that imposes the death penalty on individuals who commit their crimes as juveniles.

The imposition of the death penalty on juveniles is not without international criticism. Eleven countries—Belgium, Denmark, Finland, France, Germany, Italy, Netherlands, Norway, Portugal, Spain, and Sweden—have voiced their objection of this continued practice across the United States.[102] The United Nations Human Rights Committee contends that the United States "undermine[s] the effective implementation of the Covenant [International Covenant on Civil and Political Rights] and tend[s] to weaken respect for the obligations of the State parties."[103]

The legality of capital punishment for juveniles is left up to each individual jurisdiction. In the case of *Thompson v. Oklahoma* (487 U.S. 815, 1988), the Supreme Court ruled that executing youths under the age of 16 was unconstitutional and "the chronological age of the minor is itself a relevant mitigating factor" (*Eddings v. Oklahoma* 455 U.S. 104, 1982).

Public calls for the death penalty for juvenile offenders are made in response to high-profile juvenile homicides. Several politicians appear to be in a contest to see who can appear to be the toughest. The governor of New Mexico publicly stated that he favors the death penalty for juveniles as young as 13. The governor of California indicated personal support for the death penalty against 14 year olds, and a Los Angeles district attorney stated that he favored the death penalty for children "no matter what their age." A Texas state representative contemplated introducing legislation under which 11 year olds who commit murder could be sentenced to death.[104]

In 1998, the case of Michael Domingues was brought before the Nevada Supreme Court. Michael Domingues was convicted in 1994 for a crime he committed when he was 16 years old—the murder of his next-door neighbor and her 4-year-old son in their home. His case was appealed based on the violation of international law and the U.S. ratification of International Covenant on Civil and Political Rights (ICCPR). The Nevada Supreme Court voted that the death sentence was legal and binding. The justices stated that "many of our sister jurisdictions have laws authorizing the death penalty for criminal offenders under the age of eighteen and such laws have withstood Constitutional scrutiny."[105] The Court reached this conclusion by looking at other U.S. states rather than examining international opinion or practice. The justices also ignored the fact that in 1998, fourteen states and two federal jurisdictions (civilian and military) enacted legislation that prohibits the death penalty for any juvenile offender.

According to a long-standing principle of international jurisprudence, which the United States chooses to ignore, the nation-state is subject to international law. According to United Nations, the U.S. policy on executing juvenile offenders violates international laws and treaties signed or ratified by the United States.[106] In 1955, the United States ratified Article 68 of the Fourth Geneva Convention (1949), "Relative to the Protection of Civilian Person in Time of War," which states, "the death penalty may not be pronounced on a protected person who was under 18 years of age at the time of the offense."[107] Thus, for nearly five decades, the United States has protected all civilian youthful offenders in protected countries from the death penalty during war or armed conflict, yet U.S. policies and practices deprive youth in this country of protection during peace. The International Covenant on Civil and Political Rights was signed by the United States in 1977 and ratified in 1992.[108] According to the provisions in this Covenant, youth should be separated from incarcerated adults and receive appropriate treatment (Article 10), and the death penalty must not be imposed for crimes committed by juvenile offenders (Article 6). The U.S. submission to the Human Rights Committee examining compliance with ICCPR states that the United States reserves the right to treat juveniles as adults in exceptional circumstances: "the policy and practice of the United States are generally in compliance with and supportive of the Covenant's provisions regarding treatment of juveniles in the criminal justice system. Nevertheless, the United States reserves the right in exceptional circumstances to treat juveniles as adults."[109] This "treatment" includes imprisoning children with adults and imposing the death penalty.

The Inter-American Commission on Human Rights also found the United States in violation of international law,[110] as did the United Nations Special Rapporteuer, which "emphasizes that international law clearly indicates a prohibition of imposing the death sentence on juvenile offenders. Therefore, it is not only the execution of a juvenile offender which constitutes a violation of international law, but also the imposition of a sentence of death on a juvenile offender by itself."[111] Nevertheless, the Republican National Committee chairperson called on the U.S. administration to publicly renounce this report and ensure that none of the U.S. debts to the United Nations was paid until the report was formally withdrawn and apologized for.[112]

Further, the United States resists international human rights commitments for children in its failure to ratify the Convention of the Rights of the Children (CRC). A total of 192 countries ratified the convention; two countries did not—the United States and Somalia. Article 6 of the Convention states that all children must be guaranteed the right to survival, life, and development. Article 3 says that the "best interests of the child" should be a primary consideration. These laws apply to all juveniles, including those who are accused or convicted of violating the law.[113]

The general perception that human rights are an international issue and not only a domestic issue is predominant in state jurisdictions. Within the United States, state and local jurisdictions have a low level of awareness of international human rights standards. Hence, human rights seem not to be taken seriously in the United States. When defense attorneys bring international human rights issues into the courtroom, judges and prosecutors dismiss treaties and international laws, stating that international law is irrelevant because it is not a state law. This demonstrates a serious gap between federal and state governments concerning international obligations taken by the U.S. government. The United Nations (1998) documents that the United States cannot claim to represent countries at the international level and ensure that human rights obligations are fulfilled.[114]

The vast majority of juvenile offenders executed in the United States before 1972 were sentenced to death and executed while still teenagers. The current application of the death penalty means that most juvenile offenders will be well into their adult years by the time they are executed. Perhaps the fact that it is not actually a child who is strapped down and killed makes it easier for society to stomach this human rights violation. The fact remains, however, that such prisoners are being executed for crimes they committed as juveniles. Many have been sentenced to death by juries that were not in the position to fully consider mitigating factors and the youths' backgrounds.

For instance, on October 14, 1998, Dwayne Allen Wright was executed in the Greensville Correctional Center, Virginia. Dwayne Wright grew up in a poor family in a neighborhood characterized by illegal drug activity, gun violence, and homicides. Dwayne's father was incarcerated when Dwayne was 4 years old. His mother, suffering from mental illness, was unemployed for most of his life. When he was 10, his older brother was murdered; then Dwayne developed serious mental problems. He did poorly at school and for the next seven years spent time in hospitals and juvenile detention facilities. He was treated for major depression with psychotic episodes; his mental capacity was evaluated as borderline retarded, his verbal ability, retarded; and doctors found signs of organic brain damage. Many appealed to the state governor to give Dwayne clemency. These included appeals from the American Civil Liberties Union, Reverend Jesse Jackson, and Senator Edward Kennedy. The American Bar Association president reportedly wrote: "A borderline mentally retarded child simply cannot be held to the same degree of culpability and accountability for their actions to which we would hold an adult." Dwayne Wright's attorneys obtained affidavits from two jurors in his 1991 capital trial who stated that they would not have sentenced him to death had they known of brain damage suffered at birth that left Dwayne prone to violent outbursts. One juror stated, "Had I been told the truth about Dwayne during his trial, I never would have voted to impose a death sentence."[115]

On January 10, 2000, Douglas Christopher Thomas was executed in Virginia. Questions still remain about his responsibility for the crime he was convicted of—killing his girlfriend's mother. Witnesses came forward before his execution to reveal that his codefendant (his girlfriend, Jessica Wiseman) admitted that she had killed her mother. Further, psychologists chosen by the Commonwealth of Virginia found that Thomas's intellectual deficits and emotional disturbances mitigated the criminal behavior. In fact, the Commonwealth's psychologist opposed Thomas's execution.[116]

SUMMARY

With changes in the labor market structure and several other structural changes in society during the nineteenth century came changes in conceptions of and responses to youthful deviance. The first indication of such changes came with the house of refuge movement during the first half of the nineteenth century. These institutions functioned to control and reform children of the poor (especially Irish immigrants in the New York House of Refuge). The general aim of "reform" was to inculcate "habits of industry" and respect for authority, which would help maintain the existing class structure.

With more changes in the social structure came more reforms of the juvenile justice system during the last half of the nineteenth century. Youth became more and more dependent, with the age of adolescence setting in, and many were relegated to the surplus labor population ("redundant workers"). With thousands flocking to large cities in the Northeast and Midwest, unemployment and vagrancy became widespread. Juvenile delinquency became a problem for reformers as the juvenile system as we know it today began to take shape. One of the most notable changes was the establishment of the juvenile court system and industrial and training schools. Thus, by 1900 to 1910 the basic structure of the modern juvenile justice was created, with the *parens patriae* doctrine and the medical model of deviance providing the philosophical and theoretical justification for state intervention into the lives of "wayward" youth.

We examined the various components of today's juvenile justice system. Juvenile laws, which undergird the system, include prohibitions of a wide variety of behavior applicable to those under a certain age (usually 18). Juvenile court procedures differ in many ways from the adult system, yet like the adult system, the juvenile court places a premium on the efficient processing of cases (as can be seen, for instance, in the subtle forms of plea bargaining). And despite Supreme Court rulings (e.g., *Kent* and *In re Gault*), juveniles still have few of the rights accorded to adults, especially at the intake stage. The juvenile laws and the philosophy of *parens patriae* seem to reinforce the dependent status of youth and their relationship to the adult world as analogous to property.

The juvenile correctional system, particularly training schools, is not much different in most respects from adult prisons. Training schools house mainly youth from the lowest segments of the class structure and contain a disproportionate number of nonwhite youths.

Juvenile justice functions to regulate and control primarily youths who are among the economically marginal or part of the surplus population of "redundant workers." As illustrated so well by the study of the Saints and the Roughnecks, the juvenile justice system tends to help maintain a class society.

This chapter also examined the controversial topics of certification, the death penalty for juveniles, and the violation of basic human rights of juveniles. We noted how racially biased the certification process is, subjecting proportionately far more minorities to the adult system. The mere existence of the death penalty for certain juveniles is by definition a violation of the Convention of the Rights of the Children, passed overwhelmingly by the United Nations yet rejected by the United States and Somalia.

KEY TERMS

adjudication 342	*In re Winship* 330	*parens patriae* 325
Ex Parte Crouse 328	intake division 339	*People v. Turner* 328
house of refuge 330	*Kent v. United States* 329	status offenses 329
In re Gault 330	*McKeiver v. Pennsylvania* 330	training school 349

NOTES

1. Shelden, R. G., S. K. Tracy, and W. B. Brown. *Youth Gangs in American Society* (2nd ed.). Belmont, CA: Wadsworth, 2001.

2. Ibid. See also Chesney-Lind, M., and R. G. Shelden. *Girls, Delinquency and Juvenile Justice* (2nd ed.). Belmont, CA: Wadsworth, 1998.

3. This section is adapted from Shelden, R. G. *Controlling the Dangerous Classes: A Critical Introduction to the History of Criminal Justice.* Boston: Allyn and Bacon, 2001, ch. 5.

4. Platt, A. The Child Savers (rev. ed.). Chicago: University of Chicago Press. 1977; Empey, L. *American Delinquency.* Homewood, IL: Dorsey Press, 1982.

5. Sutton, J. R. *Stubborn Children: Controlling Delinquency in the United States, 1640–1981.* Berkeley: University of California Press, 1988.

6. Rendleman D. R. "Parent Patriae: From Chancery to the Juvenile Court." In F. L. Faust and P. J. Brantingham (eds.), *Juvenile Justice Philosophy*. St. Paul, West, 1974, p. 63.

7. Rothman, D. J. *The Discovery of the Asylum.* Boston: Little, Brown, 1971; Krisberg, B., and J. Austin. *Reinventing Juvenile Justice.* Newbury Park, CA: Sage, 1993; Shelden, *Controlling the Dangerous Classes,* ch. 5.

8. Empey, *American Delinquency,* p. 59.

9. Brenzel, B. *Daughters of the State.* Cambridge, MA: MIT Press, 1983, p. 11.

10. Informal systems of control have always been reserved for the more privileged youths; the less privileged have been subjected to formal systems of control. However, if we examine history closely, with few exceptions it has almost always been the case that minority youth have been much more likely to be viewed not as "juvenile delinquents" (i.e., "malleable" and thus "redeemable") but as "hardened criminals" (not redeemable, for by definition "adults" are more fixed in their ways and less redeemable). Little wonder that such a great proportion of those certified or waived to adult court in recent years (i.e., viewed as "unredeemable" adult criminals) have been minorities.

11. Bernard, T. J. *The Cycle of Juvenile Justice.* Oxford: Oxford University Press, 1992, pp. 49–55.

12. Pickett, R. *House of Refuge.* Syracuse: Syracuse University Press, 1969; Platt, *The Child Savers.*

13. Bernard, *The Cycle of Juvenile Justice.*

14. Shelden, R. G. "Confronting the Ghost of Mary Ann Crouse: Gender Bias within the Juvenile Justice System." *Juvenile and Family Court Journal* 49: 11–25, 1998.

15. *Ex Parte Crouse,* 4 Wharton (Pa.) 9 (1838), pp. 9–11.

16. Ibid., p. 11.

17. Bernard, *The Cycle of Juvenile Justice,* pp. 70–72; "People v. Turner," in Faust and Brantingham, *Juvenile Justice Philosophy.*

18. Bartollas, C. *Juvenile Delinquency* (5th ed.). Boston: Allyn and Bacon, 2001, p. 5.

19. Chesney-Lind and Shelden, *Girls, Delinquency and Juvenile Justice.*

20. Krisberg and Austin, *Reinventing Juvenile Justice,* p. 66.

21. Ibid.

22. Mnookin, R. H. *Child, Family and State: Problems and Materials on Children and the Law.* Boston: Little, Brown, 1978, p. 546.

23. Bartollas, *Juvenile Delinquency,* p. 426.

24. Faust and Brantingham, *Juvenile Justice Philosophy,* p. 229.

25. Bartollas, C., and S. H. Miller. *Juvenile Justice in America* (2nd ed.). Englewood Cliffs, NJ: Prentice-Hall, 1998, pp. 11–12.

26. The latest report, from which the data reported in this section are derived, is *Juvenile Court Statistics, 1997.* Washington, DC: Office of Juvenile Justice and Delinquency Prevention, May 2000. Note that the data are already three years old when the report is issued.

27. The vast majority of juveniles who are arrested and referred to juvenile court never become serious, chronic offenders, and a very small percentage become adult offenders. See Bartollas, *Juvenile Delinquency.*

28. Shelden, Tracy, and Brown, *Youth Gangs in American Society.*

29. All figures quoted here are from U.S. Department of Justice. *Juvenile Court Statistics, 1997.* Washington, DC: Office of Juvenile Justice and Delinquency Prevention, May 2000. Online (www.ncjrs.org/html/ojjdp/jcs_1997).

30. Krisberg and Austin, *Reinventing Juvenile Justice,* pp. 86–87.

31. Krisberg and Austin, ibid., p. 88.

32. Pope, C., and W. Feyerherm, "Minority Status and Juvenile Justice Processing: An Assessment of the Research Literature" (Parts I and II). *Criminal Justice Abstracts* 22 (213). 1990; Bishop, D., and C. E. Frazier. "The Influence of Race in Juvenile Justice Processing." *Journal of Research in Crime and Delinquency* 25: 242–263 (1988).

33. Bishop and Frazier, ibid., p. 258.

34. For additional sources on the drug war see the following: Currie, E. *Reckoning: Drugs, the Cities, and the American Future.* New York: Hill and Wang, 1993; Tonry, M. Malign Neglect: Race, Crime, and Punishment in America. New York: Oxford University Press, 1995; Chambliss, W. J. "Crime Control and Ethnic Minorities: Legitimizing Racial Oppression by Creating Moral Panics." In D. F. Hawkins (ed.), *Ethnicity, Race, and Crime.* Albany: State University of New York Press, 1995; Lockwood, D., A. E. Pottieger, and J. A. Inciardi. "Crack Use, Crime by Crack Users, and Ethnicity." In D. F. Hawkins (ed.), *Ethnicity, Race, and Crime.* Albany: State University of New York Press, 1995.

35. Miller, J. *Search and Destroy: African-American Males in the Criminal Justice System.* New York: Cambridge University Press, 1996, p. 8.

36. Ibid., pp. 84–86.

37. U.S. Department of Justice, *Juvenile Court Statistics, 1997.*

38. McGarrell, E. "Trends in Racial Disproportionality in Juvenile Court Processing: 1985–1989." *Crime and Delinquency* 39: 29–48 (1993), quoted in Miller, *Search and Destroy,* p. 258.

39. Fellner, J. "Stark Racial Disparities Found in Georgia Drug Law Enforcement." *Overcrowded Times* 7(5): 11 (October 1996).

40. Sampson, R. J. "SES and Official Reaction to Delinquency." *American Sociological Review* 51: 876–885 (1986).

41. Bartollas and Miller, *Juvenile Justice in America,* p. 144.

42. Jankowski, M. S. *Islands in the Street: Gangs and American Urban Society.* Berkeley: University of California Press, 1990.

43. Walker, Spone, and DeLone, *The Color of Justice,* p. 144.

44. Chambliss, W. J. "The Saints and the Roughnecks." In W. J. Chambliss (ed.), *Criminal Law in Action.* New York: Wiley, 1975.

45. Ibid., p. 74.

46. Ibid., p. 77.

47. Ibid., p. 78.

48. Bartollas, *Juvenile Delinquency,* p. 492.

49. Bartollas and Miller, *Juvenile Justice in America,* pp. 179–180.

50. Krisberg and Austin, *Reinventing Juvenile Justice.*

51. Ibid., pp. 126–127.

52. Shelden, R. G. "Detention Diversion Advocacy: An Evaluation." Washington, DC: U.S. Department of Justice, Office of Juvenile Justice and Delinquency Prevention, 1999.

53. Brown, W. B. "The Subjective Nature of Decision Makers in the Domain of Objective Sentence Processing." Unpublished doctoral diss. University of Nevada–Las Vegas, 1992.

54. Bartollas and Miller, *Juvenile Justice in America,* p. 182.

55. Krisberg and Austin, *Reinventing Juvenile Justice,* p. 101.

56. Bartollas and Miller, *Juvenile Justice in America,* p. 186

57. Bortner, M. A. *Inside a Juvenile Court: The Tarnished Idea of Individualized Justice.* New York: New York University Press, 1982; Thornberry, T. P. "Race, Socioeconomic Status and Sentencing in the Juvenile Justice System." *Journal of Criminal Law and Criminology* 64: 90–98 (1973), and "Sentencing Disparities in the Juvenile Justice System." *Journal of Criminal Law and Criminology* 70 (Summer 1979).

58. Peterson, R. D. "Youthful Offender Designations and Sentencing in the New York Criminal Courts." *Social Problems* 35 (April 1988).

59. Chambliss, "Crime Control and Ethnic Minorities." See also Chambliss, W. J. *Power, Politics and Crime.* Boulder, CO: Westview Press, 1999.

60. Sarri, R., and Y. Hasenfeld (eds.). *Brought to Justice? Juveniles, the Courts, and the Law.* Ann Arbor: National Assessment of Juvenile Corrections, University of Michigan, 1976, pp 148–149, 159.

61. Ibid., p. 210.

62. Krisberg and Austin, *Reinventing Juvenile Justice,* p. 109.

63. Miller, J. *Last One Over the Wall: The Massachusetts Experiment in Closing Reform Schools* (2nd ed.). Columbus: Ohio University Press, 2000, p. 232.

64. Bartollas and Miller, *Juvenile Justice in America,* pp. 315–320; Bartollas, Juvenile Delinquency, p. 300.

65. Office of Juvenile Delinquency and Juvenile Justice. *Juvenile Offenders and Victims: 1999 National Report.* Washington, DC: U.S. Department of Justice, 2001, p. 186.

66. Walker, Spohn, and DeLone, *The Color of Justice,* pp. 223–224; U.S. Department of Commerce. *Statistical Abstract of the United States.* Washington, DC: U.S. Government Printing Office, 1975, p. 419; see note 69 for the source of the 1997 numbers.

67. Sickmund, M., and Y. Wan. "Census of Juveniles in Residential Placement Data Book." Online (www.ojjdp. ncjrs.org/ojstatbb/cjrp/index.asp).

68. Ibid.

69. Krisberg and Austin, *Reinventing Juvenile Justice,* pp. 126–128.

70. California Youth Authority figures obtained from the Center on Juvenile and Criminal Justice, San Francisco. Online (http://www.cjcj.org/cyapop.gif).

71. Sickmund and Wan, "Census of Juveniles in Residential Placement Data Book."

72. Shelden, R. G. "If It Looks like a Prison" *Las Vegas City Life,* August 13, 1999.

73. For a particularly gruesome account of actions within one of these "correctional" institutions see the movie *Sleepers* (starring Brad Pitt, Robert DeNiro, and Dustin Hoffman).

74. Vinter, R. D., et al. (eds.). *Time Out: A National Study of Juvenile Correctional Programs.* Ann Arbor: National Assessment of Juvenile Corrections, University of Michigan, 1976.

75. Barker, G. E., and W. T. Adams. "The Social Structure of a Correctional Institution." *Journal of Criminal Law, Criminology and Police Science* 49: 417–499 (1959); Polsky, H. Cottage Six. New York: Russell Sage Foundation, 1962; Jesness, C. F. *The Fricot Ranch Study.* Sacramento: State of California, Department of the Youth Authority, 1965; Street, D., R. D. Vinter, and C. Perrow. *Organization for Treatment.* New York: Free Press, 1966.

76. Bowker, L. *Prisoner Subcultures.* Lexington, MA: Heath, 1977, p. 100.

77. Bartollas, C., S. H. Miller, and S. Dinitz. *Juvenile Victimization: The Institutional Paradox.* Beverly Hills: Sage, 1976.

78. Miller, Bartollas, and Dinitz, *Juvenile Victimizatton Revisited: A Study of TICO Fifteen Years Later* (forthcoming), cited in Bartollas and Miller, *Juvenile Justice in America,* pp. 348–349.

79. One obvious problem that immediately arises but is rarely discussed is that if, say, a 15-year-old is certified as an adult, does that mean he or she can vote, drop out of school, purchase alcohol, leave home, or do anything an adult can do? In actual fact he or she cannot, *even if placed on probation by the adult court before age 18.*

80. Bartollas, *Juvenile Delinquency,* pp. 441–442.

81. U.S. Department of Justice, Office of Juvenile Justice and Delinquency Prevention. "Delinquency Cases Waived to Criminal Court, 1989–1998." Washington, DC: U.S. Department of Justice, September 2001.

82. Bortner, *Inside a Juvenile Court.*

83. Bartollas and Miller, *Juvenile Justice in America,* pp. 214–215.

84. Bishop, D., C. E. Frazier, L. Lanza-Kaduce, and L. Winner. "The Transfer of Juveniles to Criminal Court: Does It Make a Difference?" *Crime and Delinquency* 42: 187–202 (1996).

85. Bishop and Frazier, "The Influence of Race in Juvenile Justice Processing"; Bishop, D. M., and C. S. Frazier. "Transfer of Juveniles to Criminal Court: A Case Study and Analysis of Prosecutorial Waiver." *Notre Dame Journal of Law, Ethics and Public Policy* 5: 281–302; Fritsch, E., and C. Hemmens. "Juvenile Waiver in the United States, 1979–1995: A Comparison and Analysis of State Waiver Statutes." *Juvenile and Family Court Journal* 46: 17–35 (1995); Feld, B. C. *Bad Kids: Race and the Transformation of the Juvenile Court.* Oxford: Oxford University Press, 1999.

86. Bishop, D. M., C. S. Frazier, and J. Henretta. "Prosecutorial Waiver: Case Study of Questionable Reform." *Crime and Delinquency* 35: 179–201 (1989).

87. Feld, *Bad Kids,* p. 190.

88. Griffin, P., P. Torbet, and L. Szymanski. *Trying Juveniles as Adults in Criminal Court: An Analysis of State Transfer Provisions.* Washington DC: U.S. Department of Justice, Office of Justice Programs, Office of Juvenile Justice and Delinquency Prevention, 1998.

89. Torbet, P., and L. Szymanski. *State Legislative Responses to Violent Juvenile Crime: 1996–1997 Update.* Washington, DC: Office of Juvenile Justice and Delinquency Prevention, 1998.

90. Griffin et al., *Trying Juveniles as Adults in Criminal Court.*

91. Feld, *Bad Kids.*

92. Snyder, H. N. *Juvenile Arrests, 1998.* Washington, DC: Office of Juvenile Justice and Delinquency Prevention, 1999.

93. Sickmund, M., H. N. Snyder, and E. Poe-Yamagata. *Juvenile Offenders and Victims: 1997 Update on Violence.* Office of Juvenile Justice and Delinquency Prevention. Washington DC: U.S. Government Printing Office, 1997.

94. Strom, K. J., S. K. Smith, and H. N. Snyder. *Juvenile Felony Defendants in Criminal Courts.* Washington, DC: Bureau of Justice Statistics, 1998.

95. Struckman-Johnson, C., D. Struckman-Johnson, L. Rucker, K. Bumby, and S. Donaldson. "Sexual Coercion Reported by Men and Women in Prison." *The Journal of Sex Research* 33: 67–76 (1996).

96. Howell, J. C. *Juvenile Justice and Youth Violence.* Thousand Oaks, CA: Sage, 1997.

97. Amnesty International. *Betraying the Young: Human Rights Violations against Children in the U.S. Justice System.* AMR 51/57/98. New York: Amnesty International Publications, 1998.

98. Strieb, V. L. "The Juvenile Death Penalty Today: Death Sentences and Executions for Juvenile Crimes, January 1973–June, 1999." Online (http://www.law.onu.edu/faculty/streib/juvdeath.pdf).

99. Feld, *Bad Kids,* p. 236.

100. Strieb, "The Juvenile Death Penalty Today."

101. Ibid.; see also American Bar Association. "Three Juveniles Scheduled to Die in the First Month of the Millennium." Online (http://www.abanet.org/crimjust/juvjust/deathpenalty.htm), 2000.

102. United Nations. *International Covenant on Civil and Political Rights.* Geneva: Office of the United Nations Commissioner for Human Rights, 1997.

103. United Nations. *Question of the Violation of Human Rights and Fundamental Freedoms in any Part of the World, with Particular Reference to Colonial and Other Dependent Countries and Territories, Mission to the United States of America.* Geneva: United Nations, Economic and Social Council, 1998.

104. Amnesty International, *Betraying the Young.*

105. Ibid.

106. United Nations. *Question of the Violation of Human Rights.*

107. Amnesty International, *Betraying the Young.*

108. United Nations, *International Covenant on Civil and Political Rights.*

109. Ibid., p. 28.

110. Paul, W. G. *America on the Threshold of Setting a Shameful Record.* Presidential Statements. American Bar Association, 1999.

111. United Nations, *Question of the Violation of Human Rights,* p. 10.

112. Amnesty International. *On the Wrong Side of History: Children and the Death Penalty in the U.S.A.* AMR 51/58/98. New York: Amnesty International Publications, 1998.

113. See previously cited United Nations reports (1997, 1998).

114. United Nations, *Question of the Violation of Human Rights.*

115. Amnesty International, *On the Wrong Side of History.*

116. American Bar Association, "Three Juveniles Scheduled to Die in the First Month of the Millennium."

CHAPTER FOURTEEN

WOMEN AND THE CRIMINAL JUSTICE SYSTEM

WOMEN AND THE LAW: A HISTORICAL OVERVIEW

Several stereotypical images of women have helped shape not only the law but the definitions of what behaviors and what kinds of persons are considered criminal: (1) woman as the pawn of biology (i.e., she is controlled by biological forces, such as the menstrual cycle, beyond her control); (2) woman as passive and weak; (3) woman as impulsive and nonanalytical (i.e., she acts illogically and therefore needs guidance from the more analytical men); (4) woman as impressionable and in need of protection (i.e., she is childlike and gullible and needs protection from men); (5) the active woman as masculine (i.e., whenever she breaks away from the traditional roles, her behavior is deemed unnatural or even masculine); (6) the criminal woman as purely evil (i.e., a woman who "falls from grace" is truly evil because women are inherently pure); (7) the madonna–whore duality (a woman is either a paragon of virtue or a seductress).[1] Stereotypes of female criminals have persisted since the nineteenth century. One recent observer notes that women prisoners today are viewed as "tramps" and as "cheap women," as "wild," "loose," "immoral," and "fallen," as having broken not only social laws but unwritten moral laws as well. In popular films they are often portrayed as "amazons" or "bull dikes," "crude nymphomaniacs," or even "psychopaths."[2]

Given these images, it is not surprising to find that there is a tradition in law, going back as far as ancient Rome and Greece, that holds that women are perpetual children and the only adults are men. In ancient Greece, for instance, only men could be citizens in the political arena, and most of the slaves were women (and women in general were treated as slaves). In Rome the status of women and slaves was improved somewhat as they were incorporated into the family under the rule of **patria potestas** ("power of the father"). This term implied not so much to a family relationship but rather to a *property relationship*. The woman had to turn any income she received over to the head of the household and had no rights to her own children, no rights to divorce, or, for that matter, no rights to life outside of the family. According to Roman law, unlike slaves, women could not be emancipated. A woman's relationship to her husband was designated by the concept of *manus,* or hand. From this is derived the modern practice to ask a woman's father for "her hand in marriage."[3]

Such control of women is consistent with the system known as **patriarchy.** In her excellent treatment of this subject, Gerda Lerner defines *patriarchy* as "the manifestation and institutionalization of male dominance over women and children in the family and the extension of male dominance over women in society in general. It implies that men hold power in all the important institutions of society and that women are deprived of access to such power." The legal institution is one among these various institutions mentioned by Lerner that are ultimately controlled by men and by extension are used to control women. Lerner describes it best by an analogy with a stage in a theater:

> Men and women live on a stage, on which they act out their assigned roles, equal in importance. The play cannot go on without both kinds of performers. Neither of them "contributes" more or less to the whole; neither is marginal or dispensable. But the stage set is conceived, painted, defined by men. Men have written the play, have directed the show, interpreted the meanings of the action. They have assigned themselves the most interesting, most heroic parts, giving women the supporting roles.[4]

Continuing the analogy, Lerner notes that as women become more aware of this inequality, they begin to protest, asking for more roles, more equality in determining what is assigned. At times they may "upstage the men," and at other times they may "pinch-hit" for a male performer. Yet even when they win equal access to desired roles, they must first "qualify" according to terms set by the men, who are the judges of whether women measure up. Preference is given to women who are "docile," and those who act differently are punished— by ridicule, ostracism, exclusion. In time, women realize that getting "equal" parts does not translate into "equality," as long as the script, stage setting, props, and so on are controlled by men.[5]

Although women's subordinate status existed before capitalism emerged as a dominant mode of production (contrary to the strictly Marxist interpretation),[6] it is nevertheless true that capitalism has made things worse. This is because "capitalism rewards the impulses of exploitation, accumulation, competitiveness, ruthless self-interest, individualized aggrandizement, scarcity psychology, and indifference to the sufferings of the disadvantaged." Capitalism also "relies on sexism as a diversionary force" by focusing on issues other than class inequality, such as abortion and sexual morality, rather than a "critical examination of who gets what, when, and how." Further, under capitalism "wealth is accumulated by expropriating the labor power of the worker," and both sexism and racism make this that much easier. Women, moreover, are often blamed by conservatives for what ails the society; they are convenient scapegoats (charges that too many women are in the workforce demanding equal pay, or too many are "welfare queens," etc.).[7]

Perhaps more important, women are viewed as "commodities." Parenti describes "commodification" as "the process of objectifying and transforming the female appearance and body to fit marketable (that is, marriageable) standards." Women have gone through hundreds of different procedures over the years (stretching lips and necks, flattened breasts during certain times and expanded at other times, painted nails and lips, etc.)

mainly to "gain the attention and approval of men, to persuade men to 'buy' them either as wives or workers."[8]

Much of Roman law was eventually incorporated into English common law, which in turn was copied (with few significant changes) in America. For several years the only law book used was Blackstone's *Commentaries on the Laws in England,* originally published in 1765. American family law incorporated Blackstone's famous dictum that the husband and wife are as one and that one is the husband.[9]

Not surprisingly, in early American law the wife could not sue, execute a deed, and engage in any other similar practices, without consent of her husband. Women were denied the vote until 1921 and in general laws that were "designed to protect the interests of 'persons' simply did not apply to women." In fact, the Supreme Court ruled in 1867 that a woman who had completed law school and had passed the bar in Illinois nevertheless had no right to practice law! Using the prevailing logic of the time, the Court stated that the "natural and proper timidity and delicacy which belongs to the female sex evidently unfits it for many of the occupations in civil life" and the "destiny and mission of women are to fulfill the noble and benign offices of wife and mother.[10]

Throughout colonial America a woman had no identity independent of her relationship with her father or her husband. The husband had rights over his wife that resembled in many ways the rights of masters over their slaves. Even if a man killed his wife, he would be treated under the law with far more leniency than his wife would experience if she killed him. In fact, a man who killed his wife was treated almost the same as if he had killed an animal or a servant. Colonial law was often very specific about women, and some crimes were, in effect, "women's crimes" and were severely punished. For instance, the crime of being a "common scold" was applied "to a woman who berated her husband or was too vocal in public settings." The most appropriate punishment for scolding was the "ducking stool" and "branks." The former was a chair on which the female offender sat and was ducked in a pool of water several times, for the purpose of drowning her. The latter was a type of metal headgear placed over the head of a woman who was accused of scolding. If the woman tried to move her tongue to speak, sharp spikes would dig into her.

The witch hunts in the late seventeenth century stand as classic examples of the use of the legal system to punish women who dared challenge the male power structure. Most of the so-called witches were merely women who were outspoken in their views or had a great deal of informal power either as healers or as community leaders.[11]

Although woman played an active role in efforts to pass the three "Civil War Amendments" to the Constitution (Thirteenth, Fourteenth, and Fifteenth Amendments), these amendments, which extended "equal protection" to all "persons," ignored women.[12] In other words, these "equal rights amendments to the Constitution simply did not apply to women. Not until 1971, in the case of **Reed v. Reed** (404, U.S. 71, 92 S. Ct. 251, 30 L.Ed.2nd 225, 1971) did the Court say that under the U.S. Constitution women were "persons"! Before this time, the prevailing attitude was perhaps best reflected in an 1869 Illinois Supreme Court decision. The court stated that "God designed the sexes to occupy different spheres of action, and that it belonged to men to make, apply, and execute the laws."[13] The law obviously singled out women in the case of the crime of prostitution, making no mention of male "clients." Even in cases where the law supposedly "protected" women as victims of rape, abduction, seduction, and carnal abuse, the "victim" had to "prove that she had, in fact, been a victim," that "she had led a chaste and virtuous life prior to the crime against her."[14] In fact, there was once a law, in Mississippi, that granted the right of husbands to beat their wives, a law upheld by that state's supreme court in 1824. The law was overturned by the U.S. Supreme Court in 1874.[15]

The feminist movement of the nineteenth century led to several significant changes in the legal status of women. The **Married Women's Property Acts** gave women certain property rights previously denied, and the issue of domestic violence led to the passage of laws in some parts of the country, as it was for the first time considered a crime. In the first part of the twentieth century, women made some gains in the workplace. Yet despite these new laws, women's gains were often illusory. The law and legal system remained male dominated, and women continued to be treated as second-class citizens.[16]

Various sentencing laws, until the later 1970s, singled out women for differential treatment. One such law, in New Jersey, stipulated that women offenders should serve longer sentences than males convicted of identical crimes, on the assumption that female criminals "were more amendable and responsive to rehabilitation and reform" and thus required "a longer period of confinement in a different type of institution." This is from the case of *State v. Costello* in 1971. A similar case was heard in 1973. In *State v. Chambers* the New Jersey Supreme Court ruled that the state's sentencing laws violated the Fourteenth Amendment to the Constitution. Not until the new law went into effect in 1979 were such sentencing practices ended.[17] Differential treatment of female juvenile offenders is documented later in this chapter.

WOMEN AND CRIME

Several generalizations can be made at the outset about women and crime. First, women commit far less crime than men do. As we saw in Chapter 1, women constitute about one-fifth of all the arrests, a percentage that has not changed much over the years. Second, the crimes women commit are far less serious than those men commit. In 1999, women constituted around 11 percent of arrests for homicide, around 1 percent of the arrests for rape, and about 10 percent of the arrests for robbery. Although they accounted for almost 20 percent of the arrests for aggravated assaults during 1999, this figure was largely attributable to the greater attention devoted by the police to domestic violence. Third, there are very significant gender differences in the overall patterns of crime, although in many cases we can conclude that the crimes women commit are pretty much the same as the crimes men commit, especially when we consider property crimes. Fourth, given the preceding generalizations, it should come as no surprise that the "careers" of female offenders are of a much shorter duration than the "careers" of male offenders. Fifth, women are far less likely than men to end up in prison, although their rate of imprisonment has increased significantly in recent years.[18] Let us now explore some of these generalizations in more detail. Table 14.1 shows the arrests police made in 1999, according to gender.

Patterns of Female Crime

One pattern needs to be noted at the outset—namely, the fact that for centuries women have been arrested largely for relatively minor offenses. This pattern can be traced as far back as fourteenth-century England and especially in the offenses of women "transported" from England to Australia during the late eighteenth and early nineteenth centuries. Most of these offenders were poor women (servants, maids, and laundresses) who had been convicted of petty theft (mostly shoplifting) or prostitution. Most of them experienced sexual abuse aboard these "convict ships," and about one-third died along the way. In the American colonies these offense patterns continued, although we must add the "crime" of being an "unruly woman" to the list, along with such heinous offenses as fornication and adultery. Later in the nineteenth and well into the early twentieth century we find women—the vast majority of whom lived on the margins of society and were disproportionately immigrants and racial minorities—being arrested for public-order offenses along with minor theft.[19]

In more recent years, most of those patterns have continued. Women generally have been arrested for such offenses as larceny–theft (which has consistently been ranked number one of all offenses committed by women, including juveniles; the most common offense within this category is shoplifting[20]), fraud (mostly what is known as "welfare fraud"—a reflection of the poverty of these women), drugs, disorderly conduct (which in many cases is actually prostitution), and a host of other minor offenses subsumed under the category "all other offenses."[21] There have been a few noteworthy changes, however.

TABLE 14.1 Persons Arrested, by Gender, 1999

OFFENSE	MALE (%)	FEMALE (%)
TOTAL	78.2	21.8
INDEX CRIMES		
Homicide	88.6	11.4
Rape	98.7	1.3
Robbery	89.9	10.1
Aggravated assault	80.3	19.7
Burglary	87.1	12.9
Larceny–theft	64.5	35.5
Motor-vehicle theft	84.4	15.6
Arson	85.6	14.4
Violent crime	83.0	17.0
Property crime	70.4	29.6
Total index	73.9	26.1
PART II CRIMES		
Other assaults	77.5	22.5
Forgery and counterfeiting	61.6	38.4
Fraud	56.4	43.6
Embezzlement	50.8	49.2
Stolen property	84.3	15.7
Vandalism	84.7	15.3
Weapons	92.2	7.8
Prostitution	39.2	60.8
Sex offenses (except rape and prostitution)	92.9	7.1
Drug-abuse violations	82.4	17.6
Gambling	87.6	12.4
Offenses against family and children	77.9	22.1
Driving under the influence	84.1	15.9
Liquor laws	78.0	22.0
Drunkenness	87.3	12.7
Disorderly conduct	77.0	23.0
Vagrancy	81.6	18.4
All other (except traffic)	79.4	20.6
Suspicion	79.2	20.8
Curfew and loitering	69.5	30.5
Runaways	40.8	59.2

Source: U.S. Department of Justice, Bureau of Justice Statistics. *Sourcebook of Criminal Justice Statistics,* 2000 (Online).

One new trend is the increase in arrests for such offenses as aggravated assault, "other assaults," offenses against the family and children, and drugs. The first three can be attributed mostly to the increased attention given by law enforcement to the issue of "domestic violence." It is ironic that women have historically been the victims of violence within the home (along with children), yet in arrest situations the police have been arresting both partners in the majority of cases.[22]

Space does not permit a detailed examination of the background variables associated with women offenders, but the important role of prior victimization in their lives should be mentioned. Studies of women who kill repeatedly note that the majority killed someone they knew intimately, such as a husband or boyfriend. And a good number of these cases (depending on the study, ranging from 40 to 78%) had experienced abuse; many of them fit the battered-woman syndrome. Over half of all women prisoners have experienced some form of abuse, more than one-third experiencing sexual abuse. As so many studies demonstrate,[23] one of the pathways leading women into a life of crime and repeated contacts with the criminal justice system is victimization by the men in their lives. The all-too-typical scenario has been described by Daly as one involving a horrible home situation that leads to running away, which in turn leads to surviving on the streets by using their bodies as the major source of income, which just happens to be a main source of further victimization either by male clients or intimate male friends.[24] An almost identical scenario was found in Miller's study of a group of women offenders in Milwaukee. For the women in her study, there were abusive parents (who were also often alcoholic), and their lives of crime typically began with running away, after which they became involved in the lives of a variety of abusive men.[25]

Class, Race, and Women Offenders

As with their male counterparts, any analysis of women, crime, and criminal justice must consider the interrelationship of class and race. Hundreds of studies covering more than a century confirm that class and race are strong predictors of crime and play significant roles in the processing of offenders through the criminal justice system.[26] Indeed, even a cursory review of the literature shows that the vast majority of female offenders, especially those who end up in prison, are drawn from the lower class and are racial minorities.[27]

Women's crime cannot be separated from the overall social context within which it occurs. In recent years the plight of women has not improved a great deal. Women have entered the labor force in increased numbers in recent years (to around 60% versus less than 40% in the 1950s), but their employment is largely in traditional "female" occupations, especially in retail trade and service occupations. Women still constitute over 80 percent of all nurses, 75 percent of all teachers (except colleges and universities), almost 80 percent of all secretarial and administrative support positions (clerical work, cashiers, etc.), and about 80 percent of all hairdressers and other "personal service occupations." Furthermore, although gains have been made, women still earn less than men, and their "gains" have come largely because so many men have been eliminated from the labor force. In 1960, 89 percent of all married men and 32 percent of married women were in the labor force; in 1994, the male percentage had decreased to 77 percent, and the female percentage had increased to 61 percent. Also, almost half of all working women (47%) work part time, compared to 32 percent of men.[28]

More important, increasing numbers of households are being maintained by women with children. In 1960 only 6 percent of all families with one or more children was headed by a woman; by the 1990s this figure had jumped to 18 percent. Not surprisingly, race plays a role here, for just over 40 percent of African American families are headed by a woman, compared to only about 14 percent of white families.[29] More important, however, is the fact that more than one-fourth of all children live with only one parent (almost 90% live with their mothers). Moreover, about 44 percent of all African American children and 42 percent of Hispanic children live in poverty, compared to only 17 percent of white children.[30]

Women in these situations are far more likely to be living in poverty: whereas in 1959 only 20 percent of all poor families were headed by women, by the 1990s more than half were headed by women. About two-thirds of *all* people living in poverty today are women. This fact is what is sometimes known as the **feminization of poverty,** which may be somewhat misleading, suggesting that this problem is racially neutral. Poverty, however, hits racial minorities (especially minority women) far more than whites: 29 percent of all African American families and 30 percent of Hispanic families live in poverty, compared to only 8.5 percent of white families.[31]

One specific example of the role of class and race is demonstrated in a very detailed and sophisticated study by Daly of a sample of women offenders in a court system in New

Haven, Connecticut. From a larger sample of 397 cases, this study focused in depth on 40 men and 40 women who were sentenced to prison—they went through all of the stages of the criminal justice process. Of the 40 women, 24 (60%) were African American, 5 (12%) were Puerto Rican, and the remainder (28%) were white. Half of the women were raised in single-parent families, and only 2 of the women were described as growing up in "middle class households." Most of these women were described by Daly as having grown up in families "whose economic circumstances were precarious"; in about two-thirds of the cases the biological fathers were "out of the picture" while they were growing up. Only one-third completed high school or the equivalent GED (General Education Diploma). Two-thirds "had either a sporadic or no paid employment record," and over 80 percent were unemployed at the time of their most recent arrest.[32]

SENTENCING PATTERNS, THE "WAR ON DRUGS," AND WOMEN

When it comes to the criminal justice system's response to female offenders, it is often difficult to separate class, race, and gender. The prevailing view, however, has been that the system acts in a "chivalrous" manner toward female offenders, consistently giving them more lenient treatment than male offenders. Many scholars have believed that criminal justice officials are lenient because they want to "protect" women offenders, perhaps because they remind them of their wives or mothers. Unfortunately there is little research to support this view.[33]

Perhaps the most outrageous form of judicial sexism comes from the crackdown (no pun intended) on pregnant women addicted to drugs, especially crack cocaine. A recent study by Siegel notes that there has been a concerted effort to criminalize pregnancy in the case of women addicted to drugs, as if arresting them and putting them in prison would cure their drug problem! Siegel cites the racial bias in such a crackdown by observing that in Florida in 1989 more than 700 pregnant women in public and private clinics were tested for drugs. There was virtually no difference by race in the percentage who tested positive (15.4% of the white women tested positive versus 14.1% of the African American women). African American women, however, were almost ten times more likely to be reported to the authorities for drug abuse.[34]

Chivalry is largely a racist and classist concept, for lenient treatment is typically reserved for white women from the higher social classes. Moreover, any lenient treatment granted to women is due largely to the fact that their crimes are so minor compared to men's and their criminal careers are not nearly as lengthy as men's, two variables that are highly predictive of treatment in the criminal justice system.[35] Field observations of police officers confirm the suspicion that "demeanor" also plays a significant role. A detailed analysis of field observations of over five thousand police–citizen encounters in twenty-four cities found that although offense type is important, age, race, and demeanor all played important roles. Significantly, it was discovered that female offenders who were young, African American, or hostile did not receive any preferential treatment, while white women who displayed a calm and deferential attitude received lenient treatment by the police.[36] Additional support for the argument that African American female offenders are treated more harshly came from a study in California of a sample of all felony cases in 1980. It was found that the odds of women being arrested ranged from a high of 1 in 42 for African American females in their 20s to a low of 1 in 667 for white females 70 years or older.[37]

The most dramatic illustration of the lack of chivalry toward African American and other minority women comes from examining who gets sentenced to prison. And this has been, in recent years, a direct result of the "war on drugs." This "war" has had a dramatic impact on the criminal justice system and on women, especially the dramatic growth in the prison population.

There is no way we can separate the phenomenal growth in prison populations from the "war on drugs," a war that has targeted huge numbers of African Americans. Although there is little relationship between race and illicit drug use, African Americans are far more likely to be arrested and sent to prison. Among women, the poor in general and African Americans in particular have been singled out. As of 1991 about one-third of women offenders had been sentenced on drug offenses, compared to around one in ten in 1979. Further, more than one-third of the women doing time in prison on drug charges had been convicted of drug *possession*.

If this is not bad enough, a large percentage of women sentenced to prison on parole violations did *not* commit any new crimes but rather *were returned for not passing their urine tests*. The federal prison system has been notorious for the sentencing of drug offenders, males and females alike. In 1984 a total of 28 percent of female offenders in federal prisons were drug offenders; by 1995 their percentage had more than doubled, to 66 percent.[38] During the last couple of decades of the twentieth century the proportion of women convicted of felonies in federal court who were given probation declined from about two-thirds to around one-fourth, and, the average time served by women on drug offenses rose from 27 months in 1984 to 67 months in 1990.[39]

A study of sentencing trends in three states (California, Minnesota, and New York) by the Sentencing Project (a Washington, D.C., research group) found that between 1986 and 1996 the number of women sentenced to prison increased tenfold, and drug crimes accounted for half of this increase (for men, drugs accounted for about one-third). These states differed significantly: in New York, drugs accounted for 91 percent of the increase in women incarcerated, compared to 55 percent in California and 26 percent in Minnesota. In New York, twice as many women were sent to prison for drugs in 1996 as in 1986, in 1986 one of every twenty women arrested for drugs was sent to prison, and in 1996 one out of every seven was. This trend paralleled drug arrests in New York: total arrests for women increased by only 15 percent during this time, but drug arrests jumped up by 61 percent (drug convictions accounted for 82% of the overall increase in convictions of women in state courts). As usual, race figured predominantly, as 77 percent of Hispanic women, 59 percent of African American women, but only 34 percent of white women were sentenced for drug crimes during this period.[40]

Another state that has taken a super-tough stance on drugs is Florida. Here's one quite dramatic statistic: in this state, during the 1980s, admissions to prison for drugs increased by a whopping 1,825 percent for all offenders, but for female offenders the increase was an astounding 3,103 percent![41]

It is important to underscore one salient point about these drug arrests: contrary to popular views, drug offenders arrested and sent to prison are rarely drug "kingpins." The vast majority are low-level users and dealers. (The word *dealer* or *trafficker* is value-loaded if you consider the fact that alcohol, tobacco, and many prescription drugs are far more dangerous than any of the "illegal" drugs, causing more than 500,000 deaths each year. Therefore, it is our contention that the biggest "drug traffickers" in the world are the corporate producers of these dangerous substances. But, of course, they have the power to keep such substances perfectly legal.) Most of the women who do get involved in the illegal drug business do so in conjunction with a man with whom they are intimate. And when it comes to the so-called sentencing guidelines there is virtually no consideration of the social context of these drug offenses, such as the poverty, the coercion from males, and the fact that the majority of these women are single parents. Our society creates social conditions that make involvement in drug markets almost inevitable and then turns around and punishes those who get caught up in this world. But, then again, this might be understandable when we consider that these women are part of the "surplus population," a group no longer needed for corporate profits.[42]

Much of the increase in women prisoners comes from the impact of mandatory sentencing laws, passed during the 1980s crackdown on crime. Under many of these laws, mitigating circumstances (e.g., having children, few or no prior offenses, nonviolent offenses) are rarely acknowledged. One recent survey found that just over half (51%) of women in state prisons had none or only one prior offense, compared to 39 percent of the male prisoners.[43]

Thus, this society's recent efforts to get tough on crime has had a most negative impact on female offenders, as more and more are finding their way into the nation's prison system. Largely because of the war on drugs, the number of new women's prisons has dramatically increased in recent years. Between 1940 and the end of the 1960s, only twelve new women's prisons were built. In the 1970s, seventeen were built; in the 1980s, thirty-four![44]

Next, we discuss the history of women's prisons from the early nineteenth century to the present day, and then we examine the daily reality of life inside a women's prison.

WOMEN'S PRISONS

Historical Origins

Recall from Chapter 11 that the modern prison system did not emerge until the late eighteenth and early nineteenth centuries. Prior to the mid-nineteenth century, however, women offenders usually were housed within the same quarters as the men, though kept separate. Reports of early jails and workhouses note the often deplorable conditions in which men, women, and children were all thrown in together, along with the mentally ill and both petty and serious offenders. In 1853, however, one of the first attempts was made to separate women offenders from men. So-called houses of corrections were established to provide "industrial schools" for young women.[45]

In colonial America few women offenders were incarcerated, which is not surprising because few men were incarcerated either. Of the white women who were arrested, most were charged with violations of minor religious law (e.g., violation of the Sabbath, adultery). They were held in local jails for trial, and the usual punishment was some sort of "public" reprimand, such as whipping or the "stocks and the pillory."[46] For African American women the situation was quite different, for the majority were legally slaves and or indentured servants.[47] Most violations of laws by these women were handled informally within the plantation, but occasionally the slave owners had to rely on the local criminal justice system. In such cases they often used what were called "Negro Courts," set up specifically for slaves who violated laws that were applicable to slaves but not whites. The "crimes" (often considered felonies) they were charged with included "striking the master three times" (punishable by death). Sentences of death or even incarceration were rarely imposed on slaves because such action would have cost the owners money. Not until after the Civil War did African Americans begin to appear in penal institutions in large numbers, most as a result of "Jim Crow" laws and "Black Codes." Many were subjected to the "convict lease" system.[48]

As we noted in Chapter 11, the early American jails were often extensions of the earlier workhouses and poorhouses. By 1835 there appeared several institutions with separate quarters for women offenders, notably in Maryland and New York. Newgate Prison (New York), opened in 1797, was the first institution for felons only. Women offenders were housed in an area separate from men.[49]

Treatment of prisoners, both male and female, changed dramatically around the 1820s with the founding of the Auburn State Prison, originally housing both men and women, though in separate quarters. Overcrowding soon set in (a condition that continues to plague prisons), and there was little interest in the women offenders, who at that time were viewed with particular distaste. Conditions were so bad that the prison chaplain once remarked that it was bad enough for male prisoners, "but to be a female convict, for any protracted period, would be worse than death."[50] When Newgate was closed in the 1820s, the men were all eventually transferred to Auburn prison, and the women were sent to Bellevue Penitentiary in New York City. However, conditions were so horrible at Bellevue, that a women's prison was built at Mount Pleasant, New York, on the grounds of the infamous Sing Sing Prison, and opened in 1839.[51] Around the same time a "women's annex" was built on the grounds of the Ohio Penitentiary and opened in 1837. At this time it was widely believed that women offenders should he treated more harshly than their male counterparts. This belief was justified by the argument that the female offender was more depraved than her male counterpart because, having been born pure, she had "fallen" farther from grace than he; in fact, she was often blamed for the crimes of men![52]

Most of the activities female prisoners performed in these early prisons (activities still performed today) were designed to "fit them for the duties of domestic life." At first there was little or no separation of male and female prisoners. Several reformers, such as Elizabeth Fry (1780–1845), a Quaker, Dorothea Dix (1802–1887), Clara Barton (1821–1912), and Josephine Shaw Lowell (1843–1905), began to advocate separate facilities and other changes. One of the first results of reform activities was the hiring of female matrons, beginning in Maryland after the Civil War. The majority of nineteenth and early-twentieth-century prison reformers were not only women but members of the upper class. As Freedman's study of these nineteenth-century reformers shows, the roster reads like a who's who of the American elite—not an uncommon occurrence, for most reforms were carried out by members of the elite.[53]

Separate facilities for women emerged following the 1870 meeting of the National Congress on Penitentiary and Reformatory Discipline in Cincinnati. One of the resolutions of this conference was that the goal of prisons should be *rehabilitation* rather than punishment. In 1873 the first prison for women was opened, the Indiana Women's Prison. Watterson notes that

> It embraced the revolutionary notion that women criminals should be rehabilitated rather than punished. Young girls from the age of sixteen who "habitually associate with dissolute persons" and other uneducated and indigent women were ushered into the model prison apart from men and isolated from the "corruption and chaos" of the outside world. The essential ingredient of their rehabilitative treatment would be to bring discipline and regularity into their lives. Obedience and systematic religious education would, it was felt, help the women form orderly habits and moral values.[54]

Several other women's prisons were opened over the next forty years, including the Massachusetts Prison at Framington (1877), the New York Reformatory for Women at Westfield Farm (1901), the District of Columbia Reformatory for Women (1910), and the New Jersey Reformatory for Women at Clinton (1913). These institutions were intended to be "separate, home-like institutions" where women "would have an opportunity" to "mend their criminal ways" and "learn to be good housewives, helpmates and mothers."[55]

Freedman suggests that four factors contributed to the rise of the women's prison movement between 1870 and 1900: (1) an apparent increase in female crime after the war and an increase in women prisoners; (2) the women's Civil War social service movement; (3) the emergence of charity and prison reform movements in general, many of them emphasizing the problem of crime and the notion of rehabilitation; and (4) the beginnings of a feminist movement that emphasized a separatist approach and a reinterpretation of the notion of the "fallen woman." The alleged "crime wave" among women following the war primarily involved the wives and daughters of men who had died in the war. The large number of deaths during the war created a class of poor women who began to be arrested for mostly public-order offenses and offenses against morality, such as "lewd and lascivious carriage, stubbornness, idle and disorderly conduct, drunkenness, and vagrancy, as well as fornication and adultry." Several reformers placed the blame for the rise of female criminality on the attitudes and sexist practices of men. Josephine Shaw Lowell complained that many women "from early girlhood have been tossed from poorhouse to jail, and from jail to poorhouse, until the last trace of womanhood in them has been destroyed." She condemned law officers who regarded women "as objects of derision and sport" and who "wantonly assaulted and degraded numerous young women prisoners." Many specifically blamed the "double standard" whereby men condemned female sexual activity while condoning their own and, moreover, arrested and imprisoned prostitutes but not the men who enjoyed their services. Finally, reformers complained of male guards in prisons where women were confined. Investigators found that women "may be forced to minister to the lust of the officials or if they refused, submit to the inflection of the lash until they do."[56]

Reformers argued that women prisoners would be treated more fairly and would stand a better chance of being reformed if they were confined in separate institutions controlled by women. Reformers countered male resistance by arguing that "the shield of a pure woman's presence" would enable them "to govern the depraved and desperate of her own sex."[57] The first reformatories relied on "domestic routines" and, upon release, women were placed in "suitable" private homes as housekeepers. These institutions, and most to follow, were designed according to the "cottage plan." Separate housing facilities were as nearly as possible like an average family home in order to teach these women to become good homemakers. Although the women reformers often claimed to be staunch feminists, the organization of prison life they created was perfectly suited to keep women in their traditional "place." In fact, the design won the approval of many skeptical men, one of whom commented, "Girls and women should be trained to adorn homes with the virtues which make their lives noble and ennobling. *It is only in this province, that they may most fittingly fill their mission.*"[58] The end result, of course, would be to perpetuate women's traditional roles of dependency as housewives and maids. Even a cursory look at women's prisons today reveals that little has changed, especially the treatment of women as children and training them to continue their domestic roles.

What really stands out in the early development of women's institutions is the over-representation of African Americans, which varied widely by region. For instance, in the 1880s, the percentage of women prisoners who were African American ranged from 7 percent in the Northeast to 85.8 percent in the South. By 1904, the proportion of African Americans in northern prisons had increased to 18 percent, while in the South the percentage was 90. By 1923 both percentages had decreased somewhat, to 15.4 and 79.6, respectively. This decrease may be attributed to the rise of reformatories, which were much more likely to house white inmates. Indeed, in 1923 almost two-thirds (64.5%) of the women inmates in custodial prisons were African American, compared to only 11.9 percent in reformatory institutions. Ranges by specific institutions were marked. Between 1860 and 1934, fully four-fifths of the inmates at the Tennessee Penitentiary for Women were African American, in contrast to only 3 percent at the Albion State Prison in New York. Not surprisingly, the early prison system reflected the segregation in the general society. African American women were housed in prisons where there was little or no hope of any sort of rehabilitation (i.e., "custodial" prisons); white women were placed in "reformatories" where there was at least a formal commitment to rehabilitation.[59]

The federal prison system for women developed much later than the state prison system. Women convicted of federal crimes were generally sentenced to state prisons, but as the number of female inmates grew after the Civil War, efforts were made to open the federal system to women. The first of the federal prisons for women only was in Alderson, West Virginia. When it opened in 1927, it housed 50 women in fourteen cottages. By 1929 there were more than 250 inmates, most of whom had violated various drug laws (the Harrison Act of 1914 outlawed several kinds of drugs) and the Volstead Act of 1919 (Prohibition). Largely in response to the rise of organized crime (which was a direct result of Prohibition), legislation passed in 1930 created the federal Bureau of Prisons, which authorized the construction of several new prisons.[60]

The proportion of women in prison who are African American has continued to increase over the years. Historically, African American women have been most likely to be incarcerated in southern prisons. For instance, in 1880 African American women constituted 86 percent of the female inmates in the South, compared to only 7 percent in the Northeast, 29 percent in the Midwest, and 20 percent in the West. In 1904 the percentages had increased in every region: the South led the way at 90 precent, followed by the Midwest with 48 percent. By 1978 African American women constituted half of the total female prison population.[61] Their percentages declined somewhat by the end of the 1980s and early 1990s, largely as a result of an increase in Hispanics, but also as a result of more white women being sentenced on drug charges.

Women's Prisons Today

Women constitute around 20 percent of all those arrested and about 6 percent of those in prison, but their numbers and their rate of incarceration have been dramatically increasing during the past twenty years. As of December 31, 1999, there were 90,668 (compared to only 8,850 in 1976) women in federal and state prisons, constituting 6.6 percent (versus 3.6% in 1976) of all prisoners.[62] These figures represent a numerical increase of 924 percent from 1976 through 1999, and the proportion of women increased by 83 percent during that period. Moreover, as indicated in Table 14.2, the incarceration *rate* of women rose from 8 per 100,000 in 1975 to 59 per 100,000 in 1999, an increase of 638 percent!

These increases do not match the increases in women's crime as measured by arrests, except if we consider the impact of the "war on drugs" along with greater attention to domestic violence. Between 1976 and 1999 there was a very dramatic change in the criminal justice system's response to female drug use—and to all illegal drug use, as well as to domestic violence. The increased attention to domestic violence led to an increase in arrests of women for both aggravated assault and "other assaults."[63]

A Profile of Women in Prison

The "war on crime" and "war on drugs" have really been, in effect, a war on women and minorities. Like male prisoners, most women in prison are poor and uneducated, but more women prisoners than males are minorities. Also, about 80 percent of women prisoners have children. Table 14.3 shows some background characteristics of women in prison, according to a survey by the American Correctional Association. Most of the women are racial minorities with little education; one-third of them have less than a high school education. The occupational histories show that nearly every inmate worked at some time or another, mostly in low-skill, low-wage jobs in the service and retail trade industries. The profile further reveals that most of these women were not "career criminals"; about 60 per-

TABLE 14.2   Incarceration Rates of Men and Women in State and Federal Institutions, 1925–1999

YEAR	TOTAL	MALE	FEMALE	RATIO
1925	79	149	6	24.8:1
1935	113	217	8	27.1:1
1945	98	193	9	21.4:1
1955	112	217	8	27.1:1
1965	108	213	8	26.6:1
1975	111	220	8	27.5:1
1985	202	397	17	23.4:1
1999	476	914	59	15.5:1
PERCENTAGE INCREASE				
1975–1985	82.0	80.5	112.5	
1985–1999	135.6	130.2	247.1	

Source: Maguire, K., and A. L. Pastore (eds.). *Sourcebook of Criminal Justice Statistics—1995.* Washington, DC: U.S. Department of Justice, Bureau of Justice Statistics, 1996, p. 556; Beck, A. J., "Prisoners in 1999." Washington, DC: Bureau of Justice Statistics, 2000.

TABLE 14.3   A Profile of Women Prisoners

CHARACTERISTIC	PERCENTAGE	CHARACTERISTIC	PERCENTAGE
1998 DATA		**WORK EXPERIENCE**	
Current offense		Service occupations	45
Drugs	34	Sales/clerical occupations	34
Violent	28		
Homicide	11	**PERCENT EVER RECEIVED**	
Property	27	**WELFARE**	60
Fraud	10		
Larceny	9	**MOST COMMON OFFENSE,**	
Public order	11	**FIRST ARREST**	
		Larceny–theft	19
Race		Drug-abuse violations	16
White	33	Fraud/forgery/embezzlement	13
African American	48		
Hispanic	15	**PRIOR ARRESTS**	
Other	4	One	26
		2–4	35
Age		5 or more	36
24 or less	12		
25–34	43	**TIMES INCARCERATED,**	
35–44	34	**INCLUDING CURRENT**	
45–54	9	Once	46
55 and older	2	Twice	40
Marital status			
Never married	47		
Married	17		
Separated or divorced	30		
1987 DATA			
Percent never had a driver's license	28		
Percent never had a checking account	33		
Percent with at least one child	79		
Percent under 18 when had first child	42		
Of those with children, percent where someone other than father has custody	92		
Percent with other family member ever in prison	48		
Percent ever ran away from home	46		
Percent ever physically abused	53		
Percent ever sexually abused	36		
Percent used alcohol daily or once/twice a week	41		
Percent used heroin daily or once/twice a week	25		
Percent used cocaine daily or once/twice a week	32		
Percent used marijuana daily or once/twice a week	33		
Percent high school grad or more	43		

Source: 1987 data: American Correctional Association. *The Female Offender.* College Park, MD: American Correctional Association, 1990. 1998 data: Pollock, J. M. *Women, Prison, and Crime* (2nd ed.). Belmont, CA: Wadsworth, 2002, p. 54 (citing Bureau of Justice Statistics data).

cent had fewer than five previous arrests, and about one-fourth (26.3%) had been arrested only once. For almost half (45.8%) this was the first time they had ever been incarcerated. The most common offense on their current sentence was, not surprisingly, a drug offense (20.7%); murder was second (15%), larceny–theft third (12%).[64]

The data in Table 14.3 also reveal that most had been married at some time but the majority were now either divorced or separated. Indicative of the low social status of many women inmates is the fact that around 30 percent never had a driver's license or a checking account and 60 percent had received welfare assistance at one time or another. As already noted, most had at least one child, and about 30 percent had three or more children. It is also significant that 42 percent had their first child when they were under 18, and another 26 percent had their first child when they were 18 or 19 years of age. Research suggests that having children as a teenager puts one at high risk for greater involvement in criminal behavior. Further, such a situation places the children at risk as well. Note that in almost every case, someone other than the child's father has custody of the child, usually grandparents or the mother's siblings.[65]

What is also of interest is the personal background of these women. Almost half had another family member who had been in prison, which is another strong predictor of criminality.[66] Indicative of a negative family life is the fact that so many had run away and were abused. In fact, the percentage who were abused is a somewhat low number, given what some other researchers have found through other data.[67] And in fact, the American Correctional Association survey on which these data are based also surveyed a sample of incarcerated juvenile females, and those data reveal a far greater pattern of abuse. For instance, among the juveniles an astounding 80 percent had run away at least once, and 39 percent reported that they had run away 10 or more times! Also, over half (54%) had attempted suicide at least once. A greater proportion of the juveniles had been physically abused (62%) and sexually abused (54%) than was the case for the adults.

As for substance abuse, the figures show a pattern of rather extensive abuse. Alcohol abuse was common for these women; 41 percent used alcohol either daily or once or twice a week. However, for juveniles such abuse was even greater; 60 percent used alcohol either daily or once or twice a week. One-fourth of the adult women used heroin frequently, and around one-third used cocaine and marijuana. Among the juveniles, the abuse of heroin was minimal and the use of cocaine was roughly the same as adults'. Marijuana use, however, was far more prevalent; almost half (47%) used it "daily," and another 17 percent used it once or twice a week.

Finally, it is interesting to note that for the adult women, the majority were not "career criminals" (if we based this term on the usual proof of such a status, namely, five or more arrests), and almost half (45.8%) had no prior prison sentences—that is, they were "first timers." This is probably indicative of the "war on drugs" and its effect on women drug users: it has, in effect, criminalized those who in previous years would never have been sent to prison but instead would have been placed on probation, if they were arrested at all.[68]

Now that we have reviewed what women in prison "look like," it is perhaps appropriate that we turn to the subject of what prison life is like for them. In the next section we explore the prison from a rather unique perspective, one derived largely from the work of Kathryn Watterson. This is life within the "concrete womb."

The "Concrete Womb"

Both males and females who go to prison suffer a number of pains of imprisonment. For women, however, there are some important qualitative differences. Watterson notes that a process referred to, interestingly, as "reception" introduces a female inmate to the "**concrete womb**." The words of a deputy sheriff at the Los Angeles County Jail for women aptly describes the "reception" procedures used at this institution:

For a new booking the officer types up a booking slip while another officer has the inmate in custody. She gives her a number and then goes through her purse to search for contraband. After everything is complete, the inmate is sent through number three gate and delivered to a female deputy, still in full view of the control center and hall leading to the administrative offices. At that time the deputy gives her a pat search. She removes her wig, rings, shoes and socks. Anything such as a leather belt, drugs or medication is taken. She can keep up to ten dollars—but no *more than two dollars in* change. More than two dollars in change is not allowed because it could be put into a sock and used as a weapon.

This is where I am generally assigned. The pat search means I also look in your ears, your nose and mouth. I search your bra and around your waist and look up your pants leg. If they have dentures I ask them to remove the dentures and look at this for contraband possibly being concealed under it. Then we put them into one of the *two* holding blocks.[69]

The institutionalization process in women's prisons (and to a certain extent in men's prisons also) is, says Watterson, "synonymous with forced dependency. The controls of prison which attempt to regulate lives, attitudes and behavior are synonymous with those used during infancy." The role of the prison system over prisoners is like that of parent to child. The prison teaches you to he manipulative, to lie, to be dependent, not to love others, and not to trust others. You learn to take orders and with the inevitable acceptance of the custodial regime comes an erosion of self-determination, independence, and a sense of responsibility. Watterson quotes a lieutenant at Riker's Island, New York City, who refers to a 40-year-old woman as "my problem child."[70]

Men in prison form a number of informal groups, gangs, and cliques. These relationships are often short-lived, and really close attachments are rare. For women, however, one of the most common adaptations to life in prison is the formation of "families," a fact that has been amply documented, in both adult and juvenile institutions.[71] The major reason for this is that the majority of women have husbands and children on the outside and do not generally receive much support from them. Perhaps the most important factor has to do with traditional women's roles. For women, the family is the center of life (with children and husbands), at least this is what they have been socialized to believe. One of the ways in which women have chosen to adapt to the prison world is modeled after the outside world in which they have been socialized—namely, re-creating family life, even though their "families" are likely to have been highly dysfunctional and abusive.[72] In women's prisons, therefore, there exists a sort of "pseudo-family system," with all the traditional roles: fathers. sons, daughters, grandfathers, etc. Some women play the role of "husband" and wear their hair short, wear slacks, and walk and talk in a masculine way. Others play the role of "wife," "grandmother," and even "sons" and "daughters." Watterson writes: "In the context of prison society, it is not shocking to meet someone's institutional wife or grandfather. On several occasions while visiting prisons, I met a woman's entire prison 'family' and saw the interweaving of wife, grandmother, son, wife-in-law, daughter." Most of these "families" evolve in a natural way as an inevitable adaptation to the deprivations of prison life.[73]

Some of these family relationships can become quite competitive and exploitative. Hefferman makes the following appropriate comments:

the women playing the role of "dad" or "stud" are often the objects of active competition and recipients of extensive support. It was asserted, however, that some of the "husbands" would not hesitate leaving one partner to play an initially active role in attracting a new "wife" if she "had the looks and the money." Later in the relationship the "wife" would be expected to supply material support and services.[74]

There are other relationships in women's prisons. There are couples who "go steady" and perhaps even get "married" and "break up," just as people on the outside do. Also, as in male prisons, there are various homosexual roles in women's prisons. The terms applied to these roles depend on the particular type of homosexual role one plays. For example, "the true fern" is the prisoner who plays the role of woman in a lesbian relationship; the male role might go by such names as "true bitch" or "big hard daddy."

For women in prison, in contrast to men in prison, the close bonds of a "family" help to alleviate the pains of imprisonment. Such relationships, though not without problems of their own, help to create the kind of ideal family many of them never had on the outside. Because of this, many women never want to leave. Some, upon release, do things that will automatically bring them back to prison. As one female prisoner stated: "It's that security. It's that instant gratification coming back and having everybody holler and say, 'Look, Pat's back,' all happy to see you."[75]

The "concrete womb" is reinforced every day within women's prisons, sometimes subtly and sometimes not so subtly. Take for example the "programming" available in the typical women's prison. Although many modern women's prisons offer some college courses and some training with computers, most of the programming reinforces traditional female roles. A survey in the mid-1980s found the following programs: sewing, food services, secretarial training, "domestic" programs (unspecified), and cosmetology. A few offer typical "masculine" training in auto repair, welding, plumbing, and so on, but prisons offering such training are in the minority. Some of the "training" provides a form of cheap labor for corporations. In Arizona, for example, inmates help book reservations for the Best Western hotel/motel chain.[76]

It should come as no surprise that many, if not most, of the women incarcerated in American prisons have had plenty of experiences with the juvenile justice system. Young girls and their experiences with this system is the subject explored in the next section.

YOUNG WOMEN AND THE JUVENILE JUSTICE SYSTEM[77]

Keeping Girls in Their Place: The Development of Institutions for Girls

Recall from Chapter 13 that prior to the nineteenth century the deviant behavior of young people was handled largely on an informal basis. Do not infer from this that all was well with the treatment of youths in previous centuries. Children were subjected to some extreme forms of physical and sexual abuse. Strict laws governed the behavior of children; however, in the United States, these laws were used only infrequently.[78] Although entirely separate systems to monitor and control the behavior of young people began to appear during the early part of the nineteenth century, differential treatment based on age did not come about overnight. The roots of the juvenile justice system can be traced to much earlier legal and social perspectives on childhood and youth. One of the most important of these, for girls, was the legal doctrine known as ***parens patriae.***

Parens patriae ascribed to the state the role of parent or, more especially, father. Traditionally, women as well as children have been subject to a patriarch's authority. The idea of patriarchy also reinforces the sanctity and privacy of the home and the power (in early years, almost absolute) of the patriarch to discipline wife and children. Further, the notion of *parens patriae* assumes that the state can legally act as a parent, exercising many of the implicit parental powers possessed by fathers. Therefore, government leaders eventually utilized *parens patriae* to justify extreme government intervention in the lives of young people. Arguing that such intervention was "for their own good," "for their own protection," or "in the best interests of the child," the state during the eighteenth century became increasingly involved in the regulation of adolescent behavior.

As we explained in Chapter 13, juvenile institutions known as houses of refuge were constructed during the early nineteenth century. They were ostensibly designed to provide education, religious instruction, training for future employment, and parental discipline. In other words, they were to be schools with a "homelike" atmosphere rather than prisons. The rhetoric of the founders and managers of houses of refuge, however, fell far short of the reality experienced by the youth held in these facilities. A look at one of the most significant court challenges to the refuge movement, and one that, perhaps not surprisingly, involved an adolescent female, provides additional insight into the origins of the juvenile justice system.

The *Ex Parte Crouse* Case

Filed in 1838, *Ex Parte Crouse* arose from a petition of *habeas corpus* filed by the father of the minor Mary Ann Crouse.[79] Without her father's knowledge, Mary Ann had been committed to the Philadelphia House of Refuge by her mother on the grounds that she was "incorrigible." Her father argued that the incarceration was illegal because Mary Ann had not been given a jury trial. The justices of the Pennsylvania Supreme Court rejected the appeal, saying that the Bill of Rights did not apply to juveniles. The ruling was based on the *parens patriae* doctrine since justices assumed many parents were unfit.[80]

As noted in Chapter 13, the court assumed that the Philadelphia House of Refuge had a beneficial effect on its residents because it was considered a "school."[81]

What evidence did the justices consult to support their conclusion that the Philadelphia House of Refuge was not a prison but a school? Sadly, only testimony by those who managed the institution was solicited. A more objective review of the treatment of youths housed in these places might have led the justices to a very different conclusion. There was an enormous amount of abuse within these institutions. They were run according to a strict military regimen. Corporal punishment (girls in one institution were "ducked" underwater, and boys were hung by their thumbs), solitary confinement, and a "silent system" were part of the routine.[82] Work training was practically nonexistent, and outside companies contracted for cheap inmate labor. Religious instruction was often little more than Protestant indoctrination (many of the youngsters were Catholic). Education, in the conventional meaning of the word, was almost nonexistent.

Significantly, though, judges in the nineteenth century, when asked to review the care of juveniles, were reluctant to examine too closely state intervention into minors' lives if it was justified in familial terms. Ironically, such reviews were not undertaken even if a parent so requested (as in the *Crouse* case). The remainder of the nineteenth century witnessed intensification of the notion of the state as parent, and even greater threats to girls' rights.

The Child-Saving Movement, the Juvenile Court, and Girls

The **child-saving movement,** along with the juvenile court, had a special meaning for girls. The child-saving movement made much rhetorical use of the value of such traditional institutions as the family and education: "The child savers elevated the nuclear family, especially women as stalwarts of the family, and defended the family's right to supervise the socialization of youth."[83] But while the child savers were exalting the family, they were crafting a governmental system that would have authority to intervene in familial areas and, more specifically, in the lives of young people in ways that were unprecedented.

The concern of the child savers went far beyond removing the adolescent criminal from the adult justice system. Many of their reforms were actually aimed at "imposing sanctions on conduct unbecoming youth and disqualifying youth from the benefit of adult privileges."[84] Other students of the court's history have expanded on this point. They assert that the pervasive state intervention into the life of the family was grounded in colonial laws regarding "stubborn" and "neglected" children. Those laws incorporated the thinking of their time, that "parents were godly and children wicked," yet most child savers actually held an opposite opinion, that children were innocent and either the parents or the environment was morally suspect. Although the two views are incompatible, they have nevertheless coexisted in the juvenile court system since its inception. At various times one view or the other has predominated, but both bode ill for young women, because girls and their moral behavior were of specific concern to the child savers. Scientific and popular literature on female delinquency expanded enormously during this period, as did institutions specifically devoted to the reformation of girls.[85]

The child-saving movement was keenly concerned about prostitution and such other "social evils" as white slavery. Ironically, although child saving was a celebration of women's domesticity, the movement was not without female leaders. Privileged women found in the moral purity crusades and the establishment of family courts a safe outlet for their energies. As the legitimate guardians of the moral sphere, middle-class women were seen as uniquely suited to patrol the normative boundaries of the social order. Embracing rather than challenging these stereotypes, women managed to carve out for themselves a role in the policing of women and girls. Many early activities of the child savers revolved around monitoring young girls', particularly immigrant girls', behavior to prevent their straying from the path of virtues.

Just exactly how women, many of them highly educated, became involved in patrolling the boundaries of working-class girls' sexuality is a depressing but important story. Initially, as Odem's history of the period documents, middle-class women reformers were focused on regulating and controlling male, not female sexuality. Involved in the social purity movement, these reformers had a Victorian view of women's sexuality and saw girls as inherently chaste and sexually passive. If a girl lost "the most precious jewel in the crown of her womanhood," to their way of thinking, it was men who had forced them into sexual activity.[86] The protection and saving of girls, then, led these women to organize an aggressive social movement aimed at raising the age of consent (which in many parts of the country hovered at 10 or 12 years of age) to 16 or above. The pursuit of claims of statutory rape against men was another component of this effort, and such charges were brought in a number of cases despite evidence in about three-quarters of the cases Odem reviewed in Los Angeles that the girls entered into sexual relationships with young men willingly. Led largely by upper- and upper-middle-class women volunteers, many of whom were prominent in the temperance movement (like Frances Willard), this campaign, not unlike the Mothers against Drunk Driving campaign of later decades, drew an impressive and enthusiastic following, particularly among white citizens.

African American women participated in other aspects of Progressive reform, but Odem notes they were less than aggressive in the pursuit of statutory rape complaints. She speculates that they rightly suspected that any aggressive enforcement of these statutes was likely to fall most heavily on young African American men (while doing little to protect girls of color), and Odem notes that this is precisely what occurred. Of the very small number of cases in which stiff penalties were imposed, Odem found evidence that African American men were not infrequently sent to prison to reform their "supposedly lax and immoral habits" but white men either were not prosecuted or were given probation.

Efforts to vigorously pursue statutory rape complaints, though, ran headlong into predictable, staunch judicial resistance, particularly when many (but not all) cases involved young working-class women who had chosen to be sexually active. Eventually, as Odem's work documents, reformers (many of them now professional social workers) began to shift the focus of their activities. The "delinquent girl" herself became the focus of reform, and "moral campaigns to control teenage female sexuality" began to appear. Reformers during this later period (1910–1925) assumed that they had the authority to define what was "appropriate" conduct for young working-class women and girls, which of course was based on middle-class ideals of female sexual propriety. Girls who did not conform to these ideals were labeled as "wayward" and thus "in need of control" by the state in the form of juvenile courts and reformatories and training schools.[87]

Women reformers played a key role in the founding of the first juvenile court in Los Angeles in 1903 and vigorously advocated the appointment of women court workers to deal with the "special" problems of girls. This court was the first in the country to appoint women "referees," who were invested with nearly all the powers of judges in girls' cases. Women were also hired to run the juvenile detention facility in 1911. The logic for this was quite clear: "in view of the number of girls and the type of girls detained there...it is utterly unfeasible to have a man at the head of the institution," declared Cora Lewis, chair of the Probation Committee, which established Juvenile Hall. The civic leaders and newly hired female court workers "advocated special measures to contain sexual behavior among working class girls, to bring them to safety by placing them in custody, and to attend to their distinctive needs as young, vulnerable females."[88]

The evolution of what might be called the "girl-saving" effort was then the direct consequence of a disturbing coalition between some feminists and other Progressive-era movements. Concerned about female victimization and distrustful of male (and to some degree female) sexuality, prominent women leaders, including Susan B. Anthony, found common cause with the more conservative social purity movement around such issues as the regulation of prostitution and raising the age of consent. Eventually, in the face of stiff judicial and political resistance, the concern about male sexuality more or less disappeared from sight, and the delinquent girl herself becomes the problem. The solution: harsh "maternal justice" meted out by professional women.[89]

Girls were the losers in this reform effort. Studies of early family court activity reveal that almost all of the girls who appeared in these courts were charged with immorality or waywardness. The sanctions for such misbehavior were extremely severe. For example, the Chicago family court sent half the girl delinquents but only a fifth of the boy delinquents to reformatories between 1899 and 1909. In Milwaukee, twice as many girls as boys were committed to training schools.[90] In Memphis, females were twice as likely as males to be committed to training schools.[91]

In Honolulu in 1929–1930, over half the girls referred to juvenile court were charged with "immorality," which meant there was evidence of sexual intercourse; 30 percent were charged with "waywardness." Evidence of immorality was vigorously pursued by both arresting officers and social workers through lengthy questioning of the girls and, if possible, men with whom they were suspected of having sex. Other evidence of "exposure" was provided by gynecological examinations that were routinely ordered in most girls' cases. Doctors, who understood the purpose of such examinations, would routinely note the condition of the hymen. Girls were twice as likely as men to be detained for their offenses and spent five times as long in detention on average as their male counterparts. They were also nearly three times more likely to be sentenced to the training school. Indeed, half of those committed to training schools in Honolulu well into the 1950s were girls.[92]

Not surprisingly, large numbers of girls' reformatories and training schools were established during the Progressive era, in addition to places of "rescue and reform." For example, twenty-three facilities for girls were opened during the 1910–1920 decade (in contrast to the 1850–1910 period, when the average was five reformatories a decade), and they did much to set the tone of the official response to female delinquency. These institutions were obsessed with precocious female sexuality and were determined to instruct girls in their proper place.[93]

According to Pisciotta, there was a slight modification of the *parens patriae* doctrine during this period. The "training" of girls was shaped by the image of the ideal woman that had evolved during the early part of the nineteenth century. According to this ideal (which was informed by what some have called the "separate spheres" notion), a woman belonged in the private sphere, performing such tasks as rearing children, keeping house, caring for a husband, and serving as the moral guardian of the home. In this capacity, she was to exhibit qualities like obedience, modesty, and dependence.[94] The man's domain was the public sphere: the workplace, politics, and the law. Men, by virtue of their public power, were the final arbiters of public morality and culture. This white middle-class "cult of domesticity," was, of course, very distant from the lives of many working- and lower-class women, who by necessity were in the labor force. Pisciotta notes that the ideal woman was like a "Protestant nun."[95] The institutions established for girls set about to isolate them from all contact with males while training them in feminine skills and housing them in bucolic settings. The intention was to hold the girls until marriageable age and to occupy them in domestic pursuits during their sometimes lengthy incarceration. The child savers had little hesitation about such extreme intervention in girls' lives.

Envisioned as a "benevolent" institution that would emphasize treatment rather than punishment, the juvenile court turned out to be a mixture of the two orientations. The confusion can be traced to the mixed legacy of the court—on the one hand, a puritanical approach to stubborn children and parental authority; on the other, the Progressive era's belief that children's essential goodness can be corrupted by undesirable elements in their environments.

Nowhere has the confusion and irony of the juvenile court been more clearly demonstrated than in its treatment of girls labeled "delinquent." Many of these girls were incarcerated for noncriminal behavior during the early years of the court.

Controlling Girls

The first reform school for girls was the State Industrial School for Girls in Lancaster, Massachusetts, established in 1856. This "school" was intended for the "gentler sex" and "with all the details relating to employment, instruction, and amusement, and, indeed, to every branch of domestic economy."[96] Such rhetoric would eventually find its way into the other girls' training schools. The Home of the Good Shepherd, established in 1875 in Memphis, Tennessee, was designed for the "reformation of fallen…women and a home or house of refuge for abandoned and vicious girls." Moreover, because the girls had "fallen from grace," they needed to be saved for the "preservation of the State's young manhood."[97] Lancaster's first superintendent, Bradford K. Peirce, echoed this sentiment: "It is sublime to work to save a woman, for in her bosom generations are embodied, and in her hands, if perverted, the fate of innumerable men is held."[98]

Lancaster, a model for all juvenile training schools, was to save children from "perversion through conversion," according to Brenzel. "Loving care" and confinement in an atmosphere free from the "sins and temptations" of city life would redirect girls' lives. What sorts of crimes had the girls committed? Over two-thirds had been accused of moral rather than criminal offenses: vagrancy, beggary, stubbornness, deceitfulness, idle and vicious behavior, wanton and lewd conduct, and running away.[99] Of the first ninety-nine inmates at Lancaster, only slightly over half (53 percent) were American-born. Of the immigrant group, most spoke English and many were Irish. Significantly, at least half of the girls had been brought to Lancaster because of the actions of parents and relatives.[100] Clearly, early training schools were deeply concerned with female respectability and hence worked to control the sexuality of lower- and working-class adolescent girls.

These institutions for girls strove for a family-like atmosphere, from which, after having been taught domestic skills, girls would be released to the care of other families as domestic workers. Gradually, however, vocational training in appropriate manual skills (sewing and the cutting of garments), age-group classification, and punishment characterized the institutional regime. By the late 1880s, Lancaster had devolved into a "middle place between the care of that Board [Health, Lunacy, and Charity] and a Reformatory Prison." Lancaster's original goal of establishing a "loving family circle" had been supplanted by "harsh judgement, rudimentary job training and punitive custody."[101]

Juvenile Court and the Double Standard of Juvenile Justice

The offenses that bring girls into the juvenile justice system reflect the system's dual concerns: adolescent criminality and moral conduct. Historically, they have also reflected a unique and intense preoccupation with girls' sexuality and their obedience to parental authority. What happened to the girls once they arrived in the system?

Relatively early in the juvenile justice system's history, a few astute observers became concerned about the abandonment of minors' rights in the name of treatment, saving, and protection. A evaluation of several hundred cases in the Wayward Minor Court in New York City during the late 1930s and early 1940s found that there were serious problems with a statute that brought young women into court simply for disobedience of parental commands or because they were in "danger of becoming morally depraved." The study warned that the "need to interpret the 'danger of becoming morally depraved' imposes upon the court a legislative function of a moralizing character." Noting that many young women were being charged simply with sexual activity, the author of the study asked,

"What is sexual misbehavior—in a legal sense—of the nonprostitute of 16, or 18, or of 20 when fornication is no offense under criminal law?"[102]

A study of the Los Angeles Juvenile Court during the first half of the twentieth century supplies additional evidence of the juvenile justice system's historical preoccupation with girls' sexual morality, a preoccupation that clearly colored the Los Angeles court's activity into the 1950s. Odem and Schlossman reviewed the characteristics of the girls who entered the court in 1920 and in 1950. In 1920, 93 percent of the girls accused of delinquency were charged with status offenses; of these, 65 percent were charged with immoral sexual activity (though the vast majority—56 percent—had engaged in sex with only one partner, usually a boyfriend). The researchers found that 51 percent of the referrals had come from the girls' parents, a situation they explained as working-class parents' fears about their daughters' exposure to the "omnipresent temptations to which working class daughters in particular were exposed to in the modern ecology of urban work and leisure." The working-class girls had been encouraged by their families to work (in fact 52 percent were working or had been working within the past year), but their parents were extremely ambivalent about changing community morals, and some were not hesitant about involving the court in their arguments with problem daughters.[103]

Odem and Schlossman also found that the Los Angeles Juvenile Court did not shirk from its perceived duty. Seventy-seven percent of the girls were detained before their hearings. Both pre- and post-hearing detention were common and "clearly linked" to the presence of venereal disease. Thirty-five percent of all delinquent girls and over half being held for sex offenses had gonorrhea, syphilis, or other venereal infections. The researchers noted that the presence of venereal disease, and the desire to impose treatment (which in those times was lengthy and painful) accounted for the large numbers of girls in detention centers. Analysis of court actions revealed that although probation was the most common court response—61 percent were accorded probation—only 27 percent were released on probation immediately following the hearing. Many girls, it appears, were held for weeks or months after initial hearings. Girls not given probation were often placed in private homes as domestics, or they were placed in a wide range of private institutions, such as the Convent of the Good Shepherd or homes for unmarried mothers. Ultimately, according to Odem and Schlossman, about 33 percent of the "problem girls" during this period were sentenced to institutional confinement.

It is obvious these court officials were quite obsessed with the sexuality of these young women. Odem notes that after a girl was arrested, "probation officers questioned her relatives, neighbors, employers, and school officials to gather details about her sexual misconduct and, in the process, alerted them that she was a delinquent in trouble with the law." After this, the girls were usually detained in juvenile hall and further questioned about their sexual behavior. They were asked to give a complete sexual history, starting with their first act of intercourse, and they were pressured to reveal the names of all their partners, the exact times and locations of sexual activities, as well as the number of times they had had sex. Further court discipline was leveled at those who did not give complete information.[104]

Studies continue to pick up on problems with the vagueness of contemporary status offense categories, which are essentially "buffer charges" for suspected sexuality. Consider Vedder and Somerville's observation in the 1960s that although girls in their study were incarcerated in training schools for the "big five" (running away from home, incorrigibility, sexual offenses, probation violation, and truancy), "the underlying vein in many of these cases is sexual misconduct by the girl delinquent."[105] Such attitudes were also present in other parts of the world, such as Australia.[106]

Another study, conducted in the early 1970s in a New Jersey training school, revealed large numbers of girls incarcerated "for their own protection." When asked about this pattern, one judge explained, "Why most of the girls I commit are for status offenses. I figure if a girl is about to get pregnant, we'll keep her until she's sixteen and then ADC (Aid to Dependent Children) will pick her up." Still another study reviewed the handling of cases of ungovernability in New York in 1972 and concluded that judges were acting "upon personal feelings and predilections in making decisions." Included among the evidence were statements made by judges—for example: "She thinks she's a pretty hot number; I'd be worried about leaving my kid with her in a room alone. She needs to get her mind off boys." Another judge remarked that at the age of 14 some girls "get some crazy ideas. They want to fool around with men, and that's sure as hell trouble." Another admonished a girl, "I want you to promise me to obey your mother, to have perfect school attendance and not miss a day of school, to give up these people who are trying to lead you to do wrong, not to hang out in candy stores or tobacco shops or street corners where these people are, and to be in when your mother says."[107]

Studies of the processing of girls' and boys' cases between 1950 and the early 1970s documented the impact of these sorts of judicial attitudes. Girls charged with status offenses were often more harshly treated than their male or female counterparts charged with crimes. These studies continued to document the fact that girls charged with status offenses were far more likely to be incarcerated than boys charged with status offenses and even in some cases more likely than boys charged with more serious crimes.

In short, studies of the juvenile courts during the past few decades suggest that court personnel participated directly in the judicial enforcement of the sexual double standard. Such activity was most pronounced in the system's early years, but there is evidence that the pattern continues, in part because status offenses can still serve as buffer charges for sexual misconduct. Some of the problem with status offenses, although they are discriminatory, is understandable. They are not like criminal cases, regarding which judges have relatively clear guidelines. Standards of evidence are delineated, elements of the crime are laid out in the statutes, and civil rights are, at least to some extent, protected by law.

The **double standard of juvenile justice** was indirectly challenged in the 1970s by passage of the **Juvenile Justice and Delinquency Prevention Act,** which encouraged states to divert and deinstitutionalize status offenders. Despite some gains in the early years of this movement (such as a decline in the number of girls in detention centers and training schools), studies of courts in the later 1980s and early 1990s show that juvenile justice is far from gender-blind. Moreover, challenges to deinstitutionalization during the 1980s and 1990s indicate that the gains made in eradicating gender bias are in serious jeopardy—and could even be reversed. As juvenile courts approach their centenary, it is unfortunately still all too easy to find evidence that girls coming into the system—and not just in the United States—are receiving a special, discriminatory form of justice.[108]

SUMMARY

In this chapter we discussed how women have historically been given second-class treatment within both the adult and the juvenile justice systems. This stems from women's subordinate status, dating back to early Greek and Roman history and continuing throughout American history. This history especially shows that women of color and poor women have felt the brunt of the criminal justice system. Recent data on women in prison show tremendous increases in their rate of imprisonment, due chiefly to the "war on drugs."

The history of the juvenile justice system in the United States demonstrates that sexism has pervaded the institution since its inception. The roots of this pattern can be traced to colonial embellishments of the *parens patriae* doctrine, and it is probably no accident that the first and most significant legal challenge to this doctrine, *Ex Parte Crouse,* involved the incarceration of a girl on the grounds that she was "incorrigible." The *Crouse* case also illustrates that the evolution of the contemporary juvenile justice system was accelerated by the growth of institutions for delinquent and wayward youths, starting with houses of refuge and concluding with the establishment of training and reform schools. These schools were set up largely to save young people from the temptations of city life and precocious sexuality, and there they were taught domestic skills and moral precepts.

The establishment of the first juvenile court, in 1899, capped years of effort by people described as child savers to extend state control over the lives of youth. Girls were the losers in the reform movement as vast numbers were referred to juvenile courts for immorality and waywardness in the early years. Enormous numbers of girls who appeared before the courts in the first few decades were detained, tried, and ultimately institutionalized for their offenses.

By midcentury, juvenile courts were still involved in controlling girls' sexuality, but the pattern was a little less distinct. Instead of being charged with "immorality," girls in the juvenile courts of the 1950s and 1960s were being charged with status offenses like running away, which court observers called buffer charges for sexual misconduct. Girls continue to be arrested for this and other noncriminal status offenses, a pattern that also appears in other countries.

KEY TERMS

child-saving movement   373
chivalry   363
concrete womb   370
double standard of juvenile
   justice   378
Ex Parte Crouse   373

feminization of poverty   362
Juvenile Justice and Delinquency
   Prevention Act   378
Married Women's Property
   Acts   359
parens patriae   372

patria potestas   358
patriarchy   358
Reed v. Reed   359
State v. Costello   360
State v. Chambers   360

NOTES

1. Rafter, N., and E. A. Stanko (eds.). *Judge, Lawyer, Victim, Thief: Women, Gender Roles and Criminal Justice.* Boston: Northeastern University Press, 1982, pp. 2–4; Pollock, J. M. "Gender, Justice, and Social Control: A Historical Perspective." In A. V. Merlo and J. M. Pollock (eds.), *Women, Law, and Social Control.* Boston: Allyn and Bacon, 1996, p. 4.

2. Watterson, K. *Women in Prison: Inside the Concrete Womb.* Boston: Northeastern University Press, 1996, p. 33.

3. Eisenstein, Z. R. *The Female Body and the Law.* Berkeley: University of California Press, 1988, pp. 58–59; Terkel, G. *Law and Society: Critical Approaches.* Boston: Allyn and Bacon, 1996, pp. 6–7.

4. Lerner, G. *The Creation of Patriarchy.* New York: Oxford University Press, 1986, p. 239.

5. Ibid., pp. 12–13.

6. For the classic statement of this position see Engels, F. *The Origin of the Family, Private Property and the State.* New York: International Publishers, 1972 (originally published in 1884); a good critique of this thesis is provided in Lerner, *The Creation of Patriarchy,* ch. 1.

7. Parenti, M. Land of Idols: Political Mythology in America. New York: St. Martin's Press, 1994, pp. 149–150. For a discussion of how and why capitalism promotes selfishness, greed, the need for power and control, and so on, see Heilbroner, R. L. *The Nature and Logic of Capitalism.* New York: Norton, 1985, esp. chs. 2 and 3.

8. Parenti, *Land of Idols,* p. 150.

9. Eisenstein, *The Female Body and the Law,* pp. 58–59.

10. Chambliss, W. J., and T. F. Courtless. *Criminal Law, Criminology, and Criminal Justice.* Belmont, CA: Wadsworth, 1992, p. 31.

11. Pollock, "Gender, Justice, and Social Control," pp. 7–9.

12. Turkel, *Law and Society,* pp. 177–178.

13. Feinman, C. *Women in the Criminal Justice System.* New York: Praeger, 1980, p. 58.

14. Ibid., p. 60.

15. Eitzen, D. S., and M. B. Zinn. *In Conflict and Order* (8th ed.). Boston: Allyn and Bacon, 1998, p. 335.

16. Turkel, *Law and Society;* Faludi, S. *Backlash: The Undeclared War against American Women.* New York: Anchor Books, 1991; MacKinnon, C. *Toward a Feminist Theory of the State.* Cambridge, MA: Harvard University Press, 1989; Sokoloff, N. J., and B. R. Price (eds.). *The Criminal Justice System and Women* (2nd ed.). New York: McGraw-Hill, 1995, pp. 23–25.

17. Feinman, *Women in the Criminal Justice System,* pp. 60–61.

18. Donziger, S. *The Real War on Crime;* Chesney-Lind, M. *The Female Offender.* Thousand Oaks, CA: Sage, 1997.

19. Boritch, H., and J. Hagan. "A Century of Crime in Toronto: Gender, Class and Patterns of Social Control, 1859–1955." *Criminology* 28: 567–599 (1990); Chesney-Lind, The Female Offender.

20. Chesney-Lind, M., and R. G. Shelden. *Girls, Delinquency and Juvenile Justice* (2nd ed.). Belmont, CA: Wadsworth, 1998.

21. Miller, E. *Street Woman.* Philadelphia: Temple University Press, 1986; Steffensmeier, D. "Trends in Female Crime: It's Still a Man's World." In B. R. Price and N. J. Sokoloff (eds.), *The Criminal Justice System and Women* (2nd ed.). New York: McGraw-Hill, 1995.

22. Chesney-Lind, M. *The Female Offender.* College Park, MD: American Correctional Association, 1990;

Ferraro, K. "Cops, Courts, and Woman Battering," in Price and Sokoloff, ibid.

23. There are numerous studies of the abuse of women and the connection with subsequent criminality. See, for instance, Miller, *Street Woman;* Sheffield, C. J. "Sexual Terrorism: The Social Control of Women." In B. B. Hess and M. M. Ferree (eds.), *Analyzing Gender: A Handbook of Social Science Research.* Newbury Park, CA: Sage, 1987; Stout, K. "A Continuum of Male Controls and Violence against Women: A Teaching Model." *Journal of Social Work Education* 27: 305–319 (Fall 1991); Walker, L. E. *The Battered Woman.* New York: Harper/Perennial, 1980.

24. Daly, K. "Women's Pathways to Felony Court: Feminist Theories of Lawbreaking and Problems of Representation." *Review of Law and Women's Studies* 2: 11–52 (Fall 1992), at p. 14.

25. Miller, *Street Woman;* see case summaries in Chesney-Lind and Shelden, *Girls, Delinquency and Juvenile Justice,* ch. 10.

26. For reviews see the following: Hawkins, D. F. (ed.). *Ethnicity, Race, and Crime.* Albany: State University of New York Press, 1995; Mann, C. R. *Unequal Justice: A Question of Color.* Bloomington: Indiana University Press, 1995; Walker, S., C. Spohn, and M. DeLone. *The Color of Justice* (2nd ed.). Belmont, CA: Wadsworth, 2000; Reiman, J. *The Rich Get Richer and the Poor Get Prison* (6th ed.). Boston: Allyn and Bacon, 2001; Chesney-Lind, *The Female Offender.*

27. Daly, "Women's Pathways to Felony Court"; Miller, *Street Woman.* A survey by the American Correctional Association (Chesney-Lind, *The Female Offender*) found that among adult women in prison, whites constituted only 43 percent of those incarcerated at the time of the survey, African Americans 41.5 percent, and Hispanics 10 percent.

28. U.S. Bureau of the Census. *Statistical Abstract of the United States, 1995.* Washington, DC: U.S. Government Printing Office, 1996, pp. 405, 435; Folbre, N., and the Center for Popular Economics. *The New Field Guide to the U.S. Economy.* New York: New Press, 1995.

29. *Statistical Abstract, 1995,* p. 434.

30. Eitzen and Zinn, *In Conflict and Order,* p. 270.

31. Folbre, *The New Field Guide to the U.S. Economy;* Eitzen and Zinn, ibid., pp. 268–269.

32. Daly, "Women's Pathways to Felony Court," pp. 23–24.

33. Moyer, I. L. (ed.). *The Changing Roles of Women in the Criminal Justice System* (2nd ed.). Prospect Heights, IL: Waveland Press, 1992, pp. 71–72.

34. Siegel, L. "The Pregnancy Police Fight the War on Drugs." In C. Reinarman and H. G. Levine (eds.), *Crack in America: Demon Drugs and Social Justice.* Berkeley CA: University of California Press, 1997, p. 251.

35. Moyer, *The Changing Roles of Women in the Criminal Justice System.*

36. Visher, C. A. "Gender, Police Arrest Decisions, and Notions of Chivalry." *Criminology* 21: 15–28 (1983).

37. Wilbanks, W. "Are Female Felons Treated More Leniently by the Criminal Justice System?" *Justice Quarterly* 3: 517–529 (1986).

38. Pollock, J. M. *Women, Prison, and Crime* (2nd ed.). Belmont, CA: Wadsworth, 2002, p. 7.

39. Chesney-Lind, *The Female Offender,* pp. 147–148.

40. Mauer, M., C. Potler, and R. Wolf. "The Impact of the Drug War on Women: A Comparative Analysis in Three States." *Women, Girls and Criminal Justice* 1(2): 21–22, 30–31 (2000), cited in Pollock, *Women, Prison, and Crime,* pp. 5–6.

41. Donziger, *The Real War on Crime,* p. 151.

42. For further elaboration of this theme see Shelden, *Controlling the Dangerous Classes,* and Reinarman and Levine, *Crack in America.*

43. Donziger, *The Real War on Crime,* p. 152.

44. Ibid., p. 148.

45. Collins, C. F. *The Imprisonment of African-American Women.* Jefferson, NC: McFarland, 1997, p. 4.

46. Ibid., p. 5.

47. Sellin, J. T. *Slavery and the Penal System.* New York: Elsevier, 1976.

48. Shelden, R. G. "From Slave to Caste Society: Penal Changes in Tennessee, 1840–1915." *Tennessee Historical Quarterly* 38: 462–478 (Winter 1979).

49. Rafter, N. H. *Partial Justice: Women, Prisons, and Social Control* (2nd ed.). New Brunswick, NJ: Transaction Books, 1990, pp. 4–5.

50. Freedman, E. B. *Their Sisters' Keepers: Women's Prison Reform in America, 1830–1930.* Ann Arbor: University of Michigan Press, 1981, p. 16.

51. Rafter, *Partial Justice,* p. 6; Watterson, Women in Prison, p. 196.

52. Freedman, *Their Sister' Keepers,* pp. 17–18.

53. Ibid.; see also Platt, A. *The Child Savers* (rev. ed.). Chicago: University of Chicago Press, 1977.

54. Watterson, *Women in Prison,* p. 198.

55. Ibid.

56. Freedman, *Their Sisters' Keepers,* pp. 14, 59–60.

57. Ibid., p. 61.

58. Ibid., p. 62, emphasis added by Freedman.

59. Rafter, *Partial Justice,* pp. 142–146; Collins, *The Imprisonment of African-American Women.*

60. Collins, ibid., p. 21.

61. Ibid., p. 46.

62. For 1976 data see Shelden, R. G. *Criminal Justice in America.* Boston: Little, Brown, 1982, p. 347. For 1999 data see Beck, A. J. "Prisoners in 1999." Washington, DC: Bureau of Justice Statistics, 2000.

63. Chesney-Lind, *The Female Offender.*

64. American Correctional Association, *The Female Offender.*

65. Dryfoos, J. *Adolescents at Risk.* New York: Oxford University Press, 1990.

66. Ibid.

67. Chesney-Lind, *The Female Offender.*

68. Ibid.

69. Watterson, *Women in Prison,* p. 66.

70. Ibid., pp. 77–79.

71. Giallombardo, R. *Society of Women: A Study of Women's Prisons.* New York: Wiley, 1966, and *The Social Order of Imprisoned Girls.* New York: Wiley, 1974; Ward, D. H., and K. S. Kassebaum. *Women's Prisons.* Chicago: Aldine, 1965; Hefferman, E. *Making It in Prison: The Square, the Cool and the Life.* New York: Wiley, 1972; Hefferman, E. "Making It in a Woman's Prison: The Square, the Cool and the Life." In R. M. Carter, D. Glaser, and L. T. Wilkins (eds.), *Correctional Institutions* (2nd ed.). Philadelphia: Lippincott, 1977; Owen, B. *In the Mix: Struggle and Survival in a Women's Prison.* Albany: State University of New York Press, 1998.

72. Watterson, *Women in Prison,* pp. 285–308.

73. Ibid., p. 288.

74. Hefferman, "Making It in a Woman's Prison," p. 222.

75. Watterson, *Women in Prison,* p. 63.

76. Pollock-Byrne, J. M. *Women, Prison, and Crime.* Belmont, CA: Wadsworth, 1990, p. 93.

77. Most of the material in this section is drawn from Chesney-Lind and Shelden, *Girls, Delinquency and Juvenile Justice.*

78. See Shelden, *Controlling the Dangerous Classes,* ch. 6 and citations therein.

79. For a more detailed look at this case see Shelden, R. G. "Confronting the Ghost of Mary Ann Crouse: Gender Bias in the Juvenile Justice System." *Juvenile and Family Court Journal* 49: 11–25 (1998).

80. Pisciotta, A. "Saving the Children: The Promise and Practice of *Parens Patriae,* 1838–98." *Crime and Delinquency* 28: 411 (1982).

81. Ibid.

82. Shelden, *Controlling the Dangerous Classes.*

83. Platt, *The Child Savers,* p. 98.

84. Ibid., p. 199.

85. Teitelbaum, L. E., and Harris, L. J. "Some Historical Perspectives on Governmental Regulation of Children and Parents." In L. E. Teitelbaum and A. R. Gough (eds.), *Beyond Control: Status Offenders in the Juvenile Court.* Cambridge, MA: Ballinger, 1977, p. 34; Schlossman, S., and S. Wallach. "The Crime of Precocious Sexuality: Female Delinquency in the Progressive Era." *Harvard Educational Review* 8: 65–94(1978); Odem, M. *Delinquent Daughters: Protecting and Policing Adolescent Female Sexuality in the United States, 1885–1920.* Chapel Hill: University of North Carolina Press, 1995.

86. Odem, ibid., p. 25.

87. Ibid., pp. 4–5.

88. Odem, M., and S. Schlossman. "Guardians of Virtue: The Juvenile Court and Female Delinquency in Early 20th Century Los Angeles." *Crime and Delinquency* 37: 190–192 (1991).

89. Odem, *Delinquent Daughters,* p. 128.

90. Schlossman and Wallach, "The Crime of Precocious Sexuality," p. 72.

91. Shelden, R. G. "Sex Discrimination in the Juvenile Justice System: Memphis, Tennessee, 1900–1917." In M. Q. Warren (ed.), *Comparing Male and Female Offenders.* Newbury Park, CA: Sage, 1981, p. 70.

92. Chesney-Lind and Shelden, *Girls, Delinquency and Juvenile Justice,* ch. 7.

93. Schlossman and Wallach, "The Crime of Precocious Sexuality," p. 70.

94. Pisciotta, A. "Race, Sex and Rehabilitation: A Study of Differential Treatment in the Juvenile Reformatory, 1825–1900." *Crime and Delinquency* 29: 254–268 (1983).

95. Ibid., p. 265.

96. Brenzel, B. 1975. "Lancaster Industrial School for Girls: A Social Portrait of a 19th Century Reform School for Girls." *Feminist Studies* 3: 41 (1975). See also Brenzel, B. *Daughters of the State.* Cambridge, MA: MIT Press, 1983.

97. Shelden, "Sex Discrimination in the Juvenile Justice System," p. 58.

98. Brenzel, *Daughters of the State,* p. 4.

99. Ibid., p. 81.

100. Similarly, many girls in the Home of the Good Shepherd in Memphis had been brought into the juvenile court because of running away, incorrigibility, or various charges labeled by the court as "immorality," including "sexual relations" that ranged from sexual intercourse to "kissing and holding hands in the park" (Shelden, "Sex Discrimination in the Juvenile Justice System," p. 63). Schlossman and Wallach arrived at the same conclusion: "immorality" seems to have been the most common charge against females. Included under the rubric were "coming home late at night," "masturbating," "using obscene language," "riding at night in automobiles without a chaperon," and "strutting about in a lascivious manner" ("The Crime of Precocious Sexuality," p. 72).

101. Brenzel, *Daughters of the State,* pp. 153, 160.

102. Tappan, P. *Delinquent Girls in Court.* New York: Columbia University Press, 1947, p. 33.

103. Odem and Schlossman, "Guardians of Virtue," p. 196.

104. Odem, *Delinquent Daughters,* pp. 143–144.

105. Vedder, C. B., and D. B. Sommerville. *The Delinquent Girl.* Springfield, IL: Charles C. Thomas, 1970, p. 147.

106. Naffine, N. *Female Crime: The Construction of Women in Criminology.* Sydney, Australia: Allen and Unwin, 1987, p. 13.

107. Documented in Chesney-Lind and Shelden, *Girls, Delinquency and Juvenile Justice.*

108. Ibid., pp. 138–144.

CHAPTER FIFTEEN

MAKING CHANGES
Reforming Criminal Justice and Seeking Social Justice

Over 150 years ago Karl Marx made an astute observation about society's response to crime, forewarning of what we have come to call the **crime control industry:**

> The criminal produces not only crime but also the criminal law; he produces the professor who delivers lectures on this criminal law; and even the inevitable text-book in which the professor presents his lectures as a commodity for sale in the market.... Further, the criminal produces the whole apparatus of the police and criminal justice, detectives, judges, executioners, juries, etc.... Crime takes off the labour market a portion of the excess population, diminishes competition among workers, and to a certain extent stops wages from falling below the minimum, while the war against crime absorbs another part of the same population. The criminal therefore appears as one of those natural "equilibrating forces" which establish a just balance and open up a whole perspective of "useful" occupations.[1]

Any attempt to "reform" the criminal justice system, to make it "better" at achieving "justice" or reducing crime by any significant amount must confront this fact. In short, the criminal justice system—the crime control industry—has, ironically, a vested interested in *not* reducing crime to any great extent. True, we may try to make the current system more "efficient" at capturing and convicting criminals, but that does not generally result in any significant reduction in the overall rate of crime. Indeed, we have already shown that despite huge increases in expenditures on the criminal justice system over the past twenty years or so, the overall rate of crime has changed little.

Before we make some of our own recommendations for change, it may be appropriate to briefly review what research has shown has *not* been effective in producing positive changes in the criminal justice system. In his book *Sense and Nonsense about Crime and Drugs,* Samuel Walker rather effectively debunks some of the most common solutions that have been offered.[2] In the following section we will summarize some of these solutions.

WHAT DOESN'T WORK

Walker begins by noting that not only are most crime control proposals "nonsense" but most of the ideas behind the solutions "rest on faith rather than facts."[3] Here are some examples:

1. *Add more police officers.* During the early years of his administration, President Bill Clinton made much ado about adding 100,000 more police officers. But as so many studies have documented, there is no correlation between the number of police officers and the crime rate. Similarly, adding more detectives to a police department has not resulted in any change in the crime rate.

2. *Increase the response time after a crime has been committed.* There is no evidence that this will alter the crime rate to any significant degree, mostly because the vast majority of crimes are "cold" by the time someone reports them.

3. *Repeal or modify the exclusionary rule and the* Miranda *warning.* Far from "handcuffing" the police, these two rules have had a positive effect on the way police do business, adding a degree of professionalism to police work. Besides, the "exclusionary rule" applies to a small proportion of all cases.

4. *Selectively incapacitate "career" criminals.* In general, the use of incarceration to reduce crime, whether it involves the popular "selective incapacitation" or simply "gross incapacitation," does not produce any significant reduction in crime.

5. *Make sentences "mandatory."* So-called mandatory sentences, such as the infamous "three-strikes laws," have no impact on the crime problem. In fact, they actually make matters worse by locking up low-level offenders and causing severe overcrowding in most prisons, all at a terrible cost to taxpayers.

6. *Concentrate on prosecuting "career criminals."* This proposal is based on the assumption that a few "career criminals" commit a disproportionate amount of crime and locking them up for long periods of time will cause the crime rate to go down. This is absolutely not true, according to many studies.

7. *Abolish the insanity defense and plea bargaining.* Because the insanity defense is so rarely used, abolishing it can't possibly have a significant impact on crime. Plea bargaining does not "let criminals off the hook" as conventional wisdom suggests. Abolishing it would have no impact on crime, and studies suggest that in places where it has either been abolished or reduced, there has been no impact on crime.

8. *Limit the appeals criminals can file.* This is another simplistic solution, with no basis in fact, for few criminals file appeals.

9. *Use diversion to reduce crime.* Most diversion programs, as implemented, have little or no impact on crime because (a) they concentrate mostly on low-level offenders and (b) they tend to "widen the net" by bringing more offenders under the watchful eyes of the criminal justice system. (One of the exceptions is the Detention Diversion Advocacy Project (DDAP), described later in this chapter.)

10. *Boot camps will reduce crime.* This is another common myth, although it "sounds good" and "feels good" and much ado has been made by politicians wanting to sound "tough on crime." The fact is that these programs have practically no impact on crime.

As Walker suggests, such recommendations are indeed based on "faith" rather than hard data. Generally speaking, vague promises to get tough on crime by, for instance, declaring a "war on crime" or a "war on drugs" or a "war on gangs" (not to mention a "war on terrorism") fail miserably.

Before any meaningful reforms can be attempted, before there is any serious attempt to reduce crime and suffering in the United States, and before we can make the criminal justice system more effective at reducing crime, we must address the larger social context of crime and criminal justice in American society. Any effort to achieve *social justice* will first require addressing a serious matter—the incredible amount of social inequality in our society. It may be impossible to achieve equal justice in a society with so much inequality. It is to this problem that we now turn.

ADDRESSING THE PROBLEM OF SOCIAL INEQUALITY

We mentioned in Chapter 1 the extent of inequality in American society today, noting how much it has increased during the past two decades. We repeatedly point out throughout this book the effect such inequality has not only on the nature and extent of crime but also on the response by the criminal justice system. The effect is summarized nicely by the title of Reiman's book, *The Rich Get Richer and the Poor Get Prison.* Because racial minorities fare the worst, when we speak of social inequality, we almost by definition speak of *racial* inequality. These twin issues must be seriously addressed before we take on the more general issue of achieving "justice"—however it is defined.

As these words are being written (February 2002), unemployment rates and other negative social indicators are rising. Much of these increases stem either directly or indirectly from the September 11, 2001, terrorist attacks. Millions have been put on the unemployment rolls, yet corporate profits (along with the usual "bailouts"—especially the airline industry) continue to remain high. At the same time, prisons and jails continue to overflow. Moreover, the federal budget being proposed by President Bush shows an increase in military spending, with little extra going for domestic problems.

Before we continue, let's take a look at one of the most commonly overlooked effects of widespread imprisonment—namely, the effect it has on unemployment rates, especially for African Americans. As many critics have noted, the "official" unemployment rate always underestimates the extent of the problem (we wonder whether this is done intentionally) by ignoring those who have part-time work but want full-time work and those who have given up looking. However, another large group excluded from these figures: those in prison or jail. With an estimated 2 million prisoners, this is a sizable number. For African American men, the unemployment rate becomes an astounding 40 percent![4]

Most of the rise in incarceration rates stems directly from the "war on drugs." We begin our recommendations for seeking social justice with what to do about this unjust "war."

ENDING THE "WAR ON DRUGS"

The "war on drugs" has had a devastating toll on American citizens, especially the poor and racial minorities. The negative consequences of this "war" have been far-reaching: the exploding prison population, the targeting of racial minorities (and their disenfranchisement), the enormous costs to taxpayers, little or no impact on drug use. Before any meaningful changes can come about and before any sort of "justice" can be achieved—however "justice" is defined—we recommend the end of the "war on drugs" or, at the very least, a sort of "ceasefire" until other options are studied and tried.

As a result of the more than twenty-five years we have spent researching the problem of crime, including the drug war, we have arrived at some interesting conclusions about this "war." One conclusion is that it is very beneficial to some groups, especially various businesses and the "drug warriors"—law enforcement agencies being paid enormous sums of money to fight the "war." (Fighting any "war" benefits a number of people, whether it be the "war on poverty," "war on gangs," or the "war on terrorism.")

The drug war has helped create and perpetuate a prison-industrial complex, which in turn is the result of an economic system driven by a "free market" philosophy that places profits above people. In this "free market" everyone is "free" to earn a buck any way they can. The fact that it may be illegal is often beside the point; the fact that it may be downright unethical is largely irrelevant. One of the key aspects of a capitalist, "free market" economic system is that the production and distribution of "commodities" are the major goals. Commodities create profits, pure and simple. And the production and distribution of commodities are based on the "law of supply and demand," which dictates that where there is a demand for a commodity, someone willing to take the risks will engage in the act of supply. And when the commodity has been considered a "vice" and attempts are made to limit access to it by the criminal justice system, there appears to be even a greater demand. Such has been the case with all sorts of "vices"—prostitution, gambling, alcohol, drugs …you name it. When we have made attempts to reduce either the supply or the demand of something that is desired through the law, we have always had drastic consequences and have always failed miserably.

What many do not seem to understand is that by making something illegal that is at the same time highly desired by the general public, we open up all sorts of opportunities for not only bribery (the usual scandalous variety where cops receive payoffs to look the other way, judges fix things if they get that far, etc.) but also a great deal of money made very legitimately via working in the criminal justice system. Indeed, largely as a result of fighting the drug war, the "criminal justice industrial complex" (of which the prison is one part) has become a booming business. Currently we taxpayers shell out in excess of $150 billion per year for the police, the courts, and the correctional system—up from a paltry $11 billion thirty years ago. Fighting the drug war is big business. The same can be said of the "war on gangs."

The fact is, we do not seem to be winning the drug war. At least, we are not winning in the usual sense of the word: the drug problem is not getting any better, people are finding it easier and easier to obtain drugs, street prices of illegal drugs have dropped considerably, and hardly a dent has been made in the amount of drugs coming into the country. But in another sense many are in fact "winning"—if we define *winning* as making huge profits, the expansion of drug war bureaucracies, and so on. Aside from the jobs created and the money made actually "fighting" the war (lucrative contracts to build prisons, providing police cars and various technology to fight crime, drug testing, etc.), there is plenty of money to be made on the supply side.

Part of the problem is that drugs are a huge business enterprise. Consider these facts:[5]

■ A United Nations report notes that drug trafficking is a $400 billion per year industry, equal to about 8 percent of the world's trade. One example: one kilo of raw opium in Pakistan averages $90 but sells for $290,000 in the United States. Another example: there are about $7 billion in drug profits coming out of Colombia each year (legitimate exports are only slightly greater at $7.6 billion); Colombian cartels spend about $100 million on bribes to officials each year; 98 percent of Bolivia's foreign exchange earnings from goods and services came from the coca market in 1993.

■ The estimated economic cost of alcohol abuse is around $148 billion, compared to drug-abuse costs of around $97 billion. Concerning this $97 billion, 60 percent of the costs are related to law enforcement and imprisonment; only 3 percent were from the victims of drug-related crime.

■ And speaking of costs: in 1969 the Nixon administration spent $65 million on the drug war; in 1982 the Reagan administration spent $1.65 billion; in 1998 the Clinton administration requested $17.1 billion (more money for drug war bureaucracies).

The most recent data show that as of November 2001 the combined total money spent at the state and federal levels was $34 billion.

■ Our government steadfastly continues to focus on the supply side rather than the demand side of the equation, with horrible results. Interdiction efforts intercept only 10 to 15 percent of the heroin and 30 percent of the cocaine. United States expenditures to counter drug operations in Colombia came to $625 million between 1990 and 1998, yet during this time Colombia was able to pass Peru and Bolivia as the number-one producer of coca.

It looks as if the "spirit of capitalism" helps perpetuate the demand for and the supply of drugs. Drugs, whether legal or illegal, are profitable commodities—profitable for the supplier, the seller, and the "drug warriors" who are supposedly trying to "win" this "war." But these "drug warriors" are not really interested in truly "winning" in the sense of eliminating the drug problem or even reducing it to any significant degree.[6] After all, careers are at stake, as are promotions and other perks. Further, we must consider the thousands of businesses, large and small, that benefit from the existence of jails and prisons. Consider the number of contractors needed to build a prison or jail (engineers, architects, builders, electricians, mortgage companies, those providing security measures such as locks and fences, furniture, computers, etc.) and then those who benefit from everyday maintenance (suppliers of linen, food, medical supplies, etc.). Billions of dollars are to be made in the "prison industry," not to mention salaries and benefits for those working in the system (police officers, court workers, judges, prison guards, etc.). Then, too, there are the education and training for the next generation of "drug warriors" in various criminal justice programs in more than three thousand colleges and universities, plus law enforcement training academies.

In other words, the "war on drugs" is too profitable to end, for too many people and too many government agencies, and corporations are reaping profits from this war. In spite of the obvious obstacles that may lie in the way of ending this war (and remember that it is really in the best interest of the average citizen to end this "war"), we nevertheless insist that some attempt be made to do so.

The first thing to consider is the options that are available. Do we simply legalize all drugs? Do we legalize them with some regulations and restrictions (e.g., minors prohibited from using)? Do we legalize only some drugs (e.g., marijuana)? Do we "decriminalize" some or all drugs by limiting the penalties or some other options? Do we involve the criminal justice system in only indirect ways, such as having drug courts or drug treatment sentences instead of jail or prison (as stipulated in a recent California referendum, known as Proposition 36)? First, let's review some myths and realities about drugs and crime.[7]

Myths and Realities about Drugs and Crime

First, we must be aware of the extent of illegal drug use (leaving aside the widespread use of both tobacco and alcohol—the two most dangerous drugs in the world, responsible for perhaps 500,000 deaths each year). Most experts on drug use have come to the conclusion that there are *two drug problems,* one related to the general population, the other related to those living in extreme poverty, including those caught up in the criminal justice system. In recent years, while the use of illegal drugs by the general population has declined, there has been a significant increase in drug use among the poorest segments of our society.

The connection of drugs to crime is a complex issue, but generally we can say that there are three aspects of the drug–crime connection. First, there are *drug-defined crimes*—possession and sale of illegal drugs. Second, there are *drug-related crimes,* such as those (e.g., robbery) committed to support one's habit or violence associated with the pharmacology of the drug. Third, there are *crimes associated with drug usage,* meaning that the offender was using drugs around the time the crime was committed but the crime was not directly caused by drug use.

What is important to note is that while the majority of high-rate offenders use drugs, most started their criminal careers *before* the onset of drug use, and some started their criminal careers and their drug use about the same time. It must also be stressed that *the overwhelming majority of those who used an illegal drug sometime in their lives became neither drug addicts nor career criminals.* Thus, reducing illegal drug use will not guarantee a lowering of the crime rate.[8]

What about the dangerousness of illegal drugs? It is beyond the scope of this final chapter to explore the harmfulness of the various drugs on the market—both legal and illegal. We know for a fact what alcohol and tobacco usage does to individuals, their families, and their communities. The extent of the harm done by substances that have been made illegal is not known with any degree of certainty, although some studies document the negative long-term consequences of the use of such drugs as cocaine and heroin, especially heroin.[9] Nevertheless, one set of statistics underscores the dramatic differences between tobacco and alcohol on the one hand and illegal drugs like cocaine and heroin on the other. Every year, on average, there are between 400,000 and 450,000 tobacco-related deaths, between 80,000 and 150,000 alcohol-related deaths, roughly 100,000 deaths from prescription drugs, and between 4,000 and 5,000 deaths are related to cocaine and heroin. And how many deaths are attributed to marijuana? Zero![10]

There is continuing controversy over marijuana use. Although marijuana is not a totally benign substance, the negative consequences of marijuana use are far less than most other drugs. To be sure, there are some harmful effects, such as the ingestion of carbon monoxide (one marijuana cigarette delivers three times more tar to the system than one tobacco cigarette).[11] However, most hard-core tobacco smokers go through a pack a day or more, compared to the typical casual marijuana smoker. And contrary to popular myth, marijuana is not a "gateway" drug—leading to the use of more serious drugs. Most of those who use marijuana do not progress to the harder drugs. Besides, THC (the main ingredient for marijuana) "ranks lowest in addictive potential of all commonly used substances, even below caffeine," according to drug-use researcher Tom Clark.[12]

We have not learned some of the valuable lessons of history about using the criminal law to attempt to control something that is in great demand.[13] First, we have to consider the law of supply and demand, which says that when you have a large demand for a product (e.g., drugs, alcohol) or a service (e.g., prostitution), there will always be someone willing to provide it, despite the risks involved. Second, any effort to prevent the supply from getting to those who demand these goods or services inevitably results in the creation of criminal syndicates and widespread evasion by those who want what is offered. Third, any attempts to enforce these laws will have some very negative side effects, such as corruption within the criminal justice system (especially the police), the violation of individual rights, and turf wars between rival street gangs,[14] not to mention widespread disrespect for the law. Fourth, any intensification of law enforcement efforts will result in many people either substituting other illegal products or transferring the "service" to people who are more willing to take the risks—after all, the profits are always quite high.

A Modest Proposal

Short of legalizing all drugs (which may be the ultimate solution but is politically infeasible for the foreseeable future), we recommend at the very least two things. First, legalize marijuana, with some restrictions for youth (as there are for alcohol). This makes the most sense to us, because about half of all drug arrests are for marijuana, mostly possession.[15] In the year 2000 (the latest figures available as of this writing), 46.5 percent of all drug arrests in the United States were for marijuana, and almost 90 percent were for simple possession. Of course, even this modest proposal will receive considerable resistance, especially from those in charge of enforcing the drug laws and those profiting from the prison-industrial complex. The usual argument is that such a policy would mean that we condone the use of marijuana, to which we reply, So what? We condone the use of alcohol and, until recently, we condoned the use of tobacco. We can discourage use of marijuana—and other drugs as well—by using the methods that were so successful in reducing the demand for tobacco. Further, because there is no evidence that marijuana use leads to any serious problems (with some exceptions, to be sure)—and no one dies from it—why criminalize it?

Second, for those addicted to drugs, treatment options should be made available.[16] There are plenty of relatively successful treatment options. It is clear that providing treatment instead of jail or prison is much more cost-effective. One study noted that every dollar spent on drug treatment results in an overall $3 social benefit (less crime, more employment, etc.). One illustration is the **Treatment Alternatives to Street Crime (TASC) project.** Under this plan, instead of going to jail or prison, an offender is placed under community-based supervision in some drug treatment program.[17]

Expanding Diversion Programs, Avoiding Net Widening

As noted in Chapter 10, diversion has been in practice throughout the history of criminal justice. In recent years more specific programs have been devised to prevent offenders from encroaching even further into the criminal or juvenile justice system. Diversionary programs have a strong theoretical background based firmly on labeling principles (see Chapter 4). These principles have evolved from Tannenbaum, who initially wrote in 1938 on the "dramatization of evil," and from Becker's notion that social groups create deviance by labeling acts as "deviant" and treating persons so labeled as "outsiders," and from Lemert's classic statements about labeling leading to "secondary deviance."[18] Thus, the legal interaction by the juvenile justice system may actually perpetuate crime or delinquency by processing cases that might otherwise be ignored, normalized in their original settings, or better dealt with in more informal settings within the community.

One of the most immediate responses to the labeling perspective was the 1967 President's Commission on Law Enforcement and Administration of Justice report, which called for the creation of "youth services bureaus" to develop alternative programs for juvenile offenders in local communities and many different programs for adult offenders. The establishment of these youth services bureaus began a move toward diverting youths, especially status offenders and other nonserious delinquents, away from the juvenile court. These bureaus were quickly established in virtually every community regardless of size.[19]

It should not be surprising that conflicting expectations, findings, and conclusions emerged from such a widespread, disjointed, and complicated social experiment. Many studies show that diversion programs are successful in reducing subsequent deviance. These findings are balanced, however, by findings of no impact. There are, in addition, reports that find diversion programs to have detrimental properties.[20]

Proponents of diversion programs cite numerous studies, such as the diversion project in Colorado that involved comparisons between an experimental group of diverted youths and a control group who received regular juvenile justice system handling. The Colorado program administered individual, parental, or family counseling to the diversion cases, resulting in significantly lower recidivism rates.[21]

The most successful diversion projects have been those that provide the most intensive services, which is consistent with Dryfoos's findings that successful programs offer comprehensive services.[22] Especially important is the use of experienced youth workers. A project in St. Louis found that the most experienced youth workers were able to bring about greater behavioral changes than inexperienced youth workers.[23]

The issue of increased or decreased recidivism rates is coupled with the concerns over prejudice, discrimination, civil rights violations, and net widening. The issue of net widening has perhaps received the most attention. Ideally, a true diversion program (and the original concept behind diversion) seeks to take those who would ordinarily be processed within the juvenile justice system and place them into some alternative program. Suppose you normally have 1,000 youths processed within the juvenile justice system. A true *diversion* will occur if you take, say, 300 of these youths and place them in alternative programs. **Net widening** will occur if the alternative programs serve 300 youths who were *not* among your original 1,000. In the latter scenario, instead of processing 1,000 youths (300 in diversion programs and 700 within the juvenile justice system), you instead process 1,300 (1,000 + 300), and you have a net gain, or a net widening, of 300 youths.

Most of the research on diversion programs centers on juvenile offenders. However, the same concepts can easily apply to adults. The key is the provision of needed services and keeping as many offenders out of the criminal justice system as possible. One excellent example of such a program is the **Detention Diversion Advocacy Project (DDAP),** begun in San Francisco.

A Model Program: The Detention Diversion Advocacy Project.   The original Detention Diversion Advocacy Project was begun in 1993 by the Center on Juvenile and Criminal Justice (CJCJ) in San Francisco. The major goal is to reduce the number of youths in court-ordered detention and provide them with culturally relevant community-based services and supervision. Youths selected are those who are likely to be detained pending their adjudication. DDAP provides an intensive level of community-based monitoring and advocacy that is not presently available.

Disposition case advocacy is the approach being used in this program. It has been defined as "the efforts of lay persons or nonlegal experts acting on behalf of youthful offenders at disposition hearings."[24]

Clients are primarily identified through referrals from the public defender's office, the probation department, community agencies, and parents. Admission to DDAP is restricted to youths currently held, or likely to be held, in secure detention. The individuals selected are those deemed to be "high risk" in terms of their chance of engaging in subsequent criminal activity. The selection is based on a risk assessment instrument developed by the National Council on Crime and Delinquency. The target population is persons whose risk assessment scores indicate that they would ordinarily be detained. This is what Miller terms the "deep-end" approach.[25] This is very important, for by focusing on *detained* youth, the project ensures that it remains a true diversion alternative and does not engage in net widening. Youths are screened by DDAP staff to determine whether they are likely to be detained and whether they present an acceptable risk to the community.

Client screening involves gathering background information from probation reports, psychological evaluations, police reports, school reports, and other pertinent documents. Interviews are conducted with youths, family members, and adult professionals to determine the types of services required. Once a potential client is evaluated, DDAP staff presents a comprehensive community service plan at the detention hearing and requests that the judge release the youth to DDAP custody.

Because the project deals only with youths who are awaiting adjudication or final disposition, their appropriateness for the project is based on whether they can reside in the community under supervision without unreasonable risk and their likelihood of attending their court hearings. This is similar in principle to what often occurs in the adult system when someone is released on bail pending court hearings (e.g., arraignments, trial).

The primary goal of DDAP is to design and implement individualized community service plans that address a wide range of personal and social needs. Services that address specific linguistic or medical needs are located by case managers. Along with the youth's participation, the quality and level of services are monitored by DDAP staff. It should be noted that the purpose of multiple collaboratives is to ensure that the project is able to represent and address the needs of the various communities within San Francisco in the most culturally appropriate manner. Because youth services in San Francisco have been historically fragmented by ethnicity, race, and community, a more unified approach is being tried with DDAP. It has become a neutral site within the city and is staffed by representatives from CJCJ and several other community-based service agencies.

Shelden conducted an evaluation of this program, which consisted of comparing a group of youths referred to DDAP with a similarly matched control group that remained within the juvenile justice system.[26] The results showed that after a three-year follow-up, the recidivism rate for the DDAP group was 34 percent, compared to a 60 percent rate for the control group. Detailed comparisons holding several variables constant (e.g., prior record, race, age, gender) and examining several different measures of recidivism (e.g., subsequent commitments, referrals for violent offenses) showed that the DDAP youths still had a significantly lower recidivism rate. There may be several reasons for the apparent success of this program. From the data collected here and information from previous research, three reasons seem of paramount importance.

First, the caseloads of the DDAP caseworkers are extremely low in comparison to normal probation officers. The DDAP workers average about 10 cases each. Regular probation officers in major urban areas have caseloads ranging from 50 to 150. Smaller caseloads typically result in more intensive supervision, and more intensive supervision means that caseworkers are constantly "on top of things" with regard to their clients. Indeed, with small caseloads they can spend more "quality time" with their clients *in the field* (e.g., in their homes, on street corners, at school), rather than endless hours in an office making phone calls and doing paperwork and other bureaucratic chores.

Second, DDAP is a program that is "out of the mainstream" of the juvenile justice system—that is, it is a true "alternative" rather than one of many bureaucratic extensions of the system. This means that normal bureaucratic restrictions do not generally apply. For instance, the qualifications for being a caseworker with DDAP are not as strict as you might find within the juvenile justice system (age restrictions, educational requirements, arrest records, "street" experience, etc.). From casual observations of some of these caseworkers, researchers have been impressed with their dedication and passion to helping youth. Moreover, the backgrounds of these workers were similar to the backgrounds of some of their clients (similar race, neighborhood of origins, language, etc.).

Third, the physical location of DDAP seems user friendly and lacks the usual macho appearance of the formal system. There are no bars, no concrete buildings, no devices for screening for weapons as you enter the building, no "cells" for "lockdown," and so on. Further, the DDAP workers are not "officers of the court" with powers of arrest and the usual accouterments of such occupations (e.g., badges, guns).

There could also be a possible fourth explanation—but one we can only speculate on at this time because we lack the data to draw such a conclusion. It could be that given the small caseloads, DDAP caseworkers are more likely than regular probation officers to be "on top of the case"—that is, to be in constant contact with the youth and thus be able to "nip in the bud" potential problems. Also, when police officers facing a possible arrest situation learn that the youth is a DDAP case (presuming the officers know about DDAP), they may decide to contact the caseworker, who might be able to persuade the officers that the situation could be handled without a formal arrest. We have no way of knowing whether this occurs with any degree of regularity. If it does, such a procedure may be a positive sign, because youths from more privileged backgrounds are often treated this way by the police if they believe that someone in authority can "handle" the youth informally. Many youths have been saved the stigma of formal juvenile processing by such intervention by significant adults in their lives.

Though certainly not a "magic bullet," DDAP has much promise. As already noted, some of the basic principles behind this program (case management, etc.) can easily be applied to adults. It shows the way toward dealing with many criminal matters in the community, rather than within the justice system. In terms of cost savings alone, it is worth a try.

We would be remiss if we did not note that there are limitations to any proposals that are offered as an alternative to using the criminal justice system as a response to crime, because these proposals fail to get at the root causes of crime. There is only so much tinkering with the justice system that can be done, if for no other reason than the fact that we are dealing with a "revolving door" whereby we rehabilitate one offender and escort him or her out the back door, only to make room for another coming in the front door. For addressing some of these root causes we offer the following nationwide reforms.

BROAD-BASED NATIONAL STRATEGIES TO REDUCE CRIME[27]

The criminal justice system represents a *reactive* approach to the problem of crime. In other words, the system merely *responds,* after the fact, to crime. Certainly there are ways in which this response can be made more productive. But a better approach would be to make a serious attempt to be *proactive*—that is, to try to *prevent* crime before it happens. Because there are numerous *social* causes of crime (after all, this is certainly a *social* rather than merely an individual problem), it is necessary not only to find these causes but then to act on them by alleviating them as much as possible.

Over the years, many researchers have offered versions of how such responses should be structured. One example is offered by the criminologist Elliot Currie.[28] He suggests five general categories for a national strategy to address the general problem of crime, which by definition also focuses on the gang problem. First, he recommends early educational interventions. These would include programs such as Head Start, based on the assumption that delinquency is related to poor school performance and dropping out, which in turn are related to lack of preparedness for school, especially among lower-class minorities.

Second, the United States should expand health and mental health services, with a special focus on high-risk youths. Such services would include prenatal and postnatal care. This is based on evidence that the most violent youths suffer from childhood traumas of the central nervous system, exhibit multiple psychotic symptoms, and have experienced severe physical or sexual abuse.[29]

Third, Currie suggests family support programs, especially for families dealing with child abuse and other forms of domestic violence. Abused children are far more likely than nonabused children to become abusers themselves. Some recent research indicates that the majority of prison inmates, especially violent ones, experienced severe physical, emotional, or sexual abuse or some combination of all three.

Fourth, Currie recommends doing something constructive with offenders after they have broken the law. In other words, do not merely warehouse them in a correctional setting. He notes that an ingredient found in virtually all successful rehabilitation programs is improving skills—work skills, reading and verbal skills, problem-solving skills, and so on.

Fifth, there is a pressing need for drug and alcohol abuse treatment programs. Currie notes that most recent approaches to the "war on drugs" have tried to halt the manufacturing and distribution (the supply side) of drugs, rather than the use (the demand side) of drugs. The effects of this "war" have not only been a failure to reduce the problem but also a tremendous growth in the prison population. Most of the increase in the prison population in the last ten to fifteen years is due to the increase in drug convictions and sentences.

On a more general level, Currie suggests that we as a society need to reduce racial inequality, poverty, and inadequate services and that, perhaps most important, we need to prepare the next generation better for the labor market of the future. With this in mind, he outlines four goals for the decades ahead: (1) reduction of inequality and social impoverishment, (2) an active labor market policy that aims at upgrading job skills, (3) a national family policy (e.g., a family leave law), and (4) economic and social stability of local communities, because we need to prevent the frequent moving of capital and employment opportunities, which has forced so many families to relocate in order to seek better jobs; this relocation has weakened the sense of community and the development of networks that would provide support. In addition, he suggests the need for a national research agenda to study the effectiveness of these policies in order to find what works.

Mark Colvin has also written about the need for national strategies.[30] One of his major assumptions revolves around the concept of social reproduction, which refers to the process engaged in by institutions—mostly families and schools—that socialize children and prepare them for productive roles in society. His main thesis is that these institutions have largely failed to give growing numbers of young people social bonds to legitimate avenues to adulthood. The result is that many are becoming marginal to the country's economic institutions. This has been caused by a failure to invest in human development and human capital. This failure has resulted in a growing crime rate and increasing expenditures for welfare and prisons. There is a need for a "national comprehensive program aimed at spurring economic growth, human development, and grass-roots, democratic participation in the major institutions affecting our lives and those of our children."[31]

Colvin argues that neither conservative deterrence approaches nor liberal approaches to rehabilitation have been very effective, mainly because they are reactive policies. Clearly, widespread preventive measures are in order. Some prevention programs do not work because of a lack of funding or a failure to address the larger problems in society, or because they often appear to target specific groups (e.g., high-risk poor children) at the expense of middle-class taxpayers. A comprehensive approach must aim at broader economic and human development programs that affect large segments of the population (e.g., the Social Security system versus welfare for the poor). The United States must do what other industrialized nations do and consider seriously the need to develop human capital for the continued overall well-being of society. In the United States the system is so privatized that public or social needs are often undermined by private investment decisions that result in moving capital all over the world but cost jobs here at home.

We need to redirect our focus away from the question of "what to do about crime" to "what to do about our declining infrastructure and competitiveness in the world economy." Further, there is a need to establish an educational-industrial complex to replace the already declining military-industrial complex. Today, our national security threat comes from within, a result of our domestic decline.[32]

Education is the key here. However, as Colvin notes, education must be more than what the term has traditionally meant—namely, formalized public schooling leading to a diploma. He says that education "must include families, schools, workplaces and communities." The educational-industrial complex must "reduce the marginalization of young people." Colvin offers eight specific proposals:[33]

1. *Short-term emergency measures.* These are needed to reduce immediate problems such as joblessness and human suffering. Programs such as Civilian Employment Training Act (CETA), income subsidies for poor families, and other War on Poverty–type programs are included here. However, Colvin stresses the importance of simultaneously starting more comprehensive programs that affect a broader spectrum of people.

2. *Nationwide parent-effectiveness programs.* These types of programs should be required in the senior year of all high schools and also be offered to adult education classes in high school for new parents. Supplement these with parent-effectiveness counseling programs. The model used in Oregon by Patterson and his colleagues could be followed.[34]

3. *Universal Head Start preschool programs.* For parents who can afford them, programs for certification and training should be offered. Certified preschool programs should also include free day care programs. These have proved to be very effective in preventing delinquency.

4. *Expanded and enhanced public education.* This includes several interrelated proposals: (a) increase teachers' salaries; (b) change certification to open up the profession to noneducation majors so specialists (especially in math and science) can teach (having to take a year of often-silly education courses at their own expense can discourage otherwise qualified people from entering the teaching profession); (c) increase the school year to 230 days (from the 180-day average) to compete with Germany and Japan (which average 240 days per year); (d) focus especially on problem-solving skills; (e) offer nontraditional courses such as "outward bound" and apprenticeships; (f) use peer counseling and student tutoring; (g) eliminate tracking; (h) award stipends for attending school and bonuses for good grades to eliminate the

need for students to work (this would also open up many unskilled jobs for unemployed adults); (i) establish nonviolent conflict resolution programs; and (j) get students more active in school policies, to help prepare them for participating in democracy as adults.

5. *National service program.* Upon completing high school, a youth should have the opportunity to complete two years of national service and be given educational and vocational stipends upon completion. This service could include health care, nursing, environmental cleanup, day care services, care for the elderly, and so on. This program could provide much-needed labor for public works projects. It would be good for young people to participate in the improvement of their communities, and communities could take advantage of the energy of these youths to help rebuild.

6. ***Enhancement of workplace environments.*** Young people must have hope that they are headed for a good-quality job. There need to be labor laws that emphasize workplace democracy to create noncoercive work environments. This helps to attract and reward creative individuals who are needed to compete in a global economy.

7. ***Programs for economic growth and expanded production.*** First, investments need to be aimed toward what is good for the general public rather than toward profit for the wealthy few who are interested mainly in short-term profits. Second, there should be more investment in research and industrial techniques.

8. ***Progressive income-tax system.*** The wealthy are now paying proportionately less than they paid thirty years ago. According to Robert Reich, "Were the personal income tax as progressive as it was even as late as 1977, in 1989 the top tenth would have paid $93 billion more in taxes than they did. At that rate, from 1991 to 2000 they would contribute close to a trillion dollars, even if their incomes fail to rise."[35]

A variation of the proposals offered by both Currie and Colvin comes from Margaret Phillips and is a good example of a theory-based intervention.[36] Phillips elaborates on the importance of unemployment as a key factor related to crime. Her goal is to show why there is a connection between these two variables. Her thesis is that the stress associated with poverty and feelings of powerlessness (which are correlated) results in the tendency to be present oriented—that is, unable to plan for the future because of a belief that your life is out of control. This is part of the irresponsibility typically associated with crime and delinquency.

Phillips notes that most theories fall somewhere within the old "nature versus nurture" debate. She gives an interesting account of what was nearly a perfect laboratory test of this debate, in which a strike at the Hormel Meatpacking Company in Austin, Minnesota, in the mid-1980s was broken when the company reopened by hiring workers from outside the town. Many local workers were left jobless, and the rates of crime—especially domestic violence—and alcohol and drug abuse rose noticeably. These increases were explained by a ripple effect common after plant closures, when crime in general—and domestic violence in particular—increases, along with suicides, stress-related illnesses, and drug and alcohol abuse. What is perhaps most interesting is that there is a corresponding decrease in citizen participation in civic activities, which decreases the amount of informal social control. Phillips concludes by noting that there is abundant evidence that poverty and economic dislocation play an important role in crime, as well as in the lack of self-control.[37]

Phillips's theory tries to combine the role of environmental (especially socioeconomic) factors with individual responsibility and powerlessness. She defines powerlessness and its linkage with irresponsibility in the following manner:

> The essence of powerlessness is the feeling that nothing one does matters; taking responsibility for one's acts assumes the understanding that one's acts have consequences. Taking control of one's life implies the understanding that one can have some control over the future. Thus empowerment is a prerequisite for taking responsibility, and the most basic kind of empowerment is economic, the ability to support oneself and a family.[38]

This would logically lead us to consider full employment as a solution to the crime problem. It even suggests a Works Progress Administration (WPA) project like what occurred in the 1930s.

Next, Phillips outlines the link between powerlessness and irresponsibility. She begins by noting that if there is such a thing as a criminal personality type, then such a person would tend to be present oriented and irresponsible. This kind of person sees himself or herself as having little or no control over the future and is therefore extremely tied to the present. This theme can be seen, at least implicitly, in the techniques of neutralization noted by Sykes and Matza (see Chapter 4). Many delinquents see themselves as effects, rather than as active doers. This leads to irresponsibility, which in turn leads to what Matza called "drift," a condition that places one at risk of becoming a delinquent.[39]

Phillips then turns to an area seemingly unrelated (and usually considered off-limits) to sociologists—namely, medical evidence that links poverty and lack of security to fatalism and various physiological effects. Quoting studies by an epidemiologist and a biologist, she notes that there is a connection between the symptoms of stress and the lack of control over one's fate. Stress stems from such things as a lack of nurturing, not knowing what tomorrow will bring, seeing people suffering and dying on a regular basis, and being subjected to criminal victimization. These stressors are especially pronounced in a society of scarcity (which includes many inner-city ghettos). A person's psychological defenses become limited, and one is unable to develop a sense of autonomy and inner psychological strength to cope. When scarcity exists, a normal psychological defense mechanism is to view one's own situation as uncontrollable and oneself as helpless. This in turn leads to attempts to control others (via various sorts of crime, especially violence).[40] It is easy to understand why delinquents from these kinds of backgrounds would be so present oriented. Yet it is important to view such characteristics as a result of the stress produced by poverty, discrimination, and oppression, obviously pointing to political and economic solutions.

What is also emphasized is still another characteristic of these individuals and another outcome of the stress associated with poverty—namely, the decrease in the degree of trust. This results in the tendency to view others as potential enemies.[41] It has also been long recognized that there is a higher incidence of stress-related mental illness in the lower classes. The longitudinal study by Werner and Smith reinforces these ideas. Those high-risk children who led fairly stable lives came from families with at least two years between children and had someone in the family with whom they could bond closely. They also had good support networks and developed a belief that they had some control over their fate. In short, they had someone they could trust.[42]

Phillips next focuses on some common causes of feelings of powerlessness (in addition to poverty itself and the corresponding lack of resources). The main causes are as follows:

1. *Joblessness and underemployment.* There is a need for jobs with livable wages.
2. *Population size.* There is a need to develop small neighborhood units so that people will become more empowered (the "safety in numbers" idea).
3. *Alcohol and drug abuse.* Not only is this a way to escape stress, but also such abuse itself results in a lack of control. Addiction, having numerous causes in itself, in turn creates irresponsibility and crime. There is a desperate need for more resources for both treatment and prevention.
4. *Low IQ.* Hard-core offenders, especially those in prison, have lower than average IQs. Resources for special education programs early in life would help.
5. *Child abuse.* Families most at risk are those with low income and low educational levels and those experiencing stress. Such abuse is strongly correlated with crime—a high percentage of inmates experienced severe abuse throughout childhood and adolescence.[43]

Phillips offers several interrelated proposals to address these problems. She begins by noting that programs are needed that empower people—programs that help individuals learn to be responsible and able to help themselves independently. Prisons (including the popular boot camp programs) fail to do this. Some alternative sentencing programs may help (victim–offender reconciliation, probation programs that require substance-abuse treatment, etc.). On a national level, Phillips suggests that some of the following types of programs might well succeed:

1. *Full employment.* Examples include WPA-type programs and "reindustrialization from below" (like the old Tennessee Valley Authority of the 1930s).
2. *Welfare reform.* The inclusion of programs that would provide transitional publicly funded jobs.
3. *Raising the minimum wage.* Although Phillips does not mention this, Ron Huff has noted in his discussions with gang members that, when asked what kind of wage would attract them to regular jobs, the answer was usually about $7 per hour.[44]
4. *Health care insurance for all.*
5. *Low-income housing for the homeless.*

One way to achieve some of these lofty goals is to have corrections departments and other professional associations endorse proposals like full employment and the channeling of the nation's resources to health care, education, and drug and alcohol treatment. These professionals can explain to policy makers exactly why such programs are needed.

To find out what made the difference between staying out of trouble or not, future research might compare recidivists with successful parolees and probationers in terms of differences in their perception of control. There is some anecdotal evidence from successful parolees/probationers who have mentioned such reasons for success as "finding religion," strong family support, and getting a good job. In her conclusion Phillips states that the key to solving the problem is empowerment, which begins with having meaningful work at livable wages and developing tools that assist offenders in taking some control over their lives.

RESTORATIVE JUSTICE

An emerging idea that has great potential is known as **restorative justice.** The aim of this approach is to end the pain and suffering of the victims of crime—not just the victims of "normal" crimes but the victims of all crimes, all forms of human rights abuses. The usual response to crime—especially violent crime—is a desire to "get even" by seeking "just deserts" against offenders. But this response has always proved to be counterproductive. In fact, it goes against virtually every religious tenant.[45] As Gandhi and Martin Luther King Jr. taught and demonstrated, the only way to end violence is *not* to reciprocate in kind. In other words, to end the cycle, just stop the violence. King, in his acceptance speech for the Nobel Peace Prize in 1964, said: "The choice today is not between violence and non-violence. It is either non-violence or non-existence."[46]

There is certainly some truth to the idea that the only way to rid oneself of hurt and anger is through forgiveness. Indeed, the English poet Alexander Pope (1688–1744) wrote, "To err is human, to forgive divine."[47] Unfortunately, forgiveness seems out of step in our current political/economic system. Forgiveness would be more in line with a political/economic system "that sees acknowledgment of a harm-done, and apology for it, and forgiveness offered in return, as processes that are personally healing for all involved and simultaneously restorative of community."[48]

The underlying aim of restorative justice is to cease further objectification of those who have been involved in the violent act—the victim, the offender, the families connected to these two individuals, and the community at large. Restorative justice lets all of the individuals involved engage in a healing process through traditional mediation and conflict resolution techniques, in order to "help those affected by the harm dissolve their fears, and hates, and resentments and thereby recover a sense of their former selves." Through this process the person most directly harmed "is able to achieve a greater sense of inner-healing and closure for any traumatic loss of trust, self-worth, and freedom...[while] the harmed person might also achieve a modicum of reparation for his or her losses as well as be able to reduce his or her fears of being harmed."[49]

Proponents of restorative justice know full well what a difficult sell it is within a capitalist society. As Sullivan and Tifft observe, the change needed "transforms all of our conceptions of political economy, that is, how we view power and money, and how we assess human worth." But we come to see the "money-surplus complex" for what it really is—namely, a game of power and control over others.[50]

SOME CONCLUDING THOUGHTS

In this chapter we provided a brief outline of some specific recommendations that might help reduce the crime problem. We deliberately omitted the usual recommendations that attempt to make the criminal justice system more "humane" or "fair" or "less biased." How can we achieve equal justice in an unequal society? To make the existing justice system more "efficient" (as many recommend) is to miss the point, for we would make the system more efficient at making more arrests of the poor and racial minorities and sending more people to prison. In order to achieve "justice," restorative or otherwise, we need to confront and overcome some of the ugly realities of modern American capitalism.

This is not to say that good people are not needed to work within the system, for indeed they are. Many who work in the criminal justice system are conscientious and dedicated and fully understand the inequities within the larger society and within the justice system itself. One of Shelden's former students who works in a juvenile court once said, "I hate the system, but I love my kids." We both have heard from police officers who have reinforced the idea that the police institution is like an "army of occupation" within the ghettos. We both have met many people who work inside jails or prisons and hate what these institutions do to people—both those incarcerated and those who work there. A prison guard once said something like "We are all doing time here. But we [the guards] just do it in eight-hour shifts."

We have no "magic bullets" that would make the problem go away. No one does. But we are hopeful that you realize that this is the reality that faces you as you prepare for a career within the criminal justice system or for some other career. In either case you may be able to have some impact on the crime problem—a positive impact on specific individuals with whom you come in contact. This in itself can be rewarding. But you must also realize that for every individual that you help "go straight" there are hundreds, perhaps thousands, you will not be able to reach and millions more who are likely to come into the system in the future.

Because crime is still very much with us, perhaps in the new millennium we should be looking elsewhere for answers. In recent years many criminologists have been searching in other directions for answers. One direction has been in the area of philosophy and various Eastern religions, such as Buddhism, and some of the views of Native Americans. Many of us have begun to seriously examine some of the more recent writings of Richard Quinney, whose latest works point us in the direction of "peacemaking" by seeking peace within ourselves and various nonviolent and noncoercive alternatives to crime, consistent with the restorative justice idea.[51]

Although we do not claim to have all the answers, after about thirty years of studying and teaching about the subject of crime and delinquency, we are convinced that fundamental changes need to be made in the way we live and think before we will see any significant decrease in these problems. In discussing delinquency, for example, it is important to note that we are always talking about the "problem of delinquency" or the "problem of youth" or that youths in trouble need to change their attitudes, their behaviors, their lifestyles, their methods of thinking, and so on. It seems that it is always *they* who have to change.

What is invariably included in this line of thinking is the use of labels to describe these youths (and adult offenders too). The labels keep changing, along with changing times. As Jerome Miller noted, we began with "possessed" youths in the seventeenth century, then moved to the "rabble" or "dangerous classes" in the eighteenth and late nineteenth centuries, and to the "moral imbeciles" and the "constitutional psychopathic inferiors" in the early twentieth centuries. We continued through the twentieth century and into the twenty-first with the "psychopaths" of the 1940s and the "sociopaths" of the 1950s and finally to recent labels such as "compulsive delinquent," the "learning disabled," the "unsocialized aggressive," and the "socialized aggressive," and the "bored" delinquent. "With the growth of professionalism, the number of labels has multiplied exponentially," Miller observed. He suggests that the problem with these labels is that it seems to be a way "whereby we bolster the maintenance of the existing order against threats which might arise from its own internal contradictions." And it reassure us "that the fault lies in the warped offender and takes everyone else off the hook. Moreover, it enables the professional diagnostician to enter the scene or withdraw at will, wearing success like a halo and placing failure around the neck of the client like a noose." More important, we continue to believe that harsh punishment works, especially the kind of punishment that includes some form of incarceration, so that the offender is placed out of sight and, not coincidentally, out of mind.[52]

But there is a problem here. Throughout the past two centuries we have continued to succumb to the "edifice complex." We love to build "edifices," no matter what they are called (a new courthouse, a new prison, a new correctional center, a new police station, etc.). Perhaps it is because politicians like to have some kind of permanent structure to leave behind as a legacy so they can tell the people who voted for them to look at this or that building as "proof" they have done something about crime. Or perhaps it is because they are so profitable and are part of the huge crime control industry.

We believe otherwise. We believe that we need to quit looking solely at the "troubled youth" or "criminals" as the main source of the problem, or even at their "troubled families" and "troubled communities." It is time that those of us among the more privileged sectors of society consider that we are just as much part of the problem; perhaps more so. In short, if anyone wants to know where the answers lie and where to begin to look for solutions, we think it prudent that all of us begin by simply looking in the mirror. We should begin by asking ourselves: Is there anything that *I* can do differently? Is there something wrong with *my* attitudes, *my* beliefs, *my* actions that may contribute to the problem? If we want some answers, begin by searching *within ourselves*. This is the message from many who espouse some of the philosophies of the East. A quotation from one such source seems appropriate, *Peace Is Every Step;* a book written by a Vietnamese Zen master and poet Thich Nhat Hanh:

> When you plant lettuce, if it does not grow well, you don't blame the lettuce. You look into the reasons it is not doing well. It may need fertilizer, or more water, or less sun. You never blame the lettuce. Yet if we have problems with our friends or our family we blame the other person. But if we know how to take care of them, they will grow well, like lettuce. Blaming has no positive effect at all, nor does trying to persuade using reason and arguments. That is my experience. No blame, no reasoning, no argument, just understanding. If you understand, and you show that you understand, you can love, and the situation will change.[53]

Later in his book, Hanh describes young prostitutes in Manila:

> In the city of Manila there are many young prostitutes; some are only fourteen or fifteen years old. They are very unhappy. They did not want to be prostitutes, but their families are poor and these young girls went to the city to look for some kind of job, like street vendor, to make money to send back to their families. Of course this is true not only in Manila, but in Ho Chi Minh City in Vietnam, in New York City, and in Paris also. After only a few weeks in the city, a vulnerable girl can be persuaded by a clever person to work for him and earn perhaps one hundred times more money than she could as a street vendor. Because she

is so young and does not know much about life, she accepts and becomes a prostitute. Since that time, she has carried the feeling of being impure, defiled, and this causes her great suffering. When she looks at other young girls, dressed beautifully, belonging to good families, a wretched feeling wells up in her, a feeling of defilement that becomes her hell.

But if she could look deeply at herself and at the whole situation, she would see that she is the way she is because other people are the way they are.... No one among us has clean hands. No one of us can claim that it is not our responsibility. The girl in Manila is that way because of the way we are. Looking into the life of that young prostitute, we see the lives of all the "non-prostitutes." And looking at the non-prostitutes and the way we live our lives, we see the prostitute. Each thing helps to create the other.... [T]he truth is that everything contains everything else. We cannot be, we only inter-be. We are responsible for every thing that happens around us.[54]

The thrust of Hanh's book is that before we can achieve peace on earth, which includes a world without crime and suffering, we have to develop peace within ourselves. How else can we make the world a better place, unless we make our own lives better? How can we tell the "criminals" in our midst how to live their lives if we do not set good examples? As Richard Quinney has written: "If human actions are not rooted in compassion, these actions will not contribute to a compassionate and peaceful world. If we ourselves cannot know peace, be peaceful, how will our acts disarm hatred and violence."[55] Without such hatred and violence, there would be no need to even have, much less need to control, the "dangerous classes." There is a lot of work to do.

KEY TERMS

crime control industry   382
Detention Diversion Advocacy
   Project (DDAP)   389

net widening   389
restorative justice   395

Treatment Alternatives to Street
   Crime (TASC) project   388

NOTES

1. Marx, K. "The Usefulness of Crime." In D. Greenberg (ed.), *Crime and Capitalism* (2nd ed.). Philadelphia: Temple University Press, 1993, pp. 52–53.

2. Walker, S. *Sense and Nonsense about Crime and Drugs* (5th ed.). Belmont, CA: Wadsworth, 2001. Consult Walker's book for the evidence supporting the claims made in this section.

3. Ibid., p. 18.

4. Western, B., and K. Beckett. "How Unregulated Is the U.S. Labor Market? The Penal System as a Labor Market." *American Journal of Sociology* 104: 1030–1060 (1999).

5. The following information is taken from *Drug War Facts*, 2000.

6. Miller, R. L. *Drug Warriors and Their Prey: From Police Power to Police State*. Westport CT: Praeger, 1996.

7. Two main sources were consulted for the following discussion: Walker, *Sense and Nonsense about Crime and Drugs*, ch. 13; Inciardi, J. *The War on Drugs III*. Boston: Allyn and Bacon, 2002, ch. 10.

8. Walker, *Sense and Nonsense about Crime and Drugs*, pp. 254–255.

9. Inciardi, *The War on Drugs III*, pp. 283–285; see also Clark, T. "Heroin: The Problem with Pleasure." Online (http://world.std.com/~twc/heroin.htm), and "Keep Marijuana Illegal—For Teens." Online (http://world.std.com/~twc/marijuan.htm).

10. These data are taken from the following sources: "Governor Pushes Legalization of Drugs during U. of Mexico Speech." *Daily Lobo*, September 25, 2000; Duhigg, C. "Tokin' Reformer." *The New Republic*, April 3, 2000; Pierce, N. "Prison Reform: A Moment to Seize?" *Nation's Cities Weekly*, March 6, 2000. See also the Website of the Lindesmith Center on Drug Policy (www.drugpolicy.org).

11. Inciardi, *The War on Drugs III*, p. 282.

12. Clark, "Keep Marijuana Illegal."

13. Walker, *Sense and Nonsense about Crime and Drugs*, p. 262,

14. See Shelden, R., S. Tracy, and W. B. Brown, *Youth Gangs in American Society* (2nd ed.). Belmont, CA: Wadsworth, 2001.

15. *Drug War Facts*, 2000 (http://www.drugwarfacts.org/marijuana.htm).

16. Documented in both Inciardi, *The War on Drugs III*, ch. 10 and pp. 305–308, and Walker, *Sense and Nonsense about Crime and Drugs*, ch. 13.

17. Inciardi, ibid., pp. 306–307.

18. Tannenbaum, F. *Crime and the Community*. New York: Columbia University Press, 1938; Becker, H. S. *Outsiders: Studies in the Sociology of Deviance*. New York: Free Press, 1963; Lemert, E. *Social Pathology*. New York: McGraw-Hill, 1951.

19. President's Commission on Law and Administration of Justice. *The Challenge of Crime in a Free Society.* Washington, DC: U.S. Government Printing Office, 1967.

20. Polk, K. "Juvenile Diversion: A Look at the Record." In P. M. Sharp and B. W. Hancock (eds.), *Juvenile Delinquency.* Englewood Cliffs, NJ: Prentice-Hall, 1995.

21. Pogebrin, M. R., E. D. Poole, and R. M. Regoli. "Constructing and Implementing a Model Juvenile Diversion Program." *Youth and Society* 15: 305–324 (1984); see also Frazier, C. E., and J. K. Cochran. "Official Intervention, Diversion from the Juvenile Justice System, and Dynamics of Human Services Work: Effects of a Reform Goal Based on Labeling Theory." *Crime and Delinquency* 32: 157–176 (1986).

22. Dryfoos, J. *Adolescents at Risk.* New York: Oxford University Press, 1990.

23. Feldman, R. A., T. E. Caplinger, and J. S. Wodarski. *The St. Louis Conundrum.* Englewood Cliffs, NJ: Prentice-Hall, 1983.

24. Macallair, D. "Disposition Case Advocacy in San Francisco's Juvenile Justice System: A New Approach to Deinstitutionalization." *Crime and Delinquency* 40: 84 (1984).

25. Miller, J. *Last One over the Wall: The Massachusetts Experiment in Closing Reform Schools* (2nd ed.). Columbus: Ohio State University Press, 1998.

26. Shelden, *Detention Diversion Advocacy.*

27. The following section is taken from Shelden, Tracy, and Brown, *Youth Gangs in American Society,* ch. 8.

28. Currie, E. "Confronting Crime: Looking toward the Twenty-First Century." *Justice Quarterly* 6: 5–25 (1989). See also Currier, E. *Crime and Punishment in America.* New York: Metropolitan Books, 1998.

29. See also Dryfoos, J. *Adolescents at Risk.* New York: Oxford University Press, 1990.

30. Colvin, M. "Crime and Social Reproduction: A Response to the Call for 'Outrageous' Proposals." *Crime and Delinquency* 37: 436–448 (1991).

31. Ibid., p. 437.

32. Ibid., pp. 439–440.

33. Ibid., p. 446.

34. Patterson, G. R., P. Chamberlain, and J. B. Reid. "A Comparative Evaluation of a Parent-Training Program." *Behavior Therapy* 13: 636–650 (1982).

35. Reich, R. B. "The Real Economy." *The Atlantic* 267 (1991), 51.

36. Phillips, M. B. "A Hedgehog Proposal." *Crime and Delinquency* 37: 555–574 (1991).

37. Phillips, "A Hedgehog Proposal," p. 558.

38. Ibid., pp. 558–559.

39. Sykes, G., and Matza, D. "Techniques of Neutralization." *American Journal of Sociology* 22: 664–670 (1957); Matza, D., *Delinquency and Drift.* New York: Wiley, 1957.

40. Sapolsky, R. M. "Lessons of the Serengeti: Why Some of Us Are More Susceptible to Stress." *The Sciences* (May/June 1988), pp. 38–42; Sagan, L. A. *The Health of Nations.* New York: Basic Books, 1989.

41. See Jankowski, M. S. *Islands in the Street: Gangs and American Urban Society.* Berkeley: University of California Press, 1990.

42. Werner, E. E., and R. S. Smith. *Vulnerable, but Invincible: A Longitudinal Study of Resilient Children and Youth.* New York: McGraw-Hill, 1982, p. 563.

43. Currie, E. *Confronting Crime.* New York: Pantheon, 1985.

44. Huff, C. R. "Youth Gangs and Public Policy." *Crime and Delinquency* 35: 524–537 (1989).

45. Restorative justice, it is not practiced much, despite the fact that most religions preach this and similar principles. In the name of Christianity a multitude of horrors have been committed worldwide (see Ellerbe, H. *The Dark Side of Christian History.* San Rafael, CA: Morningstar Books, 1995). Thus, restorative justice will be hard to sell to some Christians.

46. Quoted in Seldes, G. (ed.). *The Great Thoughts.* New York: Ballantine Books, 1996, p. 253.

47. Ibid., p. 376.

48. Sullivan, D., and L. Tifft. *Restorative Justice as a Transformative Process.* Voorheesville, NY: Mutual Aid Press, 2000, p. 6.

49. Ibid., p. 9.

50. Ibid., p. 34.

51. Quinney, R., and J. Wideman. *The Problem of Crime: A Peace and Social Justice Perspective* (3rd ed.). Mountain View, CA: Mayfield, 1991; Quinney, R. *For the Time Being.* Albany: State University of New York Press, 1999.

52. Miller, J. *Last One over the Wall* (2nd ed.). Columbus: Ohio State University Press, 1998, p. 234.

53. Hanh, T. N. *Peace Is Every Step.* New York: Bantam Books, 1991, p. 78.

54. Ibid., pp. 97–98.

55. Quinney, R. "Socialist Humanism and the Problem of Crime: Thinking about Erich Fromm in the Development of Critical/Peacemaking Criminology." Unpublished manuscript. Northern Illinois University, 1995, p. 10.